The Last Titan

JEROME LOVING

The Last Titan

A Life of Theodore Dreiser

UNIVERSITY OF CALIFORNIA PRESS

BERKELEY   LOS ANGELES   LONDON

*The publisher gratefully acknowledges the
generous contribution to this book provided
by Edmund and Jeannie Kaufman as members
of the Literati Circle of the University of
California Press Associates.*

University of California Press
Berkeley and Los Angeles, California

University of California Press, Ltd.
London, England

© 2005 by the Regents of the University of California

Library of Congress Cataloging-in-Publication Data

Loving, Jerome.
    The last titan : a life of Theodore Dreiser /
  Jerome Loving.
        p.   cm.
    Includes bibliographical references and index.
    ISBN 0-520-23481-2 (alk. paper)
      1. Dreiser, Theodore, 1871–1945.   2. Novelists,
  American— 20th century—Biography.
  3. Journalists—United States—Biography.
  I. Title.
  PS3507.R55Z6655   2005
  813'.52—dc22   2004016270

Manufactured in the United States of America
14   13   12   11   10   09   08   07   06   05
10   9   8   7   6   5   4   3   2   1

The paper used in this publication meets the minimum
requirements of ANSI/NISO Z39.48–1992 (R 1997)
(*Permanence of Paper*).

Like Walt Whitman, another shaggy outsider,
Dreiser elbowed himself into the company of
Leading American Authors without
the proper credentials.

DANIEL AARON

TO MARY LOVING

———————

TO THE MEMORY OF DENNIS CREIGHTON

CONTENTS

PREFACE

IN THE WINTER OF 1903, a tall, slightly undernourished man in his early thirties, whose glasses added to the look of someone unfit for manual labor, approached the car barn of Philadelphia's streetcar company at Eighth and Dauphin to apply for a position as a conductor. Finding its offices closed for the day, he proceeded north to Reading Terminal on Market Street. In threadbare clothes and down to his last fifty cents, Theodore Dreiser also possessed two streetcar tickets for travel between downtown and the suburb of Wissahickon, where he lived in a rooming house he could no longer afford. Nothing had seemed to go right for him since the commercial failure of his first novel, *Sister Carrie*, published a little more than two years earlier. At that moment his situation resembled that of his most famous fictional creation, George Hurstwood, who ultimately commits suicide in a Bowery flophouse. Indeed, although Dreiser at last received payment for some magazine articles he had written and was able to return to New York the next month, he almost followed Hurstwood to an early grave. Instead, at the brink of despair, chance encounters with his brother and a canal boatman pushed him onto the path of mental and physical recovery. Dreiser lived to write a second literary masterpiece as well as a body of fiction that remains securely placed in the American literary canon.

Most celebrated for *Sister Carrie* (1900) and *An American Tragedy* (1925), Dreiser was the last big voice to come out of the American nineteenth century. He lived his first twenty-nine years in the century—and the shadow—of Melville and Whitman, and he emerged from that influence as a belated romantic in the age of realism and naturalism that he himself helped to define. Most of his novels are set in the nineteenth century; even the action of *An American Tragedy*'s tale of crime and punishment is vaguely placed between the era of the Robber Barons of the 1880s and the materialism of the 1920s. Like those Robber Barons, most of Dreiser's literary characters aspire to a life of wealth or at least "conspicuous consumption," and some, such as his overreaching Frank Cowperwood of *The Financier* (1912), *The Titan* (1914), and *The Stoic* (1947), achieve it. (Conceived as a cautionary tale during the first decade of the twentieth century as American universities began to establish schools of business to encourage ethical behavior in commerce, the trilogy is today equally applicable to our own era of corporate corruption.)

My working title during the first years of researching and writing this biography was "Lacking Everything But Genius," a phrase taken from the critic Mark Van Doren. It evoked what I initially thought was the essence of this twelfth-born child of impoverished parents who stumbled into greatness in spite of personal and educational impediments. But I came to see that it actually perpetuated a view of Dreiser I did not accept, that of the "Indiana peasant," a caricature first developed by his longtime friend (and sometime enemy) H. L. Mencken. Although Mencken had begun as an avid and astute champion of *Sister Carrie, Jennie Gerhardt* (1911), and *The Titan,* he became disenchanted with many of Dreiser's later works. A social conservative and Depression Republican, he also came to disapprove of Dreiser's multiple liaisons with women (even though at one point the two writers dated and ultimately exploited a pair of sisters) as well as his bohemian associations in Greenwich Village.

Nevertheless, the two men's friendship endured, and after Dreiser's death in 1945, Mencken considered writing a biographical study. Instead, what might have been Mencken's life of Dreiser became W. A. Swanberg's *Dreiser,* published in 1965. Dedicated to the memory of Mencken, "who knew Dreiser at his best and worst, and fought for the best," it was the most exhaustive biography to that date and still stands today as the most influential account of Dreiser's life. Yet this "Story of a Tormented Life" (as the dust jacket boasted) distorted many of the facts of Dreiser's life, mainly by presenting the novelist's character in a skewed context. Swanberg, whose earlier biographies had not been of artists but of outsize and rogue figures such as General Sickles, Jim Fisk, and William Randolph Hearst, never missed an opportunity to characterize his subject as suspicious, superstitious, contentious, lecherous, greedy, and egotistical. Furthermore, Swanberg was no literary critic and was thus unable to appreciate the reason his subject deserved a biography in the first place. His treatment of Dreiser's major works consisted mainly of bare outlines and quotes from a few reviews. As a result, his readers had to wonder how this apparent sociopath could have written not one but two of the novels ranked among the twentieth century's hundred best by a Random House panel of leading American writers in 1999.

Nonetheless, in undertaking a full-length critical biography of Dreiser, I owe a debt not only to Swanberg's research but to that of three other Dreiser biographies. Dorothy Dudley's *Forgotten Frontiers: Dreiser and the Land of the Free* (1932), though at best an impressionable memoir, was apparently done with Dreiser's cooperation and contains material available nowhere else. Robert H. Elias, who met Dreiser while a graduate student in English at Columbia University and knew him for eight years, wrote the first critical biography in 1948; *Theodore Dreiser: Apostle of Nature* was groundbreaking in the use of Dreiser's papers, but its brevity does not allow for the full story of Dreiser's life. The most recent life, Richard Lingeman's two-volume *Theodore Dreiser,* published in 1986 and 1990, viewed Dreiser more as a cultural figure than a literary one, with an emphasis on the social and political activities that made him a controversial figure in his time.

But even as I drew from each of these earlier biographies, as well as from the upsurge of criticism on his work since the centennial of his birth in 1971, I came to see that Dreiser, often recognized as the "Father of American Realism" and the first major American writer who was not of British heritage, needed a new biographical framework. It was time for a biography in which this controversial life was put back onto the context of his great literary achievements. For while he certainly had his personal faults and stylistic lapses (which critics continue to overemphasize at the expense of his art), Dreiser as a storyteller possessed the rare gift of genius lacking nothing.

ACKNOWLEDGMENTS

FIRST, I WOULD LIKE TO acknowledge the help of the late Roger Asselineau of the Sorbonne. A friend for more than a quarter of a century, Roger was my audience of one as I wrote the first draft of this biography. A biographer himself and a leading European authority on American literature, he had a lifelong fondness for Dreiser and his breakthrough realism that opened the twentieth century in U.S. literature. I am also indebted to Richard Lehan, Keith Newlin, Jay Parini, and Robert D. Richardson for reading the final draft of this book. At the outset of this work and indeed throughout it, two leading Dreiserians, Thomas P. Riggio and James L. W. West III, generously advised me; they also read all or parts of my work-in-progress. Two other prominent students of Dreiser and American Realism, Donald Pizer and Frederic Rusch, kindly allowed me to peruse a draft of their forthcoming edition of Dreiser's interviews with the press over his lifetime.

Others who assisted me in one way or another are Harold Aspiz, Renate von Bardeleben, Susan Belasco, Mack Bradford, Stephen C. Brennan, Julia Roop Cairns, Dominick F. Callo, William Bedford Clark, James M. Cox, Carl Dawson, Robert Dowling, Yvette Eastman, Clare Eby, Vincent Fitzpatrick, Robert H. Elias, Ed Folsom, Tedi Dreiser Godard, Miriam Gogol, Susan Goodman, the late Norman S. Grabo, Yoshinobu Hakutani, Terence Hoagwood, Alison Cameron House, Clara Clark Jaeger, Karen Kalinevitch, Justin Kaplan, Richard Lingeman, David C. Loving, Edward Martin, Jay

Martin, Terence Martin, Dan McCall, John J. McDermott, Philip McFarland, J. Lawrence Mitchell, T. D. Nostwich, Thomas Rotell, Victoria Rosner, Edward Sandoval, Kenneth Silverman, David H. Stewart, Alan Trachtenberg, Mark and Maggie Walker, and Waldemar Zacharasiewicz.

I would like to thank my student research assistants during the years of this endeavor: Amanda Jo Atkins, Jennifer Chenoweth, and Erin Fleming. For help in special collections, I thank Nancy Shawcross and John Pollack of the Dreiser Papers at the Van Pelt–Dietrich Library at the University of Pennsylvania, where copyright is held and permission to quote is granted for all of Dreiser's unpublished writings; and Rebecca Cape of the Lilly Library at Indiana University, where the second largest collection of Dreiser papers can be found. I am also indebted to the special collection departments of the Alderman Library at the University of Virginia, the Kroch Library at Cornell University, and the Newberry Library in Chicago. Closer to home, I thank John Fitzpatrick, Pat Fox, and Cathy Henderson at the Harry Ransom Humanities Research Center at the University of Texas at Austin; and Steven Escar Smith, Director of the Cushing Memorial Library and Archives at Texas A&M University, where I was also assisted by the interlibrary loan department of the Sterling C. Evans Library.

Parts of chapters 6 and 7 appeared in a slightly different form in "Notes from the Underground of *Sister Carrie*," *Dictionary of Literary Biography Yearbook: 2001*, ed. Matthew J. Bruccoli (Farmington Hills, Minn.: The Gale Group, 2002), 360–66.

Financial support for the research and writing of *The Last Titan* came from the John Simon Guggenheim Memorial Foundation, the National Endowment for the Humanities Summer Stipend Program, the Research Foundation at Texas A&M University, and the Office of the Dean of Liberal Arts at Texas A&M University.

At the University of California Press, I have once again benefited from the wisdom and energy of Associate Director and Acquisitions Editor Stanley Holwitz. My thanks also to my editors there, Mary Severance and Ellen F. Smith.

My favorite recipient of thanks is the same one I have gratefully acknowledged in every book I've written, my wife and colleague at Texas A&M, Cathleen C. Loving.

ONE

Hoosier Hard Times

Life was a strange, colorful kaleidoscopic welter then.
It has remained so ever since.

A HOOSIER HOLIDAY

SINCE HER MARRIAGE IN 1851, Sarah Schänäb Dreiser had given birth almost every seventeen or eighteen months. Twelve years younger than her husband, this woman of Moravian-German stock had eloped with John Paul Dreiser at the age of seventeen. If the primordial urge to reproduce weren't enough to keep her regularly enceinte, religious forces were. For Theodore Dreiser's father, a German immigrant from a walled city near the French border more than ninety percent Catholic, was committed to propagating a faith his famous son would grow up to despise. Sarah's parents were Mennonite farmers near Dayton, Ohio, their Czechoslovakian ancestors having migrated west through the Dunkard communities of Germantown, Bethlehem, and Beaver Falls, Pennsylvania. Sarah's father disowned his daughter for marrying a Catholic and converting to his faith. At 8:30 in the morning of August 27, 1871, Hermann Theodor Dreiser became her twelfth child. He began in a haze of superstition and summer fog in Terre Haute, Indiana, a soot-darkened industrial town on the banks of the Wabash about seventy-five miles southwest of Indianapolis.

His mother, however, seems to have been a somewhat ambivalent parent even from the start. After bearing her first three children in as many years, Sarah apparently began to shrink from her maternal responsibilities, as such quick and repeated motherhood sapped her youth. Her restlessness drove her to wish herself single again. She may also have missed the secu-

1

rity and approval of her angry parents. As Dreiser tells it in *Dawn* (1931), a memoir of his youth, she even wished herself dead or, in a bolder fantasy, her children. One evening, while visiting what family still welcomed her—a brother in North Manchester, Indiana, Dreiser recalled from family legend—"she went to the door and stood looking out at a clearing which surrounded the farmhouse." There she saw coming out of the woods "three lights, bobbing lightly to and fro" in procession. They seemed to approach her before vanishing over a rail fence and into the woods. "Right away," Dreiser quoted his mother, "I knew that those were my three children and that they were going to die!" The deaths of Jacob, George, and Xavier did indeed follow, one after another in the next three years, and the remorseful Sarah threw herself at the feet of the God her favorite son would come to view as an inscrutable combination of beauty and terror. If only she could become a mother again, she begged the Almighty, she would never again fail to meet her responsibilities.[1]

Her prayer was answered: the first of her next ten children arrived soon thereafter. Paul, who adapted the family name to Dresser and achieved fame as the author of such songs as "On the Banks of the Wabash" and "My Gal Sal," was born in 1857. He was followed by Marcus Romanus, or Rome, in 1860; Maria Franziska, or Mame, in 1861; Emma Wilhelmina, or Emma, in 1863; Mary Theresa, or Theresa, in 1864; Cacilia, or Sylvia, in 1866; Alphonse Joachim, or Al, in 1867; Clara Clothilde, or Claire (also "Tillie"), in 1868 or 1869; Theodore, or Theo, in 1871; and Eduard Minerod, or Ed, in 1873.[2]

Sarah's superstition, combined with John Paul's Catholic fears of God's retribution, naturally made an impression on young Theodore. Yet even though he sometimes consulted Ouija boards and fortune-tellers as an adult, he never seems to have allowed such suspicions to invade his fiction to any serious extent. Indeed, previous biographers have tended not to see his superstition in the context of the late nineteenth century, when spiritualist movements in America and England flourished and reports of the doings of Madame Blavatsky and other mediums filled the newspapers of the day. Dreiser recalled an episode from his infancy when his mother feared her sickly child was close to death. Opposite the crowded family dwelling in a German neighborhood on South Ninth Street resided an enfeebled woman thought to be a witch. She gave illegal medical advice to the German community and was often consulted in emergencies. One night, when Theo's demise appeared imminent, Sarah sent young Mame across the street to fetch the aged recluse. The woman refused to enter the Dreiser house because of Mr. Dreiser's strict religious views, but she told Mame to have her mother measure the ailing child from head to toe and from fingertip to fingertip: "If the arms are as long as the body, bring the string to me." Finding the measurements satisfactory, the old woman then announced that Theodore Dreiser would not die. But to complete the healing, he must be taken out during the full of the moon for three successive nights and positioned so that the light would "fall slant-wise" over his face. Each night Sarah was to bless her child with the following words, in German: "Whatever I have, take away. Whatever I am doing, increase it!" "As a result of this remarkable therapy," Dreiser recalled almost fifty years later, "I am reported to have improved. In three months I was well."[3]

Dreiser, who as an adult endured almost annual bouts of bronchitis, remembered himself not only as sickly, but as a "mother child" who was afflicted by vision problems that previous biographers have identified as a "cast" in his right eye, a condition in which one eye does not focus because of a misalignment of the optical muscles. He was also a homely child with protruding teeth who clung to his mother's skirts and cried easily. "It always seemed to me," he recalled, "that no one ever wanted me *enough*, unless it was my mother." Not only did he miss his mother for the rest of his life after her death, but as a boy he lamented that as a late child he had missed seeing her in the prime of her beauty, now recorded only in the memories of his elder siblings.[4] Dreiser considered his mother a poet, "after her fashion," who, though she endured a poverty-stricken life, continued "to contemplate beauty—her only earthly reward, as I came to know." Sarah's frequent daydreaming would suggest in part the model for Carrie Meeber in *Sister Carrie* (1900), who ultimately dreams—as Dreiser writes of her in his first novel—"such happiness as you may never feel."[5]

Although it seemed to the young Dreiser that his mother never sat down, whether it was taking in laundry from wealthy families on Wabash Avenue or, as she eventually did in Sullivan, Indiana, running a boardinghouse, Sarah Dreiser evidently toyed with the feelings of her children in order to command the obedience and allegiance that their father never received. One evening, young Theo came upon his mother wearing "a white dressing-sacque" with "a pair of worn slippers on her feet." When the boy ran his hand over her toes, which extended from the slippers, she asked the question that rang in the author's memory for the rest of his life: "See poor mother's shoes? Aren't you sorry she has to wear such torn shoes?" As he burst into tears, he remembered, "she took me up on her lap and held me against her soft breasts and smoothed my head. Then I felt even more helpless and pitiful than before, for it was within the power of my mother's voice to make me cry at any time."[6] Dreiser's lifelong sympathy and tenderness for the poor, certainly grounded in the hard-luck existence of his youth and ultimately leading him to the religion of socialism, was probably born that day.

Sarah's histrionic ways may also have helped lead three of the boys in the family to the stage: Theo, whose first literary ambition was to be a playwright; Paul, the eldest, who composed sentimental songs in the Gay Nineties era of Broadway; and Ed, the youngest, who became an actor of some prominence in New York. One of his mother's "tricks," Dreiser remembered, was to threaten to leave the children when they were misbehaving—sometimes even leaving the house and hiding outside. "If no contrition on our part was visible, she would produce her shawl and Mennonite bonnet, and packing a small basket, would hang it on her arm and start to go." This raised "a storm of wails and tears" from the children until she relented. When finally she did leave them by death's door in her mid-fifties, Dreiser continued to fear her loss in dreams for the rest of his life. "I can see her now," wandering about their humble home, he wrote in *Dawn,* with "shreds of slippers on her feet, at times the typical Mennonite bonnet pulled over her face, her eyes wide and expressive, bestirring herself about the things which concerned her home and family."[7] Dreiser never found a woman's love to fill the void his mother left, although his quest for that mother-lover led him through a lifelong series of affairs.

What his mother thought of her own marital relationship cannot be told, although his parents evidently remained loyal to one another for thirty-eight years, despite hardships and long separations. Certainly from his children's perspective John Paul Dreiser was not always an easy man to love or admire. At twenty-three he had fled Mayen, a small town near Coblentz in Germany, in order to avoid conscription into the Prussian army. John Paul's memories of his youth seem to have been mixed. In *A Traveler at Forty* (1913), Dreiser recalled that he had heard of Mayen ever since he was three or four and "dandled on my father's knee." With typical German pride in the fatherland, John Paul Dreiser spoke of his native village's loveliness—"how the hills rose about it, how grape-growing was its principal industry, how there were castles there and grafs [counts] and rich burghers, and how there was a wall about the city which in his day constituted it an armed fortress, and how often as a little child [his father] had been taken out through some one of its great gates seated on the saddle of some kindly minded cavalry-man and galloped about the drill-ground." But other memories were less pleasant. The senior Dreiser, who left behind twenty-one siblings and half-siblings, had lost his mother early on and became an unwelcome stepson when his father remarried. Once, he told Theo, he was whipped for steal-ing cherries from the overhanging branches of a tree belonging to a neigh-boring priest. While he was secretly feasting on his forbidden fruit, his step-mother had informed on him. (Years later, when Dreiser visited Mayen in 1912, it reminded him of Terre Haute: "Now I can see why my father and so many other Germans from this region settled in southern Indiana. It is like their old home. The wide, flat fields are the same.")[8]

After he left Mayen, John Paul spent some time in Paris, then sailed for New York City, where he arrived in 1844. He worked in woolen mills in New York and Connecticut before moving west to Dayton, Ohio, where he met Sarah and eloped with her to Fort Wayne, Indiana. He worked in a small woolen mill there, and by 1858 the couple had moved to Terre Haute, where their fortunes seemed to improve. By this time, they had had their first child after the loss of the three boys, and John Paul was a mill super-visor. Sometime in the 1860s, Dreiser's father prospered even more, be-coming a mill owner in the nearby coal-mining town of Sullivan. There he made enough money to afford to donate the land for St. Joseph's, the town's first Catholic Church. But fate, which so often intervenes in the lives of Dreiser's fictional characters, intervened here. The woolen mill burned down in 1865, and John Paul was seriously injured by a falling beam during its re-building a year later. Although he invested in another Sullivan mill in 1870, his proprietorship did not last long, either because of economic conditions or as the result of the head injury he had suffered in 1866. By 1871, when Dreiser was born, the now chronically unemployed John Paul was fifty years old and the father of nine living children. Ed, the youngest, would arrive two years later.[9]

John Paul frequently spoke German at home, relied heavily on the German-American community wherever the family lived, and was pro-foundly religious. Like the withered patriarch in *Jennie Gerhardt* (1911), he feared any and all gossip about his children. And like Gerhardt, he believed he would be punished for their sins. Dreiser, along with his brothers and sisters, probably knew enough German to comprehend their father, but, again like the Gerhardts, he and the others no doubt responded in English.[10] We can fairly trust this second novel for a general view of Dreiser's home life, for he drew directly upon his life in his early fiction—and not so indirectly afterward. Indeed, he seems to have found almost nothing more interesting than his own life and his encounters with the world. This obsession with himself shows very much in *Dawn,* where no detail, it seems, is treated routinely. The picture of Gerhardt as a doddering old man who took odd jobs and worked as night watchman parallels roughly the depiction of Dreiser's father in *Dawn.*

———

By the time Dreiser entered school, the family had moved several times within Terre Haute, mainly out of economic necessity: from Ninth Street to Twelfth, Fourteenth, and Thirteenth streets. On Fourteenth Street, near Walnut, they occupied rooms in a boardinghouse. There the shy Theo marveled at "a certain woman—a vulgar showy creature, probably—who moved about this place in silks, satins and laces, a jeweled and perfumed lady with a wealth of light yellow hair."[11] Possibly she was a prostitute, for the Dreiser family soon chose to move to a smaller house on Thirteenth, and Sarah began to take in washing. Whatever the case, the peripatetic family was to encounter more than its share of prostitutes living next door or even under its very roof.

One of Dreiser's most galling memories of childhood was having to attend Catholic schools, whose pupils, he later thought, were routinely brainwashed with "psychopathic balderdash." But John Paul insisted—over the muted objections of his wife and in spite of the family's lack of money—that all his children be educated in parochial schools, which charged tuition while the public schools were free. Dreiser and the youngest of his siblings, Claire and Ed, were enrolled in the German adjunct of Terre Haute's St. Joseph's Roman Catholic Church on Ninth Street. "I often think," he wrote in bitter reflection of the experience, "of the hundreds of thousands of children turned out of the Catholic schools at twelve or thirteen years of age, with not a glimmer of true history or logic." The classrooms were austere: their bare floors and hard wooden desks much scarred by knives and stained with ink. Worse yet, the classes were packed with as many as fifty students. On a dais before them sat a seemingly ancient nun in black, her oval face framed by "a great flaring white bonnet."[12] On his very first day at school, he remembered, this hooded figure paced the class through its ABCs in German, pointing to each letter with a long wand also used for corporal punishment. Other than recitation, the order of the day for the young students, though never perfectly enforced, was absolute silence.

Dreiser remained a harsh critic of the Catholic Church all his life, yet his curiosity about it, or about the beliefs that organized religion commanded, never abated. After visiting a cathedral in France in 1912, he was astounded "that the faith of man had ever reared so lovely a thing." In Rome he even participated in a papal audience, and he sometimes substituted superstitious practices for prayer. Later, his bitterness toward the Church shifted from memories of what its dictates had put his parents and siblings through to the belief that "the gold-encrusted, power-seeking, wealth-loving Papacy" exploited the ignorance of the lower classes and Third World peoples. "No wonder," he wrote in the wake of the Russian Revolution of 1917, "it became the first business of the Russian Communists to rip out root and branch the eastern or Asiatic extension of this . . . designing and serpentine organization!"[13]

Closer to home, Dreiser believed that one of the first victims of his father's slavish allegiance to the Church was his brother Paul, whose early rebelliousness eventually led to several scrapes with the law. In 1872, at age fourteen, husky and already well on the way to achieving his adult weight of more than three hundred pounds, Paul was sent to St. Meinard's Seminary in southwestern Indiana, near Evansville, to study for the priesthood. The accounts vary as to how long he lasted, possibly two years, but he eventually made his way to Indianapolis. There he was able, his brother recalled, "to connect himself with an itinerant cure-all company, a troupe or wagon caravan which traveled gypsy fashion" from town to town, entertaining the locals and trying to sell them Hamlin's Wizard Oil. Although this experience whetted his appetite for the stage, Paul was back in Terre Haute a few years later and in trouble with the law. Apparently, he was charged with the burglary of a saloon, and his debt-ridden father had to come up with $300 to pay his son's bail.[14]

The rest of the siblings also seemed to find trouble to be their main teacher, no doubt, according to Dreiser, because of the perceived hardships their father's Catholic faith brought to the family. Possibly only two of the ten children grew up to be religious in any sense. In full adulthood, after many mistakes with men, Mame became a Christian Scientist. The even wilder Sylvia, who gave birth out of wedlock, also adopted the religion of Mary Baker Eddy and became a "full-fledged" Practitioner, or healer.[15] Generally, however, the girls in the family fared no better in youth and early adulthood than their brothers, as all of the Dreiser brood seemed to follow their eldest brother out into the world and into trouble. The most troubled and troublesome was the second-eldest son, Rome, "short," Dreiser noted with some bitterness in *Dawn*, "for Marcus Romanus, a very noble handle for so humble a mid-western boy." As a teenager Rome had apprenticed as a printer and showed the promise of the newspaper man his brother Theodore would become for a time.[16] But something happened to him along the way. He took to showing off, to drinking, wearing flashy clothes, and going about with loose women. Like several of Dreiser's protagonists, he sought the American Dream of success but settled for its sham materialism. He also fell in love with long distance. He would be involved in the railroad business all his life, working as a butcher on trains whenever he could hold a job—but the alcoholic Rome spent much of his time in and out of saloons and local jails.

In 1879, by the time Dreiser was seven or eight, the family split up because of economic hard times. Sarah may also have wanted to get away from the general gloom her husband seemed to cast over the children, especially the youngest and most impressionable of them, because of his business failures and rigid Catholicism. John Paul remained in Terre Haute as a general handyman in a local woolen mill and tried to keep a rein on the older girls—Mame, Emma, Theresa, and Sylvia—who were fast falling, one after another, into the perils of unsupervised adolescence and older men. With Paul and Rome already on the road and Al apprenticed to his mother's brother on the farm in North Manchester, Sarah took the three youngest children, Claire, Theo, and Ed, south to Vincennes—a provincial "French-looking" town also on the Wabash, but different from Terre Haute, Dreiser remembered, with its cobblestone "streets narrow and winding, the French love of red and white predominating."

Here, to save money, the Dreiser foursome moved in with a woman later remembered as "Sue Bellette," whom Sarah had befriended in Terre Haute when the French orphan worked there as a seamstress. Now Madame Bellette was married to the fire chief of Vincennes and lived above the firehouse, where there also was room for the Dreisers. Apparently, at the behest of influential town leaders who could insure his continued employment, the fire chief had allowed prostitutes to visit his fire station's bunk rooms during the wee hours, for trysts with the local politicians or firemen. After his marriage, he determined to stop the practice, but Sue, having been birthed if not brought up by a French prostitute—so Dreiser's mother later told him—"would have none of it." Sarah soon quarreled with her former protégée over the immoral situation and departed with her children in tow after only five weeks—but not before young Theo, "being a restless, early-rising child," one morning saw "one of these daughters of desire, a corn-haired blonde, her pink face buried in a curled arm, lying on the bed allotted to one of the firemen serving on the night shift."[17]

Sarah took the children to Sullivan, a town that mixed family memories good and bad, since it was here that John Paul had enjoyed his only clear success, as a mill owner in the late 1860s, and here that he had failed once and for all with the mill fire and his head injury. To make that memory even more bitter, there now stood prospering in place of John Paul's shattered dream another mill built exactly like the first. Parts of the town, however, were shabby and run down, and unlike Terre Haute and Vincennes, the Wabash did not grace the town, only a creek called the Busseron. Dreiser found the place far less interesting than Vincennes.[18]

Initially, Sarah moved in with the family of Thomas Bulger, an Irishman who had known John Paul when he owned his mill there. Like the senior Dreiser, Bulger was, in Dreiser's words, "a priest-ridden Catholic," with a wayward son who wasn't as lucky as the initially wayward Paul Dresser. By the turn of the century, Jimmy Bulger would become a bank robber. He was convicted of murder for killing a man during a holdup in Cobleskill, New York, and was executed in 1903 at Dannemora Prison under the name of "Whitey" Sullivan (called "'Red' Sullivan" in *Dawn*). On the morning he was led to the electric chair, Dreiser later recalled, "he confessed his evil ways, received communion, and so, if we believe the noble religionists, passed pure and regenerate, into the presence of his Maker!" Perhaps some of Dreiser's pity for the young Irishman as well as his rage against the Church bled into his sympathetic depiction of Clyde Griffiths, the convicted murderer in *An American Tragedy* (1925), whose father, Asa, is also a religious zealot.[19]

After a week or two with the Bulgers, Sarah found "a small white five- or six-room house" in the northeast corner of Sullivan near the railroad yard and round house of the E. & T.H., a line that ran between Evansville and Terre Haute. The rent was seven dollars a month for a shabby, somewhat run-down place with no furnishings. It bordered on a large vegetable garden, which Dreiser and his mother began to cultivate. Later, income was derived from renting rooms to railroad and mine workers, although some of them skipped out without paying during particularly hard economic times. Dreiser also remembered helping Ed and Claire pick up spilled pieces of coal from the nearby train tracks in order to heat their home. Sarah and the three children remained in Sullivan for the next two or three years, with occasional (and at times disruptive) visits from John Paul. After a year, the older sisters were in frequent rebellion against their Terre Haute existence under the father's watchful eye. Despite his fierce religiosity and his fear for his family's reputation, John Paul's influence over family matters waned with his diminished ability to contribute to his family's upkeep.

It was in the Sullivan house that Dreiser adopted his mother's practice of retreating to a rocking chair to think and to dream. All the rest of his life the rocker was his favorite chair. In the early morning, he rocked and sang to himself or hummed while looking out at the trees and birds. This future chronicler of the snares of the city had his fertile imagination first stimulated through an early and intense appreciation of nature. He took long and solitary walks. "At first," he recorded in *Dawn,* "my mother could not understand why I wished to be so much alone or why my aloneness should require such exaggerated periods of time, although she never suspected mischief in my case and later told me so. I was just odd, she said, different."[20] One day, he followed a bumblebee all the way across a wheat field, tracking it from flower to flower. On other days, he observed a wasps' nest under an eave, fish in the water, and finally at night a bat hanging upside down. He began to ponder the strangeness of life.

It was also in Sullivan that the boy first discovered literature. Readers of Dreiser's deterministic fiction such as *Sister Carrie* and *An American Tragedy* will be surprised to learn that his first literary influences were the romantic ones of Washington Irving, Nathaniel Hawthorne, and Ralph Waldo Emerson. They might be equally surprised to know that the first book to influence this impoverished son of America was not by Karl Marx, but Thomas E. Hill: *Hill's Manual of Social and Business Forms,* first published in 1878 and in successive editions thereafter. Billed as a "Guide to Correct Writing," it was a veritable almanac and encyclopedia on the subject of success in postbellum America. Ever since the New England lyceum movement before the Civil War, Americans had been encouraged to educate themselves on proper decorum and diction in a new and promising republic. Self-help books and pamphlets abounded, advising, for example, young apprentices not to smell their meat at the dinner table before consuming it. The emphasis was upon helping oneself up the ladder of success through good manners and textbook locution, a far cry from the illicit behavior and colloquial diction of Dreiser's hard-boiled heroes and heroines.

Dreiser remembered the *Manual*'s peddler, a "Professor Solax," perhaps the first model for Charles Drouet, the traveling salesman in *Sister Carrie*. "A small, trig, dandified man," the professor wore "a cutaway coat and high silk hat, with shoebrush whiskers and Jovian curls." The bulky book cost a whopping $3.50, but the Dreisers got their copy in exchange for the drummer's room and board while he sold his product to others in search of the American Dream around the shabby village of Sullivan. This living arrangement came about because of the professor's interest in Dreiser's sister Sylvia, who had come to Sullivan to escape her father. The attention this nubile adolescent paid the middle-aged dandy alarmed Mrs. Dreiser, who pleaded with her daughter to keep "her place." Later, Dreiser learned that "she and the Professor had often met outside, and finally he begged her to run away with him." She didn't, Dreiser later recalled, because "she feared that he had a wife somewhere (by this time this had come to mean an obstacle to her) and she did not go."[21]

Dreiser never forgot *Hill's Manual,* respectfully dedicated "To the Millions who would, and may, easily and gracefully express the Right Thought." He and Tillie (as Claire now preferred to be called) fought over it, both of them in search of the right thought and the right sound. The "leather portfolio" had pictures of model penmanship, the proper sitting positions while writing, poems, demographic charts, samples of all kinds of letters, including one "To a Young Man Addicted to Intemperance," and love letters. "Of all letters," this future serial lover of women and lifelong writer of love letters to them no doubt read in the section on "Letters of Love," "the love-letter should be the most carefully prepared" because it is the "most thoroughly read and re-read, the longest preserved, and the most likely to be regretted in after life." Further, the book offered advice on how to hold a knife and fork at meals and the proper way to eat soup ("Darksome mysteries all at the time, and since," Dreiser remembered). Interestingly, it also included an illustrated section on the "Etiquette of Traveling" on trains, which is where Dreiser met his first wife and Drouet meets Carrie.[22]

The Dreisers' last winter in Sullivan was difficult. With renters running off without paying, the boardinghouse venture finally failed. Sarah feared eviction. To make matters worse, in January or February of 1882, John Paul Dreiser was out of work again, and his daughters gradually abandoned their jobs as housemaids for selected Catholic families in Terre Haute. In fact, three of the four had come to Sarah for motherly relief, especially from their father's endless, and evidently self-defeating, lectures about attending Mass and avoiding temptation. Sylvia had been soon followed by Emma, who eventually went to live with brother Al, now in Chicago. Finally, Mame arrived in the family way after a brief affair with an older man in Terre Haute. "Colonel Silsby" (as he would be immortalized in Dreiser's autobiography) had given her his blessing and directions to the nearest country doctor who performed abortions. The doctor, it turned out, had died years before. Sarah delivered the child, a boy who lived not an hour. "While I was almost unconscious," Mame told her brother many years later, "Mother took it and buried it at the side of the house quite deep down where it still lies."[23]

Just when it looked as if there were nowhere to turn, Paul, now successful as a "strolling minstrel" and songwriter, reappeared to save the day. Dreiser later recalled that when he thought of Paul, he thought of Thomas Gray's lines in "Elegy Written in a Country Churchyard" about the "unknown Miltons and Caesars" who were missed by fortune or fate. For the dedicated determinist who believed that everyone possessed a "chemism," a term invented by the pseudoscientists of his day to describe the ratio between will and instinct in a particular personality, Paul "was one of those great Falstaffian souls who, for lack of a little iron or sodium or carbon dioxide in his chemical compost, was not able to bestride the world like a Colossus." When he returned to help the family, Paul was twenty-four and the author of *The Paul Dresser Songster* (he had changed his name to "Dresser" because it was suitable to his stage life: it was more pronounceable and less revealing of his first-generation German-American immigrant heritage, which remained quite disparaged in that day). The gaudy ten-cent pamphlet of comic songs even featured the ebullient lyricist's picture on the cover.

Paul was Santa Claus to the eleven-year-old Dreiser and his family. He heaped cash on his mother for rent and food as well as clothing for his youngest siblings, who often had been sent home from school because they had no shoes. Paul was a welcome contrast to the wandering Rome, who came home occasionally but seldom brought anything but need and usually disappeared once he had satisfied himself and exhausted the family with tales of his pointless explorations around the nation. Paul, on the other hand, delivered more goods than even his father could supply. Sarah was his magnet, and, according to Dreiser, Paul's "loving, helpful arms" never failed to come to her support from that time until her death.

Paul left after a few days, but plans were set in motion for a more permanent kind of help. Sarah and her three youngest children would remove to Evansville, a largely German-American town on the Ohio River. Here, Paul would soon be living and working at the Apollo Theater. First, his current girlfriend, Anna Winter (alias Sallie Walker, the actual namesake for "My Gal Sal," and called Annie Brace in the published version of *Dawn*), visited the family briefly in Sullivan. Twenty-seven or twenty-eight and "very dark as to hair and eyes," Anna quickly charmed Sarah with the happy expectation that her eldest son had finally found a good girl and might settle down.

Eagerly, Sarah and her brood moved to Evansville in May. Going from a town of twenty-two hundred to one of thirty thousand was a big change for the family. Sarah set up housekeeping in a brick cottage in the midst of the bustling burg at 1415 East Franklin Street. What she may not have known, not at the outset certainly, was that Anna, who regularly sent the family groceries, was not exactly the good girl she had hoped but in fact ran one of Evansville's more upscale whorehouses. Once again, a prostitute had entered the life of the impressionable Theo—and his mother. Yet when Sarah learned the truth this time, she did not take the evasive action she had in Vincennes. Although she was aware of the benefits of keeping on the right side of society, there was also a wild streak in this woman, who after all had run away from her Mennonite parents to marry a Catholic, whose rigid views she would eventually resist. She might sigh and cry over the failures of her children, but she never blamed them, because she believed they couldn't help themselves in a world of uncontrollable circumstances. When they reached adulthood, she never pried into their affairs, and so Paul's arrangement with his "Gal Sal" was at least tolerated or politely overlooked.

The Evansville house Paul found for them (and where he paid the rent) was far and away superior to their austere accommodations in Sullivan. Unlike the drafty, empty house there that had had to be furnished with discarded furniture, this one was more completely and comfortably appointed. "No shabby makeshifts and leavings here, as at Sullivan," Dreiser fondly remembered in *Dawn*. "Instead, in the dining-room a shining new table with a complete set of chairs, and in the parlor, not only parlor furniture but a piano! . . . Quite like one who has seen a fairy wave her wand and work a miracle, stood my mother, looking at it all from first one doorway and then another. And behind her, patting her shoulder, because she was crying, my brother Paul."[24] Paul, the sentimental songmaker, was crying, too.

If the young Dreiser's lot was improved at home, he still had to contend with the parochial schools. Evansville had three prosperous German Catholic churches. Its adjacent parochial schools, however, were austere and overcrowded. And here too German, not English, was taught; boys and girls were instructed separately. The boys' education was largely the responsibility of one Ludwig von Valkenburg, who was also the church organist and all-around factotum. Over him and the school stood the Reverend Anton Dudenhausen. "Stout, pompous, aggressive," Dreiser remembered, perhaps with some hyperbole, "this priest had the presence and solidity of a ferocious bull. The mere sight of him terrified me, so much so that when he was anywhere near . . . I lost all self-possession and stood agape, wondering what terror, punishment or deprivation might not be in preparation."[25] Younger brother Ed, too, hated the school, possibly even more than Theo. At first, he refused to enter the schoolhouse.

Despite these schoolroom horrors, Theo, Ed, and Tillie apparently got on well enough. This wing of the Dreiser family, headed by the indefatigable Sarah, lived in Evansville for one year, until the early summer of 1883. Then, some months before their departure, word leaked to Sarah's Evansville neighbors that Paul's girlfriend was connected to a house of ill repute, thereby socially stigmatizing the other Dreisers. As if this whiff of scandal were not enough, the itinerant and pugnacious Rome rolled into Evansville, showing the wear and tear of his latest debaucheries. Finding that Paul was well-respected, at least among saloon types, he bragged of his sibling connection, borrowed money from Paul's friends that he did not repay, got into drunken brawls, and finally landed in the Evansville jail. At about the same time, Paul contracted syphilis, possibly from one of Anna's girls, and turned to his mother for help. "I recall his coming to my mother and weeping over his condition and her advising that they offer up masses to God and prayers to St. Joseph and the Virgin Mary accompanied by flowers in order that he might be speedily cured," Dreiser wrote in a passage that was later excised from *Dawn*.[26] Paul and Anna broke up that spring, mainly because of his dalliances with her employees, and the Dreiser household in Evansville broke up with it.

With nowhere else to go, Sarah moved to Chicago, where the nineteen-year-old Theresa had a third-floor walk-up of six rooms at West Madison and Throop streets. Before long, John Paul, once again or still unemployed, had joined them, along with Mame and Emma, while Paul went back on the road, with either another minstrel show or a theatrical group. Chicago had a population of more than a half-million and was just becoming the great metropolis of the Midwest when the future author of urban realism got his first look at it. Dreiser, raised in mostly German communities, had never before encountered such ethnic diversity. Their Chicago neighborhood counted first-generation immigrants from just about everywhere—Germans, Swedes, Czechs, Poles, and Irish. At first Theo found a job as a cash boy in a store; then he and Ed worked as newsboys for the summer, but Sarah ultimately decided that Chicago was not affordable or right for her three youngest children and packed them up to move back to Indiana.

It was during this brief stay in Chicago, however, that the twelve-year-old Theo first came to appreciate his father. It had been four or five years since Dreiser had actually lived with his father for any length of time, and as a result, the boy was well on his way to becoming a "lapsed Catholic." (He was still in his middle teens when he made his last confession.)[27] But in spite of John Paul's fanatical devotion to the Church, he now struck his son as sincere, honest, and intelligent, as well as clever in his assessments of and remarks about their neighbors. In addition, for the first time Dreiser felt sorry for his father, not only as a dupe of Catholicism but—and worse—as a victim in so-called democratic America of economic forces beyond his control. Later, while writing *Dawn,* he suspected that his father had been clinically depressed.

The adolescent Dreiser also became more acutely aware of the opposite sex at this time. Looking back on his pubescence from middle age, he confessed that "for the second, third and fourth decades of my life—or from fifteen to thirty-five—there appeared to be a toxic something in form itself—that of the female of the species where beautiful—that could effect veritable paroxysms of emotion and desire in me." His experience in Chicago was tentative, however. He became interested in a girl on his block—"a gay, shapely, buxom, young hoyden of perhaps ten or twelve."[28] But before he could get anywhere with the girl, a rival cornered him and struck him, cutting his lip. Dreiser was not a strong youth, tall and gangling, then neither physically nor temperamentally able to defend himself, and so he retreated. Afterward, he was enraged and mortified, at both his attacker and his helplessness to defend himself.

In September of 1883, the Hoosier odyssey of Dreiser's youth and adolescence took him to Warsaw, in the northeastern part of the state, not far from where Sarah's brother and his family lived. Thirty-five miles to the east lay the city of Fort Wayne, where Dreiser's parents had lived as newlyweds. Warsaw had several lakes, and two of them—Center and Pike—came close enough to shape some of its street configurations. The town's many venues for boating, fishing, and swimming made it a popular summer resort. Dreiser remembered Warsaw—where he lived between the ages of thirteen and sixteen—as "one of the most agreeable minor residence towns" he had ever known. The Kosciusko County courthouse, a magnificent structure of native sandstone towering 160 feet and topped with a square clock tower with faces on all four sides, stood at the center of a public square bounded by Main, Buffalo, Center, and Lake streets. Later, Dreiser recalled how charmed he had always been by the scene, especially the sound of the great bell in the clock tower. Two blocks down Buffalo Street stood Center Lake, with "a handsome boat-house offering all manner of small boats for hire."[29] His mother's parents, aunts, or uncles had lived in the vicinity, and his mother even owned several acres of land somehow left to her by her estranged parents. For the first time in his life, Dreiser felt that he and his siblings *belonged* somewhere.

One clear improvement in Warsaw was that Dreiser got to attend public school for the first time. As ever, John Paul had insisted on a Catholic education, but this time Sarah stood up for her children on the issue. As a Catholic convert (a fact her son played down in his memoirs) she had originally supported her husband on this choice. But his financial failure in Sullivan and their subsequent hard times had gradually worn down her religious allegiance; by the time she and the three children left Chicago for Warsaw, she was closer to the "pagan" Dreiser liked to remember. They were no longer going to pay for an inferior school, Sarah now asserted, when they could get a superior one for free. In fact, the public school was right next to the house they rented after discovering their first choice was next door to—yes—prostitutes. Instead of the grim welcome of a nun looking to discipline him, Dreiser found a pretty young woman of twenty. And he found for the first time a curriculum devoid of what he considered to be the superstition of the Roman Catholic Church. Instead of medieval warnings about how either the Jews or all non-Catholics were going to hell, he was ushered into the secular world of learning, including American literature, which until the rise of Theodore Dreiser was essentially a Protestant literature produced by writers of English stock. From his "plump, rosy, fairhaired" young teacher, the future author formally met Nathaniel Hawthorne, Ralph Waldo Emerson, William Cullen Bryant, John Greenleaf

Whittier, Henry Wadsworth Longfellow, Washington Irving, James Fenimore Cooper, William Dean Howells, and—Dreiser's lifelong favorite—Edgar Allan Poe.[30]

Theodore's grades for 1883 were in the middle B range. The record for his first year at West Ward Public School No. 4 reveals that he was best at reading (94.3 percent), geography (92 percent), and writing (87 percent). He was less than a B student in mathematics (77 percent), spelling (78 percent), and grammar (79 percent). His school attendance was regular, and his deportment was "good." Ed's grades were slightly lower; his overall average for the 1885–86 school year was 80 percent—though he excelled in math with a 96 percent.[31]

In recalling the names of the American writers of the Romantic era he had read, Dreiser thought that for all his "modest repute as a realist, I seem . . . somewhat more of a romanticist than a realist."[32] In fact, Dreiser in his literary maturity was both, in a blending of the ideas of the nineteenth and twentieth centuries. As his final philosophy suggests, evidenced in the material that was posthumously organized and published as his *Notes on Life* (1974), he and his fictional extensions lived in a world whose universal beauty was also a form of terror to the individual. Critiques of Dreiser's work usually focus on its Darwinian determinism, in which people are whisked along by the forces of heredity and environment. Or—as lately—it is seen psychologically, since it begins properly with the beginning of the twentieth century and eventually the age of Freud. But Dreiser had his beginnings in the age of Emerson and its nineteenth-century essentialist claims for an ordered universe, instead of the accidental, relativistic universe of many twentieth-century intellectuals. His first heroine, Carrie Meeber of *Sister Carrie,* goes where her predecessors in American literature do not in terms of breaking social taboos about marriage and the place of the woman. Yet at the end of her story, there is the same Romantic desire for a more ordered, even logocentric world in which the human condition has a happy ending, qualified though that desire may be by a sense that ultimately it never can be satisfied.

———

It may have been Poe's claim that every great work of art is about the death of a beautiful woman that inspired Dreiser to see the "formula (female)" as symbolizing the last trace of the possibility of total fulfillment. Personally, he confessed, it had led him to "the invasion of homes, the destruction of happy arrangements among others, lies, persuasions, this, that. In short, thus moved, I have adored until satiated, so satiated, indeed, as to turn betimes in weariness, even disgust, and so fleeing."[33] Like Poe, Dreiser was always in search of the woman who could love him as much as he remembered his mother had, and this led him, as he freely admitted, through the life of an emotional nomad.

This ideal woman had to embody the flesh and the spirit in the roles of lover and teacher. His mother had been his first "lover," and his first wife (also named Sara, without the "h") was a schoolteacher. (His later lovers began almost exclusively as literary admirers and became in many cases his editors and typists.) The first teacher to touch his heart, and perhaps his libido, however, was his first public school instructor, a young divorced woman named May Calvert. Dreiser spells her name "Mae" in *A Hoosier Holiday* (1916), a nostalgic account of a visit to the state in 1915. When he returned to Warsaw and entered his old schoolhouse, which he was amazed to find still standing, he was haunted by the sounds and sights of his first year in a public school and especially the memory of May.

"You see," he wrote, "hitherto, I had been trained in a Catholic school . . . and the process had proved most depressing—black garbed, straight laced nuns. But here in this warm, friendly room, with girls who were attractive and boys who were for the larger part genial and companionable, and with a teacher who took an interest in me, I felt as though I were in a kind of school paradise." By the time of his return to Warsaw, he had been mistakenly told that May Calvert had died, and that belief merely served to fortify his memory of the "blooming girl" who "at that time seemed one of the most entrancing creatures in all the world." He remembered her deep-blue eyes, light-brown hair, and "rounded, healthy, vigorous body," along with the fact that in her class he had sat in the fifth seat from the front in the second row from the west side of the room.[34]

Sometimes the young teacher would pinch the young man's cheek or even run her hands through his dark hair, as we learn in *Dawn*, where her name is spelled correctly as "May." Dreiser also hinted in *Dawn* that this handsome young woman of twenty came close to crossing the line in her encouragement. Toward the end of the year, while he was reading aloud after school a passage from Irving's "The Legend of Sleepy Hollow," she praised the performance. Flushed and drawn to this woman, he wanted to hold her, but did not dare. She put her hand on his shoulder, then around his waist. (This last detail was removed when the manuscript of *Dawn* was edited for publication.) "I snuggled up to her, because I thought she was lovely," he admitted. (But for all her charms and her young pupil's already evident skill in writing, she failed to impart the basic rules of spelling and punctuation, skills Dreiser would never master.)

Interestingly, another female in that classroom to fascinate him was a "Cad" Tuttle. In the holograph of *Dawn,* she is Carrie Rutter, whose "full brown eyes and rounded chin and heavy, shapely neck were richly sensuous." Perhaps this young lady also contributed to one of the classics of American literature. In *Sister Carrie,* Drouet refers to Carrie as "Cad." (Dreiser also remembered other attractive females in the class, sometimes cynically. There was Maud Rutter, Carrie's sister, "soft and plump and blonde, the type sure to be fat at forty.")[35]

Lustful as his thoughts sometimes were, he was still shy around girls. He occasionally stuttered in their company and generally thought himself unattractive to the opposite sex. (When he was an adult, some women described him as ugly.) He suspected in surer moods that his sense of inadequacy might be a reaction to the beating he had taken in Chicago. May Calvert probably sensed his shyness and took advantage of it. Dreiser's own initiative in this regard was to masturbate, in spite of both the Catholic proscription against such "self-abuse" and the medical myths about the practice.

Dreiser claimed that he first found a partner in sex one April evening in Warsaw. The anecdote is not in the holograph of *Dawn,* but appears in both its first typescript and the published volume.[36] Dreiser was around fourteen and his alleged partner fourteen or fifteen, a stocky baker's daughter of some "mid-European" background, definitely lower on the Warsaw social register than the girls he described from Miss Calvert's class. One day when he found her alone at the bakery, one playful remark led to another until she dared Dreiser to catch her as she ran out of the store and down a nearby alley. He caught up with her in a secluded area, they stumbled, and he found the girl underneath him. She continued to lead the way by helping him unbutton his trousers. After a fit of Catholic guilt and fear of eternal damnation if he died before going to confession, he also brooded on just what kind of girl she was. Obviously, she was not "a good girl," but one of the type his father, if not his mother, had warned him to avoid. In addition, this first-generation American thought her parents "common— restaurant-keepers, bakers, foreigners."[37] Once his sense of guilt had passed, he turned to the more practical fear that the girl had given him a sexually transmitted disease.

Soon Dreiser had found his first real girlfriend—Myrtle Weimar ("Trego" in the published version of *Dawn*), a dark-haired beauty whose father owned one of the two or three drugstores (and soda fountains) in town. The thought of being near her or perhaps kissing her during a game of Post Office at an upcoming party sent him into a paroxysm of sexual fantasy. Yet even deep in the throes of first love, he was also keenly aware of other pretty girls in May Calvert's classroom. Sex, he was beginning to realize, was not the same as love. The search for female love, true love or the surrogate for mother love, he would later conclude, was for him almost always somehow the search for sex.

Following his great discovery of books, as well as sex, in May Calvert's seventh-grade class, Dreiser began to realize that he was no longer the boy he had been in Evansville. He read constantly and began to articulate his feelings and observations. His family also soon sensed his intellectual superiority—perhaps astonished by his near-photographic memory. His father in particular seemed to detect the subtle changes in his son's development during his infrequent visits from Terre Haute. John Paul "authorized" the purchase of cheap sets of the works of Washington Irving, and soon thereafter agreed to similar acquisitions of Dickens, Thackeray, and Scott. Not even May Calvert's disappointing successor at Warsaw Central High, "a stern, dark, sallow woman" named Luella Reid, could dampen Theodore's interest in books and the worlds they opened to him.

Freed from the limitations of parochial schools, he and his youngest sister and brother seemed to flourish, although Ed, according to Dreiser, was not much of a reader outside of class. They had gotten to where they could sidestep their gypsy lifestyle and make some claim to respectability, an image Sarah dearly wanted, at least for her younger children. The older siblings, however, frequently threatened to shatter this image with visits from a disheveled Rome or the unwanted pregnancy of one or another of her older daughters. Furthermore, it was about this time that Emma became involved with L. A. Hopkins, a married man who worked in Chapin & Gore's saloon on the South Side of Chicago.

Hopkins and Emma planned to run away together, and to finance this, Hopkins stole $3,500 and some jewelry from the safe of the saloon. Before they could flee, his suspicious wife hired a Pinkerton detective and eventually surprised the couple in bed. Caught in the act, Hopkins exclaimed, according to the *Chicago Mail* of February 17, 1886, "My God! ma . . . is that you!"[38] The news of this adultery easily reached Warsaw, where the Chicago papers were read more than the local ones. To make matters worse, because Mame and Sylvia were acquainted with Hopkins through Emma, Mrs. Hopkins initially implicated them with Emma in snaring a married man.

Either Dreiser or his editors excised this information from the autobiography, along with the fact that Hopkins—like George Hurstwood of *Sister Carrie,* who steals from his employers' safe after it is too late to replace the money—was driven to his crime both by "semi-intoxication" and "his exceeding passion" for another woman. In this sense, both men steal by "accident." Hopkins had been a faithful employee of the saloon for many years and was about forty when he fled Chicago with the stolen money and his paramour Emma, who like Carrie was initially tricked into running away with her lover. Hopkins and Emma also ended up living together in New York.[39]

Dreiser's father, if he ever heard the full story of Emma's alliance with Hopkins, would have been outraged, but Sarah and her partial family had already suffered enough without his patriarchal rancor and managed to keep the details from him. Once again, as in Evansville, the family's hard-won cover of respectability had been ripped away. To reduce their sense of shame, Mame and Theresa asserted that Emma (described in one newspaper account of the theft as "a dashing blond [*sic*], with an abundance of auburn hair and good features") had married Hopkins. Although Emma was never directly implicated in the theft, certainly she was singled out as the woman who broke up Hopkins's marriage and the reason he stole.

Then Sylvia, who was living in Warsaw, got pregnant. Her lover and the father-to-be was remembered in *Dawn* as Don Ashley, the son of a Warsaw solid citizen, and a womanizer. His good looks and social position had swept Sylvia off her feet, and Sarah may have hoped for a connection to Warsaw respectability through Ashley. Anxious that her children do better in life than she had, she was as easily fooled by Ashley as Sylvia was. One day, she even permitted Sylvia to entertain her young man at home without a proper chaperone. When confronted months later with the news of her pregnancy, the wily seducer quickly left town on the false promise to send for her when it was financially feasible. Sylvia briefly contemplated an abortion, but their family doctor and a friend of the Ashley family lectured her about "duty and virtue," while saying nothing about young Ashley's duty except to label him a scamp.[40] (This family episode no doubt influenced Dreiser in the writing of the scene in *An American Tragedy* where Roberta Alden is similarly lectured by a doctor who performs abortions for more socially prominent citizens.) Later, when it became clear that Ashley was never to be seen again, Paul Dresser returned on one of his saving visits, though this time the family spirits were resistant to the usual effect of his glorious descents. It may have struck poor Sylvia as wickedly ironic—surely it did her precocious brother Theo—that Paul was now famous for the song, "The Letter That Never Came."

Sylvia was mortified and angry. She may have tried to abort her fetus with various medicines, a vial of which her prying brother Theo had found hidden in one of her bureau drawers. Like Mame when she was threatened with becoming an involuntary mother, Sylvia had hidden the fact from her parents as long as she could. When the secret was finally out, Sarah—to avoid the raised eyebrows and stares of her Warsaw neighbors—quickly sent her daughter to New York, where Sylvia waited out her pregnancy at Emma's flat on West Fifteenth Street. The infant, who was named Carl Dreiser, was soon sent to Warsaw because Sylvia did not want him. Dreiser remembered the five-month-old's "endless care." The man who would remain childless never forgot the infant's "constant wailing" and the many hours he had been assigned to "'mind' it." The family pretended to neighbors that the child was just another belated sibling, but their ears were burning with their neighbors' gossip. Later, Dreiser described his nephew as "an extremely sensitive and ruminative child whose life was darkened by an intense and almost pathologic desire for affection which he never received" from his mother.[41] Around the same time, a third daughter, Theresa, broke up with her lover and arrived in Warsaw in tears. She, at least, had not become pregnant.

When Dreiser was in ninth grade, Sarah moved her enlarged family across the street to a brick house of fourteen or fifteen rooms known as "Thrall's House." Although it had ample room, it had no indoor plumbing, merely an outhouse covered over with grapevines. Even though John Paul was working and contributing what he could afford, there simply wasn't enough money coming in. Having to support unwed daughters, however temporarily, and occasionally having to host the unwelcome Rome, Sarah found it necessary to find cheaper quarters and more space. Yet the house had a garden and fruit trees, and young Dreiser, lost in his own adolescent world of romance and reading, absolutely loved living there. At least he remembered it that way in *Dawn*.

At this time Dreiser encountered another teacher who was to stand out in his memory. Tall, gangling, and with protruding teeth, Mildred Fielding had grown up as poor as her student in the mill town of Malden, Massachusetts, but had managed to escape the poverty of her youth and become a teacher. At thirty-five or so, she was unmarried and considered in those days "an old maid." Whereas the already divorced May Calvert may have been physically, as well as pedagogically, attracted to Dreiser, Mildred Fielding was more professional in her attentions and perhaps even more insightful in detecting her student's extraordinary talent. Having come from an unstable family herself, she could empathize with Dreiser about his embarrassment over family scandals. One day, she pulled him aside and told him, "I can see that you are not like the other boys and girls here. You are different, Theodore. Very sensitive. Your mind is very different."[42] She warned him not to become distracted by the petty gossip of Warsaw society, which sometimes targeted Sarah and her family—advice that no doubt contributed to Dreiser's later disregard for social standards when it came to his private life or sexual behavior.

Miss Fielding was not alone in perceiving Dreiser's difference from the other students. "A small paper I wrote in our literature class—a description of a local scene—brought me direct encomiums," he remembered. He was even encouraged by the superintendent of schools in Warsaw, "a lean, pedagogic, temperamental and enthusiastic man" who advised him to read Shakespeare. Miss Fielding also encouraged his hunger to learn, which far surpassed her other students' willingness to study for the usual social rewards. Like most great artists, his genius consisted of being a generalist about life. "Life," he said, "did not appeal to me so much on its technical or purely structural and trade aspects as it did on its general forms and surface appearances." He was made, he thought, to be a general, albeit close, observer of life—"of the form and motion of things, their effect upon and import to the individual as well as society at large."[43] Yet it was not until many years later that he even dreamed of becoming a writer. In the long interlude, he fretted over his lack of a particular skill or talent with which to support himself.

Despite the fact that Dreiser's reputation for being somehow gifted now went beyond the family and was even acknowledged by his peers at school, he decided to quit and go to work. Without influential family connections in a small town such as Warsaw, however, his chances for success in any line of business were sharply limited. Furthermore, his family's dubious reputation wouldn't have helped advance him locally. To escape his family's poverty and tarnished name, he felt compelled to strike out on his own. He was already heated up by the American Dream of success, the reward for anyone in America willing to work hard and be good. (In fact, he first hired himself out to a farmer, but the work was too exhausting for someone accustomed to heavy reading and only light physical labor.) Some of his friends were already heading out for new opportunities in Chicago and elsewhere. Restless and tired of the small-town feel of Warsaw, as he tells it in *Dawn,* one day he announced, "Ma, I am going to Chicago."

Although initially shocked by his plan, his mother had always been temperamentally in favor of change, probably because her life had been so difficult. But when she reassured him that he could always come back, he responded, without any reason for certainty, that he would never return. In *Sister Carrie,* Caroline Meeber at about the same age makes a similar leap into the abyss as she boards a train from Columbia City, Wisconsin, bound for Chicago. (Dreiser probably had in mind Columbia City, Indiana, about twenty-five miles southeast of Warsaw.) For his return to Chicago in 1887, Dreiser boarded the nonfictional train at Warsaw and began again in the same urban wilderness that greets Carrie.

TWO

A Very Bard of a City

*Here was the Negro, the prostitute, the blackleg, the gambler,
the romantic* par excellence.

THE TITAN

WHEN DREISER RETURNED TO CHICAGO in the summer of 1887, he found a city that stretched north and south for twenty-four miles along Lake Michigan and westward from the lake over almost ten miles of potential and half-completed development. Cable cars already served this urban frontier while New York City, its rival, still depended on horse-drawn public transportation. The cable car system was almost single-handedly the work of Charles Tyson Yerkes, the "Cable Czar" who became the model for Frank Algernon Cowperwood in Dreiser's "Trilogy of Desire"—of which *The Financier* (1912) and *The Titan* (1914) brought that most appropriate American tradition known as the "business novel" to its apex. Chicago was also the home of such post–Civil War moguls as George Mortimer Pullman, Philip Danforth Armour, Gustavus Franklin Swift, Marshall Field, Richard Warren Sears, and Aaron Montgomery Ward. Their conspicuous success and social doings, well chronicled in the society pages, hypnotized midwestern America and helped import the American Dream of success from the northeast.

"Before I was out of my teens," Dreiser recalled in a 1929 biographical sketch, "the entire country suddenly awoke to a consciousness of its vast resources." Those waking up to the opportunities of Dreiser's Midwest were the sons and daughters of immigrants, fellow first-generation Americans to whom, he said, "Europe was only an intangible memory referred to by their fathers as 'the old country.'" They found themselves in the grip of "an almost universal desire for material betterment [that] swept the land, one of its manifestations being an influx from the country towns and villages to the cities."[1] And the main city that drew them was Chicago, reborn out of the ashes of the Great Fire of 1871, the same year Dreiser was born.

Chicago at the end of the nineteenth century was a city of contrasts. This home to millionaires also housed some of the worst slums in the nation. Three-fourths of Chicago's residents were immigrants or children of immigrants, most of whom lived in rundown dwellings overcrowded with extended families. Beautiful parks and wide, tree-lined boulevards may have graced parts of the city, but many of its commercial and residential streets were littered with horse manure and, frequently, dead dray animals. Few streets were paved, and most were edged with boardwalk-like structures that in places rose to a hazardous curb several feet above the street. Chicago had a saloon on almost every corner and the second largest distilling industry in the country, even as it was fast becoming the temperance capital of the nation. (The lake city was home to both the evangelist Dwight L. Moody and Women's Christian Temperance Union president Frances E. Willard.)[2] Prostitution thrived throughout the city with the help of a bribed police force.

As the young Dreiser's train reached the South Side of the city, "with its sudden smudge of factory life against the great plains," his car filled to standing-room capacity with laborers making their morning migration. The tranquillity of his ride from Warsaw, during which he had indulged himself in visions of success and prosperity, was instantly overtaken by the clatter of Italians, Germans, Poles, and Czechs speaking their different native tongues and polluting the air of the car with vile-smelling pipes. He felt suddenly inducted into this army of toilers, if only until the train reached its final destination. With only a few dollars and one bag containing "a single change of underwear and socks," his own prospects in Chicago seemed limited. Yet as he stepped off the train, the gritty grandness of the city beckoned. "In me are all the pulses and wonders and tastes and loves of life itself!" he remembered in *Dawn*. "I am life! This is paradise!"[3]

"Paradise" soon consisted of a dollar-fifty-a-week front bedroom in a rooming house on West Madison Street, not far from where the family had lived in Chicago years before, and a job as a dishwasher at five dollars a week in a nearby Greek restaurant run by one John Paradiso. The neighborhood around it at Halstead Street near Van Buren pulsated with life—though there were also the lifeless, left lingering in its streets and alleys.

Dreiser was fascinated with its vitality and variety—its street markets and streetwalkers, its shoppers and malingerers side by side in the surge of big city life. The unglamorous little restaurant in which he worked three meals a day, seven days a week, was dirty and "fly-specked," with low ceilings and three rows of tables lining a rectangular room. Although his sisters Theresa and Mame and his brother Al were already sharing an apartment in Chicago, Dreiser—who liked his brothers and sisters "fairly well according to their merits as individuals, but never more so"—was determined, at least at first, to make it on his own, even in the heat of July in a smoky kitchen.[4]

One day in August, however, Theo finally decided to pay a visit to his siblings. He found only Theresa at home; Al was temporarily working in Milwaukee, and Mame, who had taken up with a man named Austin Brennan and was now supposedly married to him, was away for the summer. Theresa herself indicated she felt like visiting her mother in Warsaw—but at that moment Sarah, along with what grown children still clung to her for emotional support, was probably already on her way to Chicago. By September most of the Dreiser clan, including Theo and John Paul, had assembled in multiple rooms on Ogden Avenue near Robey Street.

Young Dreiser, now turning seventeen, was embarrassed to tell his family that he worked in a lowly Greek restaurant washing dishes, so he told them he was employed in a fashionable haberdasher's shop on Halstead Street that (like the restaurant) was open on Sundays.[5] Eventually, he quit that job for one with an enterprise that cleaned and repaired stoves. The work was hard and dirty and required heavy lifting; he lasted only one day. Next he worked briefly for Ed Davis, a "literary-minded" painter of background scenery for photographers—and the beau of his sister Theresa. This job didn't last long either (mainly because Theo talked too much; his more stolid brother Ed replaced him), but recognizing his interest in books, Davis recommended Christopher Marlowe and Walt Whitman, two writers Dreiser admitted he came to appreciate only "years later."[6]

Al, who had returned to Chicago to join the family, but lost the job he had found in a hardware store, was also looking for work at this time, and the two Dreiser boys made the rounds of the unemployed together. This search brought into focus for Dreiser "that keen appreciation of the storms and stress of life that later may have manifested itself in my writings. . . . For so often I was touched by the figures of other seekers like myself and Al—their eyes, worn faces, bodies, clothes, the weariness of them in line at so many doors!"[7] In October of 1887 another brother came to Dreiser's assistance—not the noble Paul, but the shiftless Rome. Through his railroad connections, Rome managed to get his younger brother a job as a car tracer at a whopping forty-five dollars a month. Although Dreiser got sick and lost the job after two days, on the first day he got a taste of his brother's class anger—and self-defeating ways. Escorting Theo to hunt down a car far out, Rome insisted on stopping for a morning whiskey. Later, on the train en route to their destination, he complained of the rich—the Armours, Swifts, and Pullmans—who were fast piling up gigantic fortunes while "other men toiled at the bottom for their 'sissy sons and daughters.'" As they rode along, Rome furtively jabbed away at the car's velvet upholstery with a small pen knife.[8]

By late in the year, Dreiser had found a job in the shipping department of an enormous wholesale hardware concern, Hibbard, Spencer, Bartlett & Company, located on the Chicago River. (It was also around this time that the family moved to cheaper quarters at 61 Flourney Street.) At the warehouse he learned of industrial spies and met fellow "box rustlers" who hoped to be elevated to traveling salesmen for the firm. He also saw some of those "sissy" rich boys Rome spoke of, sons of the owners, graduates of colleges that "Dorse" (Dreiser's family nickname of the moment) had scarcely heard of, come in "from the east somewhere" to learn the business from the top down. But the biggest impression on this future chronicler of the contrasts between rich and poor was made by Christian Aaberg. This Danish immigrant was a womanizer, a broken-down drunk, and a philosopher, kept on at the warehouse at the sufferance of one of the owners. "My Gott, how I have lived!" he regularly exclaimed to his young new friend. "My Gott, how drunk I was yesterday! Oh, these women! These devils of women!"

Aaberg spoke to him of Ibsen, Strindberg, and Goethe, among others, while they loaded boxes, stacked pots and pans "or buckets or bolts or rivets." He was also among the first to weaken Dreiser's Catholic faith, even suggesting that the crucifix was originally a phallic symbol. He spoke to Theo by the hour of history recorded, Dreiser remembered, not in "the silly, glossed, emasculated data of the school libraries . . . but [in] the harsh, jagged realities and savageries of the too real world." Aaberg also brought home to Dreiser the European notion that the mind alone made up the essential difference "between the masses and the classes."[9]

"Working Chicago," with its hardy diversity and colorful street scenes, inspired poetry, Dreiser thought—even though this high school drop-out preferred art galleries to libraries during his off hours and free Sundays. Dreiser was "burning with desire" to go ahead in the world, and about him at this very time—"as luck would have it"—was the great metropolis of

Chicago. By 1889 preparations were underway for the city's world's fair to celebrate the four-hundredth anniversary of the discovery of the New World. When the celebration, which held up grand visions of the coming twentieth century, arrived a year late in 1893, the excitement was such that no one seemed to notice. At the same time John D. Rockefeller was turning a small Baptist school into the University of Chicago, and Yerkes was taking his streetcar lines to the West and North sides. The young Dreiser was not alone in imagining that one—almost anyone—could actually rise and take part of this material splendor, if only he were good enough or smart enough.

Yet for Dreiser, the most poetic sight remained that of his mother, now in her mid-fifties—overweight and graying—and long divested of "the delicacy of her youth." To her son, however, her soul shone through as sweetly as "any girl's." Dressed in her modified "Moravian habit of black, with the nun-like collar," she moved from the dark of early morning to the dark of night about their rented rooms performing her "servant-like labors." The character of "Sister" Sarah would contribute to the portrait of "Sister Carrie," the girl next door whose innocence is lost in the crush of the mundane. Carrie never stops dreaming of a better life even when down, but Sarah's hopes for a "superior home" were fading away by this time. To some extent, despite the sympathy he could feel for him, Dreiser blamed his father. "I can see him now," he bitterly recalled, "in his worn-out clothes, a derby or soft hat pulled low over his eyes, his shoes oiled (not shined) in order to make them wear longer, . . . trudging off at seven or eight every morning, rain or shine, to his beloved mass."[10] He took to religion, his son thought, the way others took to drink or drugs.

Even as he felt sadness at his parents' plight, their brightest son was also beginning to look at their never-ending dilemma philosophically, matching it up with life around him, its twists and turns of fate that seemed to order success or failure for no apparent reason. Curiously, indeed almost perversely in view of his family's failed dreams, he began to think that life was more dramatic than any fiction could paint it. He worked on at Hibbard, Spencer, Bartlett & Company with no real future in sight until the summer of 1889, rising six days a week at 5:45 A.M. and getting home at dusk. The working conditions were marked by poor ventilation, and his weak lungs were hurting from cleaning out dusty bins. His health, he told a friend back in Warsaw, was "decidedly" poor.[11] Then, reminiscent of Paul's jubilant appearances out of nowhere during bleak times, Dreiser relates in his autobiography that relief and salvation now arrived in the person of Mildred Fielding, his teacher in Warsaw. She had become a principal in one of Chicago's outlying high schools, but she had not forgotten the dreamy boy in Warsaw who so impressed her with his intellectual curiosity and obvious potential. Hearing that the family had relocated to Chicago, she went to Flourney Street, where she found Sarah. She had an idea, a plan, that had perhaps been simmering in her mind since the Warsaw days.

Miss Fielding was prepared to send her former student to college and, as reported in *Dawn*, to pay all the expenses. "Now Theodore," she said to him after going to the warehouse and drawing him aside, "I have come here especially to do this, and you must help me. I have the money." He was to attend the Indiana State College in Bloomington, her alma mater; she knew its president personally and would see that Theodore was admitted as a special student in spite of the lack of a high school diploma. In the published autobiography, Dreiser remembers being offered a "year or two," but the manuscript version says "one year," which is probably right. He wrote in both the manuscript and the published version that Fielding agreed to pay the yearly tuition of $200 and provided her scholar with a monthly allowance of $50 for room, board, and all other expenses. This intervention of an English teacher in the development of literary genius, however, may be as much romantic fancy and distorted memory as fact. Much earlier than the composition of his autobiography, he remembered it differently. Writing to a friend in 1901, he said that while working at the hardware store, "I discovered I could go to college for a year for $200, and made an arrangement with a friend of mine to advance me half of this. The rest I earned and in 1889 adjourned to Bloomington."[12] Though the friend may well have been Mildred Fielding and he may have gained admission through her intervention, this is a more mundane rendition. Whatever the case, Sarah ruled that he could expect no family support for such an enterprise, even though she must have been delighted that, unlike his siblings, her son was—for a while at least—finding an intellectual way out of the workaday world.

Whenever he reflected on his year at what is now Indiana University, Dreiser wrote in *Dawn*, "I have to smile, for aside from the differing mental and scenic aspects of the life there as contrasted with what I had left, its technical educational value to me was zero, or nearly so." But this is perhaps best seen as the bitter reflection of one to whom college was barely available and who, in the end, did not stay. Even though he entered college in the fall of 1889 as a special student who could have chosen a more flexible course of study than the degree student's, he followed the baccalaureate program in the selection of his freshman classes. Like the underprivileged Clyde Griffiths of *An American Tragedy,* who fears that he has no viable future outside his uncle's factory and his cousins' social circle, the underprivileged Theodore Dreiser seized upon this rare, almost fabulous, opportunity to rise out of the poverty encircling himself and his sisters and brothers. With no high school diploma, no money, and no apparent skills, he had been headed downward, not up; at best, he might have hoped, like his coworkers at the warehouse, to become a traveling salesman. To prepare for this remarkable change of fortune, he read books—*Tom Brown at Rugby, Four Years at Harvard,* and *A Collegiate's Remembrances of Princeton.* With a cheap suit and little else in the way of proper clothing for a college freshman, he set out for Bloomington that fall.

Indiana University in those days was a far cry from either Rugby or Princeton, or from its status today as a major American university. Its student body numbered around three hundred (though Dreiser gives a higher number in his autobiography); the town's streets were unpaved and muddy; and the college curriculum still clung to old-fashioned pedagogy over research-oriented faculty interests. But change had been set in motion with the appointment of David Starr Jordan as the institution's president in 1885. Jordan was an effective lobbyist and fund-raiser who by the end of his first year in office had spoken in all ninety-two counties of the state and was working effectively with the legislature. By the fall of 1889, when Dreiser arrived, the "new" campus boasted a library constructed of native limestone and six or seven buildings (two or three of which still grace the campus). Jordan had also begun to fill in the ranks of the old guard professors with promising young faculty members. Himself a specialist in zoology, he first strengthened the sciences with Charles Henry Gilbert (zoology), John Casper Branner (geology), Douglas Houghton Campbell (botany), and Joseph P. Naylor (physics). In the humanities he hired Orrin Benner Clark (English), Gustaf Karston (romance languages and philology), and Earl Barnes (history), among others.

But at Indiana, as at most nineteenth-century colleges and universities, the humanities curriculum consisted almost exclusively of classical languages and literatures. English courses (but not much literature in English, certainly no American literature, which wouldn't reach the American college curriculum until the 1920s) were usually taught by clergymen professors who—entrenched in the classics themselves—were less than enthusiastic and sometimes rigidly supercilious about English as a legitimate academic subject. At Indiana there was no "Professor of English" per se in the years following the Civil War but instead pedagogically bloated titles such as "Professor of English Literature and Theory and Practice of Teaching" or "Professor of Elocution," reflecting America's love of oratory in the nineteenth century. By the time Dreiser became a student, at least the beginnings of change to more diversified curriculum appeared in the form of Jordan's new hire for English, Orrin Benner Clark, who was also secretary of the faculty. Clark was less than kindly memorialized in *Dawn* as "Arthur Peddoe Gates, Litt.D., Ph.D., an osseous, skeleton-like creature, who taught English Literature, Anglo-Saxon, and the Study of Words. . . . As my father to religion, so this man to bookish knowledge."[13]

Although Clark took a liking to the young student, Dreiser nevertheless regretted in his later reminiscence that for all the professor's deep learning he apparently lacked one important ingredient. "I truly believe this man toiled by night as well as by day," he recalled, "trying to extract wisdom and understanding from his tomes, when the least gift of imagination, the tiniest spark, would have saved him from years of toil." Like many of his colleagues in this small college atmosphere, Clark gave "literary evenings"; Dreiser thought the professor read Shakespeare "abominably." This may be a judgment he could only make in hindsight, however. Along with many of his literary contemporaries born in the latter half of the nineteenth century (Frank Norris, Stephen Crane, Hamlin Garland), Dreiser merely dabbled in formal learning and put little faith in its mimicry of and obeisance to the European models of the university. It all smacked of Old World adoration—garnering, he thought, more quantity than quality of information, "stored eventually in the dry, dusty bins of libraries."[14] Certainly the stubbornly American Walt Whitman and Mark Twain, with their emphasis on vernacular and workaday themes, were not held in high regard by the prevailing literary and academic circles when Dreiser was in college.

At only twenty-two, Clark was hardly older than his student, but he looked much older—a "tall, frail, graceful . . . willowy, candle-waxy man . . . with a head that hung like a great heavy flower on a thin stem." Personally, Dreiser thought him just another American average raised up under exotic and rarified conditions so that he probably never experienced a youthful period, skipping it for the altar of high culture. The impression was first overwhelming and then somewhat stifling to the blue-collar freshman, who would never learn to spell right or use apostrophes with contractions. In

Clark's Anglo-Saxon class, Dreiser received an "x" ("passed without grade") during the first trimester. Clark also taught him Philology in the second term and The Study of Words [*sic*] in the third term of the freshman's year, where he earned a "1" ("low pass") and a "2" ("good"), respectively.

English literature is not among the nine courses in which Dreiser enrolled—although he states in his autobiography that his Anglo-Saxon course included "English literature." He mentions Walter Deming Willikus (Edward Howard Griggs), a graduate of the college who had returned to Bloomington as an "Instructor in English" from a postdoctorate at Princeton.[15] Dreiser may have attended one or two literary or "musical" evenings at Griggs's "pea-green house" near the campus where he noticed the professor's wisp of a wife. He also took Elementary Latin during the first term, earning a grade of "1." It was taught by the school's vice president, Amzi Atwater, "an ardent Presbyterian" identified in *Dawn* by his actual name. A more pious, "prayerful-looking" man Dreiser did not think he had ever met. Atwater was a perfect fit for his era and ideology in American higher education, another clergyman professor who saw learning as a vague extension of the teachings of the Bible. Tall and sanctimonious, he wore a heavy black goatee that jutted out whenever "he turned his face heavenward, as he frequently did."[16] Put off by Atwater's high manner and moralistic tone, Dreiser went steadily down hill. As with Clark, he had Atwater for two more courses, Latin and Virgil's Aeneid, during the second and third terms. Both grades were "x." (Although he was vice president, Atwater may have been one of the faculty President Jordan was trying to work around and eventually replace, yet Atwater remained while a few years later Jordan left to become president of Stanford University).

It is not altogether clear from *Dawn* just who taught Dreiser his other three courses; he mentions other professors either by fictitious or real names, or a misremembered mix (such as "Willard Pelton Green" for Rufus L. Green, Associate Professor of Pure Mathematics). Green probably taught him Preparatory Geometry ("1"), Freshman Geometry ("=," meaning a conditional pass), and Freshman Algebra ("1"). Later Dreiser testified that he never could see the "import" of any of these courses.

———

Like Emily Dickinson in her one year of college (and just about every other freshman since), Dreiser seems to have derived more knowledge from his college compatriots than from the professors. Upon his arrival, he found a room with board not far from the campus. The walk to classes was no more than ten or fifteen minutes, and he remembered the crisp September and October days, the serenity and foliage so different from the relentless pace and treeless streets of the city he had so recently left. After the "vitality and urge" of Chicago, Bloomington was like coming into a soundproof chamber to rest. And no sooner had he slipped into its hypnotic lull than he found himself also charmed by the sight of a girl next door, a student at the college.

Petite, with blue eyes and pink cheeks and daily framed by the long window of her room at which she studied, she could be seen across the garden of Dreiser's rooming house. As he too studied by his window, they exchanged furtive glances. He was entranced by the scene of this attractive young woman in her "brilliant window-niche" (as Poe, his favorite author, once described his Helen) and sexually charged when she loosened her blond hair and let it fall about her books. After about a week of this welcomed distraction, his "feeble old landlady" smirkingly informed him as he "brooded" over his studies that the young woman had requested help with one of her classroom assignments. Dreiser was painfully shy and unsure of himself, but apparently the young woman, of a "commonplace, a small-town working-class family," was nothing short of a flirt, and he later said he could never forget her. Yet the help so cheekily requested involved a knowledge of Latin grammar. Without any "trace of grammar in my system," he recalled in *Dawn*, "I stood trembling before another Waterloo."[17]

But Dreiser's first Helen was evidently more interested in romance than Latin and quickly finessed the situation as Dreiser stood awkwardly before her, tongue-tied with nervousness. Never mind the lesson. Was he from Fort Wayne, where she knew a boy? But Dreiser, his mind drifting into flight, couldn't think of anything clever to say to her. "It never occurred to me," as he remembered the incident and its aftermath slightly differently in *A Hoosier Holiday*, "to tease her, or to tell her how pretty she looked, or frankly to confess that I knew nothing of Latin but that I liked her. . . . That was years beyond me."[18] Dreiser, now almost his eventual full height of six feet one-and-a-half inches but underweight from the long hours and harsh working conditions of the hardware store in Chicago, eventually slunk back to his room in defeat, mortified by his bashfulness and inability to take advantage of the opportunity. He determined to do better next time, but it never came. No more did his Helen present herself "statue-like" in her window, carefully opening the shutters and espying him. Now she seemed, as she passed his rooming house on her way to classes, perfectly absorbed in something—or someone—else.

In *Dawn* Dreiser names his roommate William Levitt; in *A Hoosier Holiday,* he is called William Wadhams, a "gallant roysterer." His real name was Bill Yakey—and he was soon spooning over the fence with the girl and taking her for Sunday carriage rides. Yakey was a law student and also one of the stars of the football team. Gregarious and good looking, he was the center of interest among his fellows. Their room became a regular gathering place. Dreiser, while glad to have this extrovert on his side, so to speak, also began to worry that he would never get a girl now with such competition. A few years later he remembered Yakey as "not so much of a friend."[19] He was unquestionably more experienced and at ease with girls. After taking the young hoyden as far as he could towards the bedroom, Yakey promptly dismissed her as a "cute little bitch" who was trying to "string" him along.

All this activity while the future lover of so many women stood agape in silent admiration and envy. There was another girl of fifteen or sixteen directly across the street, whom the lusty Yakey evidently ignored. She was a dark-haired doctor's daughter, as shy as Theo himself. Whereas the attraction of the first girl had been decidedly physical for Dreiser, this one suggested in the retrospect of middle age Dante's Beatrice, whose physical appearance or sexuality in *La Vita Nuova* represents merely the first step on the ladder of love and spirituality. She was truly "the girl next door" who would not give up her virginity without a commitment, but Dreiser failed here almost as quickly as he had with the flirt. After tearing up ten or fifteen versions, he finally sent a note asking her to meet him on campus. She never answered, and they never met.[20] (Dreiser would later find another Beatrice in his first wife and spend the rest of his life regretting it.)

It is not surprising that no fraternity ever offered the lank and cheaply dressed kid from Chicago a bid, though Dreiser thought he might have come close to receiving an invitation to join Delta Tau Delta. He consequently fell in with students from working-class backgrounds like himself, who were more than likely paying their own way through school. One was Howard Hall, as he is called in the holograph and final version of *Dawn,* who took "a very small hall bedroom" on the third floor of Dreiser's rooming house. Hall was from Michigan, a blond-haired youth as thin as Dreiser. To increase their needed bulk, the two lifted weights together. Hall planned to become a lawyer even though a "speech impediment . . . promised to prevent his pleading before any jury." After two years he returned home to work in a local law office for "four or five years" before dying from consumption at age twenty-four.[21]

Another college chum called Russell Ratliff (in *A Hoosier Holiday* and the holograph of *Dawn* and "Sutcliffe" in the printed version) was an idealist and reformer who, Dreiser testified, exercised a "serene and broadening influence" on him, more than any other student he came to know in college. Ratliff was a poet, a philosopher, a vegetarian, and an orator with the roundness and eloquence of "a youthful [Robert] Ingersoll"—the famous lawyer-agnostic of the day, who championed unpopular social causes such as penal reform and the plight of the poor. It was probably at this time and with this influential friend that Dreiser's social awareness of the developing contest between the haves and the have-nots in late-nineteenth-century America—not simply his self-pity about having begun poor or his sympathy for others like himself—was born. As impoverished as Dreiser had been in his youth, he came to see his "unearned" talent as a writer, and the class status it gave him, as salvation from the psychological damage his family poverty inflicted on many of his siblings.[22]

Ratliff's interest in philosophy brought the work of Herbert Spencer to Dreiser's attention. One of the philosophical fathers of literary naturalism, which holds that man is both product and victim of heredity and environment, Spencer questioned the logic of religious dogmatists by arguing that man is controlled by chemical forces that ultimately dictate individual fate; yet in an attempt to reconcile religion with science, he also suggested that some of us were chemically superior, or chosen by God for success. Ratliff may also have been responsible for introducing Dreiser to Darwin and other naturalists. For years after Bloomington he often wondered what had become of Ratliff, how his chemistry, or "chemism," had served him in the experiment called life. He eventually heard from his old friend in the 1890s when he wrote approvingly of Dreiser's magazine work. By then Ratliff was working for "some Indian agency."[23]

Ratliff and Hall, along with Yakey as a "counter-irritant," exercised "considerable influence" over Dreiser during his first, and only, year of college. They caused him, he said, "to seek for the wellsprings of life and human actions more carefully than I ever had before." For Dreiser, they were proof of what Mildred Fielding had told him in Chicago, that "this college world was little more than a realm in which one might find oneself intellectually— if one had an intellect—a table spread with good things of which one could partake if one had an appetite. The curriculum—a mere bill of fare. The professors and instructors—waiters who served what was provided but who could neither eat nor digest for you."[24]

Together these friends opened each other's eyes. They went on field trips together, belonged to literary societies, and once visited a local high school spelling bee, where Dreiser recalled that some of the winners were attractive country maidens. With Hall and Ratliff, Dreiser also joined the college spelunking society. Not only was Bloomington, and all of Monroe County, the center of the limestone industry, marked by deep quarries, but the area was also underlain with a series of tortuous natural caves. One of the earliest photographs of Dreiser shows him with a group of student cave explorers posing solemnly with their staffs and holding balls of twine used to trace their return to the surface during an exploration. During one excursion the three friends broke off from a larger party to investigate a cave on their own. They got lost after outpacing the length of their twine, played out along the various ledges and through prehistoric doorways, some hardly large enough to admit passage. All they had left was the lights attached to their hats. In those days these were either miners' lamps fueled by calcium carbide or some kind of oil lamp. Such illumination was often unreliable, and if the lights went out and matches got damp, as they usually did underground, explorers were cast into utter darkness. Dreiser speaks of having taken "half a dozen or more candles," which would have been even more precarious. Evidently, their light held, for the three finally groped and scraped their way to safety after hours of panic and increasing hunger and thirst. This threat of a "premature burial" gave Dreiser nightmares that continued "for a long period thereafter."[25]

One other college chum mentioned significantly in *Dawn* is Day Allen Willy (David Ben O'Connor in both the holograph and published versions), a well-to-do law student and the son of a judge in Northern Indiana. Willy was always up for action and ready to pay Dreiser's share of the cost, even on a Thanksgiving trip to Louisville, where they hoped to spend the night with two young women Willy knew. Dreiser also needed to consult an oculist there because the long hours of college reading were apparently straining his good eye. They got to Louisville—careful not to sit next to the girls until their train cleared Bloomington—only to discover (since the out-of-town newspapers typically didn't reach Bloomington until late afternoon, after they had boarded their train) that a cyclone had nearly devastated the city. Dreiser was also devastated (again) when he proved to be too shy or hesitant with Kathie Millership, the name he gave to the girl he was supposed to entertain—while Willy apparently encountered no difficulties in romancing his date. The eye appointment scheduled for the next day was postponed for twenty-four hours because of the storm. While his three companions returned to Bloomington, he waited alone in his hotel room, mortified once more that he was a miserable failure with women yet consumed with "sex hunger."[26]

He was hardly more successful on a similar, if more pecuniary, mission in Chicago during Christmas vacation, when Willy visited and the two went to a brothel. Willy, who was staying at the expensive Palmer House, again footed most of the bills. This time the hot anticipation of sexual adventure ended with mutual disenchantment over the coarseness of the prostitutes. Dreiser nevertheless managed to fondle the "rounded solid flesh" of one of these women, even though he lacked the necessary five dollars to take her upstairs. He was saved from embarrassment by Willy, who appeared to declare that there was nothing "worthwhile" in the house. They tried other houses in the red light district on the South Side, and Willy eventually found satisfaction. He would have paid for his friend's indulgence as well, but Dreiser stubbornly abstained, claiming that the entire process had been ruined for him because of a lack of independent means.

While at home that Christmas, he became aware of the widening gap between himself and his siblings, whose interests were exclusively practical. After his college exposure, all at home except his dear mother seemed slightly remote. Finding his father out of work once again, he looked upon the all too familiar dilemma not as the sorrowful son but now as the student of psychology or biology "interested in the life history or processes of any given species."[27] There must have been just the slightest sadness, therefore, when he remembered that his privileged tenure as the observer, the college student to whom the "real world" could be regarded as hypothetical, had already reached its midlife and would terminate in the spring.

For he tells us in *Dawn* that he decided in December to quit after one year and make his way alone "as before." This decision may have been tentative at first; he fails to mention that, according to the *Indiana Student* of January 1890, he stated that he hoped to return for his sophomore year. Furthermore, in the holograph of *Dawn* he reveals that in truth he did not see how it would be possible to "secure another year." When he visited his benefactor in Chicago during his Christmas vacation, Miss Fielding told him she had merely wanted to expose her former student to the possibilities of higher learning and perhaps professional life. "Men do go to college late in life," she told him, "and you might like to do that some day."[28]

To compensate for the reality that awaited him, he began to tell himself that he had never belonged at college in the first place. Nevertheless, his year away from working-class strife had lifted him out of his milieu long enough to see it unemotionally or objectively for the first time. Before, he had never felt solitary when surrounded by family members; now he experienced "a sense of mental loneliness." There is no question that Dreiser would have remained at Indiana a second year had it been possible, even if his mediocre grades didn't seem to warrant any more time there. Following the last of his exams, he sat around in his room, wondering whether he should linger on a day or two to savor "the spring and these last sweet days." Sartorially at least, he left Bloomington in as shabby a state as he had arrived, lacking the spring suit other students donned and waiting beside his old trunk for the train to take him back to the mean streets of Chicago.

Within three weeks of his return, Dreiser found a job in a real estate office on Ogden Avenue at three dollars a week. This was the dubious business venture of Andrew Conklin, whose first name was changed to "Asa" in *Dawn*. ("Asa" Conklin, as Dreiser acknowledges in his autobiography, was in part the basis for the father of the fated Clyde, the religious Asa Griffiths who, with his wife, runs a storefront mission in Kansas City at the opening of *An American Tragedy*.) Having invested his last $500 in a Chicago real estate market that was clearly booming, Conklin tried to conduct the business while his wife ran their shabby religious retreat, equipped with "a small organ, a set of hymn books, some chairs, a desk or rostrum, some mottoes or quotations from the Bible, a picture of Christ or a map of Palestine, or both." With the foregoing, they "set up in religion for themselves."[29] Conklin also advertised his business, mainly a leasing agency, as dealing in insurance and loans, but he had no money for either without an underwriter, which he was unlikely to find.

Conklin was one of the thousands of Civil War veterans living on a slim pension for "some alleged war injury." He had no more idea of how to run a business than the young Dreiser, who kept the "books" with a system devised totally on his own. Yet there was a horse and buggy, and before long Dreiser had secured, so he remembered, over forty houses and apartments to rent and ten lots to sell. He also used the buggy to take his aging mother out in the fresh air. During his working rounds, he met with all sorts of adventures and temptations, from women seeking to marry Dreiser off to their daughters to mothers who were more interested in the young man for their own purposes. His feelings of sexual impotence began to subside. Mainly, these flirtations involved older women, in their thirties or more, but the match that almost completely cleared him of his sense of inadequacy was with an Italian woman in her teens who nearly seduced him in the back room of the real estate office. She promised to return to finish the job, based he thought on his handling of himself, but she never did.

One day there appeared at the office a character right out of the pages of Mark Twain and Charles Dudley Warner's *The Gilded Age* (1873). Colonel Thomas Bundy, whose *carte de visite* claimed that he specialized in "Real Estate, Mines, Insurance," closely resembles Colonel Beriah Sellers of that novel, which depicted the same post–Civil War greed in which Dreiser was growing up. Reminiscent as well of Twain's Duke and Dauphin, the two frauds who sail the Mississippi in search of easy prey in *Adventures of Huckleberry Finn* (1884), Bundy at first impressed Dreiser and Conklin as much as Twain's con men impress the runaway slave Jim—if not Huck. "Mr. Conklin is a novice, I can see that," the Colonel told Dreiser. The office needed more furniture and rugs—a rolltop desk and chair as well as a railing to set off the bookkeeper's area. And like Twain's Colonel Sellers in his faith in future railroad lines, Bundy saw nothing but prosperity ahead when a street-car line was induced to pass by their soon-to-be-acquired properties. Young Dreiser was at first a fellow optimist. Like the fictional Carrie, who in her wild imagination far outspends the four-dollar-a-week salary she expects from working in the Chicago shoe factory, her future creator at about the same age immediately "had visions of a splendid salary, the best of clothes, myself hobnobbing with successful people; theatres, restaurants, mansions, money, girls!"[30]

Glibly claiming the publisher of the *Christian Age* in St. Paul as his brother, the Colonel had been looking around, and now he had found the perfect opportunity. Conklin was thrilled, and so was Bundy, who slickly took advantage of such gullibility. Before a day had passed, he was sending Dreiser out for "cigars, stationery, laundry he had left, saying I was to say they were for Mr. Bundy and they were to be charged." He ate at the best neighborhood restaurants on Conklin's credit as he pretended to advance the real estate business, not even bothering to pay his landlady. Whether all this is real as it is related in *Dawn* or partially a reflection of Dreiser's admiration for Mark Twain's satire is a question to go forever unanswered. But Conklin, Bundy & Co. soon floundered, and Conklin in his despera-

tion went so far as to accuse Bundy of stealing—to which the Colonel retorted, in either Dreiser's imagination or memory, "What do you mean,
stole? Ain't I a partner here?" Ultimately, Conklin lost his investment, sank
into debt, and died in 1891.[31]

In his defeat, Conklin resembled not only Asa Griffiths, but John Paul
Dreiser, who had failed at just about everything he tried after he lost his
mill in the 1860s. Now a largely pathetic figure at sixty-nine, he seemed to
have little to do other than try to keep up the spirits of his once energetic
wife. But that task was getting harder. Sarah showed signs of being ground
down—rather quickly. Before, it had been a rare moment when she had sat
down or rested, but now, on one of his increasingly rare visits home because of his road trips, Paul noticed that his mother was not looking well
and suggested that his sisters pitch in more on the housework. The only
existing photograph of Sarah, taken sometime in her last years, shows a
woman with her hair pulled tightly back from her rounded face (she weighed
more than two hundred pounds when she died). She gives just the glimmer of a smile—or perhaps it is the frown of life-long disappointment.

Eventually Sarah became bedridden and was under several doctors' care
for weeks. In her weakening state, she seemed to fret most over her wandering son Rome, even though he had so often disrupted their small-town
existence in Indiana. Frantic but futile efforts were made to find him when
the end seemed certain. Dreiser was home for lunch on the day she died,
joining his sisters Mame, Theresa, and Claire, and brother Ed in their vigil.
When Sarah attempted to return to bed after being helped to the toilet, she
collapsed in Theodore's arms as he rushed to her side, her weight bringing
them both to the floor. John Paul ran upstairs to her bedroom and "began
to blubber in a forlorn, exhausted, and uncontrollable way." She died not
long after, surrounded by her husband and five of her children. Besides
Rome, Al and Paul were away from the house.

In fact, Paul was about to go on stage at a matinee in the city, and the
family didn't want to distract him with news that would have been threatening to anyone's performance, but most certainly to that of Sarah's oldest
son. (His mother would live again and again in his songs; already Paul was
moderately famous and had written "I Believe It for My Mother Told Me
So.") When he returned home, he could only stare at his mother's corpse,
stunned out of all words. Al had almost the same reaction when he came
home, mumbling that he just couldn't cry and asking himself why. It appears that the boys in the family were more deeply affected by the passing
of their mother than their sisters were. Yet both sexes knew in their hearts

what Dreiser himself felt and what Al expressed upon hearing from Ed that their mother had just died: "Well, that's the end of our home."[32]

Her death at age fifty-seven on November 14, 1890, gave Dreiser, he said more than a quarter of a century later, "the most profound, psychologic shake-up I ever received." He experienced something mystical in her departure, watching his mother's "very weak and pale" look transformed into a clear and healthy lightness "as though she were thinking or trying to say something to me, but through her eyes alone."[33] If the debacle that surrounded the publication of *Sister Carrie* ten years hence wasn't the lowest point in Dreiser's lifetime, the loss of his mother surely was.

Sarah's burial added bitterness to the memory etched in Dreiser's mind. Because she hadn't been the best of Catholics (missing Mass while nevertheless urging her children to attend) and because Mame and Theresa had purposely subverted the Catholic process of extreme unction through deathbed confession in their mother's case, the young clergyman John Paul summoned allegedly refused to allow Sarah a Catholic burial. The parish priest, whatever his sense of right and wrong, was probably within his doctrinal rights, but Theodore—who along with the majority of his siblings by this time had determined to put away Catholicism for good—was enraged and never forgave the Church, even though the diocese soon reversed the initial decision and granted their father's wish for Sarah to be buried in St. Boniface's Roman Catholic Cemetery on the North Side.

"You would have thought," Dreiser wrote in *Dawn,* still seething from the incident almost thirty years later, that the priest would have immediately taken pity on his church-ridden father for his "slavish and pleading devotion" to the Church and dispensed with its technicalities, which also included a refusal to bless the body because Sarah had possibly died in a state of mortal sin. "But not so," the ever-grieving son wrote. "This low-browed, dogmatic little Bavarian, panoplied with the trashy authority of his church, chose instead to come to our door, and disregarding the pleas of my father, if not the rest of us, show how savagely Mother Church would repay by stern denial of her hieratic pomp and meaningless formulas the spiritual lapses which it condemned."[34]

———

Rome returned to Chicago after the funeral. Informed of his mother's death, he told Theo that she had communicated with him in a dream, asking why he wasn't there when she died. "That's why I'm here," he muttered in what Dreiser remembered as his brother's "heavy, guttural, Gargantuan weeping," which caused him to cry, too. For all her wiles and ambivalences, Sarah had still managed to be the calm center of a storm of sibling rivalries and general rebellion at the father's strict rule. After she died, the family remained together for only three or four months. John Paul now had little or no influence over the way his children lived their lives, with the possible exception of Al, Theresa, and later Claire, when she fully outgrew her prolonged adolescence. He further annoyed them, or at least the religiously disenchanted of them, by repeatedly making reference to Sarah's religious shortcomings and insisting that the family make weekly contributions to light votive candles and have Masses said so that she might get out of purgatory sooner. This was galling to them, especially on the heels of having to pay installments towards the Church funeral that had been so reluctantly authorized.[35]

Dreiser himself felt absolutely anchorless. Conklin's real estate company was failing, and he hadn't been paid for weeks. It was Christmas time, but there was little to cheer about in the family with Sarah gone from its midst. He quit, and despite the grim prospect of tramping the streets of the city in search of another job, he experienced a vision in which he conceived of life as a living tableau. The "artistry of any passing scene—a boat, a sail, a crowd, a tower, a flock of pigeons," he recalled of this embryonic period in his literary development, "was sufficient to hold me for moments or hours." He marveled at the ordinary details of life, the way they charged the atmosphere with "such brilliant life-pictures." As he returned home that day, full of wonders but with no job, he imagined the beautiful women waiting "with kisses" for those who were gainfully employed.[36]

In January or February of 1891 he found a job at eight dollars a week, driving a wagon for a laundry on Madison Street on the West Side. It was a well-established business whose success rested partly on the practice of turning over its driver positions so that employees wouldn't be around long enough to steal customers away to a competing business when they quit for higher wages. The Munger Laundry Company, therefore, preferred younger drivers like Dreiser. He noticed and was attracted to the young laundry girls. Smartly dressed young men waited outside for the prettier ones, but Dreiser in his teamster uniform of old clothes and hat felt at a disadvantage.

He worked for Munger for the next four months, in what he called, in spite of his lowly status as a driver, "a kind of Adamless paradise." How marvelous it would be, he sighed, to have the money and good clothes with which to approach beautiful women. Some of them were so attractive, he wondered why they had to work at all. One who did was Nellie Anderson (Nellie MacPherson in *Dawn*), who came from a religious Scotch Presbyterian family. She wasn't the prettiest girl in the laundry but the one with whom Dreiser with his poor resources thought he could easily win. As the cashier for the company, Nellie collected from all the drivers, five or six of them, at the end of each day. Usually Dreiser was one of the last to return from his delivery rounds, occasionally after the other drivers had departed. One night he and Nellie did inventory after hours, and he could scarcely resist the urge to embrace her. On another evening soon afterward he kissed her, she resisted nominally, and they became a couple. Yet when he later met her parents and sister Lilly, he found himself equally attracted to the sister.[37]

That spring he was recruited by three Jewish businessmen who owned the Barnhardt Brothers' Troy Laundry on Ogden Avenue, closer to where Dreiser lived. Ordinarily, they sought older drivers who could deliver new customers from their last place of employment, but for some reason they made an exception in Dreiser's case, offering him ten dollars a week. He enjoyed the job at first, driving a newer rig around Chicago, but the experience turned out poorly and either fueled or initiated Dreiser's stereotyped view of the greedy Jew. Evidently, the brothers expected Dreiser to recruit more new business than he did. Moreover, their delivery and pick-up business covered a wider city area than Munger's and often took him downtown where the heavy traffic made the driving hazardous and arduous. After three months, in which his anti-Semitism smoldered, he was fired after he collided with another wagon, even though that driver was at fault. "Jews, for the moment at least, were anathema to me," he wrote in *Dawn*. (He was not then aware, as he insisted he was in 1931, when this volume of his autobiography was published, "of the possible beauty of the individual soul in any race, Jew as well as Gentile."[38] This realization, however, would not save him from a very public imbroglio a few years after that.)

After his experience with the two laundries, he decided it was time to find something with more future in it. He was hired as a bill collector at the Lovell Manufacturing Company on Lake Street, at the increased salary of fourteen dollars a week. The business was actually a front for or secret branch of a larger Pennsylvania company that sold household items on time, charging inflated prices for the cheap merchandise. Dreiser knew firsthand of such companies because his mother's furniture had been once repossessed for nonpayment. At the time Sarah left Chicago in 1883, it was illegal to take furniture purchased on time across state lines until the bill was paid in full. The family had had to forfeit hundreds of dollars and arrived to an empty house in Warsaw.[39]

This bitter memory may have clouded Dreiser's judgment in his new job. One day he decided to withhold—with the intention of repaying—twenty-five dollars from the rent receipts to buy himself a new overcoat and hat to go with his other new clothes. No longer the shabbily dressed wagon driver, he had become very conscious of his appearance, was dating Nellie rather regularly now, and was always on the lookout for other romantic conquests. It was about two weeks before Christmas. His employer, who was fond of young Dreiser, confronted him with indisputable evidence of his "theft." (Later in *Sister Carrie* and *An American Tragedy* the same question of intent lingers about the crime.) Mortified and even fearful of going to jail, he was let go but was expected to repay the amount, which he apparently did. "God," he wrote in *Dawn,* "I have never taken a dime since!"[40]

Somewhat surprisingly, his concern about going to jail was second to his cringing worry that his father would find out. It was bad enough to have to come home and announce that he had been laid off "because of business" and probably wouldn't find another job until after the New Year, quite another that he might follow his brothers Paul and Rome into the criminal courts. What if his father inquired at the Lovell Company the same way he had gone to Conklin after he had stopped paying his son? Dreiser's anxiety here suggests that, whatever he thought of John Paul's religion, the father was still a moral authority to his son. He doesn't mention it, but as a lapsed Catholic, not simply an "inoculated Catholic," as he later described himself, Dreiser might even have considered going to confession over the theft. Although he was "through" with the Church, the Church apparently was not quite through with him. Indeed, throughout his description of himself as a Catholic, there is a striking absence or evasiveness—never a word about having made his First Holy Communion or confirmation, important junctures in any young Catholic's life, or his possible service as an altar boy.

But Dreiser was by now pretty much finished with youth, and with that had gone possibly the last vestiges of his Catholicism. As he watched his father fret about the house, preoccupied mainly with religious concerns, he saw the end not only of his conventionally religious consciousness but also the integrity of the family that had nourished it. Claire and Mame, the youngest and oldest sisters, were at odds over various issues, including

Mame's condescending attitude toward her siblings following her marriage to Brennan, a reformed alcoholic who came from a well-to-do family in Rochester, New York. (The couple, in fact, was never bound by more than a common-law marriage, although it lasted until Brennan's death in 1928.)[41] Whenever Mame and Austin, who had moved to Brennan's hometown, came to Chicago, for weeks at a time, they had stayed with the Dreiser family, usually in the best rooms, to the consternation of other family members. The family turmoil increased when Mame accused Theo of another theft. During her illness, Sarah had received a postal order from Paul for ten dollars. Wanting for whatever reasons to keep the money a secret, she sent Theo to the post office with permission to cash it. Afterward, the terminally ailing woman forgot and denied receiving the check when Paul wrote again to inquire about it. Following her mother's death, Mame tried to initiate an official inquiry at the post office, thereby threatening her brother with a federal offense. Infuriated because—so he insists in *Dawn*— he was innocent of the charge of theft this time, he rarely spoke to his eldest sister for the next fifteen years.[42]

By March 1891, such apprehensions and quarrels without Sarah's intervention broke up the family. Angry at Mame, Dreiser sided with Claire against her, and followed Claire and Ed to a "rival home" on Taylor Street, only a few blocks from Flourney Street. The other sisters also jumped ship. Only Theresa and Al remained, Al saying the only decent thing was to keep a home for his aged father. The distraught father's pleas for family unity fell on deaf ears. The "decent" thing to do, as it would be to so many of Dreiser's fictional characters, was simply unattractive. Dreiser marched out along with the rest, in spite of his abiding sense of the unfairness of it all. Much later, in *Newspaper Days,* he would recall this moment with sadness and remorse. Perhaps still ringing in his ears so many years after his father's death in 1900 was the old man's "Dorsh, I done the best I could."

THREE

This Matter of Reporting

*Imagine a dreamy cub of twenty, soon to be twenty-one, long,
lank, spindling, a pair of gold-framed specs on his nose, his hair
combed à la pompadour, a new spring suit, consisting of a pair of
light check trousers and bright blue coat and vest, with a brown
fedora hat and new yellow shoes, starting out to connect
himself with the newspaper press of Chicago.*

NEWSPAPER DAYS

THE TAYLOR STREET LIVING ARRANGEMENT lasted barely more than a
month, for Claire proved to be neither housekeeper nor cook. Ed moved
to the nearby home of the DeGoods, whose daughter he was seeing, and
Theo followed soon after. Claire subsequently relocated to a rooming house
on Ogden Place. The brothers shared a room for a dollar-fifty a week and
paid twenty-five cents apiece for whatever meals they ate with the family.
Dreiser continued working with the Corbin Company, another installment
collection agency, a job he had found about the time the Flourney Street
household had broken up. But he had already set his mind on becoming a
journalist. In fact, by the Christmas season of 1891 he worked part-time for
the *Chicago Herald*—but not as a reporter.

He answered its ad on December 17: "YOUNG MEN—TWO, OF GOOD AD-
DRESS; must be good penmen; salary $1.50 per day."[1] Dreiser and more than
a dozen other young men were hired for a holiday campaign the *Herald* was
running called "Santa Is Jolly." On Christmas day thousands of toys were
handed out to children who had sent their wish lists to Santa Claus in care
of the newspaper. (Just what good penmanship had to do with wrapping
and doling out Christmas presents remains unclear.) In his autobiography
Dreiser misremembered the advertisement as suggesting the possibility of
a permanent position, but of course he received no such "promotion."

"Here was I," he recalled, ". . . a victim of what socialists would look upon as economic error, almost as worthy of free gifts as any other, and yet lined up with fifteen or twenty other economic victims—as poorly off as myself—all out of a job, many of them almost out at the elbows." When Dreiser wrote this sentence in his autobiography twenty-some years later, he was living in Greenwich Village and surrounded by what his friend H. L. Mencken called "the red ink fraternity." Yet underlying all his thinking since his year at Indiana University when Russell Ratliff had introduced him to the various socioeconomic philosophers, was the idea of an inequity that was not only social but cosmic. It underscores the pathos of both George Hurstwood's fatal Bowery descent and Clyde Griffiths's doom in the electric chair. Having been exposed to Huxley and Nietzsche, Dreiser was early on aware of what he regarded as the post–Civil War drift of the country "to monopoly and so to oligarchy."[2]

Chicago in the 1890s was an exciting place to be a newspaperman, second only to New York. It could boast of such journalistic lights and column humorists as Eugene Field, George Ade, Finley Peter Dunne, and Brand Whitlock. By April 1892, Dreiser, unable any longer to resist the call from the Fourth Estate, simply quit the Corbin Company, without having found another job. Determined now to enter journalism, come what may, he had saved $65 to underwrite his search and vowed not to abandon the quest unless threatened by starvation. After a first fruitless survey of the various Chicago papers, he decided to focus all his energies on just one. He picked the poorest in the city, the *Daily Globe,* figuring that, with no experience and really no idea of what a journalist actually did, his best chance lay with the least competitive newspaper. The *Globe,* which was owned and controlled by a local politician, was located on Fifth Avenue, directly across from Chicago's best newspaper at the time, the *Daily News.* Dreiser came to the newsroom every day, as if he worked there (some of the reporters thought he did after a while), and John Maxwell, then a copyreader there, encouraged him to hang on until a position came open.

Dreiser did eventually get himself hired as a reporter for the *Globe,* mainly by agreeing to sell door-to-door a college memoir by one of the editors, which then led to a trial reporting assignment. Harry Gissell, an "intimate of the city editor," had privately and pseudonymously printed a third-rate memoir entitled *The Adventures of Mickey Finn* and was in need of a sales canvasser. In exchange for selling at least 120 copies of the book within the next week, Gissell promised he would see that Dreiser received a tryout as a reporter on the *Globe.* (With the Democratic presidential convention to be held in Chicago that June, there was a reasonable chance new reporters would be needed.) Since the book concerned Gissell's days at Hyde Park High School, Dreiser was to seek out as many as possible of the three hundred graduates in the author's class with the promise that the book "related to scenes with which they were all familiar." Dreiser reluctantly accepted the challenge from "this little yellow-haired rat of an editor." He claims in his autobiography that he met the sales quota that led to his first true newspaper job at fifteen dollars a week.[3]

He was initially hired as a reporter only for two weeks, to cover the Democratic convention, which was meeting at four Chicago hotels, including the Palmer House, where Day Allen Willy had stayed during their Christmas escapades in 1889. Dreiser had hardly a clue as to how to carry out his reportorial duties, claiming his phrenological "bump of politics was not very large." His mind, he claimed in looking back on his first involvement in politics, "was too much concerned with the poetry of life to busy myself with such minor things as politics."[4] But his youthful curiosity and a little serendipity led to the discovery that former President Grover Cleveland would be the nominee over New York governor David Bennett Hill. Actually, the information was available to the larger newspapers through a news service the *Globe* could not afford, but Dreiser picked it up for his paper in a chance interview with Supreme Court Justice Melville Weston Fuller, whom Cleveland had appointed during his first term. Having once been a newspaperman himself, the judge took pity on the inexperienced reporter.

Young Dreiser had a lot to learn about journalism; fortunately for literature he never learned enough. Some years before, he had tried writing in the style of Eugene Field, who wrote the popular "Sharps and Flats" column of whimsical humor and colloquial verse for the *Daily News*. In a sense, Field, who is best remembered for his sentimental poem "Little Boy Blue," was to literature what Paul Dresser was to music, and Dreiser himself was suckled on this kind of lowbrow popular culture as he grew up in the small towns of Indiana. He had even sent a few of his efforts to the humorist, hoping—in vain—for his response and possible encouragement. While he was canvassing all the newspapers for a job, he visited the offices of the *News*, where Field was pointed out to him. Young Dreiser was relieved that the great man could not know he was the one who had sent him "unsolicited slush," but in fact it may have been from Field that Dreiser first came to appreciate the literary value of the colloquial dialect that sparkles so through his short fiction and autobiographical writings.

But at the *Globe,* Maxwell told him repeatedly, "You're not to write general stuff." And during the Democratic convention Maxwell complained, "That's literature—not news stuff. Did you see any particular man?"[5] Still Dreiser found himself more interested in the sordid conditions than in the politicians who were supposed to clean them up. He had noticed the grimy neighborhood between the Chicago River and State Street, passing through it daily on his way downtown from his room at Ogden Place near Union Park. (He would later place the fictional Carrie there after she moves in with Drouet.) The area was dubbed "Cheyenne" because its crime suggested the lawless western town of Cheyenne, Wyoming. In the poem "At Cheyenne," Eugene Field had suggested it would take "Young Lochinvar," the romantic hero of Sir Walter Scott's *Marmion,* to clean up the Chicago neighborhood. But the budding realist already knew better.

"The belated pedestrian," Dreiser wrote in the *Globe* of July 24, "who goes into the district bounded by State, Van Buren, Sixteenth streets and the river literally steps into the bedrooms of scores of sleepers, who on hot nights stretch their weary limbs on the hard pavements." He described the manifold nationalities, all struggling indigents, most prominently Greek and Italian "banana peddlers and organ grinders," and the streets and incredibly overcrowded tenements ("a dozen in a single room") resounding "with the babel of tongues endeavoring to speak intelligently the English of Uncle Sam." He described how these men and women and their human litters—fifty families for fifty rooms—squeezed sardine-like into three-story buildings during the winter and how "the first breath of heat [drove] them, as water drives rats, from their dens." He did not shy from including sketches of drunken men in the streets and casually clad women in the windows, the domestic violence, the ill-lighted streets and broken pavements.

Throughout "Cheyenne, Haunt of Misery and Crime" can be heard for the first time that deterministic and yet compassionate narrative voice that leads us through Dreiser's greatest works. Here were future Americans, and this democrat from poverty was implicitly asking how America would ultimately accommodate them. It was already too late, he thought, for the current tenants of Cheyenne, if not their children. In the meantime nature also ignored their plight. "Over them," Dreiser wrote of these Chicago poor, "all the night wind softly breathes and the stars look down in their serene purity. On they sleep with white faces upturned from the pavement."[6] Even God was oblivious of their suffering.

Already Dreiser was distinguishing himself from the Social Darwinism of most writers and social philosophers of the 1890s, who fused a moralistic hierarchy onto the "survival of the fittest" model in *On the Origin of Species* (1859). The true traits of survival, they held, were anything but the result of chance and were to be found in the moral will and manners of the American middle class—that is, white Anglo-American males instead of the immigrant classes of Irish, Germans, and Italians. These unwashed newcomers to American society were generally considered inferior. (Consider, for example, the Irish dentist in Frank Norris's *McTeague* [1899], who succumbs to his hereditary alcoholism when his luck turns sour.) Dreiser, coming himself from "suspicious" German stock, seldom made these socially constructed distinctions. This difference from the Howellsian mode, in which manners or middle-class culture mattered, was what made Dreiser's sterner realism initially unpalatable. In his view, the social world reflected the cosmic picture in which all were subject to forces beyond their control: "The young are born blind and deaf to experience and failure. The old scarcely live long enough or gain sufficient wisdom or experience to see what a vast force it is that controls them—what tools and fools they have been. How truly ridiculous, in the face of great forces of nature, all strutting by a man or a woman is."[7]

Accordingly, in spite of the determinism of Dreiser's piece on the Cheyenne neighborhood, he ends it by exhorting "human pity" to "extend a helping hand." He wanted the helpless to be helped even though they might be the flotsam and jetsam of nature's elimination of the weak. Thus was born the determinist and the reformer, Dreiser's lifelong contradiction—to be simultaneously the observer of nature's law of survival and the apologist for its victims. He was "still sniffing about . . . the Sermon on the Mount and the Beatitudes as alleged governing principles" as he entered the hard-boiled world of journalism. Coming from a religious upbringing that insisted upon such absolutes as good and evil, right and wrong, he encountered everywhere as a journalist a world of vice and corruption. He worked in it side by side with reporters who were cynical and iconoclastic, who did not believe in a fixed moral order that, Dreiser had believed, "one contravened at his peril."[8]

Dreiser's tenure as a Chicago reporter was probably destined from the first to be short-lived. Once the Democratic convention was gone from the city, there were more than enough *Globe* reporters to cover the crime scene at Cheyenne and other hot spots in this urban mix of immigrants and con men. Nonetheless, in September and October, he was assigned to report on the city's fake auction shops where bids were artificially raised to lure in and trap undiscerning strangers. The police, who were involved in or at least aware of the scheme, finally had to act against the perpetrators because of the notoriety created by the newspapers. The likely collusion of police and criminals served to reinforce Dreiser's cynicism about phony or unfair social standards and conventions. Furthermore, he could not have missed the irony in the fact that the very newspaper that sent him out to expose criminal activity was owned by a celebrated politician who ran a string of prostitution and gambling houses, also with the cooperation of a corrupt police force.[9]

During the summer the city editor who had hired Dreiser was replaced by John T. McEnnis, now an alcoholic but once an up-and-coming newspaperman in St. Louis. He affected a western style of dress that later reminded Dreiser of Bret Harte, especially because of his wide-brimmed hat. Dreiser recalled that McEnnis "furthered my career as rapidly as he could, the while that he borrowed a goodly portion of my small salary wherewith to drink."[10] Like Maxwell, McEnnis liked and encouraged him. He regaled the young reporter with stories of the great newspaper editors of the day, such as Charles A. Dana of the *New York Tribune* and Joseph B. McCullagh of the *St. Louis Globe-Democrat,* and declared that Dreiser's talents mandated that he move east to New York—but first by detouring to McCullagh in St. Louis. Through a mutual friend who had just moved from St. Louis, he told McCullagh about Dreiser, and within weeks Dreiser received a wire that a job on the *Globe-Democrat* was waiting for him at twenty dollars a week. The salary was above average for new reporters, but the *Globe-Democrat* was known to pay its staff superior wages.

Dreiser took the train south to St. Louis in late October. Before he left Chicago, however, he had to disentangle himself romantically. By that summer, he had become involved with three different women. There was still Nellie Anderson, but he had also become interested in a young woman on Wabash Avenue by the name of Winstead. And more important than Miss Winstead was Lois Zahn, whom he had met shortly after meeting Nellie. While the Dreiser family was still together on Flourney Street, Claire had brought Lois home one night. Lois had another, older beau, a telegraph operator, but she managed to keep him in the background while she responded to Dreiser's advances. He ultimately became so deeply infatuated with her that he broke up with Nellie and only occasionally saw Miss Winstead. He also declares in the unabridged edition of *Newspaper Days* that

Lois was his first sexual partner, thereby casting doubt on the story in *Dawn* of the baker's daughter in Warsaw.[11] (But, then, Dreiser seems uncertain throughout his autobiography exactly when he experienced his first real sexual intercourse.)

That opportunity with Lois Zahn came about shortly before his departure for St. Louis. One evening the couple retreated to Theo's rented room, and "in the glow of a cheap lamp," they fell into the "creaky yellow-pine contraption" that was his bed. But their passion was preempted by Theo's early ejaculation. Still fretting over the imagined effects of his teenage masturbation, he regarded this accident as evidence of "impotence" or even sterility.[12] Afterward, he said he felt closer to Lois, yet subsequently spent time with Miss Winstead and finally left the city without even saying goodbye. As he had approached Lois's house late one night to do so (thinking vaguely he would send for her once established in St. Louis), he found her with her telegraph operator and left without announcing himself.

Before he left the *Chicago Globe,* Dreiser wrote a few more straight news stories and "even essayed a few parables of my own," which Maxwell published after much scrutiny and scowling. One of the parables was "The Return of Genius," published under the name of Carl Dreiser on October 23, 1892. (For some unknown reason, "Carl" was Maxwell's nickname for Dreiser, but Theo told his family that he had signed it in honor of Sylvia's illegitimate son, Carl, now six years old and possibly back in the care of his reluctant mother.) The tale anticipates Dreiser's idea of himself in *The "Genius,"* at least in its autobiographical dash: "There was born, once upon a time, a great Genius. His younger years were spent in poverty and sorrow. Yet his brain teemed with noble thoughts and grand purposes."[13] Its tone also bears a strong resemblance to Dreiser's self-portrait in *Dawn,* where he tells us that his mother and siblings suspected he was different and perhaps somehow gifted.

In "The Return of Genius," the god of genius comes to the young man as he pines for wealth, pleasure, and enduring fame. The visionary promises to fulfill his wishes, provided the genius agrees never to see or hear of his fame. He is ensconced in a silver mansion with every convenience, but he eventually feels isolated from the world and society. He is warned in vain when he determines to abandon his Faustian paradise that doing so will ensure that his name is forgotten. Dreiser's moral here is not altogether clear. One biographer suggests that to Dreiser achievement had become meaningless apart from an imperfect world. Another suggests it reveals Dreiser's recognition that daydreaming alone was useless; life demanded action.[14] Yet the fact that the protagonist is designated a genius may be more significant than the outcome of the story. At twenty-one Dreiser already knew he was destined for something out of the ordinary. He suspected that he could write, although he sometimes underplays this ability in his autobiography. He was also beginning to think that his talent, like the gift of the silver mansion, had little to do with anything but chance. Life was something of a fable in which the "god of genius" was yet another fickle agent of fate.

Dreiser arrived in St. Louis on a Sunday afternoon and registered at the Silver Moon Hotel, which had been recommended by McEnnis and was right around the corner from the *Globe-Democrat* at Sixth and Pine. It was already dark by the time he checked into his austere hotel room and walked around the heart of the river city. Its decrepit brick buildings contrasted sharply with Chicago's new spirit of growth as it prepared for the World's Fair. And its Sunday quiet reflected more than the Sabbath. By that fall of 1892, "the Mound City" (as it was known for its pre-Columbian burial sites) had a population of almost half a million. Since 1890, however, it had experienced a dramatic decline in industrial growth, mainly because the new national system of railroads had replaced river traffic on the Mississippi as the means of bringing raw material such as Texas cattle to St. Louis for processing and distribution. Also, smaller railroad hubs like Kansas City, Kansas, were becoming more attractive sites for slaughterhouses and meatpacking centers. Lighter industries such as clothing, construction, and canning, as well as the city's largest enterprise, brewing, also began to decline. And the economic depression of 1893 was just around the corner. Despite its rapid growth as an industrial and commercial hub in the 1880s, the manufacturing growth of St. Louis would increase by only two percent in the following decade.[15]

St. Louis also lagged behind Chicago in newspapers, having only a few, including the two Dreiser would work for—the *Globe-Democrat* and the *Republic*. In a turnabout from the Civil War days, the first was Republican and the second Democratic. Postbellum Missouri was almost completely Democratic, but the *Globe-Democrat* offered its voters a formidable antagonist in its editor, Joseph B. McCullagh, whom Eugene Field described in "Little Mack":

This talk about the journalists that run the East is bosh,
We've got a Western editor that's little, but O gosh!
He lives here in Mizzoora, where the people are so set
In ante-bellum notions they vote for Jackson yet;
But the paper he is running makes the rusty fossils swear,—
The smartest, likeliest paper that is printed anywhere!
And best of all, the paragraphs are pointed as a tack
And that's because they emanate
From little Mack.[16]

"In architecture," Field continued, McCullagh was "what you'd call a chunky man," and Dreiser depicts him as "a short, thick, aggressive, rather pugnacious and defensive-looking person of Irish extraction, who looked when I saw him as though he were quite capable of editing this and a dozen other great papers at one and the same time." Dreiser didn't know it when he arrived in St. Louis, but McCullagh came from an even poorer background and bigger family than his own. Born in Dublin in 1842 as one of sixteen children, McCullagh had immigrated to the United States at age eleven. By the time he was sixteen, he had settled in St. Louis and within a year won a job on the *St. Louis Democrat.* He distinguished himself with his reporting during the Civil War, and after the war, when the *Democrat* merged with the *Globe,* he rose to the position of editor, a job he held until his death by probable suicide in 1896. (A heavy cigar smoker who became chronically asthmatic, he was said to have either fallen or thrown himself from his third-story sickroom.) The editor had a genius for instigating news and political debates, and was a crusader against gambling and the sale of alcoholic beverages. He anticipated the "yellow journalism" of the 1890s that Joseph Pulitzer had taken to New York from St. Louis, but he didn't always approve of its applications. He was neither exactly for labor nor against it, though he usually opposed strikes.[17]

The *Globe-Democrat* consisted partly of out-of-town news, stories from around the nation with a smattering of international reports. McCullagh's editorial columns were made up of a series of short one- and two-sentence paragraphs on various topics, which were pointedly and often sarcastically argued. Full of advertising, the daily issues of the paper ran to thirty-six pages; on Sunday there were three different sections. It published features on spiritualism almost daily, a subject that continued to grasp the national and international imagination throughout the 1890s. There was a regular weekly column on Germany entitled "From the Fatherland." The newspaper also ran columns of exhaustive facts on different places and subjects. On January 15, 1893, there is one on physiognomy, in which "very large, thick lips are a sign of sensuality," and "blue eyes belong to people of an enthusiastic turn of mind." There were approving stories about ex-rabbis converting Jews to Christianity and arguments aimed at the lower immigrant classes in which man was disgraced by his "animal functions" only when they "are turned to riot, are perverted or exaggerated and made monstrous."[18]

Stories about lynchings in the neighboring Southern states were also common—and would later inspire Dreiser's short story "Nigger Jeff," in which a cub reporter witnesses a lynching and then visits the condemned man's mother. In one report dispatched to the *Globe-Democrat* about the lynching of a black man accused of raping and murdering an eight-year-old girl in Paris, Texas, the condemned man foolishly returns to the town after his escape "looking for his mother." Though the details in general do not match closely those in Dreiser's short story, the horrible vigilante action was reported vividly enough to make a strong impression on any reader, especially one as young as Dreiser with his emerging sympathy for the impoverished perpetrators of crime, including American blacks in the Jim Crow era. According to the dispatches, two thousand people jeered and cheered as the dead girl's father, brother, and two uncles took turns shoving red-hot irons under the feet of the accused who was pinioned to a stake. Afterward, they thrust the irons into the man's eyes and ears and finally burned him at the stake. The incident was reported in newspapers around the country, and the governor of Texas, James S. Hogg, demanded (in vain) the arrest and conviction of the active members of the lynch mob.[19]

By the time Dreiser met the already overweight and asthmatic McCullagh, the editor was seldom absent from his sedentary post. The only other chair in his small office, presumably for guests, was always piled high with newspapers and editorial copy. As Dreiser stood awkwardly amidst the office debris on his first day on the job, he felt discouraged by McCullagh's dismissive welcome: "'Um, yuss! Um, yuss,' was all he deigned after I had given my name and the fact that he had telegraphed for me," he remembered in *Newspaper Days*. "'See Mr. Mitchell in the city room—the city editor. Your salary will be—um—um—twenty dollars to begin with' (he was chewing a cigar and mumbled his words), and he turned to his papers." To top off McCullagh's disappointing welcome, Tobias Mitchell, the city editor, sent Dreiser out on the traditional cub reporter initiation, to report the news from a vacant lot.[20]

For the first time Dreiser was living wholly on his own, not across town from family members now but in a different city three hundred miles away. He found a room ("It was a hall bedroom—one of a long series that I was to occupy") on Pine Street around the corner from the newspaper building, whose offices were on the sixth floor. He remembered the first weeks as the loneliest he had ever experienced. In Chicago he had enjoyed friends and family; now he had not even a girlfriend. He began to regret his behavior toward Lois and thought of writing her but then had second thoughts that the renewed relationship would suggest marriage and its elusive twin, fidelity, two fugitive states throughout Dreiser's adult life.

His regular assignment for the *Globe-Democrat* became the police station and criminal court—his specialty, as it turned out, throughout his newspaper days. To Dreiser, the courtroom (as he would ultimately suggest in *An American Tragedy*) was the last place the poor and uneducated were likely to receive justice in an imperfect world. "By degrees" he made friends with all the staff at the paper, including one unidentified African-American. One of his colleagues, Bob Hazard, had written a novel after the example of Émile Zola, the father of French naturalism. Since it told the "truth" about life in all its sordid detail, Hazard was certain it couldn't be published in America. Yet Hazard's ambition sparked Dreiser's own interest in creative writing, though he initially hoped this would manifest itself in playwriting.

One day he wandered into the newspaper's art department and met Peter McCord, an illustrator who was to become one of his best friends. "Nearly every turning point in my career," Dreiser noted in *Newspaper Days*, "has been signalized by my meeting up with some man—not woman—of great force."[21] A first-generation American and a Catholic like Dreiser, this St. Louis native had lapsed in his faith but had not given it up completely. Another close companion from the paper was Dick Wood, also an illustrator, whose talents were inferior to McCord's. At first, Wood seemed to resent Dreiser's intrusion into his own friendship with McCord, but gradually, they became a trio, meeting often in Wood's "so-called 'studio,'" and dreaming of careers as professional artists and writers. Dreiser was intrigued by the semi-bohemian life the two illustrators appeared to lead, and before he knew it, he was writing poetry for the first time.

Dreiser's break on the *Chicago Daily Globe* had been at the Democratic convention of 1892. On the *Globe-Democrat* he claims to have been the first reporter on the scene at a horrible train mishap near Alton, Illinois, about twenty-five miles north of St. Louis. Train wrecks were commonplace in the late nineteenth century because cars ran in different directions on the same track and depended on the alertness of switchmen, who were often poorly trained and usually only part-time employees. One day when Dreiser was the first to arrive at the editorial room, word reached him of this latest catastrophe. With the city editor absent from the office, he said he took it upon himself to rush to the scene and try to scoop the story, which was actually only half played out by the time he (or at least someone from the *Globe-Democrat*) reached Alton Junction. The collision had involved oil-tank cars, which after being pushed off the tracks continued to give off fire and smoke until they exploded, throwing debris for hundreds of yards in all directions.

Dreiser says he was about fifteen hundred feet away when the tanks exploded. Many more people were injured in this phase of the disaster, especially the curious who had come out of their houses in neighboring Wann. "I saw dashing toward me," he recalled in his autobiography, "a man whose face I could not make out clearly, for at times it was partially covered by his hands." The victim was on fire and flailing his hands in the air when he wasn't grasping his face. Dreiser tried to smother the flames with his coat, but it was too little too late. Yet his reporter's instincts were at once activated. While the injured and dead were en route by a special train to Alton, Dreiser made a list of the names and injuries for the story he would write. But before he could get away to write it, he was surrounded in Alton by anxious friends and relatives. Consequently prevented from rushing back to St. Louis to write his story, he stood before the crowd and read off the names and injuries to the worried and grief-stricken crowd.[22]

"One of the most appalling and disastrous wrecks that has occurred in years," Dreiser wrote that evening under the leader "Burned to Death" in the *Globe-Democrat* of January 22, 1893, "followed the negligence of a switchman on the Big Four road at Wann, Ill., yesterday morning." The story, more than five thousand words in length, is remarkable for its Balzacian detail, though the narrative itself seems to lack some of the Dreiserian pace. It provided not only all the names of the dead and injured but an hour-by-hour account of the accident, with nothing left out except the obvious negligence of the railroad itself. Newspapers could criticize the police, but rarely corporate America before the advent of the muckrakers and yellow journalists at the turn of the century. He followed up the next day with "Sixteen Dead," almost as long as the first report. Here Dreiser was not squeamish in relating the medical situation. "Their eyes are burned out. Their ears are great, swollen sores, or mere crusts," he wrote. "They have breathed in the flames and the fumes of the burning oil, and, as a consequence, their mouths and throats are raw and bleeding."[23]

Dreiser found Dick Wood's illustration for the first story disappointing, commenting that it lacked all "spirit or meaning." It was a crude representation in which the figures approaching the wreck looked like cartoon caricatures of human forms; the train itself was hardly recognizable as such. Wood's lackluster performance did nothing, however, to diminish McCullagh's warm reaction to Dreiser's achievement. The reporter he had summoned from Chicago at McEnnis's suggestion seemed to have lived up to his recommendation. "I wanted to say to you that I liked that story you wrote very much—very much indeed," the editor-in-chief told Dreiser in an uncharacteristic show of cordiality. "I like to recognize a good piece of work when I see it. I have raised your salary to twenty-five dollars."[24] McCullagh then reached into his pocket and drew out a yellowed twenty dollar bill, which he handed over as a bonus.

The story of the train wreck and subsequent bonus comes, of course, from *Newspaper Days*. Famous people often write autobiographies in part to preempt the inevitable more critical biographies with favorable facts that sometimes stray into fiction. Such memoirs are particularly useful in controlling any early parts of a biography, where contradictory facts are hazy or more often unavailable. Doubtless, Dreiser distorted parts of his autobiography, either consciously or unconsciously. McCullagh did not live to confirm or deny the story as told in *Newspaper Days,* but one of Dreiser's fellow newspaper reporters cast some doubt on this tale of heroic on-the-scene reporting. Arch T. Edmonston wrote Dreiser at the beginning of the Great Depression, when Dreiser was rich and famous as the author of *An American Tragedy,* claiming that he had been the reporter sent to Alton Junction to cover the story and that Dreiser covered it only from St. Louis. In 1929 Edmonston was sick and out of work and asking for a loan, so there is no reason he would have lied in his letter or claimed something which would annoy his potential benefactor.

"We 'did' a railroad wreck together," Edmonston wrote. "It was in Illinois a few miles East of St. Louis. You 'did' the St. Louis end of it—the old Union Depot, and I hastened to the scene in an old 'sea going hack,' taking a telegraph operator with me, and finally wired in about 2000 words." (Although there were three different railroad companies running trains between St. Louis and Alton, travel by boat may have been more expeditious, especially after a wreck.) The main problem with believing Edmonston, whose own memory by this time may have been unreliable, is that he recalls that he and Dreiser were colleagues not on the *Globe-Democrat,* but the *St. Louis Republic,* which all other evidence indicates Dreiser did not join until long after any major train wreck occurred, as Edmonston put it, "in Illinois a few miles East of St. Louis."[25]

Since Dreiser was never a newspaper editor or a full-time columnist with a byline, it is often a challenge to identify his journalism. He wrote neither the Broadway editorials of Walt Whitman, whose democratic catalogs eventually surfaced in *Leaves of Grass,* nor the comic hyperbole of Mark Twain, whose correspondences from the Holy Land revealed his early suspicions about the "damned human race."[26] Most of what has been identified as his reporting (based either on his penchant for detail or on cross-references to items in *Newspaper Days*) focused on police and court stories of domestic violence, rapes (then euphemistically called "outrages"), and kidnappings or visiting celebrities, including famous clairvoyants passing through town, plus the usual run of assignments doled out by the city editor. Dreiser claimed to have interviewed the famed boxer John L. Sullivan, but the only recovered piece in the *Globe-Democrat* about Sullivan is a condescending description of the great man's uninterrupted inebriation, a tone decidedly too harsh for the younger Dreiser's pen.[27]

There were opportunities—however limited—for the future fictionist's creative energies which contain unimpeachable evidence of Dreiser's authorship. In addition to his regular reportorial duties, he was assigned a column, which had been passed around the office, called "Heard in the Corridors." The idea may have been an offshoot of the formal newspaper interview, which McCullagh is credited with inventing. A similar informal mix of fiction and fact, called "About the Hotels," ran in the *Chicago Globe,* where McCullagh's influence operated through McEnnis. There Dreiser had already written three or four such pieces in which a traveling salesman or a local celebrity is interviewed in a hotel lobby. One column features Dreiser's college roommate by name, and another dwells on Poe and spiritualism.[28]

It was from writing "Heard in the Corridors" and other interview pieces that Dreiser acquired an early fondness for the setting of the hotel lobby furnished with rocking chairs that would become George Hurstwood's last sanctuary in *Sister Carrie,* before his clothes give him away as down and out. The "Heard in the Corridors" interviews, some real, most fabulous, take place in the following St. Louis hotels: the Laclede, Lindell, Southern, Richelieu, and St. James. Often he introduced real people known to him, such as his brother Paul, into these fictitious conversations. Recurring subjects in the column were superstition, man's best friend, mother love, religion, the moral dangers of the American Dream or success, realism, the economy, socialism, legendary or unsolved crimes, reformers and social panaceas, mortality, and local color items of general interest.

Dreiser's subjects here come from the same sentimental world of Paul's songs about longings for home or mothers who have died while waiting for their wandering sons or daughters to return home. Among the stories for the column of December 24, 1892, Paul is interviewed about a Connecticut mill accident, perhaps linking their own father's mill work in Connecticut and his mill accident in Indiana. On another subject, published on February 20, 1893, the hotel interviewee speaks of the painful effect of a letter from his dead mother ("written to me months before when at school"), uncovered as he repacked his trunks. Dreiser clearly was reaching into his family past for his fictions long before *Sister Carrie.* In "Heard in the Corridors" he also used a version of his near premature burial while spelunking outside Bloomington (December 30, 1892). We find as well the seeds of later attitudes. One on government control of industries in Russia regrets only that the state is controlled by a czar instead of the people (January 2, 1893).

Not long after his (or Edmonston's) stories on the train wreck, the position of dramatic editor on the *Globe-Democrat* came open. It too had been passed around the office, Hazard having already done the job once. At the time, the job of drama critic was not considered an important post by newspapers. Following the Civil War, local acting troupes had given way to touring companies that followed the spread of railroads. And with this change, American drama—still in its fledgling state before the twentieth century—became big business in which melodramas, society plays, and farce-comedies predominated. By the mid-1890's, *Century Magazine* bitterly lamented that "Tragedy, high comedy, the historical and romantic drama have been virtually banished from the state, or find few worthy interpreters, and have been replaced to a large extent by worthless melodramas, the extravagant buffooneries of so-called farce-comedies, or the feverish and unwholesome society play, in which the most vicious topics are discussed openly under the pretense of solving problems."[29]

Dreiser, as he readily confessed in *Newspaper Days,* hadn't known the difference. The closest he had probably ever come to a stage by the 1890s was seeing his brother Paul perform in burlesque shows in Evansville and Chicago. Where there was respectable drama, it favored old standbys of the last forty years—dramatizations of Harriet Beecher Stowe's *Uncle Tom's Cabin,* Lew Wallace's *Ben Hur,* or Washington Irving's "Rip Van Winkle." Dreiser saw the beloved actor Joseph Jefferson star in the last, which played in St. Louis during the week of December 12, 1892. Another play making the popular rounds was *Under the Gaslight* by Augustin Daly. Daly, with his real-life settings and mushy plots, became the father, or at least grandfather, of modern American drama.[30] (The play, which portrays life in New York City, is the same one in which Carrie Meeber first performs in *Sister Carrie.*)

Emboldened by his success with the train accident, Dreiser went over the city editor's head to ask for the job. This would come back to haunt him, but he couldn't conceal his ultimate dislike for Tobias Mitchell (as he could not throughout his life for anybody he disliked). He imagined he was now McCullagh's protégé and so approached the cigar-chewing editor directly. Characteristically succinct and to the point, the great editor told him, "Very well. You're dramatic editor. Tell Mr. Mitchell to let you be it." According to Dreiser's account, he got the job at the end of January 1893. He reviewed not only plays but individual performances, such as that of "Black Patti," or Sissieretta Jones, whose popular singing had made her a star in Europe. In his review of April 1, Dreiser may have irritated the largely Southern sensibilities of his St. Louis readers with his admiration for the black soprano by lavishly proclaiming that her "singing reminds one of the beauty of nature and brings back visions of the still, glassy water and soft swaying branches of some drowsy nook in summer time." At any rate, as he remembers it in his autobiography, he was laughed at by his colleagues at the *Globe-Democrat,* and McCullagh, as editor of the paper, became the target of ridicule from the *Republic.*[31]

This generosity toward a black performer probably didn't help him at the *Globe-Democrat,* but what hurt him more directly is that Mitchell, annoyed at how Dreiser had gone around him to get the dramatic assignment, kept piling on other assignments as if Dreiser weren't now doing that job. As it was, with more than one troupe of actors appearing in the city at the same time, there already wasn't enough time for Dreiser to see an entire show. He had to rely—as was the common practice among newspapers in those days—on advance notices and plot summaries for his reviews. And then one night Mitchell struck his fatal blow.

On the last Saturday night in April, when all the St. Louis theaters were booked, Mitchell sent him on what was essentially another "vacant lot" assignment. He was dispatched to the scene of an alleged streetcar holdup on the western edge of St. Louis. Accordingly, he filed three dramatic reviews based on press accounts and advance notices and set out for the scene of the crime. Nobody knew anything about a holdup when he got there, and by the time he returned to the center of the city it was too late to check with the theaters to make sure the companies had actually performed—it was a common occurrence for storms to wash out roads or low bridges and thus prevent companies from arriving in time to perform, and it had rained violently that evening.

He thought of checking with his counterpart at the *Republic,* but didn't, later comparing this psychic paralysis to Poe's "imp of the perverse," where we fail to act to save ourselves. (Buried in Poe's anticipation of the Pre-Raphaelite Movement and the aesthetic one championed by Oscar Wilde, another hero of Dreiser's, are the deterministic themes that underscore Dreiser's later fictions and masterpieces.) In fact, two of the touring companies for whom Dreiser had written notices (not three, as remembered in *Newspaper Days*) were missing in action that night. In one of those reviews, of *Uncle Tom's Cabin* scheduled for Pope's Theater, he remembered calling the performance "unworthy" and "top-heavy"; the meaning of the last adjective is unclear in the text of *Newspaper Days.* In the review itself, appearing in the *Globe-Democrat* of May 1, the only performance deemed "unworthy" is that of Peter Jackson, one of several famed pugilists of the day (among them John L. Sullivan) who were introduced into plays regardless of their acting talent in hopes of drawing big audiences. Jackson, an Australian black heavyweight, played "Uncle Tom." The "top-heavy" comment was probably directed at the anticipated audience, which tended to overfill the theater's balconies and galleries whenever a prizefighter appeared on stage, especially in blackface.[32]

Dreiser claimed he was so embarrassed by the fiasco that rather than face McCullagh he sheepishly left him a note of apology and resignation. He envisioned himself as the laughingstock of St. Louis. He was right to a certain extent, for this time, unlike with the "Black Patti" incident, he didn't have to exaggerate the response from the competing newspapers.[33] They came out in the city's afternoon newspapers with satiric barbs the same day his bogus reviews appeared. Dreiser claimed that McCullagh was sorry he had resigned. This may sound self-serving, but it was a common practice for drama critics to crib from the advance publicity; no doubt it had happened before.

———

Dreiser picked up his reporter's life almost without missing a beat. Within a week he was hired by the *Republic* at eighteen dollars a week, seven less than what he had been getting on the *Globe-Democrat*. He got on with its city editor, H. B. Wandell, better than he had with Mitchell, yet he remembered Wandell as a narrow-minded and self-serving Machiavellian who would do just about anything to get the story first. A "mouse-like" little man with piercing hawk eyes and "dark, swarthy skin," he cackled mirthlessly whenever he was ahead of the competition.[34]

Here too Dreiser's testimony is contested by another survivor from his autobiographical past. Tobias Mitchell, for example, was probably dead by the time *Newspaper Days* was first published (in 1922, with the title *A Book About Myself*), but Wandell was exceedingly alive and incensed at Dreiser's extended remarks about him. Describing himself as still "an editorial writer, actively engaged," he threatened to sue Dreiser's publisher, Boni & Liveright. More significantly, he described Dreiser in his St. Louis days as "vile, licentious, dishonorable and ignorant" and never a true newspaperman. "He was a cheap and super-sexative [*sic*] faker, always with the libidinous uppermost in his mind—at least that was the general opinion held of him here—a parasite and a leech." Wandell's testimony may be exaggerated because of his anger, but his comment about sexual excess may throw into clearer focus Dreiser's portrait of himself as sex-starved. In other words, Dreiser may have developed his reputation as a womanizer as early as 1893, a time when he still described himself as shy around women. "Women," he confesses in a moment of greater candor in his autobiography, "were not included in my moral speculations as among those who were to receive strict justice—not pretty women."[35]

Dreiser worked for the *Republic* for about nine months, until February or March of 1894, but he doesn't have that much to say about the experience. It was generally a continuation of his assignments on the *Globe-Democrat*, though the *Republic* appears to have been more interested in local news, scandals, and exposés. One of his compatriots remembered Dreiser as "better as a writer than in getting the news." The articles attributed to him, or suspected to have been written by him, in his collected journalism for this period show him reporting on domestic murders, train robberies, hangings, lynchings, spiritualists—the usual run of sensational newspaper stories of that day that were often hyped up for maximum effect.[36]

One of the spiritualists investigated by the *Republic* makes a fleeting appearance in *Sister Carrie*—Jules Wallace, a hard-drinking Irishman whom the paper set out to embarrass in the fall of 1893. Wandell assigned Dreiser to hang about the site of the spiritualist's performances and his residence in the hope of digging up some dirt. Dreiser managed to learn from Wallace's landlady, who had spied on her raucous tenant through a keyhole, that the medium had used his room for group sex. She claimed to have seen Wallace and two associates cavorting with partially nude women. And to support her testimony, this "moralist" had purloined a card left by one of the women for Wallace and turned it over to Dreiser.

When Dreiser went to the address in an upscale neighborhood to confront the woman in question, she fell to her knees and begged him to drop the matter. She even tried to bribe him with sex when he refused her pleas to drop the matter and said he had no choice but to turn the evidence over to his city editor. As it turned out, Wandell did not pursue this angle of the campaign against Wallace because, as Dreiser hints in the manuscript of his autobiography (material that was not included in the published version in 1922), Wandell may have compromised himself by accepting the woman's sexual advances. We might applaud Dreiser for his professionalism, as well as his disinclination to take sexual advantage of a desperate woman, but whatever his other shortcomings in dealing with women, Dreiser probably never coerced anybody into sex. On the other hand, in turning over the evidence to Wandell, Dreiser—the future author of "immoral literature"—was enforcing the puritanical mandates of society he afterward so vigorously and vociferously opposed. His view of the matter at the time was simply that he "had done a very clever piece" of reporting.[37]

During his fourteen or so months in St. Louis, Dreiser moved three or four times, and in at least two of these rooming houses, his landlady, older than himself, became his sexual partner. While living at the corner of Tenth and Walnut, he got involved with a woman who reminded him of his mother. Like Sarah Dreiser, "Mrs. Zernhouse" was large, buxom, and peasantlike. Also like Sarah, she was of Germanic background, and her late husband had been the victim of a factory accident. Dreiser often visited her room after a late-night assignment. Sometimes Mrs. Zernhouse waited for him in his room and once surrendered herself to him stimulated by the knowledge that he had shared his bed with a younger woman earlier in the day. Later he recalled Mrs. Z's "blazing orgasms." In another rooming house, on Chestnut Street just beyond Jefferson, he took up with "Mrs. X," who was a little younger than Mrs. Z, but more promiscuous. Dreiser, however, wanted more than sex—not "this kind of woman but an ineffable poetic something. . . ."[38] In spite of his sexual restlessness, he still subscribed to the very conventional idea of true love—and he soon believed he had found it.

As a way to take advantage of the long awaited Chicago World's Fair, formally the Columbian Exposition, the *Republic* had staged a statewide contest to find the favorite teacher in each of Missouri's school districts. The winners, mostly young women, were to be sent to the Chicago Fair for two weeks, all expenses paid. One might wonder here whether the randy Wandell was not putting the fox in the henhouse when he assigned the "supersexative" Dreiser to accompany the young ladies and write up their adventures for the paper. Whatever the case, Dreiser was delighted to find himself on the way to Chicago in a lavish Pullman car surrounded by what he would call in his dispatches back to the *Republic* the "Forty Odd"—a "bevy" of young ladies and their relatives, mainly nubile younger sisters.[39] It is on just such a train to Chicago that Charles Drouet meets Carrie Meeber in the opening pages of *Sister Carrie*—and his train ride is based in part on the one Dreiser took from St. Louis to Chicago in 1893: in that Pullman filled with marriageable young women, his future wife, Sara Osborne White of Montgomery City, Missouri, stood out for her innocent looks and quiet charm.

Jug, as she was called for her beautiful hair, the reddish-brown color of an earthen jug of the song, hailed from a family almost as large as Dreiser's, with seven girls and three boys. Their economic backgrounds were also similar, she having grown up in rural Missouri. Jug had become a contest winner, she told him, because her friends bought hundreds of the *Republic* issues advertising the competition and clipped the coupons. What a wonderful thing, he thought, to have such loyal friends. Jug wore her hair clasped in a bun behind her head. She had a slightly weak chin, but this was offset by a soft mouth and large liquid eyes. Her lithe figure and gentle half smile sent Dreiser into near spasms of desire. He sensed almost immediately that there was an unspoken bond of sympathy between them. Yet at the same time, he as readily imagined himself with several of the other beauties on the train, including the less inhibited Annie Ginity, who easily responded to Dreiser's advances, and Jug's younger sister Rose, who didn't.

Like many of the twenty-seven million visitors to the World's Fair that year, Rose paid her own way from out of town, even though she could hardly afford to do so. Indeed, the anticipation over the fair was so great and widespread that some people even mortgaged their homes to be able see the sights at Jackson Park on the shores of Lake Michigan. Designed to celebrate the four hundredth anniversary of Columbus's discovery of the New World, the Exposition also celebrated by implication America's full recovery from the Civil War and the idea that through its technology America was destined to become the world's leader in the twentieth century. Perhaps tellingly, the fair opened a year late for the anniversary, just as America was entering the depression years of 1893–97, but during its run, optimism remained high. Certainly, as Dreiser noted in his autobiography, it was seen as a clear symbol for Chicago's own metamorphosis. "Here all at once, as it were, out of nothing, in this dingy city of six or seven hundred thousand, which but a few years before had been a waste of wet grass and mud flats, and by this lake, which a hundred years before was but a lone silent waste, was now this vast and harmonious collection of perfectly constructed and snowy buildings, containing in their delightful interiors . . . the artistic, mechanical and scientific achievements to date."[40]

The main part of the White City (so-called for its white neoclassical domed structures made out of plaster and fiber) consisted of a long basin with exhibition halls, including an Administration Building and a Court of Honor. The Grand Basin was elaborately connected by bridges and waterways to a series of terraced lagoons designed by Frederick Law Olmstead, famed as the designer of New York's Central Park. Here were found more enchanting buildings and statuary. The two main sculptures of the exhibition, Daniel Chester French's *Republic* and Frederick William MacMonnie's *Columbian Fountain,* stood in the middle of the basin. Tourists thought French's mammoth creation resembled the Statue of Liberty, while the Administration Building reminded Exposition visitors of the Capitol in Washington. The grand architecture, as one historian notes, represented "a return not to the Rome of the Caesars but to the chaste classicism of Thomas Jefferson." The palatial aura of this neoclassical city—its idealized gardens and lighted white buildings—made an impression on Dreiser that later translated into Carrie Meeber's infatuation with the mansions along Chicago's north shore in Chicago.[41] An ancillary feature of the Fair— certainly another indelible literary impression for Dreiser—was the new fast paced "El," or elevated train, constructed by Chicago's transit king, Charles T. Yerkes.

When he wasn't busy escorting one or another of the schoolteachers (including Miss White) around the Exposition grounds, Dreiser took the cable car out to the west side of town to visit his father, whom he hadn't seen for almost a year. More than once they toured the astonishing exhibits at the fair together, including a simulated German village, but the old man wasn't up to much walking around the picturesque concourses, and father and son no doubt took advantage of the launches that ran over more than two miles of watercourse. He found his father "thin as a grasshopper, brooding sadly with those brown-black German eyes." Now in his seventies, John Paul Dreiser still stood tall and erect, looking with his cape like a Prussian soldier. This, as well as the rest of his quasi-military uniform, was largely made of material from Paul's discarded clothes. He fretted endlessly about money and wondered whether Theo could actually afford their outings. Father and son got along now because Dreiser no longer openly fought his father's cloying Catholicism. He simply lied when asked whether he had kept up the Church sacraments. He learned that Al and Ed hadn't come near their father in months, and Dreiser left him at the end of his Chicago stay with a nagging sense of guilt.[42]

Before he left, he saw his two brothers and perhaps reproached them for ignoring their father. Ed was still driving a laundry wagon, and Al was working for an electric plant. Neither felt he was getting ahead in Chicago, and both soon answered Theo's invitation to join him after he returned to St. Louis. But the depression had now begun to set in, and after six weeks of searching they were back in Chicago. Ed eventually migrated to New York City to pursue an acting career. But Al, a morose, brooding man, would ultimately vanish from the life of Theodore Dreiser. While in St. Louis he had vocally disapproved of Theo's connection with "Mrs. X"; it is possible he had once like his brother Paul contracted a venereal disease.[43] Al had aspirations and longings for "a higher intellectual life" and eventually tried advertising in Chicago, writing on one occasion Bromo Seltzer jingles that did not sell.

Dreiser, too, ached for something better than the arduous routine of newspaper reporting with its late-night hours and low pay. Even though he felt he had already distinguished himself on the *Republic,* his salary remained at the same pitiful eighteen dollars a week, less than half that earned by his friends McCord and Wood. Once back in St. Louis, he courted Jug by mail with long letters he later classified as his "first and easiest attempt at literary expression."[44] He longed to get her into bed, and it was in the thrall of this not so chivalrous point of view that he proposed marriage to her in November and they became engaged. Jug visited Theo in St. Louis from time to time, but she wouldn't allow him to visit her in Florissant, where she taught, some twenty miles northwest of downtown St. Louis. The betrothal lasted five years, and the resolutely elusive Jug did not surrender her virginity until she became Mrs. Dreiser.

Paul came to St. Louis in January 1894 as part of the cast of *The Danger Signal,* which played at the Havilin. He met Dreiser's newspaper friends, including McCord and Wood, and later Jug, whom he would never like. In fact, Paul viewed Jug as mired in midwestern convention whose mediocrity would stifle Theo's development as a writer, and he tried to dissuade his brother from continuing the engagement. Theo should at least remain single long enough to try out his talents on New York.[45] For his part, Dreiser clung to the idyllic notion of having Jug and a little cottage somewhere, yet in his restlessness, continued to see "Mrs. X" and the young teacher Miss Ginity on the sly. He wanted only Jug, he thought, but there was no other way to satisfy his sexual hunger; Jug wouldn't even consent to sit on his lap.

One day a newspaperman "blew in" from Chicago and got a job on the *Republic.* Like Dreiser, Winfield Hutchinson was engaged to a type of girl-next-door but could not afford to get married yet. Hutchinson longed to start a country newspaper in Grand Rapids, Ohio, where he had been raised. Dreiser, as he later recalled, felt so uncertain as to his "proper future" that he was soon converted to the idea of becoming his partner in the enterprise. Not long after Hutchinson lost his job on the *Republic* "over his inability to imagine something properly one night," the two new friends departed separately for Ohio.[46] Dreiser was on the open road once again, leaving yet another city and yet another woman behind. But this woman was his fiancée, and Jug promised to wait for him. He promised, too, but was already cultivating doubts about having and holding the same woman.

FOUR

Survival of the Fittest

*How was it, I now asked myself, after nearly three years
of work in which I had been a reporter, a traveling correspondent,
a dramatic editor, and a staff feature man doing Sunday and
daily features, I should now once more be called upon
to do this wretched reportorial stuff?*

NEWSPAPER DAYS

ALTHOUGH DREISER DIDN'T KNOW IT for certain as his train from St. Louis pushed through Indiana to the northwest corner of Ohio ("over the Clover Leaf route"), he had begun a journey whose final destination would be New York. By the time he left St. Louis in early March of 1894, the attraction of that "great and glowing centre" of America had been well planted by his brother Paul. He could not have known that he was also within four or five years of, not journalistic success, but literary greatness. Writing to a friend from his Sullivan days, he drew a self-portrait that reveals a measure of his self-confidence: "when you look at [my picture], you will see egotism written in every lineament; a strong presentment of self love in every expression. I have a semi-Roman nose, a high forehead and an Austrian lip, with the edges of my teeth always showing. I wear my hair long, and part it in the middle, only to brush it roughly back from the temples. Then I'm six feet tall, but never look it, and very frail of physique. I always feel ill, and people say I look cold and distant. I dislike companionship as far as numbers go, and care only for a few friends."[1]

In his autobiography Dreiser maintains that he left St. Louis entirely on his own initiative, armed even with a letter from the *Republic* (presumably from H. B. Wandell) to help him find another newspaper job. Although he evidently did have an invitation to start the country newspaper with Winfield Hutchinson in Grand Rapids, it is not improbable that Dreiser was fired from the *Republic* by Wandell, who, as we have seen, rather sourly remembered Dreiser as not much of a newspaper man. Interestingly, Dreiser was careful to follow up the claim of this letter of recommendation in the autobiographies by mentioning later that—for reasons unexplained or unexplainable—he never used it as he sought newspaper jobs in Toledo, Cleveland, Buffalo, Pittsburgh, and New York.[2] He also asserts that the *Republic* offered him an increased salary as an incentive to remain in St. Louis. As near to broke as he was, it hardly seems likely that he would have set out for the unknown just then.

He may have left St. Louis in part to get away from Jug, whose determined resistance to his advances seemed to contribute to increasingly regular moods of depression, an affliction he suffered from during several periods in his life. Yet in manic relief from those moods, he wrote prodigiously to his "honey pot" while still in St. Louis and afterward, longing for her presence and occasionally accusing her of indifference. At the same time, however, he also tried to initiate a romantic correspondence with Emma Rector, the daughter of old family friends living in Indiana. (One wonders whether Dreiser was bipolar. The manic phase of this condition is usually accompanied by lower inhibitions and a correspondingly raised libido. This would also help to account for his sustained bursts of energy as a novelist later on.) Like his "varietistic" protagonists from George Hurstwood to Clyde Griffiths, Dreiser loved most what he couldn't have. Perhaps Jug would, at least literally, hold on to him the longest because she held out the longest. Even his eventual second wife, Helen, whose intimate attachment outlasted all the other Dreiser women, was jolted out of paradise early and regularly in their twenty-five-year association.

Grand Rapids ("Ohio, not Michigan," Dreiser reminds the reader of *A Hoosier Holiday*, as if to italicize his uneasy sense of going off to nowhere) sat on the Maumee River in the northwest corner of the state, about fifteen miles from Toledo. The river, he recalled, was "a wide and shallow affair, flowing directly through the heart of the town and tumbling rapidly over grey stones, a spectacle which had suggested the name of the town."[3] Its beauty impressed him far more than the town itself, or for that matter his prospects there. Consisting mostly of one- and two-story framed dwellings and brick storefronts, Grand Rapids sat in rural surroundings dotted with gaunt oil wells whose industrial hue made them stand out in the still snow-covered landscape. After he and Hutchinson had inspected the newspaper office and equipment to be purchased—a bleak affair that had been inoperative for more than a year—they queried the local merchants to gauge the advertising potential. The merchants, including a druggist, a banker, and a stable owner, stared at the two "as if we were adventurers from Mars." The town fathers weren't even sure they wanted a newspaper in Grand Rapids to read, much less one in which to advertise. Moreover, they wanted to know what the politics of such a newspaper would be and whether its editors, or at least the newcomer Dreiser, were "good moral boys and whether we would work hard for the interests of the town and against certain unsatisfactory elements."[4]

Having grown up in the narrow-minded and economically deprived towns of Indiana, Dreiser soon suspected that their newspaper scheme would not have worked on any basis. Even so, the two prospective editors also looked over a more expensive paper for sale in nearby Bowling Green. By then Hutchinson himself seemed discouraged. By mid-March, Dreiser decided to move on, thinking that he might settle for another reporter's position in Toledo. Although he did not wish to settle down in this city of one hundred thousand—by now he wasn't even sure he wanted to continue in the field of journalism—he thought Toledo might be pleasant for six months or so.

Dreiser never forgot his train ride to Toledo along the beautiful Maumee, with its sloping banks and occasional waterfalls and rapids. And though he would try later, he would also never forget a young man he met there, the new city editor of the *Toledo Blade,* who was destined "to take a definite and inspiriting part in my life." Arthur Henry, who claimed to be a direct descendant of Patrick Henry, had previously worked in Chicago, where he had covered Cook County politics for the *Herald* with the future novelist Brand Whitlock. When he came to the *Blade* the previous November, he was already engaged to Maude Wood, an independent-minded young woman who worked as a reporter on the paper; the couple married in May 1894.[5] His Napoleonic profile and cherubic countenance gave him a look at once of accomplishment and youthful innocence. (He was, in fact, four years older than Dreiser.) Henry confided his dreams of becoming a poet and a novelist and had already written some poems. What Henry didn't tell his new friend was that he was already the author of one novel, *Nicholas Blood, Candidate* (1890).

Anticipating the genre of novels favoring the activities of the Ku Klux

Klan, the most popular of which would be Thomas Dixon's *The Clansman* (1905), *Nicholas Blood, Candidate* capitalized on the Negrophobia that had developed in the United States since the Civil War and Reconstruction. As much a screed as a novel, it takes place in Memphis following the passage of the Fifteenth Amendment in 1870, which gave black males the constitutional right to vote. "Does anybody doubt that America has among her possibilities a Reign of Terror?" the epigraph asks. "We have 8,000,000 children of the night among us, and, like the shadows of a dark and stormy night, they spread swiftly. . . . Let us look at them." Nicholas Blood alarms the white citizens of the city when he runs unsuccessfully for mayor. Among the stock characters are northern whites—second-generation abolitionists— who relocate in the South and initially give blacks the benefit of the doubt, until they are dissuaded by tales of their barbarous conduct. One disillusioned Yankee tells his former Confederate foes: "Before the war I cursed you, and you deserved it then. After the war I called you bloodthirsty lords and damned tyrants. I used to hold up the poor colored brethren to view as an oppressed and lamb-like race."

But Blood destroys these beliefs when he turns violent after his political defeat. He kills one white man as he walks down Beale Street and later rapes the man's daughter while she is visiting her old mammy in the black section of the city. The tale is addressed to those northern whites who still think of blacks as passive and submissive, as they appeared as slaves. (Indeed, the lynching era was largely fueled by white fears about blacks who would no longer be "properly" raised under slavery.) Another victim of black barbarity in this book is Philander Matthews, who thinks black rule is inevitable, if also undesirable. Finally, the white woman's honor is avenged by the stereotyped white hero, Thomas Judd, a Yankee and a former abolitionist whose motto is that the "negro is the greatest problem in America, but I know very little of him." Judd throws Blood off a high balcony after the black fiend and his cohorts have set fire to the city. The story ends with the warning that blacks are multiplying much faster than whites in Memphis and elsewhere in the South, which is now "at last awakening from its long sleep."[6]

It is impossible to know whether Arthur Henry truly harbored these racist sentiments or was simply availing himself of an opportunity to write a formulaic novel in Jim Crow America. Perhaps it was both, but by the time he met Dreiser, he was apparently embarrassed about the book, and he later falsely claimed that no copies of it had ever been distributed.[7] In the nineteenth century—easily as late as the 1890s—educated or socially enlightened whites like Henry and the future author of "Nigger Jeff" didn't hate or fear blacks in the manner of the narrator in *Nicholas Blood,* but they were probably part of the consensus that perceived blacks as genetically inferior to whites and thus an emerging social problem. As late as 1945, Henry's first wife described the book as simply "a story of the negro menace to whites," which Arthur had written as a "side issue" while on assignment in the South for *Frank Leslie's* magazine.[8]

When Dreiser presented himself at the *Blade,* Henry made immediate use of the itinerant reporter—whom he later recalled as looking "gaunt, rugged, a little dishevelled from his travels" the day the two met. Toledo was in the throes of a streetcar strike that threatened to turn violent. Learning that the streetcar company was going to run a strike-breaking car on the lines the next day and having no reporter on hand to send on what might be a dangerous assignment, the city editor offered Dreiser the assignment on a per diem basis. As Henry remembered it, Dreiser "rode with the car and returned with the story. I read it, rushed it to the composing room, hovered over it and read the proof myself so that no loyal proof-reader could carry it to the Owners of the paper and have it killed or changed. It was a great story and nearly cost me my job."[9]

The Toledo streetcar strike was one of two that would influence the scenes in *Sister Carrie* where Hurstwood becomes a scab, but it was not nearly as violent as the Brooklyn streetcar strike of 1895, which Dreiser only read about. In Toledo the strikers threw rotten eggs and mud at those who crossed the picket line; in Brooklyn they threw brickbats and stones. He took generally a neutral point of view in his story of March 24, but his sympathy was clearly with the strikers—which is probably the reason for Henry's having to shepherd the story through the press room.[10] The assignment marked the first time Dreiser had reported on labor unrest, a problem that was to grow worse throughout the 1890s in the United States.

Henry and Dreiser were drawn to each other immediately. "If he had been a girl," Dreiser wrote in *Newspaper Days,* "I would have married him. . . . We were intellectual affinities at the time at least, or thought we were. Our dreams were practically identical."[11] In fact, as his future novels, if not also *Nicholas Blood, Candidate,* indicate, Henry was a rank sentimentalist and—with the exception of *The Unwritten Law* (1905), which Dreiser directly influenced—the very opposite of the realist Dreiser became. Dreiser stayed in Toledo about a week or ten days and wrote a few more pieces for the *Blade* on consignment. Henry wanted him to stay, but in spite of their seemingly "joint chemistries" there was no room on the newspaper. Henry suggested that Dreiser continue east to Cleveland and perhaps to Pittsburgh in search of work and promised to telegraph him as soon as there was an opening on the *Blade,* which he thought would not be long.

———

In Cleveland Dreiser found essentially what he had seen in St. Louis—dark, narrow streets and houses "small and mean," full of "dirty, ill-dressed children" and "slatterns in lieu of women." Here, however, such bleak streets were offset by the conspicuous consumption of the rich across town. Young Dreiser marveled at the new mansions on Euclid Avenue of John D. Rockefeller and Tom Johnson. In spite of his sincere pity for the poor and exploited, this Hoosier from hard economic times as sincerely imagined himself someday becoming a part of this splendor of money. Like Clyde Griffiths, he remembered "envying the rich and wishing that I was famous or a member of a wealthy family, and that I might meet some one of the beautiful girls I imagined I saw there and have her fall in love with me and make me rich."[12] Yet he was already twenty-three and getting nowhere, it seemed.

He found another job reporting on consignment, at three dollars a column for the *Cleveland Leader.* It might have been significant for his literary development because the slot was to be not straight reporting but writing "human interest" stories for the Sunday issues. But the city editor of the *Leader* had no imagination and nixed Dreiser's ideas for features one after another. Dreiser suggested a piece about the newly rising suburbs, but the Sunday editor frowned on the idea as giving out free advertising to real estate developers. He proposed "the magnificence of Euclid Avenue" and was told it had been done before. So too a "no" about the great steel works coming to Cleveland. Finally, the editor allowed him to write a story about a chicken farm on the edge of the city. By the end of a week, he had earned only $7.50. He spent most of his Cleveland time in the public library, reading a book on Russia and Laurence Sterne's two-volume *Sentimental Journey through France and Italy* (1768), the latter recommended by the romantic Henry.[13]

After about a week, Dreiser traveled to Buffalo, partly because he wanted to visit Niagara Falls. The town did not impress him, and he found no work there in spite of the fact that Buffalo had four newspapers. He could get only the promise of a job on one of them weeks in the future. At the Falls he sensed the relative smallness of man, overwhelmed and always in danger of being consumed by giant cosmic or physical forces. "Standing out on a rock near the greatest volume of water, under a grey sky," he recalled, "I was awed by the downpour and then finally became dizzy and felt as though I were being carried along, whether I wanted to or not."[14] It was in this mood that he boarded a train for Pittsburgh only an hour after passing the railroad station and espying a sign announcing that day's cut-rate price on the ticket to the Steel City, "Pittsburg, $5.75."

By now the United States had entered its second year of the worst economic depression of the century. As Dreiser's train headed for Pittsburgh, so did Coxey's Army on its march from Ohio to Washington to demand that President Cleveland implement a public works program to relieve unemployment. The ragtag army of unemployed, one of several that formed in the aftermath of the Panic of 1893, wouldn't find much sympathy in the nation's capital, where Jacob S. Coxey and his "lieutenants" were ultimately humiliated by being arrested in Washington for stepping on the grass. And Pittsburgh, where the great Homestead steel strike of 1892 had been crushed, wasn't any friendlier to the economic outcasts. In a headline of March 26, 1894, the *Pittsburgh Dispatch* called "General" Coxey's band of protesters "The Funniest Thing That They Ever Saw." Yet the human fallout from the depression—fueled not only by labor unrest but by a splurge of overspeculation on Wall Street, agricultural failures, and agitation for the replacement of gold with silver to back the nation's currency—wasn't about to go away. Thousands of businesses across the nation had collapsed, and homeless gangs roamed the country.[15]

Pittsburgh had a population of about 240,000 when Dreiser reached the triangle of a city bounded by the Allegheny and Monongahela rivers where they join to form the Ohio. Across one river to the north lay the rival city of Allegheny (today designated simply the "North Side") and to the south loomed Mt. Washington, whose elevation was reached by ten or more inclines, or vertical trolleys. It was dusk when his train pulled in, but the time of his arrival wouldn't have mattered, for Pittsburgh frequently seemed dark or overcast even at noon because of the pall from its many blast furnaces. Most of the buildings and church steeples were blackened by smoke and grime.

More than any other city except New York, it was Pittsburgh that stirred Dreiser's evolving literary imagination. Looking back as the author of *Sister Carrie* on the seven or eight months he spent there, he thought it had been a perfect city "for a realist to work and dream in."[16] He had approached it by rail through "the brown-blue mountains" of western Pennsylvania and had never before seen such a hilly terrain. Along the way he stared out his train window at soot-faced miners with their oil lamps and lunch pails, their shacks and raggedly dressed children, reminding him of the coal miners he had known as a child in Sullivan. This was his first glimpse of the poverty he was to find among the coal and steel laborers of Pittsburgh, conditions that led to continued strikes in the coal industry in nearby Uniontown as well as in eastern Pennsylvania and Ohio.

In Pittsburgh Dreiser also encountered for the first time various eastern European nationalities. The king of American steel, Andrew Carnegie, or his "chairman," Henry Clay Frick, had routinely averted labor strikes by replacing one immigrant group with another, promising each in turn the sky for what turned out to be impossible wages for twelve hours' work, six or seven days a week. "I did not then know," Dreiser later wrote, "of the padrone, the labor spy, the company store, five cents an hour for breaker children, the company stockade, all in very full operation at this time. All I knew was that there [had] been a very great strike in Pittsburgh recently; that one Andrew Carnegie as well as other steel manufacturers—the Olivers, for one, and Frick—had built fences and strung them with electrified barbed wire in order to protect themselves against the 'lawless' attacks of 'lawless' workingmen."[17]

Here, too, the future realist, or naturalist, was stunned by the immense and immediate contrast between rich and poor. Not long after his arrival, he rode a streetcar a mile or two along the Monongahela River to the company town of Homestead. Pinkerton guards now protected the Carnegie Steel Company, located on the river's edge in front of a cluster of dilapidated houses. He observed sullen and despondent workers, ousted from the enormous plant over a year ago, after the strike. They huddled on their front stoops or idled about the barren streets and empty store fronts. Poles, Hungarians, Slovaks, and Lithuanians fresh from the cauldron of Europe's crowded capitals had been imported to take their places. When Dreiser returned to Pittsburgh and ventured into its East End, he found the absolute antithesis of Homestead in the homes of their new American masters. He entered the exclusive neighborhood of the Fricks, the Thaws, the Olivers, the Thompsons, and the Phippses, whose imposing mansions lined Fifth

Avenue in the area of Schenley Park. "Never, I think," he wrote in his autobiography, "owing perhaps to Homestead and a world of low small yellow shacks which lay to the right of this thoroughfare as I walked east, did the mere possession of wealth—a great house and grounds, a carriage and the like—impress me so keenly."[18]

Today, Pittsburgh is marked indelibly by the presence of these moguls—memorialized by Frick Park, two Carnegie libraries, and the Phipps Conservatory next to Carnegie Mellon University. In fact, by 1890 Carnegie had already built in Allegheny the first of the hundreds of libraries he gave to America. At the time, it wasn't clear whether Allegheny or Pittsburgh would prevail as the major city, and Carnegie picked the wrong one. But, as we shall see, his miscalculation played an important part in the literary apprenticeship of Theodore Dreiser. By 1894 Carnegie was also completing his largest library, in the Oakland section of Pittsburgh. Dreiser recalls in his memoirs admiring its white limestone, today somewhat darkened by the many years in which the steel industry once rendered Pittsburgh "black as night."

Dreiser rented a room on Wylie Avenue in what is today a black ghetto designated as the Hill District (part of which was torn down some years ago to make room for a sports arena). It was an easy cable car ride downtown to the corner of Smithfield and Diamond (now Forbes) streets, where a number of newspapers were clustered together in different buildings. Pittsburgh boasted at least two morning and two afternoon papers, probably more. Dreiser started with the morning papers and visited the *Times,* where he was cordially informed there were no openings. The *Dispatch,* however, seemed more promising. He was interviewed by Harrison Null Gaither, the soft-spoken city editor, who wore an artificial hand, or "gloved dummy." There was no work at the moment, but Gaither expected a vacancy soon and urged the applicant to hang around for a week or ten days. Dreiser indicated that he could wait, but no longer than three or four days. Gaither promised him eighteen dollars a week if the job materialized. In the meantime Henry cabled from Toledo with an offer of a job on the *Blade* at the same salary. At that price, neither offer attracted him; he had already made more in St. Louis. Somehow—Dreiser is vague on this in his memoirs—

he allegedly changed the "$18" to "$25" on Henry's telegram and used it to persuade Gaither to make a firm offer and pay the higher salary.[19]

Before he reported for work on the *Dispatch,* he crossed one of several bridges over the Monongahela and boarded an incline to the top of Mt. Washington and Grandview Avenue, where the vista quite astonished this product of the flatlands of southwestern Indiana. Years later, after he had feasted on the views of "New York from the heights of the Palisades and the hills of Staten Island, also on Rome from the Pincian gardens, and on Florence from the region of San Miniato, as well as on Pasadena and Los Angeles from the slopes of Mt. Lowe," he recalled he had nowhere else beheld

> a scene which impressed me more, not only for the rugged beauty of the mountains which encircle the city on every hand, but for the three rivers which run as threads of bright metal, dividing it into three parts, and for the several cities which here joined together as one, their clambering streets presenting a checkered pattern emphasized here and there by the soot-darkened spires of churches and the walls of the taller and newer and therefore cleaner office buildings.

Godlike almost, the future determinist looked down on the "clambering streets" of Pittsburgh. He was within only a few years of writing "The Shining Slave Makers," where the protagonist falls asleep and wakes up as an ant.[20]

The *Dispatch* was published in a three-story building not nearly as elegant as that which housed its morning competitor. It had a twelve-page format during the week and extended sections on Sunday. In politics it was xenophobically anti-labor. A fellow reporter by the name of Martyn spoke to Dreiser of the appalling wages, even for skilled laborers. "But you can't say anything about that in Pittsburgh," he told him. "If I should want to talk I would have to get out of here. The papers won't use a thing unfavorable to the magnates in any of these fields." In reporting a strike in the Connellsville coke region that spring, the *Dispatch* headlines spoke of "Mobs of Foreigners" who could "scarcely speak English" and the "Good Work of the Armed Deputies." The subsequent jailing of the strikers (for "rioting") was considered "A Good Haul."[21] One of Dreiser's first assignments was to interview Speaker of the House Thomas B. Reed at the Monongahela House about the "menace" Coxey's Army posed. Reed was a strong supporter of

Carnegie's plutocratic ways, and in *Newspaper Days* Dreiser remembers him as denouncing the fledgling labor movement. Curiously, the *Dispatch* article attributed to Dreiser reports Reed's fear that Coxey's Army was evidence of a general unrest in the country which Washington was so far ignoring. Even later, he wrote a favorable report on Reed's career in *Success* magazine.[22]

Dreiser's "beat" was Allegheny on the north side, covering city hall and the police station, which were housed in the same building at Federal and Ohio streets. The complex faced Ober Park and stood next to the Allegheny Market House, a white structure of shops and food stands now replaced by a modern mini-mall. Allegheny City Hall was demolished in the late 1930s, but Carnegie's first library nearby still stands, having undergone extensive restoration in the 1970s and now looking much as it did when it was constructed in 1890. The gray-granite edifice with a five-story clock tower housed a library and a music hall. The library itself featured a mahogany-lined reception and reference room on the second floor with a twenty-six-foot-high domed ceiling of stained glass. The immortal names in literature were engraved on a scroll around the edge of the ceiling. Behind the circular desk in the middle of the room were two levels of bookshelves, or open stacks (they are closed today).

In one of the great American ironies—which also accounts for the funding of the country's fledgling colleges and universities in the late nineteenth century—this product of poverty, ignorance, and superstition was uplifted and educated through the benevolence or "blood money" of one of the country's leading financial titans, himself an immigrant and self-made man. "What pleased and impressed me most about this institution," Dreiser remembered, "was its forty or fifty thousand volumes so conveniently arranged so that one could walk from stack to stack." Here, while supposedly "on duty" at the courthouse, he frequently hid himself in window nooks and alcoves furnished with chairs and read book after book. He mentions Smollett, Fielding, Sterne, and Dryden, but the writer who impressed him most in Andrew Carnegie's first library was Honoré de Balzac. It was in the several books from *La Comédie Humaine* he read that spring and summer that Dreiser thought he had finally discovered the true nature of life— or its dramatic spectacle. "By the merest chance," he picked up *The Wild Ass's Skin* and instantly became enamored of the grand master. "Through him I saw at a glance a prospect so wide that it fairly left me breathless— all Paris, all France, all life through French eyes, and those of a genius." Other romances by Balzac that Dreiser read included *The Great Man from the Provinces, Père Goriot, Cousin Pons,* and *Cousin Bette.* Perhaps Balzac's use of "Father" and "Cousin" in his titles in some way suggested the use of "Sister" in Dreiser's first novel.[23]

Dreiser thought that Balzac's Human Comedy exhausted "every aspect of the human welter." He also fancied (in his autobiography, at least, written after he had visited Europe) that Pittsburgh, with its many bridges and canal-like rivers to the north and south sides, resembled Paris and the Seine, with its numerous bridges linking the Left and Right Banks. The parallels between the two cities went deeper than the physical because Pittsburgh was also a dynamic urban laboratory just waiting for its Balzac. Here was another realist's paradise, but where were its artists? He thought it a wonder that Pittsburgh had not already produced "a score of writers, poets, painters and sculptors instead of—well—how many?" Yet Dreiser later told Mencken that from the time he discovered Balzac almost all the way through to the composition of *Sister Carrie,* he "never had the slightest idea" of becoming a novelist. His first literary ambition was to write a comic play. Nonetheless, for Dreiser, reading Balzac in Pittsburgh constituted an epiphany. "It was," he recalled, "as if a new and inviting door to life had been suddenly thrown open to me."[24]

A writer Dreiser doesn't mention but one who may have begun to influence his writing as early as Pittsburgh was Stephen Crane. By 1894, he could have heard about the naturalist's new brand of Bowery Journalism or even perused its literary metamorphosis in *Maggie, Girl of the Streets* (1893) or "An Experiment in Misery" (1894). In a sketch about Allegheny Hospital that appeared in the pages of the *Dispatch* of April 28, 1894, Dreiser contrasted the beauty of the morning sunshine with the routine death of a patient. Just as in Crane's cruel depictions of nature's aloofness from human suffering, Dreiser wrote in "Hospital Violet Day" of one of the patients who had died on a spring day on which "for the first time, violets came in quantity": "Poor Fintz! . . . When the light shone bright he coughed blood, and when all the patients had been arranged by windows, or wheeled to the court below, long-suffering Fintz died."[25]

That summer he wrote of a potter's field located on the way to the Ohio River community of Bellevue, two or three miles from downtown Pittsburgh. It had neither a name nor anyone to watch over it. There were no visitors to walk "its barren paths. Those who lie there came tagged and written upon from the river's slime and the garret's discouraging want, victims of the same unerring forces that make beautiful the neighboring mausoleums. . . . These sleepers are the potter's brood." Already we can discern in Dreiser's observations the footsteps of an apathetic God, supremely indifferent about the human condition. Our only relief comes in the fact that we don't feel "the desolateness of that mound of the future, which shall be one's own and over which the elements shall sweep in their varying moods, as though we had never been."[26]

Dreiser definitely read Hamlin Garland. In a letter to the prairie naturalist in 1903, in response to belated praise of *Sister Carrie,* he wrote, "Years ago (1894) when a newspaper writer in Pittsburgh I made the acquaintance of 'Main Traveled Roads' in the lovely Carnegie Library of Allegheny while lounging away the long afternoons of my 'city hall' assignment. I have never forgotten it. Like the other beautiful things of life those fresh flowered stories of yours became identified with my dearest remembrances and I have always followed your work with interest. Only a year ago I read 'Rose of Dutcher's Coolly.'"[27] *Rose of Dutcher's Coolly* (1895), like *Sister Carrie,* was about a young woman who went to Chicago to escape the country and its stifling routine. It too had become a target of the censors.

In *Newspaper Days* Dreiser recalls writing other human interest pieces that anticipate the pathos of his best writing. His reading of Balzac, along with the "very picturesque nature" of Pittsburgh, he claimed, helped him to "achieve a series of mood or word pictures anent the most trivial news matters." In one little allegory, he recalled, he thought of a common housefly as a worthy subject. "He was arriving about now; being young and ambitious and having freshly crawled out of some breeding-pit somewhere, he alighted on the nearest fence or windowsill, brushed his head and wings reflectively and meditated on the possibility of a livelihood or a career of sorts. What now, pray, could be open to a young and ambitious fly in a world all too crowded with flies?" In fact, the story, called "The Last Fly of Fly Time," was set in the fall, when winter is approaching to doom all flies, however young and ambitious. Appearing in the *Dispatch* of October 3, it describes the fly almost as dramatically as Old Fintz or the anonymous dead in a potter's field. Harassed by the flypaper trust, the relentless pursuit of the housewife, and singed wings from flying too near hot dishes, as well as the inevitable end of fly season, "the fly is a suicide by inheritance."[28] Perhaps it was true of man, also.

Once he had landed his job, Dreiser moved his residence to Mt. Washington. He spent a major part of his time downtown in and around the *Dispatch* building, when he wasn't on assignment at the North Side. And possibly inspired by Crane's *Maggie,* he ventured again into working neighborhoods and now also into the red light districts. One of the latter could be found directly behind his building. His colleague Martyn was his guide to the mill districts, but Dreiser, driven by loneliness, conducted his own interviews with prostitutes. There is "a type of girl between fifteen and twenty-three or -four," he wrote later, "who for reasons of poverty or the hope of finery takes to the streets, and a few of these I made friends with."[29] He records doing business with at least two of them, an olive-skinned brunette and a red-head. He remembered little about them (though he recalls one "large and soft and white, with big hips and small feet and hands").

He was halted dead in his tracks, however, by a third "with indifferent yet haunting blue eyes" that he never forgot. He met her on the streets late one rainy night. When they reached her shabbily furnished room, he was astonished at her beauty—"a face so delicate and intelligent and a body so gracefully and delicately formed that I was almost breathless with delight." But there was one problem. As she disrobed, he noted track marks on one of her arms. "She was a dope fiend—a consumer of cocaine or heroin or what not, via the needle." Overcoming his shock at the young woman's wretched circumstance and no longer interested in her sexually, he, who had grown up around prostitutes in Sullivan, Vincennes, and Evansville, addressed her as a brother, beginning a "hortatory and moralic [*sic*] discourse anent the error and pity of all this." He gave her three dollars—two more than sex would have cost him and all the money he had on his person—and went home, thinking "of her and the old house and the bare room and the punctured arm."[30] What did he know about life, anyway, he demanded of himself, to be preaching to this desperate young woman?

A short time later he "interviewed" Andrew Carnegie at the Duquesne Club for the *Dispatch;* that is, he was permitted to listen to a prepared speech at which reporters were allowed no note taking and took away only a copy of the speech to use in their stories of the event. At the time Dreiser may have thought back to the beautiful girl with needle marks or to the mill workers packed into tiny dwellings, overcrowded with boarders taken in to assist with the rent—all this so "that Mr. Carnegie might give the world one or two extra libraries with his name plastered on the front." Later on, Dreiser used the handout as the basis of yet another fake interview with Carnegie for *Success* magazine. Here, because of the ideology of the magazine, he was diametrically different in his treatment of the great man. The industrialist is quoted in an article attributed to Dreiser as saying he believed a time was fast approaching "when true success in life would be recognized as consisting neither of wealth nor fame, but having been useful to mankind."[31]

New York, the ultimate stage on which this American naturalist would observe and dramatize the indignities of life, was now only a night train ride away. The idea of going there soon—when he was financially ready perhaps—was becoming stronger. He was already perusing some of that city's glitzy magazines. One was the *Standard,* "a theatre and chorus girl paper" with alluring photographs. Another, more serious, was *Munsey's,* also devoted to theater life in the great metropolis. These whetted his appetite and toughened his nerve. It was about this time that a letter arrived from Paul demanding to know why he was still "piking" about the West and urging him to visit New York that August.

———

Before Theo heeded Paul's summons, however, he first went west—to St. Louis and then to the town of Danville, seven miles from the nearest railroad station in Montgomery City, Missouri. There in the "backwoods" lived Jug's family: Archibald White, his wife, and whatever of their ten children who were still unmarried, including that summer Jug herself. Dreiser later wrote more than one version of his impressions of his wife's somewhat eccentric father and the Danville farm he visited several times. In *Twelve Men* (1919), the image was definitely favorable. "One might have taken him to be Walt Whitman," he wrote in the sketch entitled "A True Patriarch," "of whom he was the living counterpart."

If to his children he was something of a dominating patriarch, White was to his neighbors a born democrat who, Dreiser remarked, "treated a Jersey cow with the same dignity of bearing and forcefulness of manner that characterized him when he stood before his fellow-citizens at a public meeting." He was known as a friend to the sick, the poor, the widowed, the orphaned, and the insane, and might have echoed Whitman's general call in the Preface to his 1855 edition of *Leaves of Grass* to "[l]ove the earth and the sun and the animals." It seemed to Dreiser during the week or more that he stayed with the White family that it cradled "the spirit of rural America"—from the democratic dreams of Jackson to the courage of Lincoln.[32]

Dreiser liked to remember himself and his love as locked into a "chemic lust" for each other, but the facts of that summer visit seem to indicate that Jug had not retreated from her resolve to abstain from premarital sex. Although by now, as he recalled, he enjoyed "repeated fondlings," such erotic previews were regularly squelched by Jug's fears that her parents would discover them or perhaps by her mortification at the thought of having sex in her parents' very home. Jug's virginity survived the week-long assault, but its survival—Dreiser later concluded—drove another nail in the coffin of their eventually doomed relationship.[33] Certainly he felt then that there was no use in spending any more time in Missouri. He had requested several weeks' unpaid leave from the *Dispatch,* and it was past time to head east again, this time all the way to New York.

Along the way, he saw his old *Globe-Democrat* friends in St. Louis, Peter McCord and Dick Wood. He also made a brief stopover in Pittsburgh to refresh himself and collect clean clothes. Then the overnight train to Jersey City, where Paul was waiting to take him across the Hudson River by ferry. As the two brothers boarded the vessel, the would-be playwright and future novelist imagined himself crossing the proscenium arch of a stage for the first time. Making their way through the bustling city to the brownstone on West Fifteenth Street, where Paul was staying with Emma Dreiser and her common-law husband, L. A. Hopkins, Theo realized that he had not seen his sister since 1890, when their mother had died. At thirty-one, the once lithe and sensuous beauty who had taken Hopkins away from his first wife and children, had grown stout and was now herself the mother of a boy and a girl, both under four. And Hopkins was beginning to look and act like the fated Hurstwood, for whom he was the primary model.

Any bad omens the couple suggested were quickly forgotten as Paul showed his little brother the sights of New York. They walked across Fifteenth Street and up Sixth Avenue to Twentieth Street, where they headed east across Broadway towards Fifth Avenue. Just beyond Broadway on Twentieth stood the offices of Howley, Haviland, and Company on the third floor. Paul was now in the sheet music business. "After years of essaying life as a comedian and song writer in the middle west," Dreiser wrote in a biographical memorandum, he had become an established song writer with the publications of "The Letter That Never Came" and "I Believe It For My Mother Told Me So." Pat Howley and Fred Haviland had been clerks in other music companies. In fact, Howley had worked for Willis, Woodward and Company, which had published "My Mother Told Me So" and had alerted Paul to the fact that the company was cheating him on royalties. This revelation moved Paul to sever his ties with that company and establish a formal connection with Howley and Haviland.[34]

The enterprise was just then getting underway, but Paul was customarily full of optimism. The fact that Howley was a hunchback also gave the superstitious Paul hope that it would be a grand success. Haviland was still working for the celebrated Ditson music company, with offices in New York and Boston, and using the position secretly, according to Paul, to aid their new company "in disposing of some of their published wares." Mostly, the new firm sold Paul's songs. Haviland, who was about twenty-seven, "shot out questions and replies as one might bullets out of a gun," Dreiser remembered: "'DidyaseeDrake? Whaddesay? AnynewsfromBaker? Thedevilyasay! Yadon'tmeanit.'"[35]

On the way to Paul's office, Dreiser experienced Broadway for the first time. Within a year he would produce a Whitmanesque catalog of the famed avenue. He marveled at its surging crush of humanity and its store windows, alive with a dazzle of paintings, furniture, clothing—whatever one could want and imagine, he thought. Thousands of people, perhaps a hundred thousand a day, passed up and down, staring into the lushly filled plate-glass windows or walking by each other as utter strangers. Some of the buildings were a block in length. "And the carriages!" he recalled in his memoirs, "and the well dressed people!" Within five years, these impressions would become Carrie's uneasy thoughts while living with Hurstwood in New York. "The walk down Broadway," he wrote in *Sister Carrie*, "then as now, was one of the remarkable features of the city. . . . Men in flawless topcoats, high hats, and silver-headed walking sticks elbowed near and looked too often into conscious eyes. Ladies rustled by in dresses of stiff cloth, shedding affected smiles and perfumes. . . . The whole street bore the flavour of riches and show, and Carrie felt that she was not of it."[36]

"Broadway Paul," as he probably should have been hailed, was clearly at home on the stretch of Broadway between Union Square and Forty-Second Street. Dreiser recalled in his memoirs the many famous addresses Paul took him by on their stroll uptown that day—Tiffany's still at Fifteenth; Brentano's Bookstore at Sixteenth; Sarony's photography studio between Fifteenth and Sixteenth; the Century Company, which would later publish *A Traveler at Forty,* on the north side of Union Square at Seventeenth Street; Lord and Taylor, whose great building stood next to the one which housed Paul's business; and so on up the avenue to Thirtieth, where Augustin Daly's famous playhouse then stood. Here, too, Dreiser was visiting his future, for he has Carrie Meeber play the role of Laura in Daly's *Under the Gaslight.*

At Delmonico's, recently moved from Fourteenth Street and Fifth Avenue to Broadway between Twenty-Fourth and Twenty-Fifth, his good brother Paul hailed, "chipperly and genially, some acquaintance who happened to be in charge of the floor at the moment. Here as elsewhere he was known." The waiter greeted Paul warmly, which strongly impressed his kid brother, who had long ago heard of this "sanctum sanctorum of the smart social life of the city." It was the same at the newly opened Metropole Hotel at Forty-Second and Broadway. Here gathered daily the representatives of the boxing, gambling, and theatrical worlds—all decked out in loud clothes, diamond pins, straw hats, and "hot" socks. This was yet another visit to the future, for Hurstwood flourishes in the same sartorial extravagance as manager of Fitzgerald and Moy's in Chicago. Here Hurstwood first stood in the flesh. It was "Paul" this and "Paul" that, Dreiser recalled in *Newspaper Days:* "'Why hello, Dresser. You're just in time. Have a drink.' . . . Then drinks, cigars, my brother telling and paying and har-haring as freely as any. I felt as though I were in the heart of fairyland itself."[37]

Paul Dresser was not only a friend to the successes but to the failures as well—punch-drunk ex-prizefighters or long-haired thespians down on their luck. In "My Brother Paul," a veritable love letter to his late brother, Dreiser remembered that although Paul was a "Jack Falstaff, with his love of women" or a stand-up comic and songwriter who mildly mocked the current butts of humor (the Irish day laborer, the Negro, and the Jew), sympathy was truly his outstanding characteristic. When Dreiser asked his brother one day why the needy should always appeal to him, he was simply told that he ought to know "how it was."[38] His brother couldn't stand to see people suffer. No doubt he had Paul also in the back of his mind as he wrote about Charlie Potter in the short story, "A Doer of the Word" (1902), who works only for others. Paul was surely a wellspring for Dreiser's own deep compassion for the human condition.

His visit to New York lasted only days, a week at most, but through Paul Theo obtained "an excellent sip" of the city in which he was to live almost without interruption for the next forty-five years. Before he returned to Pittsburgh, however, he became possibly more familiar with Paul and his cronies than was altogether comfortable. One day as he sat with his brother and friends at a curbside cafe, two women, looking like prostitutes, passed by. One of Paul's pals suggested they were "French," implying not nationality but the probability that they engaged in oral sex. When young Dreiser challenged the assertion that the women were of French origin, his naïveté was greeted with a gale of laughter. Before the evening was out, Paul and his cohorts had arranged to initiate Dreiser in what he had apparently considered a forbidden aspect of sexual foreplay. In an episode that was suppressed until the 1995 scholarly edition of *Newspaper Days,* he remembered it as "a wild, blood-racking, brain-scarifying experience"— and he worried for weeks afterward that he might have caught "a low and shameful disease."[39]

When he returned to Pittsburgh in the late summer of 1894, the city had lost much of the romance he had imagined he found in it. New York seemed more like Balzac's Paris than this now dreary steel and coal center. This new mood was perhaps enhanced by his discovery of Herbert Spencer's *First Principles* (1893). Just as New York had blown away Pittsburgh, Spencer, whom he now read with far more depth and experience than he had in his year of college, "quite blew me to bits intellectually."[40] He also read Thomas Huxley's *Science and Hebrew Tradition* (1893) and *Science and Christian Tradition* (1894). The total impact of these volumes, he said, was to destroy the last traces of his adherence to conventional religion. But where Huxley's effect was to negate traditional religious views, Spencer gave Dreiser a new religion, as it were. Essentially, the synthetic philosopher held that a higher power was manifested through nature, or physical matter, but unlike transcendentalism, which saw nature as merely an emblem of spirit, his doctrine emphasized nature itself.

Because the spirit was "unknowable," only nature could be known, and it was evidenced by the evolutionary movement of life, or force. This evolutionary force operated on the world as a series of chemical reactions over which man, as part of the chemistry, had no control. Spencer reduced man to a chemical atom, or combination of same, which reacted to other chemical formulas or human personalities or situations to produce what we call chance or fate. Man's options, therefore, consisted not in free will but merely in the necessity of acting out the particular "will" or chemism he or she chanced to receive, mainly through the combination of heredity and environment. There was, however, one element in Spencer's "survival of the fittest" (his coinage, not Darwin's) that is altogether missing from *On the*

Origin of Species; and that was a moral component. For Spencer, the world was evolving towards perfection as its forces and counterforces came into balance.

In the words of Donald Pizer, "Men at present are still guided by egotism, Spencer believed, because society was still dominated by an older form of evolution, but men were increasingly recognizing the greater social efficacy of conscious altruism and 'harmonious cooperation.'" Another authority on Dreiser, Richard Lehan, is impressed that someone like Dreiser without philosophical training could have so readily understood Spencer, whose *First Principles* is not an easy book to read or comprehend. Possibly Dreiser was helped along in his reading by the fact that he found what he was looking for all along: a system of thought that would explain away the pathos of the human condition. Dreiser put it best in *Sister Carrie:* "Our civilisation is still in the middle stage, scarcely beast, in that it is no longer wholly guided by instinct; scarcely human, in that it is not yet guided by reason. . . . We see man far removed from the lairs of the jungles, his innate instincts dulled by too near an approach to free will, his free will not sufficiently developed to replace his instincts." Man was only halfway along in his evolution towards perfection, frequently torn between the demands of instinct and the morality of will. Man is but "a wisp in the wind" among the forces "which sweep and play throughout the universe."[41]

Before he left New York, Dreiser had already decided he would return there to live permanently. He went back to Pittsburgh and his job on the *Dispatch* in order to save as much money as he could—enough to sustain him in New York while he searched for another newspaper job. During the next four months, he was able to lay aside $240 by doing without new clothes and even regular meals. Later he thought he had done himself some physical damage, which told on him during his first and most difficult year in New York.[42] He returned to New York in late November 1894. This time there was no big brother to whisk him about, for Paul was, as usual in winter, on the road. Instead, Dreiser was greeted only by the gloomy Hopkins and—yet again—a sister in distress.

Dreiser was ill-prepared for a family burden at this juncture. He had his own worries. "I was haunted by the thought that I was sure to fail," he remembered. "And in addition that very remarkable book of Balzac's, *The Great Man from the Provinces,* so recently read, in which was recorded the poignant failure of such a youth as myself, was weighing on me to a degree."[43] With Paul away, Emma had rented his room, but there was still space for Theo in what must have been a large apartment. Hopkins had lost his connection with Tammany Hall, which was under investigation and beginning to lose power and influence in the city. In Dreiser's view, Hopkins looked "played out." Once a fairly aggressive and resourceful man, he sat around the apartment, waiting for something to happen.

Within a day or so of his re-arrival, Dreiser set out to conquer the great newspaper world of New York. He had been hearing about it now for more than three years, since he had first joined the Fourth Estate in Chicago— tales of the great Joseph Pulitzer of the *World* and the famed Charles A. Dana of the *Sun*. He was immediately shocked to discover that, unlike newspaper offices in the West, New York's were summarily closed to casual inquiries about employment. At one paper after another, the *Herald*, the *Sun*, the *Times*, and the *World*—most of them facing City Hall Park at Chambers Street and Broadway—he encountered "buffers" or "lookouts," thugs in business attire stationed outside every editorial office to mouth the words "no vacancies."

At first he couldn't bring himself to challenge these hired ruffians or push past them. Actually, he felt a general fear of New York, which he found most intimidating and somewhat paralyzing. It was also December, and the cold winds were not just meteorological but financial, for it was now the very depth of the depression following the Panic of 1893. Thousands of men thrown out of work loitered about the city. One day, at the height of his frustration and feelings of helplessness, Dreiser walked over to City Hall Park. There he stared back at the great buildings of the newspapers that had ignored him and then around at the bedraggled company in the park. "About me on the benches of the Park was—even in this grey, chill December weather—that same large company of 'benchers' so frequently described as bums, loafers, tramps, idlers—the flotsam and jetsam of the great city's whirl and strife," he recalled. He thought of his chances of becoming one of them, then of his sister's dilemma and the spectacle of the once successful Hopkins. The city seemed so heartless and cruel. "And it was then," he wrote, "if ever, that the idea of Hurstwood was born."[44]

———

He returned to Emma's warm apartment, his long face all too clearly revealing his day. This was the first of several periods in Dreiser's life in which—like the ill-fated Hurstwood—he felt the pull of a serious depression over the downward turns of fate. Now he took refuge in a rocking chair and fretted. He was nearing the brink of an emotional abyss that would temporarily overwhelm him before another decade was out. Emma tried to cheer him up, saying that New York wasn't as bad as he feared and that Paul had said he was a talented writer. Surely, he would find a newspaper job here.

He resolved to try the *World* again, the paper that had most interested him. The next day, after another false start, he barged past the sentries into the editorial room, which was full of tobacco smoke and reporters: "most of them in shirt sleeves, a number of them operating typewriters or writing by hand, and in many instances smoking."[45] As the two watchdogs caught up with him, a young man of apparent authority intervened. Dreiser insisted that he needed a job, that he had worked as a reporter in the West— and he was hired on the spot, as a space-rate reporter at $7.50 per column. Dreiser's angel in this instance was Arthur Brisbane, then managing editor of the *World* and soon to become editor of Pulitzer's main competition in the world of "yellow journalism," William Randolph Hearst's *New York Evening Journal.*

Dreiser had gotten lucky, but this upturn wouldn't last long. Although he survived the customary "vacant lot" assignment to a graveyard in Elizabeth, New Jersey, he failed to make a living wage on the newspaper. He resented the privileges of the regular reporters, for he had to put in the same number of hours, which in his case ran till three in the morning. Actually, many more reporters than Dreiser realized worked on "space," but they were toughened veterans of Pulitzer's rat race and many made decent livings. (Stephen Crane and Lincoln Steffens had also made their living as "space" reporters before Dreiser, as they honed their writing skills toward literature.)[46]

But New York, with its overworked charities, bedhouses (rooms let out to prostitutes by the hour or day), streetwalkers, and run-down tenements, threatened his will to succeed. He felt that the world must be arranged differently in the minds of his competition, for everyone around him seemed to miss the pathos of so many down-and-out victims of the economic depression that winter. "How was a sniveling scribbler such as myself to make his way in a world such as this?" he asked himself. Whenever he went out on an assignment, usually the most trivial, whose "facts" he wasn't even allowed to write up himself, he remembered, "I carried with me this sense of my immense unimportance, fortified by what I had read in Spencer and what I saw here."[47] In the meantime, his Pittsburgh savings had begun to disappear as he helped his sister with household expenses. (There is no evidence that Emma was unreasonable in her needs, but the situation may have laid the seed for the exploitation of Carrie when she first lives with her sister and brother-in-law in Chicago, or during her time in New York with the run-down Hurstwood.)

There are only four *World* articles attributed to Dreiser in the collected journalism, and none of them is dated beyond February 16, 1895. The grimness of their subjects probably didn't surpass what he had written about in Pittsburgh, but now Dreiser wasn't that far away from the pitiful condition of many of those he reported. One piece dated December 13 was about "disorderly women," or prostitutes, in the tenements similar to Emma's place on West Fifteenth Street. Another focused on tenement violence. A third concerned a woman named Emma who, like Crane's Maggie, died "a daughter of the slums." The fourth, interestingly enough, was about a "shabbily dressed man" who took his life the same way Hurstwood does in *Sister Carrie*.[48]

Readers of that novel in 1900 were shocked that Dreiser, while punishing Hurstwood with death, left Carrie unpunished (if also unfulfilled) at the close of his novel. What was truly shocking, however, in the words of Robert Penn Warren, "was not so much the things he presented as the fact that he himself was not shocked by them."[49] His formative years, as we have seen, had been full of Hurstwoods and Carries. Dreiser was the first great American novelist from the wrong side of town. His fictions about the social brutality of life had none of the "redeeming" features of the work of his fellow naturalists such as Crane and Frank Norris.

In both Crane's *Maggie* and Norris's *McTeague* (1899), for example, the main characters are flawed enough to be blamed for their own downfalls. Crane depicts the Irish of the East Side as hopeless brutes. And Norris almost laughs through his narrative about the working-class immigrants on Polk Street in San Francisco. It is no wonder that William Dean Howells, whose own realistic fictions nevertheless subscribed to Victorian standards of timidity and gentility, disliked *Sister Carrie,* while at the same time encouraging the work of both Crane and Norris.[50] He believed—even after having his eyes opened by the police riots in Haymarket Square in 1886— in the principles of Social Darwinism in which the "moral" prove to be the most likely candidates for survival. In his view, Carrie and Hurstwood, whose social status suggests only a one- or two-generation remove from immigrant status, no more deserve to be saved from themselves than the genetically defective Irish in *Maggie* and *McTeague*. The important difference was that Crane and Norris shared Howells's belief in the moral superiority of a certain class, mainly Anglo-American. Dreiser, on the other hand, as the son of an immigrant, did not. For him, man—all of humankind—was still only halfway between animal instinct and the ideal of human morality, and so a lack of humanity was to be expected.

Evidence close at hand that winter of man's hopelessly amoral condition was the fifty-year-old Hopkins, who had become unfaithful both to Emma and to the idea of supporting their two children. For some years, before Dreiser's arrival, the couple had operated a prostitution ring out of their own apartment on West Fifteenth Street. Because they had returned most of the money Hopkins had stolen to finance his running away with Emma, he had persuaded her that prostitution was their "swiftest road to fortune. . . . As easy, unmoral money began to roll in E[mma] indulged in furs, jewels, and gaudy knick-knacks in the way of furniture and household decoration. Carriage rides in the park were her daily delight. Believing herself safely placed in the matter of love and fortune she indulged in the luxury of two children which long before she had learned how to prevent." In the printed text of *Dawn,* this information is replaced by the assertion that Emma was shocked at the idea of renting out their rooms to prostitutes when it was brought up during her brother's visit. But Emma—the model for Sister Carrie—may have briefly been a prostitute herself in Chicago before meeting Hopkins. Dreiser opines in another suppressed section of *Dawn* that while in Chicago she "was obviously selling her virtue for cash," quickly adding that she "subsequently fell in love [with Hopkins] and made tremendous sacrifices for her children," which was true.[51]

Emma was still in love with Hopkins after ten years together, but at the same time she was afraid he would someday hurt her or their children in a fit of despair. Eventually, she agreed to her brother's plan to escape her brooding husband once and for all. Accordingly, Dreiser came home one day and announced that he was giving up the reporter's game in New York and going back to Pittsburgh. In the meantime, he rented a room for himself on East Fourth Street, which, ironically, turned out to be in a bedhouse. From there he had a friend in Pittsburgh forward his letter addressed to Emma back to New York. It said that he had reestablished himself in Pittsburgh and had room for Emma and her two children. At first Hopkins refused to let her go but soon relented. He himself moved to a cheap hotel.

Actually, Emma moved to a flat on West Seventeenth Street, where she lived with her children for several years. Hopkins's fate is not clear, and Emma may have never seen him again. One source suggests that he went back to his wife in Chicago. But in his memoirs, Dreiser gave his brother-in-law a Hurstwood obituary: "I know I never saw him but once after, a most washed-out and deteriorated-looking person, and then he did not see me. A few years later, as [Emma] learned, he died—still working for the same hotel." In *Sister Carrie,* the "gloomy Hurstwood" on the brink of his final descent broods "in his cheap hotel . . . not wholly indifferent to the fact that his money was slipping away."[52]

FIVE

Editorial Days

New York is a Christian city, if anyone should inquire of you.
It has 2,000,000 residents and 546 churches.

EV'RY MONTH, OCTOBER 1895

DREISER DROPS ALMOST COMPLETELY from sight between December 1894 and September 1895. Decades later he completed two autobiographical volumes, *Dawn* and *Newspaper Days*, but these followed his life only through 1894. Although he had plans for two more volumes, he never wrote them. What little we know about this missing period comes from an unpublished fragment titled "A Literary Apprenticeship," which may have been the start of the third volume and which he apparently began some years after finishing *Newspaper Days.* In it he states that he still worked for the *New York World* between January and "late February or the early days of March," but misremembers the year as 1894 instead of 1895. He speaks of his dreams of becoming a real writer instead of a reporter—uppermost in his mind were the "meteoric" literary successes of Rudyard Kipling and Richard Harding Davis.[1]

The main subject of "A Literary Apprenticeship," however, is not Dreiser's inspiration leading up to *Sister Carrie,* but his frustrated efforts to establish himself as a writer outside of newspaper work. Even while he remained on the *World,* he wasn't allowed to write up his own stories. One of his final assignments before he left the newspaper was to cover the morgue on East Twenty-Sixth Street, along with the neighboring Bellevue Hospital, whose mentally ill patients were guarded by "hobbling ghouls of caretakers."[2] The hospital was caught up in the graft of Tammany Hall, and Dreiser considered writing an exposé of the misapplication of its medical resources and offering it to a magazine. He became aware of other possibilities as he walked around the Bowery, where he soon lived in a hall bedroom nearby. Here he struggled to write what he thought the magazines would publish. He even tried to interview Mark Twain, whom he encountered on the street one day.[3] But at this time his freelance efforts met with no success.

The drifters and derelicts that filled the Bowery in the continuing depression no doubt provided grist for what would be his first novel, however. Even the healthy could find no work, and, like George Hurstwood, thousands of homeless men slept on gratings and huddled against doorways to warm themselves against the sleet and winter gusts. Once he stopped writing for the *World,* Dreiser himself began to feel "down and out." He told Dorothy Dudley, his first biographer, "I got terribly depressed. My money was dwindling, I thought, my gosh, I would have to go back to newspaper work."[4] Near Houston Street a few days later, he struck up an acquaintance with a young Italian girl, "pretty and gracious." When he told her he had no money, she took him to her room nearby, over her father's restaurant. Her parents liked him, she said, and would provide him a room for nothing next to hers. He fancied they were looking for a son-in-law. He allegedly lived with this family for a short time, perhaps until the spring, undecided, he told Dudley, "whether to accept her offer [of marriage?] and thus escape from misery and solitude." He wondered whether Italian in-laws would be better than Jug's Methodist ones, more accommodating of his exotic dreams of himself as a writer. But Italian also meant Catholic, and his rejection of his father's religion was by now irrevocable. And even as he lived off the Italian family and their daughter's infatuation for him, Dreiser may also have been corresponding with Jug. Their extant letters date only from 1896, but the content of the earliest ones suggests lost letters from the previous year.

It was during this period that Dreiser decided to write another play. While he was drama critic on the *St. Louis Globe-Democrat,* he had drafted a comic opera called *Jeremiah I.* Perhaps suggested by a reading of Twain's *A Connecticut Yankee* (1889), the play concerned an Indiana farmer who is magically transported to Aztec Mexico, where he becomes a bully. This time Dreiser either wrote or intended to write "Along the Wabash," which he described as a "comedy drama" when he filed for copyright in 1895 at the Library of Congress. The play has never been found (indeed, may have never been written), but its title curiously anticipates Paul's most famous song, "On the Banks of the Wabash," written two years later.[5] Dreiser later claimed partial authorship of that song.

Dreiser the hopeful dramatist was, of course, more than capable of dramatizing his own difficult days and may have exaggerated his situation in the winter of 1895. He was probably never truly in the same peril as those he saw every day in the Bowery, because even then he had relatives nearby to lend a hand. Emma might not have been much of a resource after she left Hopkins, but there was always Paul. He was back on the road for the winter but probably never out of touch. And he was scheduled to return to New York that spring, as he had the previous year, when Theo had visited. As Robert H. Elias has observed, initially it was Dreiser's relationship to Paul, not his own talent as a writer, that helped him survive in New York.[6] Coarse in manners, grossly overweight, hardly educated beyond the popular culture of the day, and ever attired in the gaudy uniforms of newfound Broadway success, Paul was not only a practical source of help but in some ways an emotional surrogate for the mother they both still mourned.

Until recently, our knowledge of Paul came largely from his brother's sketches, especially "My Brother Paul," written in 1919. Apart from his songs, Paul left no writings except for an article, crafted no doubt with Theo's help, in the *Metropolitan* of November 1900 (coincidentally, the same month in which *Sister Carrie* first appeared). Entitled "Making Songs for the Millions," it revealed that Paul had been cheated out of the profits of his very first song. In 1886 he had given the lyrics of "The Letter That Never Came" "to a man whom I no longer love" to score it for the piano. When he returned to New York after a tour on the road, he saw his song published under the other fellow's name in the *New York Clipper*. Everywhere he went he heard his song.

> A letter here for me? was the question that he asked
> Of the mailman at the closing of the day—
> He turned sadly with a sigh, while a tear stood in his eye,
> Then he bow'd his head and slowly walked away.[7]

"Another man was getting the money," he recalled, "and I was getting the laugh."

Paul had arrived in New York "an absolute stranger," but apparently the threat of poverty did not scare him the way it did his brother. In fact, when it came to adversity, the fat man seemed to float through it like a butterfly. On the day he learned his song had been stolen and was down to his last sixty-five cents, he "knocked around all night" on Broadway, choosing breakfast over a bed. A rough-and-tumble type, he never fully comprehended his younger brother's darker and more nuanced view of the world. Possessing only one year, if that, of formal music study, he disdained what he called "high-class music"—not only because it was beyond him but because it represented a social class that deemed him and his Tin Pan Alley colleagues inferior. Like brother Rome in his class anger, if not in his shiftless approach to life, Paul wore his commonality as a badge of honor, much preferring—he wrote in the *Metropolitan* article—a "broiled steak with plenty of bread and butter" to any posthumous recognition of his musical talent.[8] As it turns out, he probably would not have received any posthumous recognition, outside the annals of Tin Pan Alley, without his brother's touching reminiscences and the collection of many of his ballads as *The Songs of Paul Dresser* (1927), which Theo edited.

Paul's songs were about people who love and lose because of their selfishness or their impatience for the material comforts denied them during their impoverished childhood. As we know, several of the Dreiser sisters had their heads so turned, and in "Just Tell Them That You Saw Me," written in 1894, somebody's sister has gone off to the big city and fallen into prostitution. She can't face her family—and especially her mother, a figure informing many of Paul's songs—and so she tells a former schoolmate about to return home:

> Just tell them that you saw me,
> She said, They'll know the rest,
> Just tell them I was looking well, you know,
> Just whisper if you get the chance to mother dear, and say,
> I love her as I did long, long ago.

The song was a huge success that year and established Paul with Howley and Haviland. Some of his other better-known titles include "The Pardon That Came Too Late," "I Can't Believe Her Faithless," and "The Lone Grave." The latter was reminiscent of what Dreiser himself had already written about potter's fields and lonely deaths in Pittsburgh, a story he would shortly revise and publish under the title of "Forgotten."[9]

Dreiser had been trying his hand at both fiction and magazine articles, apparently without success, throughout the winter of 1895. By spring he was nearly broke but not prepared to marry back into the Catholic Church or to return to Pittsburgh, St. Louis, or even Jug, still more or less patiently waiting for him in Missouri. Once again his rescue came through Paul. Dreiser went around to the East Twentieth Street offices of Howley, Haviland, and Company, to see his brother, only to discover he hadn't yet returned from his winter's road trip. He had an interesting proposal for the music sheet company, but he thought he would need Paul's support in getting the owners to agree to it. Paul wasn't an official partner there until 1901, but his music was one of the company's main sellers and his opinion would weigh in favorably, so Dreiser hoped. The idea was for the company to start a magazine to advertise its merchandise. Other music companies, such as Ditson, where Fred Haviland had been employed, had such magazines, the forerunners of today's house organ in an American business. With the growth of Howley, Haviland, and Company, Dreiser argued, this would be the next logical step in the firm's development.

On his return, Paul agreed, and he easily persuaded Howley and Haviland not only that this would be a fine idea but that his brother, with his newspaper experience, would be an able editor. Dreiser was soon installed in a small office on the second floor, just large enough for two chairs and a table. There he conducted the business of the new magazine, which he called *Ev'ry Month*. While young Dreiser edited copy or talked with contributors, the music business in the main office went ahead as usual. Young women hastily addressed and folded circulars, and others pounded typewriters, while men in green eyeshades worked over desks and messenger boys carried packages in and out of the establishment. In one corner at a piano there might be a blond in "a gorgeous hat and gown" trying out one of the firm's new songs with an accompanist. In another corner, Paul might be standing at a second piano, thrumming out the tune to another sad, nostalgic tale. Not only was the place noisy, but it was also filled with tobacco smoke, which filtered up to the garret of the editor, who rarely smoked.[10] If the noise was a distraction, it was also a constant reminder that the raison d'être of the magazine was primarily to sell the company's wares.

But Dreiser had bigger ideas for his new magazine, whose first issue appeared in October 1895. Its moderate success (eventually reaching a circulation of 65,000) marked not only an upswing in business for the firm but a major step forward in Dreiser's literary development. Initially subtitled "An Illustrated Magazine of Popular Music, the Drama, and Literature" (later changed to "The Woman's Magazine of Literature and Music"), it hosted a large, thirty-two- to forty-eight-page format consisting of four newly released songs each month along with an editorial section called "Review of the Month" (later "Reflections"), reviews of current New York plays, poems, and short stories. Some of these were written by Dreiser's former newspaper colleagues Peter McCord, Dick Wood, and Arthur Henry, but, at least for the first year, Dreiser wrote most of the copy himself. After a year of profits, Dreiser hired George C. Jenks, a former colleague at the *New York World,* to help him with some of the editorials.[11] Dreiser was paid ten dollars a week while preparing the first issue and fifteen a week once publication got underway.

The magazine was filled with sentimental songs and stories, though Dreiser's editorials were often lofty recyclings of material he got from Herbert Spencer. The cheaper halftone printing technology that was replacing woodcuts at the turn of the century allowed for an abundance of affordable illustrations, usually of pensive young women or distinguished-looking men, whose élan encouraged readers to merge their consciousness with each *Ev'ry Month* daydream. Aside from the minor help of his friends and the printed songs featured in each issue, Dreiser signed much of the copy he wrote with pseudonyms: for the "Reflections" column he was "The Prophet"; for others he used either combinations of his brothers' names ("Edward Al") or his future wife's maiden name ("S. J. White"—Sara Jug). Generally, *Ev'ry Month* gave the budding writer a ready outlet for the kind of casual reporting he often had been denied as a journalist and unleashed his imaginative curiosity in almost every direction around the city. Unlike Walt Whitman, whose newspaper office was the equivalent of Herman Melville's whaling ship, Dreiser's literary Harvard and his Yale (as the author of *Moby-Dick* called his experiences at sea) was not so much the newspaper as it was the magazine.[12]

Ev'ry Month was one of a number of magazines emerging in the 1890s that differed widely from their more serious (some now thought stuffy) forerunners, such as *Century* and *Harper's*. With their informal approach to life and their appeal to the consumer with a little recreational cash, they envisioned a world of leisure and luxury that animates the dreams of Sister Carrie. Part of that vision was conveyed by *Ev'ry Month*'s illustrations, as Dreiser frankly acknowledged in the inaugural issue of October 1895. "The actresses selected" to pose for them, he said, were not chosen for their individual distinction but simply because they were "pretty, and because they serve to adorn a page of serious matter better than anything else." Such alluring faces as that of Violet Dale, a "very promising little toe dancer," were to be found on almost every page of the first issue, allowing the viewer to "see in them the moods and expressions of other beings, not always a part of our lives, and often not even a part of the life of the world in general." It was the "formula female" that seemed to ennoble life and set the mood for its artistic expression. Of course, as the magazine of a music publisher, *Ev'ry Month* also invited readers to participate in the general nostalgia of the songs published in each issue. The first month's musical features included Theodore F. Morse's "The Arrival of the Bride" and Paul's "I Was Looking for My Boy, She Said." The first appealed to female readers still in search of the right man, while the second—"respectfully dedicated to the Veterans of the late War"—told the sad tale of a Civil War mother straining her eyes in vain to locate her still missing son among the surviving Union soldiers marching past her on Decoration Day.

> I saw an old, old woman, most feeble and most gray,
> Look closely at each vet'ran soldier's face,
> I saw the tear-drops trickling down her pinched and withered cheeks,
> As she mingled with the throng from place to place.[13]

Sentimental as it was, this song serves as a reminder that although Dreiser is viewed as mainly a twentieth-century novelist, he (and his brother) grew up under the long shadow of the Civil War.

Like any editor, especially one just starting out, Dreiser was always on the lookout for material for his editorials, and the topics in his "Reflections" range widely—and reveal much about his development as a writer. These editorials followed a general pattern of beginning with facts, statistics, and demographics and ending in literary drama. Writing as "The Prophet" and speaking with the editorial "we" allowed Dreiser to cut the ice and adopt the tone of a lifelong New Yorker, even referring fondly to "Gotham" as "innately wicked." "We are getting to be a very great people," he boasted in the November issue. "We are marrying our millionaire daughters off to foreign dukes and earls. . . . [and] chasing off to foreign capitals every springtime 100,000 strong, and spending $100,000,000 all told." He praised the Cotton States Exposition held in Atlanta that fall to showcase the restoration of the South after the Civil War. He was glad the eastern press was more receptive to this exposition than they had been to the Chicago World's

Fair, whose "White City" he well remembered. He went on to accuse New York journalists of having been envious of Chicago's accomplishment: "The glitter of the lights of days gone by upon its slender turrets and spires still makes blind with envy those sponsors of New York's reputation."[14]

Still a midwesterner at heart when he wrote those lines, Dreiser would soon come to identify with New York as the American center to which all true talent would gravitate. And it was the *Ev'ry Month* experience that effected his complete conversion. *Sister Carrie*'s plot division between Chicago and New York probably reflected Dreiser's lingering sense of duality between the Midwest and the East. Carrie's innocence is lost in the first city and replaced in the second with the kind of fantasy only a New York or a Paris can sustain. But for all the enthusiasm he felt for New York, he recognized the cost of that fantasy. He had witnessed the pathos of the hordes of down-and-outers who had migrated from the Midwest and elsewhere to Gotham, only to end up in its Bowery instead of the economic bower they might have imagined. He felt he was beginning to seize upon the true drama of life, which he thought the newspapers—especially "that slime-wallowing, barrel house organ, *The World*"—completely missed. The time was soon to come, he hoped, when "there will not be any room [in newspapers] for long articles concerning 'what we have done,' nor endless words relative to the movements of people in society. Citizens will not be hounded by verbose reporters, anxious to make a sensation of something, no matter what." Moreover, "this degrading system of making spies and freaks of individuals and then calling them newspaper men, of delegating them to crawl through the sewers and up smoke-stacks, will be discredited."[15]

Such reporters of life, the fraternity of mere "space-writers" to which he had briefly belonged on the *World,* should turn their attention, proclaimed "The Prophet," from palaver about reform to the true reformations even then taking place. Dreiser, the future determinist who would record in microcosmic pictures the meaningless ebb and flow of life in the city, seemed here almost to anticipate a kind of Christ figure, that Central Man who haunts the work of nineteenth-century American literature from Emerson to Whitman, the culmination of which can be found in the "Captain" of *Sister Carrie,* who appears each night on Broadway to help the homeless find shelter from the icy chill of winter. In the October issue Dreiser had declared that stories about such uplifting examples of reformation were overdue. Now in the second issue he spoke of reports from the New Mexico border "of a man, who, walking lowly among the poor, was possessed of almost miraculous power." Desiring no compensation whatever, "he walked among the sick and the maimed, and all who looked into the deep sympathy of his eyes arose strong in body." Dreiser was referring to Franz Schlatter, the Denver fakir and self-styled messiah, who eventually disappeared into Central America. If indeed he was the real thing, Dreiser hinted with a skepticism that was directed at both the "messiah" and "the lame, halt, and blind in New York" he might save, "He has come . . . among a people who are gallivanting after nothing but gold and fame." Even art in America, he argued in that same issue, too often worshipped at the altar of success rather than self-exploration. "Quite distressing it is to me," wrote the Prophet, "to observe young men and women laboriously engaged in copying reproductions of exhumed Grecian marbles of heroes and Goddesses, when American heroes and Goddesses are thronging Broadway, and not maintaining unnatural poses either."[16]

Indeed, instead of national introspection, America was also obsessed with the "new"—anything other than its present or past. In the Christmas issue of *Ev'ry Month* Dreiser noted how time dissolves man's material monuments—how quickly such cities as New York, Chicago, and St. Louis were sweeping away the old to make way for the new. In New York, "places austere with historic memories are being assaulted with pick and shovel . . . and carted away and dumped in gullies somewhere north of Harlem. Places once frequented by Washington, . . . neighborhoods strolled over by Irving and Poe, and mentioned in some of our most delightful American sketches, are being completely transformed." Certainly, the transformation of many of New York's "gorgeous chambers turned into sweatshops where pale women sew from dawn into the long night," was proof of the cruelty of some of the changes taking place.[17]

That December one of his earliest literary models, Eugene Field, died suddenly at age forty-five, and here the literary picks and shovels were soon brought to bear, as critics now reassessed his poems as hopelessly sentimental, including his most famous work, "Little Boy Blue." "Regardless of the squabble that is now progressing as to the infantile value of Field's poetry," Dreiser insisted, "this 'Little Boy Blue' of his will remain renowned when those who are now arguing have been buried and forgotten." He thought that there was "an ebb and flow of heart" in the ballad about the dead boy whose faithful toys stand "each in the same old place / Awaiting the touch of a little hand." When Ralph Waldo Emerson, another of Dreiser's favorite American authors, lost his five-year-old son to sudden death, he too had stared—though unsentimentally—at his son's playthings as the only earthly evidence of the bliss the boy had brought him. Later in the essay "Experience," Emerson echoed what he had told a friend only days following the death, that "I chiefly grieve that I cannot grieve."[18] Field might wonder "what has become of Little Boy Blue / Since he kissed [his toys] and put them there," but it was Emerson the Transcendentalist who through his belief that nature was nothing more than a mere emblem of the Oversoul, or higher reality, expressed a kind of determinism that would become Dreiser's lifelong paradox, for his heart went out to human suffering that was nonetheless regarded as inevitable. But for now, in the heady nineties, with the wealth of the new magnates dwarfing Irvingesque quaintness, it seemed to Dreiser that death was forever upstaged by the gaudy spectacle of life.

And nowhere, he noted, was that gaudy spectacle more compelling than on Broadway, where there was "everything: windows adorned with rare paintings and crowded with aged bric-a-brac; windows filled with rarest gems and gaudiest trifles, all displayed 'neath a hundred electric bulbs to attract attention." On Broadway, Dreiser wrote in close imitation of Whitman, whose poetic catalogs first put the avenue into American literature, "surges the cosmopolitan, dallying crowd, and all night the stream of humanity flows past, crowding itself here before a poster and there before a window, where some latest gew-gaw is to show, nothing being quite too trifling to fail to attract some one idler."[19]

Dreiser may well have been aware that Whitman had started his great literary career as an editorialist, writing his catalogs of Broadway and New York in the *Aurora* in the 1840s, for by 1895 the Walt Whitman Fellowship, headed by Horace Traubel of Philadelphia, was already holding its publicized annual meetings in New York. These "Whitmaniacs" were generally socialists who subscribed to largely impractical panaceas such as Henry George's "Single Tax" (which Whitman himself admired as romantic folly). Their political agenda would have attracted Dreiser, whose imagination kept coming back to those bleak Bowery scenes he witnessed almost daily. In the June 1896 issue, he asked whether it was better to be "a strong man with average knowledge or a weak man [physically speaking] with great knowledge." In other words perhaps, whether to be of the people or about them. In defining the first, Dreiser drew—almost verbatim—from Whitman's "I Sing the Body Electric" about the octogenarian father of five sons, which came right out of Whitman's Long Island background to surface in the first edition of *Leaves of Grass:*

Emma Dreiser, the model for "Sister Carrie."
(Van Pelt–Dietrich Library, University of Pennsylvania)

Sara Schänäb Dreiser: "It always seemed to me that no one ever wanted me *enough,* unless it was my mother." (Van Pelt–Dietrich Library)

Dreiser's father, John Paul, in Rochester, New York, not long before his death in 1900. (Van Pelt–Dietrich Library)

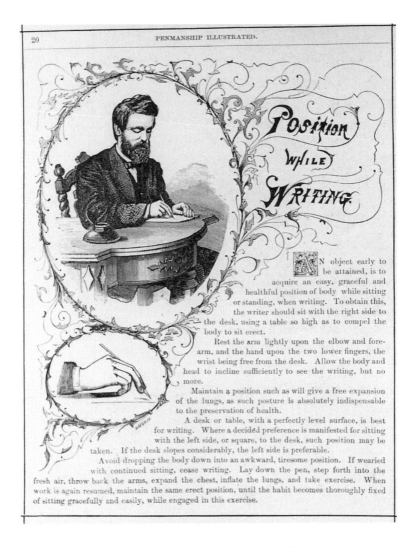

Dreiser's first lesson in writing, from Thomas E. Hill,
*Hill's Manual of Social and Business Forms: Guide to
Correct Writing* (Chicago: Moses, Warren and Co., 1880).

Dreiser (back row sitting, fourth from left) with members of the spelunking club at Indiana University, 1890. (Lilly Library, Indiana University)

The Chicago family residence on Flourney Street where Dreiser's mother died in 1890. (Van Pelt–Dietrich Library)

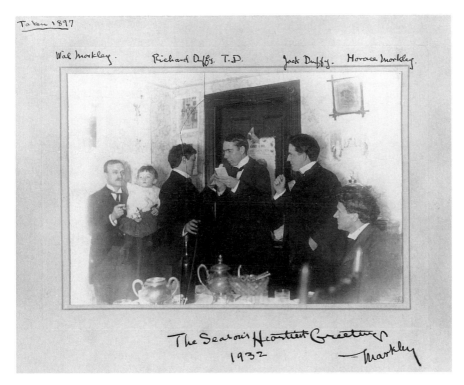

The Carnegie Library in Pittsburgh—where Dreiser first read Balzac.
(Historical Society of Western Pennsylvania)

Dreiser (center) with Richard Duffy (third from left) and others in 1897.
(Van Pelt–Dietrich Library)

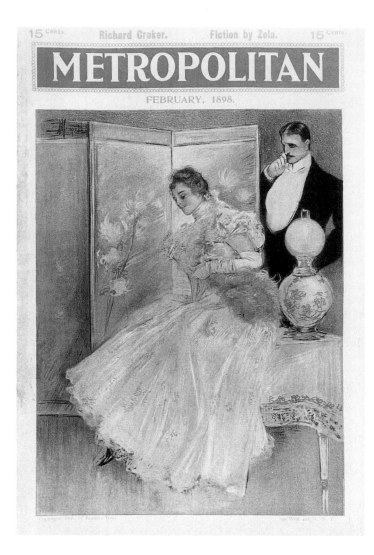

A typical cover for one of the magazines in which Dreiser
frequently published in the late 1890s. (Van Pelt–Dietrich Library)

Paul Dresser, author of
"On the Banks of the Wabash,"
in *The Metropolitan Magazine*
for November 1900.
(Van Pelt–Dietrich Library)

Arthur Henry in Toledo, Ohio, shortly
before the publication of *Sister Carrie*.
(Lilly Library, Indiana University)

Frank Norris, a champion for *Sister Carrie*.
(Library of Congress)

Question on proof

Sister Carrie.

CHAPTER I.

The maquet attracting: a waif amid forces.

When Caroline Meeber boarded the afternoon train for Chicago, her total outfit consisted of a small trunk, ~~which was checked
in the baggage car,~~ a cheap imitation alligator skin satchel, ~~holding
some minor details of the toilet,~~ a small lunch in a paper box and a
yellow leather snap purse, containing her ticket, a scrap of paper
with her sister's address in Van Buren Street, and four dollars in
money. It was in August, 1889. She was eighteen years of age,
bright, timid and full of illusions, ignorance and youth. Whatever
touch of regret at parting characterized her thoughts, it was certainly not for advantages now being given up. A gush of tears at her
mother's farewell kiss, a touch in the throat when the cars clacked
by the flour mill where her father worked by the day, a pathetic sigh
as the familiar green environs of the village passed in review, and the
threads which bound her so lightly to girlhood and home were irre-
trievably broken.

To be sure, ~~she was not conscious of any of this. Any
change, however great, might be remedied.~~ There was always the next
station where one might descend and return. There was the great
city bound more closely by these very trains which came up daily.
Columbia City was not so very far away, even once she was in Chicago.
What, pray, is a few hours - a hundred miles? ~~And then her sister
was there.~~ She looked at the little slip bearing ~~the latter's~~ her sister's address and wondered. She gazed at the green landscape, now passing
in swift review, until her swifter thoughts replaced its impression
with vague conjectures of what Chicago might be, like. ~~Since infancy
her ears had been full of its fame. Since the family had thought of~~

The first page of the typesetting copy of *Sister Carrie,*
with corrections. (Van Pelt–Dietrich Library)

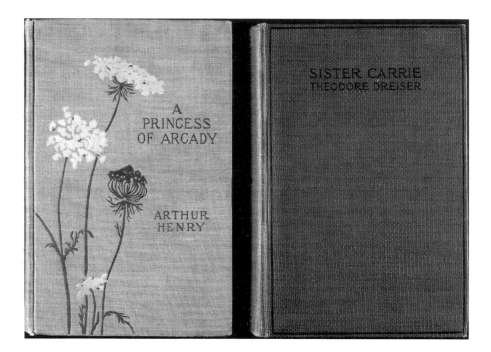

Arthur Henry's *A Princess of Arcady* and *Sister Carrie,*
both published by Doubleday in 1900. (Van Pelt–Dietrich Library)

"Paradise Lost"—one of the dumpling islands off the coast of Connecticut, where Dreiser visited Arthur Henry in 1901. (Frontispiece for *An Island Cabin,* New York: McClure, Phillips, and Company, 1902)

William Muldoon's Sanitarium in Olympia, New York, where
Dreiser was a patient in 1903. (Edward Van Every, *Muldoon:
The Solid Man* [New York: Frederick A. Stokes, 1929])

Peter McCord's caricature of Dreiser in 1907, when Dreiser
had his appendix removed. McCord was the basis for "Peter"
in *Twelve Men*. (Van Pelt–Dietrich Library)

Sara Osborne White ("Jug"), Dreiser's first wife, around 1912.
(Van Pelt–Dietrich Library)

Dreiser as magazine editor, around 1908.
(Lilly Library, Indiana University)

H. L. Mencken in 1913, at the height of his friendship with Dreiser. (Enoch Pratt Free Library, Baltimore)

Thelma Cudlipp around 1910. (Van Pelt–Dietrich Library)

The love of Dreiser's life: Kirah Markham
(Elaine Hyman). (Van Pelt–Dietrich Library)

I knew a man, a common farmer, the father of five sons,
And in them the fathers of sons, and in them the fathers of sons.

This man was of wonderful vigor, calmness, beauty of person,
. . . .
He was six feet tall, he was over eighty years old, his sons were massive,
   clean, bearded, tan-faced, handsome,
They and his daughters loved him, all who saw him loved him,
They did not love him by allowance, they loved him with personal love,
He drank water only, the blood show'd like scarlet through the clear-
   brown skin of his face.

"Here is the strong man, say, the common farmer and father of five sons,"
Dreiser wrote. "Here he is, a man of wonderful vigor, calmness, and beauty
of person. . . . He is six feet tall, he is over eighty years of age, his sons are
massive, clean, bearded, tan-faced and handsome. They, and his daughters
love him . . . , not by allowance but with a personal love. He drinks water
only, and through the clear, brown skin of his face his pure blood shows
scarlet."[20]

In his sketch, Dreiser also borrowed Whitman's frequent contrast between
the individual who goes with nature's flow (like the poet) and the uptight,
over-socialized, and often dyspeptic types whose book learning proves iso-
lating.[21] Dreiser insisted that there was "no happy medium." As a developing novelist, he suspected that Whitman's literary success came from his
realistic treatment of life, based on living life instead of merely reading about
it—and its social stereotypes and hierarchies. He thought Balzac's immersion in life had done the same thing for his art.

In fact, Dreiser paid Balzac the same compliment he gave to Whitman.
In the May 1896 issue, he as boldly plagiarized a passage from *The Wild
Ass's Skin,* concerning the dreamy youth who hopes to enter society and a
world of wealth by winning the hand of "some bright, dashing, beautiful
and wealthy girl." Balzac's *La Comédie Humaine* was as real in its depictions as Whitman was of his roughs in *Leaves of Grass.* In fact, as he had
first struggled on the *World,* Dreiser couldn't get out of his mind the failures he had read about in Balzac, who knew "how pitifully they slave for
fame." "More than one young man dreams of a brilliant future in these
sharply contrasted days of business," he wrote in *Ev'ry Month* by way of
introducing the Balzacian paradigm which he himself felt he was still acting out. "There is many a brilliant young nobody, who at twenty-six years

old imagines that he is dying unrecognized because he had not attained fame."[22]

This was certainly a self-portrait of the twenty-six-year-old editor of *Ev'ry Month,* who still fantasized about wealth through marriage, even as he poured out his heart to his "Darling Honey Girl" back in Missouri. "If you knew . . . ," he wrote Jug, "how my heart has ached only to see your face once more." He had made a second visit to see her, in the spring of 1896. On the way back from Montgomery City to St. Louis in the rain, he wrote her that "the landscape, towns and structures" were bare and dismal without her.[23] That summer he sent her an engagement ring, along with the latest issue of his magazine. "By the way," he asked, "did you receive the July [1896] no? I put your name on the cover as usual. You're the book's mascot."[24] The *Ev'ry Month* covers had the table of contents superimposed on the picture of a beautiful actress (usually gazing upward), and invariably one of the authors listed was "S. J. White."

Having sought to possess her sexually, as he had in the summer of 1894, he had returned east again in defeat. At least he could write suggestive letters that slyly invited her to give another thought to doing the great deed, pages and half pages that Jug (or her heirs) cut from his letters. "Oh, my own Jug! What a lover you are. You are Sapphic in your fire. You love as I never dreamed a woman could"—with the rest of the paragraph on the next page missing. In another letter he called her his "repentant Magdalene," but alas with the qualifier that Jug was "Magdalenic in sentiment" only. This particular comment came, he said, from a photograph of an actress posing as the "Parisian 'Chanteuse' [Cleo de Merade] who enslaved the King of Belgium." It was his only picture, he hinted, of Jug on the threshold of sex. "I look at it and it recalls the evenings in St. Louis when you unbound your splendid hair and coaxed me to kiss you."[25]

Dreiser now lived in a room at 232 West Fifteenth Street and took many of his meals at the Continental Hotel, whose cafe windows looked out on Broadway. "The crowd, street cars, vehicles and pedestrians all tend to dispel gloomy moments," he told Jug, "and so I love to lounge at tables and look out."[26] He planned to spend the winter reading Darwin, the bespectacled Dreiser told her, but by the fall of 1896 he had already begun to enhance his Spencerian impressions. (In the September 1896 *Ev'ry Month* he had pronounced all life as a helpless product of the sun.) "You would[n't] care for such study I suppose," he said, "seeing you don't believe in Evolution." He had just finished a chapter "relating to probable reasons why in nature, the male courts the female." Perhaps Jug was still too much a Christian, he implied, "but your lover is firmly grounded in the belief and gains as much satisfaction from observing the truth of it, as some would in observing the nearness of a novelistic fiction to actual life."[27] He may also have been reading about human sex in the explicit underground novels of the day, not that difficult to find in New York.

Later, as the approach of a marriage that would demand fidelity to only one sexual partner terrified him more and more, he seemed to qualify his unbounded love with the caveat that "if ever you are grieved because of me, be sure that circumstances outside the control of my will and desire, and not I, are to blame." This comment reflects more than the basic determinism he would dramatize in his novels; it also suggests his growing ambivalence regarding a benign deity. He was already caught between the past and the onrushing future in intellectual America, between antebellum ideas about morality and sexual responsibility, and the Darwinian idea—as it was being explained in the "pragmatism" of William James—that "truth" depended on necessity, which is to say, whatever worked in life.[28]

His social life became more and more tempting. There were late-night parties with fellow writers and editors of the other magazines in the city. "We had a banquet at the Arena, Saturday," he told Jug. He had heard "stories and comic and tragic recitations, together with songs, musical selections and speeches that were hilarious to the ridiculous degree. There were ten courses and eight kinds of wine, though I only drank a little." Dreiser was surely telling the truth about the drinking, for he was a moderate imbiber most of his life, but his frequent comments to Jug about other women who would welcome his company probably stemmed more from an innocent tease or effort to chastise her for her prudishness. Certainly he held up his brother Paul as no positive example. The one-time candidate for the priesthood had just returned from Terre Haute in March 1897 to announce his plans to marry an old flame, but Dreiser confided to Jug that Paul "loves all women too well generally to love any one in particular for long. He is fickle, fat and forty and worse than ever."[29]

Dreiser was also caught up in the literary whirl of New York. Reviews in *Ev'ry Month* praised such works as Hamlin Garland's *Main-Traveled Roads* (1891), which he had read while still in Pittsburgh, and Stephen Crane's *The Red Badge of Courage* (1895). "Here is a novelist for you, if you want an American," wrote "Edward Al" of Crane in the May 1896 issue. Crane expressed "the sentiments that are nothing, if not the whisperings of the oversoul." In the September 1896 issue, he published Crane's "A Mystery of Heroism," a vivid tale of the grimness of the Civil War. (In the issue of February 1897, he also had Jenks praise Crane's "The Men in the Storm.") Although Garland would later abandon Dreiser over the "pornography" of The "*Genius*," Dreiser never failed to credit the prairie realist as one of his early literary models. He put Crane even more firmly in this category. "He was among the very earliest of my purely American literary admirations and one of the few writers who stood forward intellectually and artistically at a time when this nation was thoroughly submerged in romance and sentimentality and business as it is today," he told Max J. Herzberg in 1921.[30]

Earlier that year, in the June issue, as the serialization of Twain's *Personal Reflections of Joan of Arc* in *Harper's* wound down, Dreiser also praised "this rugged old humorist" who was "something far more than a mere humorist. . . . [H]e is a great writer. Like Balzac himself he can afford to let the critic smile and dissect at leisure, serene in the consciousness that he has in some measure understood and expressed the wondrous workings of the human heart."[31] As we shall see, Dreiser was as prescient of Twain's future fame as he would be of Whitman's. Both were vernacular writers who taught him that it was all right to let his characters talk naturally— something he too would be censured for in *Sister Carrie*.

He also published his own poems, sometimes under Jug's pseudonym, sometimes under his own name. "I sing of the toiling masses," he now wrote with Whitman again on the brain, "of the hands that never cease,"

> From their labor and wretched living till the soul wings home in peace:
> For the name of the poor is legion, where the name of the rich is score,
> And the hearts of the poor are trampled by the things which the rich
>   adore.

In another he borrowed his title from a Thomas Hardy novel. "The Madding Crowd" expressed the sentimental love of "woodland ways and sylvan glades" over the "crowded marts" whose "mad temptations" and "physical tastes" lead to an early grave. He may have feared his own sense of potential debauchery, although his "tastes" did not run to alcohol. He told Jug later that year, "I take so little exercise, practically none at all, that somedays I really feel wretched for the lack of it."[32] The literary life took its toll.

When Harriet Beecher Stowe died in July 1896 at age eighty-five, he read *Uncle Tom's Cabin* (1852), possibly for the first time, and praised it in the next number of *Ev'ry Month* as the "famous story of the woes of blackmen in this gracious land of ours" who had since "been freed and provided for." (Perhaps in the rush of editorial adrenaline here Dreiser had temporarily forgotten about the lynching he had seen outside St. Louis.) It didn't matter what the critics were already saying about the novel's sentimentality and crudeness, he insisted, because the tale "was matchlessly adorned by the beauty of truth, whereas the flood of literature which daily rolls about us is finely written but hopelessly defiled by moral lies and pompous affectations." He had recently lambasted Elizabeth Stuart Phelps's *A Singular Life* (1895), an extremely popular novel described by its promoters as the best American novel since Stowe's famous book. *A Singular Life,* he railed, had nothing to do with greatness. It had "no charms" whatever. Furthermore, he declared, "Elizabeth Stuart Phelps can't write."[33]

In reviewing the British novelist Halliwell Sutcliffe's *The Eleventh Commandment* (1896), the *Ev'ry Month* editor who filled his issues with pictures of fashion-plate females complained of the tendency to present women as beings more spiritual than human. The modern reader, he insisted, was "weary of the idiocy of [such] writers who are always trying to cover up the human element in human beings and showing love as a high, thoroughly reasonable and philosophical affair. . . . If [Sutcliffe] had gathered love's meaning from hard, fanciless teachers like Spencer, Huxley and Hume, his story would not sound so unnatural and meaningless." In other words, writers of such romantic fictions were ignoring the "probable reasons why in nature, the male courts the female"—and vice versa. The British author had apparently received "his thoughts of spirituality in love from poets and mystics like Goethe and Carlyle."[34] In cold reality, there were such women as his sister Emma who exploited as much as they were exploited, and there were women such as Jug, who were submissive in everything except premarital sex. Out of their opposites the idea of Carrie Meeber no doubt took root.

Dreiser may have been thinking of his own literary chances when, in the August 1896 number, he again called on Whitman, who emphasized beautifully in his poems "the need of being strong, of entering the race with sturdy, fleet limbs, and flesh fair and sweet." In the same issue he published

"Forgotten," recycling in near-verbatim fashion "Hospital Violet Day," which he had written for the *Pittsburgh Dispatch* on May 12, 1894. The dying man, Old Fintz in the *Dispatch* story, becomes Channing in "Forgotten," but the description of "Violet Day" in the hospital is taken exactly from the *Dispatch* piece. Ellen Moers has suggested that the story also owes its theme to Paul Dresser's ballad, "The Letter That Never Came," for there is present in both the dying man's futile efforts to notify a relative or friend. In Dreiser's story, no replies ever come to the hospital from "West Virginia city," and Channing—like the man in Paul's song—dies "forgotten."[35] The larger influence here, as it had been with the story's Pittsburgh version, was Crane's "Bowery Journalism," recently raised to nobler heights in *The Red Badge of Courage*. Thrilled as he was to be running a magazine and writing what he chose to write, Dreiser retained his sympathy for those caught in the urban misery around him—and as a lifelong worrier about money, he feared it might sweep him too from his editor's chair and leave him in the gutter.

He stayed in the editor's chair at *Ev'ry Month* for nearly two years. The second year shows a faint decline in quality or Dreiserian verve at the beginning, and by the April and May 1897 issues the change is so marked that it seems that either the editorship has been erroneously attributed to him or he was being heavily overruled by Paul or, more likely, the partners, with whom he had differing political opinions.[36] Paul may have objected to the publication of Arthur Henry's "It Is to Laugh" in the April issue, which mocked Paul's brand of comic opera as merely a series of pratfalls. It described a songwriter character smashing furniture in a recent farce and advised writers accordingly to "avoid anything subtle. Your sarcasms must have teeth. Rapier thrusts at social conditions are lost. Use a club, and be sure and land on the old wounds." (Later, Henry would describe Paul in print as "a very fat man . . . hanging, as it were, over the keys [of a piano] thrumming and humming a song he was composing. . . . [It] was very sad, and in spite of his exuberant, well-fed appearance, he seemed to feel it. I surely saw a tear roll down his big fat face as, a verse completed, he sang it softly through.")[37] Just how much Dreiser himself contributed to the satire of Paul's theatrical methods in his own trade magazine cannot be known, but the fact that it appeared under his editorship suggests he was feeling a mounting frustration at his brother's success and his own static situation.

Without a doubt, however, starting with the recycled "Forgotten," Dreiser began to turn his—and the magazine's—attention from the purely literary and musical to the sociological. In September 1896 he reviewed Abraham Cahan's *Yekl: A Tale of the New York Ghetto* (1896), a vivid account of living conditions in the Jewish ghetto of New York. Cahan, a Russian émigré and militant socialist whose political views ought to have found favor with Dreiser's sense of the urban poor, was also, as Dreiser noted, the founder and editor of the *Jewish Daily Forward*. But somehow Jewish poverty didn't register with him to the same degree as the Irish or German or Lithuanian poverty he had seen in Pittsburgh. Instead Cahan's brand of Bowery Journalism presented "a picture of unrelieved sordidness and hardness for the most part, with the finer, softer traits of character entirely obscured." *Yekl,* he granted, was "undoubtedly an authentic account of the lives of people"— if only of those "who, though near neighbors, are great strangers to us."[38]

The next month he tried his hand at ghettos of the poor himself, detailing the underbelly of the glittering city. Comparing Manhattan to a flowering plant and rather tangling the metaphor, he wrote: "Down in the dark earth are the roots, drawing life and strength and sending them coursing up the veins; and down in alleys and byways, in the shop and small dark chambers are the roots of this luxurious high life, starving and toiling the long year through, that carriages may roll and great palaces stand brilliant with ornaments." The fascinating surface, he continued, "conceals the sorrow and want and ceaseless toil upon which all this is built." Then he turned to the wretched and dwarfed specimen "of masculine humanity" who was charged with vagrancy after attempting to eat garbage from a restaurant. "Thus could be written," said the future author of *Sister Carrie,* "the story of many another."[39]

With so many George Hurstwoods crisscrossing Broadway and the Bowery, Dreiser recognized that some must have come originally from the economically privileged classes, or at least the solidly middle class knocked down by the last gusts of the Panic of 1893. And indeed, there were already many examples of personal debauchery among the rich in America. By 1897 Frank Norris had drafted *Vandover and the Brute;* although it would not be published until 1914, after Norris's death, it reflected the fears of the nineties. Social Darwinists of the era still preached that the "brute" in the middle-class person could be controlled, while of course it ran rampant in the lower classes exemplified by Norris's *McTeague.* (It was about this time that Andrew Carnegie began to talk about giving away his money instead of leaving it to his heirs. He would build libraries instead of spoiling the next generation with unearned wealth.) "Like the flight of a comet, from outer darkness into outer darkness," Dreiser noted of the tragic rich, "the progress of the spendthrift up from obscurity, through gilded and glittering resorts, into the asylum and the Potter's Field, must ever arrest the attention of the eye and the mind." "They say this last one was a prince of good fellows," Dreiser continued. "Yes, while he had money. So are all the prodigals."[40]

Returning a month later to the subject of the forgotten graves he had written about in Pittsburgh, Dreiser imagined how these once "flash and flippant" good fellows so quickly disappear behind the numbered grave boards that "mingle with unnumbered weeds." The lesson, intensified by his boyhood poverty, would haunt him all his life. He was beginning to believe in hard work as the only means of success, yet also suspected that fate had the final say. Part of the equation, of course, was the spark of "ambition, or its complementary term, selfish desire, [which] is the lever that moves the world." And those with the most ambition and blessed with talent, he believed, came to New York.

Of course, many others came as well, whether to stay or to visit, including members of the Dreiser clan. Christmas 1896 was a family reunion. They all gathered at Emma's, and he ate everything, Dreiser told Jug, "from candy to imported plum pudding." Claire and Ed were visiting from Chicago; Mame and Austin Brennan brought John Paul Dreiser, now seventy-five. Also present at what was to be the last large family gathering were Theresa and Al, indeed all the children but Sylvia and the wandering Rome. Brennan, the only example of dissipated wealth here, got sick, but it was "no special cause for alarm," Theo told Jug. "He is subject to all the ailments that come to one because of high living." Mame, he said, "is more of a nurse than anything else now-a-days."[41] Paul was in his usual high spirits, showing no signs of slowing down.

———

By the late winter of 1897, Dreiser seemed unsettled. He had become well known to the magazine world in the city and was offered the editorship of "a new magazine in three colors, which H. E. Jones is going to start," he told his fiancée. "However I think I have had enough of new magazines." Either trouble was brewing with the partners or Dreiser felt he had exhausted his material for *Ev'ry Month*. Even with Jenks as his assistant, he needed more time to research his copy. He felt confined to his cramped editorial office, not only because of work but by the freezing weather that winter. "I have remained close in my office for two days," he told Jug. "This the M.D. says is not good for me, but neither is the extreme cold."[42]

By April—the month that Henry's "It Is to Laugh" appeared—something had definitely changed around the office. Between this issue and the following September, when previous biographers and critics have assumed Dreiser left the magazine, the "Reflections" column lost its title and was no longer signed "The Prophet." Its worldview shifted as well. We now hear echoes of the conventional sentiments of Paul, whose songs continued to sell to the "millions," as he would later claim in the *Metropolitan*. The April editorial in *Ev'ry Month* complains good-heartedly about the "fairer sex," and how juries are often too lenient to convict a woman for her crime. Before a dozen men, she escapes punishment because of the male's "innate sympathy for the opposite sex, which will not down." In earlier issues, the problem—as Howley, Haviland, and Company may now have recognized—was the fact that the images of realism and fantasy had conveyed conflicting moral messages. While "The Prophet" complained of the rents in the social fabric, illustrations in the magazine projected images of beautiful women, near sated with their dreams of riches and fame. Now the women who fluttered through the pages of *Ev'ry Month* were no longer subject to Darwin's implied notions about social behavior; now men were to be exonerated "for their error of judgment where women are concerned."[43]

Beginning in the spring of 1897, the searching rhetoric of Dreiser's Spencerian conscience transforms into a sermon characterized by a blend of Social Darwinism and Christianity. Every man has the innate right to "search far and wide" over the earth in search of prosperity, yet it is conceded that "so many thousands or hundreds of thousands of illiterate immigrants every year" will both reduce wages and through the ballot box "lower the moral standard of the nation."[44] Such xenophobia was possibly more the bailiwick of Paul, who changed his German surname, than of Theodore Dreiser, who would later write tenderly about Italian ghettos. Generally, platitudes replace pathos in a column that is more reactive than reflective, echoing, for example, Emerson's antebellum call for American self-reliance more than forty years after the Civil War and the nation's ascent as a world power, both industrially and intellectually. They speak of uplifting humanity through the doing of good and the favor of Providence.

It might be one's duty to arouse sympathy among the rich for those whom the undertow of adversity has swept to the lowest depths, but it is improbable that this witness of the deep divisions between the rich and poor in Pittsburgh and New York would ever believe it possible. Although Dreiser had read Cahan, he didn't have to read the muckraker Jacob Riis's *How the Other Half Lives* (1890) to know that "working sympathy" was a hopeful fantasy. Riis reports, in perhaps an exaggeration, how as many as ten thousand men a night descended on the Bowery in search of an affordable place to sleep and possibly eat. Dreiser had seen it for himself—had indeed already been a part of what Crane called "An Experiment in Misery." If we are to trust his recollections, his brother-in-law L. A. Hopkins was now one of the *misérables*.

Although he may have continued to contribute reviews, Dreiser was clearly moving out of the editor's chair by the spring of 1897. Whenever it was that he finally left, he and Paul quarreled. They would see each other only rarely over the next five years. The anger was almost exclusively on Theo's part, for Paul always thought of his brother as his brightest and most promising sibling, whose writing he had faith in long before anyone else. After *Ev'ry Month* it was becoming clear to many others that the "young man from the provinces" could write. He might not write songs for the "millions," but he would write for posterity. In the meantime, there was a living to make and—ready or not—a woman to marry.

SIX

The Writer

Outside the door of what was once a row of red brick family dwellings, in Fifteenth street, but what is now a mission or convent house of the Sisters of Mercy, hangs a plain wooden contribution box, on which is painted the statement that every noon a meal is given free to all those who apply and ask for aid.

"CURIOUS SHIFTS OF THE POOR"

DREISER BECAME A MAGAZINE WRITER. It has been said that after "fixing up other fellows' articles" for two years, he was more than prepared to write his own.[1] In fact, it was mainly his own articles he had "fixed up" in writing most of the copy for *Ev'ry Month,* and there he had learned to write— to entertain and educate. He couldn't have come of age as a freelance magazinist at a more propitious time, for the country was at the height of its transition from human brawn to mechanical power as it approached the twentieth century, and there was no end of material to write about. Americans were excited about the prospects of such labor-saving devices as the horseless carriage and electricity in the home. At the same time, however, the new technologies created new fears. They undercut the independence and identity of the artisan or mechanic. In *The Twentieth Century* (1898), Josiah Strong noted that it now took sixty-four men to make a simple shoe.[2] Love of the homespun small-town life also seemed to be giving way to infatuation with the city and its dependence on the complexity of the new order. Most of the geniuses of the age appeared to have come from simple backgrounds, but the ultimate product of their imagination and industry became lost in their practical applications. The "wizard" Edison had invented the incandescent lightbulb, but his attempts to provide the country with electricity were already being absorbed by corporations of engineers and investors such as General Electric (once "Edison General Electric") and Westinghouse.

The biggest invention was the modern American city. Its magnetism seemed to be turning America's agrarian ideal of hard work and clean living into an ideological hothouse of ambition and greed. Writers such as Abraham Cahan and Jacob Riis had already complained about urban "progress," and Stephen Crane in *Maggie* had shown city life to be potentially a helter-skelter affair, almost surrealistic in its scenes of violence and mayhem. With newspapers chasing the latest scandal and calling for spurious reforms, the magazine emerged in the late 1890s as a resource for the middle-class American who sought a more congenial explanation of the times as well as an affirmation that basic values were still the bedrock of a society intoxicated by its own advances. Essentially, *Ev'ry Month* existed to sell sheet music, making even Dreiser's now defunct "Reflections" column subordinate to the demands of commerce. But there were other magazines around—among them *Metropolitan, Truth, Munsey's,* and *Ainslee's*—livelier descendants of the purely literary journals such as *Century* and *Harper's,* and they sold their stories as their main product.

Turning to these magazines, Dreiser struck out on his own, not only because he had lost control (or been forced out) of *Ev'ry Month,* but because he felt increasingly threatened by that other genius in the family, his brother Paul. Paul's "On the Banks of the Wabash, Far Away" was written in 1897 and quickly sold over five thousand copies. By the next year the song (which would be officially adopted as Indiana's state song in 1913) was a national bestseller.[3] Its easy nostalgia took America back to when life seemed less conflicted:

> Round my Indiana homestead wave the cornfield,
> In the distance loom the woodlands clear and cool.
> Often times my thoughts revert to scenes of childhood,
> Where I first received my lessons, nature's school.
> But one thing there is missing in the picture,
> Without her face it seems so incomplete.
> I long to see my mother in the doorway,
> As she stood there years ago, her boy to greet![4]

"Yes, dearie," Dreiser told Jug, "I wrote the words as I said of 'On the Banks of the Wabash.'" When he first made this boast, in May of 1898, Jug was more interested to know who "Mary" was, for the song speaks in its refrain of walking arm in arm along the Wabash with a sweetheart by that name. "There was no 'Mary' in my life. That idea is merely introduced for effect, nothing more," he said and teased that she might "store your hate for some other purpose—perhaps the next girl I get." (In fact, "Mary" was most likely based on Mary South, the fourteen-year-old daughter of an acquaintance of Paul's in Terre Haute. The song was officially dedicated to her, before Paul had even met her. Later, after they had met and begun a correspondence, Paul in turn claimed to her that his brother had given him only the subject of the Wabash River.)[5]

Did Dreiser actually write the words to Paul's most famous song? Paul was always generous with his brother, so there is little reason to think he would deny him credit if it was due. The letter to Jug is the only time we know of that Dreiser made the claim before Paul's death. In an article he wrote for the *Metropolitan* late in 1898, he claimed merely to have been present at the time of the song's composition. But in 1916, in *A Hoosier Holiday*, he boasted, "I wrote the first verse and chorus!" In "My Brother Paul," as well as in an introduction to Boni & Liveright's *Songs of Paul Dresser*, he told the same story of a collaboration between the two in writing the song, claiming that one day, while he was still editor of *Ev'ry Month*, Paul, who was "sitting at the piano and thrumming," asked his brother to give him the idea for a song. Dreiser allegedly answered, "Why don't you write something about a State or a river? Look at 'My Old Kentucky Home,' 'Dixie,' 'Old Black Joe' . . . something that suggests a part of America? People like that. Take Indiana—what's the matter with it—the Wabash River? It's as good as any other river, and you were 'raised' beside it." And here, as in his letter, Dreiser claimed to have written the first verse and chorus.[6]

The truth is probably that Dreiser gave Paul the general idea of writing about the Wabash River but wrote at most only a line or two of the song. The fact that he wrote or planned to write a comic opera entitled *Along the Wabash* in 1895 is perhaps evidence of his interest in the river for artistic purposes, if not also of his influence on the composition of "On the Banks of the Wabash, Far Away." Yet in 1939, chastened by old age and the aged memory of Paul, he told Lorna Smith, a California acquaintance, "I only wrote part of the words. The music, title, and most of the words were the inspiration and work of my brother Paul Dresser."[7] The first three lines are vintage Paul with their emphasis on home and childhood, though Dreiser too thought often of childhood and (along with Paul) of his mother, whose ghost pervades Paul's songs. The fourth line, "Where I first received my lessons, nature's school," is possibly Dreiser's. In *Dawn* there is much devoted to the young Dreiser's infatuation with nature and the question of what it all meant or how it came to be. Paul Dresser hardly had time for nature. He was too busy with the world to notice flowers or fauna. Dreiser's various claims for anything more than a few words and the general idea, however, were probably the result of the *Ev'ry Month* tiff, a hurt that festered for many years, before finally finding a sort of middle ground in a boast that also romanticized his songster-brother—much as he would do in "My Brother Paul" and the introduction to the *Songs of Paul Dresser,* both love letters to a brother who had loved him like a father.

As "On the Banks" moved steadily toward national recognition in 1897, Dreiser's jealousy may have also manifested itself in the article he commissioned from Arthur Henry for the April issue of *Ev'ry Month.* The ever restless Henry had given up newspaper work after his marriage in 1894 and scavenged around the country for more creative opportunities, leaving his wife and their daughter behind in Toledo. In 1895, for example, he had become a publicist for the magician Hermann the Great, who unfortunately dropped dead of heart attack in his private railroad car a year later. By 1897 Henry was in New York hoping to make it as a writer, and at this early stage in his writing career *Ev'ry Month* was possibly the first magazine in which he published anything.[8] Meanwhile, Dreiser, denied a pay raise as well as complete editorial control as of the April issue, may have considered Henry's attack on Paul's style of music his parting gesture of revenge for his mistreatment, as he saw it, at *Ev'ry Month.*[9]

Henry himself was full of romantic visions of becoming a high-toned poet, standing above the fray of a culture that valued success over integrity. He was, as Dreiser later described him, "a dreamer of dreams, a spinner of fine fancies, a lover of impossible romances which fascinated me by their very impossibility." Dreiser, too, was disdainful of the popular culture after two years at *Ev'ry Month* under the restraints of its commercially minded owners. He told his friend that although he was drawing a good salary, "The things I am able to get the boss to publish that I believe in are very few." Both men hoped to write someday about the true meaning of life, but the two made curious bedfellows in the annals of American literature.[10] Both began by telling Americans what they wanted to hear. Henry had written of the romance of white superiority in his Klan novel only a few years earlier, and Dreiser, before he found his literary key in *Sister Carrie,* would soon write puffed-up autobiographical sketches for *Success* magazine, dedicated to the American materialists "who have made the century great." Dreiser, whose "Prophet" columns had scratched more than the surface of American society to contemplate its inequities and conundrums, now began his career as a freelancer by writing up the rich and famous.

The formula of success applied even to the literary famous, though today most of them are more interesting for their station in life than their place in literature. In "New York's Art Colony," Dreiser's very first freelance article, published in the November 1897 *Metropolitan,* he wrote about the artistic and literary retreat at Lawrence Park, New York, then a sylvan expanse of estates in Bronxville, only "twenty-six minutes from the heart of New York." (Perhaps to give his literary debut a weightiness he felt it lacked in the shadow of the ascendant Paul, he signed the piece "Theodore Dresser.") Lawrence Park was "the home of the literati who believe that genius and talent are best fostered by quiet." The literary outsider who lived in a rented room on West Fifteenth Street spoke admiringly of the well-appointed homes of such luminaries as the "banker-poet" Edmund Clarence Stedman; Tudor Jenks, the editor of *St. Nicholas* magazine; the now-forgotten author Alice W. Rollins; and Mrs. General Custer. At Lawrence Park he found authorship with a pedigree nestled on ninety-six acres of woods and slopes dotted with "trees, ribbed with fine rock, and starred with wild flowers." There were no fences or other signs of ownership, but admission into the community clearly depended on wealth—along with the consent of its members, who had taken up residence there on land purchased to emulate art colonies outside London and Paris.

The article's nine illustrations of homes, whose natural, uncultivated grounds merged into one another, suggested anything but the literary world in which Dreiser and Henry struggled. Here, Dreiser wrote, "one must either have talent or a *savoir-faire,* according to the literary and artistic code prevailing, to be eligible at all for such privileges as the colony extends."[11] That code had given its imprimatur to such Victorian realists as William Dean Howells and Henry James, whose most memorable depictions of life left out the vulgar and sordid details that Dreiser had seen as a journalist and survivor of the tawdrier aspects of the city just twenty-six minutes south. Stedman's surviving claim to literary fame is that he was the first writer of the genteel tradition to champion *Leaves of Grass* in the 1880s when that great work was still denied the claim of literature. Even then, he did so with a Victorian detachment that ultimately left his defense in doubt. Yet Stedman and his conventional poetry represented literary success in the 1890s, or at least its worldly rewards.

That fall Dreiser also traveled to Chester County, Pennsylvania, and the scene of the Revolutionary War battleground at Brandywine. In *Truth* he extolled the beauty of the countryside, which like Lawrence Park offered relief from the fast pace of city life.[12] The true purpose of the trip, however, was to seek out the homestead of another famous writer now nearly forgotten, America's centennial poet laureate Bayard Taylor. Once again, the focus was not so much on the writer's literary achievement but on the spoils of his success; "The Haunts of Bayard Taylor" was published in *Munsey's* magazine for January 1898. In spite of his almost fifty books and more than seven hundred newspaper and magazine articles, his distinguished career on Horace Greeley's *New York Tribune,* and his translation of Goethe's *Faust* (his only truly lasting work), Taylor, who had died in 1878, was already being forgotten two decades into America's second hundred years. "When men who are now fifty years old were boys," the admiring Dreiser wrote, "there was not a youth in the country who did not know of Bayard Taylor and hope to do as he had done." Dreiser admired Taylor most for his impoverished beginning, "that he was a poor lad who had earned his own way."[13]

This Horatio Alger scenario still appealed to Dreiser, who was also earning his own way and whose early articles suggest that he aspired to some of the respectability Taylor and the scribblers of Lawrence Park had achieved. The future chronicler of not only Hurstwood's fall but also Cowperwood's rise to wealth was not opposed to popular literary success per se. In an essay called "The Homes of Longfellow," which was written about this time but never published, he begrudged the most popular poet of the nineteenth century neither his privileged beginning in life (saying that it kept him "mindful of duty") nor his commercial success (which "stimulated him to toil").[14] Yet Dreiser could not sustain this generosity towards the rich as he approached *Sister Carrie.*

What probably changed this course, broke its nostalgic trance, were the thirty articles Dreiser wrote for *Success,* a magazine that featured interviews with and stories about those who had recently "arrived"—successful men of business, industry, science, art, and literature. First issued in January 1898, Dr. Orison Swett Marden's publication sought to demonstrate that character, energy, and endless ambition were the only keys to success in a land where all men were born free and equal. Its articles were structured by three basic questions concerning the essential quality of success (inevitably industry); where or at what level the achievers began in life (inevitably poor); and the definition of the successful person's concept of happiness (almost inevitably that hard work was its own best reward). Naturally, the stock answers were narcoleptic to any but the most avid believers in the formula "success."[15] But it was not simply the monotony of the American Dream that pushed Dreiser towards the new realism, or the naturalism of *Sister Carrie.* It was the suspicion in interviewing all these people that the picture of life in the ideal, even the democratic ideal of hard work and fair play, was a sham.

One question Dreiser usually added to the battery of stock queries touched on the debate, fueled by the rise of Social Darwinism, over whether ability was inherited or acquired. By the time of *Sister Carrie,* or in its disastrous aftermath, Dreiser was convinced that his writing talent was inherent, not taught or learned. Edison, whom he interviewed in February 1898, reinforced his suspicions about heredity and environment. When the most famous American of his day insisted that the talent to improve technology "is born in a man," Dreiser asked whether familiarity with "certain mechanical conditions and defects" might not suggest improvements to anyone. No, the inventor answered, some people might be perfectly familiar with the machinery and never see a way to improve it. The slaughterhouse and meat-packing king Philip D. Armour agreed when Dreiser interviewed him in Chicago that June.[16] Yet the very raison d'être of the magazine in which these interviews were to appear was to tell Americans that life was an even playing field. Its theme of success and self-help also ignored the role of chance, not only in terms of inherited ability but opportunity. "It never occurred to me at the time," Dreiser wrote in an undated manuscript probably from the 1920s, "that nearly everybody was nothing more than a minor point in a huge organism, and that the part of it in which one found oneself might offer very serious objections to the achievement of a great financial or mental success."[17] But obviously, it had occurred to him, for both Edison and Armour had explained to him that their success depended mainly on native intelligence and the right opportunity, or essentially chance. For Edison, his wizardly understanding of electricity surfaced not long after he saved the son of a station master who in gratitude gave him a job on the railroad and taught him how to operate a telegraph machine, while for Armour achievement owed its success to the growth of the cattle market and the outbreak of the Civil War, which produced enormous demands for pork and beef.

———

By now Dreiser was convinced that he had a talent to write, but he must have asked himself if or when it was going to intersect with the right opportunity. He was working as hard as had any of the men he interviewed, traveling to the Midwest, New England, and Pennsylvania on freelance assignments. He was writing now not only for *Success* but such other ten-cent magazines as *Cosmopolitan, Demorest's, McClure's, Metropolitan, Munsey's, Pearson's, Puritan, Truth,* and *Ainslee's,* whose editor, Richard Duffy, would become a lifelong friend. Between the fall of 1897 and the fall of 1900, when *Sister Carrie* appeared, he had in print almost one hundred articles; another eleven would appear before 1902. Many of these subscribed to the conventional values of hard work, with success as its inevitable reward. He was also writing and publishing his own poetry, which the McClure's Syndicate may have tentatively agreed to publish in book form. "I am hard at work now, for us," he told Jug in July 1898, "and hope the day is not far off when you can join me."[18] He had arranged to visit her in Missouri that spring while on his trip to Chicago to interview not only Armour, but Robert Lincoln of the Pullman Company and the department-store king Marshall Field. In the continuing vein of uncritical success stories, his article on the model town of Pullman, just outside Chicago, offered bland praise for this worker's paradise in which—he somehow failed to mention—employees (mostly immigrants) could own no property and could be evicted on ten days' notice for any conduct considered immoral. To its credit, however, the state of Pullman did seem the diametric opposite of the conditions Dreiser had seen at Homestead in 1894, and other "bleak mining and milling villages which now disgrace our national domain." He described Field as "the celebrated Western merchant, sprung from rugged Eastern soil, whose career is an example to be studied with profit by every farmer boy, by every office boy, by every clerk and artisan."[19]

Seeing Jug had renewed his excitement about her and helped numb his fears about marriage. For months before his visit, he had poured out his love, or lust, in letters to his "tempestuous little creature." For her part, Jug was growing impatient after almost five years. "You make me feel criminal, truly," he told her, "when you mourn so in words." He was weary of his

"Bohemian existence . . . of restaurants and hotel dinners" and longed for "a cozy flat" for the two of them somewhere in New York. "I have not the slightest idea of how much it would cost. Flats run here from $15 to $200 a month, so you can see the range they cover," and there was the furniture, either to be purchased or rented. He wished there "were houses already furnished for lovers" and suggested teasingly that he should "keep house with some maiden here for a few months" to learn the domestic routine. He worried then, as he would most of his life, about money, but he was making it, or beginning to. Dreiser would earn by his own estimate up to $5,000 a year as a freelancer.[20]

From his Fifteenth Street room, he told her later that summer, his view had "the sweep of a number of open rear windows, . . . and in these rooms dwell a number of lovely maidens. They are unconscious of my existence and the summer heat seems to make them reckless." Alternately scared of marriage and awash in sexual fantasies about her, he told Jug that he hadn't witnessed "such a display of beauty" since his days at the World's Fair where they had met. "Man is ever an iniquitous beast—don't you think? I suppose I am criminal in thus employing my time admiring such loveliness at a distance." But he blamed his voyeurism in part on her and wished they were already together in the state of marriage and connubial bliss. Earlier he had sent her Dante Gabriel Rossetti's "The Stream's Secret," which speaks of being "Beneath her sheltering hair, / In the warm silence near her breast." "Read this Jug slowly," he closed, "and think how it will be with us." In September, with the marriage date still not settled, he encountered a woman who looked like Jug on the New York Central while returning from one of his magazine assignments. No doubt stirring up the memory of their having met on a train, he wrote, "She did look so modest and quiet looking, but she followed me with her eyes." Like the fictional Drouet whose initial approach to Carrie on a train is borrowed from the fiction of George Ade, Dreiser took advantage of the situation, he confessed to Jug in yet another tease, and helped the young woman arrange her seat, and "so began a talk which lasted from 12:30 midnight until almost 5 AM."[21]

One would hardly know from Dreiser's magazine topics that the Spanish-American War had begun with the mysterious explosion of the *Maine* in Havana Harbor on February 15, 1898, killing 260 Americans. Lost in love and the literature of magazines, Dreiser was almost oblivious of the war. His only articles remotely connected with the national obsession, fueled by the sensationalist news coverage by the dueling papers of Hearst and Pulitzer, are about ammunition factories for *Ainslee's* and *Cosmopolitan* and one called

"Carrier Pigeons in War Time" in *Demorest's*—all appearing in July.[22] Otherwise, his published writings dwelled on such serene subjects as the "Quiet Nooks" of the naturalist John Burroughs, the "Haunts of Nathaniel Hawthorne," and various painters, sculptors, and musicians.

He also continued to publish poetry, mainly in his friend Richard Duffy's magazine. In the August number of *Ainslee's*, whose cover illustration depicts a returning wounded soldier, is found Dreiser's poem entitled "Night Song." It has nothing to do with the war but, in the mode of Rossetti, reflects on a love gone dry. "Night Song" never made it into Dreiser's three collections of poetry—and for good reason. Lacking Rossetti's gift for internal rhythm, its flat lines resemble the hackneyed lyrics of some of Paul's songs, as in this second stanza:

> Over fields lighted white by the moon,
> Comes the wind with a tune.
> Through the trees gleam the stars, and so rare
> Each caress of the air.
> Ah, my love, once so true, can it be
> All forgotten of thee.

As in "On the Banks of the Wabash," where the lover longs to stroll once again with his "Mary dear," Dreiser's night singer roams in despair of his love, who unlike Mary is not yet dead.

> But to meet, for a day, once again!
> Thus alway, I complain.
> And of you all the night voices croon
> When the world seems aswoon.[23]

Whether Jug ever saw this publication and, if so, just what she thought of its theme of lost love is not known. Nor can it be said for certain whether Dreiser enjoyed brief encounters with other women during his extended courtship; there is no direct evidence, only what is suggested by the actions of Eugene Witla in *The "Genius"* and by something Dorothy Dudley claims Dreiser told her when she interviewed him for her biography. In "The Return," appearing in *Ainslee's* two months later, he continued the theme of unrequited love, this time returning to a river not unlike the Wabash, "where the long green grass / Waves as of old." Paraphrasing Dreiser, Dudley speaks of a fellow writer, "a beautiful creature with a voice and a career before her [who] surprised him with the gift of a summer of romance in [the] Virginia mountains." Unlike Jug, she was something of a believer in free love and was willing to break her engagement with another man. She was not, however, willing to give up her writing career, and that ended everything for Dreiser, who apparently told Dudley that no household could sustain more than one writer—or egotist.[24]

Whatever the case, Sallie O. White, as Jug's name appeared on the marriage certificate, finally got the marriage she had held out for on December 28, 1898, in a Methodist ceremony conducted by the Rev. J. W. Duffy in Washington, D.C. Those in attendance included her sister Rose and possibly their brother Richard White, a midshipman finishing at the Naval Academy in Annapolis. (The couple may have honeymooned in that city.) And Dreiser finally got Jug the way he had wanted her all along—though the next poem he published, five months later in *Ainslee's,* was called "Bondage." Nonetheless, though it may not mean much in Dreiser's case, there is little or no evidence of his straying from his vows during the early years of the marriage. Perhaps with Jug, at least in the beginning, he would better withstand "the ceaseless drag of all desire."[25]

Dreiser had four articles appear the month he married, three in January, and eight in February. He continued this remarkable output throughout 1899 and into 1900, even after he had actually begun *Sister Carrie.* About the same time he started writing the novel, he interviewed William Dean Howells for *Ainslee's* and published "Curious Shifts of the Poor" in *Demorest's.* Dreiser's most important literary interview and his most serious work as a freelancer may indeed form the nexus for *Sister Carrie.*

In the interview Dreiser finds Howells on the threshold of the kind of social sympathy that only a Bowery Journalist such as Dreiser (or Crane) could ever have truly crossed. The "Dean of American Letters" (an appellation apparently first given Howells in the *Ainslee's* interview) may seem a strange bedfellow for the future "Father of American Realism." But *realism* is a somewhat elastic term. With Dreiser we are not talking about the earnest novel of manners for which Howells is most celebrated today or even the realism of the Social Darwinists such as Crane and Norris; a more appropriate term is *naturalism,* in which (1) the "moral" element does not necessarily triumph over the forces of heredity and environment; and (2) Anglican-bred individuals are just as vulnerable as any immigrant class. In the literary realism of Howells's masterpiece, *The Rise of Silas Lapham* (1885), the protagonist rises spiritually or morally even as he falls materialistically. A year following that novel's publication, however, an event occurred that would give Howells pause in his confidence about the balance of the cosmos. After the Haymarket Square Riot in Chicago, eight Knights of Labor protesters were unfairly convicted of anarchy; five were sentenced to death, and the other three received long prison terms. Howells was among the few writers to join the protest, which did not save the condemned (one committed suicide and the other four were executed), though the other three were eventually pardoned. Two years later, in 1888, Howells moved from Boston to New York to take over "The Editor's Study" for *Harper's*. The move also marked his transition from dissecting the manners of Boston society to providing a broader social basis for his fiction.

This shift found its most noteworthy literary expression in *A Hazard of New Fortunes* (1890), where the plot involves labor unrest and class conflict in New York City. Howells had also discovered about the time of the Haymarket Square riot the writings of Tolstoy, including *What to Do?* (1886), a powerful political tract that assails the state of poverty the Russian novelist found in Moscow. Interestingly, Dreiser had read *What to Do?* in college. Given his deprived background, he would have come, in either 1889 or 1899, to slightly more revolutionary—or philosophical—conclusions than Howells does in *A Hazard of New Fortunes*. Yet if Howells would never go as far as Dreiser, his book embraces, in a panoramic canvas worthy of Tolstoy, social problems ignored in his earlier works. By the 1890s, then, Howells was prepared at least for the "sterner realism" of Crane, Garland, and Norris, if not the completely amoral and race-neutral notions about man in *Sister Carrie*. In fact, he allegedly told Dreiser one day following its publication, "You know, I don't like *Sister Carrie*."[26]

Another reason Howells's view of *Sister Carrie* may have been tainted was Dreiser's subordination in the *Ainslee's* article of the master's reputation and achievement to his noble character, especially in his recent efforts to help younger writers. Here Dreiser was possibly dreaming of eventually joining the ranks of Crane, Garland, Cahan, and others (he did not read Norris's *McTeague* until after writing *Sister Carrie*) as part of Howells's stable of approved writers. In fact, he had first "interviewed" Howells in a most positive manner for the April 1898 issue of *Success,* in a piece entitled "How He Climbed Fame's Ladder." It has been argued that the interview was based mostly on material Dreiser took from Howells's *My Literary Passions* (1895) and then fleshed out with a questionnaire that the older writer may have completed and returned to *Success*. Yet there exist notes on Howells's career in Dreiser's hand that appear to have been hastily indited as in an actual interview. Whatever the case, Howells had evidently liked the harmless observations of the earlier article and invited Dreiser over to his apartment overlooking Central Park for the *Ainslee's* piece. The result of the face-to-face interview, however, was a disaster in terms of any relationship he might have fancied with Howells. Dreiser began by observing that it could be truly said of the "Dean," whom he described as "a stout, thick-set, middle-aged man," that he "is greater than his literary volumes make him out to be. If this be considered little enough, then let us say he is even greater than his reputation." Worse yet: "Since it is contended that his reputation far outweighs his achievements, let this tribute be taken in full, for he is all that it implies—[merely] one of the noblemen of literature." And finally, "It does not matter whether or not Howells is the greatest novelist in the world, he is a great character." Clearly, Howells's most important contribution to American letters was that he "has helped thousands in more ways than one, and is a sweet and wholesome presence in the world of art."

It is no wonder that Howells, who had reviewed the other naturalists, never reviewed *Sister Carrie.* We can only imagine his annoyance, even outrage, at Dreiser's cheeky condescension. Dreiser must have somehow fancied that Howells considered himself "retired," over the hill except as a mentor to the new wave of writers in the 1890s. "Do you find," he asked, "that it is painful to feel life wearing on, slipping away, and change overtaking us all?"[27]

Dreiser, for his part, naively went away from the interview that day impressed by his own vision of Howells and perhaps even imagining a camaraderie that surely never existed. "Is it so hard," he ventured to ask Howells, as if he were already a protégé, "to rise in the literary world?" He found "dispiriting" the answer that it was about as difficult as any other field of endeavor, but Dreiser was otherwise deeply moved by the older man's newfound passion for the oppressed. In his *Ainslee's* article, he made a point of mentioning *A Traveler from Altruria* (1894), in which Howells "sets forth his dream of universal peace and goodwill." He sketches there, Dreiser added, "a state of utter degradation from which the brutalized poor rise to the purest altruism." He was also "charmed" by Howells's humanity in *My Literary Passions,* including his devotion to Tolstoy's passion for social justice.

There might also have been a little jealousy of Howells leavened into all this mixed praise. Dreiser had been truly poor, not simply the son of a father in southern Ohio who never provided his family quite enough to maintain its middle-class status. He had also lived in or near the Bowery and seen desperate human suffering first hand. Ironically, he faulted Howells for resigning himself philosophically to the human condition in which all must suffer in one way or another. (The criticism was blatantly hypocritical coming from a Spencerian philosopher who saw the good if not justice in the way nature eliminates the weak.) "His sympathies are right," Dreiser conceded, "but he is not primarily a deep reasoner. He would not, for instance, choose to follow up his speculations concerning life and attempt to offer some modest theory of improvement."[28]

In "Curious Shifts of the Poor," Dreiser may have thought he came closer to reality. Although it is not exactly clear when the sketch was completed, it appeared in the same issue of *Demorest's* that featured an article on the "Twelve Handsomest Married Women in the World." In a way, the juxtaposition of such diverse subjects in the same number was no more out of sync, Dreiser might have thought, than Howells writing about the same kind of suffering from his "editor's chair" overlooking Central Park. What at the very outset drives the four sketches that make up the article (subtitled "Strange Ways of Relieving Desperate Poverty") is Dreiser's contrast of men on the skids with the gaiety and good fortune of the city's theater district nearby. "Curious Shifts of the Poor" opens with the "Captain," the mysterious do-gooder who will reappear in the finale of *Sister Carrie*. This "peculiar individual takes his stand" near Broadway nightly to find beds for the homeless by first lining them up and then asking theater patrons and other passers-by for the twelve cents required to pay for each man's lodging. This "broken, ragged" queue of stragglers with the Captain at its head is offset by "firesigns announcing the night's amusements, [which] blaze on every hand." The theaters are filling up, and "cabs and carriages, their lamps gleaming like yellow eyes, patter by. Couples and parties of three and four are freely mingled in the common crowd which passes by in a thick stream, laughing and jesting. . . . All about, the night has a feeling of pleasure and exhilaration, the curious enthusiasm of a great city, bent upon finding joy in a thousand different ways."

The Captain is stoical in his sympathy for the homeless men who shiver from the winter cold while waiting for hours to be marched away to a flophouse on Tenth Street. With military bearing, he treats them brusquely and acts in general as though he is merely performing a duty vaguely mandated by Providence. Dreiser, too, though he personally sympathizes with the plight of the poor, philosophically adopts the same stance at the conclusion of the four sketches. Their plight, he says, "should not appeal to our pity, but should awaken us to what we are—for society is no better than its poorest type. They expose what is present, though better concealed, everywhere. . . . The livid-faced dyspeptic who rides from his club to his apartments and pauses on the way to hand his dollar to the Captain should awaken the same pity as the shivering applicant for a free bed whom his dollar aids—pity for the ignorance and error that cause the distress of the world."

The second sketch zooms in on a Catholic mission on Fifteenth Street whose wooden collection box affixed to its front door advertises the fact that it provides a free meal every day at noon to all in need. "Unless one were looking up this matter in particular," Dreiser writes of the relative invisibility of the poor in America's most expensive city, "he could stand at Sixth avenue and Fifteenth street for days, around noon, and never notice that, out of the vast crowd that surges along that busy thoroughfare, there turned out, every few seconds, some weather-beaten, heavy-footed specimen of humanity, gaunt in countenance, and dilapidated in the matter of clothes." The third sketch describes Bowery men slouching towards "a dirty four-story building" where they wait in the cold for a bed for the night. The last tells of Fleischman's restaurant at the corner of Broadway and Ninth around midnight, where every night for the last twenty-three years its owner has dispensed free loaves of bread to men who dumbly line up, pass by, and vanish again into the night.

The difference between Dreiser's and Howells's attitude about such human tragedy is subtle but also significant. While they both bow to the idea "that life is difficult and inexplicable" (to quote Dreiser on Howells in "The Real Howells"), the young Dreiser's god is Herbert Spencer, while Howells's guide at mid-life is Leo Tolstoy. Although Dreiser somewhat reluctantly accepts the Spencerian—if not Darwinian—formula, he does not altogether sanction it. This ambivalence underscores the later contradiction between his activist sympathy for the exploited poor in corporate America and his belief in the survival of the fittest. Howells, on the other hand, accepts the tragedy of the human condition as part of a providential design, even as he laments its toll in individual suffering. Although his social thinking shifted as a result of the Haymarket Square incident and his reading of *What to Do?*, he had begun his literary career at the feet of Emerson and Hawthorne, who—philosophically, at least—never believed in reform movements as any panacea for the human condition. Nevertheless, his transition from realism to—not naturalism—but a more realistic view of the world may even have helped point the way for the early naturalists and so directly or indirectly for Dreiser himself. Shortly after the appearance of "Curious Shifts of the Poor" and his interview with Howells, Dreiser began *Sister Carrie*.[29]

Before he immersed himself in the composition of the first Great American Novel of the twentieth century, however, Dreiser experimented with short stories. He may have already been thinking of himself as a writer of more than magazine articles when he allowed himself to be described in the first edition of *Who's Who* (1899) not only as a "journalist-author" who contributes "prose and verse to various periodicals" but as the author of a book called *Studies of Contemporary Celebrities*. (Possibly a proposed collection of his *Success* articles, no such book ever appeared.)[30] And, as he had told Jug, there was that volume of poems slated for the press, though that too, never materialized. He may have been encouraged to some extent in the poetic endeavor by Edmund Clarence Stedman; in 1899, Dreiser wrote a second fawning piece on the "banker-poet" for *Munsey's*. (Stedman was apparently never aware that much of it was plagiarized from a piece in the *Critic* thirteen years earlier.)[31]

It was at Arthur Henry's urging that Dreiser wrote five or six stories in the summer of 1899.[32] Henry, while back with his wife in Ohio, had invited Dreiser and Jug to join them at the "House of the Four Pillars," their summer home on the Maumee River. He hoped that having his soul mate working by his side would stimulate his own writing—indeed, they might even write something together. By then Dreiser was living with his bride at 6 West 102nd Street. Arthur, who had literally "camped" in their apartment for several months before going back home, also proffered the invitation as a way to repay the hospitality Jug and Ted (as the Henrys called him) had shown Arthur while he was in New York.[33]

The Greek Revival mansion had fourteen airy rooms—space and privacy enough not only for the two couples but for the Henrys' five-year-old daughter Dottie. It was the perfect writer's retreat, far enough from town to be as quiet as its residents wished. Maude Henry, who had collaborated with her husband on a collection of fairytales, probably wrote there, too. (In later life she became the prolific author of short verse for juvenile and educational magazines.) Jug, the new bride, doted on her "Teddykins" and did the cooking for the entire household. Arthur and Ted worked all day in the basement, either writing separately or arguing this issue or that, and emerging only in the evening for dinner to notice the ladies. The pipe-smoking Arthur was variously working on either short stories or his second novel, which became *The Princess of Arcady*, published in 1900 by the same firm that issued *Sister Carrie*. Dreiser probably did not begin his novel, at least in earnest, until returning to New York that fall. But he may have gotten the urge to begin it before leaving Maumee, for as he later related, Henry not only pestered him to write short stories but also began to "ding-dong about a novel." It was Henry, Dreiser told H. L. Mencken in 1916, "who persuaded me to write my first short story. This is literally true. He nagged until I did, saying he saw short stories in me."[34]

Although there is no way of knowing for sure which of the five or six stories he wrote first, most critics agree that it was most likely "The Shining Slave Makers," an allegory in which the protagonist wakes up as an ant and witnesses the same kind of competition to survive Dreiser had read about in Darwin. He said it was immediately taken by *Ainslee's* (who did in fact publish the story in 1901). "Nigger Jeff," also written on the Maumee, was placed in *Ainslee's* as well. This story, too, is in its way about the survival of the fittest. In fact, all the Maumee stories are. "Butcher Rogaum's Door" resembles Crane's *Maggie* in that an eighteen-year-old daughter of a German butcher (like one or another of Dreiser's adventuresome sisters) is almost lost to the streets of lower New York and a life of prostitution after being locked out of the house by her father for staying out too late. "When the Old Century Was New" combines an idyllic picture of New York society in the spring of 1801 with a prediction of the formidable crush of industrialism to come in the new century. Finally, "A Mayor and His People"—based on an idealistic former mayor of Bridgeport, Connecticut, whom Dreiser had met while on a magazine assignment in the spring of 1898—is about the struggle of the common citizen and taxpayer in the vise of corporate greed and governmental mismanagement.[35] The final story from this summer mentioned by Dreiser, "The World and the Bubble," whose title seems to put it in the same class as the others in terms of the theme of illusion and reality, has never been found. (There are two essays in manuscript, both written before the Maumee stories, at the University of Virginia Library entitled "The Bubble of Success" and "Lying about Success" that argue against the American idea that hard work and honesty will lead *everyone* to success.)

Dreiser's earliest stories have been generally slighted in studies of his work, described in one source as uneven in quality, ranging from almost "worthless" ("When the Old Century Was New") to powerful ("Nigger Jeff").[36] It is true that "When the Old Century Was New" is only a few steps away from the kind of magazine articles he was writing about American life at the turn of the coming century, but it joins the others in expressing the uneasy sense of impending doom or decline that will pervade not only *Sister Carrie* but all of Dreiser's novels. The Maumee stories mark Dreiser's shift from the sugar-coated depictions of the surface of American life for such magazines as *Success* to clear-eyed portrayals of its underside, where the collateral social damage of "success" is both suggested and interpreted artistically. Dreiser had been wanting to write more truthfully about life before he got to the Maumee River, had indeed tried, but the larger magazine world wasn't as receptive even as *Ev'ry Month* had been, with the author as his own managing editor. There, as noted, he had at least been able to explore around the edges of American life. (When years later he published a heavily revised version of "A Mayor and His People," he has the narrator say at its close that he had met the mayor, a former shoemaker by trade—"in other words a factory shoehand" by the 1890s—while making "a very careful study of his career for a current magazine, which, curiously, was never published.")[37]

In one sense, *Sister Carrie* was merely the latest expression of Dreiser's need to explore this underside of American life, where hard work didn't always pay off and virtue wasn't necessarily its own reward. Carrie is an extension of Theresa of "Butcher Rogaum's Door," who also comes close to perishing in an urban jungle—as well as a reflection of the fact that Dreiser's sister Theresa did perish, at a railroad crossing in Chicago in 1897.[38] Carrie also lives in the New York foreseen a century hence from the romantic depiction in "When the Old Century Was New." Broadway will be transformed from "a lane through the woods and fields" into a crowded and faceless thoroughfare dotted with homeless men waiting in the cold for a bed for the night. Without stretching the comparison, we might also observe that life in *Sister Carrie* is about the same rat race, or ant race, as in "The Shining Slave Makers." The only extant story from that summer without direct echoes in *Sister Carrie* is "Nigger Jeff"—and even there the "curious shifts" of life are rather haunting.

———

Dreiser recalled that he wrote "The Shining Slave Makers" one afternoon in the basement of Four Pillars with Henry nearly standing over him. "After every paragraph," he wrote Mencken, "I blushed for my folly—it seemed so asinine." But Henry kept at him, and after it was finally done, he had the manuscript typed and began to submit it, at first without success. On October 9, 1899, Henry M. Alden of *Harper's* told Dreiser that "a large accumulation of short stories prevents me from using 'Of the Shining Slave Makers,'" (possibly an indication of its original title).[39] Dreiser next sent the story to the *Century,* where it was rejected in early January, this time apparently on the technical grounds that the allegory was scientifically unsound. In an angry letter to the *Century's* editor, Robert Underwood Johnson, on January 9, 1900, Dreiser ridiculed the decision, saying it was absurd to worry about the sex of ant workers while accepting the possibility of a human transformed into an ant. As to scientific fact, the veteran of magazine articles from "Electricity in the Household" to "Japanese Home Life" assured Johnson the story was correct according to Sir John Lubbock's authoritative study of *Ants, Bees and Wasps.* He also accused the magazine of employing one of its clerks instead of a literary person to read his manuscript. Johnson responded on January 13 that his story had indeed been read by one of the editors, and was rejected mainly because of the editorial board's "considerable dislike for allegory."[40] Eventually "The Shining Slave Makers" appeared in the June 1901 issue of *Ainslee's* and earned its author $75.

In the story Robert McEwen falls asleep after killing an ant one hot August day and wakes up as one of the tribe of the Shining Slave Makers who are at war with the Red Slave Makers. What follows is a personal battle for survival with echoes of *The Red Badge of Courage.* Dreiser must have seen the similarity when he revised his story for *Free and Other Stories* (1918), for he has McEwen falling into an "insane lust of combat" like that which ultimately absorbs Crane's protagonist.[41] In fact, Dreiser revised this story more than he did any of the other Maumee stories. In its revision, there is an emphasis on the need for social interdependence in a world best depicted with battle imagery—a need to share food and assist comrades. The original, however, is blindly Darwinistic. When the protagonist wakes from his dream or vision of having participated in the continual warfare of the "thousands and thousands [of ants] engaged in terrific battle," his sense of sorrow is nothing more than "a vague, sad something out of far-off things." The ants were no more important to McEwen than the fly Dreiser had written about in Pittsburgh or the prostitute with needle marks he had visited there. Life was a struggle that bordered on suicide. The fly had plunged itself into the housewife's cup of steaming coffee. The girl had sealed her own fate in the struggle for economic survival.

In discussing "When the Old Century Was New," critics usually fail to point out that it appeared in its original publication in *Pearson's* for January 1901 with the subtitle "A Love Story." Young William Walton in the first spring of the "Old Century" is in love not only with the woman who becomes his fiancée but with the coming century, which promises nothing but upward change. The story has been called a parody of the popular historical romances that upper-class magazines such as *Century* and *Harper's* published (while rejecting Dreiser's allegory about ants). But if so, it is also one with Hawthorne's "My Kinsman, Major Molineux" in that the protagonist is a naïf in the New World, dazzled by his prospects, as he strolls by the City Reservoir and through the idyllic Bowery. By the end of the nineteenth century these will become, respectively, the Tombs prison, where executions were held, and the skid row in which Hurstwood dies.[42] But the story argues that it is love, love of life and anticipation of its comforts and pleasures, that saves us, at least temporarily from the impending doom of the future. In *Sister Carrie,* Carrie dreams such dreams as she will never realize, and until the very end the down-and-out Hurstwood never quite gives up his dreams of becoming a manager again.

"Butcher Rogaum's Door" appeared on December 12, 1901, in the radical William Marion Reedy's *Mirror,* a Chicago magazine that would publish many writers of the coming Chicago Renaissance, including Dreiser's future friend Edgar Lee Masters. This story has been dismissed as "a markedly plain, melodramatic tale of a transparently didactic nature," but again this criticism fails to credit the same mood of impending disaster in life we find elsewhere in the fiction leading up to *Sister Carrie.*[43] It is also, in its German dialect, imposing father, and restless daughter, an anticipation of *Jennie Gerhardt*—and a story drawn right out of Dreiser's family past, with its tensions between John Paul Dreiser and his hedonistic daughters. Dreiser also drew upon his police reporter's experience (as he would a quarter century later in *An American Tragedy*) to give the point of view of the Irish police officers who investigate Theresa's disappearance and disapprove of the way the German immigrant is raising his daughter. When a wayward girl of Theresa's age is found dead at Rogaum's door after having swallowed acid, the old man learns that she too had been locked out of her house once upon a time, and he begins to worry whether he had gone too far in trying to teach his daughter "a lesson." On the one hand, Rogaum is insensitive to his daughter's adolescent restlessness, but on the other he is right to want to keep her from the company of Connie Almerting, a young man of dubious reputation. In the end Theresa is found safe and returned to her parents. Almerting is sufficiently frightened by the officers to stay away from her. Yet he has the last words in the story (which he doesn't quite have in its revision for *Free*), and they leave the reader with the same unease about the future. "Let him have his old daughter," Almerting shouts back at the police as they release him and adds significantly, "They had better not lock her out, though—that's all I say."[44] The abiding sense of the story is that it will probably happen again and the next time she won't be so lucky.

The animal nature of man is so strong, Dreiser is saying, that it often cannot be denied, even when the risks are certain. This understanding is most dramatically demonstrated in Dreiser's finest short story of the pre–*Sister Carrie* period, "Nigger Jeff." It is unfortunate that Dreiser chose to use the word "nigger" in his title, for, in large part because of that, the story is today no longer anthologized in college surveys of American literature. Certainly Dreiser was sympathetic throughout his life to the plight of American blacks (participating in protests of the conviction of the Scottsboro Boys in Alabama for the same crime for which Jeff Ingalls hangs in his story and leaving in his will a significant amount to fund a black orphanage), but in the late nineteenth century (and well into the twentieth) the "N-word" could be found in nursery rhymes and popular songs.[45] *The Songs of Paul Dresser* includes "I'se Your Nigger If You Wants Me, Liza Jane" and "You'se Just a Little Nigger, Still You'se All Mine All Mine." (The latter is about a parent's love and the advice that being just a black person is a burden which must be accepted for the best—that there is no use in "fussin'" because "We ain't got all de comforts like the white folks, rich an' fine.") It is worth remembering that if the songs indulge in the usual condescension and racism of their day, they also embrace blacks as humans with the same capacity for love and the same ambitions and lusts for life as whites.

> Some day among de cullud folks you'll have a great big name,
> Of course some of de white folks think dat somehow you won't do,
> But trust in de Lordy an' he'll sho' take care o' you.

Such might have been the hope of the lynching victim's mother in "Nigger Jeff," whom Eugene Davies, the newspaper reporter in the story, finds curled up in agony after the hanging. "I'll get that in," Dreiser has him exclaim in the final words of the story. "I'll get it all in."

And this is precisely Dreiser's great accomplishment in "Nigger Jeff," to get it all in. The story, whose title in manuscript is "A Victim of Justice," is based primarily on an article about a lynching just north of St. Louis that Dreiser published in the *Republic* for January 18, 1894, entitled "Ten-Foot Drop." As noted earlier, however, the short story also draws generally on the lynching era from which it comes. In the 1890s, such vigilante hangings of blacks happened frequently in America, but mostly in the South. One clue to identify the hanging outside St. Louis as the main source for the story published in *Ainslee's* for November 1901 is the fictional city editor's comment on dispatching Davies to the scene that "A lynching up there would be a big thing."[46] Actually, there are two *Republic* reports of the lynching that critics see as the basis for the story: the one for the 18th and one preceding it on January 17, entitled "This Calls for the Hemp." Both reported the story of the arrest of a black ex-convict named John Buckner for the sexual assault of two women, one black, one white, in Valley Park, Missouri, about fifteen miles from St. Louis.

The January 17 report, "This Calls for the Hemp," follows the incident up to Buckner's arrest and incarceration by the local sheriff, who initially stands up to the lynching mob. Its racist epithets ("worthless negro," "black fiend," "demon") may disqualify Dreiser as the author, though as a reporter in the 1890s he was no doubt encouraged to engage in such rhetoric. Dreiser is also rougher on the accused in "A Victim of Justice," using the archaic "varlet," meaning "rascal" or "knave," to characterize the African-American's life before the attempted rape.[47] On the other hand, "Nigger Jeff," as published in *Ainslee's* and later in *Free and Other Stories*, treats the Buckner character more sympathetically than does the first newspaper report, and the follow-up account of January 18 also seems less judgmental. "Ten-Foot Drop" dramatically reports how the prisoner was taken from the sheriff and hanged from a bridge and begins with a one-sentence paragraph that is more dramatic than reportorial: "They lynched him."

While it is possible that someone else wrote the first report, similarities between the second article and "Nigger Jeff" strongly support Dreiser's authorship. Both accounts involve the rape of a nineteen-year-old white woman. In each, the accused is found cowering in the sheriff's "cellar dungeon." "Don't kill me, boss," we read in the newspaper account. "Oh, my Lawd, boss, don't kill me," Dreiser's Jeff Ingalls pleads. Both describe the distorted look on the doomed man's face, his contorted figure as he is dragged from his hiding place, tied into a sack, and thrown in the back of a wagon for transport to his doom.

Republic: "His face was distorted with all the fear of a hunted beast. The eyes rolled wildly and great beads of sweat gathered on his forehead. Instead of pleading the miserable fellow began wailing more like an animal than a human being."

"Nigger Jeff": "The black face was distorted beyond all human semblance. . . . [He] seemed out of his senses. He was breathing heavily and groaning. His eyes were fixed and staring, his face and hands bleeding as if they had been scratched or trampled on. He was bundled up like limp wheat."[48]

Both express sympathy for the condemned man, even though he is black and guilty. In the article, it is his criminal record and suspicious actions reported by witnesses that convict him, but Dreiser's lynching victim says, "Before God, boss, I didn't mean to. . . . I won't do it no mo'." In other words, Jeff is Dreiser's first victim of the cosmic forces that will doom so many of his protagonists, from George Hurstwood to Clyde Griffiths. He is guilty of human weakness that involves sex, which symbolizes the irresistible desire for beauty. But whereas the *Republic* article of January 18 expresses no revulsion at the punishment, except to match "Nigger Jeff" in its description of the agony of the accused, the fictional Davies turns away from the sight of the bound and bleeding man, exclaiming "Oh, my God," as he bites his fingers unconsciously. But the story's deepest sympathy, like that of Paul's songs, is reserved for the victim's mother. (Interestingly, this scene is absent from "A Victim of Justice," whose plot is framed by a meditation on the forgotten dead of a potter's field.) Once the hanging has taken place and the body is returned to his mother's shanty outside of town, Eugene goes there and finds "a little negro girl," Jeff's sister. When asked why her brother had returned home, thus making his capture possible, the reply is that "he wanted tuh see motha." And it is when he finally comes upon the "old black mammy, doubled up and weeping," that he decides to "get it all in."

These are the last words of the revision for *Free*, too, but Dreiser adds something before the close in the later version which may be revealing. We must remember that "Nigger Jeff," as one of the Maumee stories, was inspired or compelled by Arthur Henry, the author of *Nicholas Blood, Candidate*, that tale, as Maude Wood Henry put it, about the "negro menace to the white people."[49] Dreiser and Henry, as we shall see, fell out hard between 1899 and 1918, when "Nigger Jeff" reappeared in *Free*. By then Dreiser probably regretted whatever commonplace racist ideas they may have shared at the turn of the century. It wasn't that his original story had been racist—far from it, but in the *Ainslee's* version he had merely observed the plight of blacks, expressed its "feeling and pathos" instead of condemning lynchings outright. In the revision for *Free* he has to articulate—perhaps apologize for—the "cruel instinct of the budding artist," and state that it "was not so much the business of the writer to indict as to interpret." Of course, the story as a whole does condemn by indirection, the way art should, but somehow Dreiser felt the need to apologize here for being an artist instead of a political activist. Certainly by the end of World War I, when *Free* with its revision of "Nigger Jeff" appeared, he was far more the activist than he had been in 1899.

Indeed, the earliest fictional seeds of his future activism can be found in "A Mayor and His People," a story that is more important for its evidence of Dreiser's political unhappiness with the way the capitalistic world worked (even as, ironically, he wrote for *Success*) than as a prototype of the new realism he would produce in *Sister Carrie*.

But another article that came out of Dreiser's visit to New England in the spring of 1898 may also offer an important insight about the immediate foreground of *Sister Carrie*. He wrote Jug from the Colonial Hotel in Concord, Massachusetts, that he had visited Boston the day before and was slated to visit Cambridge, Salem, and Lexington before his return to New York. During his trip, Dreiser picked up many visual impressions of the American literary past as represented by the homes of the Transcendentalists and Schoolroom Poets. Despite its title (reminiscent of his piece on Bayard Taylor), however, "Haunts of Nathaniel Hawthorne" clearly focuses on the man, the writer, and the crisis that led to his beginning to write *The Scarlet Letter.*[50] Dreiser was deeply impressed by his visit to the custom house in Salem, where, he noted, Hawthorne had wasted his talent before his involuntary "removal from the surveyorship through trickery and betrayal." It is clear from the article that Dreiser, who was already possibly beginning to think he was wasting *his* literary talent in magazine articles, had done his homework on Hawthorne. He alludes to most of the novels and the major short stories, and the capsule biography in which his discussion is couched suggests he had read a book-length biography, probably Moncure Conway's popular life of 1890.

Although Dreiser's article is on the surface merely an efficient and well-written summary of known facts about one of America's most famous writers, one has to wonder whether his focus on Hawthorne in the custom house immediately before he wrote *The Scarlet Letter* didn't have an influence on the writing of *Sister Carrie*. Dreiser notes that the Salem "magician," as he called him, wrote his "masterpiece" following his "betrayal." He too felt he had been "betrayed" at *Ev'ry Month,* in its way a literary sinecure like the one Hawthorne had enjoyed in the custom house. Even without reading the famous Preface in which Hawthorne complained about his treatment, Dreiser may have understood *The Scarlet Letter* as Hawthorne's protest against the inequities of society in which appearances are more important than reality. The plot of the novel is daring and even rebellious in its use of extramarital sex. Also, like *Sister Carrie,* it involves the intertwined and yet separate dramas of a woman and a man in violation of strictures based on religious ideology. Throughout most of his story, Hawthorne approves if not applauds his heroine in her defiance of the puritanical social codes, even allowing Hester Prynne to tell the neurasthenic and guilt-ridden Arthur Dimmesdale, "What we did had a consecration of its own."

In preparation for his article, Dreiser even visited the house on Mall Street in Salem where Hawthorne wrote his "masterpiece," noting just where his study had been and where he kept the manuscript of his novel. He ventured in his piece to say that "Hawthorne evidently had this story in mind sometime before he began to write it." Later Dreiser would tell Mencken that in beginning *Sister Carrie* he wrote down his title "at random" and immediately began, but he too seems to have had his story in mind, or at least the outline of one that drew clearly on his family history.[51] Could Dreiser have been thinking of himself as he wrote about Hawthorne—about his possibilities as a writer of something more enduring than a magazine article? Perhaps. Arthur Henry, we will remember, saw short stories in him. Why not a novel?

Sister Carrie

Sister Carrie *is a work of genius and Doubleday*
belongs to that species of long-eared animals which are not hares.

GEORGE HORTON TO ARTHUR HENRY, FEBRUARY 9, 1901

FRESH FROM A SUMMER ON THE BANKS OF THE MAUMEE, Dreiser took
out a piece of yellow paper and changed the course of American letters. As
a result, he is called the "Father of American Realism," but that academic
saw ignores, of course, the pioneering work of Walt Whitman, whose fifth
edition of his indefatigable book was privately published in the year of
Dreiser's birth. The next edition of *Leaves of Grass,* and essentially the last,
came under fire by Anthony Comstock and his New England Society for
the Suppression of Vice, which even attempted to have Whitman's book
banned from the U.S. mail. Dreiser, as we shall see, caught the wrath of
the second generation of that infamous censorship movement with the publication of *The "Genius,"* but *Sister Carrie* was the first heir to Whitman's
fight to tell the truth in literature. Indeed, Dreiser's title may actually come
from Whitman's era in the form of a Civil War song of the same name, in
which "Sister Carrie" (South Carolina) is chastised for leaving home (or the
Union).[1] Whitman is the true precursor of American literature in the twentieth century, but he wrote poetry instead of prose—many denied it even
the claim to poetry—which kept it out of general circulation among popular readers during his lifetime. But *Sister Carrie* was a novel, a genre more
accessible to the average reader, especially women, who made up the great
majority of American readers at the end of the nineteenth century. One of
them was allegedly Mrs. Frank Doubleday.

Dreiser probably began *Sister Carrie* in late September of 1899, shortly after returning to New York City. Henry returned, too, again leaving Maude and Dottie behind, to resume for the next month or so his residence with the Dreisers, and he either continued or began to write *A Princess of Arcady*. While Henry imagined a conventional romance in which the heroine is sent to a convent school to preserve her innocence until the proper time for marriage, Dreiser began his own fable about an American princess, "two generations removed from the emigrant," who rules only in her dreams and loses her innocence at almost the first opportunity. Henry wrote an idyll about a "nun" whose youthful sexuality is never violated, while Dreiser wrote a novel about a sister who commits adultery. It is generally thought that Dreiser was thinking exclusively of his sister Emma and not even remotely—or ironically—about a nun when he gave his Carrie the title of "Sister" at the top of his page, but Henry's use of nuns and a convent in his book may have had an associative influence. Dreiser's romantic chapter titles, which were added between the first draft and the revision published by Doubleday, suggest the moral contrast and underscore the departure of this gritty tale of two cities from the Victorian fiction of its day.

It is instructive to take a closer look at *A Princess of Arcady*. The story concerns two children, Hilda and Pierre, whom we first meet on Pilliod's Island, a paradise of vineyards and richly colored flowers on the Maumee River. They meet Minot Alexander, who visits the island with its owner (the boy's grandfather, Jean Pilliod), and who feels a strange attachment to the girl in spite of the fact that he is old enough to be her grandfather. The feeling is mutual, and the girl escorts Alexander back to her humble cottage, where her sick mother is slowly dying and her fisherman father drinks too much. The ambiguity of Alexander's feeling for the girl is vaguely associated with a love affair he had had long ago with a woman now lost to the convent, a woman named Betty, whom he still remembers as passionate and beautiful. Alexander returns to the village of Maumee, here elevated to the status of city, where he befriends Christopher Mott and his daughter Primrose, an eccentric and homely woman of thirty, who occupy gardens and greenhouses in the middle of town, one of the last holdouts against urban sprawl. Mott is an impractical man who refuses to give up his precious plants, which he considers more noble than humans. When the bank threatens to foreclose, Alexander quietly pays off the mortgage and tears up the note. In the meantime, Hilda's mother dies, and the child is put into an orphanage. By the time Alexander learns of it, Hilda has escaped and returned to the island. He adopts her on the condition that she will attend a convent school in order to grow into the ideal woman whose charm inspires not merely sexual passion but "achievements which have made epochs and kingdoms famous when the patronage of the throne alone would have failed."[2]

He writes to his old flame, now Mother Superior Pelagia at the Convent of Our Lady of Peace, to get permission to send Hilda to the convent, which is in New York City, across from the Palisades. Before Hilda leaves, however, she visits the island one last time. There she finds young Pierre carrying stones from the water's edge and fantasizing that he is building a palace for the two of them. Hilda goes away to the convent school, returning every summer to the Motts' cottage, which she now considers her permanent home. Interestingly, on her first train ride to the school, she befriends a fellow enrollee named Edna, whose beautiful mother attracts the attention of a "drummer, who wishing to look at her now and then, took a place on a vacant seat behind where she would not notice." Dreiser's *Sister Carrie,* of course, begins on a train with the same kind of "masher" or "drummer," the traveling salesman Charles Drouet, who befriends Carrie. Alexander also accompanies Hilda to the school upon her enrollment and sees for the first time in forty years his Betty, now a "black-robed figure" and a "little old lady."

Many years later, following Hilda's graduation from the convent school, she learns what has happened to Pierre. Apparently, after losing her he had become a disgruntled and disappointed young man who got into minor scrapes with the law. Hilda returns home to Maumee, where Pierre, now twenty, reformed, and the owner of Pilliod's Island following his grandfather's death, secretly watches over her at the Mott gardens—which thanks to Alexander's financial support have become a sanctuary not unlike the beautiful garden in Hawthorne's "Rappaccini's Daughter." Hilda is not cursed by paternal love in this romance, however, and so she and Pierre are soon reunited and marry to live happily ever after. The novel closes with Mott's saying to Alexander that Hilda had "come to fine flower" under his influence. When Alexander denies any direct influence, Mott agrees but says that he had "done all the best gardeners could do. You provided the good soil and shelter from the storm."[3]

While Henry was writing his novel about true love and eternal romance, he carried on an extramarital affair with Anna T. Mallon, leaving Maude to worry about the upbringing of their daughter and the mortgage on the House of the Four Pillars. Anna, who was several years older than Henry, ran a typing service at 308 Broadway. Dreiser had patronized it for his magazine articles, and Henry apparently went down to the typing pool one day on an errand for either Dreiser or himself and promptly fell in love. His dedication of his book to Anna, whom he would eventually marry, suggests that she influenced the plot of *A Princess of Arcady:* to Anna "on whose attitude toward her own convent life was founded the convent of 'Our Lady of Peace.'" Since the convent scenes cover the second half of the book, this may mean that he was halfway through his novel when he moved in with Anna that fall. Meanwhile, Dreiser was spinning his own romance in the same urban jungle that Hilda is protected against. Indeed, as we learn on his very first page, the city is the seducer as much as any drummer on a train. "The gleam of a thousand lights," he wrote, "is often as effective as the persuasive light in a wooing and fascinating eye."[4]

By the time Henry moved in with Anna, Dreiser had written the first ten chapters of *Sister Carrie.* He wrote "steadily," as he told Mencken, until the middle of October, then quit in disgust, thinking his work was "rotten." He laid the manuscript aside until December, when Henry came back to prod him again. He wrote on until the end of January before quitting once more, just before the climactic scene of the book, where the story will cease to be mainly Carrie's and become primarily Hurstwood's. "Then in February," he told Dorothy Dudley in 1930, "Arthur Henry, off flirting with some girl, came back and read it. He thought there was nothing wrong with it, told me I must go on." Possibly, Dreiser was blocked by his unpleasant memories of the *World* and that fateful day in City Hall Park when the idea of Hurstwood was first born. But if so, he recovered from the blues those memories gave him, "managed to get the thread" of his story back, and "finished it up."[5]

The plot of *Sister Carrie* involves essentially three characters who, true to Dreiser's sense of determinism, are pawns of heredity and environment. Like Henry's tale, it begins hopefully, if not romantically, with a young woman seeking her destiny, but unlike Hilda's fate, which involves nuns, priests, and a garden, Sister Carrie's destiny threatens to become a train ride to hell as she becomes involved with two male predators. The fates of all three intersect first in Chicago and then in New York to send Carrie to stardom on Broadway, Hurstwood to the soup kitchens and flophouses of the Bowery, and Drouet on his merry way, neither hurt nor helped by his interaction with the other two. Knowing nothing of Henry's chivalric code but only self-interest, like any lower creature, they are driven by the gods of money and sex to their fates. Carrie Meeber ("amoeba") moves from the country to the city, exchanging her virginity for material comfort. Her successive lovers, Charles Drouet and George Hurstwood, see her, reciprocally, as a symbol of the pleasure money and power can purchase. Carrie abandons the unmarried Drouet for the married Hurstwood, who in turn leaves his family and his position as manager of a posh Chicago saloon, steals money from his employers, and flees with Carrie to New York. There, as he eventually fails in his new investment, Carrie abandons him as well, and he soon finds himself homeless, sick, and dazed by fate in the winter of 1896.

It is difficult to see how this plot can be the Siamese twin of *A Princess of Arcady.* Yet these two books, both published by Doubleday in 1900, one an Arcadian romance, the other a grim tale of success and failure, were born together on the Maumee. Indeed, Henry helped cut and revise *Sister Carrie,* and Dreiser later claimed to have finished *A Princess of Arcady.* "At that time," he told Mencken, "Henry's interest in *Sister Carrie* having been so great his own book was neglected and he could not finish the last chapter." This may be an exaggeration or even an outright lie, for by 1916 when Dreiser made the claim, he and his friend had been estranged for many years. Furthermore, the style throughout the thirteen chapters of *A Princess of Arcady* appears to be uniformly Henry's. What the boast does suggest, aside from an opportunity to undercut the work of a former friend, is that Dreiser was as familiar with Henry's plot as Henry was with *Sister Carrie.* In fact, as he told Mencken, "Since he had told it to me so often and I knew exactly what he desired to say, I wrote it."[6]

The Princess of Arcady is also a nature book in the tradition of John Burroughs, "one of the living men," Henry once wrote, "I admire most at a distance." (Ironically, Dreiser once interviewed Burroughs for an article in *Success,* but Henry never met him.) Henry would develop his abilities as a nature writer much more directly in his next two works, *An Island Cabin* (1902) and *The House in the Woods* (1904). They are Thoreauvian recollections of his escapes from the daily grind of the city—first on an island off the coast of Connecticut, which Anna had either purchased or rented, and then in the Catskills, where the couple built a cabin. These books reflect the nineteenth-century idea that even pristine nature cannot help us if we cannot help ourselves. "Let those who think they are unhappy, because of an unfriendly world, retire to a wilderness," he writes in *An Island Cabin*, "and they will discover the source of all their sorrows is in themselves." As nature writers of such self-help books went, he was probably at least as good as most of his competitors. The *Brooklyn Eagle* called his books "delightful nature literature," and *Bookman* stated that "As a result of life so close to nature Mr. Henry brought back a more intangible yet indestructible possession in the form of fresh ideals and hopes."[7] He was a dreamer, just like Dreiser. And like him, he pursued beauty (usually in the feminine form) most of his life. In fact, there is something of Henry in Carrie's daydreamy nature. Dreiser even dedicated *Sister Carrie* to Henry, "whose steadfast ideals and serene devotion to truth and beauty have served to lighten the method and strengthen the purpose of this volume." He withdrew the dedication in later printings, however, and never again formally dedicated a book to anyone, except Grant Richards ("Barfleur") in *A Traveler at Forty* (1913) and his mother in *A Hoosier Holiday* (1916).

Henry, on the other hand, dedicated *An Island Cabin* to his by then ex-wife Maude. And while their separation was brutally sprung on Maude (in the presence of Anna), they remained friends for the rest of their lives. Henry was that lovable, and he attracted Dreiser as much as anybody else who was charmed by the man's cherubic looks and affable way. One gets the sense of his ebullience from reading his books, especially the ones following *A Princess*, where he drops all pretense of the storyteller and aspires to become the Emersonian essayist and poet. Henry had already worked out his idea of the self-reliant life in two essays, "The Doctrine of Happiness" and "The Philosophy of Hope," both utterly derivative of the transcendentalist doctrine. Dreiser's theme in *Sister Carrie* also argues that no island sanctuary exists in life, but in Carrie and Hurstwood's world the romance of self-reliance gives way almost completely to the naturalistic picture of robotic characters true to their basic needs and nothing more. When young Hilda of *A Princess* is asked whether she would like to live in the city, she answers yes, but only out of love and self-respect: "if ever the prince should come and marry me." When Carrie is asked to remain in the city by Drouet, it takes only twenty dollars—"two soft, green, ten-dollar bills" to persuade her.[8]

Dreiser's Chicago and New York experiences in the 1890s meshed to produce this masterpiece of reportorial realism, poetry, family history, and the drama of the city. He knew well the types he wrote about. He had seen many examples of Drouet on his train trips while on magazine assignments. Carrie, of course, springs in part from the character of Emma and from attributes of his other sisters. And Hurstwood, the first unforgettable tragic figure of American literature in the twentieth century and the prototype for such other unforgettable failures as F. Scott Fitzgerald's Jay Gatsby and Arthur Miller's Willy Loman, was based on Hopkins. He was also based—though Dreiser probably wouldn't have admitted it at the time—on his general sense of his father's failure in life. John Paul Dreiser barely lived long enough to be aware of the novel. He died on Christmas Day 1900, a little over six weeks after the book's publication on November 8. He was by then living in Rochester, New York, with Mame and Austin Brennan. (To save money, Dreiser wrote a personal dedication in one of his ten free author copies of *Sister Carrie* to all three of them, with the proviso that "if any of you fail to read and praise, the book reverts to me." The book did come back to him, either after Mame divided up their father's estate or following her own death in 1944, and is now part of the Dreiser collection at the University of Pennsylvania.)[9]

There is no father figure in *Sister Carrie.* Only Carrie's mother is vaguely mentioned in the beginning of the book. Certainly the married Hurstwood is no father figure. Carrie's brother-in-law Hanson, who cleans out refrigerator cars in Chicago, is a doting father but also one of the first to try to cheat her in the big city. There is no God the Father in this naturalistic tale either, only children of desire. This is not any lofty desire for the beautiful, but a basic, primitive desire for clothing, shelter, and sex, elevated to the fantastic level suggested in the magazines of the day, including *Ev'ry Month* with its exotic women. This is first illustrated in Carrie's life with the Hansons and her visions of something so much better. While Carrie looks for a job the first day, she enters one of the new department stores. Dreiser was no doubt thinking of Marshall Field's at the corner of State and Twentieth streets in Chicago, once burnt-out shells of horse-car barns in which Field set up his business after the fire of 1871 and accidentally invented the department store.[10]

As Carrie, with hardly a cent in her purse, passes down the aisles of the store displaying its latest items, she cannot help but feel the claim of every object upon her personally. "There was nothing there which she could not have used—nothing which she did not long to own. The dainty slippers and stockings, the delicately frilled skirts and petticoats, the laces, ribbons, hair-combs, purses, all touched her with individual desire." In spite of his prosperous appearance, Drouet too is intoxicated by such symbols of the good life. He "was as deluded by fine clothes as any silly-headed girl."[11] That and the company of successful men. It is associations above all that count to this salesman, or any salesman for that matter, on the lookout to succeed in the selling of his wares. He dines in the "right" restaurants and takes his nightcap at the "resort" of Fitzgerald and Moy's saloon (originally Dreiser used the real name of Hannah and Hogg's of Chicago, before the revision for Doubleday).

Here we meet George W. Hurstwood, the manager of the saloon and a social notch or two above the drummer Drouet. Everyone in this book is looking to ascend—as in all of Dreiser's novels. Carrie is satisfied with Drouet until the more burnished Hurstwood appears, just as in *An American Tragedy*, Clyde is satisfied with one girl until another more attractive one (both physically and financially) comes along. Hurstwood himself is by now about as high on the social ladder as he will ever get and serves as a sort of social referee who ranks his saloon patrons according to three essential groups in order to hold onto his position. He is a professional "Hail fellow, well met" who knows most of his customers by name. Yet he also knows his place.

> He had a finely graduated scale of informality and friendship, which improved from the "How do you do?" addressed to the fifteen-dollar-a-week clerks and office attachés . . . to the "Why, old man, how are you?" which he addressed to those noted or rich individuals who knew him and were inclined to be friendly. There was a class, however, too rich, too famous, or too successful, with whom he could not attempt any familiarity of address, and with these he was professionally tactful, assuming a grave and dignified attitude, paying them the deference which would win their good feeling.[12]

The saloon manager keeps a neat life consisting of horse, house, wife, and two children—until he meets Carrie.

Hurstwood has risen by perseverance "through long years of service, from the position of barkeeper in a commonplace saloon," but in the manner of Paul Dresser, who often, in the beginning of his career at least, accepted flat fees instead of royalties for his songs, Hurstwood may occupy a fairly imposing managerial position, "but lacked financial control." In other words, he could fall into poverty almost immediately, as Paul would go broke by 1903. This is a world of hangers-on and the sometimes lucky. Dreiser knew about both from personal experience and the American successes he had interviewed during the last two years. Emma's Hopkins had been a cashier in the saloon of Chapin and Gore in Chicago before he fled with her—and his employer's cash. Marshall Field had begun, as he told Dreiser during his interview, as a clerk in a dry goods house on South Water Street, but his luck had been different.

After Carrie has lost her job through illness and is living with Drouet at a three-room flat on Ogden Place, she meets Hurstwood, whom she sees immediately as "more clever than Drouet in a hundred ways."[13] Drouet now seems to her to have no "poetry in him," and in fact Drouet has been losing interest in Carrie until Hurstwood enters the picture. But both Drouet and Hurstwood merely hope to keep Carrie as a paramour—until both men capitulate to a deeper infatuation when they see her in an Elks' production of Daly's *Under the Gaslight* (a play Dreiser had seen during his days as a drama critic in St. Louis). Then, found out by his wife, who threatens to have his wages garnisheed with his employers' approval, Hurstwood is cornered by circumstance. Determined to have Carrie now at any cost, he steals his employers' money and flees like Hopkins to Canada and then to New York.

It is at this point in the plot that Dreiser got stuck once again, but he also became energized, because the Hurstwood section in New York is what gives this novel much of its drama and pathos. We feel a kind of detached sympathy for the bedraggled figures in Crane's "Men in the Storm" or the soldier in Garland's "The Return of the Private," but Hurstwood personifies the prosperity of the American Dream—and he flings it away for the youth and beauty of Carrie. More tragic is the fact that Hurstwood cannot help himself. The scene with the safe is a mechanical demonstration of Spencer's ideas about humans as wisps in the wind, "still led by instinct before they are regulated by knowledge." When the lock to the safe clicks shut, Hurstwood, still contemplating the act of theft, is left holding $10,800 of its funds. Dreiser asks, "Did he do it?"[14] The answer is no, but the consequences of his actions must be accepted. This is no Pilliod's Island or Mott's Garden. The island is New York on the eve of the Panic of 1893.

Sister Carrie amplifies the same sense of foreboding that informs Dreiser's earliest short stories. Hurstwood is doomed long before he finds himself tipsy in front of his employer's money. He is programmed for catastrophe. He arrogantly underestimates his wife, into whose hands he has put the legal ownership of everything they have. The first omen of danger comes from his son, who coolly informs his father in his mother's presence: "I saw you, Governor, last night." George, Jr., has seen his father with Drouet and Carrie at McVickar's Theater watching a production of *Rip Van Winkle*. If this isn't his wake-up call, the reader's comes along shortly when "a gaunt-faced man of about thirty, who looked the picture of privation and wretchedness" approaches Hurstwood on the street while he is walking with Carrie and Drouet. Drouet is the first to see him and the only one to sympathize, handing over a dime "with an upwelling feeling of pity in his heart. Hurstwood scarcely noticed the incident. Carrie quickly forgot."[15] Ultimately, Carrie will forget about Hurstwood, as will his wife and two children.

Once Hurstwood and Carrie move to New York, and Hurstwood invests in the Warren Street saloon, Dreiser traces his gradual downfall with painful detail. One way this is accomplished is by watching his money dwindle. Dreiser worried about money, as we know, most of his life, and this phobia is dramatized in the increasing shabbiness of Hurstwood's living quarters. He and Carrie begin uptown in the neighborhood where Dreiser and Jug first lived, then after three years move to the area around Fifteenth Street, where Hopkins and Emma had lived. The money count, beginning with $1,300 following Hurstwood's forced restitution of most of the stolen money, is then at $700, then to $340 after a gambling loss, then tumbling through another card game to $190 on down to $100, $50, $13, and $10. All the while, Carrie's success as a chorus girl nets a salary beginning with $12 a week, rising steadily with the decline of Hurstwood's savings. On her way up to $150 a week, she deserts him to brood by himself.[16]

In chapter 45, which reuses the title "Curious Shifts of the Poor," Hurstwood begins again with $70 after selling their furniture and deserting their flat for "a third-rate Bleecker Street hotel" on the edge of the Bowery. He comes down to his last fifty cents and finds a job sweeping up and doing odd jobs, perhaps as Hopkins did, at the Broadway Hotel near Washington Square. "Porters, cooks, firemen, clerks"—all were higher than the now almost wholly defeated Hurstwood, who gets the lowly position by telling the manager, "I came here because I've been a manager myself in my day." When he falls sick with pneumonia in February of 1896 and loses even this job, he is sent to Bellevue, where Dreiser had one of his last assignments as a reporter on the *World*. It is here that the "Captain" of the *Demorest's* essay enters the story. The fact that Dreiser drew on this article, written before he wrote the novel, confirms his own sense of gloom and doom as he constructed his tale. He not only spliced in parts of the "Curious Shifts" essay, but he restored parts that the editors at *Demorest's* had taken out.[17]

The difference between the versions in *Demorest's* and *Sister Carrie* is that one of the figures of "Curious Shifts of the Poor" emerges out of the shadows as George Hurstwood, once utterly oblivious of those whose ranks he has now joined. Although he sees Carrie once more very briefly and gets nine dollars from her, she forgets about him as quickly as she had the beggar to whom Drouet allowed a dime. He tries to see her again by going to the stage door of her theater, where he is pushed into the icy slush by the doorman. The scene shifts to Carrie in her Waldorf Astoria suite, Drouet's unsuccessful attempt to renew relations, and Hurstwood's family comfortably riding in a Pullman car on their way to a ship bound for Rome. At the same moment, Hurstwood is described as standing in a side street waiting to pay fifteen cents for his final night's rest—this scene, too, adapted from one of the vignettes in "Curious Shifts of the Poor." Dreiser originally ended the novel with Hurstwood's suicide, dating the conclusion of his penciled manuscript, "Thursday, March 29, 1900—2:53 P.M."[18]

Just how Dreiser came to extend this final chapter so that it ends with Carrie in her rocking chair alone dreaming of such happiness as she will never feel is not known, and may never be. Once the original manuscript was typed at Anna Mallon's agency, he, Arthur, and Jug edited it. He told Mencken that they reduced it by almost forty thousand words, and the scholarly editors of the original typescript estimate approximately thirty-six thousand words.[19] Dreiser was from the beginning a prolix writer, and after Dreiser Henry made most of the substantive cuts, while Jug looked after her husband's grammar, spelling, and punctuation. Henry's books show him to have been a better and more economical stylist than Dreiser, though falling well behind his friend in originality and literary substance. Dreiser may have also agreed to the cuts because they both feared it was too long for commercial publication. Henry's *A Princess* is just over three hundred pages in print; even as revised, *Sister Carrie* would run almost twice that.

Since the book's title was *Sister Carrie,* it no doubt seemed reasonable to end with Carrie somehow, and the basis of what were to be the final words already appeared in the penultimate chapter. Robert Ames (an Edison-like figure who is also a stand-in for the author), urges Carrie to consider applying her talents to serious drama, but she continues blindly as a showgirl, trapped in both the sentimental culture of her class and a lack of education. It is clear that no serious relationship between them will ever work out, because Carrie is simply too intellectually shallow for this electrical engineer. They part, and Carrie is left almost as emotionally needy as she had been in the beginning of the novel. Dreiser originally wrote, perhaps with some help, the following coda in the penultimate chapter:

> Oh, blind strivings of the human heart. Onward, onward it saith, and where beauty leads, there it follows. Whether it be the tinkle of a lone sheep bell o'er some quiet landscape, or the glimmer of beauty in sylvan places, or the show of soul in some passing eye, the heart knows and makes answer, following. It is when the feet weary in pursuit and hope seems vain that the heartaches and the longings arise.

This kind of "nature" writing and florid style could easily have been a part of *A Princess of Arcady,* so much so as to suggest that Henry influenced its composition. We know from internal evidence that Henry helped with the romantic chapter titles, which were penciled into the typescript in both men's hands as they were getting it ready to go to press at Doubleday.[20] The sentimental romantic convention to which the titles subscribe suggests Henry's idealism more than Dreiser's realism, from the first chapter ("The Magnet Attracting: A Waif Amid Forces") to the last ("The Way of the Beaten: A Harp in the Wind"). Other Henryesque titles are "The Machine and the Maiden: A Knight of To-Day" (6), "The Lure of the Beautiful: Beauty Speaks for Itself" (7), "A Witless Aladdin: The Gate to the World" (16), and "An Hour in Elfland: A Clamour Half Heard" (19). The products of what F. O. Matthiessen calls "magazine verse"—and most likely the joint project of two writers who had worked for magazines— the titles serve as a counterpart to the book's harsh naturalism, but they also cloak it to some extent.[21]

But to return to the final chapter of the Doubleday version, in which Carrie is featured following the suicide of Hurstwood. It, too, is written in the florid style of the penultimate chapter and the chapter titles. In fact, the last paragraph of the final chapter is taken almost verbatim from the coda of the penultimate chapter. Dreiser merely shifted it to the end of the Doubleday version of the book, placing "O Carrie! O Carrie" at its beginning, before "blind striving of the human heart." And then he added three more sentences that brought the passage in line with one of the leitmotifs in the novel, the rocking chair into whose arms both Carrie and Hurstwood fall whenever confused or defeated: "Know then, that for you is neither surfeit nor content. In your rocking chair, by your window dreaming, shall you long, alone. In your rocking chair, by your window shall you dream such happiness as you may never feel."[22]

It may be conjectured, therefore, that Henry helped to write the last paragraph in the last chapter of *Sister Carrie*. The paragraph appears to be in Jug's hand; she evidently made a fair copy of the paragraph taken from the original penultimate chapter, in which, as the editors of the original typescript note, she made slight changes. Of course, all these alterations, like any suggestions Henry may have made for the final paragraph, could have been agreed upon orally by Dreiser.[23] But ironically, although Dreiser, as noted earlier, claimed to have written the last chapter of Henry's novel, the opposite may have been true. Whatever the case, the extent of Henry's collaboration may be greater than has been thought. They knew each other's plots intimately, the two books were conceived together on the Maumee, and they both had female protagonists who were in one sense or another "nuns."[24]

Aside from the logic of Dreiser's title, ending the book with Carrie may also have been an effort to placate the Victorian critics by "punishing" her for her adultery in leaving her basically unhappy, if also materially enriched. But that wasn't enough for the censors in 1900. Nor had it been in 1899 when Kate Chopin in *The Awakening* felt obliged to have her adulterous female commit suicide. Only Hester of *The Scarlet Letter,* published a half century earlier, passed America's puritanical code of literature because she became the object of Hawthorne's sermon and final scolding remarks (through Dimmesdale), just as she was the object of the minister's sermon on sin on the scaffold at the beginning of the story. As we shall see, by the time Dreiser had finally written the novel he indicated to Henry he couldn't write, he was prepared to do almost anything to see it in print.

———

Once the typescript had been initially edited and its changes spliced in, Dreiser asked Henry Alden of *Harper's Monthly* to read it and advise as to its chances of publication. Alden had sent him a kind letter of rejection for "The Shining Slave Makers," and *Harper's* had just published his article on the railroad. Furthermore, Alden frequently read book manuscripts for the well-established publishing house of Harper and Brothers. Alden told Dreiser it was a capable piece of work and ought to be published, but he doubted whether any publisher would touch it because of the reigning standards of decency. Nevertheless, no doubt at Dreiser's urging, Alden passed the typescript on to Harper and Brothers, who, as Dreiser remembered in his letter to Mencken about the affair, "promptly rejected [it] with a sharp slap." Actually, the reader's report he received from the firm was not a flat-out rejection, but in the first half at least an able and accurate assessment, which finally devolved into a vague argument as to why Harper's dare not publish it.[25]

In the report dated May 2, 1900, the unknown reader or readers called it "a superior piece of reportorial realism—of highclass newspaper work, such as might have been done by George Ade." This may have been part of the "slap," but "reportorial realism" had already been published not only by Crane (albeit privately) but by Garland and even Howells in *A Hazard of New Fortunes*. The report continued to note Dreiser's "many elements of strength—it is graphic, the local color is excellent, the portrayal of certain below-the-surface life in the Chicago of twenty years ago faithful to fact." Furthermore, it found "chapters that reveal very keen insight into this phase of life and incidents that disclose a sympathetic appreciation of the motives of the characters of the story." It seems clear that in declining to publish *Sister Carrie* Harper's made a commercial—and moral—decision, not an aesthetic one. The negative side of the report is less exact in making its arguments, such as the statement that "the author has not risen to the standard necessary for the efficient handling of the theme." The key to their true meaning here comes in the statement that Dreiser's "touch is neither firm enough nor sufficiently delicate to depict without offense to the reader [i.e., 'feminine readers who control the destinies of so many novels'] the continued illicit relations of the heroine." Its parting shot took aim at the alleged weariness of parts of the plot (mainly dealing with Carrie, since the report admired the section on Hurstwood's decline) and Dreiser's uneven or colloquial style.[26] The matter of that "style" would dog him throughout his lifetime—as well as his literary reputation today.

It has been said that Dreiser was crushed by the letter, believing he had written a novel in the tradition of Balzac and Hardy (which he had), but Alden had warned Dreiser that his inclusion of illicit sexual relations would not be tolerated. Dreiser later described himself at the time as being "as green as grass about such matters, totally unsophisticated." He promptly took Alden's advice to try the newer firm of Doubleday and Page—recently reorganized from the firm of Doubleday and McClure, which had published in 1899 a novel almost as challenging to the standards of decency, Frank Norris's *McTeague: A Story of San Francisco*.[27]

Before he did so, *Sister Carrie* very likely went through another round of revisions, this time to cut out or moderate the offensive parts of the book. Henry, whose novel was already in press at Doubleday, was the logical choice for the job. Once this work was done, Dreiser took the typescript to the offices of Doubleday and Page at 34 Union Square and personally handed it to Frank Doubleday. He remembered that Doubleday looked at him "with a kind of condescending, examining smirk." The publisher had a big ego, too big for his former partner Sam McClure (who after their split had formed the house of McClure and Phillips). When he left McClure, Doubleday had taken Walter Hines Page and Frank Norris with him as part of his editorial staff.[28] He now turned over the typescript either to his partner Page or directly to Norris, because he himself was getting ready to go abroad with his wife.

About a week later, Jug's sister Rose White, who was visiting, raved to her brother-in-law about *McTeague*. Dreiser read it and admired it immensely. "It made a great hit with me and I talked of nothing else for months," he later told Mencken. "It was the first real American book I had ever read—and I had read quite a number by W. D. Howells and others." At almost the same time, Frank Norris was reading *Sister Carrie* in a cabin resort in Greenwich, Connecticut, and coming to an equally enthusiastic conclusion about Dreiser's decidedly American book. Although his reader's report is unfortunately lost, he wrote directly to Dreiser that "it was the best novel I had read in M.S. since I had been reading for the firm, and that it pleased me as well as any novel I have read in any form, published or otherwise."[29] If events had played out differently, we might be celebrating this literary intersection as another "shock of recognition" such as what Melville experienced when he crossed paths with Hawthorne or Emerson when he greeted Whitman "at the beginning of a great career."

But there were other players, not only Doubleday, but the second reader on Dreiser's submission, Henry Lanier, the firm's junior partner. While he joined Norris in recommending *Sister Carrie*, Lanier evidently had his reservations about the potential risks to the firm's reputation. For the time being, however, he kept them to himself. Meanwhile Page, who acted as third reader, liked the book almost as much as Norris. He wrote to Dreiser on June 9, "As, we hope, Mr. Norris has informed you, we are very much pleased with your novel." Congratulating him "on so good a piece of work," Page invited the author to come down to their offices the following Monday afternoon. Dreiser's prospects couldn't have looked better, and after the meeting he felt confident enough about them to leave town and accompany his wife back to Missouri to see her family.

It was about this time—between mid-June and early July—that Frank Doubleday returned from Europe. Just what happened isn't clear, even to this day. Allegedly, Doubleday took the typescript home and shared the enthusiastic reports of the book with his wife, whom Dreiser later described as "a social worker and active in moral reform." According to legend, Mrs. Doubleday read the typescript and strongly advised her husband not to publish it. Mrs. Doubleday's role in the affair, however, has never been verified; all accounts of her involvement as Mrs. Grundy come from Dreiser, who told the story at various points in his life.[30] The actual villain and possibly the catalyst to Doubleday's decision to try to get out of the firm's oral agreement with Dreiser may have been Henry Lanier, whom Arthur Henry described to Dreiser on July 14 as "a good deal of a cad . . . [who] knows nothing at all about real life . . . [and] is exceedingly conceited."

Since Dreiser was still in Missouri, Henry had gone to see Lanier at Norris's suggestion when the process for publishing Dreiser's book had suddenly and mysteriously stalled. During the interview, he and Lanier had engaged in "a warm argument" over the value of Dreiser's realism in *Sister Carrie*. Lanier insisted that Dreiser was unnecessarily "straining after realism." Interestingly, this had been the same argument his late father, the poet Sidney Lanier, had used against Walt Whitman in *The English Novel and the Principle of Its Development* (1883), where he objected to Whitman's depiction of the "rough" as the ideal or average American. The senior Lanier also stood for form in poetry, thinking "free verse" no more preferable than political anarchy.[31] It appears that Henry Lanier shared this tradition in literature with his father, objecting to Dreiser's focus on the average American who falls short of the ideal in sentimental literature. He could have stomached his colleague Norris's characters in *McTeague* because there the author himself treats them condescendingly (almost humorously) as defectives in the fantasy of Social Darwinism. Dreiser's creations, moreover, were not the kind of people, as Page would soon tell Dreiser, who would interest ladies and gentlemen, or the great majority of their readers.[32] In a word, Lanier thought Dreiser's realism was not only "strained," but false since its view of life failed to uplift the reader morally. While Lanier—as Henry told Dreiser—may have been as surprised as Norris by Doubleday's decision not to publish *Sister Carrie*, he was certainly prepared to abide by it.

———

In a strange twist, Lanier was arguing these points with someone who had upheld the same Victorian standard. Henry had, after all, written *A Princess of Arcady,* for which Lanier had probably been a reader along with his work on *Sister Carrie.* But Henry held his ground on behalf of his friend. Once the real reason for the delay became apparent, Henry urged Dreiser to return to New York at once and hold Doubleday and Page to their decision to publish the book. When he learned from Norris that Page had written a letter dated July 19 to Dreiser saying that they preferred not to publish his book after all, Henry was dumbfounded. "It has dazed me—I am amazed and enraged," he told his friend, "Doubleday has turned down your story. He did it all by himself and to the intense surprise of Norris and Lanier."[33] One has to wonder not only about Lanier's role here but also Norris's, for the author/reader found himself in a tight place. He was financially dependent on the firm for a salary as well as its intention to publish *The Octopus* (1902).

Norris, however, never lost faith in Dreiser's work. As we shall see, he did almost everything he could to promote it once the decision was reluctantly reached to issue the novel. But he does seem to have joined ranks initially with Doubleday and Page to discourage Dreiser from making *Sister Carrie* his first novel, especially at Doubleday. In breaking the bad news about *Sister Carrie* to Henry, Norris told him on July 18 that Page's letter was first held up for Dreiser's return and then dispatched to him for fear that if the firm waited any longer the delay would constitute a commitment. He tried to mollify Henry (and hence Dreiser, as would Page's letter) by suggesting that the firm would do something else in return for Dreiser's decision to yield on the question. "There is much more than a 'turning-down' of Sister Carrie" in Page's letter of July 19, he told Henry. "Page—and all of us— Mr. Doubleday too—are immensely interested in Dreiser and have every faith that he will go far." The publishers expressed faith in him as a writer and wanted to publish his *second* novel, hoping that it would be more acceptable to conventional taste. To vouch for their continued interest, they offered him an editorial position on a new magazine the firm was getting ready to publish—*World's Work.* They also promised to attempt to place

Sister Carrie with another publisher, though one wonders exactly what firms they had in mind.[34]

At first, upon receiving Henry's letter, Dreiser tried to remain calm. But it was a mere pose, for as he later remembered, the Doubleday affair "proved to be the greatest blow I was ever to have."[35] In fact, he had been actively worried ever since receiving Henry's letter about his meeting with Lanier, even asking the blacks who worked around Arch White's farm in Danville if there was a fortune-teller nearby. He had—he told "Hen" in his letter of July 23—received both Henry's letter and Page's, and he enclosed a copy of his response to Page, which spoke of the enormous embarrassment he faced in the wake of this latest decision. Word of his success was already abroad. He had, for example, received a note of congratulations from the assistant editor of the *Atlantic Monthly,* and a lecture was being arranged for him at the Player's Club on his new kind of realism. "The repute in which your firm is held," he told Page, "the warm and rather extra-ordinary reception accorded my effort by your readers—the number and enthusiasm of those interested in me—all could but combine to engender a state, the destruction of which must necessarily put me in an untoward and very unsatisfactory predicament."[36] In other words, his literary reputation would be in tatters.

Dreiser didn't say he *wouldn't* withdraw the novel, telling Henry privately that he might if he could borrow the manuscript from Doubleday and silently offer it to Macmillan for a "quick consideration." He told Page that he was "willing to rest the matter, leaving for another day my reply to your eventual decision." Perhaps in denial, he simply could not believe what was happening. Any hope of relief was dashed, however, by Page's blunt if lengthy reply of August 2. "You do not say specifically whether you will release us," Page stated, adding cruelly in response to Dreiser's fear of embarrassment over the affair: "After all, other people, even our friends, think much less of our work than we imagine they do!" This should have, and probably did, convince Dreiser that the firm didn't have his best interests at heart. He therefore ignored their offer of August 15 to try to place the novel with another publisher. By now Henry might have already looked into those prospects and found absolutely no interest. He was also convinced that Doubleday and Page couldn't be trusted, telling his friend that while his own story was being "set up," he was sorry he had signed a contract for *A Princess of Arcady,* that he would have held off and used his own book as a bargaining chip for Dreiser's. Henry, however, had another reason for his deep devotion. He considered Dreiser his literary double whom he needed to spur on his own writing. He hoped to move back in with Dreiser and Jug, so that they might write another set of books together. "I am already to begin mine—am only waiting for you," he told him. "I want to be with you when you start yours."[37]

At this point, Dreiser was just as devoted to Henry. In his letter of July 23, he had told his literary collaborator that he was "thoroughly pleased" by his support, saying that it reflected his own distress when things went badly for Henry. "Surely there were never better friends than we. If words were anything I think I would tell you how I feel." He called Henry his doppelgänger—"a very excellent Dreiser minus some of my defects. . . . If I could not be what I am, I would be you."[38] If we didn't understand before exactly why he dedicated his book to Henry, it becomes clear with these words. If it hadn't been for Henry, Dreiser might have given in to the pressure applied not only by Frank Doubleday, whom Henry described to Dreiser as thinking *Sister Carrie* both "immoral and badly written," but by his staff, which quickly closed ranks behind their leader.

Doubleday thought at first that they could simply notify Dreiser of their decision not to publish his book. After talking first with Henry and then with Page, as well as with his attorney, however, Doubleday asked Dreiser through Page to release them from their proclaimed intentions. When it was clear that Dreiser was adamant, a contract was finally drawn up on August 20. Nonetheless, Doubleday sent Dreiser a cold letter of September 4 ("Dear Sir"), which doggedly rehearsed earlier suggestions to change all real names of people and places. It had to be clear to Dreiser that the firm was going to do as little as possible to fulfill its contract, which promised the author royalties on retail sales of 10 percent on the first 1,500 copies sold, 12.5 on the next 1,500, and 15 percent on everything over 3,000 copies. The first and only press run was just 1,008 sets of sheets, of which only 558 sets were initially bound, to be sold for $1.50 apiece. (There was further binding of copies from the 1008 sets, but the exact number is not known.) Norris, who was in charge of publicity at Doubleday, did his best to stimulate sales by sending out an estimated 127 review copies. But Dreiser's first and last royalty check from Doubleday, which tracked sales between November 1900 and February 1902, was a dismal $68.40.[39]

Furthermore, when *Sister Carrie* appeared in the fall of 1900 along with *The Princess of Arcady,* the physical contrast between the two couldn't have been greater. Henry's garden-green cover was imprinted with stalks of flowers, while the flat dull red of Dreiser's book made it—in the words of one biographer—resemble a plumber's manual. It has been said that Doubleday refused to advertise *Sister Carrie*.[40] Yet there is no evidence that the firm advertised *A Princess* either. In fact, if the issues of the *New York Times Saturday Review of Books* between November and January are a reliable gauge, Doubleday didn't advertise any of its books. On the other hand, the competition—Scribner's, Macmillan, G. P. Putnam's Sons, Harper and Brothers, Houghton, Mifflin, and Company, even McClure, Phillips, and Company—ran full-page advertisements for their fall lists. The November 10 issue of *Saturday Review* would have been the time to strike for *Sister Carrie,* but the only book of lasting value to appear—under review—in the journal that day was the first variorum edition of another book suppressed in its day, *Leaves of Grass.* Some of the reviews of *Sister Carrie* actually commented on the paucity of advertising, among them the review in William Marion Reedy's *Mirror* (which would publish "Butcher Rogaum's Door" in 1902) in its issue of January 3. And on January 16, George Horton of the *Chicago Times Herald,* one of Henry's former colleagues, asked "Why a firm that can get hold of such literature should expend all their resources in pushing such cheap and trite clap-trap as 'An Englishwoman's Love Letters' must remain a puzzle to everybody not in the publishing business."[41]

The Doubleday affair would render Dreiser forever suspicious of publishers. In fact, he prepared to remember and to record it (not always faithfully) from the very beginning. He told Henry when the crisis first surfaced, "If when better known and successful I should choose to make known this correspondence, every scrap of which I have, even to letters of commendation from others, the house of Doubleday would not shine so very brightly." To this end, he accumulated a scrapbook consisting of 245 letters, including copies in his hand of Henry's letters relating to the affair, which in fact are almost the only extant evidence of his friend's assistance.[42] He would also embellish his own artistic role, telling an interviewer for the *New York Herald* in 1907, when the book was first reissued by another publisher, of his heroic struggle to complete it. "The story had to stop, and yet I wanted in the final picture to suggest the continuation of Carrie's fate along the lines of established truths," he was paraphrased as saying. "Finally, with note book and pencil I made a trip to the Palisades, hoping that the change of scene would bring out just what I was trying to express." There, he said, he stretched himself out on one of its ledges. After two hours, the inspiration finally came: "I reached for my note book and pencil and wrote. And when I left the Palisades 'Sister Carrie' was completed."[43] This account may be a cruel shorthand to both acknowledge and erase Henry's role in the ending, for his "sister" or sisters in *A Princess of Arcady* dwell in a convent facing the Palisades. We will never know what if anything Dreiser changed in transcribing Henry's letters, but this later account left his now ex-friend completely out of the picture. Their falling out in 1902 no doubt contributed to this, but earlier Dreiser may have chafed at the superior treatment Henry had received from Doubleday.

Only Norris remained unscathed, or unrevised, in Dreiser's memory of the affair, and even here he apparently made some comments in 1930 about the writer's conflict of interests. Although Dreiser also wrote a flattering introduction to a reissue of *McTeague* about the same time, their relationship was cut short when Norris died of peritonitis in 1902. A month after the muted appearance of *Sister Carrie,* Dreiser sent Norris an autographed copy, acknowledging his "earliest and most unqualified approval" and claiming that his book was an "offspring" he had "so generously fostered." For his part, Norris reiterated his admiration of Dreiser's book. "I have read most of her again," he told Dreiser in thanking him for the book. "It is a *true* book in all senses of the word."[44]

Aside from Norris's valiant statements and support, an American novel couldn't have appeared under more unpromising circumstances. The number of review copies Norris actually was allowed to send out may be exaggerated, but it was the only advertisement the book was going to receive. As a result of the Doubleday reversal, word surely got out that *Sister Carrie* was not to be celebrated, or even noticed, in the literary press. No doubt, after his experience with Dreiser, Howells had no qualms about ignoring the book in *Harper's*. Other mainstream journals that might have been expected to do reviews—the *North American Review,* the *Atlantic Monthly,* the *Critic,* the *Arena,* the *Literary Digest,* the *Review of Reviews,* and curiously enough even *Ainslee's,* where Dreiser's friend Richard Duffy was the editor—also ignored it. *Outlook, Current Literature,* and the *Nation* listed the book as published but never reviewed it.[45] Mainly, it was the newspapers that reviewed *Sister Carrie.*

Part of the legend surrounding *Sister Carrie* was that the reviews were overwhelmingly negative, but the fact is that of the handful that the first edition received between November 20, 1900, and March 9, 1901—fewer than thirty—more than a few hinted that despite the book's colloquial language and seamy plot, it was undeniably a rare example of literary genius. "Here, at last, is, in its field," wrote Horton in the *Chicago Times Herald* of January 16, "a great American novel." By "in its field," he undoubtedly referred to naturalism with its focus on the more sordid aspects of American life, such as in *McTeague,* which many condemned for its vulgarity in depicting the bestial natures of the main characters. Interestingly, one of the reasons Doubleday may have shied away from Dreiser's book was because of the adverse reviews of *McTeague* (again for its subject matter, not its power), which he had published when he was still a partner with McClure. But what struck reviewers of *Sister Carrie* was how Dreiser managed to state his case without either profanity or the use of explicit scenes like those found in the underground literature of its day.

"It is a remarkable book," said the *Louisville Times* of November 20, "strong, virile, written with the clear determination of a man who has a story to tell and who tells it." Its coverage by New York reviewers was almost nil, but the *New York Commercial Advertiser* of December 19 referred to its "extraordinary power" to tell a profound and moving story. Three days later the *Albany Journal* called it "intensely human." Up in New Haven, the *Journal-Courier* of January 12 thought its "depth of insight into human character [had] evidenced . . . a touch of Balzac's strength and penetration." And out West, the *Seattle Post Intelligencer* of January 20 called Dreiser "a new writer with endowments of a most unusual order. It seems not unlikely that, if himself so wills it, he can stand at the head of American novelists." Complaints, sometimes the predominant feature of a review, were aimed at Dreiser's style ("the English is seldom good and frequently atrocious"), the title ("this oddly named story"), and that fact that the story "was not a book to be put into the hands of every reader indiscriminately." Two reviewers recognized Dreiser's borrowing from George Ade.

Two others observed that neither the word "God" nor "Deity" occurred anywhere in its 557 pages, only "the godless side of American life." Generally, reviewers objected to the idea that life had no deeper or higher meaning than the accidental paths that Carrie and Hurstwood follow. Hurstwood's drama was thought to be the greater strength in the book, but ironically its force lay in the fact that the ex-manager falls for no better or worse reason than that by which Carrie rises. He falls down and down and nobody seems to care, not even God. Naturally, Hurstwood drew more sympathy than Carrie. To many reviewers (all male in this case), Carrie was regarded as an irresponsible shopgirl who got lucky, but Hurstwood drew their empathy. The *Hartford Courant* of December 6 thought that there was "nothing more impressive in the year's novel writing" than the description of Hurstwood's last days and death. "There is hardly such another picture anywhere of the man who has lost his grip," wrote the *Seattle Post Intelligencer,* "the man who disintegrates utterly in the face of adversity."

One bright interlude in the publishing history of *Sister Carrie* occurred when the English got to read the novel. Through Norris, a copy of the "banned" book fell into the hands of the British publisher William Heinemann, who was getting a series in American fiction under way with his "Dollar Library," in which a reprint of an American book was published every month. The book had also been brought to his attention by George A. Brett, an editor at Macmillan who wrote Dreiser an admiring letter about *Sister Carrie.* Heinemann made the offer of publication through Doubleday on May 6, 1901. The only requirement for change was that in order for the book to conform to the length of the other five books already published Dreiser would have to condense the first two hundred pages down to eighty. Heinemann had no intention of expurgating or revising the content of the book, but the end result was to produce a novel with a tighter structure and one in which the dramatic downfall of Hurstwood is more central to the overall plot. Henry once again helped his friend edit *Sister Carrie,* indeed, may have done the job himself to cut material from the first 195 pages, or up to Chapter 18, where Hurstwood, out to the theater one night with Carrie and Drouet, lies that his wife is ill.[46]

The revised novel, which appeared in 1901, sold better than the Doubleday edition, exhausting its first printing of 1,500 copies and netting Dreiser royalties of $150.[47] The bigger pay-off came, however, in the English reviews, which were much stronger than the American ones. Up until the time of Washington Irving, the English had been condescending toward American authors, but they had spent the latter half of the nineteenth century in condescension toward American critics, who seemed to overlook everyone of their countrymen who wrote unlike the English, such as Whitman and Mark Twain. Heinemann suspected a new American School of writers, perhaps thinking of Crane and Garland, with Dreiser as its latest head. "At last a really strong novel has come from America," announced the *London Daily Mail* of August 13, 1901; "Dreiser has contrived a masterpiece." The *Manchester Guardian* of the following day wrote, "Rarely, even in modern work, have we met with characters so little idealised." The *Academy* of August 24 readily admitted its ignorance of this new breed of American writers, "but *Sister Carrie* has opened our eyes. It is a calm, reasoned, realistic study of American life, . . . absolutely free from the slightest traces of sentimentality . . . and dominated everywhere by a serious and strenuous desire for the truth." The comparison with Zola in the *Athenaeum* of September 7 was quoted in the *New York Commercial Advertiser* of September 18, which had already given the original edition one of its best American reviews. Now the book was hailed as "not only one of the best novels published last year by Doubleday, Page and Company, but one of the strongest and best-sustained pieces of fiction that we have read for a long time." It also noted that while *Sister Carrie* was winning "golden opinions" from the British, it had "curiously enough attracted comparatively little notice in this country."

By the time of the English edition of *Sister Carrie,* Dreiser had already begun two other new novels. The first, to be called "The Rake," was the story of a sexual adventurer and may have been based either on his sexual exploits as a newspaperman or possibly a "rake" like Frank Cowperwood of *The Financier.* Perhaps fearing the subject offensive to the publishing industry, he turned instead on New Year's Day 1901 to write *Jennie Gerhardt,* originally entitled *The Transgressor.* Richard Lingeman speculates that it was his father's death a week earlier that prompted this novel, based not only on another sister but on his father and mother. He wrote up to forty chapters, then tore up all but the first fifteen, before he ran out of gas. He was emotionally exhausted and began to brood. It was as if his world had come to an end with the old century, collapsing on the eve of the new in a reversal of William Walton's prospects in his short story "When the Old Century Was New." Young Walton has "no inkling" of what the century might bring forth, but he is naively optimistic. His creator could see only "the crush and stress and wretchedness fast treading upon his path."[48] In fact, Dreiser was almost fatally intertwined with his fictional characters and the sense of impending doom that frequently envelops them—so much so that the author of *Sister Carrie* began to turn into the gloomy Hurstwood.

EIGHT

Down Hill and Up

Hurstwood moved on, wondering. The sight of the large, bright coin pleased him a little. He remembered that he was hungry and that he could get a bed for ten cents. With this, the idea of death passed, for the time being, out of his mind. It was only when he could get nothing but insults that death seemed worth while.

SISTER CARRIE

THE DOUBLEDAY FIASCO WASN'T THE ONLY REASON for Dreiser's low mood. His nervous breakdown had been looming for the last decade. Essentially, he never fully recovered from his mother's death. He had recreated her in *Sister Carrie,* to the extent that Carrie is a dreamer destined to be disappointed. But by now Dreiser had generalized the idea of her tragic existence into the belief that all life was slated for disappointment. How could it be otherwise? There might be order on the cosmic level, but surely not on the human, where change ultimately meant disappointment and death to the individual. Not only had Dreiser's own life led him to this view, but he stood as the heir to a chain of nineteenth-century logocentric thought ultimately overturned or at least challenged by Darwin's famous study of the species. As the last major American writer of the nineteenth century, Dreiser had also sought order in the chaos of experience but ultimately fell victim to the relativism of the approaching twentieth century.

There was also the challenge of continuing to make a living in the wake of the *Sister Carrie* debacle. Dreiser had let his magazine work slide during the composition of his novel, and he wasn't in any mood to return to such hack work in the spring of 1901. In March he had borrowed $100 from Richard Duffy of *Ainslee's,* where he was still on the rolls as a contributor.[1] He spent the month of July with Arthur Henry and Anna Mallon on one of the dumpling islands off Connecticut, opposite Noank between New London and Stonington. This was the island Anna had purchased for $300 — about a half acre of grasslands and a cabin whose construction Henry (with Anna's money) had arranged. Professing to live on two dollars a week, Henry, Anna, and her maid had set out in May to commune with nature. (Actually, Anna's companion, Brigitte Seery, served as a "chaperone" for Arthur and Anna, who would not marry until 1903.)[2] Despite Henry's romantic descriptions of the island, it was clearly a rough paradise. Naturally, everything was damp from the ocean air, including the pallets on the floor used for beds. At first the only stove for cooking was a fireplace, which blackened not only the pots and pans but the faces of those doing the cooking. For drinking water, they had to pull a large barrel with their rowboat the half-mile or so across the ship's channel to Noank and back. Frequently, the island and its tiny cabin were battered by rain.

While Anna and Brigitte were back in New York temporarily, Dreiser arrived as the serpent in Henry's Eden. For what actually happened on the island, we have two dueling accounts. The first is Henry's description of a petulant Dreiser (called "Tom") in *An Island Cabin,* a book that would heavily damage their friendship. The other is Dreiser's revenge more than a quarter of a century later: the sketch "Rona Murtha" in *A Gallery of Women* (1929), in which Henry (called "Winnie") is depicted as a self-serving romantic who takes advantage of women who love him. Certainly, Dreiser was unprepared for nature's austerity after the jolts and disappointments over his first novel. He admits in "Rona Murtha" that he was not "spiritually happy" on the island: "Wonderful as it was . . . I could never say that I was wholly happy here, not even at peace at any time, with myself, however much I might be with Winnie or the sea." Most biographers of Dreiser have accepted Henry's extended description of Dreiser as an unhappy, almost irascible guest who simply objected to the primitive accommodations. Yet even Henry admitted that Dreiser had brought his problems with him— but after saying so, he proceeds to exaggerate his friend's reactions to the island experience. "He stood by his grip on the sand," Henry introduces "Tom" upon his arrival, "and as I turned from the sky and water and distant shore line, radiant and sparkling with hues of a fair morning, I saw a cloud of uncertainty and trouble in his face."[3]

Dreiser, according to Henry, disliked the smell of the island woods. He thought they should scrub the cabin floor at once, and wash the "greasy" dishes. "When the dishes were done," Henry writes, "we went to the beach and captured the crabs for bait. As we picked them from their hiding places, Tom's wonder and interest grew. He cursed them for elusive devils, sighed over their fate." The two also disagree significantly in worldviews. Dreiser is the grouchy if uncomfortable relativist, while Henry holds forth in Emersonian splendor. "How little we know . . . ," Tom says. "Here we sit with our eyes cocked on the universe like two wise frogs croaking by their pond. . . . We look and speculate, but what can we say after it all, except to exclaim in meaningless phrases over its varying aspects. Why all this marvelous beauty?" Henry for his part insists on the significance of nature "beyond the mere tickling of our senses."[4]

The arrival of Jug a week later, along with the return of Anna and Brigitte, brought little tranquillity to the island. Called "Ruth" in *An Island Cabin,* Jug had, Henry notes, a girlish figure, a glorious mass of red hair, and bright blue eyes. Not a philosopher, she was "a complex combination of child and woman, a being of affectionate impulses and stubborn fidelity, devoted to the comfort of her husband, and managing, in some mysterious fashion, to reconcile her traditional beliefs with his unorthodox thoughts and ways."[5] Ruth's devotion to her Tom's (or Teddy's) needs, however, leads to even more strife in paradise. Once Anna ("Nancy") arrived, she joined Arthur in complaining about the way the visiting couple wanted to rearrange the kitchen, close in the porch, have meat instead of fish, and wash dishes in their scarce drinking water instead of the ocean surf.

All the while, when he wasn't grousing about something, Dreiser sat in a rocking chair and sang or hummed old German ballads. "Tom" also paints, but there is no evidence that Dreiser ever approached an easel. *An Island Cabin,* an exercise in nature writing, is mainly of interest today for what it suggests about Dreiser in the immediate wake of *Sister Carrie.* By devolving into such domestic detail, Henry effectively scuttled his original purpose. And he also pretty well jettisoned his friendship with Dreiser, who by the time he heard about his exploitation in *An Island Cabin* was already almost suicidal. Often contradicting himself, Henry later denied that "Tom" was based on his friend. "The chapters dealing with the squabbles of our little group of islanders," he wrote in a preface or appendix intended for the third edition of *An Island Cabin* to assuage Dreiser's anger, "were written solely to show how foolishly we throw away our opportunities of delight. This particular friend happened to be the one staying with me, and it was, therefore, the incidents in which he figured that were chosen to point my moral and to adorn or mar my tale." "*Tom,* as I have depicted him,"

Henry wrote, "could not have produced 'Sister Carrie,'" which he earlier describes "a great American novel."[6]

Yet in *An Island Cabin,* he wrote of Dreiser's fictional counterpart as the born poet he then believed his friend to be—"no one [is] more sensitive to the world about him, more deeply sympathetic with it, than is Tom." By early in 1904, however, when he and Anna were living in a cabin in the Adirondacks, the experience that formed the basis for his fourth book, *The House in the Woods,* his feelings were more complicated. In a letter to Dreiser dated February 17, which included a draft of the intended preface and also expressed anger at revengeful comments Dreiser had apparently made to Anna, Henry wrote: "It is very clear to me that this book is not responsible for the interruption of our friendship. That was doomed before the book was written, and the doom of it lay in the fact that you could listen to what other people might insinuate or affirm concerning me . . . in the fact that, in spite of our long intimacy, under all manner of circumstances and conditions, you could form such a vulgar and undiscriminating, undiscerning conception of my attachment for Anna, and in the fact that you could tolerate in yourself such a gratuitous animosity toward her."[7]

Later, in "Rona Murtha," Dreiser suggests that Anna was jealous of Henry's intimacy with him, but he also admits to a resentment of his friend's interest in Anna at his expense. He may have retaliated by hinting to friends, as suggested in his sketch, that Henry was exploiting Anna for her money while deserting Maude and their daughter. In the same letter, Henry assured Dreiser that "Maude and I were not separated until she was happily engaged with the Briggs Real Estate Company," making a salary with commissions of "nearly $4,000 a year." "At that time," he added, "Maude, Anna and I were on affectionate and friendly terms, and this friendship has increased till now."[8] This is probably true, for many years later Maude in her letters to Robert H. Elias, who was writing Dreiser's biography in the 1940s, regarded her late husband (who died in 1934) kindly if also as an irresponsible romantic. Anna herself did not think as fondly of Henry as Maude did, once he left her a few years later for another woman half his age. Clare Kummer, a playwright and the "Mrs. Angel" of Dreiser's "Rona Murtha," became Henry's third wife in 1910. Anna Mallon probably should have listened to her mother, who distrusted Henry from the start and cut her daughter out of her will when she married him. Anna apparently never got over her separation from Henry. In and out of mental hospitals for the rest of her life, she drowned on May 7, 1921, at age fifty-nine, in a possible suicide.[9]

Upon returning to New York, Dreiser and his wife had to give up their apartment on the West Side for a smaller place on East Eighty-Second Street, looking out onto Blackwell's (today Roosevelt) Island, which then housed the sick, criminal, and insane. He managed to overcome his acquired distaste for magazine work well enough to sell several sketches to magazines, including one based on an experience he had had while visiting Connecticut that summer. Others were based on personal friends and acquaintances, such as the graphic artist William Louis Sonntag, Jr., and Jug's father, Archibald White; these later reappeared in *Twelve Men.* He also reworked "Curious Shifts of the Poor" for *Success.*[10] With the manuscript of "The Rake" abandoned since Christmas 1900, he had worked away on what would become *Jennie Gerhardt.* Once he had forty chapters written, he had approached several publishers in search of a contract and an advance, including George P. Brett of Macmillan, who had expressed admiration for *Sister Carrie.* He also tried McClure, Phillips, and Company, which would publish the first edition of *An Island Cabin,* perhaps after Doubleday refused it because of Henry's role in the *Sister Carrie* affair. Despite the rave English reviews of the abridged edition of *Sister Carrie,* American publishers were not interested in Dreiser. "If this is your slant on life," he heard again and again, "quit, get out, it's rotten."[11]

In his continuing efforts to salvage *Sister Carrie,* he tried to purchase the plates in hopes of finding another firm to bring it out right, but Doubleday demanded $500. That fall he managed to secure a contract at J. F. Taylor, a small reprint firm looking to expand. Rutger B. Jewett, one of the editors there, believed in *Sister Carrie* (though it is possible he may have wanted a J. F. Taylor version to end differently, with Ames finally rejecting Carrie because of her immoral life), but his boss feared that Doubleday had already spoiled the market for *Sister Carrie.* In the end, they agreed to publish Dreiser's next novel, still called *The Transgressor,* as well as *Sister Carrie,* if the first were a success. J. F. Taylor then also purchased the plates to *Sister Carrie* from Doubleday for the price quoted to Dreiser. Dreiser was to receive an advance of a $100 a month for the next year to finish the book. He signed the contract on November 6, 1901, and soon thereafter gave up his New York apartment to move with Jug to Bedford City, Virginia, where he hoped he would find even cheaper living quarters and the quiet to finish his book.

At first, the change of scenery had a palliative effect on the author's bruised psyche, as well as on his physical condition. "It is very beautiful here," he told Duffy, who, aware of Dreiser's increasingly fragile state of mind, had recommended exercise. "The atmosphere is dry and clear. Mountains twenty miles away loom up so close as to seem but a few minutes' walk." But the depression had already set in too deeply, and by December, he described writing as "steady strain." It was impossible for him "to lighten it even by walking." He told his editor at J. F. Taylor that he was "straining every nerve" to write and coming up dry.[12] That Christmas, the Dreisers broke up housekeeping and visited Jug's parents in Missouri, which offered some distraction at least. He wrote Duffy from Montgomery City that Christmas Day there among the White clan was a "rout of many children— a Christmas that I like." And the sketch "Rella" in *A Gallery of Women* suggests that during the visit Dreiser developed an inordinate interest in the eighteen-year-old daughter of a neighbor of the Whites, but when the couple returned in January, by way of the Gulf Coast, to settle in Hinton, West Virginia, he was in no better spirits than before. It was at this time that Dreiser learned of the forthcoming publication of *An Island Cabin.* The book first appeared serially in the *New York Post,* beginning in January 1902, and Duffy sent him the first installment. In acknowledging it, Dreiser also acknowledged that Henry "has rather gone out of my life recently," but the first installment would not have included the part about "Tom." He also thanked Duffy for the gift of *Leaves of Grass* and predicted: "Time will put [Whitman] above all other American poets up to now."[13]

As if running from the expected protests of his latest publisher, whether over a deadline or the immorality of the emerging plot of *Jennie Gerhardt,* which may have originally resembled *Sister Carrie's,* Dreiser was on the move again in March 1902, this time to Lynchburg, Virginia. Duffy advised him not to fret about "style" as he worked on his second novel. Yet at the same time the editor was compelled to reject two of Dreiser's submissions to *Ainslee's*—"The Problem of Distribution" and "A Mayor and His People." In between these rejections, Dreiser also learned from Duffy that Henry's book had earned a large advance sale as a result of its serialization.[14] By the end of March, Dreiser moved again, this time to Charlottesville, where he remained until April or May. By now Jug, helpless in the face of her husband's depression and their dwindling funds, had gone back to her parents in Missouri. She would go back and forth as Dreiser fought his demons.

By June, mentally exhausted from his struggle to write himself out of his depression, he abandoned his novel and promised to repay J. F. Taylor the $750 he had received since the previous November. Perhaps relieved to be without Jug because he feared that too much sex was contributing to his poor health, he set out on a hiking tour to restore himself. Walking north over three hundred miles, he reached Rehobeth Beach, Delaware, by the end of the month. In July, he had settled in Philadelphia, but was no better off than before for the exercise and fresh air. Jug rejoined her husband in his rented rooms on Ridge Avenue in the suburb of Wissahickon. By now, with no more money coming in from J. F. Taylor, it became increasingly clear to the unhappy couple that one could live more cheaply than two. All Dreiser could count on now were payments for magazine work already done but still unpublished. He would soon ask Duffy for another $100, even though he still owed him $80 from the first loan. "It seems to me," Duffy told Dreiser on November 4, "that it is about time you and I got together for a talk and a walk." He sent him John Stuart Mill's autobiography, recommending the chapter entitled "A Crisis in My Life." Very likely, Duffy visited his friend in Philadelphia in December 1902 and lent him the additional money. Dreiser told Duffy in January that he had been "busy doing nothing. Nervous prostration (which I have shortened to N.P. for family use) still holds a restraining finger on me."[15]

That winter, with Jug back in Missouri again, the author of *Sister Carrie* could be found walking the streets of Philadelphia in threadbare clothing. On February 9 he tried to apply for a position as conductor, but the streetcar barn at Eighth and Dauphin was closed. He eventually walked west on Market Street and across the Schuylkill River to speak with his physician. Dr. Louis A. Duhring was on the medical faculty at the University of Pennsylvania, and though he was a dermatologist, he had agreed—because he had suffered from the same malady—to treat Dreiser for "neurasthenia." Following one of Dreiser's anxiety attacks the previous November, the doctor had prescribed opiates to help him sleep and had advised keeping a journal on his medical condition during waking hours. (This became part of what was published as his *American Diaries* in 1983.) Not very many days later, Dreiser was finally able to collect fifteen dollars from a friend named Gray and another thirty-five or forty from the *Era,* which had an office in Philadelphia and which would publish "A Mayor and His People" in June 1903.[16]

Dreiser returned to New York around the middle of February 1903. He took a room in the Williamsburg section of Brooklyn, at 113 Ross Street. It was probably at this point that, as he later told a friend, he truly "went down and down." Reduced to living in a six-by-eight-foot hall bedroom not far from the East River, Dreiser considered suicide by drowning. "The sight of the icy cold and splashing waters actually appealed to me," he recalled in an autobiographical fragment composed more than twenty years later. "It would be so easy to drop in. The cold would soon numb me—a few gulps and all would be over. All that was necessary was to slip down into this gulf and rest. No one would know. I would be completely forgotten."[17]

At first resisting the idea, he roamed the Brooklyn riverfront, picking up raw potatoes to eat from its docks. "Here in a tumble down street near the waterfront . . . I hid myself away in ye hall bedroom—daily determined to complete at least one saleable article, poem or short story. . . . I had written a book to be sure, but who cared?" In 1943, he recalled for H. L. Mencken the "*cursed life*" that had brought him, he thought, to the verge of suicide. "My pride and my anger would not let me continue . . . and yet a lunatic canal boatman ferrying potatoes from Tonawanda to the Wallabout Market in Brooklyn did. Wanting me as a companion to accompany him on his trip to Tonawanda, he stated as his excuse for his liberality or charity was that he 'thought maybe I was trying to run away from my wife.'"[18]

Saved from the act but with no more money for rent, not to mention the $4.50 a week he spent for his twice-a-day meals of milk and bread, he now decided to leave Brooklyn and try for a manual labor job on the New York Central Railroad. A few years earlier and in better days, he had interviewed its president, Chauncey M. Depew, for *Success*.[19] As he set out with "but one lone quarter," he beheld the vision of a Scotch-Irish sailor. "I have never really believed in apparitions, materializations, boggarts, or kobolds," he claimed in 1924. "Yet now and again in my life . . . there have appeared to be things in Heaven and Earth that are not dreamed of in our philosophies." He experienced the illusion as he approached the Brooklyn Bridge. "His gait and manner suggested the sea to me. He was slim and uncouth and rather shabby as to his get-up and yet amusingly loutish and waggish and decidedly more than half drunk." "Ah, well. We're very low today, but we'll be much better by and by," said the ghost as it "proceeded to execute a fairly airy and trill-ful melody to which he added a few gay steps and capers." Then he "danced on and up the street and out of sight."[20]

Crossing the Brooklyn Bridge, Dreiser looked up at the magnificence of Manhattan's tall buildings and lamented his fate. "If one only had the key, the friendly word," he thought, "how easy it would be to obtain a competence there." But success was not necessarily the fruit of hard work and honesty, as Armour, Fields, and the other captains of industry he had written about in *Success* had claimed. "It did not exactly depend on fitness. Many a man not so fit as I was rolling in luxury. It had been given to him. . . . And yet they talked of earning your bread." "How silly," he thought. "In nature no such rule held as earning anything singlehanded. Each one was favored or discriminated against before he began. I was favored. I was given to write and no one had ever taught me."[21]

He walked north to Twenty-Second Street and Fourth Avenue with the thought of appealing to a charitable society but went instead finally to the offices of the New York Central Railroad at Forty-Second Street and Fourth Avenue. Before turning to the railroad that day, he had spent an evening with Mame and Austin Brennan, who were now living in Washington Square. He had also dined with Jug's brother, Dick White, who was a lieutenant aboard the battleship *Indiana,* docked in the Brooklyn Navy Shipyard. But he asked neither of them for help, and he did not seek out Paul either. (Emma, who was also still in the area, had married John Nelson, like Hopkins another loser, and was too needy herself to have been of any assistance to her younger brother.) According to *An Amateur Laborer,* actually written in 1904, he spoke with George Henry Daniels, the general passenger agent for the New York Central, who in turn passed him on to A. T. Hardin, the railroad's engineer of maintenance of way. In "Down Hill and Up," written twenty years later, Dreiser claims that he intended to see Depew, but in fact he had retired as president in 1899. Dreiser was hired for light physical labor in early April and instructed to report the following week. Rather than return to Brooklyn, where his room was already given up, but his trunk was still stored, he decided to spend the intervening two or three days at the Mills Hotel, a way station for the indigent at 164 Bleecker Street. To do this, he pawned his watch. The pawnbroker, Dreiser told an interviewer almost forty years later, took pity on him and gave him twenty-five dollars for a watch he had bought for only eight dollars in St. Louis. With the money he purchased new shoes to replace his worn-out ones and a hat for the one that had blown off his head. He headed down Broadway to the hotel on the edge of Greenwich Village, where its rooms, or stalls, went for twenty cents a night.[22]

As Dreiser walked past the Imperial, a luxury hotel on Broadway, a cab stopped before it and two men jumped out, both of whom Dreiser recognized immediately. One was "a small, dark little hunchback," while the other was fat and ruddy. The hunchback was Pat Howley, the other was the writer's brother, Paul, still fairly well-off as the author of "On the Banks of the Wabash." Dreiser had probably seen his brother only briefly since their falling out in 1897, when he lost his editorship at *Ev'ry Month,* but it seems Paul had heard from Mame about their younger brother's emotional state and was concerned about him. When the rotund songwriter recognized his brother on Broadway that day, Dreiser recalled that he "looked at me with his big soft blue eyes—the eyes of my mother"—and cried. That day, amid the noise of Broadway, Paul looked sadly at the shabby clothes of the now 130-pound Dreiser. After some discussion, Paul forced $75 on his reluctant brother. Paul was scheduled to go to Buffalo that day, but wanted to see his brother as soon as he got back. Dreiser agreed and after more talk resumed his walk down Broadway to the Mills Hotel.[23]

One would think that with this second windfall of the day, he might have stayed at the Ritz instead of the Mills. Built in 1896 by philanthropist Darius O. Mills, it resembled the Hyatt hotels of today in that the rooms look down on a central lobby. But the similarity stops there, for the only interior source of light in its nine stories of cramped spaces came from the lobby. In "A Wayplace of the Fallen," written a year after his brief occupancy at the Mills, he remembered the rooms as "really not rooms at all . . . but cells partitioned or arranged in such a way as to provide the largest amount of renting space and personal supervision and espionage to the founder and manager but only a bare bed to the guest." The rooms were about the size of prison cells, even smaller than his hall bedroom in Brooklyn. "The atmosphere of the whole building was permeated with tobacco smoke" and after "lights out" at ten, also filled with the sound of coughing, snoring, and loud complaints about both.[24]

As promised, Dreiser went to see Paul the following Monday. After two or three nights at the Mills, the inviting lobby of the Imperial Hotel must have reminded Dreiser of the painful contrast between his own situation and Paul's. Seeing his brother's run-down condition, Paul wouldn't listen to his unrealistic talk about working for the railroad. He signed up Dreiser as a patient at William Muldoon's sanitarium in Olympia, New York, near White Plains. Since the 1870s, Muldoon, a celebrated wrestler and boxing trainer, had hobnobbed with the elite of Broadway and New York. His pals included Paul Dresser, known on Broadway to all the show-business types since the mid-1890s. Muldoon's sanitarium began as a training camp for boxers in 1900, but by 1902 had become a famous health spa catering to the rich and intemperate. Paul himself had taken the treatment at Muldoon's "repair shop." Other patrons included Pat Howley and Mame's common-law husband Austin.[25]

Paul accompanied Dreiser to White Plains the following day. On the train, they reminisced about growing up in Indiana and wondered about the fortunes of their various brothers. Al Dreiser, who had idolized Muldoon in his prime as a wrestler, was still in Chicago. Ed, the youngest, was pursuing an acting career in New York. The scapegrace Rome could be anywhere, of course, boozing and bumming his way around the country.

Muldoon was a powerfully built man of about fifty-five with the manner of a socially savvy drill sergeant. Privately, the inmates of the sanitarium called him "Buldoon." Each one of them paid approximately fifty dollars a week to be harassed and insulted back into good health. Here it was that Dreiser, although he rather disliked the experience, finally found the "doctor" who would start him firmly on the road to recovery. Most of the enrollees were alcoholics while Dreiser suffered from physical and mental exhaustion. He was nevertheless as harshly treated as the others. Like the "Captain" in *Sister Carrie,* Muldoon treated his wards like wayward children. "He seemed," Dreiser later wrote, "to have no respect for either wealth or poverty, but to have a profound contempt for weakness—physical, mental, moral."[26]

A Civil War veteran, a former New York policeman, a Shakespearean actor, and the boxing coach who had trained John L. Sullivan for his famous fight with Jake Kilrain in 1889, Muldoon presided over a fairly grueling daily schedule. One hyperbolic witness pronounced the routine to be "a mild duplicate" of what Sullivan had undergone in preparation for the Kilrain fight, which lasted seventy-five rounds. Although Muldoon never lacked for customers, he kept his classes small so as to ride herd on the inmates personally. Each day began at 6:00 A.M. in a gymnasium equipped with low stools. Here the men—about ten in a class—first performed forty-five minutes of calisthenics. They were, Dreiser recalled, "as lymphatic and flabby as oysters without their shells, myself included."[27] Following this exercise, they were required to keep in the air three small medicine balls (invented by Muldoon). All the while the "Captain" shouted commands and ridiculed their awkwardness. Next they were required to jog around the gym, do more push-ups and jumping jacks, and then head for the showers (another of the coach's inventions, according to Dreiser). Afterward, adorned with towels and a wool jacket around their heads and a bathrobe over their gym clothes, they each drank two glasses of hot water as they perspired on their wooden stools. The routine was topped off by a cold shower, after which they donned riding togs over flannel underwear—the dress for breakfast at 7:30.[28]

The tortures of the sanitarium included horseback riding and long hikes overlooking Long Island Sound. At least once Muldoon took his crew five miles out in a tallyho and ordered them to walk back home. By the end of the second week, Dreiser's appetite improved so that he had gained five pounds. He began to feel stronger. His nervousness disappeared, or at least abated, and his eyesight improved. Before, everything had seemed to be off center or at a slightly wrong angle—possibly the effect of the medicine he had been taking on either his "cast" eye or perhaps his good one. "Now I began . . . to feel as if life were not so bad. People were all wretched and greedy as I had imagined, but so was I, and why not accept the conditions?" He cynically eyed his fellow patrons, several of them relatively young men. For all of them, he thought, "Money was the main object . . . nothing but money."[29]

By the first week of June 1903, after five weeks and $256.75 of Paul's money, Dreiser returned to New York to claim his job on the New York Central Railroad. He reported a few days later to its carpentry shop at Spuyten Duyvil. The "Spike," as the carpentry shop and the other buildings there were called, sat on land extending out into the Hudson opposite the mouth of the Harlem River, a mile or two north of where the George Washington Bridge is today. It was a beautiful spot then, just across from the Palisades and surrounded by expensive yachts, right next to a spa for the rich. Here the "neurasthenic author" was assigned to R. P. Mills, supervisor of buildings, who provided Dreiser with the following letter to F. A. Strang, the shop foreman at Spuyten Duyvil:

This will introduce you to Mr. Dreiser whom you will put to work doing general labor around the shop and outside, paying him fifteen cents an hour [or $1.50 a day for the ten-hour shift]. He is a man recommended to me by Mr. Hardin and is completely run down mentally. Mr. Hardin requests that we keep him busy at general labor in order to build him up physically. You will put him to work at once at the amount specified.

Obviously, Mills was trying to please Hardin, his superior, who in turn was possibly reacting up the line to the influence of Depew, who now sat on the railroad's board of directors. Interestingly, Depew, whose reputation for clean living was part of his public signature as a popular orator of his day, had also been once a patient at Muldoon's.[30]

After presenting his letter to Strang's assistant, Dreiser looked for a room to rent nearby, but most of the cottages there were vacation homes. He found a room in Kingsbridge, one train stop to the south and three minutes away. It was part of the "summery" cottage of a woman by the name of Hardenbrooks, who lived with her daughter, a nephew, and a cousin. Dreiser was charmed with everybody but the cousin, whom he found "cold" and indifferent. In Dreiser's autobiographical novel The "Genius," the protagonist has an affair with the landlady's daughter, but there is—notwithstanding an earlier biographer's surmise—little or no indication that Dreiser was interested in this woman, whom he described as "a weary-looking lady, rather pale." And in September, Jug rejoined her husband there.[31]

On the morning after securing his place with Mrs. Hardenbrooks, Dreiser rose at 5:45, after a night of tossing and turning, and prepared to enter the world of manual labor he had left as a teenager in Chicago, hardly more than a decade ago. Loyal to the Muldoon routine, he performed jumping jacks and drank "three or four" glasses of the prescribed hot water and then—as if he were reporting for a white-color job—took a bath and dressed for breakfast. At the carpentry shop, he was assigned to "two brawny sons of labor who looked for all the world like twins so much were they dressed alike." Dreiser himself was somewhat inappropriately dressed for manual labor, even though his suit was by now threadbare. The author of Sister Carrie was made to carry heavy ash posts, eight feet long and six to eight inches wide. Despite his time at Muldoon's, he was in no shape for this kind of lifting. As he strained to lift one of the posts over his shoulder, he felt a sharp pain across his back and down his legs.[32]

The two men he worked with were friendly and tried to show him the "trick" of heavy lifting, but they (and later others) also vied for his assistance in order to minimize their own labors. Once the three had lugged and dragged all the posts to the second level of the shop, Dreiser was assigned to sweep up sawdust and shavings. At noon he gloomily ate a sack lunch seated on a pile of lumber. The workers had descended from the second floor and elsewhere—"painters, carpenters, tinsmiths and whatnot, and lined themselves up in a row on lumber piles and benches." They spoke mainly of work and the threat of being laid off, and indeed the experience as a whole gave Dreiser fresh insights on the laboring class. Yet he was also revolted by their "pointless political argument[s], so barren of ideas that it was painful."[33]

Twenty years later, with hindsight and a humor for which Dreiser is not generally known, he described his fellow workers at the carpentry shop as laughable pawns of big business. Malachi Dempsey was "so ignorant" he did not even know the meaning of "Europe." "His church, his flat, his pipe, six children at thirty-four years of age, and his wife, last and least, constituted his world." Another, Big John Peters, at three hundred pounds, with flesh cascading over his hidden belt line, "was as genial and unimportant as a child." Always cheerful, Big John would admire the yachts on the Hudson and often remark: "Woodenja think them fellas would feel poorty good sittin' out there on the poop deck of them yachts smokin' their perfectos, eh? Wooden that be swell for you and me, eh sport?"[34]

Dreiser returned to Kingsbridge exhausted from his first day. Even the view of the Hudson in the approaching sunset as the train whisked him the mile south from the railroad yard did little to raise his spirits. Forgetting for the moment his recent joblessness and poverty as well as the lessons he had learned at Muldoon's, it now seemed to him that he had fallen about as low as one possibly could without dying: "To be compelled to rise thus every morning at six or rather five-thirty, to eat a lonely and rather desolate breakfast and to hustle out through a damp atmosphere while others were still drowsing seemed the height of hardship to me." Things got worse when the regular shop foreman returned two days later—"a relentless unfeeling creature [who] would sometimes smile in a coarse and it seemed to me cruel way, exclaiming the while, 'that's the ticket.' Sometimes he would pitch in himself, for show's sake largely . . . only to work the men up to a great pitch. . . . Then he would go off somewhere and rest while they would work on."[35]

Although he later wrote with relative detachment of his experiences at the "Spike" in *Free,* Dreiser especially resented the demeaning labor of having to crawl under tables and around machinery to sweep up wood shavings. After about six weeks of this routine, he asked R. P. Mills to transfer him to a plumbing crew. Apparently, it was not only the foreman who wore on Dreiser's nerves, but his brother Paul, who kept tabs on him and tried to cheer him with jokes about his being the "all-around Supt. of the tie lifting gang of Gorillas." At the end of August, Dreiser joined Mike Burke's masonry crew, which was based at Spuyten Duyvil and serviced operations between New York City and fifty miles out on three railroad divisions. For the remainder of 1903, Dreiser worked on Burke's twelve-man crew of Italian immigrants ("nagurs," according to Burke) as it built concrete platforms, sidewalks, culverts—anything, as Dreiser eventually noted in a sketch of Burke, "that could be made out of crushed stone and cement, or bricks and stone." Since he could not perform the heavy lifting the toughened crew undertook, he became Burke's clerical assistant, keeping tabs on material ordered for each job—paperwork the Irish foreman-mason considered a necessary nuisance.[36]

F. O. Matthiessen and others have viewed Burke as Dreiser's salvation at this point in his career because of the example the foreman set for persistence in the face of life's obstacles. At first, Dreiser viewed Burke as a bully, but he soon came to see that the foreman's verbal abuse of his crew of Sicilians was mainly affectionate bluster. His men felt no threat whatever, and in fact loved the gruff Irishman for his paternal interest in them. In 1924, in an essay for *Hearst's International* entitled "The Irish Section Foreman Who Taught Me How to Live," Dreiser recalled that this illiterate foreman's example had been a source of strength and encouragement as he determined to return to the world of literature:

> This is the attitude and this is the man—and his policy and his viewpoint are mine from this day forth. I will not whine and I will not tremble anymore, come what may. I may not be able to write or win in my own field, but I will be able to do something somewhere, and that will have to be enough—will have to do. For by the living God, this man and his men in their way are as happy and useful as any and as good as any.

Because there exist several conflicting versions of the Burke story, it is risky to base biographical assertions too firmly on the relationship. But it may be significant that Dreiser wrote this statement about Burke's character and the inspiration it gave him in 1924 as he was writing *An American Tragedy* and found himself stymied by indecision several times over how to launch the tale.[37]

Dreiser retired as "an amateur laborer" in December 1903, bidding goodbye to Mike Burke and his crew on Christmas Eve. He literally wrote himself out of "the workaday world" with *An Amateur Laborer* during the winter and spring of 1904. The progress of his life, he noted in one of the fragmentary parts of the manuscript, which he never published himself but mined for other work, had been "in the main filled with commonplace, ordinary human beings, and yet hemmed about and colored by such contrasts of poverty and luxury, such a world of beauty and indifference that even now, as I write it, my eyes all but filled and I am filled with emotions too deep for words." Shortly before turning to *An Amateur Laborer,* he had written an article called "The Toil of the Laborer," which was turned down first by *McClure's* and then by five other magazines; it was finally published in the *New York Call,* a socialist news sheet, on July 13, 1913. Here he wrote of what he had learned from the manual laborer, whose fate he had shared for eight months. "Working with day laborers and attempting to do what work they did," he later recalled, "I gradually began to realize the immense gulf which lies between the man who is an ordinary born and bred working man of the pick and shovel and the one who is not."[38]

During his time in the labor pool, Dreiser had kept up some of his contacts with the literary world, mainly through Duffy, in the hope of returning in some way to the world of writing. Yet it was Paul who once again came to the rescue—even though his own situation was increasingly uncertain. By this time, he was a full partner in the sheet music business, and he and Howley had bought out Haviland. This, however, was the beginning of the end financially. During the fall of 1903 Paul had already been moonlighting to keep afloat and was writing a vaudevillian farce with Robert H. Davis, the editor of the *New York Daily News.* Knowing that the paper was getting ready to launch a Sunday supplement, Paul requested that Davis promise to hire Dreiser after the first of the year.[39] So it was on the strength of Davis's word to Paul that Dreiser finally left the railroad, and he and Jug moved to 399 Mott Avenue in the Bronx.

Dreiser started writing for the *Daily News* supplement in January, but that feature of the paper was canceled by June 1904, and his record of publications there suggests his job was only part-time. He was barely back in any game of writing, doing pieces based on his experience with the railroad, many of which did not find publication until many years later, in either *The Color of a Great City* (1923) or *Chains* (1927), both omnium-gatherums published by Boni and Liveright. His "Just What Happened When the Waters of the Hudson Broke into the North River Tunnel" appeared in the *Daily News* on January 27. This report on the travails of constructing the Holland Tunnel became the basis of one of his best short stories, "St. Columba and the River." Two months later, on March 27, the supplement ran "The Cradle of Tears," which described New York's institutions for abandoned infants. "It is a place," Dreiser wrote, "where annually twelve hundred foundlings are placed, many of them by mothers who are too helpless or too unfortunately environed to be further able to care for their children; and the misery which compels it makes of the little open crib a cradle of tears." "The Story of a Human Nine-Pin" (April 3), which would later resurface in *Tom Watson's Magazine* (in 1905) and *The Color of a Great City* as "The Track Walker," was about "a peculiar individual" who constantly risks his life inspecting railroad tracks for a pitiful wage. A week later the *Daily News* carried "The Love Affairs of Little Italy," an almost farcical sketch in which Dreiser compares old world love rivalries in an Italian-American neighborhood on the East Side above Ninety-Sixth Street to the violence in *Romeo and Juliet* or *Carmen.* "This, truly, in so far as New York is concerned," he wrote, "is the region of the love feud and the balcony."[40] Running through all of these pieces is the theme of the exploitation of immigrants. With the German-Americans of his generation fast becoming absorbed into the American middle class, the Sicilian had become the latest "nagur" of American labor.

Completely unemployed by June, Dreiser turned again to the magazines, but it would be a long summer and well into the fall before he found anything. In the meantime, he read the book version of *An Island Cabin* and seethed over Henry's characterization of him. Henry's explanation did little to ameliorate his sense of wrath and betrayal. The Swanberg biography, which generally skewed the story of Dreiser's personal relations, has led scholars to think he was always the one at fault in the various quarrels and misunderstandings he had with friends and associates. Henry had been a true friend, but he then took advantage of Dreiser at one of his lowest points. He betrayed him as surely as he did his first wife, Maude, and as he would eventually betray his second wife, Anna. He and Dreiser would never be the same again, though they would have casual and sometimes professional connections through the 1920s, when Henry may have attended (with his daughter, Dottie) one or more of Dreiser's lavish parties at his Fifty-Seventh Street residence after the success of *An American Tragedy.*

By contrast, Richard Duffy remained Dreiser's friend for the rest of his life, and it was he who now told Dreiser that Street and Smith, the publishing house that owned *Ainslee's,* was looking for an assistant editor. The titles in its boys' libraries included *Diamond Dick, Luck and Pluck, Brave and Bold,* and *Nick Carter.* Dreiser was hired initially at fifteen dollars a week to edit the boys' books, but his salary was upped to thirty-five a week when he took the helm of the newly founded *Smith's Magazine*. Dreiser worked for Street and Smith between September 1904 and April 1906, and as editor of its newest magazine, he got the circulation up to 125,000. But the urge to write instead of edit was always just below the surface. "I am an editor at present . . . ," he told a recent enthusiast of *Sister Carrie,* "but longing to do but one thing—write." He came to know Charles Agnew Mac-Lean, who was the editor for Ormond Smith's pulp fiction series. MacLean talked to Dreiser about the possibility of reissuing *Sister Carrie* and arranged to purchase the plates from J. F. Taylor for $550, but this latest attempt at a comeback for the book was not to be. In his editor's chair at Street and Smith Dreiser also first met Charles Fort, whose *The Book of the Damned* (1920) and other books he would later champion (to the astonishment of all except John Cowper Powys, a writer and a friend of Dreiser's, who more than shared his casual interest in extraterrestrial possibilities). He published in *Smith's* some of Fort's Lannigan stories, which were apparently based on real-life incidents.[41]

While editor of *Smith's Magazine,* he also wrote and had published pieces in *Watson's Magazine,* where Duffy had moved as editor, having left *Ainslee's* when he was denied a partnership in the firm of Street and Smith. One of these was "The Rivers of the Nameless Dead." Here Dreiser began the life-long practice of basing his fictions on a public incident or crime, an approach that would culminate in *An American Tragedy.* "The body of a man was found yesterday in the North River at Twenty-fifth street," the epigraph said, quoting a New York newspaper. Behind that stark bulletin lay for Dreiser the disappointment and suffering of so many (almost including himself in 1903) who had given themselves to the rivers surrounding Manhattan because the "beautiful island is not possessed of happiness for all." "Such waters" were neither kind nor cruel—merely "dark, strong, deep, indifferent." "The Track Walker" also depended on a grim incident worthy of a journalistic headline ("body mangled by a passing train").[42] That Dreiser arranged for these stories in *Watson's* to state under the author's byline that he was the "Author of 'Sister Carrie'" further shows that almost five years after its publication, he still held out for its rebirth.

As her husband struggled along, editing and writing, Jug was probably again frequently back in Missouri for economic reasons. Money woes were no doubt on his mind when he published "The Silent Worker" and "The Loneliness of the City" in *Watson's* that fall. The first discussed ironically the "beauty of wealth" in which the investment of ten thousand dollars is the equivalent to one man's labor every day of the year, "including Sundays." "Think of it! One man working for you, day after day, in rain or shine, whether there be good times or bad," forever "silent" in terms of whether he is sick or has a family to support. No laborer in 1905, of course, would have earned $10,000 a year, no matter how many hours and days a week he put in. The second starts out with the same kind of hyperbole about economic conditions, this time in terms of their psychological effect on the lonely crowd. "I live in a neighborhood," he wrote, "which is an excellent illustration of this. There are perhaps a hundred people in our apartment house in the Bronx, a thousand, or it may be two or three thousand, in our block. They live in small, comfortably furnished and very convenient apartments, but they live alone." Dreiser appears here to be developing another literary tool, that of the psychological, which would also reach its apex in his second masterpiece. "We cannot forever crowd into cities and forget man for mammon," he concluded. "There will come a day, and an hour, in each and every individual life when the need of despised and neglected relationships will weigh heavy on the soul."[43]

Relationships probably weighed heavily on Dreiser that fall. Paul Dresser, who had been reduced to "bankrupstcy" by the end of 1903, died on January 30, 1906, of either a cerebral hemorrhage or a heart attack—a death possibly complicated by the effects of the mercury treatment he had received for syphilis in the early 1880s.[44] He was only forty-nine. (Others in the family who lived more conservative lives lasted much longer, not only their father, but Mame, who lived sensibly in her maturity, and Ed, in adulthood the most "normal" of the siblings.) As Paul's health failed, he had moved in with sister Emma, at 203 West 106th Street. Hardly a month before his death, he had written his eldest sister on stationery with the letterhead "The Paul Dresser Publishing Company," his last effort to recover financially, after the failure of Howley and Dresser: "Well Mame I am still on earth & things are running along slowly." But Paul was no businessman. Little or none of his sheet music was selling, he said, because of the Christmas season and its demand for "books, toys, etc." His latest songs, reflecting the state of his health, were morbid instead of gay and nostalgic. His last song was entitled "The Judgment Is at Hand." Dreiser first heard of his brother's death in a phone call from Emma. "And yet," Dreiser wrote in the essay "My Brother Paul," "two years before he did die, I knew he would. . . . He emanated a kind of fear. Depression and even despair seemed to hang about him like a cloak."[45]

The "Fat Man" died penniless, and almost friendless as far as any of his Broadway cronies coming forward to help with the funeral expenses.

Dreiser, of course, was just getting back on his feet and had nothing to contribute. But by this time Ed was married to Mai Skelly, a former show business protégée of Paul's. With the help of Mai's mother, Margaret, and the White Rats, a fraternity of New York actors, they scraped up the money for the funeral, and Paul was buried, initially in the Skelly family plot on Long Island. Since Mai, as well as Ed ostensibly, was a devout Catholic, Paul the one-time seminarian and lifelong if irregular Catholic, received a solemn High Mass at St. Francis Xavier's on Sixteenth Street that would have made his father proud. The priest even read the lyrics to his last song. His niece recalled that "all Broadway" was in observance. The mourners included Louise Dresser, the stage name for Louise Kerlin, whom Paul had "adopted" after hearing her sing one of his songs in 1899. Known as Paul Dresser's "sister," she had become famous in the intervening years, singing "On the Banks of the Wabash" and other sentimental ballads in vaudeville.[46] The *New York Times* of January 31, 1906, reported that when she heard "by telephone that her brother had died," she was about to go on stage at Proctor's Fifty-Eighth Street Theater and canceled her performances for the rest of the week. (In the same year as Paul's death, however, she managed to replace her songwriter "brother" by marrying another almost as famous, Jack Norworth, the author of "Shine On, Harvest Moon.") Paul's obituary noted that he had written "The Blue and the Gray," whose subtitle—ever apropos of Paul—was "A Mother's Gift to Her Country."

Almost two years later Mame had Paul's body removed to St. Boniface Cemetery in Chicago, to lie beside their parents. Carl Dreiser, the unwanted child of Sylvia, who as an adolescent at the turn of the century had possibly been under Paul's supervision in New York, told Dreiser in 1908 that Paul's grave still lacked a tombstone. Carl himself had gone to Chicago a year earlier to try to turn around his luck with a failed life. "I am working every day," he told his Uncle Theodore, "but I sometimes get lonesome and discouraged & feel like giving up everything." He spoke of attending business college, but instead, at twenty-two, he committed suicide.[47]

———

In April 1906, Dreiser left *Smith's* for the new *Broadway Magazine*. It was then owned by Thomas McKee, the Doubleday and Page lawyer who had advised the publishers that they were legally required to publish *Sister Carrie* even in the absence of a written contract. The magazine was conceived as a "white-light" publication that reported on the scandals of the theatrical profession as well as "telling on the great and powerful" in general. But McKee wanted to clean up its image and broaden its coverage. When Dreiser applied for the job on April 10, he stressed his experience as a magazine editor who could produce columns featuring "eminent personalities," plays of the month, the arts, "a department of beautiful women," and such special topics as "Are the Dead Alive?" "Are We Tending toward Socialism?" and "Do American Women Drink Too Much?" He asked for a beginning salary of forty dollars and fifty after six months if he fulfilled his promise to raise circulation.[48]

Even though muckraking was on the rise—Upton Sinclair's *The Jungle* was published that year—Dreiser promised in the June issue to rid *Broadway* of "the cheap, the vulgar, and the commonplace policy which once guided it." "No one," wrote the author of that "dirty book" called *Sister Carrie,* "need to work here any longer for anything but that which is sweet and refreshing, and clean."[49] In an effort to place success ahead of politics, he pushed the magazine's circulation from twelve thousand to almost six figures. As his salary increased accordingly, he and Jug moved from the Bronx to Morningside Heights. He was now the editor of a magazine that catered to the middle-class sensibility. Not only were his contributors on the bland side, but Dreiser himself seemed to be taking a holiday from his feeling of injustice in the world, possibly even recycling earlier work. In his first issue, he published a one-page essay entitled "The Beauty of the Tree," which suggests artistic if not intellectual atrophy: "How, when we are tired of activity, the fixed condition of the tree appeals!" In the August issue, he published "The Poet's Creed," bloated sentiment worthy of Bayard Taylor, an earlier poetic model:

> I would not give the bells that ring
> For all the world of bartering;
> Nor yet the whisper of the leaves
> For all the gold that greed conceives.
>
> To me the grass that grows in spring
> Is sweeter than Fame's offering;
> And, ah! the smile of kindly worth
> Than all the wealth of all the earth.

In "Fruitage," a poem appearing the following February, our good deeds are "better than roses . . . perfect as the morning dew." Like *Ev'ry Month,* the covers of *Broadway* featured dazzling young women dressed to the hilt or young men in tuxedoes smoking cigarettes and eyeing beautiful women.[50]

Dreiser was now, however, able to afford to purchase the plates of *Sister Carrie* from MacLean for $550, the same price MacLean had paid for them, and the ice that had effectively suppressed the book appeared to be breaking up. Even John Phillips of McClure, Phillips, and Company, who had been so adamantly against him after its appearance now confided that he had changed his mind. The book that William Dean Howells made a point to ignore now seemed eminently republishable.

That effort was mainly spearheaded by Ethel M. Kelly, an assistant editor at *Broadway,* and Flora Mai Holly (Dreiser's first literary agent). "The book," he later told Holly, "was in the doldrums until you came along with the suggestion that you thought you could market it." Kelly, an attractive young woman of "the Wellesley–Mt. Holyoke–Bryn Mawr school of literary art and criticism," was most enthusiastic about *Sister Carrie* and may have put Dreiser in touch with Holly. The latter placed the novel with the small new firm of B. W. Dodge Company, named for its owner, Ben Dodge, a "lovable alcoholic" who had bolted from Dodd, Mead, and Company. The deal was a complicated scheme in which Dreiser became a stockholder in his new publisher's company, with the title of "director."[51] The B. W. Dodge edition of *Sister Carrie* was published on March 18, 1907, in an initial run of approximately three thousand copies, which sold out in ten days.

Evidently, the promotion for the book alluded not only to the Doubleday suppression but vaguely to Mrs. Doubleday's supposed participation in it, for several of the reviews in 1907—of which there were many more American ones than in 1901—alluded to her, not by name but as the publisher's wife, "grandmother or maiden aunt or somebody like that." There were voiced again cries against the author's colloquial diction, the narrowness of his title (one reviewer pointing out that "the heroine of the book is not a nun as her title would seem to indicate"), and the fact that *Sister Carrie* was not a "pretty story." Yet this time, there was a chorus of support for Dreiser's unpretentious realism, his straightforward way of telling a well-known tale without the slightest trace of sentimentality. The *Los Angeles Times* of June 16 pronounced *Sister Carrie* "somber, powerful, fearlessly and even fearfully frank, and above all, realistic beyond the usual domain of the American school of realism." The *New Orleans Picayune* of July 1 thought its realism "deeper" than that of Howells and "more broadly typical of American life" than Edith Wharton's *House of Mirth,* the story published two years earlier of a fallen woman who drops from a higher place in society than Carrie. Frederic Taber Cooper, in the *Forum* of July 1907, thought that the story of Hurstwood "from the first hour of his meeting with Carrie to the final moment when he turns on the flow of gas . . . is fiction of a grim, compelling force that has the value of many sermons." It was also acknowledged that the book had never been given a fair hearing when it was first published.

One of the most remarkable reviews of the B. W. Dodge edition was written by Harris Merton Lyon, a writer of short stories whom Dreiser had recently met as editor of the *Broadway* and whom he later memorialized as "De Maupassant, Junior" in *Twelve Men.* At the time, Lyon, twelve years younger than Dreiser, was—as Dreiser described him—"in leash to the French school of which de Maupassant was the outstanding luminary." In the sketch, he lamented that his young friend eventually sold out to the school of popular American literature before dying of Bright's disease at age thirty-four in 1916, leaving behind a wife and two children. But in 1907 Lyon was full of enthusiasm for serious literature and made his review a plea for American realism for which *Sister Carrie* was at present the only evidence of "a broader American intellectual freedom." "No wonder England, no wonder France, no wonder Germany looks patronizingly down upon us," Lyon wrote in the *Houston Daily Post* of June 9, "a nation of grown men and women for whom publishers must expurgate books before we are allowed to read them!" But the time was soon coming, he prophesied, and he cared not whether it was to be "twenty-five years or within a century—when the United States will have to 'stand for' if it comes to the point of compulsion—an American Tolstoi, Turgenieff, Flaubert, Balzac, Nietzsche, Wilde, de Maupassant."

The review was not altogether favorable, however. Lyon was an impulsive, perhaps even angry young man, according to his description in *Twelve Men,* so it probably did not surprise Dreiser when his review came with a few barbs. The main complaint was that Dreiser had not elected to correct his errors in style and usage. While *Sister Carrie* was a most remarkable performance for "a man under thirty," it was "to his lasting discredit that, upon its present reissue, he lacked the energy, the concentration, the pride of his work which should have impelled him to use his more mature powers in correcting his disheveled youthful technique. He should have edited this new edition of 'Sister Carrie' with infinite pains." Dreiser had, however, done some minor editing: he altered the passage borrowed from George Ade and, of course, removed the dedication to Arthur Henry. At least one other reviewer held that Dreiser should have cleaned up his prose in the second edition, but Lyon took what today might seem an astonishing suggestion (in spite of Dreiser's sometimes clumsy or tedious phrasing) even further and no doubt earned his nickname, which is ultimately ironic, in *Twelve Men*. "If he had the craftsmanship of Maupassant," Lyon proclaimed, "his 'Sister Carrie' would be ten times more powerful." But no de Maupassant stylist could reach as low on the American social ladder as Dreiser, who by the very insignificant or lower-class nature of his characters was taking the first truly major step in literary democracy since Whitman and Twain. To be criticized for splitting infinitives or "using vulgar commonplaces here and there, when the tragedy of a man's life is being displayed," he told an interviewer from the *New York Times* the next week, "is silly."[52] Anyway, using de Maupassant's style to tell a tale of immorality in America had already been tried, without commercial success, by Kate Chopin in *The Awakening*.

———

If Dreiser had been simply known as the author of *Sister Carrie* before 1907, he was now quietly famous for it. By September his publisher had sold more than 4,600 copies, earning the author more than $800. A year later, Grosset & Dunlap took over the book, purchasing both unbound sheets and plates from Dodge. The firm reprinted 10,000 copies and sold over half of them in 1908. In the meantime, Dreiser was getting restless at the *Broadway*. His renewed reputation may have contributed to his desire for a bigger challenge (and salary) in the magazine world. An editor friend of Dreiser's at *Munsey's*, John O'Hara Cosgrave, perhaps sensing the situation, recommended him to George W. Wilder, president of Butterick Publications. Wilder's firm issued three American fashion magazines primarily dedicated to selling tissue-paper dress patterns, the *Delineator*, the *Designer*, and *New Idea for Women*. Wilder, a flamboyant businessman always on the lookout for publicity for his magazines, which boasted a combined circulation of 1.8 million, wanted an idea man as much as an editor. Dreiser, with both his success as a magazinist and his reemerging reputation as a writer, seemed a perfect match. Dreiser met with Wilder in his offices atop the Butterick Building just above Washington Square at Spring and MacDougal Streets in June 1907 and was hired at a salary of $7,000 a year.[53]

Installed in a large office heavy with woodwork and polished black furniture, Dreiser at first controlled only the *Delineator* but was editor-in-chief of all three magazines by 1908. The magazines worked (on a much larger scale, with more than 42,000 manuscripts a year under consideration to one extent or another) in the same way as *Ev'ry Month* had. That is, they sold a particular product by publishing features that encouraged the purchase of the company's product and its ethos, in this case dress patterns and the glory of clothes and fashion. Dreiser brought in as contributors such recognizable names as Woodrow Wilson, Mrs. William Howard Taft, Jack London, and William Jennings Bryan (whose efforts for the silver standard Dreiser had admired in the 1890s). Even Arthur Henry was called up for duty to furnish the lyrics for some sentimental songs. Other former friends and associates who contributed included Peter McCord, now married and working as an illustrator for a newspaper in New Jersey, and Joseph H. Coates, editor of the *Era,* to which Dreiser had contributed in 1903.[54] The novelist-turned-editor had learned his editor's lessons well at *Broadway,* for under his watch nothing was allowed in the Butterick publications that might offend. Usually 150 pages in length and filled with drawings of women's clothing, *The Delineator* was dedicated, Dreiser wrote in the September issue, not only to the female's mastering her own sartorial destiny but "to strengthening her in her moral fight for righteousness in the world." "The *Delineator* buys things of an idealistic turn," he told one correspondent. "We like sentiment, we like humor, we like realism, but it must be tinged with sufficient idealism to make it all of a truly uplifting character."[55] The author of *Sister Carrie* was still on holiday from the nether world of realism.

Since most of the *Delineator* readers were mothers, many of newborn children, one of the first series Dreiser commissioned focused on the proper care and feeding of infants. It was in this endeavor, ironically, that he first met Henry Louis Mencken, nine years his junior. Mencken, a newspaperman with a book on George Bernard Shaw already to his credit, had read *Sister Carrie* in 1901 and may have even been the author of a review in the *Baltimore Sun* of June 26, 1907, comparing the novel to the late Frank Norris's *McTeague* in terms of having "the same power and brutality."[56] The child care articles were published under the name of Dr. Leonard K. Hirshberg, not a pseudonym but the name of an actual Baltimore pediatrician who drew up rough drafts that Mencken silently rewrote. Before the Age of Spock in America, the articles insisted, among other things, that babies needed to cry at least twenty minutes a day for the mere sake of exercise. In the essay "The Nursing Baby," mothers were told that the infant was "an extremely delicate organism" that should be handled with care and as seldom as possible: "The young mother who, in the excess of her pride and love, cuddles her baby to her breast and showers kisses upon it by the half-hour makes a pretty picture, it must be admitted, but it cannot be maintained that the little one is benefited by the caresses." On the contrary, "her every kiss helps to make it nervous and irritable and prepares the way for disease." The articles instructed that there were different kinds of crying the mother ought to learn to recognize. They also advised that "the young wife ought not to take the advice of the grandmothers and women in the neighborhood" and "the mother should not make a slave of herself waiting on the child, but clothe it in some comfortable manner and let it fight out its own troubles."[57]

Just how Dreiser squared this advice with his own excessive need for motherly affection as a child is not known. Nor is it altogether clear why the cigar-smoking, beer-drinking bachelor Mencken was squandering his talent on such a topic, but he was already in search of horizons beyond mere newspaper work. Not only was Dreiser, a known literary quantity, the general editor of a magazine enterprise as influential as *Ladies' Home Journal,* but because of his complicated Dodge contract for *Sister Carrie,* he was, in addition to his editorial duties for Butterick, now part owner and editorial director of B. W. Dodge Company. Dreiser was Mencken's first big literary connection in New York, which would lead him in later years to his coeditorship with George Jean Nathan of *The Smart Set.* In September Dreiser had expressed the interest of his publishing firm (quite without his partner Dodge's compliance) in Mencken's next book, on the German philosopher Friedrich Nietzsche.[58] The two corresponded formally for almost a year over the baby series and finally met sometime in the spring of 1908. No record of Mencken's impressions survives, but in the 1920s Dreiser remembered meeting in his well-appointed editor's office "a taut, ruddy, blue-eyed, snub-nosed youth of twenty-eight or nine whose brisk gait and ingratiating smile proved to me at once enormously intriguing and amusing."

"More than anything else," Dreiser recalled "he reminded me of a spoiled and petted and possibly over-financed brewer's or wholesale grocer's son who was out for a lark. With the sang-froid of a Caesar or a Napoleon he made himself comfortable in a large and impressive chair which was designed primarily to reduce the over-confidence of the average beginner." Wearing yellow shoes (still fashionable in Baltimore if not then New York) and a bright tie, the Baltimore cigar maker's son soon won over completely the great man from the provinces of Indiana. "All thought of the original purpose of the conference was at once dismissed," Dreiser remembered fondly, "and instead we proceeded to palaver and yoo-hoo anent the more general phases and ridiculosities of life, with the result that an understanding based on a mutual liking was established, and from then on I counted him among those whom I most prized—temperamentally as well as intellectually."[59]

Dreiser wrote in *Twelve Men* and elsewhere that his life took several important turns and that the change was always signaled by his meeting a man, not a woman.[60] There had been Peter McCord and to a lesser extent Dick Wood in St. Louis, where he got the first hint of his literary aspirations. And there had been Arthur Henry in Toledo and New York, who had driven him to realize his singular talent in one of its finest moments. Now the man Mencken extended his influence, or at least he would try.

Return of the Novelist

For all his floundering round in the commercial world
he remained an artist still.

THE "GENIUS"

DREISER FOUND MENCKEN AT A TIME when he was losing others. Paul, of course, his ever reliable brother, had died. And even though Dreiser used Arthur Henry's contributions in the *Delineator* from time to time, their friendship too had all but died. His 1908 meeting with Mencken also coincided with the loss of another longtime friend and soul mate. Peter McCord died November 10 of pneumonia in Newark, where he was living with his wife and two children and working as an artist and cartoonist for the *Evening News.* He was only thirty-eight, a year older than Dreiser. They had known each other since their *Globe-Democrat* days. Dreiser left St. Louis in 1894, but the Missouri native had remained until 1898, when he relocated to Philadelphia to work for the *North American,* then the city's leading newspaper. Two years later he moved to Newark, and the two old friends—who had no doubt also seen each other in Philadelphia during Dreiser's crisis there—took up their companionship again on a regular basis, meeting for dinner in homes now appointed with wives instead of the bohemian atmosphere of Peter and Dick Wood's atelier in St. Louis.

In *Twelve Men,* where McCord is the basis for "Peter," its opening sketch, Dreiser described his friend as wonderfully crazy—crazy like a poet. "I always felt," Dreiser wrote, "as though I were in the presence of a great personage, not one who was reserved or pompous but a loose bubbling temperament, wise beyond his years or day, and so truly great that perhaps because of the intensity and immense variety of his interests he would never shine in a world in which the most intensive speculation, and that of a purely commercial character, was the grand role." Dreiser, interestingly, was able to make the transition into the world of money, at least for a time as we shall see. But Peter died leaving his wife and children in relative poverty. When Dreiser came forward to manage or oversee the funeral arrangements, he must have been reminded of the difficulty he had encountered when he buried his mother in Chicago in 1890. McCord's mother came east to see that her Catholic son was given a burial "in consecrated ground" as well as a proper funeral Mass. But Peter "had never been a good Catholic," Dreiser recalled in *Twelve Men*, "and there was trouble" with the presiding priest. As he had done on behalf of his mother, he "threatened the good father with an appeal to the diocesan bishop on the ground of plain common sense and courtesy to a Catholic family, if not charity to a tortured mother and wife. . . . All along I felt as if a great crime had been committed by some one, foul murder. I could not get it out of my mind, and it made me angry, not sad."[1]

It was around this time that Dreiser first realized that he had moved away from another friend of St. Louis days—his wife, Jug, who was now also employed at Butterick in a minor capacity. More than two years older than he and nearing forty, the conventional Jug must have seemed an impediment to his sense of freedom as an artist, if not as the respected chief editor of three fashion magazines. Many years later, he told his niece Vera, Ed's daughter, that he had remained with Jug much longer than he should have—that she had by her hidebound nature deprived him of experiences he felt he as an artist required. She objected to various types of individuals and artists whom he entertained, or tried to, at home. Jug barred alcoholic beverages, even wine, from her home. She may have also had racial reservations, for Vera told W. A. Swanberg that in "wanting to discuss matters with certain people, TD barred no one because of race, color, creed, etc. There were times when he was expecting certain people when Jug went so far as to put a sign on the door DO NOT DISTURB. TD said she made [a] rumpus like this several times." Once in later years, while having lunch at the Algonquin Hotel with a friend, she felt compelled to get up from their main course and leave when the actor Paul Robeson sat down with friends at an adjoining table.[2]

Jug was nevertheless for years Dreiser's emotional and domestic anchor. While narrow in her worldview, she was also well-read and something of a romantic—"truly cultured" and "charming," according to Vera. Jug mothered Dreiser much the way his own mother had. She handled money better than he did—sometimes too well, for he once found her holding back household money for a secret savings fund. Perhaps like Angela Blue, her counterpart in The "Genius," the former Sara White had hoped that a pregnancy would stabilize their deteriorating relationship. But Jug never got pregnant. For one thing, Dreiser practiced coitus interruptus. For another, there is the possibility that he was sterile.[3] It is not known whether Dreiser—like Eugene Witla of The "Genius"—enjoyed extramarital trysts during the early years of their living together as husband and wife. But after ten years their union was becoming a marriage in name only for him and a matter of nervous surveillance for her. If he had cheated on her, Jug may have reacted the way Angela does after Eugene has strayed and been caught. "While she said nothing, agreed that she would forget, Eugene had the consciousness all the while that she wasn't forgetting, that she was secretly reproaching him."[4] Their life together would go on a little longer, until somebody as youthful and compelling as a Carrie Meeber came along.

Meanwhile, Dreiser was a busy man. Not only was he working for Butterick, but on the side he purchased the failing Bohemian Magazine in the spring of 1909. He told Dorothy Dudley that he had hoped to use the magazine as a home for material that he couldn't use in the conventional Delineator, Designer, or New Idea for Women.[5] Dreiser's Bohemian survived for only four monthly issues—from September to December. Mencken contributed "In Defense of Profanity" to the November issue, a piece that although initially humorous in its point that the savage is "utterly incapable of effective swearing" because his vocabulary is so limited and thus unimaginative, ultimately falls flat in its argument. "When he arrives at that pinnacle of anger which just precedes the resort to assassination, he calls his enemy a cow or a rat—a banal, and even pathetic exhibition of will without deed. The annihilating crash of a civilized man's profanity is beyond him." Mencken turns more serious when he points the finger of responsibility for the prohibition of profanity at clergymen and women—"the principal opponents of profanity, like the principal foes of alcohol." He cites the fifth chapter of Zechariah, which is the Biblical basis for hundreds and thousands of "homilies against swearing," saying that the verses condemn perjury ("Him that sweareth falsely by my name"), not profanity.[6] Mencken would be more successful in arguing against the literary philistines.

Dreiser got contributions from other writers, popular in their day but forgotten in ours, novelists such as Willard Huntington Wright and George

Bronson Howard; the list also included George Jean Nathan, the drama critic and future collaborator with Mencken on *The Smart Set*. But as in his *Ev'ry Month* days, Dreiser may have written much of the copy for the *Bohemian* himself. The collections of short pieces (such as Mencken's on swearing) appear under the general heading of "At the Sign of the Lead Pencil," and much of it has Dreiser's touch. He complains under "In the Days of Discovery" about inherited wealth, saying the United States will not have "puffed-up inheritors" on the one hand and "millions of bond slaves on the other." Yet it is also in this issue that Dreiser expresses an admiration for supermen such as he would create in Frank Algernon Cowperwood, who earned their own way by their natural gifts. "It may be," he wrote under the subheading of "The Day of Special Privileges," "that [certain] men are born to rule, that they come stamped with the imprint of hierarchies and powers of which our philosophies know nothing. At any rate, they come. Does any one really, honestly suppose that a man like J. P. Morgan or Thomas F. Ryan [the New York streetcar magnate and financier] can be ruled by the same principles and ideas which govern the carpenter or the cobbler in the back street?"[7] Dreiser's concern was twofold: that the great and gifted individual not be overregulated or stifled by society; and that a society of carpenters and street cobblers not be exploited by the unleashed power of such individuals. In *The Titan* Cowperwood improves public transportation, but he also takes financial advantage of the people through his monopolistic control.

By contrast, the themes of the *Delineator* stayed closer to such domestic subjects as children and motherhood. Editing both the *Bohemian* and the *Delineator* (which was his primary editorial assignment, with other editors supervising *Design* and *New Idea for Women*) may have cemented his life-long pattern of standing up for the poor and exploited while admiring the captains of industry. In his day job he was content to exploit the public sense of home and hearth. One early issue of the *Delineator* under Dreiser's editorship—in the column "Concerning Us All"—assailed the fashionable preference of the teddy bear (the result of President Theodore Roosevelt's popularity) over the doll baby as the principal toy given to young girls. "When your little girl asked for a doll and you gave her a Teddy Bear," wrote the man who thought he was actively depriving his wife of a child, "your action was fraught with a consequence that is only excusable on the ground of your ignorance." Rather than merely replacing one toy with another, "You really were supplanting one ideal with another. . . . Take away a little girl's dolly and you have interfered with the nascent expression of motherhood."[8] Other subjects closer to "home" included a series on "Woman's Suffrage" (promising a number of "differing viewpoints" but suggesting at the outset such Menckenesque headings as "Woman's Broom in Municipal Housekeeping" and "The Funny Side of Woman's Suffrage," "Simplicity in Dress" [but not fashion], and "Bright Sayings of Children").

Dreiser's most successful editorial campaign to keep the *Delineator* in the national spotlight was the Child Rescue program "for the child that needs a home, and the home that needs a child." With more than two million married women without children in the country and orphans filling up its institutions, the *Delineator* undertook, beginning with its November 1907 issue, to bring the two together. It furnished pictures and descriptions of orphans for whom homes were needed, promising to assist in the adoptions. The program stumbled slightly at first when the president of the printing trade union in New York pointed out the hypocrisy of a magazine that would seek to find homes for children while also denying its printers a fair wage and an eight-hour day, thus threatening the homes of their children. "Is it not fairer as well as wiser," the trade union asked, "to protect the home of the child rather than help him find another home after his own has been taken from him?" Otherwise, the campaign was an unmarred public relations coup, with thousands of would-be parents responding to the featured waifs. In the company of James E. West (a prominent citizen and himself an orphan) and other officers of the Home-Finding Society, Dreiser visited the White House on October 10, 1908, to inform President Roosevelt of its activities. He returned to Washington on January 25, 1909, for a conference the president held on the welfare of "the children who are destitute and neglected but not delinquent."[9]

Dreiser was now part of the New York glamour scene he had once eyed without hope, comfortably situated at a salary that would climb to possibly $10,000 a year. Soon after the White House conference, he was included among the dignitaries at a banquet at the Plaza Hotel for the American Civic Alliance (where he was soon made a member and served as secretary). Invited guests included President-elect William Howard Taft, New York governor Charles Evans Hughes, J. P. Morgan, Admiral Dewey, and Andrew Carnegie, whom Dreiser had tried unsuccessfully to interview in the 1890s. Literary members of the Alliance included Hamlin Garland, Julian Hawthorne, and William Dean Howells, another difficult interviewee of Dreiser's in the previous decade, as we have seen.[10] His energetic and worshipful staff at Butterick included William C. Lengel, an attorney from the Midwest who was trying to become an actor in New York. To make ends meet, Lengel became Dreiser's private secretary and then assistant editor. When Lengel first met Dreiser, he thought he looked more like a college professor than the editor of a fashion magazine. His "large, finely modeled head" was covered with "a rather obstinate, unruly growth of hair of the color of wet straw." His eyebrows were bushy, and his cast eye was set lower than the good one. Lengel read *Sister Carrie* soon after being hired. "From that day on," he told Swanberg, "I was Dreiser's slave."[11]

In giving the *Boston Globe* a prospectus of the coming year's features for the *Delineator,* Dreiser added confidentially to its editor Charles W. Taylor, Jr., "Of course the famous Butterick fashions will, as ever, charm the feminine heart. God bless the ladies! My dear boy, what would you and I do without them. . . . Never forget that it is The Delineator that decides how they shall appear to you and me." Working for—indeed leading—"the Fashion Authority of the World" left its impression on the future literary works of Theodore Dreiser. Having access finally in his life to well-appointed homes and apartments, fine restaurants, and the general swirl of the fashion and arts scene, he would better be able to imagine the life of somebody higher on the social scale than Carrie Meeber or Jennie Gerhardt—for example, Jennie's lover Lester Kane, who hails from the upper reaches of society. One of his ablest future editors (and lovers) once commented that Dreiser was naive "in his conception of the rich and poor and the gap between them. That was one of the weaknesses of his novels. His rich people sounded childish."[12] There is more than a little truth to this observation. The background characters in his Cowperwood trilogy seem at least a little wooden in the enjoyment of their creature comforts, but Dreiser also came up against or worked for men like his fictional titan. His boss at Butterick, a corporation that employed 2,500 workers in one building, George W. Wilder, was—though a family man—no doubt as professionally aggressive as the fictional Cowperwood.

Long out of threadbare suits and no longer living in cold water flats, Dreiser—who would become a sporty dresser—now sometimes parted his hair in the middle and wore fashionable suits with stiff collars and bright vests. His spectacles gave him the look of a studious yet worldly man of letters and the city. Yet in most of his photographs of this period, he appears to gaze beyond his comfortable situation to a satisfaction or fulfillment that is ever illusive. As Mencken continued his contributions beyond his ghost-writing of the child care pieces, the interaction between these two men of letters in the world of women and fashion would often rise to higher levels. Discussing Mencken's "The Decay of Churches," Dreiser questioned the statement as to whether individuals ought to countenance a theory "that their fate is determined by the arbitrary moods of the Gods." They shouldn't, he argued, "but how about the fixed rules? And isn't seeking knowledge (scientific) a form of prayer? Aren't scientists & philosophers at bottom truly reverential and don't they wish (pray) ardently for more knowledge?" Mencken, an atheist while Dreiser was never more than an agnostic, replied that scientific investigation differs from prayer because when one studies nature without religious ideology "he is trying to gain means of fighting his own way in the world, but when he prays he confesses that he is unable to do so."[13]

Socially, Dreiser was also getting a little bored—certainly with Jug. In the fall of 1909, he met the seventeen-year-old daughter of Annie Cudlipp, who was an assistant editor at Butterick. Three years earlier Annie had moved from Richmond to Staten Island with her daughter, Thelma, and two sons, Jerome and Olaff. Thelma, the youngest, studied at the Artists League in Manhattan. She and her mother became part of Theo and Jug's social circle, which included Fritz Krog, Robert Amick, and Franklin Booth—all younger than Dreiser and fellow writers or artists. Frequently, this group would gather for weekends or Saturday evenings at the Cudlipp residence on Staten Island, where they would go dancing at the Yacht Club. Krog had worked as an editor for Dreiser on the *Bohemian,* and Mrs. Cudlipp hoped to pair him up with her daughter. But he was apparently no match for the older, surer, and richer Dreiser, whose eminence held the group together. "Theo loved to dance," Thelma remembered more than fifty years later. He also "enjoyed his affluence, his power at Butterick."[14]

By the spring of 1910 Jug had fallen ill with rheumatic fever. She turned over her social role to Annie, who apparently saw no reason to mistrust Dreiser, her boss at Butterick, and so proved to be an inadequate chaperone for her daughter. Thelma, too, claimed that she was unaware of Dreiser's romantic interest in her, though there is evidence to think that this old-age view of her adolescent self was a defense against impropriety. At least one witness has testified that "Thelma was likewise gone on" Dreiser. One night while dancing at the Yacht Club, Dreiser suddenly asked her whether she enjoyed dancing with him as much as with the younger men in their party. Thelma indicated that he must know she preferred him, but she intended the response, she later said, as completely platonic because she had always felt "perfectly safe" with him. At this point, he asked her to call him "Theo," and then he kissed her.[15]

At first, her mother thought nothing of his subsequent doting on Thelma, but as it became apparent that Dreiser was getting ready to leave his wife over her daughter, Annie Cudlipp went into swift action. Either by trickery or with Thelma's cooperation, she dispatched her daughter to Saluda, North Carolina, to be watched over by friends who also intercepted Dreiser's urgent love letters. Meanwhile, she issued Dreiser an ultimatum: either he give up his pursuit of Thelma or she would disclose the whole matter to the Butterick management, where she knew that Erman Ridgway, one of the officers above Dreiser in the company, was having an affair with a young female employee by the name of Ann Watkins. Dreiser refused, and as a result he was asked to resign his position to avoid scandal for the company. Mrs. Cudlipp took a year's leave of absence from her job and sailed for England with Thelma.[16] Dreiser went to pieces, perhaps approaching the emotional instability of 1903.

He had fallen hard in love but was effectively denied his prize by a woman who, it turned out, could be more irrational than he in his worst moments, for Mrs. Cudlipp later committed suicide, as did her two sons. (Thelma eventually married twice, the second time to Charles S. Whitman, who became governor of New York and who apparently abused her both mentally and physically.)[17] By October 1910 Dreiser had separated from Jug, even without benefit of Thelma, his "Flower Face," a term of endearment he had once applied to Jug. From the Park Avenue Hotel on October 3, he told Thelma: "You now see before you a homeless man." He wondered why she hadn't written, but of course his letters never reached her, at least not at the time of the crisis. Her mother had feigned her approval of a marriage if he and Thelma waited one year. When it almost instantly became clear that she had no intention of agreeing to anything of the sort, Dreiser got panicky and suffered several sleepless nights. "I am so worried and harassed I scarcely know which way to turn," he told Thelma in another dead letter. "Sweet you don't seem to understand that it is proximity that is essential to me—nearness to you." A few days later, he wrote her mother that Jug had suggested over the phone that he return to her for ten days ("as a boarder at the apartment") so that she "be allowed, in appearance at least, to desert me." But Mrs. Cudlipp would have none of it, and Dreiser was already reduced, it seemed, to the little boy in Indiana who once fainted when his mother pretended to leave her children. "Oh, Honeypot be kind—be kind to me," he pleaded with Thelma in a letter read only by her mother, "you said once you would once be mother & sister and sweetheart to me. I am a little pleading boy now in need of your love, your mother love." For the second time in his life, Dreiser contemplated suicide.[18]

Dreiser's emotional breakdown, if that's what it was, didn't last long. What saved him this time was his writing, whereas in 1903 it was his writing— or the poor reception of *Sister Carrie*—that had damned him. Four days after prostrating himself before his teenaged beauty, he told Mencken he was considering "several good things." He might have thought of getting another editor's job, but "first-off I should finish my book." Incredibly, he did just that. On February 24, 1911, he told Mencken he had not only finished *Jennie Gerhardt* but was halfway through another, which would become *The "Genius"* in 1915. "I expect to try out this book game," he told his friend, "for about four or five books after which unless I am enjoying a good income from them I will quit." Mencken replied that it was "Bully news!" reminding him of his opinion ("I have often said so in print") that *Sister Carrie* was one of "the best novels this fair land has ever produced." And to encourage Dreiser even further, he told him: "Whether you know it or not, 'Sister Carrie' has begun to soak in."[19] Dreiser evidently believed it. In a most remarkable burst of activity, bottled up for the last decade, he finished a draft of *The "Genius"* that spring and almost immediately began his fourth novel, *The Financier* (1912), which set out to fictionalize the entire career of the traction king Charles T. Yerkes, Jr. Ultimately Dreiser reworked the tale, extending it to *The Titan* (1914) and *The Stoic* (1947) and cutting *The Financier* by one third for its 1927 edition, the one still reprinted today.

By the time he told Mencken he had finished *Jennie*, he had moved—in the late fall of 1910—from his hotel on Park Avenue to 608 Riverside Drive, where he rented a room in the home of Elias and Emma Rosenthal. Elias Rosenthal was an attorney and a patron of the arts; his wife was a writer. Together they embraced the world of art as it reflected the more fashionable and glamorous aspects of New York in such magazines as the *Delineator*. In the receding memory of the assassination of President McKinley in 1901, this art scene also included socialists. It was possibly in the company of the Rosenthals—and that of their attractive twenty-year-old daughter Lillian, a musician—that the newly "single" Dreiser had attended the Anarchists' Ball in Greenwich Village on Christmas 1910. There he met a young writer by the name of Sinclair Lewis. "Red" Lewis and Dreiser were to have a stormy relationship during their literary careers. Whether Dreiser was ever aware of it, the often sarcastic Lewis had already criticized him for editing a ladies' magazine, saying "'Sister Carrie' is not the sort of lady who is readily associated with household recipes and a children's page."[20]

He also met the diva of the event, Emma Goldman, then at the pinnacle of her career as an anarchist, notorious for her personal history as well as her flamboyant lectures against capitalism. Not only had she possibly been associated with McKinley's assassin, Leon Czolgosz; she had also been the lover of Alexander Berkman, who had tried to assassinate Henry Clay Frick following the Homestead strike in Pittsburgh in 1892. Dreiser, as we will recall, had arrived in that city almost in the immediate aftermath of the strike, and his impressions of the spectacle of penniless steel workers locked out of the Homestead plant would remain with him throughout his life. Goldman, just two years older than Dreiser at forty, had also shared another site of social injustice, the penitentiary of Blackwell's Island in the East River. Living opposite the island in a shabby flat in 1901, he and Jug had watched their prospects dwindle with the suppression of *Sister Carrie*. Emma had served a year there in 1904 after being convicted on charges of inciting to riot. Dreiser would have a future with this anarchist as well as with Lewis, who was then only dabbling in the movement. For now, as one witness at the ball reported, Dreiser and Goldman got into a discussion on "the advancement of anarchism." The recent editor-in-chief of Butterick Publications, in the words of one of the guests that evening, "waggled his scrawny forefinger, and looked superiority through his heavy, gold rimmed, scholastic eye glasses; but Emma sent back hot shot—speaking as quietly as the haus frau she seemed to be" as she insisted on the "complete and immediate emancipation" of the people from the old bonds of religion and government.[21]

Indeed, the mindset of Dreiser as he returned to his tale of an impoverished maiden seduced by two princes of capitalism was one of polar opposites in his pity for the poor and his fascination of the rich. The plot of *Jennie Gerhardt* involves two powerful men who philander from their positions of political influence or wealth, a United States senator and the second son of a prosperous carriage manufacturer in Ohio. Dreiser had done the same more or less, or tried to, as the powerful chief editor at Butterick with Thelma, and now he was ready to take that experience back into his book. One might suspect that the youth of Thelma Cudlipp contributed somehow to the songs of innocence in Jennie's character. The scholarly consensus is that Jennie's original character in the novel's earliest known draft (1901) was that of a coarse, self-centered woman, much like her predecessor in *Sister Carrie*. Her character was then softened into the sentimental hero she becomes in the 1911 publication of the novel, supposedly because Dreiser feared that his second novel would otherwise suffer the fate of his first, and so did his editor at Harper's.

Recently, however, Thomas P. Riggio has argued, using the 1901 manuscript, that Jennie's original character lacked the crudeness and egoism of Carrie. Moreover, the males in her life were never as lascivious and as rakish in their original rendering as had been assumed. The theory of the characters' original decadence is based almost solely on a letter Dreiser wrote to George P. Brett of April 16, 1901, saying that he had made "an error in character analysis." Riggio suggests that—in the wake of the disastrous fate of *Sister Carrie*—Dreiser's act of self-censorship had already been achieved in the 1901 manuscript.[22] His comment to Brett, then, may have been a ruse to ensure the nervous editors at Macmillan (who eventually opted not to publish the novel) that *Jennie Gerhardt* would pass muster with the fading but nevertheless still flickering moral "standard of the evening lamp."

The primary model for *Jennie Gerhardt* is Mame, who in her adult years became a loyal and loving "wife" to the dissolute Austin Brennan and a "saint" to her own family members, including Dreiser, who had by now forgotten their quarrel of 1890 following their mother's death. It was she who finally took in their father after his other children had largely abandoned him in Chicago. When John Paul Dreiser died in her home in Rochester in 1900, she was also caring for Sylvia's son, Carl, who was fourteen at the time. In the novel, Old Gerhardt becomes softened in his dogmatic ways and emotionally attached to his granddaughter Vesta much as old man Dreiser apparently related to his bastard grandson.[23] Mame's own illegitimate child was stillborn; the father was the "Colonel Silsby" of *Dawn*, who becomes Senator George Sylvester Brander in *Jennie Gerhardt*.

If fiction can in any way be trusted as biography, we probably have the most faithful picture of the Dreiser clan in *Jennie Gerhardt*. Its author redraws here the close immigrant family circle in which the patriarch speaks to his children in German, and they reply in English. Like John Paul, Old Gerhardt, we are told in the novel, "insisted that the parochial schools were essential, and there, outside of the prayers and precepts of the Evangelical faith, they learned little." "Mrs. Gerhardt was no weakling" even though she wears the same "thin, worn slippers" Dreiser would remember on the feet of his mother in *Dawn*. And like Marcus Romanus, nicknamed "Rome," who often stood in front of the Terre Haute House with a toothpick in his mouth to give the impression he had just eaten in the hotel's restaurant, Jennie's brother Sebastian, nicknamed "Bass," loved to hang about the Columbus House in the neighboring state of Ohio: "He would go downtown evenings . . . and stand around the hotel entrance with his friends, kicking his heels, smoking a two-for-five-cent cigar, preening himself on his stylish appearance and looking after the girls."[24]

Though Dreiser was forty, he was still drawing heavily on his family background. Even his Maumee stories, while based on the city and his reporter's experiences, were mostly rooted in family memories. Dreiser would nearly exhaust this autobiographical source in *The "Genius"* before tapping into more worldly experiences in *The Financier* and *The Titan,* but he would also come back to it in later sketches and novels. Essentially, *Jennie Gerhardt* draws from both his family and his experience in the wider world and consists of two stories. The first concerns the seduction of eighteen-year-old Jennie by the fifty-two-year-old Brander. He dies not long after impregnating her, and her father banishes her from their home as hardly better now than a streetwalker and thus a bad influence on his five other children. With the help of her brother Bass, she moves to another part of town in Columbus and eventually on to Cleveland after giving birth to her daughter, Vesta, who remains with Mrs. Gerhardt in Columbus. This is essentially the story Dreiser had written back in 1901 and returned to briefly in 1904.

The other story brings in with Lester Kane the worldliness Dreiser had absorbed over the last decade, especially as head of the Butterick publications. It is yet another tale of seduction in which Jennie now develops into the altruistic heroine so praised by some of Dreiser's reviewers—who nevertheless complained that the author ought to have found a more dignified subject than that of a kept woman. Kane meets Jennie in Cleveland, where she is a maid in a house in which he is a guest. Eventually, they live together without marrying because Kane cannot or will not marry below his social station. His wealthy father discovers his alliance and stipulates in his will that Lester must either marry the girl or leave her. If he marries her, he will receive $10,000 a year for the rest of his life. If he doesn't but continues to live with her, he will be cut off from his inheritance entirely in three years. There is one other option, which Lester finally chooses, and that is to leave Jennie altogether and claim his full inheritance. He marries an old flame from his station in life, leaving Jennie alone with her daughter. Vesta dies of typhoid at age fourteen (the age Carl was when John Paul Dreiser died in 1900), and Jennie adopts first a girl and then a boy and settles into the role of nurturing, much like Hester Prynne at the conclusion of *The Scarlet Letter*. Like Hawthorne's fallen woman, Jennie is there in the end to comfort her man, the same one who had seduced her and ultimately scorned her.

Unlike *Sister Carrie,* in which the Carrie and Hurstwood stories almost break that novel into two discernible story lines, the dual plots in *Jennie Gerhardt* dovetail into one. In fact, they serve in tandem to retell Hawthorne's classic tale of "human frailty and sorrow." As the mother of Vesta, Jennie is first "married" to the Senator, a much older man, like Hester's Roger Chillingworth, who is dead to her in the sense of any true emotional ties. She then finds a younger man in Lester. Although Jennie already possesses a child, when the reader first meets Dimmesdale at the beginning of *The Scarlet Letter,* Hester is pregnant with his child. Like Hester with Dimmesdale, Jennie ultimately comes to realize that she can never have her lover and so dedicates herself to relieving the misery of others. And there are other, stricter parallels. Both Hester and Jennie live in isolation from society with daughters who become a symbol of both their fall and their rise. They are both despoiled by upstanding citizens: Dimmesdale is the minister his Puritan congregation looks up to for moral leadership, and Brander is a federal legislator entrusted with the people's vote. Both mothers live ultimately for their daughters in order that their offspring not suffer for their sexual sins. And Pearl and Vesta are also subtle but constant reminders of the sins of passion that brought them into existence. One critic who has observed many of these parallels also insists that the similarity of the two novels ends here, but so does the essence of *Jennie Gerhardt*.[25] What Dreiser seems to have otherwise added were merely the social frills from the world of the *Delineator* (the sketch of Jennie in the frontispiece of the first edition resembles in dress and demeanor the *Delineator*'s model of the all-around wholesome but also vulnerable female) and the cynical view of high society from one of its own that Dreiser may have taken from Edith Wharton's *The House of Mirth* (1905). He credited this book in his "Literary Apprenticeship" as an influence on him as he composed *Jennie Gerhardt*. Two years later he pronounced Wharton's masterpiece "the greatest novel I ever read by an American woman."[26]

Dreiser essentially wrote three novels in 1911. He revised and finished *Jennie Gerhardt*. He wrote a complete draft of *The "Genius"* (the original title was without the quotation marks). And he wrote more than half of *The Financier* that fall before making his first European sojourn in November 1911. *Jennie* contained the seeds of the other two novels as surely as *Sister Carrie* had launched the main idea in its successor. For we have in Dreiser's first two novels the dramas of "The Flesh & the Spirit" (the title for *Sister Carrie* that the Doubleday editors preferred). Carrie is ready to give herself almost without thinking, whereas Jennie sacrifices her body, in the words of Richard Lehan, "for those she loves—for something beyond her—in a way that would seem foolish to Carrie." Dreiser continued the autobiographical impulse in *The "Genius"* and moved in *The Financier* beyond his family saga and his own young manhood and first marriage to the world of money. Dreiser's first financier is not Frank Cowperwood, however, but Robert Kane of *Jennie Gerhardt,* Lester's older brother, who favors monopolies. With Lester out of the company, Robert makes himself president and proceeds with Cowperwood-like efficiency and ruthlessness: "Armed with the voting power of the entire stock of the company, and therefore with the privilege of hypothecating its securities, he laid before several of his intimate friends in the financial world his scheme of uniting the principal carriage companies and controlling the trade."[27] This, of course, is not the business novel of William Dean Howells, whose Silas Lapham ultimately conspires against himself to save his self-dignity. Dreiser's businessman here is cold-hearted, scheming, and unrepentant.

Even before he finished *Jennie,* he searched for a publisher, first at Macmillan and then at Harper's, where Ripley Hitchcock—famous in the trade for editing such well-known authors as Woodrow Wilson, Joel Chandler Harris, and Rudyard Kipling—eventually persuaded that firm to publish *Jennie* as long as Dreiser agreed to a thorough in-house editing of the manuscript. Hitchcock had also handled Crane's *The Red Badge of Courage* and *Maggie,* where he had been responsible for expurgations that may have altered or softened the author's naturalistic views. Dreiser didn't know this at the time, or ever, but he probably had no choice but to agree to this form of self-censorship. Even though his *Carrie* had been revived, the reputation it gave him was still largely limited to the literary world of fellow writers and editors. He could boast of no box office success and no doubt felt fortunate indeed to have a house such as Harper's willing to publish him. Hitchcock and his staff reduced the manuscript by approximately sixteen thousand words.

One critic argues that the editing transformed it from "a blunt, carefully documented piece of social analysis to a love story merely set against a social background." This may be more than a slight overstatement, but the book was certainly sanitized of its offensive parts along with its typical Dreiserian redundancies. Dreiser was always too blunt for his era, even as a realist, and he always needed an editor. When Lester, for example, debates whether to remain with Jennie once he finds out about Vesta, Dreiser wrote and Hitchcock and company struck: "He took his customary way [with] her there at the apartment the same evening that he thought these things out." In other cases, of course, only verbosity was sacrificed.[28] When Mencken saw the cuts, he told Dreiser that they irritated him at first but on second thought was inclined to the idea that not much damage had been done to the story. More candidly, he thought Dreiser probably required the larger canvas. "The chief virtue of Dreiser" he told Harry Leon Wilson, "is his skill at piling up detail. The story he tells, reduced to a mere story, is nothing." Actually, Mencken read the manuscript twice, both before and after the editing at Harper's, and suggested no substantive changes, but the novel had also been read by others before going to Harper's. Both Fremont Rider, who had worked with Dreiser at B. W. Dodge Company as well as at Butterick, and Lillian Rosenthal, who had already become Dreiser's occasional lover, recommended that he change the original happy ending, in which Jennie and Lester marry. He even showed the completed manuscript to Jug, who as she had done with *Sister Carrie,* tried to clean up the diction and joined the other editors in recommending the excision of suggestive passages.[29]

The book appeared that fall to generally favorable reviews. The climate for realistic literature had improved since the appearance of *Sister Carrie.* Reviewers had not forgotten that novel, of course, but now they expected Dreiser to tell the unalloyed truth and thought it probably ought to be told. What saved it from the old denunciation was that in spite of her sins, Jennie is—unlike Carrie—wholly unselfish. Indeed, some critics thought she was "really too unselfish to be virtuous."[30] Edward Markham wrote in the *New York American* of October 25, 1911, that Jennie "never becomes wholly degraded in spirit" but rather "develops into a forgiving and ministering woman." Yet the reviewer could not let pass the obligation Jennie owed to her own sense of womanhood. "Is a woman ever justified in smirching her womanhood, in staining her virtue, in order to help her relatives—even to save them from starvation?" he asked. The answer was a resounding and ironclad "No." It was the old "love the sinner, hate the sin" insistence that before Freud prevailed in even the most liberal of the post-Victorian critics. For the *Detroit Free Press* of November 4, the story probably should not have been told because it tells a tale "repugnant to all our ideals and standards." But even this reviewer could not condemn Jennie as "unmoral" for acting as she does in the face of so much adversity. The *New York Times* of November 19 generally agreed that Dreiser's novel presented a "naked picture" of life, "but no one can for a moment question the real life about us is more naked than the story."

Dreiser made an important concession in this story that would in one way reappear in *An American Tragedy*. He punishes his protagonist for succumbing to the forces of heredity and environment. Carrie may be confused, but she is not left so abandoned by the world as Jennie. Eugene Witla in *The "Genius"* will also survive by making a few concessions in the end, and Frank Cowperwood will not be soundly defeated until *The Stoic*, which Dreiser never completely finished himself. For this reason, the *New York Daily Tribune* of October 21 thought in its review of *Jennie* that *Sister Carrie* "remains to this day one of the most powerful productions of uncompromising realism in American literature." Hurstwood, of course, is punished in the novel, but it is mere chance that he goes downward while Carrie rises. This is the point: life to Dreiser was mostly if not exclusively (and it is this lingering doubt that makes him so profound) a matter of blind chance—with morality or unselfishness ultimately having nothing to do with it. Therefore, the *Tribune* reviewer felt *Jennie* was not as compelling as *Sister Carrie*.

None of the contemporary reviewers of *Jennie* saw the parallel with *The Scarlet Letter*, but they found literary sources in Hardy's *Tess of the D'Urbervilles*, Flaubert's *Madame Bovary*, Zola's *Nana*, George Moore's *Esther Waters*, and Tolstoy's *Anna Karenina*. Actually, Mencken mentioned Hawthorne's novel in his review for *The Smart Set*, but only for its similarly high achievement, not for any similarity of plot. He hailed *Jennie Gerhardt* as "the best American novel I have ever read, with the lonesome but Himalayan exception of 'Huckleberry Finn.'" He placed the book ahead of not only Hawthorne's novel but Howells's *The Rise of Silas Lapham*, James's *What Maisie Knew* ("to drag an exile unwillingly home"), Norris's *McTeague*, and Wharton's *The House of Mirth*, among others. He placed it ahead of *Sister Carrie* as well, which he faulted for its two almost disparate plots. "In the midst of the story of Carrie, Mr. Dreiser paused to tell the story of

Hurstwood—an astonishingly vivid and tragic story, true enough, but still one that broke the back of the other. In 'Jennie Gerhardt' he falls into no such overelaboration of episode." The fact that Mencken preferred *Jennie Gerhardt*, which lacks the compelling story of *Sister Carrie*, suggests his myopia in fully appreciating Dreiser's genius—probably equaled only by Crane in America—in dramatizing such a brutal picture of inhumanity that is all too human.

We have in this review the seeds of future discontent between these by then fast friends and advocates of a truly veristic American literature. For in his preference for *Jennie Gerhardt*, Mencken was objecting to more than the two plots in *Sister Carrie*. This son of middle-class parents in the largely German Baltimore was a literary progressive but also a social conservative who extolled Jennie's strength of character, which Carrie entirely lacks. Jennie's story, he wrote in *The Smart Set*, "loses nothing in validity by the fact that life is meaningless, a tragedy without a moral, a joke without a point." *Jennie* was not a moral tale—it had no more moral than a string quartet or the first book of Euclid, he said—but in fact this naturalistic novel does have a moral or at least the concession that good exists in places in the universe, regardless of whether it is triumphant.[31] As we shall see, Dreiser was to find this glimmer of goodness in the worst scenarios—with his play *The Hand of the Potter* (1916), for example, which Mencken would roundly condemn.

Mencken also reviewed the novel in the *Baltimore Evening Sun* of November 27 and the *Los Angeles Times* of December 10. At the end of November, *Jennie Gerhardt* had sold almost 5,000 copies; by the end of the year, 7,712. This was certainly a marvelous contrast to the initial figures for *Sister Carrie*, yet both Dreiser and Harper's were somewhat disappointed, the latter even fearing that Dreiser's reputation from his first novel was dampening the sales of the next. For Dreiser the disappointment was partly financial; he had hoped to travel to London to continue his research on the Yerkes saga, but he felt it was beyond his means. Even though he had written almost three books in the last year, the idea of returning to the world of editing was never far from his mind. It was at this time that a monocled English publisher named Grant Richards entered his life.

———

Richards, a sophisticated Edwardian at home in the best salons and hotels of Europe, had in 1901 made the first of his annual visits to the United States in search of American manuscripts to publish in England. He was particularly enamored of the novels of Frank Norris, especially after the publication of *McTeague,* to which Richards had secured the English rights. At a luncheon that spring, he and Norris discussed the future arrangement of his other Doubleday books in England, when Norris suddenly announced that he could tell Richards about "an author worth two of me."³² He was referring, according to Richards, to Dreiser and the difficulty he was having with Doubleday, who had not yet given in to the idea of publishing *Sister Carrie.* That would place their meeting in 1900 instead of 1901, so there is some reason to doubt Richards's complete accuracy in his characterization of Dreiser and their affairs. Richards was also a friend of Doubleday and his wife, but in his memoirs he repeated the Dreiser assertion that Neltje Doubleday had been instrumental in the Doubleday suppression of *Sister Carrie.* It was at this time that Richards first read the novel, but he did not make an offer on it because Heinemann was already committed to its truncated version.

Richards also read the first twenty chapters of *Jennie Gerhardt* two years after first meeting Dreiser in 1906 (not 1911 as it has been stated in earlier biographies).³³ Not long after that novel finally appeared in 1911, the two men met once again. Informed that Richards would reach New York in early November, Dreiser left an inscribed copy of *Jennie Gerhardt* at his hotel shortly before he arrived. In a note giving his address and telephone number so that they might breakfast following his arrival, Dreiser wrote: "I hope if you are interviewed you will say something definite about me and Jennie. It seems almost impossible to make my fellow Americans understand that I am alive." When the two met the following day, Richards, in spite of Dreiser's sour note, took it for granted that the author of the new book with such positive reviews ought to be in the best of spirits. Yet even though the book was being reviewed fairly well, Dreiser did not feel it was going to bring him a great deal of money—or the fame he craved and had deserved since 1900. He was also balked in completing *The Financier,* promised to but not yet contracted by Harper's, because he could not afford to follow the career of Yerkes to Europe where it had come to an end with the mogul's death in 1905.³⁴

Besides a genuine admiration of his talent and a sincere desire to encourage its continued development, Richards was possessed of the not-so-concealed motive of getting *The Financier* away from Harper's and into the hands of the Century Company, where he was informally connected. Accordingly, he first pulled Dreiser out of his funk and persuaded him to insist on an advance from Harper's for *The Financier*—on the not entirely remote chance that the firm might balk and lose it to Century. But after seeing the first thirty-nine chapters of *The Financier,* Harper's (which was also reissuing a thousand copies of *Sister Carrie*) gave Dreiser a $2,000 advance as well as another $500 against future royalties on *Jennie Gerhardt.* This by itself was probably enough to bankroll Dreiser's European visit, but Richards also arranged for Century to put up $1,500 for three travel articles for its magazine and an option on a possible book on his impressions of Europe, which would become *A Traveler at Forty* in 1913.[35]

"Things are moving around here in a peculiar way," Dreiser told Mencken on November 11. "I may go to Europe on the 22nd of the month for the Century Company—London, Paris, Rome & The Riviera!" Confidentially, he acknowledged that the company would like to get his future books. Richards had done his job well, as Dreiser seemed a new man almost overnight, though the ups and downs of his shifting moods were nothing new. The smooth-talking Englishman even suggested Dreiser had a good chance for the next Nobel Prize in literature, but no American was to win this prize for many years. (Dreiser's only sense of consolation in this regard may have been that it was won in 1912 by a German, Gerhart Hauptmann.) Mencken merely ignored Richards's wild suggestion about Dreiser's winning the prize when he congratulated his friend on the trip and said he hoped to be in London in the spring himself.[36]

The Century Company held a send-off party for Dreiser, and he and Richards sailed for England on the *Mauretania* on November 22, 1911. Dreiser would remain in Europe until the following April and visit not only England, but France, Italy, Switzerland, and Germany. And he would return with plenty of copy for the three *Century Magazine* articles as well as the book. Indeed, he kept a diary while abroad and also wrote part of the 103 chapters of the draft version of *A Traveler at Forty;* these were reduced to 53 for publication. Much of the excised material contained "woman stuff," as Dreiser told Mencken, but the manuscript was also simply too long and redundant in its Dreiserian way of piling fact upon fact. The Century editors (strongly encouraged by Richards, who sought to protect his privacy) objected "like hell" to his accounts of interviews or outright trysts with prostitutes. They also felt there was in general too much attention paid not only to the seamy side of European life but its rampant poverty among the laboring classes. Furthermore, the majority of the poverty was found in England, where Dreiser exhibited symptoms of his later Anglophobia. In one observation admitted to the printed chapters, Dreiser writes that he "never saw such sickly, shabby, run-down-at-the-heels, decayed figures in all my life."[37]

Dreiser began the original *Traveler* with a description of his current residence at 3609 Broadway, near the new 145th Street subway station ("six pretty rooms and a bath"), but *Century* editors wisely cut everything to the sentence, "I have just turned forty." It probably seemed unlikely that Dreiser would have something new to say about Europe since so many Americans before him had made the Grand Tour; he was, however, no gentleman in that nineteenth-century sense but more like the irreverent Mark Twain in *The Innocents Abroad* (1869). This was particularly true with England, whose inhabitants he noted "have this executive or managerial gift. . . . They go about colonizing so efficiently, industriously." And he claimed a certain superiority about America's servant class. British servants didn't "look at one so brutally and critically as does the American menial," who seems to say with his eyes that he is his master's equal or better. "The American clerk," Dreiser wrote a little later in his book, "always looks his possibilities—his problematic future; the English clerk looks as if he were to be one indefinitely."[38]

Also unlike most travel book writers, Dreiser recounts the tale of his meeting with a prostitute in Piccadilly Square not long after his arrival in London. The published version, "Lilly: A Girl of the Streets" is chapter 13 of *A Traveler at Forty,* condensed and somewhat expurgated from what was originally two chapters on the subject. Interestingly, when Mencken read Dreiser's "travel book," he correctly thought that parts of it represented "the best writing you have done since 'Jennie Gerhardt,'" but he also detected "a note of reticence," in which Dreiser began "affairs which come to nothing." In this "affair" Dreiser meets two women, pays off one with a shilling to get rid of her, and takes the other, a Welsh woman of about nineteen (and pregnant, as she later reveals), to a run-down building with private rooms divided by cheap partitions. He is firm, almost bossy, with her—expressing his disbelief in her story about having a middle-class family background and branding her tale about what happens to patrons who pay too little as "one of the oldest stories of the trade." He does not engage her services but agrees to pay her if she accompanies him to a restaurant where he plies her with questions about her life on the streets. Afterwards, he buys her a box of candy, pays her three pounds, and returns her to her "shabby room." In an echo of Whitman's "To a Common Prostitute," Dreiser writes, "I had tried to make her feel that I admired her a little and that I was sorry for her a little."[39]

In the completely excised eighty-fourth and eighty-fifth chapters, the narrator becomes sexually involved with another prostitute. In Berlin, on March 26, 1912, he met Hanscha Jower, "large, soft, innocent, mild eye— like one of Rubens' women." About thirty, she reminded him of "an un-Americanized Jennie Gerhardt." In Germany in those days the street woman was not allowed to approach a man with the proposition of her body. Yet "Any man may accost any unaccompanied woman," we are told in the unpublished pages of *A Traveler at Forty.* "If she does not want him she does not speak." Dreiser, the *flaneur,* watches Hanscha go down the street and is finally convinced of her profession in the way she circles back around another segment of the Alexander Platz. This leads to the inevitable. "We undress," he writes in his diary, "and I find her charmingly formed, quite the most charming I have seen for some time." He finds her nature aglow with a "keen but simple understanding of the order of things." In his manuscript, he described Hanscha as a "girl or woman [of] the type that I think I understand best of all: a vague, wondering soul that does not understand life at all"—that is, an earth mother who intuits her way through life the way Sarah Dreiser had navigated her way and that of her three youngest children. Unlike Lilly, "you would not have assumed for a moment that [Hanscha] was a street-girl—as distinctly she was not at heart."[40]

Afterward he hears the story of her family life and background—"her German story"—the familiar one he had already put into *Jennie.* "Her father was a carpenter and her mother—well, just a mother." She had started to learn the trade of weaving, as Dreiser's older sisters had at one point or another during their time with their father in Terre Haute. The pay was terrible, though that probably wouldn't have made any difference. "But there was a young blood in town," Dreiser writes in chapter 85 of his typescript, "who fell in love with her, or with whom she fell in love, and who over-persuaded her." Like Sylvia, Hanscha had left her bastard child in the care of her mother and tried working in the mills. The work was dirty. Occasionally, she sold her body for extra cash and eventually became a prostitute.[41] "It is so easy for those born in satisfactory circumstances to moralize," Dreiser concludes. This woman and her circumstance touched him to the core of his deeply sympathetic reaction to life. As a result, the story of Hanscha Jower belongs in the published canon of Theodore Dreiser. For it has the canvas that the "Lilly: A Girl of the Streets" has not—room enough for Dreiser to engage almost self-consciously his inborn empathy with those central characters who people his best work. Not the outside moralistic observer the Century editors made him in the "Lilly" episode, here Dreiser is freely enamored of both the woman's flesh and spirit.

While still in England, Dreiser spent three weeks at Richards's country home at Cookham Dean, Berkshire, and afterwards at the Capitol Hotel in London. He visited Oxford, Canterbury, and other tourist sites. At Oxford he learned from "Barfleur" (Grant's pseudonym in *A Traveler at Forty*) where Walter Pater and Oscar Wilde had lived. (He later met Wilde's literary executor in Rome.) At Oxford the Indiana college dropout hadn't changed his opinion of the knights of the academy. "Here as elsewhere," he wrote in the printed book, "I learned that professors were often cads and pedants— greedy, jealous, narrow, academic." He also toured the smoky environs of London's East End and was glad for the change of countries by January 11, when he crossed the Channel at Dover. He was greeted, he wrote of his arrival in Calais, with "a line of sparkling French *facteurs* looking down on the boat from the platform above—presto! England was gone. Gone all the solemnity and the politeness of the porters who had brought our luggage aboard, gone the quiet civility of ship officers and train-men, gone the solid doughlike quiescence of the whole English race." Finding the French so animated and colorful after the "gray misty pathos of English life," Dreiser felt as if he had suddenly returned to America.[42]

On their way to Paris, he and Richards stopped in Amiens, whose august cathedral drew from the ex-Catholic the astonishment "that the faith of man had ever reared so lovely a thing." In the City of Light, Dreiser found the debonair Richards, who was currently between wives, as at home in the French cafés as he was in English drawing rooms. In the Café de Paris, "Barfleur was in fine feather and the ladies radiated a charm and a flavor which immediately attracted attention." A few days later Richards had to return to London for two weeks, and Drieser plunged into the treasures of Paris himself, seeing the Musée de Cluny and the Louvre, and taking a car out to Père Lachaise—"that wonderful world of the celebrated dead."[43] But as he pondered the lives and deaths of its famous inhabitants—including his cherished Balzac—he also fretted over his financial situation. Sales of *Jennie* continued to climb, but at a slower pace. He told Richards, who by December had made clear his hopes of publishing all future works by Dreiser, "I am not going to be a best seller or even a half seller. . . . Critical approval won't make a sale & critical indifference won't hinder one. I haven't the drag on the public—that's all."[44]

Upon Richards's return to Paris, the two men traveled to the Riviera and Monte Carlo, where they were joined by Sir Hugh Lane, a Dublin art collector whom Dreiser watched gamble away sums that made his own meager but nevertheless painful losses at the gaming tables seem almost insignificant. After a visit to Nice with Richards and Lane, he and Richards went on to Italy, seeing on the way to Rome that most popular of sites for American tourists—the Leaning Tower of Pisa. Later on Dreiser remarked that, so far as he could tell, the principal idea of visiting Europe for most Americans was to say that they had been abroad. He stayed two weeks at the Grand Continental Hotel and again took in the usual tourist sights himself. He found St. Peter's architecturally overwhelming but not artistically beautiful. One of the last things he did was to participate in a papal audience. His father, of course, had subscribed to papal infallibility, and here at least the son wasn't altogether so brazen in his disbelief and disapproval of the Church as he had been on other occasions and would be again. Naturally, he condemned "the true history" of the Church and even joked quietly with other members of the audience while waiting for the appearance of Pope Pius X. Yet when that particular Holy Father, whose opposition to both ecumenism and modernism earned him an early sainthood, "scarcely looked" at him, Dreiser seemed to feel—if ever so fleetingly—a sense of his own "critical unworthiness."[45]

In Florence he visited the Uffizi, the Pitti, and the Belle Arti and walked along the Arno. "I should always think of the Arno," he wrote, "as it looked this evening. . . . I should always see the children playing on the green banks, quite as I used to play on the Wabash and the Tippecanoe." He visited, among other Italian cities, Milan, Venice, and Perugia before passing through Switzerland to the Fatherland. Dreiser reached Germany by March 12, and shortly—after a mistaken detour to Mayence—arrived at his father's birthplace in Mayen. Mayen was a still partially walled city of eight thousand inhabitants, "somewhere between the Moselle and the Rhine at Coblenz"— and still almost totally Catholic, having been one of the earliest German towns to convert to Catholicism in the fourteenth century. He wrote Mencken on March 25, "I struck my father's birth place yesterday and found real German beer to say nothing of a quaint old village which is 900 years old." The only relatives he found, however, were in "the local graveyard," which had actually been turned into the city park. Some of the Stations of the Cross remained along the central pathway, and there were also a few old gravestones. One of the relations he found among them, to his "real shock," was Theodore Dreiser (1820–1882). "I think," he wrote in *A Traveler at Forty,* "as clear a notion as I ever had of how my grave will look after I am gone and how utterly unimportant both life and death are, anyhow, came to me." He also located the grave of John Dreiser, one of his father's twenty-one siblings by three wives.[46]

After visiting the other, newer cemetery in search of antecedents, he wandered into the town to find it rudely updated by "another type of life." The medieval city had largely given way to such modern artifacts as a Singer Sewing Machine business, a bookstore featuring only relatively new books and current titles, a newspaper office, and a movie theater. Aside from the town castle built into the mammoth city wall, which he visited, not that much of the past, not even a Dreiser grave with a birth date before 1800, remained. After spending the night in a hotel just outside the gates of the old city, he left Mayen "with a sorrowful backward glance." He had found no living Dreisers, only his ancestral home. But he had found St. Clement's, the church his father had attended as a boy, along with the house of the priest and possibly the "identical cherry tree" under which young John Paul Dreiser had eaten the forbidden fruit and been subsequently exposed by his stepmother. According to local legend, the church's twisted steeple (a construction flaw replicated when Mayen was rebuilt following World War II) had been the work of the devil himself, who had agreed to finance the construction of the church because he thought the townspeople were building a pub. When he discovered it was to be a church, he twisted the tiled bell tower.[47]

The following day he was in Berlin, where he would met Hanscha Jower. He told Richards that he was again becoming anxious to return to the States. Earlier, he had threatened to go home, saying, "No more Europe on the worry basis for me."[48] Although Richards had helped plan the finances for his trip in which he could cash letters of credit at hotels along the way, Dreiser ultimately thought Richards had gotten him over his head financially. He went on to Amsterdam and then to Paris, where "Barfleur" gently chided him for not trusting his future earning power in his books. It was not just a question of running out of money before he got home, however, but of not having much left of the funds advanced by both Century and Harper's on which to live once there. He passed up a planned walking tour of the South of England to take a boat home from Dover in mid-April.

Dreiser boarded the *Kroonland,* sailing under the American flag, on April 13, but not before seriously flirting with the idea of taking the *Titanic,* one of the faster "smart" boats which had left on its first and fated voyage on April 9. Later, he told his friend Floyd Dell, "I missed the Titanic by two days thank heaven & I was so anxious beforehand to see how it would be on a new boat like that." But since money was a concern, Richards suggested the slower boat.[49] On April 16, the *Kroonland* learned by wireless that the *Titanic* had hit an iceberg off the coast of Newfoundland, and almost two-thirds of the 2,800 passengers were reported to have drowned. Actually, there were only slightly more than 2,200 onboard, out of which 1,513 perished, but that fact certainly wouldn't have eased the terror of those currently at sea on other vessels and possibly headed over the same sea route. Indeed, the reported dead, and even the actual count, far exceeded the *Kroonland*'s total passenger capacity of 1,162.

The captain ordered that the news be kept secret until the ship reached New York, but one of the gentlemen aboard, Herr Salz, "busy about everything and everybody," Dreiser recorded in his typescript, "had gleaned it as a sea secret from the wireless man" by providing him cigars. Dreiser was seated with several other passengers in the card and smoking room as Salz entered the compartment, "very mysterious-looking." When he insisted that the men among them come out on deck so that the ladies could not hear him, one joked that "perhaps Taft had been killed, or the Standard Oil Company has failed." The "whole, healthy, debonair manner" of the group changed instantly upon receiving the news. The overtaking gloom thickened further when one noted that their ship had another week left on the same deadly seas. "The terror of the sea," Dreiser recalled, "had come swiftly and directly home to all. I am satisfied that there was not a man of all the company who heard but felt a strange sinking sensation as he thought of the endless wastes of the sea outside—its depths, the terror of drowning in the dark and cold." As he went to his berth thinking of the horror of it all, he felt a great rage "in my heart against the fortuity of life." The women on board eventually heard the news but pretended not to know. Previously gregarious passengers became suddenly reserved, and others seemed almost manic in making repeated reference to the catastrophe. "The philosophers of the company," he wrote, "were unanimously agreed that as the *Titanic* had suffered this great disaster through carelessness on the part of her officers, no doubt our own chances of safely reaching shore were thereby enhanced."[50]

It wasn't until they reached Sandy Hook at the entrance of New York's harbor that they finally heard the full story from the boarding pilot, his pockets bulging with newspaper reports of the tragedy. Many passengers crowded into the smoking room for the last time to devour the news, Dreiser recalled. "Some broke down and cried. Others clenched their fists and swore over the vivid and painful pen pictures by eyewitnesses and survivors. For a while we all forgot we were nearly home." But as the ship docked, the fast friendships bound together on "the great deep" dissolved back into the interests of "individuals of widely separated communities and interests," as the tragedy of the *Titanic* was largely forgotten by that generation. Dreiser, too, looked ahead to his prospects and wondered whether he would ever make a decent living as a realistic writer in a land so focused on make-believe. Since its only reality, he thought, was its cult and culture of money, he may have felt reassured that he was now finishing a book to be called *The Financier.* As his ship entered the harbor, he saw the mammoth buildings of the city. "They were just finishing the upper framework of the Woolworth Building," he recalled, "that first cathedral of the American religion of business."[51]

TEN

Life after the Titanic

Mr. Dreiser calls on no exterior glamour for aid;
the Fact is glorious enough for him.

INDEPENDENT, MARCH 27, 1913

THE *TITANIC* DISASTER TOOK THE LIVES of several American millionaires, including the namesake for John Jacob Astor, worth $150 million according to the initial Associated Press report of April 16, 1912. Another millionaire with a now famous name to go down into history this way was Benjamin Guggenheim, worth $95 million. Just a year earlier he had abandoned his wife and children for a mistress in Paris and was on his way back to America to pay them a visit. The report also listed (erroneously) Colonel Washington Roebling of Brooklyn Bridge fame, allegedly worth only $25 million, but the engineer who had perfected the suspension bridge lived until 1926. Theodore Dreiser, practically broke after his European trip cost more than Grant Richards had promised it would, might well have been among the drowned if he hadn't been so short of funds. He returned on the *Kroonland,* much inferior in comfort and status to either the *Titanic* or the *Mauretania,* which had taken him abroad. To some critics in America, had they known how close he came to taking the wrong boat, it might have been better if he had perished on the *Titanic* than to continue to pollute American literature with stories about fallen women. But Dreiser was finished with women as principals in his fiction, if not with uncompromising realism. Indeed, he was largely finished with autobiography as fiction after The *"Genius,"* whose publication was to wait its turn in the rush of the novelist's midlife renewal of his literary energy. He was now prepared to write novels that would culminate the muckraking effort of the last decade to expose the shame of American business, while also celebrating one of its more outspoken conspirators.

That June, five months before the appearance of *The Financier,* he told Montrose J. Moses of the *New York Times* that *Jennie Gerhardt* was "an accomplishment of the past." He vowed never again to write "another book like it," and he never did. He was now promoting *The Financier,* the novel he had finished immediately upon his return from Europe, as a major departure from his earlier works. He looked, Moses recorded, "very much like the Man from Home. . . . Seated in a rocking chair, which moved back and forth whenever we were traveling fastest, he now and then emphasized a point with his goldrimmed glasses, in between whiles folding his handkerchief four times in length and then rolling it into a tight ball to clinch an argument." "Maybe I sound disloyal," he told Moses, "but Jenny's [*sic*] temperament does not appeal to me any longer." As he told a reporter from the *New York Evening Post* in a 1911 interview, one reason he had written "chiefly about women" in the past, was that woman "symbolizes the essentially artistic character of the universe more than man does. . . . But, of the two, man symbolizes power." In his new novel, which was then still to be dubbed by his publishers as merely "Part 1" of *The Financier* with Parts 2 and 3 to appear at six-month intervals, he said that "the note of the plot will come from the man, and [a] man shall be the centre of the next three or four novels." He also suggested that another reason he could no longer write about a woman after *Jennie* was possibly "because I know more about women now."[1]

After the failure of his relationships with Jug and Thelma, and perhaps after his experience with some of the women he had met in Europe, he may have lost his faith in the idea of Jennie's innocence, if not of Carrie's durability. It is even possible that Jennie was at least in part Dreiser's ploy to succeed in the marketplace after the devastation of *Sister Carrie* and to take advantage of the feminist movement that was increasingly apparent during the first decade of the twentieth century. Whatever the case, his representation and perhaps his understanding of women shifted. In *The "Genius,"* Dreiser deconstructed the utility of the former Sara White's virtues in the character of Angela Blue. From now on, women would become more or less a commodity to him, even as they remained a lifelong emotional necessity. The women in the life of Frank Algernon Cowperwood of *The Financier,* like those of his real-life model, Charles Tyson Yerkes, Jr., swirl around him like leaves in a storm. While most of Cowperwood's financial activities in the first volume were taken directly from the subject's biographical record, Dreiser felt freer to imagine the financier's personal and sexual adventures. Another way of putting it is that Dreiser lived vicariously through his buccaneering businessman, and out of his immersion in this sexual overreacher's life, both real and as imagined in *The Titan*, evolved his own lifetime pattern as the serial lover of women.

By the time he returned from Europe, he had taken up with Anna P. Tatum, a pertly articulate twenty-nine-year-old Wellesley graduate from Fallsington, Pennsylvania, and the first of a number of mistresses with typing skills. Like several of her successors, she seems to have found Dreiser homely but irresistible because of his compelling literary gifts and his Ames-like way of talking to women. Shortly before his departure for Europe, she had written out of the blue to tell him, almost breathlessly, how deeply "The Mighty Burke" had stirred her. Appearing in *McClure's* of May 1911, the story is one of Dreiser's first literary uses of his 1903 experiences as "an amateur laborer." But her major reason for writing, she continued, was to praise *Jennie*, which she found "magnificently constructed—like a great piece of music."[2] In praising his work, however, she had also come to quarrel with it. This was another trait or requirement of the Dreiser women: generally, they had to be more than physically attractive. They had to be intellectuals, readers of literature, and more often than not they were frustrated or would-be writers as well.

Anna, who was bisexual, thought that Dreiser depicted men better than women. "I do not believe there are any real Jennie Gerhardts," she told him. "Jennie is, I think, your idealization." Annoyed, he suggested that she send future criticism to his publisher. But Anna wasn't to be put off, and before long she had read *Sister Carrie*, whose heroine she considered "a little beast." Yet unlike Jennie, Carrie was true. When Dreiser conceded he was better at characterizing a "worldly type of women," she promptly agreed because she thought "at bottom you don't *like* women. You like men infinitely better and understand them 75 percent better." Busy as he was at the time in the creation of a male character whose personality dominates everyone around him, Dreiser no doubt concurred. Anna told him of another man, her father, whose Quakerism and religious ways had not shielded him from normal human suffering and ultimately domestic tragedy. The story, which eventually became the basis for *The Bulwark* (not published until 1947), would haunt Dreiser the rest of his days as he approached this elusive project from shifting philosophical points of view. Anna also read the manuscript version of *The "Genius"* and pronounced it "the most intimate searching and impressive portrayal of an unhappy sex relation that I am aware of in any literature."[3] There is no evidence that Anna assisted him with *The Financier,* although she may have come in on the tail end of the writing—or editing—process. She definitely helped him with *The Titan* as she and Dreiser lived together off and on from the time of his return from Europe until he went to Chicago for two months in early 1913.[4]

By the spring of 1912, Harper's had sold almost thirteen thousand copies of *Jennie Gerhardt,* along with over a thousand copies of their reissued *Sister Carrie.* The sales were a little disappointing to Dreiser and may have been more so to his publishers. Harper's, fearing that publishing three books under one title ("The Financier") was a potential marketing nightmare, decided to give each volume its own name and not to formally advertise the series as a trilogy. There was also the challenge of the first volume's excessive length. At the end of the summer, Dreiser asked for Mencken's literary judgment, describing himself as "just crawling out from under 250 galleys of the Financier." Because he ultimately came to the conclusion that Dreiser's main gift was the piling up of detail to achieve verisimilitude, Mencken suggested relatively slight cuts. The book, as published on October 24, 1912, ran to 780 pages filled with hugely long paragraphs.[5]

Mencken was mistaken to exonerate Dreiser of having "laid on too much detail," meaning irrelevant detail. It was more than a minor blemish "on a magnificent piece of work"—something that Dreiser later realized and that later yet led him to produce a shorter revised edition. As we shall see, Mencken would make a number of mistakes in judging Dreiser's art. Here he insisted that Dreiser had made Cowperwood as real as one could hope to make the subject of an actual biography, which *The Financier* and its sequels approach in their faithfulness to the public record of Yerkes's life. This was true enough—also the assertion that he had produced the best novel of business and politics ever written. But it was uncharacteristically romantic of Mencken to conclude that after almost eight hundred pages the "irrelevant details" become "in a dim and vasty way, relevant. As you laboriously set the stage, the proscenium arch disappears, the painted trees become real trees, the actors turn into authentic men and women."[6]

Carl Shapiro later described *The Financier* as "a planned work of art," but this observation also suggests what is wrong or lacking in the book to which Dreiser devoted more preparation than he had any of his earlier books.[7] He had become a prodigious researcher to write it, but in doing the actual writing, he felt himself more or less limited to the biographical and historical grid of his real financier's life. In the earlier, more family-based novels, there was less will and more whim in the actions of his characters. There Dreiser was able to summon the great powers of his imagination instead of restricting himself to the actual record. Dreiser never knew, for example, what exactly happened to Hopkins as he led Hurstwood to his slow, humiliating death. And Jennie was not just Mame but a character based on a combination of Mame, whose illegitimate child was stillborn, and Sylvia, whose unwanted son Carl survived. Moreover, in devoting himself to a figure like the wealthy Yerkes, Dreiser had seemingly abandoned his most enduring topic—that of the not-so-divine average American whose poverty sated the voracious appetite of big business in the age of the Robber Barons. Not only is Cowperwood not a victim of a society (though he is, ironically and ultimately, a victim of his own genius at making money), he doesn't even start out poor. Neither had Yerkes.

Admirers of *Sister Carrie* and *An American Tragedy* find it odd that Dreiser should have devoted so much time and effort to this Tamburlaine of American business. The theory that Dreiser identified with both the weak and the strong as pawns in the struggle for the survival of the fittest doesn't quite explain his attraction to Yerkes and the subject of the American businessman. The answer lies first in his poverty while growing up and second in the dramatic contrasts he witnessed as a young adult between the rich and poor in America. He had worked in Chicago in the middle 1880s as a newspaper vender with his brother Ed when Yerkes was at the apex of his financial power in that city. The future novelist had returned to Chicago at the end of the decade when the arrogant industrialist was embroiled in the city's streetcar strike of 1888. As a reporter in Pittsburgh in 1894, he had witnessed the systematic manipulation of impoverished immigrants by the Carnegie Steel Company, and it was here that he had first become fully aware of "the stark implication of the domination of money in a democracy."[8] Later, in 1897, he had interviewed for *Success* such parvenu dynasts of American business as Philip D. Armour and Marshall Field (models for two of Cowperwood's antagonists in *The Titan*). Here, too, were possibilities for the novelist following the economic depression of the 1890s—if he could just lift its public relations curtain enough to reveal the heart and soul of American big business.

Sometime in the late nineties, Dreiser had written a meditation entitled

"The Supremacy of the Modern Business Man." He notes in this unpublished essay the history of the aristocratic prejudice against trade in Europe, but in democratic America it had flourished because of the absence of "hereditary honors." He pronounced this new American as the "master of a hundred millions and heir to nothing." He had become the new aristocrat in capitalistic America who commands "more men in his industrial army than once the petty German kings had under their banners." Yet this heroic image is potentially compromised by the fact that the modern businessman, unlike those in the professions, has as his primary goal to make money. It is a danger, Dreiser writes, that can make the businessman "the most sordid of all men."[9]

Until the turn of the century, these economic buccaneers could count on the newspapers—as Dreiser discovered in Pittsburgh and expressed in *The Financier*—for protection. But the subsequent climate for reform following the economic depression of the 1890s spawned the muckraking efforts of David Graham Phillips, Lincoln Steffens, Ida Tarbell, and Upton Sinclair, among others. Phillips, who was assassinated for one of his exposés in 1911, depicted the typical financier as a cold-blooded opportunist in such thinly plotted novels as *The Master Rogue* (1903). Steffens's *The Shame of the Cities* (1904) unmasked illegal alliances between business and city governments. Tarbell excoriated John D. Rockefeller, Sr., in scathing journalistic indictments and in her *History of the Standard Oil Company* in 1904. Sinclair found the same success in exposing the Chicago meat-packing industry's exploitation of the immigrant in *The Jungle* (1906). Robert Herrick's preachy realism rehearsed the ruthlessness of the Chicago financier in *The Memories of an American Citizen* (1905). Meanwhile, the final work of Dreiser's former editor and champion of *Sister Carrie,* Frank Norris, focused (albeit sentimentally and romantically) on the same dangers of greedy business practices in a democracy in *The Octopus* (1901) and *The Pit* (1903), the first two volumes of his planned trilogy of how the world's food supply was manipulated at all stages of its production, sale, and distribution. Dreiser, as we know, had not read *McTeague* before he wrote *Sister Carrie,* but one wonders how aware he was later of Norris's attack on big business as he came upon the idea of Cowperwood.

Gone forever in American literature was the romantic portrait of the bungling but honest businessman in Howells's *The Rise of Silas Lapham* or the rich man of conscience in James's *The Portrait of a Lady.* The "realism" in which an individual suffers defeat with his dignity yet intact was now considered unrealistic. Such representations had been more accurate in an earlier era, before the Civil War, when the merchant operated largely with his own capital instead of heavily mortgaged assets whose endangerment weakened his ethical resolve. His profit margin had been narrow and the inventory turnover slow, but with the expansion of banking practices as well as the development of transportation and communications after the war—the railroad, the telegraph, and the telephone—the competitive pace picked up considerably, so much so that the entrepreneur of the late nineteenth century was often compelled to engage in the legerdemain of high finance and questionable labor practices.[10] In 1908, as Dreiser began his serious research into Yerkes's career, the Harvard Business School was founded to remap the ethical path of American capitalism, disseminating its "casebooks" to the nation's universities and "business colleges."

In 1906—just one month before Paul's death, an event that also helped to unmoor Dreiser from family ties in his fiction—Charles Yerkes died of Bright's disease after failing in his attempt to monopolize the London Underground. His death set off a rash of articles in newspapers and periodicals about his controversial career as his financial empire fell apart and lost its influence. One story at that time that surely reinforced Dreiser's gut feeling about the rich as a subject for fiction as well as his choice of Yerkes is preserved among the Dreiser papers at the University of Pennsylvania. Noting that the paucity of great American fiction was not due to the lack of material, "The Materials of a Great Novel" suggested that the "Yerkes affair alone presents enough raw material to lay the foundations of another Comèdie Humaine if the novelist capable of using it had the courage of his genius." It went on to outline Yerkes's career, which covered three essential stages or cities—Philadelphia, Chicago, and London—and concluded with a shudder at the thought that either Mr. Howells or Mr. James might ever venture to tell this story.[11]

This was apparently the spark for the American Balzac's "Trilogy of Desire." Also influential was Charles Edward Russell's 1907 essay in *Everybody's Magazine*, which traces the rise and fall of Yerkes in Philadelphia and Chicago; a year later the same information was the basis of two chapters in Russell's *Lawless Wealth*, published by Dreiser's old firm of B. W. Dodge. (It wasn't until 1916, however, that Dreiser dipped into Gustavus Myers' *History of Great American Fortunes* [1910], a volume often cited as an influence on "The Trilogy of Desire.") Between 1906 and 1910, while editing magazines which celebrated American materialism, Dreiser studied the careers of at least a dozen notable financiers. As he zeroed in on Yerkes, he consulted a collection of clippings on the first leg of his career in the archives of the *Philadelphia Ledger,* called to his attention by Joseph H. Coates, the editor of the *Era* who had befriended him in Philadelphia in 1902. As a bibliography in Dreiser's notes for *The Financier* suggests, he consulted several volumes on the history and workings of the American stock market. He also read Edwin LeFèvre's 1911 essay entitled "What Availeth It?"—also in *Everybody's*—which carried the story of Yerkes's first youthful experiment in finance.[12] This Dreiser expanded upon in chapter 3 of *The Financier.* Usually, the first ten years of the twentieth century are considered Dreiser's lost decade as far as his art was concerned. But, as his documented research efforts for what was to become the Cowperwood trilogy as well as the cluster of novels and travel books that soon flowed from his pen suggest, he was never very far from the writer's game.

And just as he had experimented with the pathos of *Sister Carrie* in "Curious Shifts of the Poor," he expressed the underlying idea for *The Financier* first in a magazine article. Life in "The Trilogy of Desire" is largely reduced to the fact that the world is divided into the strong and the weak, and the weak are either consumed by the strong or somehow survive as parasites or "factotums" (as Dreiser is fond of calling them). *The Financier* opens and closes with animal imagery suggesting this law of nature. Young Cowperwood first learns the hard truth about life at a local fish market. There in an aquarium in the window a lobster first wears down, gradually amputates, and ultimately devours a squid. When it finally does, Frank concludes: "That's the way it has to be, I guess. . . . Things lived on each other—that was it." In a 1906 article entitled "A Lesson from the Aquarium," Dreiser had coyly observed that the activity of stort minnows, hermit crabs, and shark suckers reveals "a few interesting facts" about "our own physical and social condition." In watching one animal dominate another or position itself to make up for weakness, he asked "what set of capitalists, or captains of industry . . . would not envy the stort minnows in their skill in driving enemies away? . . . What weakling, seeing the world was against him, and that he was not fitted to cope with it, would not attach himself, suckerwise, to any magnate, trust, political or social (we will not call them sharks), and content himself with what fell from his table?"[13]

——

The plot of *The Financier* can be summed up by reviewing the life of Yerkes as found in Dreiser's notes. Born in 1837, Yerkes grew up in Philadelphia as the son of a Quaker-educated banker. Like Henry Worthington Cowperwood of the novel, Yerkes's father was known for his honesty and "old school" manner. His son attended Central High School and began his formal business life as a clerk in the Philadelphia flour and grain commission. At twenty-one Yerkes married the older Susanna Gamble (as Frank marries the older and widowed Lillian Semple) while also opening his own stockbroker's office. During the Civil War he profited greatly and afterward entered into a secret arrangement with the city treasurer to manipulate municipal bonds. Following the Chicago Fire of 1871, which set off a financial panic around the country, Yerkes was unable to meet his loan commitments. As a result, his conspiracy with the city treasurer (Joseph F. Marcer in real life, George W. Stener in the novel) was exposed, and both Yerkes and Marcer were convicted of larceny and fraud and incarcerated in the Eastern District Penitentiary of Pennsylvania. Sentenced to two years and nine months, Yerkes was pardoned along with the city treasurer on September 27, 1872, after serving seven months. (Dreiser keeps Cowperwood in prison for thirteen months.) After losing most of his money, Yerkes managed to recover because of the 1873 failure of Jay Cooke and Company and, eventually divorcing his wife for a younger woman, went west in 1880, ultimately to Chicago, where he began his financial career anew.[14]

Cowperwood's career in *The Financier* follows this scenario almost to the letter, but such memorable characters as Edward Malia Butler and his daughter, Aileen, whom Cowperwood seduces, were drawn from Dreiser's own experience as well as his research. Butler is based on one Colonel Edward Butler Dreiser met while he was a reporter for the *Globe-Democrat* in St. Louis. Butler spoke in a thick Irish brogue and, also like his fictional counterpart, probably began his climb to political power in the city as an illiterate "slop man, a man who could come with a great wagon filled with barrels and haul away the slops from your back door." The St. Louis Butler, who made his way into Steffens's *The Shame of the Cities,* took a liking to the young Dreiser the same way the fictional Butler is drawn to young Cowperwood. In both cases the young men do not consume alcoholic beverages. Dreiser's use of Butler as well as having young Cowperwood share his own youthful abstinence suggests the mixture of autobiography and biography in *The Financier.* It also underscores Dreiser's personal identification with Yerkes (or Cowperwood) in spite of his financial abuse of the poor.[15] Aileen Butler is based on Mary Adelaide Moore, the daughter of a Philadelphia chemist and the second Mrs. Yerkes, who was rumored to have visited Yerkes in the prison on Fairmount Avenue. The two wives of Yerkes are also partly based on Dreiser's first wife Jug (also older than her husband and just as conservative as Cowperwood's first wife) and Thelma Cudlipp, whose youthfulness and sexual burnish seem to suggest the beautiful (if over-fashionably dressed) Aileen.

Without Dreiser's personal additions to the Yerkes story as well as his fantasized identification with the hero, the plot would have been unbearably stiff and documentary. As it is (even in its 1927 version), the novel is drawn out with the irrelevant details Mencken at first complained about—especially the heavy repetition of Cowperwood's complex financial dealings, which strains the attention span of the average reader of novels. But with such fully realized characters as Butler and his daughter Aileen, the reader can gain a clear picture of the personal complications in the life of someone as rapacious as Cowperwood. (Butler is livid when he discovers his daughter is having an affair with Frank and vows revenge, which sends the financier to prison.) We might pity the old man as an angered father, but not as a leading citizen in league with corrupt politicians. Pity for the egotistical Cowperwood (whose motto is "I satisfy myself") is out of the question, except possibly when he is committed to solitary confinement of the Eastern Penitentiary, drawn in graphic detail by Dreiser.[16]

One could perhaps argue that Cowperwood is less compelling than even some of the minor characters in the book. He is stoically fearless—unrealistically described more than once as "jaunty" in the face of almost certain disgrace and imprisonment. Cowperwood's father in his bankruptcy and disgrace over his son's criminal conviction is more believable. Stener, one of those parasites or blood-suckers who try to slip through life without fully confronting it, is also more colorfully drawn. We see the once confident politico reduced to crying at home in his bathtub—as his "political carcass was being as rapidly and effectively picked clean and bare to the bone as this particular flock of political buzzards [Stener's former conspirators] knew how to pick him." Even the other prisoners sentenced for petty offenses at the same time as Cowperwood and Stener show more human tenderness and vulnerability than the protagonist. Notably, one of them, a common horse thief, resembles Dreiser's ne'er-do-well brother Rome: "obviously of German extraction but born in America, of a stocky build, all of five feet ten inches, with light, straight yellow hair and a skin that would have been ruddy if he had been well fed."[17]

Cowperwood, as noted, is a victim in the cosmic sense. Although there is nothing of Hurstwood's vulnerability or Jennie's innocence, Dreiser makes it clear that the gifted financier can no more resist his fate than any of the weaker personalities in his story. At the end of this novel, after invoking as he did in the opening another sea image—this time the Darwinian one of the Black Grouper, which survives "because of its very remarkable ability to adapt itself to conditions"—Dreiser brings on stage the three prophetic witches from *Macbeth* to suggest that life is ultimately no better for the strong than for the weak. (Dreiser himself occasionally consulted readers of tea leaves, though Cowperwood is not superstitious.) The witches find—for both Macbeth and Cowperwood—only "sorrow, sorrow, sorrow."

Reviews of *The Financier* were on the whole favorable, but, mainly because of its excessive length and detail, sales were fewer than for *Jennie Gerhardt*. Mencken set the tone in his review in the *New York Times* of November 10. Although conceding to the usual complaints about the author's awkward style ("he never so much as takes the trouble to hunt for a new adjective when an old one will answer as well"), he praised its grand scale in dramatically inscribing the American scene at the time of Yerkes's Philadelphia ascent. Noting the plethora of tales about municipal corruption over the last few years, he argued that no other writer "has brought its prodigal details into better sequence and adjustment, or made them enter more vitally and convincingly into the characters and adventures of his people." On the west coast, the *San Francisco Bulletin* of November 16 claimed that Dreiser was the only living American novelist whose works "may be spoken of in the same breath with those of the great European realists." *Harper's Monthly* for December wrote that "not even the many notable critics who bestowed so much extravagant-seeming praise upon *Sister Carrie* and *Jennie Gerhardt* could well have seen in these books the promise of such a novel."[18]

Reviews in the Midwest (except for the faithful William Marion Reedy's ecstatic one in his *Mirror*) and the South were less comfortable with the amoral Cowperwood. "Greed and graft are glorified," wrote the reviewer at the *St. Louis Post-Dispatch* of November 16, "conservatism in morals caviled at, the 'grasping legality of established matrimony' contrasted rather unfavorably with illicit love that is not tainted with guile or gain." The *Charlotte Observer* of January 12, 1913, conceded that Dreiser rivaled Balzac and the French School in general by showing that "Christianity and religious teachings" had little to do with the control of passion and morality. If *The Financier* had a moral at all, the reviewer concluded, it must be that "life is finely adjusted and easily unbalanced." The *St. Joseph* [Missouri] *Press* of January 31 tried its best to see the novel as a warning to "young men of the acquisitive temperament." "Some day," Mencken promised Dreiser as the two prattled back and forth as the reviews came out, "I am going to write an essay on the moral mind: its inability to see anything save a moral spectacle. . . . At the moment they propose a law making copulation a felony."[19]

By the end of the novel Cowperwood remains unscarred and (ultimately) unpunished. In *Sister Carrie,* Dreiser (or Arthur Henry) had written an ending to soften the fact that Carrie ends up rich in spite of her sins. In *The Financier* he may have been urged by an editor at Harper's to bring in Shakespeare's witches to counter the impression that Cowperwood was getting off too easily. For his complete downfall and death were beyond the scope of volume one, and his imprisonment is more effective as an argument against cruel and unusual punishment than it is as a form of censure for Cowperwood. The chapters on the Eastern District Penitentiary are as moving in their description of the prisoner's degradation and deprivation as they are exact in the physical description of the castle-like house of detention. Its Quaker innovations intended to change the behavior of inmates through "confinement in solitude" had long since been condemned by Alexis de Toqueville and Charles Dickens on their visits to the famous prison. (With its spoke-like floor plan prisoners could be kept under constant supervision through the use of a panopticon.) Dreiser had obviously visited the prison, which first opened in 1829, during one of his research trips to Philadelphia, if not earlier while living there during his nervous breakdown.

In fact, the novel may mark the beginning of Dreiser's reputation as a champion of penal reform. Not long after the publication of *The Financier,* he signed a petition asking President Woodrow Wilson to grant clemency to Julian Hawthorne. The son of the famous novelist had been sentenced to one year in the federal penitentiary in Atlanta for the Cowperwoodesque scheme of selling $3.5 million worth of stock in nonexistent gold and silver mines in Canada. Dreiser wrote a letter in support of Julian's bid for an early release. Published in the *St. Louis Star* of July 12, 1913, it expressed his hope that the newly elected Wilson, "a broad-minded, artistic and clement person," would pardon Hawthorne. (He did not. After Julian was released at the end of 1913, he wrote a book about his prison experience, entitled *The Subterranean Brotherhood* [1914].) Later, Dreiser wrote an introduction to Walter Wilson's *Forced Labor in the United States* (1933).[20]

Even though *The Financier* didn't sell as well as *Jennie Gerhardt,* with receipts dwindling considerably three months after publication mainly because of reviewers' complaints about its length, Dreiser's literary reputation grew only stronger. He was in good company at Harper's, which published in the same fall list for 1912 Albert Bigelow Paine's three-volume biography of Mark Twain and Arnold Bennett's *Your United States.* Several reviewers considered Dreiser the only major American author then doing his best work. Dreiser's most serious competition came mainly from Europe, although Edith Wharton's seventh novel, *The Reef,* also appeared that fall. In her case, the *New York Times* did not find a reviewer as friendly as Mencken had been to Dreiser. Evidently still smarting over the questionable tragedy of Lily Bart in *The House of Mirth* (a woman "who failed so pathetically to qualify as a milliner after she had shilly-shallied away her chances of marrying either for love or for money"), the reviewer more or less dismissed *The Reef.*[21] Penetrating fiction about women—like the quest for realism in fiction generally—had a long way to go in 1912, in spite of, or perhaps because of, suffragist rallies held that year in New York City.

Dreiser led the fight for unvarnished detail not only in fiction but, as we have seen, in his European travel book, to be called *A Traveler at Forty.* Per the agreement with Century negotiated through Grant Richards, Dreiser was to provide Century with three travel articles for its magazine and a full-length travel book if the editors liked the magazine pieces, which they very much did. Yet the articles and especially the book had to be cleansed of "woman stuff." Earlier, Douglas Z. Doty, one of the senior editors at Century, had warned Richards that Dreiser had a reputation for being both "risky" in his choice of materials and "a difficult fellow." In the end, however, he and Century president William W. Ellsworth had to caution Richards about removing too much from the book, details that might embarrass Richards and his friends. "Why should you not be embodied, like a fly in amber, in this classic?" Ellsworth asked him. "You knew what Dreiser was doing when he started, and that he meant to tell the story of everything that happened to him. Please do be kind."[22]

Indeed, Dreiser's travel book went beyond the author's own trysts with prostitutes to suggest in thinly disguised references similar activities by Richards and his friends. "As I read," Richards recalled, "I discovered that

George Moore [the Anglo-Irish novelist who aimed at graphic effect] at his frankest was, compared to Dreiser, the essence of discretion." Doty allowed Richards to make excessive cuts, but restored some of them.[23] Yet the published book still represented only half of the original manuscript, described by Richards as almost a million words in length. Before Richards returned to England in 1913, Dreiser visited him in his room at the Knickerbocker Hotel. The Englishman may indeed have had Dreiser's interests in mind as much as his own when he tried to acquire more than *Traveler* for Century, but he may also have protested too much as to what Dreiser truly owed him for the European tour. At the hotel during their final meeting, Richards first tried to put him off because of the offensive chapters, he said, but also probably because he now fully realized that he would not get Dreiser on an exclusive contract. He was all the more bitter about it when he reminded himself that he had not only engineered Dreiser's trip to Europe, but had endured his constant fear of running short of money and was rewarded not only with the author's insensitive remarks in *Traveler* about himself and his friends but an impudent letter in July in which Dreiser rebuked his European host for misleading him about the cost of their trip. "My money was in your hands," he reminded Richards. "You told me you would 'arrange' it, did you?" An angry Richards shot back in August that he had endured "a rather bad half hour" after reading the letter, considering that he had gone to so much trouble for his American guest. His only consolation was that Dreiser had warned him in the beginning that he was suspicious and mistrusting by nature.[24]

Dreiser knew that he had tried Richards's patience and indicates as much in *A Traveler at Forty*. In an interview with the *New York Times,* he said that *Traveler* could not have been written without Richards's help, and compared the Englishman's influence on the book to Arthur Henry's (without mentioning the latter's name) in *Sister Carrie*. Otherwise, he was never persuaded that Richards was anything more than a useful contact to British publishers who might produce the English edition of books first published in America, as Heinemann had done with *Sister Carrie*. "His chief characteristic," Dreiser had thought throughout their relationship, was the publisher's "strong sense of individual and racial [i.e., national] superiority"—"not an uncommon trait in Englishmen." He nevertheless regretted that their relationship was ending badly. When he appeared at Richards's "narrow" hotel room as he was packing for his return to Europe, Richards recalled, "we each waited, like nervous dogs, for the other to begin, I folding my clothes and putting them away, he leaning back in his chair, interminably folding and unfolding his handkerchief. In effect, I believe, we neither of us spoke and, after a space, he departed."[25]

Remarkably, Dreiser was able to finish *A Traveler at Forty* by January 1913, having just completed the 320,000-word first volume of his trilogy and shortly before that an almost equally long manuscript of *The "Genius."* Within weeks of his farewell meeting with Richards, he traveled to Chicago to pick up the thread of his research on Yerkes for *The Titan.* Either immediately before or right after the trip, however, he wrote a short story called "The Lost Phoebe." Turning from the concupiscent Cowperwood (who becomes even more so in *The Titan*), he told the tender story of Old Reifsneider and his wife, Phoebe, who after a long marriage are—like Dreiser's parents—parted by the wife's death. The picture of Old Reifsneider is also reminiscent of the doddering Old Gerhardt, based of course on his own father in his last decade. And Dreiser himself had only recently wandered about another countryside in search of his father's homeland in Mayen. In describing Reifsneider's illusions, which compel him to roam the countryside day and night in search of the ghost of his wife, he may have been recalling how his father was emotionally at sea after the death of Sarah Dreiser. Continuing this theme, at this time he also wrote a sketch entitled "The Father."[26]

Dreiser remained in Chicago from early December to the middle of February of 1913. After many years' absence, he found the city in the midst of what is now called "the Chicago Renaissance." He saw two of its earliest writers—Hamlin Garland, who had belatedly praised *Sister Carrie* in 1903, and Henry Blake Fuller, whose *Cliff Dwellers* (1893) and *With the Procession* (1895) Dreiser counted among his influences as early examples of native realism. He had first met these two writers almost ten years earlier in New York as he concluded his days as an "amateur laborer." He met John Cowper Powys, who was lecturing in Chicago at the time. The Anglo-Welsh writer with frizzled hair and a hulking physique was to become Dreiser's closest of friends. Powys later recalled that "Dreiser was old when I met him, forty or fifty, huge, bulbous, with a crooked, flabby face, and one eye lid that drooped. He was a great, a noble, a gargantuan squire of dames." Dreiser also encountered the lawyer-poet Arthur Davison Ficke; Lucian Cary, a critic for the *Chicago Evening Post* who had hailed *The Financier* as a great novel; and Margaret Anderson, soon to become the founding editor of the influential *Little Review*. And he may at this time have first met Sherwood Anderson, still reluctantly writing advertising copy and dreaming his way toward his magnum opus, *Winesburg, Ohio* (1919). Anderson later dedicated *Horses and Men* (1923) to Dreiser ("in whose presence I have sometimes had the same refreshed feeling as when in the presence of a thoroughbred horse") and credited his early novels with having "started me on a new track" with regard to *Winesburg*. Their relationship can be documented from 1916, when Anderson asked for Dreiser's help in finding a publisher for his first novel, *Windy McPherson's Son,* but this request suggests a connection already existed.[27]

He also met Edgar Lee Masters, the Chicago attorney and former partner of Clarence Darrow. A stubby bear of a man, Masters read law instead of poetry in order to support his family and remained married to a woman he no longer loved. A poet without much success for many years, his poems bitterly expressing the disappointment of small-town life, Masters would soon become an overnight literary entity following the publication of his *Spoon River Anthology* (1915). Masters had written Dreiser shortly before his Chicago visit to praise *The Financier* as well as *Sister Carrie* and *Jennie Gerhardt:* "I believe no American writer understands the facts of modern American life as well as you do." He remembered the day he first met Dreiser, who had called at his law office "to get the names of lawyers, editors and businessmen who knew Yerkes." Dreiser arrived wearing a heavy coat with a fur collar, "and looked distinguished. His eyes were full of friendliness and a kind merriment. I noticed his buck teeth, which were very white and well cared for, and I studied his long fingers when he took off his gloves." In spite of the ex-Hoosier's "staccato way of talking, his elisions disposed of by saying, 'Don't you know,'" the lawyer was instantly impressed with "the power of his mind, and with the vast understanding that he has of people, of cities, of the game of life." He and Dreiser saw each other several times over the course of Dreiser's stay in the city. Masters learned that his new friend was writing an autobiography. Dreiser also spoke of his idea for *The Bulwark* and of a "philosophical work that he was about to write."[28]

Also living in Chicago at this time and editing *Building Management* news was Will Lengel, who had been Dreiser's assistant at the *Delineator.* Lengel had gone west after Dreiser's dismissal, but he had kept in touch with his "father," as Dreiser became to him over the years. He was forever trying to get back to New York and asking his old boss if his future plans might include his talents. When Dreiser indicated his intention of possibly visiting Chicago, Lengel quickly spread the word. "I spent a great afternoon yesterday at the Chicago Post with Floyd Dell and some of the Post boys. . . . I don't know of a writer in the country who has the staunch and loyal personal following that you have. . . . They were overjoyed when I told them you contemplated a visit to Chicago. They want to see just how you get your handkerchiefs accordion plaited."[29]

Dreiser had already met Dell briefly in New York in 1911. The twenty-six-year-old editor of the literary review of the *Chicago Evening Post* had lauded *Jennie Gerhardt* in a long and glowing review as "a bigger, finer thing" than *Sister Carrie.* The two had subsequently begun a correspondence, and at the time of Dreiser's departure for Chicago Dell was already or soon to be reading a draft of *The "Genius."* Though married, Dell was enjoying an open affair with Kirah Markham, who was five years his junior and was to appear as Andromache in an upcoming production of Euripides' *The Trojan Women* at Maurice Browne's Little Theater. This half-Jewish beauty with olive skin, dark hair, and seductive eyes, whose real name was Elaine Hyman, was the liberated daughter of a jeweler who gave her the means to follow her whims as well as artistic interests in drama and painting. Dreiser, who was not easily drawn into conversation except in the presence of the opposite sex, became almost immediately infatuated with the actress. By the time of his departure, the two were lovers on the verge of an intense and frequently anguished three-year love affair. Dreiser later described her as "tall and graceful, her tallness youthful and classically statuesque, her grace pantherlike in its ease and rhythm."[30]

Many of the people whom Dreiser met in Chicago could be found at Maurice Browne's experimental theater in the new Fine Arts Building on Michigan Avenue. Every Sunday evening friends of the theater gathered for "tea"—to hear an invited speaker or perhaps a visiting poet or novelist. Browne himself was a compelling personality, described by Powys as "a maniacal Messiah of theatrical art," a reference to Browne's courageous rebellion against the commercially viable melodramas and musical comedies that monopolized the American stage before (and after) Eugene O'Neill. During his stay in Chicago, Dreiser attended Little Theater sessions in the company of Masters or Lengel. He was treated as a formidable celebrity. "The novelist sat solidly on a chair too small for his big body, motionless," save for his handkerchief folding and unfolding, Browne remembered. Once, while he did so, he was engaged in a discussion in which his opponent's "mind darted round him like a terrier round an elephant. Dialectically,

Dreiser was defeated on every point; but with stolid and imperturbable tenacity he pushed his opinion forward step by step, as overwhelmingly as a glacier." The pipe-smoking Powys noticed that Dreiser didn't smoke, which he thought "in itself de-humanizes anyone."[31]

———

Kirah Markham played not only in Browne's production of *The Trojan Women* but later made a cameo appearance in *The Titan* as Stephanie Platow. There she is part of the "Garrick Players" at the same Little Theater in Chicago; her father is a wealthy furrier instead of a jeweler. Like Kirah, she is tall, dark, and alluring. And perhaps also like Kirah, Stephanie sleeps around; before becoming Cowperwood's lover she has affairs with Gardner Knowles (Dell), drama critic at the *Post*, and Lane Cross (Dreiser himself), an artist who acts as stage director for the dramatic group. In the end she turns out to be more unfaithful than Kirah, who mostly teased Dreiser about other men and hoped he would give her a child some day.[32] When the financier finds Stephanie with another member of the players, he ends the affair. In real life, Dreiser eventually requested that Kirah remain faithful to him while he managed brief affairs with other women, and she is possibly the only woman who—though she apparently loved him as much as did Jug, Thelma, or any of the women who followed Dreiser into the 1920s and 1930s—ultimately refused to remain with him under this double standard. It is not known how early in their three-year relationship Dreiser made these demands. He may have been testing her as early as 1914, before they began living together in New York later that year. If so, at the same time he was also putting her into his novel as the more sexually active Stephanie.

The plot of *The Titan* involves a series of mistresses as Cowperwood becomes the sexual varietist that Dreiser himself became in the life allotted to him after the sinking of the *Titanic*. Indeed, one wonders whether the two names—of the novel and the ship—weren't loosely related in Dreiser's mind as he searched for the second title in his planned trilogy. Where *The Financier* develops Cowperwood from youth to middle age in Philadelphia, *The Titan* chronicles his adventures in Chicago, alternating between financial conquests and sexual triumphs. (Indeed, Stuart P. Sherman, a professor at the University of Illinois and one of the author's major nemeses following the publication of *The "Genius,"* called *The Titan* "a huge club-sandwich composed of slices of business alternating with erotic episodes.") With respect to business, Dreiser followed the Yerkes record almost without deviation, depending on actuality for his fictional reality. For the rest, he seems to have freely mixed in his own fantasies with personal experiences. While *The Financier* suffers from its redundancy of detail, *The Titan,* outside of its impressive documentation and dramatization of Chicago politics and business in the 1880s and 1890s, is simply boring. "I do not know how many seductions there are in this book," wrote Ford Madox Ford (then still writing as Ford Madox Hueffer) from England. "I have counted eleven to the credit of the hero; and I see there are some more seductions toward the end. I have not been able to finish the book."[33]

In his *Smart Set* review of *The Titan,* Mencken would try to address this problem on the grounds that literary art required a new standard under which the truth about life would be freely depicted. He condemned "the best-sellers of the moment, shot from the presses in gaudy cataract," but he was in fact defending Cowperwood against the charge that he lacked all humanity or heart. Other reviewers who complained that the novel wanted not only beauty but authentic tragedy, Mencken implied, were looking for a protagonist in the same romantic tradition, called "realism" since the rise of Howells and James in America and George Eliot in England. Even "among the Titans who have made industrial civilization," it was thought, Dreiser might have selected "one who now and then quickened in affection to his fellow-man." Yet Dreiser had already heard such palaver about rich men—indeed *from* them when he conducted the interviews for *Success* in the 1890s. He believed that most men and women, regardless of social level and circumstance, operated on the principle of the Lobster and the Squid. The *new* realist, or the naturalist, Mencken insisted, subscribed to only two articles: (1) that the novelist describe human beings as they actually are; and (2) that "he is under no obligation to read copybook morals into their lives."[34]

It was to be the Darwinian and not the Social Darwinian point of view in literature. Upon his entrance into Chicago, Cowperwood parleys his first coup in the public utilities field into a near monopoly of the city's streetcars, bribing his way through underlings until rival financial titans gang up to deprive him ultimately of a long-term franchise and thus destroy his traction empire. The newspapers, as was the case with Yerkes, also turn against him to the point that the financier abandons Chicago to seek new fortunes in New York and ultimately London (which became the basis of *The Stoic*). As with his experience in Philadelphia, the vehemence of his enemies is enhanced by the fact that he seduces the daughter of one of the influential entrepreneurs, Hosmer Hand, who joins forces with Timothy Arneel (Philip Armour), Anson Merrill (Marshall Field), and Norman Schryhart (Levi Leiter).[35] During these adventures in high finance, Aileen—never sophisticated enough for Chicago society, which ignores the couple anyway because of Frank's Philadelphia history—steadily declines into alcoholism as Cowperwood ignores her first for a series of other women and then finally for Berenice Fleming, who is based on Emily (or Emilie, as she came to spell it) Grigsby. Her story became a part of the public record of Charles Yerkes at his death. Here Dreiser's fidelity to fact raised legal concerns that would soon come back to haunt him.[36]

By May of 1913 Dreiser had drafted sixty-two chapters of *The Titan*. Kirah remained in Chicago, sending him erotic letters as he wrote Cowperwood's seduction scenes. As Dreiser put the finishing touches on his portrait of his randy financier, Kirah's letters alluded to the tender lines of love in "Out of the Cradle Endlessly Rocking." "Twice today," she told him four days before a visit to New York in late May, "have I read the seashore memories of Walt Whitman's that I love so, and wept, wept, wept over the beauty and sorrow of it all." She had recently attended a Walt Whitman Fellowship meeting in Chicago accompanied by her father and Clarence Darrow.[37] With *The Titan* completed, Harper's now worried that it would conflict with *A Traveler at Forty*, which Century was bringing out at the end of 1913. Thus, they decided to hold volume two of the Cowperwood chronicle until the winter of 1914.

In the meantime, there was the lingering matter of *The "Genius,"* now being read not only by Dell but others in Chicago, including Lengel. On March 31, Dell, calling it "a very bad book," advised against publication. The same day Lengel, who recognized "the originals of various characters" based on Thelma Cudlipp, her mother, and others associated with the *Delineator* days, wrote to say that publication of the manuscript would "do more damage to your career than to help it."[38] Dreiser, of course, had heard before the advice about a book hurting his career—from Doubleday on *Sister Carrie*.

Before he could push forward with *The "Genius,"* however, he ran into trouble with *The Titan*, now in galley sheets. "Harper's, after printing a first edition of 10,000 copies . . . , have decided not to publish," Dreiser told Mencken from Chicago on March 6, 1914. "Reason—the realism is too hard and uncompromising and their policy cannot stand it." "If this were Sister Carrie," he calmly added, "I would now be in the same position I was then." Doran and Company considered taking over the book, but rejected the idea on March 16. He learned from Anna Tatum, who was now acting informally as his agent, that George H. Doran not only personally disliked him but thought his presentation of Yerkes in *The Financier* had been unfair to the average businessman. In fact, there was another reason that both publishers were wary of *The Titan:* as word of Dreiser's use of her history with Yerkes as the basis for Berenice Fleming got into the press, Emilie Grigsby threatened to sue. On March 23, however, Dreiser found through his friend Lengel a second English publisher with an American office—John Lane and Company would publish *The Titan* almost immediately.[39] Once again, not only with the Century Company's publication of *A Traveler at Forty* in 1913 but with Heinemann's publication of *Sister Carrie* in 1901, the British had come to the rescue.

Notwithstanding, Dreiser's history with the British, as we shall ultimately see, was a troubled one. Like Whitman, he rejected their aristocratic airs, yet the English were the first ones to recognize their geniuses. Certainly John Lane became Dreiser's publisher with alacrity, once it was clear that Grigsby probably would not sue. Meanwhile, even though Harper's had washed their hands of *The Titan,* they still insisted on their claim to *The "Genius"*—which, as J. Jefferson Jones, managing editor at the American office of John Lane, told Dreiser that April, "cannot be called a Sunday-school story." Jones added "and thank Heaven for it," but he would later have to eat those words.[40]

While both Dreiser and Jones negotiated with Harper's over which firm would publish Dreiser's future work, the house of John Lane published *The Titan* in May 1914. Dreiser received a $1,000 advance and the promise of royalties of 20 percent. Because of its historical accuracy and candid depictions, Mencken considered it Dreiser's best book since *Jennie,* perhaps his best so far, even though it lacked the emotional appeal of *Jennie.* Despite the fact that it was almost two hundred pages shorter than *The Financier* (Harper's had urged him to produce a shorter sequel), *The Titan* sold far fewer copies than its predecessor. The author was naturally disappointed and may have recalled his promise to Mencken right after leaving the *Delineator* to quit "this book game" if he wasn't "enjoying a good income" from it. Three years and (including *A Traveler at Forty*) three books later he had yet to reach "the place where I will make a living wage out of my books."[41]

He thought of returning to magazine writing, and indeed at this stage in his career he was hatching ideas almost as fast as a weekly magazinist. By the summer of 1914 he had already drafted more than half of *Dawn*, the first volume of his autobiography. He had written or completed *Jennie Gerhardt, The Financier, A Traveler at Forty, The Titan,* and *The "Genius"*—all but one out within the last three years. Right around the corner lay *A Hoosier Holiday* (1916), at 513 pages. And somewhere in one of the manuscript boxes that followed him through life was the unfinished manuscript of *An Amateur Laborer* as well as the stories and sketches that would eventually be published in the next decade in *Free and Other Stories, Twelve Men,* and *The Color of a Great City.* "I have many schemes or plans," he told Mencken that summer with understatement, "but only one pen hand."[42]

Inspired by the experimental drama he had recently seen in Chicago, he also returned to his early ambition to write plays.[43] Beginning in early summer of 1913 he wrote a number of one-act plays, the first of which was "The Girl in the Coffin." Some of these drew on actual events, others on fantasy, imagination, and the strains of distant memory recovered in the act of writing his autobiography. "The Girl in the Coffin" was based on the strike by eight hundred employees of the Henry Dougherty Silk Company in Paterson, New Jersey, beginning in January 1913, in which the nationally known labor activist "Big Bill" Haywood played a central part. Actually, Dreiser probably took up the subject after seeing the socialist John Reed's dramatic reenactment of the event, "The Paterson Strike Pageant," which was performed in front of fifteen thousand people in Madison Square Garden on June 7. Although his sympathies always went to rank and file workers like his father and brothers, the play is not primarily political but rather focused on the human imperfections that corrupt even the best of intentions. Although there is a street band playing the "Marseillaise," as there was in the Paterson strike, the focus is on poor Mary Magnet, who, like so many Dreiser girls both real and fictional, meets up with the wrong fellow and suffers the consequences.

In "The Girl in the Coffin," the seducer turns out to be the nationally known strike leader John Ferguson, who is to visit the mill town outside New York City to rally the strikers. Mary lies in the coffin dead of unstated causes. "In *my* belief," says one of the gossiping neighbors of the girl's father, William Magnet, the local foreman of the striking workers, "it's some rich fellow she met up to the city. Many a Saturday night when work was over she's been seen to take the train. I understand she spread round the report she was goin' to business college up there."[44] In fact, Mary has died from a botched abortion. Current censorship codes would have prevented Dreiser's broaching the idea, but the hint is clear enough. Her father is so overcome with grief that he cannot be persuaded to fulfill his strike duties, which involve translating Ferguson's speech to the Italian workers.

To bring Magnet around, Ferguson first appeals to his sense of brotherhood in the fight for fair wages. When that fails, he tells Magnet his own sad story. Here Dreiser works out more of his personal anxieties and anger in his fiction as he had with Kirah in writing *The Titan*. For Ferguson's story comes chapter and verse from Dreiser's marriage with Jug and the tensions of their current relationship. For many years he resented the fact that Jug persisted in identifying herself as "Mrs. Dreiser." "I didn't stay with her. . . ." Ferguson likewise complains. "A good living is all she gets out of me. It's all she ever will get. Except my name. She hangs on to that. And my freedom. She's got that locked up safe enough, or she thinks she has. She claims I'm not good enough to marry any other woman." Later, Dreiser would be grateful that he could use Jug's steadfast refusal to grant him a divorce as an excuse not to marry his current flames. But now, in the summer of 1913 before the affair with Kirah began to show signs of frustration, he may have thought he wanted to marry again.

The point of Ferguson's story is that he took a mistress who has recently died. "She did love me anyhow, this other woman," he tells Magnet, "whether I was good enough or not. She didn't get a living out of me. She didn't get my name." Ferguson is grief stricken, too, but nevertheless ready to perform his labor duties. Ultimately, Ferguson's story gives Magnet the will to put aside his pain and perform his duty, too. After he exits the stage to do so, one of Magnet's neighbors slips Ferguson a ring. Earlier Magnet wonders what happened to the ring his daughter had worn of late. "She said I was to give you this," the old woman says to the labor leader in the play's last line. "She said I was to say she died happy." "The Girl in the Coffin" found many admirers, not only when it was first published in *The Smart Set* in the fall of 1913, but when it was produced several years later.

In July 1913, Dreiser moved to 165 West Tenth Street in Greenwich Village, an area that was home now to socialists and anarchists, whom Mencken despised. "There was never a time in my youth," Mencken wrote in the 1940s, "when I succumbed to the Socialist sentimentalities that so often fetch the young of the bourgeoisie." Accordingly, he never seemed to tire of criticizing Dreiser for his own socialist sympathies born out of a childhood of poverty. "While he lived uptown with Sara [Jug]," Mencken recalled in another memoir with some bitterness after the two men had broken off their relationship for a decade, "he led a thoroughly bourgeois life, and there was no sign in his carriage of the Bohemian, though he was already practicing a Latin Quarter promiscuity, but once he got down to 10th Street he took to the life of art, and was soon a painful figure to his old friends."[45] This is somewhat unfair. While Dreiser did enjoy "a Latin Quarter promiscuity" there, he was less formally interested in its political visions than he would become in the radical politics of the 1930s. He associated primarily with Villagers whose intellectual reputations survive to one or another extent today—though these, too, not simply the lesser figures, were surely the targets of Mencken's ridicule. Floyd Dell had moved there to write for the *Masses,* then edited by Max Eastman. Others included the writer Hutchins Hapgood, the anarchist John Reed and his protégé Lincoln Steffens, the birth-control advocate Margaret Sanger, the poet Louis Untermeyer, Sinclair Lewis, and Waldo Frank, editor of *The Seven Arts.* Soon after he settled there, Ficke and Powys joined the community. Dreiser visited the Liberal Club, a popular neighborhood meeting place for artists and writers on MacDougal Street. There such progressives as Horace Traubel on Whitman, Jacques Loeb on the latest sex theories, and others were cycled through as speakers.[46]

Though Mencken delighted in castigating the literary philistines, he was becoming ever more politically conservative and ever observant, at least in public, of conventional morality. For his part, Dreiser was comfortable flouting convention. When Kirah joined Dreiser on West Tenth Street in the winter or spring of 1914, Mencken thought her Village friends "tin-pot" socialists and found her bohemian way of decorating their ground-floor flat distasteful and impractical. He couldn't help contrasting Jug's "folksy flats in 123rd Street and upper Broadway" with Kirah's campy arrangement of their two-room flat with its ceiling-high windows and double coal fireplaces. "The furniture was all arty and half a dozen paintings by Kirah hung on the wall." The building was old (it is long since torn down), reflecting the general neglect of the neighborhood, which had been abandoned by the upper middle class in New York's huge development northward in the nineteenth century. Mencken also objected to the dim lighting. Kirah provided the flat with candles that "were always guttering and going out." At about the same time John Cowper Powys, who lived a few blocks east of Dreiser on Tenth Street and Patchin Place, told his brother Llewelyn that he wasn't sure whether Kirah was Dreiser's "wife or his tart."[47]

It was in this art nouveau austerity, where his Italian neighbors turned out to be counterfeiters, that Dreiser, emboldened by the critical success of

"The Girl in the Coffin," wrote in the summer of 1914 six more one acts, dashing them off in succession the way he had his Maumee stories in 1899. These symbolic dramas were collected, along with "Girl," in *Plays of the Natural and the Supernatural* (1916). He was also stimulated in his playwriting by the Washington Square Players, a group of for the most part amateur actors who first practiced their experimental theater in the Liberal Club, and at least once in Dreiser's apartment, before opening to the public with a bill of one-act plays in the spring of 1915.[48]

Dreiser's were closet dramas, "reading plays" as he told Mencken, who published some of them in the *Smart Set*.[49] As with "The Lost Phoebe," it is somewhat puzzling as to exactly where they came from, for the realist for whom the Fact was glorious enough in *The Financier* and *The Titan* delved into what would later be termed the Theater of the Absurd to speculate on the meaning of life. Their themes on the "equation inevitable" anticipated his philosophical essays in *Hey, Rub-a-Dub-Dub* (1920). Dreiser told Mencken in sending him three of them that they represented "merely the effort at drama outside the ordinary limits of dramatic interpretation."[50] The editors of Dreiser's collected plays speculate that a seeming brush with death was the catalyst for at least one of them. While Dreiser was back in Chicago seeing Kirah, who had temporarily returned there because of his infidelities, he underwent surgery to remove a painful carbuncle on his neck. The surgeon, Kirah's family doctor, underestimated the time the operation would take. As Kirah later told the biographer W. A. Swanberg,

> Working with laughing gas Dr. Julia [Strong] realized it was going to take longer than she had anticipated and ordered oxygen. A nurse went to the store room and found it locked. . . . In the end it was brought from another building and by that time Theo was turning blue and we were all, doctor, nurses and I, chaffing his hands and feet to restore circulation. When the tank of oxygen was finally brought and administered he rose up on the operating table roaring with gargantuan laughter. "I got it, I've got it on you all, the secret of the universe, the same thing over and over, God damned repetition!"[51]

The literary result of this perhaps minor medical crisis was "The Laughing Gas," an expressionistic drama that depicts simultaneously the patient's physical struggle to survive the operation and his unconscious mind in dialogue with a spirit (the nitrous oxide) about the meaninglessness of life. The first expressionistic play staged in America, it anticipates the work of Eugene

O'Neill and Thornton Wilder in enacting continuous and simultaneous action on stage.[52]

In "The Blue Sphere," his next exercise in this experimental genre, the action concerns a deformed child, unwanted and unsupervised by his parents, who flits about the house in pursuit of an imaginary ball, or blue sphere. As the child in its chase moves closer and closer to nearby railroad tracks, a fast mail train moves inevitably toward the fatal scene of impact. The child will in fact be murdered, for the ball is controlled by the Shadow, which is purposely trying to kill the child because it is a freak of nature. Dreiser's interaction with Sanger may have had an influence here. Later, in response to a request from Sanger to write something in support of her cause, he argued that birth control was inherent in nature itself—that beings of higher intelligence produced fewer offspring in the natural "tendency to overcome useless waste with intelligent care."[53]

There is no indication—outside his mother's much regretted wish in the 1850s that her first three children were dead—that Sarah's surviving children were anything but loved in spite of the family's poverty, but life for the Dreiser family in Indiana would have been economically easier with birth control. The house next to the tracks in the play resembles the one next to a railroad yard in Sullivan in which Dreiser lived as a child. It was, as noted, around this time that he was recalling that period in *Dawn*.[54] Dreiser supported Sanger's cause, but as a former Catholic he may also have experienced pangs of doubt, if not guilt. After all, he was his mother's twelfth child. When the child in "The Blue Sphere" is killed by the train, the conductor reluctantly approves because the child was one of nature's mistakes. Yet the engineer is beside himself with the horror of it all. "I saw its face!" he yells. "I tell you! A beautiful child! I can never forgive myself for this."

"I didn't make myself" is a refrain implied throughout Dreiser's work, beginning with the rapist in "Nigger Jeff" who pleads with his lynchers for mercy because he couldn't help himself and continuing in these plays— and beyond. "In the Dark" features another American minority of the day, the "Eyetalians" or "nagurs." (In "The Mighty Burke," Dreiser had demonstrated among other things his familiarity with and sympathy for Sicilian immigrants whose poverty made them work—and be treated—like gorillas on street gangs and railroad crews such as the one at Spuyten Duyvil. He also wrote about Italian immigrants in "The Toilers of the Tenements" and "The Love Affairs of Little Italy," which appeared in *The Color of a Great City*.) This play is about an Italian fruit peddler who has murdered his brother. During the action, the dead man's ghost darts about the stage, "unconscious of duality." When the killer is apprehended and fellow spirits of the deceased "sweep and swirl" around him, he denies responsibility for his crime in the same pathetic fashion of Jeff Ingalls when confronted with the crime of rape: "No meana to kill. No maka da strong word, no maka da first blow!" pleads the Italian. Both figures are biologically trapped. Dreiser's sense of determinism would build as he moved toward his second masterpiece about somebody—another nobody—who also commits murder by accident.

Dreiser was working out something new in the summer and fall of 1914, in the wake of *The Titan*'s relatively poor sales. Ironically, he had written the Nietzschean story of Cowperwood while also thinking about *The Bulwark* and the role of religion in life. "The Spring Recital" is about the folly of religion. Set in a prosperous New York church, the satire features an organ recital attended only by four parishioners, the low attendance indicating the waning of religious belief in the twentieth century. The performance is, however, also attended by the wraiths of past ages who testify to their disappointment when they died and experienced no heavenly vision. This disillusionment is shared by two dead lovers, whose only interests remain physical satisfaction and sexual beauty, and "a barrel house bum a dozen years dead, but still enamored of the earth," who proclaims, "You thought you'd find out somepin' when yuh died, huh? Well, yuh got fooled, didn' jah? . . . Har! Har! Har!" Throughout, the organist is entirely oblivious of this supernatural activity. He concludes that it is useless to perform for only four people and retires after half an hour to a local beer garden for something more intoxicating than the rituals of religious belief.

The final two plays in his collection, "The Light in the Window" and "Old Ragpicker" are inferior to the others. The first presents a house in a fashionable district whose lighted window allows the less fortunate to observe a wealthy couple assumed to be happy. In fact, the wife is miserable because her mother-in-law wants her son to divorce her and marry a woman more socially acceptable. Laura Kindelling is cut from the mold of Aileen Butler and Jennie Gerhardt. Indeed, the husband's situation is a replay of Lester's dilemma in having to choose between Jennie and Letty, the divorcée from his own social rank. Dreiser's depiction of the rich couple is unremarkable, indeed hackneyed in its treatment of the rich; but as usual he is masterful in expressing his empathy with the have-nots as well as in his scorn for the middle-management types who, like shark-suckers, would attach themselves to the rich and famous.

"Gee!" the Messenger Boy exclaims, "I wish I could live like dat! It must be nice to be rich." The observation of the Brisk Department Store Manager, however, is clearly preemptive, indicating his own expectations in climbing the ladder of success. "Now, that is what I call a lovely home. . . . Hard-earned, no doubt. After all, prosperity depends on moral order and honesty." This had been the message of the industrial giants Dreiser had interviewed in the nineteenth century. Now—after a decade of muckraking in the twentieth—it wasn't believed so much anymore and was easy to satirize. Even the Young Scribbler, "an assistant magazine editor and self-imagined poet," is taken in by the scene. He looks at the beautiful but unloved wife and imagines himself marrying rich—Dreiser's dream before (if not after) he moved to New York and became a magazine editor and "self-imagined poet."

"Old Ragpicker" is hardly more than a dramatic sketch of a homeless person who has lost his position and middle-class happiness after his factory with three hundred employees burned down. It had produced woolen blankets. John Paul Dreiser's Indiana mill had made wool, and it too, as we remember, burned down and caused his ruination as a businessman. No doubt this play also comes out of the memories Dreiser was turning over for his autobiography. He was summing himself up. For otherwise he had written himself out. Most of what he would write and publish for the next decade was largely part of that summary. Possibly his worst exercise in autobiography would be *The "Genius,"* which cost him dearly in terms of his literary reputation at the time (and perhaps today). It would, however, ultimately be his second-biggest money maker.

ELEVEN

The Genius Himself

There is more than a hint here and elsewhere of the roman à clef.

NEW YORK WORLD, OCTOBER 2, 1915

IN THE SUMMER OF 1915, Dreiser threw a party for Edgar Lee Masters at his Tenth Street apartment upon the publication of *Spoon River Anthology*. Its gallery of characters features "Theodore the Poet," who

> . . . watched for men and women
> Hiding in burrows of fate amid great cities,
> Looking for the souls of them to come out,
> So that you could see
> How they lived, and for what.[1]

Among the guests for the August 5 reception was Franklin Booth, whose impressionistic pen-and-ink sketches illustrated magazines ranging from the *Masses* to *Ladies' Home Journal* and *Good Housekeeping*. This fellow native of Indiana was one of the founders of the commercial art movement, and it had made him a fairly wealthy man. He and Dreiser had been acquaintances for the last ten years, since the days when Booth sketched for a New York newspaper and Dreiser wrote for the magazines. Booth had just purchased a new sixty-horsepower Pathfinder touring car and was about to make his annual pilgrimage back to Indiana. He asked his host whether he would like to come along. Dreiser's only outlay, aside from food and lodging for himself, would be half the cost of the tires they would inevitably ruin along

America's hard-packed dirt and macadam roads in those early years of the automobile. Their journey, which became the subject of *A Hoosier Holiday* (1916), would be one of the earliest recorded auto road trips in America.

Dreiser was immediately interested in the venture. The idea of returning to Indiana as he wrote his autobiography was irresistible. The experience would also give him an excuse to write a book other than the third volume of his Cowperwood trilogy, which seemed commercially unwise after the disappointing sales of *The Titan;* it would also let him off the hook for a while with *The Bulwark,* which he had mentioned to his editors at John Lane but was far from getting ripe enough for publication. After telling Booth he would let him know for sure in a few days, he asked the John Lane Company for an advance of $200, which was granted in exchange for a signed contract on *Plays of the Natural and the Supernatural.* He then discussed the idea with Kirah, who was working on a poster for the upcoming publication of *The "Genius."* She had no interest in making the two-thousand-mile motor trip in what today would be considered an open vehicle.[2]

The Indiana-made Pathfinder crossed on the ferry to New Jersey on August 11. Its driver, named only "Speed" in *A Hoosier Holiday* as well as in the notes for the travel book, was a "lithe, gangling youth" who reminded Dreiser of the blond streetcar conductor in Edward Goodman's *Eugenically Speaking* (1914), a one-act comedy recently performed by the Washington Square Players. Their cross-country route was laid out only as far as northeastern Pennsylvania because the Manhattan auto club to which Dreiser applied for directions had refused him because he was not a member. To avoid a scene, however, the "smug attendant" had given Dreiser one of the company maps outlining "The Scenic Route" to Scranton. The trio was joined for the first day's journey by Booth's chief studio model—"one of those self-conscious, carefully dressed, seemingly prosperous maidens of some beauty who frequent the stage and the studios." Booth—as a Christian Scientist or "dreamy metaphysician" who knew nothing of "so-called sin"—was perhaps the perfect soul mate and fellow traveler for the man who was soon to visit the origins of his long-smoldering Catholicism.[3]

Once into Pennsylvania and approaching Scranton, from which their female companion returned to New York by train, they learned that the Keystone State's roads were rumored to be not very good. Also, if they chose the most direct route west, there would be many hills to climb in traversing the state. (Today the route is made easier by a number of tunnels in the western part of Pennsylvania.) With good roads, Dreiser noted, the automobile could presumably "roll on forever at top speed" (forty to forty-five miles per hour), but embark upon poor roads with ruts and their delicate machine (which, as Booth predicted, suffered repeated blow-outs and flats even on good roads) would eventually fall apart. Dreiser doesn't say much about the dangers of the highway, which seem alarming almost one hundred years later, except to note at one point that with a "little mud and water . . . you are in danger of skidding into kingdom come." They were soon persuaded to cut north to Binghamton, New York, before heading west again. On their way out of Pennsylvania, dismissive of its inferior roads, Dreiser and Booth took consolation in the fact that neither could recall any major contribution to American history made by a native of the state. William Penn ("a foreigner") and Benjamin Franklin were briefly mentioned—"But where are the poets, writers, and painters?" This comment, one of Dreiser's several undigested or passing criticisms of American culture in the book, raised the eyebrows of at least one Pennsylvania reader who was soon to become Dreiser's editor, and typist, and mistress.[4]

Dreiser raised even more eyebrows by his barely concealed irritation at the nation's growing xenophobia, especially toward citizens with origins in Germany. With the war in Europe already a year old, Germany was testing the will and patience of the supposedly neutral American people with its submarine blockade of England and the sinking of the *Lusitania* on May 7, 1915. As they left Scranton, Dreiser found "no evidence of that transformation of the American by the foreigner into something different from what he has ever been—the peril which has been so much discussed by our college going sociologists." Rather, if there was change, it was in the way American culture seemed "to be making the foreigner into its own image."[5] Once back inside the state of New York and hoping to visit Niagara Falls, they considered taking the Canadian route, which would have brought them out at Detroit. But according to Dreiser, Canada was no less xenophobic during the war than the United States. He feared that because of the war and his German surname, they would have to submit to a rigorous inspection of their luggage. "The war! The war!" he wrote in his book. "They were chasing German-American professors out of Canadian colleges, and making other demonstrations of hostility towards all others having pro-German leanings. I, with my German ancestry on one side and my German name and my German sympathies—what might they not have done to me! We didn't go." (Dreiser's impatience with anyone favoring the British was already showing—as it would show again years later when he made a fateful trip to Canada during World War II.) When this passage appeared in the first edition of *A Hoosier Holiday,* the complaints were so strong that the John Lane Company quickly issued a second with a substitute passage tipped in.[6]

Even without Dreiser's colorful vitriol regarding World War I, *A Hoosier Holiday* is a magnificent travel book in which he reinvents or rediscovers Whitman's spirit of the "Open Road" as the Pathfinder makes its bumpy way across Middle America. One night, as the auto party sped out of Owego, New York, just west of Binghamton, Dreiser waxed poetical, almost mystical:

> There are certain summer evenings when nature produces a poetic, emotionalizing mood. Life seems to talk to you in soft whispers of wonderful things it is doing. Marshes and pools, if you encounter any, exhale a mystic breath. . . . Every cottage seems to contain a lamp of wonder and to sing. Every garden suggests a tryst of lovers. A river, if you follow one, glimmers and whimpers. The stars glow and sing. They bend down like lambent eyes. All nature improvises a harmony—a splendid harmony—one of her rarest symphonies indeed.[7]

Even for this literary naturalist, nature sometimes worked wonders. Yet unlike Whitman's love for his divine average in the occupations he surveys in *Leaves of Grass,* Dreiser's affection in his catalog of the working class is bittersweet:

> Dear, crude, asinine, illusioned Americans! How I love them! . . . How they rise, how they hurry, how they run under the sun! Here they are building a viaduct, there a great road, yonder plowing fields or sowing grain, their faces lit with eternal, futile hope of happiness. You can see them religiously tending store, religiously running a small-town country hotel, religiously mowing the grass, religiously driving shrewd bargains or thinking that much praying will carry them to heaven . . . and then among them are the bad men, the loafers, the people who chew tobacco and swear and go to the cities Saturday nights and 'cut up' and don't save their money![8]

Nevertheless, America was his "darling Yankee land—'my country tis.'"

The Pathfinder made its way across the northern part of Ohio, passing through Toledo, where Dreiser had first met Arthur Henry, and Grand Rapids, where he had once considered forming a partnership to run a small-town newspaper. Then it was across the Indiana border into "Boyland." Their route crisscrossed the state in order to pass through all of the places where Dreiser had lived as a child (one of the promises he had secured from Booth). They first went to Warsaw, where many memories were clearly unlocked, although the only record of Warsaw in Dreiser's notes is a local newspaper clipping describing his teenage hometown as the "City of Beautiful Churches." (Dreiser's diary notes for his book stop between August 15 at Erie, Pennsylvania, and August 20, when they entered Wabash, after driving south from Warsaw.) This first stop after an absence of almost thirty years was perhaps the most difficult because he was not prepared for the change, which transcended mere landscapes and the haunts of youth. "It is all very well to dream of revisiting your native soil and finding at least traces, if no more, of your early world," he wrote in *A Hoosier Holiday,* "but I tell you it is a dismal and painful business. Life is a shifting and changing thing." One of the lakes north of town was now encircled by a casino and resort cabins instead of the beautiful trees he remembered. Other old monuments were missing: the bookstore, the small restaurant with an oyster counter, a billiard and pool room—though there were three new churches. He visited the Grant House and Thralls Mansion, where he and his "poet mother" and two siblings had lived. The second house looked "very tatterdemalion," now a tenement infested with four families instead of one.[9]

When the Dreisers lived there, he had had his own room. Now that room was occupied by a Mr. Gridley, who promptly volunteered the information that his son had been killed in the war at the Dardanelles. Later, while visiting his old school nearby, Dreiser found the old man telling Speed and Booth the same "moving details of his son's death and the futility of the campaign at the Dardanelles." As "he of my former room" retailed the story again, a small boy from somewhere in the neighborhood "stood with his legs very far apart, his hands in his pockets, and merely stared and listened." The scene was possibly amusing except for the third sidewalk local—"a short, dusty, rotund, rather oily-haired man who announced that he was the owner of the property which had formerly sheltered me, and who by virtue of having cut down all the trees and built the two abominable houses in front seemed to think that he was entitled to my friendship and admiration."[10]

As they descended to Indianapolis, they passed through Kokomo, "where James Whitcomb Riley once worked in a printer's shop." Dreiser notes here in his book that he understood that the beloved Hoosier writer, who died just before Dreiser's book went to press, had "no love for my work." At Carmel, where Booth kept his summer studio behind his parents' house, they paused for a few days' rest, and Speed turned the chauffeur duties over to a crippled boy named Bert, whom Booth had more or less adopted. They then set out for Terre Haute, where they wandered up and down the streets looking for Dreiser's birthplace and the other houses in which he lived, but too much had changed for him to recognize anything for sure. Here, in reminiscences for the book, he buried Rome prematurely as he would also do in *Dawn*, saying that his brother died of alcoholism in a "South Clark Street dive in Chicago, about 1905."[11] Even though in the city of Dreiser's beginning a more up-to-date hotel was affordable, they stayed at the Terre Haute House for nostalgic reasons. Booth sketched the city from across the Wabash. In Sullivan, twenty-five miles directly south, Dreiser posed for a photograph with ragged neighborhood urchins dressed much like himself at their age before the house in which he had lived. "I thought," he mused, "of my mother walking about in the cool of the morning and the evening, rejoicing in nature. I saw her with us on the back porch . . . [myself] listening to stories or basking in the unbelievable comfort of her presence."[12]

In Vincennes, another twenty-five miles south, he found the firehouse in which they had lived briefly with Sue Bellette, but for some reason he does not mention—as he does in *Dawn*—the fact that his mother's friend was running a whorehouse out of the building. When they moved onto Evansville, Dreiser—or his editor—also neglects to give the reason his family felt it necessary to leave that city, which again involved prostitution— the business of Paul's girlfriend and inspiration for "My Gal Sal."[13] Perhaps with the war on and the American demonization of the Germans, Dreiser was revising his history a little. In Bloomington, he discovered his old college so grown, not only in size, but in "architectural pretentiousness as to have obliterated most of that rural inadequacy and backwoods charm" he had once enjoyed. He could find only a few buildings he remembered, and he wondered to himself where all the young women he had known (or had wished to know) and the professors who had taught him had gone. "What is life," he asked himself, "that it can thus obliterate itself? . . . If a whole realm of interests and emotions can thus definitely pass, what is anything?"

It was Thursday, August 26, the eve of Dreiser's forty-fourth birthday.[14]

They took the wrong road at first on their run back up to Indianapolis and Carmel, hitting a small pig along the way. In Carmel Dreiser became attracted to the daughter of one of the neighbors of Booth's parents. Murrel Cain was a sixteen- or seventeen-year-old schoolgirl who wore her hair in a bob and looked athletic in the photograph she gave Dreiser—of herself in a bathing suit. "Tell me you think you love me . . . ," he wrote later from Savannah, Georgia, "at least until you see me again anyhow." Booth was to remain at his western studio for a few months; Dreiser was to take the train back to New York. He had heard America singing. "Oh, the whistling, singing American, with his jest and his sound heart and that light of humorous apprehension in his eye! How wonderful it all is! It isn't English, or French, or German, or Spanish, or Russian, or Swedish, or Greek. It's American." At least in America one could dream—in spite of the fact that life possibly led nowhere. America was a psychic wonderland in which "we were conceived in ecstasy and born in dreams."[15]

That fall Joyce Kilmer, then a staff writer for the *New York Times,* interviewed the popular but now forgotten writer Will N. Harben on the future of the novel. Maintaining it was doomed, Harben blamed the popularity of the automobile, the growing interest in the airplane, and the book's future arch enemy, moving pictures. The Georgia spinner of rural romances also told the *New York Times* that he was not in sympathy "with the theories of some of our modern realists." Insisting that it was almost impossible to think of the American novel without thinking of Howells, Harben said that the average realist "doesn't believe that emotions are real." The greatest materials for the novelist, he said, were to be found in the emotional and spiritual side of nature, or "the soul of man."[16] No doubt his interviewer agreed. Today, with a rest stop on the New Jersey Turnpike named after him, Joyce Kilmer is otherwise remembered for *Trees and Other Poems* (1914), particularly its title poem, doggerel for popular consumption then and now ("Poems are made by fools like me, / But only God can make a tree"). A thoroughgoing sentimentalist who dedicated this poem to his mother-in-law, he probably hadn't hurt his literary career by marrying the daughter of Henry M. Alden, editor of *Harper's Magazine.* (Alden, we will recall, had once turned down Dreiser's ant story and discouraged him about the publishing prospects for *Sister Carrie.*) Kilmer's spirituality, however, fit right into the scheme of things literary in 1915. He was a romantic in the mold of George Gearson in "Editha," Howells's short story about the dangers of romantic sentiment in the Spanish-American War—and like Gearson, Kilmer became an early casualty of war. In the summer of 1918, he bypassed the officers' corps to enlist in the "Rainbow Division"—one of the first American units dispatched to France—and was killed in the Second Battle of the Marne.

When *The "Genius"* was first published in the fall of 1915, the best-selling books included Zane Grey's *The Rainbow Trail*, Rex Beach's *Heart of the Sunset*, and Harben's latest, *The Inner Law*. It was not only this American bent for romance that greeted the publication of *The "Genius,"* but the nation's political climate, which grew increasingly hostile toward "hyphenated" Americans—many of whom were not shy about expressing their sympathy for the Fatherland. The German-American population was a distinct minority in 1915, comprising about 10 percent of the population. Americans were glad to be staying out of the war, but with Wilson, a lover of English civilization, in the White House, and the majority of Americans having antecedents in the British Isles, sentiment quickly grew for the English. To make matters worse, as far as Dreiser was concerned, the American ambassador to Great Britain was none other than the pro-British Walter Hines Page, Doubleday's former partner during the suppression of *Sister Carrie*.

The "Genius" in this America was seen as the literary equivalent of another German U-boat, threatening to undermine traditional Anglo-American standards of decency and morality. Vigorously opposed to "this hypnotism which is going on in art, in which whatever is opposed to the righteous forces of the will is celebrated," Mrs. Elia W. Peattie of the *Chicago Tribune* of December 4, repudiated the idea that *The "Genius"* was, as one reviewer had suggested, the American prose-epic. Peattie, a former contributor to the *Delineator* when Dreiser was editor, vowed: "I will never admit such a thing until I am ready to see the American flag trailing in the dust dark with stains of [the blood of] my sons, and the Germans completing their world rule by placing their governor general in the White House." N. P. Dawson, another lover of the courageous poetic idealism that Kilmer in his death would come to represent, expressed in the *New York Evening Globe* of October 30 her sincere hope that Dreiser's new novel "will immediately appear in a German translation. That's how kindly we feel toward the Germans!" Such chauvinistic reviewers rose eagerly to condemn *The "Genius."* "*Sex-land uber alles* would seem to be Theodore Dreiser's national anthem," commented *Life* magazine on November 15, 1915. Using the battle imagery spilling over from the war, the reviewer continued: "There was 'Sister Carrie,' 'Jennie Gerhardt,' 'The Financier,' 'The Titan,' and at no time, in any of them, was it very far to Tipperary. But now, in 'The Genius,' [sic] he actually goes into action on the fictional front . . . singing 'sex-land' in close formation of fine type all along the line!"[17]

Like Mencken, Dreiser was pro-German in his sympathies, but also decidedly anti-British regardless of the war. In paying back Ford Madox Ford for his belittling remarks about *The Titan* in a review of *The Good Soldier* (1915), Dreiser blamed that extracted German's British leanings for his failure to tell an honest story in spite of its realistic methods. "It is all cold narrative, never truly poignant," he wrote in *The New Republic* that year. "The whole book is indeed fairly representative of that encrusting formalism which, barnacle-wise, is apparently overtaking and destroying all that is best in English life." He may have continued to admire the English for their support of *Sister Carrie,* though his trip to England had left him less receptive to the British in general. Now he resented their "sniffy reverence for conventionalism and the glories of a fixed condition." About the same time, he spoke elsewhere of "the despicable British aristocracy." Dreiser's growing antagonism toward the British melded with Mencken's quips about German military superiority and his celebrations of German victories. Planning, he said in one letter to Dreiser in early 1915, to study German so "that I may spend my declining years in a civilized country," he cheered the German victory at the Battle of Soissons, where the French lost more than nine thousand soldiers.[18]

What the two friends didn't share, however, was the same opinion of Dreiser's latest novel—his worst yet in Mencken's opinion but, as Dreiser ultimately decided, his favorite if he had to choose one over all the rest. After accepting several of his one-act plays for *The Smart Set,* Mencken had repeatedly asked to see the text of *The "Genius."* (As already noted, for most of its composition it did not have quotation marks around its presumptive title. Dreiser told Mencken that he added them because there was another book of the same title, but reviewers assumed he was signaling a flaw in its hero, Eugene Tennyson Witla. Other working titles were "This Matter of Marriage," "The Glory of Eugene," "Eugene Witla," "The Hedonist," "The Dreamer," and "The Sensualist.")[19] When Dreiser finally did dispatch part of the manuscript in early December 1914, he was still "pruning" out stylistic blemishes he knew his friend would detect. By the end of the month, Mencken had read the entire 320,000-word typescript. Keeping up the bonhomie about German military might and their shared heritage, he preferred to speak to Dreiser in person about *The "Genius."* The two met over the matter in Dreiser's apartment, where Mencken recalled years later they had

had a "friendly row" that chased Kirah out of the apartment "horrified by the thought of two Christians murdering each other." Yet in all probability, Mencken was circumspect. They still considered each other good friends, and Dreiser had presented him with the manuscript of *Sister Carrie*. A little more than a year later, Mencken claimed that it wasn't the questionable or—as it was ultimately called—pornographic content of *The "Genius"* that bothered him, but its weakness as a work of art. He tried to downplay his dislike for the novel by telling Dreiser that it was "still my blind spot."[20]

The *New York Times* of October 10, comparing *The "Genius"* unfavorably with Sinclair Lewis's *The Trail of the Hawk,* described it as "a study of the artistic temperament, but really of only one abnormal weakness, that of ungoverned sexual passion and its effects on the life and work of an otherwise great artist." Dreiser later claimed that he had no particular artist in mind when he wrote the novel, only the "Ashcan" school of painters, several of whom he had known as magazine illustrators and whose "slice of life" focus reflects Dreiser's realism or naturalism in his own fiction. They were the "New York Realists" who led the revolt against the genteel tradition in American art during the first two decades of the twentieth century. Among those he may have used as models was William Louis Sonntag, Jr., who had illustrated *Ev'ry Month* when Dreiser was editor and whom Dreiser would memorialize as W.L.S. in *Twelve Men.*[21] Other possibilities include the Ashcan painters George Luks, John Sloan, Robert Henri, Everett Shinn, and William Glackens, who illustrated *A Traveler at Forty.* He may also have drawn from Alfred Stieglitz, whose "The El in the Storm" and "Winter on Fifth Avenue" Dreiser had singled out for praise in *Success* and *Ainslee's* respectively (both in 1899)—photographs that may have suggested the driving snowstorm Hurstwood endures during his decline in *Sister Carrie.*[22]

The primary model, of course, was Dreiser himself, whose autobiography was also well underway with the composition of *Dawn.* Indeed, Dreiser had been trying to fictionalize his life since the turn of the century. In 1943, he told Mencken that he had written thirty-two chapters "of what was to be *The 'Genius'*" in 1903 and then destroyed them in 1907 or 1908 to clear the way for the resumption and eventual completion of *Jennie Gerhardt.* Another autobiographical novel attempted even earlier was "The Rake."[23] This last was possibly to be based on his sexual escapades as a reporter, but *The "Genius"* was the book that finally fictionalized the sexual "varietism" of Theodore Dreiser.

Divided into three "books," as *An American Tragedy* would be arranged, the novel was patterned after Dreiser's life, but more loosely in Book I ("Youth") than in the other two ("Struggle" and "Revolt"). The first part recounts the life of the protagonist growing up in a middle-class family in Illinois instead of the hard-scrabble upbringing Dreiser experienced in the small towns of Indiana. We follow Eugene Witla to Chicago, where he becomes a newspaper illustrator and an evening student at the Art Institute. His sexual initiation, his jobs in a hardware store and a real estate office, and as a delivery man for a laundry roughly parallel Dreiser's Chicago experiences as described in the autobiographies. Ruby Kenny of the novel, for example, is Alice Kane in *Newspaper Days* and Lois Zahn in reality.[24] After two years in Chicago, Eugene returns to visit his parents and meets Sara White's counterpart in Angela Blue, visiting from Wisconsin, also a schoolteacher and older than her beau (by five years instead of Jug's nearly three). Soon following their mutual attraction, he proposes marriage, but like Dreiser goes off to pursue his career for several years, during which he comes to regret (and undermine) his commitment. After working as an illustrator in New York and developing into a realist of the Ashcan School, Eugene returns to the Midwest to marry Angela when she threatens suicide after having given into his sexual longings.

Book II takes up the next 300 pages of the 736-page novel and concerns Eugene's rise as a painter, his nervous breakdown, and his rise again as general editor of a magazine conglomerate similar to Butterick Publications. It follows Dreiser's marriage so closely that he feared Jug would burn the manuscript if she knew about it. Just as Dreiser was attracted to Jug's sister, Eugene is attracted to Angela's sister, but Jug would have been infuriated to learn that the sister is made into an active flirt in *The "Genius,"* certainly not the case with Rose White or, for that matter, probably any of Archibald White's conservatively bred daughters. More than likely, however, Jug never read *The "Genius."*[25] Book III covers the Thelma Cudlipp episode from start to finish, even down to Dreiser's echoing some of his frantic love letters to the eighteen-year-old. This is Suzanne Dale, who is put beyond Eugene's reach by her irate mother; Mrs. Dale also causes him to lose his job with the United States Magazines Corporation. In a last-ditch effort to keep her husband, Angela allows herself to become pregnant but dies in childbirth. Like *Jennie Gerhardt*, *The "Genius"* first had a happy ending in which Eugene and Suzanne find each other again, but Dreiser switched it to one in which, when they meet, they pass each other, "never to meet [again] in this world." Instead, Eugene discovers Christian Science, and the story ends on a philosophical note.[26]

The novel is too long for its story. It is tedious and melodramatic in too many places, downright unrealistic in others (for example, in the depiction of the near-nymphomaniacal Carlotta Wilson, with whom Eugene trysts while working for the railroad). It was clearly an act of literary self-indulgence, more of Dreiser's fictional and nonfictional summing up of himself as he struggled to make a living solely by his pen. But the novel is also epical in its strength and scope, dramatizing impressively the art scene in America in transition from New England gentility to the raw Whitmanesque celebrations of the self. Mencken's reviews of Dreiser's novels and of this one in particular in *The Smart Set* for December 1915 are usually credited for making the central argument for Dreiser's panoramic and epical qualities ("It is rambling, formless, chaotic—and yet there emerges out of it . . .").[27] But in this case it was Dreiser's recent friend John Cowper Powys who not only articulated Dreiser's new American strength but securely linked it to Whitman's.

The transplanted Englishman noted that like Whitman, Dreiser had found his first "profoundly appreciative hearing in England"—as though both writers were so large that one needs the perspective of the Atlantic "as a modifying foreground." Dreiser's Balzacian details Powys compared to Whitman's long poetic catalogs. And in terms of style, or the lack of it, Powys correctly pointed out that most of what comes under criticism with Dreiser—as indeed it did with Whitman—was his use of the vernacular. This and his attention to detail were part of the essential quality of an epic. Yet readers and critics were misled by "certain outstanding details—the sexual scenes, for instance, or the financial scenes" and so missed Dreiser's "proportionate vision." With reference to *The "Genius,"* Powys might have pointed to the very first scene in the book subsequently designated as "obscene" by the New York Society for the Suppression of Vice, the same watch-and-ward alliance that had threatened *Leaves of Grass* in the 1880s. Here Eugene kneels before his girlfriend Stella to tighten one of her skates:

> She stood before him and he fell to his knees, undoing the twisted strap. When he had the skate off and ready for her foot he looked up, and she looked down on him, smiling. He dropped the skate and flung his arms around her hips, laying his head against her waist. "You're a bad boy," she said.

Dreiser captures in this brief passage not only the passion but the entire culture of sex and its taboos at the end of the American nineteenth century. "To the European mind," Powys wrote, "there is something incredibly absurd in the notion that these Dreiser books are immoral." Not only were they not immoral, but they were religious. "It [Dreiser's religious sentiment] is felt and felt very powerfully; but it is kept in its place. Like Walt Whitman's stellar constellations, it suffices for those who belong to it, it is right enough where it is." And it was balanced, he thought, by the body, which was inexplicably tied in its urges to something spiritual. "If one is interested in the 'urge—urge—urge,' as Whitman calls it, of the normal lifestream as it goes upon its way, in these American States," Powys concluded, "one reads Dreiser with a strange pleasure."[28] Overall, Powys could have chosen a greater Dreiser novel to celebrate this way, yet The "Genius" in its swaggering disregard for the American ban on sex in literature was the immediate successor to Whitman's book, the first one to be "banned in Boston."

This was one of the favorable reviews, of course, and they divided almost evenly between the positive and negative, few occupying any middle ground. It took an academic to make the strongest negative review, and that was Mrs. Peattie's friend in Urbana, Professor Stuart Sherman of the University of Illinois. Just in case somebody wasn't completely aware of it, Sherman noted that Dreiser was the first non-Anglican American to produce major American literature. But he didn't mean it as a compliment. It was to remind his readers during the war that Dreiser was "born of German-American parents" in Indiana. His five books constituted "a singularly homogeneous mass of fiction" in which Sherman found neither "moral value" nor "memorable beauty."[29]

This was the voice of Puritanism making its last cry in a new wilderness. "College professors, alas, never learn anything," Mencken later observed in response to Sherman's attack, but Sherman's was also the voice of Realism against the inroads of Naturalism.[30] Sherman was the first academic critic to assess Dreiser; the rest had largely ignored him and his fellow naturalists in favor of the great literary lights of the last century, not only realists such as the (still living) Howells and James but the antebellum romantics who had inspired them. These were not the writers F. O. Matthiessen identified in The American Renaissance (1941) for elevation in the mid-twentieth century (Melville, Hawthorne, Poe, Emerson, Thoreau, Whitman) as much as such Schoolroom Poets as Henry Wadsworth Longfellow, James Russell Lowell, John Greenleaf Whittier, and Oliver Wendell Holmes— the trinomial "gentleman" of the American Renaissance who were more clearly linked to New England Brahmanism and middle-class conventions.

"The real distinction between one generation and another is in the thing which each takes for its master truth," Sherman observed. Dreiser and his fellow naturalists had simply come up with a new theory, the Darwinian idea that all life is exclusively and selfishly devoted to its adaptation and survival. In the cases of both Darwin and the naturalistic writers, once they had formulated their general law, they looked exclusively for evidence to support it. "Let us then," Sherman wrote, "dismiss Mr. Dreiser's untenable claims to superior courage and veracity of intention, the photographic transcript, and the unbiased service of truth; and let us seek for his definition in his general theory of life, in the order of facts which he records, and in the pattern of his representations." Dreiser's theory presented men and women not only with the will to survive but the will to pleasure wherever they found it: "The male of the species is characterized by cupidity, pugnacity, and a simian inclination for the other sex. The female is a soft, vain, pleasure-seeking creature, devoted to personal adornment." But there was another theory, a better one Sherman thought, that presented men and women more ideally and hopefully, even under realistic conditions.[31]

Dreiser, of course, was striking out for new territory in fiction when he reflected Eugene's psychosexual conflicts, laying the groundwork in the twentieth century for the psychological naturalism of such writers as Sherwood Anderson and William Faulkner. Freud is not mentioned, but his ideas were already in the air—hotly discussed and debated at the Liberal Club in Greenwich Village—and Dreiser would read him in the late teens and early twenties. "His hero is really not Sister Carrie or the Titan or the Genius," the critic Randolph Bourne acutely noted, "but that desire within us that pounds in manifold guise against the iron walls of experience."[32] But psychology was but another name for naturalism, as far as Dreiser's opponents were concerned. Both theories rendered the once-ethical person helpless and unattractive.

Dreiser spent the winter of 1916 in Savannah, Georgia, where he rented a room for $2.50 a week at 103 Taylor Street West. He went south ostensibly to rid himself of a persistent case of the grippe, but perhaps another reason to get out of town for a while was that his relationship with Kirah was deteriorating toward its eventual collapse. She had already left him at least twice because of his infidelity, the second time in June of 1915. In any event, he was looking for a quiet and comfortable place to work on *A Hoosier Holiday*. Like *A Traveler at Forty*, this travel book had a personal dedication, this time to his mother. Chastened by her memory and the travel book's focus on youthful innocence, it generally lacked what was now expected in every Dreiser book. To many readers and reviewers of *A Hoosier Holiday*, which appeared at the end of 1916, Dreiser had finally produced "a book in which the sex urge does not reign supreme." It is true that chapter 60 reflects back on his college trip to Louisville, which involved several loose women, but the story lacks the specificity he later made public in *Dawn*. Furthermore, at Mencken's suggestion, he changed the name of Day Allen Willy, one of his companions on the Louisville excursion and "now a highly respectable Baltimorean and a God-fearing man," to simply "W."[33]

But even as Dreiser was cleaning up his act, as it were, forces were mounting to make him pay for his excesses in *The "Genius."* That summer, as sales of the novel reached eight thousand copies, Professor Sherman's objections were acted upon by the New York Society for the Prevention of Vice, which threatened Dreiser's publisher, John Lane, with criminal prosecution if they did not withdraw the book from the market at once.[34] The complaint had originated in Cincinnati after John F. Herget, a Baptist minister, acting on an anonymous tip, alerted F. L. Rowe, the secretary of the Western Society for the Prevention of Vice in Cincinnati, that *The "Genius"* was "filled with obscenity and blasphemy." Rowe in turn complained to John Sumner, recently appointed executive secretary of the New York Society and successor to Anthony Comstock, who died that year. Armed also with some of the offending pages torn by an irate reader from the copy in the New York Public Library, Sumner quietly confronted J. Jefferson Jones at the John Lane Company on July 25, 1916. Sumner sought to avoid the method of his predecessor, whose theatrics had mainly provided offending books with "free advertising." (Comstock's assault on *Leaves of Grass* had given Whitman the greatest sales of his lifetime.) Three days later, the American director who had been so eager to get the book away from Harper's immediately conceded to Sumner's demand, leaving the book—and Dreiser—in limbo. "This book was selling the best of any," Dreiser told Mencken in characteristic exaggeration of his sales (which were nevertheless mounting), "and now this cuts me off right in mid stream. Don't it beat hell."[35]

His tone suggests that he initially took the whole matter somewhat lightly. "Am perfectly willing to break the postal laws and go to jail myself," he joked. "It will save me my living expenses this winter." Either he was confident that only a few changes would have to be made (as it turned out seventy-five pages of *The "Genius"* were earmarked as "lewd" and seventeen as "profane"), or he hoped the Society for the Prevention of Vice was already beginning to lose credibility with the American public and could be bluffed or compromised. Mencken initially suggested such a compromise, having himself done so after he had run afoul of the society briefly with the publication of the *Parisienne,* one of several saucy magazines he and Nathan put out on the side mainly to support *The Smart Set.* The threatened charges against *The "Genius"* were twofold: the first involved Section 1141 of Article 105 of the New York Penal Code, which forbade the sale or distribution of "any obscene, lewd, lascivious, filthy, indecent, sadistic, masochistic or disgusting book, magazine, pamphlet," and so on. The second invoked Section 211 of the U.S. Criminal Code against sending obscene material through the mail.[36]

The whole matter ceased to be amusing when bootleg copies of the suppressed novel began selling for fifty dollars apiece. The fact that Jones had wilted so readily when confronted with the remote chance of criminal prosecution and the possibility of jail now began to enrage Dreiser. Just as the publisher of *Leaves of Grass* in 1881 had withdrawn the book without any charges actually being filed, no charges were ever filed in the case of *The "Genius."* By the end of 1916, in fact, it was becoming clear that neither the U.S. District Attorney for New York nor the Postmaster General was interested in pressing charges.[37] Jones tried to placate Dreiser but in effect said one thing and did another, never calling Sumner's bluff by reoffering *The "Genius"* for sale. His indecision, indeed reluctance to get further involved in the case, ultimately compelled Dreiser, in a desperate effort to free up his book again for sale, to file a "friendly" lawsuit against the John Lane Company in order to force the matter into an official decision as to whether the novel was obscene. He sued his publishers for $50,000 for violating his contract. By complying with Sumner's order, John Lane had given credence to the idea that Dreiser was guilty of obscenity. Yet their refusal to keep publishing the book had no defensible basis without a legal decision against him. If he could get a court to rule that *The "Genius"* was not obscene and thus win the suit, he could get them to either reissue the book or turn it over to Dreiser to find another publisher. The Appellate Court that considered the case, however, sidestepped the sticky matter of ruling on an obscenity case by dismissing Dreiser's suit on a technicality in 1918: since no criminal charges had ever been filed against the book by Sumner, there was no formal question of obscenity to consider.[38]

Not long after Sumner's initial confrontation with the John Lane Company in the summer of 1916, Dreiser informed Mencken that there was an effort underway to organize a "Committee of One Hundred" to assist in the defense of The "Genius." Mencken was agreeable as long as the effort didn't contain any "professional radicals," meaning Greenwich Village socialists. This interest soon led to Dreiser's turning to the Authors' League of America to support a petition against the suppression. The League's support, it was hoped, might embolden Jones to be more combative with Sumner. Dreiser had scorned the League's efforts to enlist him as a member in 1913, claiming that their interests lay solely in protecting "second serial & moving picture rights" instead of challenging the moral strictures of the era.[39] Now with his publisher apparently deserting him, he was forced to swallow his pride and accept any help the League might provide. The problem was that more than a few of the writers asked to sign the petition didn't consider The "Genius" a very worthy cause, either because of its perceived literary weaknesses or its excessive focus on what was considered illicit sex. As a result, the final draft of the petition noted that the undersigned "may differ from Mr. Dreiser in our aims and methods, and some of us may be out of sympathy with his point of view."[40]

One of those for whom even this stipulation was not enough was Hamlin Garland. He had praised Sister Carrie to Dreiser in a 1903 letter and received him when he came to Chicago in 1913 to research The Titan. In fact, Garland had held a favorable opinion of Dreiser until the summer of 1913. When he nominated Dreiser for election to the National Institute of Arts and Letters that year, he learned that another member of the society, Robert Underwood Johnson, strongly objected. Johnson had resigned from the editorship of Century Magazine after it agreed to publish Dreiser's excerpts from A Traveler at Forty. Their unedited versions, Johnson told Garland, contained accounts of "illicit relations with five different women, with disgusting details." Garland agreed that such a sex-obsessed man would not make a good member of the institute, but it was the vulgarity of The "Genius" that sealed his ultimate disapproval. When asked to sign the Authors' League petition, he wrote Eric Schuler, its secretary, opposing the action. Mencken appealed to him, reminding Garland of the trouble he had had with Comstock over Rose of Dutcher's Coolly, but Garland would not relent. The Prairie Realist who had known Whitman personally and defended him publicly in the wake of his battle with the censors complained in the manuscript of his literary reminiscences, Companions on the Trail (1931), that Dreiser's realism had been based essentially on his sexual problems.[41]

Many, of course, did sign, through the efforts not only of Mencken but of Harold Hersey, assistant to Schuler and a clerk of the copyright office of the Library of Congress, who had written Dreiser a fan letter in 1915 about *Sister Carrie.*[42] The five hundred or more signers included Jack London, fellow Hoosier Booth Tarkington, George Ade, Henry B. Fuller, Arnold Bennett, H. G. Wells, Amy Lowell, Willa Cather, Robert Frost, Ezra Pound, Sherwood Anderson, Sinclair Lewis, Edgar Lee Masters, Edwin Arlington Robinson, Carl Van Vechten, Horace Traubel, Max Eastman, John Reed, and Ida Tarbell. The dissenters counted Howells, Ellen Glasgow, Brander Matthews, and the best-selling author Rex Beach, who was also a member of the executive committee of the League.[43] One other prominent writer to decline was the author of "Trees." "It may interest you to know," Mencken told Dreiser on December 16, 1916, "that Joyce Kilmer, the eminent critic of the New York Times, has refused to sign the protest. May the good God help Joyce."[44]

If Kilmer, a recent Catholic convert, had lived long enough to read Dreiser's next challenge to American decency, he would have been sure that God was on his side. Mencken read it in manuscript that month and was furious at Dreiser for wanting to publish something so *verboten,* if not in fact actionable under current criminal codes on obscenity, this while Mencken himself dutifully worked to gather signatures from reluctant supporters of the League petition.[45] *The Hand of the Potter,* Dreiser's only four-act play, took up the story of a sex offender whose behavior is considered philosophically and sympathetically. According to its epigraph, he took his title and theme from the *Rubáiyát:* "What! did the Hand then of the Potter shake?" The reference is to two of the children of Aaron Berchansky, a thread peddler living on the lower East Side. Of his ten children, four of whom are already dead, Masha is "a lame embroideress," and Isadore is a child molester. The idea of God as a potter prone to mistakes may have come from *Dawn,* then in manuscript. There Dreiser recalls an old potter with a small shop on Vine Street in Evansville. "He sat before an open window, winter and summer, his wheel or whirling platform before him, shaping clay into pitchers, cups, saucers, bowls and the like," Dreiser wrote. "It was my first introduction to the mystery of form."[46]

The plot itself was closely based on an actual sex crime that occurred in New York in the summer of 1912. The nude body of a twelve-year-old girl with forty-one stab wounds was discovered in a vacant lot outside the child's residence. Police arrested an ex-convict with a record for "imperiling the morals" of a fourteen-year-old girl. During a grand jury hearing designed by the district attorney to play on the feelings of the suspect's guilt-ridden parents, they confessed their belief that their son was the murderer. Still on the loose, he was found two days later in a tenement house, where he had committed suicide. He left behind several notes admitting his guilt but pleading insanity. There were similar murders in New York and elsewhere in the country in the teens that might also have inspired Dreiser, including the highly reported case in which Leo Frank was accused of the murder of a thirteen-year-old girl in Atlanta.[47] Its elements of anti-Semitism toward the accused—who was ultimately lynched by vigilantes—may have suggested the Jewish character of the Berchanskys, who are Russian immigrants but for some reason speak like German émigrés. The play relies on the stereotypical image then of the "dirty Jew," but only with reference to the family's impoverished conditions, which were shared in the same part of the city by Italians soon to be depicted in *The Color of a Great City.*

There are several parallels between the Berchanskys and the Indiana Dreisers. The character of the patriarch is one of the stronger aspects of the play, for once again we have Old Gerhardt or the reincarnation of John Paul Dreiser. And Mrs. Berchansky is as forgiving of her son's problem as Sarah Dreiser was about her offsprings' difficulties, even Rome's. The cast of characters includes a six-year-old niece called "Tillie," the nickname of Dreiser's sister Claire, one of the trio of youngest children, including Theo, who lived with Sarah after the family split up for economic reasons. In the drama, Isadore (which partially rhymes with "Theodore") lusts after this child before settling upon his eleven-year-old victim. Dreiser diverged from the facts of the actual murder to show Isadore also trying to fondle his teenaged sister Rae. One is tempted to ask whether these additions are a reflection of Dreiser's teenage sexual fantasies about his sister Tillie, two years his senior. On the other hand, this may not have been sexual at all, but merely a writer's way, à la Poe in "The Cask of Amontillado," of avenging a real person in fiction. "I have not as yet described my sister Tillie as she was then," Dreiser initially wrote in a canceled passage in the manuscript of *Dawn,* "but a blacker eyed, . . . more self-aggrandizing little magpie never lived." Two years after he wrote *The Hand of the Potter* and perhaps penned this indictment, Claire died at age forty-six of breast cancer—on May 30, 1918.[48]

As with *The "Genius,"* Dreiser may also have put some of himself into his play. According to the biographer Richard Lingeman, Mai Dreiser, Ed's wife, who strongly disapproved of Dreiser's philandering, having heard more than an earful from Jug, whom she had befriended, thought her brother-in-law ought to be sterilized.[49] Whether she read *The "Genius,"* Mai, a devout Catholic, was reportedly shocked over the moral condemnation the novel was receiving. Was it evidence that her husband's closest brother was sexually abnormal? Dreiser was aware of his sister-in-law's disapproval of him. Perhaps in this climate of family suspicions, he secretly used the play as a means of self-exploration. It contains Dreiser's first allusion in his works to the theories of Sigmund Freud, whose work was generally known by Greenwich Village writers by the middle teens. A few years later Dreiser's publisher, Boni & Liveright, issued the first American edition of *An Introduction to Psychoanalysis.*[50] Wharton Esherick, an artist whom Dreiser met in 1924, testified that it was his impression after knowing the writer for many years that Dreiser couldn't control his sexual appetite. "He was absolutely a fool with a young girl—those beautiful 16- and 17-year-olds. He always wanted to get them on his lap." Esherick added that Dreiser persisted in this conduct even in the company of the woman who eventually became his second wife. Although Dreiser's interest in pubescent girls generally did not go beyond such flirting, he did later have a sexual affair with a seventeen-year-old and may have been similarly interested in her fourteen-year-old sister.[51]

Whatever the self-revelations in *The Hand of the Potter,* it is a powerful play because it draws from the old Dreiserian well of family memories and the later one of public documents. Although the third act may distract somewhat from the dramatic action of the play with its rather tedious and largely unnecessary courtroom scene, Isadore Berchansky is clearly helpless in the face of his criminal proclivities. "It's their pretty mouths an' hair an' the way they walk an' them shirtwaists so fine" is the general refrain that defines this victim of his hormones ("Did ye know, ayther ave ye," says one of the reporters on the case, "that there's something they've called *hormones* which . . . is poured into the blood streams of every waan ave us which excites us to the m'aning ave beauty an' them things"). Dreiser's argument in the play, the one he had been elaborating since "Nigger Jeff," is that when it came to sexual desire there were certain people who simply couldn't restrain themselves. The playwright was probably instructed not only by Freud but even more so by the mechanistic theories of behavior of Jacques Loeb, made popular over the previous ten or fifteen years. Dreiser later acknowledged these twin influences during his Greenwich Village days in *A Gallery of Women.* Overestimating what the public reaction might be, Mencken in-

Dreiser in front of his childhood home in Sullivan, Indiana, during the
1915 road trip described in *A Hoosier Holiday*. (Van Pelt–Dietrich Library)

Dreiser in his West Tenth Street apartment in
Greenwich Village. (Van Pelt–Dietrich Library)

William and John Cowper Powys in 1934.
(Van Pelt–Dietrich Library)

Estelle Bloom Kubitz and Marion Bloom in 1913 in
Houston, Texas—the "Redmond Sisters" in *A Gallery
of Women*. (Courtesy of Julia Roop Cairns)

Louise Campbell: "My friends all seem to think I make a much better fashion model than a writer." (Van Pelt–Dietrich Library)

Helen Richardson (eventually the second Mrs. Dreiser) in Hollywood. (Van Pelt–Dietrich Library)

Dreiser, photographed for *Vanity Fair* following
the publication of *An American Tragedy*, 1925.
(Van Pelt–Dietrich Library)

Caricature of Dreiser at the Ritz throwing coffee in
the face of Horace Liveright, by Edward Sorel.
(*The New Yorker,* December 25, 2000)

Iroki (roughly, Japanese for "beauty"), Dreiser's country home in Mt. Kisco, New York. (Van Pelt–Dietrich Library)

Sister Mame and brother Rome Dreiser at Iroki in 1931. (Van Pelt–Dietrich Library)

Clara Clark in the 1930s.
(Courtesy of Clara Clark Jaeger)

Yvette Székely at Iroki, about 1930.
(Courtesy of Yvette Székely Eastman)

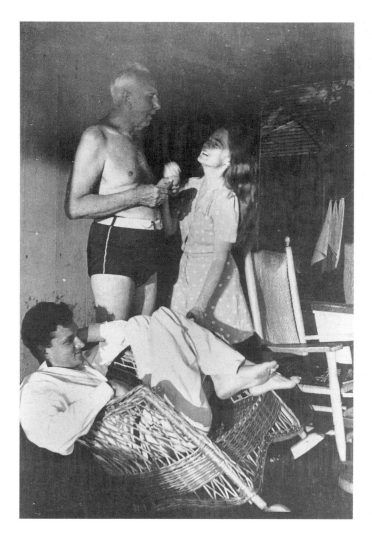

Dreiser with Marguerite Tjader and an unidentified
young man, at Iroki. (Van Pelt–Dietrich Library)

Harriet Bissell, Edgar Lee Masters,
and Dreiser at Iroki in the mid-1930s.
(Van Pelt–Dietrich Library)

Esther McCoy.
(Van Pelt–Dietrich Library)

Dreiser on his sixtieth birthday in his West Fifty-Seventh Street
apartment, New York. (Van Pelt–Dietrich Library)

Dreiser in Paris in 1938. (Van Pelt–Dietrich Library)

Above left: Sherwood
Anderson, by Alfred Steiglitz,
1923. (Art Institute of Chicago).
Above right: Hazel Mack
Godwin. (Van Pelt–Dietrich
Library). *Right*: Sinclair Lewis
and Dorothy Thompson on
their wedding day in 1928.
(Syracuse University Library)

Dreiser with Marguerite Tjader, niece Vera, and brother
Ed Dreiser, New York, 1944. (Van Pelt–Dietrich Library)

S. S. McClure, Willa Cather, Dreiser, and Paul Robeson in 1944.
(Van Pelt–Dietrich Library)

Montgomery Clift and Elizabeth Taylor in *A Place
in the Sun* (1951), the second film to be based on
An American Tragedy. (The Kobal Collection)

sisted that "Nothing is more abhorrent to the average man than sexual perversion." Equally exasperated, Dreiser could not understand his friend's "tirade" over the play. "Admittedly the idea may be badly worked out . . . ," he conceded. "But the subject! A poor weak pervert, defended or tolerated and half concealed by a family for social reasons commits a sex crime— not shown on the stage—and thereby entails a chain of disaster which destroys the home and breaks the spirit of the father and mother."[52]

"A raging, destroying bull, which insists on gormandizing all the females of a herd," Dreiser had recently written in *A Hoosier Holiday*, "is the product of nature, not of man. Man did not make the bull or the stallion, nor did they make themselves. Is nature to be controlled, made over, by man, according to some secret theory which man, a product of nature, has discovered?" As the tormented Isadore prepares to commit suicide rather than give himself up to the police, he has little control of either muscle or mind. His shoulder jerks as he swats the air and proclaims, "It's the red ones all the time, not the blacks. They won't let me alone—always followin' me around. G'wan!" His last words of hopelessness echo Hurstwood's final frustration.[53]

By the time Dreiser wrote *The Hand of the Potter* in the fall of 1916, he had changed steady girlfriends. Kirah had finally bolted in the spring to become a member of the Provincetown Players. There seems to be a consensus among Dreiser scholars that she was the only woman he ever truly loved. Certainly, it is clear that Kirah loved him—one witness noted that she was so "strongly drawn to him" that before she left town for good she would walk nostalgically past 165 West Tenth Street—but she would not stay with him on his terms.[54] And whatever Dreiser's deepest feelings, he would not change his ways. That summer Mencken, who worked for the *Baltimore Sun* and came to New York weekly in conjunction with his editorial duties on *The Smart Set,* introduced Dreiser to Estelle Bloom Kubitz, the twenty-nine-year-old sister of Marion Bloom, who had been Mencken's lover for the last three years. Estelle and Marion, six years younger, hailed from New Windsor, Maryland, farm country of rolling hills forty miles northwest of Baltimore. The sisters had escaped small-town America to make their way in the world as prototypes of the "New Woman" of the early twentieth century. They appear as minor characters in one of the fifteen sketches in *A Gallery of*

Women (1929), where Dreiser dubbed them the Redmond Sisters—"young adventurers, without background or means, as are so many of the thousands who reconnoiter the great cities and without many, if indeed any, severe or wholly unyielding moral scruples."[55]

Their past in rural Maryland sounds like something out of *Winesburg, Ohio.* Their father, a dairy farmer and former teacher, committed suicide in 1898 over his imagined sins after the descent on New Windsor of a female evangelist. Their mother, a cripple, was left at age thirty-eight with six children to raise and no money. Estelle ran away at eighteen with a German-born soldier named Hans Kubitz, whom she eventually married and accompanied to Germany. They moved back to the States and settled in Houston; in 1912 Kubitz deserted her for Mexico. Marion had also left home and established herself in Washington, D.C., where Estelle joined her. The sisters moved to New York in the winter of 1916. After Estelle linked up with Dreiser that summer, she slept over at his place occasionally but kept an apartment with her sister at 274 West Nineteenth Street. The two couples, Dreiser and Estelle and Mencken and Marion, frequently double-dated, dining at such restaurants as Lüchow's on Fourteenth Street, the Brevoort, and the Lafayette Hotel.

Estelle, a brunette whose dreamy eyes gave her appearance a certain poignance, became Dreiser's "secretary" with minimal recompense, having started by copying out reviews of *The "Genius."*[56] She was nicknamed "Gloom" because of her fondness for Russian novels, but the sobriquet also reflected her pessimistic state of mind. Like her sister (who dated Mencken into the 1920s, before he married a younger woman), she was a masochist when it came to men. Estelle complained bitterly to her sister (who was instructed to respond with dual letters, one for her eyes only) about evidence of Dreiser's infidelities. Even though he spent most of his leisure time with Estelle, he continued to engage in casual love affairs with other women. In a characteristic diary entry (for May 24, 1917), Dreiser writes: "Lill [Lillian Rosenthal] comes. Can't stay long, but we go to bed for a little while. A heavy screw. Return to my book *[The Bulwark].* Finish chapter 16 and 17. Call up Bert [another nickname for Estelle] at 5 to know about dinner. . . . Up to Bert's. We have fine meal. . . . Take a hot bath and go to bed there. One hour or so of wonderful copulation, then to sleep."[57]

They make love in "fierce rounds," fight, make up. Estelle cries and cries. All this is described in his diary, which, incredibly, *she* later typed out and gave to Mencken, possibly as a form of revenge.[58] Mencken became her confidant during the late teens and often counseled her against becoming

Dreiser's "doormat"—yet all the while, he exploited her sister Marion in the same way, if not as nonchalantly. "God in heaven," Estelle exclaimed to Marion not long after starting her affair with Dreiser. "I'm sick of it. These men, flitting lightly from one woman to another, with never a thought of what is to become of the woman they have flitted from." Such women as she and her sister, she anguished, were fools. "If they'd think, they'd know that marriage was made for them. . . . Instead, while they are young, they prattle about equal sexual and civil rights, cooking up a fine kettle of fish for their middle age." Yet almost a decade later and by then married to the successful New York food and beverage importer Arthur Phelps Williams, she told Marion, herself by this time married and deserted by a Frenchman, "I wouldn't give two cents for the whole institution of marriage" because it aimed at "penning two entirely different" people together to the point of mutual hatred.[59]

Both women were colorful writers who never developed their talents in a literary world still dominated by men. Estelle wrote best in self-descriptions that were both biting and poignant. Speaking to her sister of their mutual "friend, the honorable Theodore Dreiser," she wondered why she stayed with him. "This morning I went to a Catholic Church just off Broadway," she told Marion. "I saw the door open, and slunk in, and wasn't in one minute before I found myself crying in a dumb sort of way, for some reason, I don't know yet. . . . I saw the 'Believers' lighting candles to their departed, and I had an insane desire to light one to my own departed soul." An alcoholic eventually, if not at the time she was with Dreiser (who still did not drink much then), she ultimately returned to New Windsor, divorcing Williams, whom she caught cheating on her. She underwent a double mastectomy in 1940 and retreated for good to the family homestead, where she died a recluse in a house full of cats in 1954.[60]

While Dreiser was still deeply involved with Estelle, he received a fan letter from a literary admirer in Philadelphia. She was Louise Campbell, a married woman in her twenties who spoke fluent German. She was petite, yet another brunette, and—as Dreiser would soon discover—"a perfect little cormorant of lust." She had recently read *A Hoosier Holiday* and complained lightly about Dreiser's criticism of Pennsylvania. Otherwise, she had written to praise other works including *A Traveler at Forty,* and to whet his interest in her personally. "Ever since I came across your 'Jennie Gerhardt' I've read everything I could find that you wrote," she told him on February 24, 1917. "For the last two weeks my sister and I have been having a perfect 'orgy' reading 'a Traveler at Forty.' I read it aloud to her and we simply 'ate' every word of it." As to his other travel book, she promised to make him a list of Pennsylvania's contributions to American history. Then after admitting that she herself didn't like the Keystone State or Philadelphia that much, especially following her visits to New York, she told him that every time she read a new book of his, his writings inspired her to try to write herself. "But I seem to have more success in being decorative than intellectual. My friends all seem to think I make a much better fashion model than a writer." She signed off saying that if she ever in fact became a writer, she hoped to meet him some day.[61]

"Why wait until you are famous?" Dreiser replied immediately, adding that since he was "calmly working at above address," she might as well visit him now. As to Pennsylvania, he reminded her that he had written that he and Booth could not "recall anyone of import *at the time.*" He had once lived in Philadelphia, he told her, and wouldn't mind visiting that city again. She visited him on Tenth Street about a month later. She noted his "very large" writing desk made out of Paul's rosewood piano, which Dreiser had recently purchased from Mame. On its top she was startled to see a mouse in a small makeshift cage. He had trapped it, he told her, but when he realized it was only caught by the tail he planned to release it in the country. They had lunch that day at the Brevoort. Louise remembered that they paused outside the hotel to look up at an airplane. "This was 1917 and people really did that."[62]

Even though she had had no formal editing experience, he sent her away with a short story to read and edit for matters of grammar, spelling, and general sentence structure. Dreiser wrote easily and at any time, she later recalled, and was not intimidated by the technicalities of composition. Before long she would be typing out the manuscripts to his two long volumes of autobiography. They acknowledged their mutual attraction that day, but they may not have consummated their affair sexually until May 28. Apparently because Estelle was jealously on the alert and Louise was still married, they trysted in Trenton, halfway between New York and Philadelphia. Armed with presents for Louise as well as a bottle of disinfectant, Dreiser greeted her at the train station in the rain. Thanks to Estelle's typescript, we have the journal entry describing this blissful moment and those that followed at the Sterling Hotel, where the two lovers registered as "Mr. and Mrs. of Newark." Beforehand, at the station, Louise expressed her nervousness about her husband: "Says she didn't know till last minute whether she would come. . . . Feels she is doing wrong. Conscience troubles her and she is watched. . . . Reputation at stake. Will not come any more. I get a little angry." But once in their hotel room, all was well for the next four hours and forty-five minutes.[63] That evening, back in New York, Dreiser also had sex with Estelle, but Louise, now totally enamored of the Great Writer, would last much longer.

The Genius himself, it will become clearer, was a troubled man when it came to sex—or at least personal relations with women. He was Eugene Witla incarnate, regardless of the author's rather muted criticism of his hero's faults. In the wake of *The "Genius"* and all the grief its publication brought him, he seems to have been more sexually active than ever before. At the same time, with no money coming in from *The "Genius"* and very little from his other books, he was feeling poor again and professionally frustrated. He would turn from one-act plays back to their literary equivalent, short stories. In fact, since the suppression of *The "Genius"* he had been looking for literary ways other than the novel to make a living. It was during this dip in his literary fortunes that he met his first biographer, Dorothy Dudley. Although her life of Dreiser is largely impressionistic, it also contains firsthand information not otherwise available. The daughter of a wealthy Chicago gynecologist, and a 1905 Bryn Mawr graduate, she met Dreiser through Masters. She and Dreiser may have been lovers before she married Henry Blodgett Harvey, a Lucky Strike executive, and moved to Paris in 1925. "Do you know what woman Dreiser's living with now?" she was asked by a fellow writer in the fall of 1916. "Upon my ignorance as to that," she wrote in her book to characterize this post-*"Genius"* period, "the first and last spark of interest in 'America's foremost novelist' died."[64] Floyd Dell and others had been right in their prophecies. *The "Genius"* had seriously undercut the reputation of the author of *Sister Carrie*.

Mencken made things worse—and seriously threatened their friendship for the first time—in his *Book of Prefaces* (1917). In summing up Dreiser's career as a writer and, as he touched on each of his friend's books, passing on information about literary influences Dreiser had told him of, he described him as a "phenomenon inescapably visible, but disconcertingly hard to explain." Evidently, neither *The Hand of the Potter* nor perhaps even Estelle's unhappiness was forgotten in this act of criticism. Mencken repeated his complaint about Dreiser as a clumsy stylist who was now overstocking his books with "details that serve no purpose," but also called him a clod of a personality, untutored as to formal learning if not unwashed. Dreiser was admittedly intelligent and "a sound artist," Mencken wrote, "but there come moments when a dead hand falls upon him, and he is once more the Indiana peasant, snuffing absurdly over imbecile sentimentalities, giving a grave ear to quackeries [i.e., the socialist theories of his Greenwich Village compatriots], snorting and eye-rolling with the best of them." Mencken had probably done more as a critic for Dreiser's career than anyone else. But ever since his review of *Jennie Gerhardt,* the cracks in his praise had begun to show and then widen. Mencken felt more and more that Dreiser considered him his protégé more than his literary equal, even after he had come into his own prominence as a writer.[65] Whatever the motive, Mencken's pronouncements have had their negative impact on biographies and criticism to this day.

TWELVE

Back to the Future

Your own last letter is full of the same sweet song. Floyd Dell
has written a novel which strips me of all my alleged laurels.
Sherwood Anderson the same. Sinclair Lewis the same. Ben Hecht
the same. . . . Seriously, I get just a little tired of all this
silly palaver about the great American novel.

DREISER TO HORACE LIVERIGHT, NOVEMBER 28, 1920

WITH *THE "GENIUS"* IN LIMBO throughout 1917 and America edging closer and closer to war, Dreiser's anger with his country's puritanical ways mounted steadily. His anti-British attitude hardened, and the socialist views that would formalize by the 1930s took root during the war years (by their end, for example, he favored state control of public utilities), and the treatment of *The "Genius"* by the Anglo-American literary establishment as one more German atrocity still rankled. Mencken, who had gone to Europe at the end of 1916 for several weeks to report on the war, returned home the following spring to anti-German mobs roaming the streets of Baltimore. The United States would enter the global contest on April 7, 1917.[1] That year the Espionage Act was passed and the Sedition Act a year later, both reflecting America's anti-German sentiment. The teaching of German was summarily halted in many of the nation's high schools and colleges. Symphonies dared not play Wagner or Beethoven, and conspiracy theories abounded, leading to beatings of German-Americans and at least one lynching. This wartime xenophobia soon targeted labor agitators and socialists whose resistance to a "capitalistic war" branded them pro-German.[2] As America went to war abroad, it began to fight a cultural and economic one at home.

In "Life, Art and America," an essay published in February in *Seven Arts,* Dreiser began with a literary and cultural criticism of America and ended up almost dismissing the nation altogether. Not only did the forces of conventionality curtail artistic freedom and suppress realistic depictions of life, he thought, but America had failed to protect its citizens from a commercial oligarchy that effectively began at Plymouth Rock with the exploitation of the Indians and continued to the present in the form of the many trusts that trampled upon the rights of the average citizen. "Take, for instance, the tobacco trust, the oil trust, the milk trust, the coal trust—in what way do you suppose they help?" Interested mainly in material profit and technological advancement, America had produced no philosophers of the first rank—no Spencer, Nietzsche, Schopenhauer, or Kant. (The reception of this screed was probably not advanced by the fact that three of these philosophers happened to be German.) "Do I hear some one offering Emerson as an equivalent? Or [William] James?" As for artists, neither Emerson nor the other James was worthy of the foreign competition. Only Whitman and (incredibly) Edgar Lee Masters rose to the test. The problem lay in the fact that American censorship—Comstockery that had only recently enjoyed the force of law—suppressed not only literature but all forms of expression. Even the colleges and universities conspired to keep America conventionally minded and artistically mediocre. "The average American school, college, university, institution," he protested, "is as much against the development of the individual, in the true sense of that word, as any sect or religion."[3]

Perhaps he had in mind Professor Sherman's recent attack upon his work or the more distant example of some of his more pedantic professors at Indiana State College who figure in *Dawn*. (By then his uncut autobiography had sprawled to include what would become a second volume, ultimately titled *Newspaper Days*.) Yet he found conspiracies against the individual and indeed nature itself in all walks of American life. Soon he would write another one-act play, an overworked satire—unpublishable until it was included in his 1920 book of philosophical essays, *Hey Rub-a-Dub-Dub*—on the forces of censorship in 1918. In "The Court of Progress," the descendants of the era's opponents of contraception and saloons, examiners of lewd books, and so on meet to celebrate their vice-free society in monotonous and unending chants. In "Mr. Bottom," an excerpt from "Life, Art and America" that was published in *The Social War*, one of several progressive publications Dreiser would come to frequent, he mockingly likened the Anglo-Saxon temperament in America to the rude mechanic who wakes up an ass in Shakespeare's *A Midsummer Night's Dream*. In an essay in *Pep*, another such magazine, and reprinted in the *New York Call*, he criticized the American press for its part in the oppression of free speech and honest representation.[4]

Seven Arts was shut down later that year for violation of the Espionage Act, mainly because of antiwar articles by Randolph Bourne. Under the new law, its issues could no longer legally be mailed, but if its doom hadn't already been sealed, Dreiser's next complaint, "American Idealism and German Frightfulness," would have instantly accomplished it. To this day, it has never been published, and the manuscript is now missing from the Dreiser archive at the University of Pennsylvania, but three previous biographers and other critics either paraphrase or quote from it (or each other). Longer than "Life, Art and America" at over 10,000 words, this article—according to Robert H. Elias—"compared Germany's liberal domestic legislation with England's practices and so attacked the British that no editor would print it for fear of being charged with giving aid and comfort to the enemy and publishing a plea for violence against the United States Government."[5]

In fact, Waldo Frank and James Oppenheim, the co-editors of *Seven Arts,* had been eager to publish the article in their August issue, saying that this was "no time for putting off present impulses and the expression of present convictions." "American Idealism and German Frightfulness," they insisted, was "the logical next lead-up in the fight." In July Dreiser wrote from Westminster, Maryland, where he was visiting with Estelle, that he couldn't part with it for less than $75 or $100. He even suggested that "a banker like Herman Bahr . . . or some of his pro-German members of the Aryan club or the *Staats-Zeitung* would furnish [a more effective] means for distributing it—not so much because it is pro-German—it is not—as because it is anti-British and pro-American." Since they had furnished Dreiser with five hundred offprints of "Art, Life and America," the editors of *Seven Arts* must have been taken aback by this slight upon their circulation efforts. Moreover, Dreiser's suggestion that they associate with German sympathizers instead of merely antiwar activists ultimately frightened them off. Waldo reneged on the offer of publication, saying blandly that "Your criticisms of England are based not so much on her intrinsic faults as on the fact that she is England."[6] The essay was subsequently rejected by *Century* and *North American Review.*

One of the last important things published by *Seven Arts* was Mencken's "The Dreiser Bugaboo," which set out to fend off Dreiser's puritanical critics but also insinuated that their continued attack upon him would distract him from his best work and transform him into a professional revolutionary.[7] This idea, along with the caricature of his friend as the "Indiana peasant," was repeated and expanded in the essay on Dreiser in *A Book of Prefaces.* Neither essay broke their friendship, but the bonds were weakened.

While *A Book of Prefaces* was under consideration at John Lane, one of its editors urged Dreiser to ask Mencken to modify his estimate, but, as Dreiser recorded in his diary for August 13, "I can't influence Mencken. Get the blues from this. Bert [Estelle Kubitz] adds to them by saying that such a criticism will fix public belief, that it is always anxious to believe the worst."[8] A potential Dreiser-Mencken quarrel was a pending disaster for American literature on the front line of change in this period. Already most old-line publishers eschewed writers who were making similar kinds of assaults on American puritanism. It was ultimately left to the upstart Jewish publishers who were then generally discriminated against as editors in the established houses to publish some of the greatest writers of the twentieth century. *A Book of Prefaces* was eventually issued by the newly organized house of Alfred A. Knopf.

One of the earliest Jewish publishers unafraid of promoting new or controversial writers was Ben Huebsch, who had begun in 1902 and who would shortly publish *Winesburg, Ohio*.[9] In a letter dated March 6, 1918, he offered Dreiser the "fatherly suggestion" that "this life is too short for two such intelligent persons as you and Mencken to be at odds with each other." Dreiser responded much as he had to the editor at John Lane. He understated the situation somewhat to say that he and Mencken were "on the best of terms personally." They diverged only in Mencken's opinion of his latest work. "His profound admiration, apparently, is only for *Sister Carrie* and *Jennie Gerhardt*, works which to me represent really old-line conventional sentiment." Of course, Mencken had also publicly admired *The Titan* and *A Hoosier Holiday*, and had published some of Dreiser's experimental one-act plays as well in *The Smart Set*. Yet the two writers were already politically divided. And as Dreiser drifted further left, his literary themes began to reflect a focus more on the social ills of America than simply its oppressive literary conditions. Still insisting that there was nothing personal in their literary differences, he told Huebsch that he now considered his friend more as a critic than a comrade. Since Mencken "feels it incumbent upon him as a critic to place me in a somewhat ridiculous light, I have felt that this close personal contact might as well be eliminated, for the time being anyhow." This awkwardness if not ill-feeling was mutual. When Dreiser later offered *The Smart Set* his essay entitled "Hey Rub-a-Dub-Dub," which sounded a socialist theme, Mencken did not condemn sentiments he would have otherwise challenged but instead begged off with the excuse that it was difficult in the America of 1918 to slip in "something not downright idiotic."[10]

As one dear friend threatened to fall away, however, another one had already reappeared in his life. "Ever since first seeing your name in print," wrote May Calvert Baker from Huntington, Indiana, "I have wondered if you were 'my' Theodore Dreiser." It was his teacher from Warsaw, the one only nine years older than himself, whom he had found so attractive and affectionate. Now, almost thirty years later, she had read *A Hoosier Holiday*, in which she was reported to have died young. "You see I am not dead a bit but very much alive and still teaching the young to aspire, to strive and if possible to win." She was saddened, however, to have to infer from his book that life had been something of a disappointment to him. She thanked him for "the beautiful story of your first term in Warsaw. I am glad I was that teacher," she told him and urged him to write to "say you are glad I am not dead." Dreiser wrote back almost immediately, recalling her "pink cheeks and warm girlish smile." "I haven't been as happy as I should have been, all things considered perhaps and all due to a bad disposition I suppose. I am not as happy yet as I might be—who is?"[11]

Certainly, Dreiser's "bad disposition" contributed to his unhappiness all his life. He seems to have been almost genetically contentious, a quality enhanced by his having grown up with so many siblings and having had to fend for himself at an early age. The *Sister Carrie* debacle had sealed this irascibility in adulthood. But he had other, more practical problems. In the winter and spring of 1917 he wasn't making enough money from his writings to do more than survive. In one rather desperate act, not unknown to famous writers faced with the neglect of the general reader, he sold his books out of his home. He printed lists of his titles with the statement that "Mr. Dreiser's works have been continuously attacked by Puritans solely because America is not yet used to a vigorous portrayal of itself." Prospective browsers were invited to examine his books for themselves and "discover the reason for his present high position in American letters."[12] If they couldn't get their bookseller to order them, they could write direct to 165 West Tenth Street for copies. It was signed with the pseudonym of "George C. Baker," perhaps the resourceful Estelle's concoction as she typed up the advertisement.

Shortly before the fall publication of *A Book of Prefaces*, Dreiser informed Mencken that he had been visited at his Greenwich Village flat by "Messrs Boni & Liveright Inc. who suggest they take over all my works." Dreiser was characteristically suspicious, but after a snafu in which Frank Shay, a bookseller and publisher in the Village, failed to publish a small edition of *Sister Carrie,* he allowed the firm to become the sixth publisher of his first novel.[13] Charles Boni and his brother had operated the Washington Square Book Shop on MacDougal Street and ran a specialty publishing business before joining up with Horace Liveright, who would eventually become an important name not just in the life of Theodore Dreiser but in the annals of American literature—publisher not only of *An American Tragedy* but other such classics as e. e. cummings's *The Enormous Room,* T. S. Eliot's *The Waste Land,* and Eugene O'Neill's *The Hairy Ape* (all of which appeared in the same year, 1922) as well as Ernest Hemingway's *In Our Time* (1925). Like Dreiser's fictional Frank Cowperwood, Liveright grew up in Philadelphia and dabbled in the stock market, but, in a parallel with Dreiser himself, his first love was the theater. While still in his teens, he wrote a comic opera that got as far as the rehearsal stage on Broadway before the production ran short of funds. He settled into the securities and bond business in New York and married into money in 1911. With his father-in-law's backing, he launched a company for the manufacture of toilet paper. But he was a gambler in a number of ways. The handsome, high-living entrepreneur, who also backed several Broadway plays (all of which failed), soon entered the book business and bet on many writers whose financial return was nowhere in sight but who in many cases proved Liveright correct in his literary assessment. These included not only Dreiser but Ezra Pound, whose books never made Liveright a dime but whose European contacts introduced him to many American writers estranged from postwar America and living in Paris. Through the pioneering public relations efforts of Edward Bernays, the brother-in-law of one of Boni & Liveright's vice presidents, he sold enough books to carry the best writers until they became famous.[14]

Liveright—more than Boni, who personally disliked Dreiser—was ready to gamble on the author of *Sister Carrie.* He was also willing to publish younger writers as well as radicals such as Dreiser. His first runaway success was right around the corner, John Reed's *Ten Days That Shook the World* (1918), an example of the risks he was willing to take as a new publisher. In 1918 *The Masses* went the way of *Seven Arts,* and its editors—Reed, Max Eastman, Floyd Dell, and Art Young—stood trial for violation of the Sedition Act. Dreiser himself was full of the same kind of "dangerous" ideas, but Liveright felt that his next novel, really the first one he would have written in more than five years, would be a major literary event. He promised Dreiser that they would ultimately publish all his books in a uniform edition. "We are very eager to secure you and your books," Boni & Liveright told him, "not only because of the commercial possibilities we recognize in them, but also because we are all admirers of your work. We feel convinced that once we have your name on our list, we have gotten America's greatest novelist."[15]

These were more words of faith than fact in 1917. What they got first was a short story writer and a playwright with the publication in 1918 of *Free and Other Stories* and *The Hand of the Potter.* The latter (not actually published until September 1919 because of a pending stage production) must have been part of Dreiser's test of his new publisher's commitment. This was certainly the case for the mystical Charles Fort's *The Book of the Damned,* which the firm reluctantly published at Dreiser's insistence in 1920. Dreiser and Fort, the father of UFO spotters, shared the Spencerian notion that the development of man had reached only its intermediate stage. The ambitious publishers balked, however, when Dreiser suggested they publish John Maxwell's attempt to depose Shakespeare as the author of the plays, an effort that had pretty much run out of gas with Delia Bacon and other Shakespeare skeptics in the previous century. Both these men were names out of Dreiser's past. Maxwell (whose candidate for Shakespeare authorship was Robert Cecil) had been the cub reporter's first boss at the *Chicago Daily Globe,* and Dreiser had published articles by Fort while editing *Smith's Magazine* back in 1906. He was beginning to reach back in other ways as well.

Not only did *Free* contain many old stories, but at least three of the new ones were provoked or inspired by the old story of Dreiser's first marriage and the fact that he was still legally married. Jug reentered his life in 1917 to ask for renewed financial support. In 1914 she had signed an agreement to forgo alimony after February 1, 1915, in lieu of having received the furnishings to their apartment at 3609 Broadway, along with two residential lots they owned on Grandview Avenue in Rockland County, New York, worth at least $600, and ten acres of apple orchard in North Yakima, Washington, which Dreiser had purchased from Arthur Henry and Anna Mallon before they finally separated.[16] Jug had held onto her job at the *Delineator* for a while after Dreiser's departure, but by now she had lost that position and was asserting herself once again as "Mrs. Dreiser." Rather than meet her demands, which he could hardly afford to do, he investigated, without success, the possibilities of obtaining a divorce. Had he succeeded, of course, he would have faced another domestic dilemma, for his various lovers were bemoaning their status as simply members of his harem and lining up to one extent or another to become the second Mrs. Dreiser. Lillian Rosenthal was still in the picture and urged him to get a quickie divorce in Reno; Louise Campbell complained angrily about her husband and at the same time begged Dreiser not to throw her off; Estelle Kubitz continued to live up to her nickname of "Gloom" by brooding over his infidelities; and Kirah Markham, who had married the son of Frank Lloyd Wright, was back in town intimating her willingness to renew their relationship.

Fairly seething at Jug, he wrote and published in quick succession stories that reflected his feelings about marriage. As an added complication for both of them, Jug's sister Rose, the one Dreiser had been so attracted to when he first met the White sisters, was dying of cancer. The first two stories, "The Second Choice" and "Married," appeared in *Cosmopolitan,* which featured romantic tales with suggestive illustrations. The third, "Free," came out in the more family-oriented *Saturday Evening Post.* All together Dreiser earned from these publications around $2,000.[17]

"The Second Choice" is based on Dreiser's 1892 affair with Lois Zahn in Chicago. As he wrote this story, Dreiser was still working on *Newspaper Days,* in which he reflects his point of view of the affair he had had with the girl he left behind when he moved to St. Louis. As we have seen, shortly before his departure, he had gone by one last time to see Lois but bolted when he found her with the faithful telegraph operator whom she had encouraged in case Dreiser didn't propose to her. In the short story, he gives Lois's side of the tale. After Dreiser had settled into his new job on the *St. Louis Globe-Democrat,* Lois asked for the return of her love letters. In the story, Shirley receives the answer to a similar letter to Arthur, who has gone on to a better job in Pittsburgh, as Dreiser moved on to St. Louis. She broods over her dilemma and the fact that the ruse to reignite their courtship has failed. "Previous to him had been Barton Williams, stout, phlegmatic, good-natured, well-meaning, who was, or had been before Arthur came, asking her to marry him, and whom she allowed to half assume that she would." Barton represents the kind of conventional life and marriage that middle-class morality has in store for both sexes, but of course he is her "second choice" after Arthur appears on the scene. When it becomes clearer that Arthur has lost his enthusiasm for her once they have had sex, she reluctantly accepts her fate. "Yes, it must be—forever now, she told herself. She must marry. Time would be slipping by and she would become too old."

Her dreams were simply "too high, that's all." She enters the kitchen to find her mother bent over the stove. Taking an apron, she proceeds to set the family table.[18]

Shirley's letter does not appear in "The Second Choice," but what is supposed to be Lois's found its way into *Newspaper Days*. A postscript reads:

> I stood by the window last night and looked out on the street. The moon was shining and those dead trees were waving in the wind. I saw the moon on that little pool of water over in the field. It looked silver. Oh, Theo, I wish I were dead.

Dreiser states that he pulled it from "an old letter file," but he was obviously writing fiction here as well as in "The Second Choice." He was almost as emotionally committed to Lois in 1892 as he was to Jug a year later, and both stories—Lois's and Shirley's—may be a celebration of his escape from marriage.[19]

Although "Married" is based on the first years of his marriage to Jug, the tale is basically lifted from *The "Genius,"* where Eugene Witla has married Angela Blue, set up housekeeping in bohemian New York, and realized his mistake. Duer Wilde of "Married" is a musician instead of a painter. His last name suggests that other artist who took personal freedom too far, at least in his day. Oscar Wilde, especially his tragic history in which he was tried twice for sodomy in 1895 and committed to two years in prison, which broke him physically, had been a frequent subject of discussion among Dreiser and his friends who lived and worked around Washington Square.[20] It may have been their passing interest in the plight of the homosexual, but more likely it was related to the personal freedom of the artist in general.

Like Witla or Dreiser, Wilde is moving up in his profession only to discover that his country-bred wife does not fit into the studio life of an artist in New York. Like Jug, Marjorie is determinedly monogamous in a varietistic world—"She was for one life, one love." She disapproves of Duer's familiarity with other women. During their frequent spats on the subject, she prods him gently but persistently to maintain his dignity and to remember that he is "married." "He would learn that he was married," Dreiser tells us over and again in the story, as he had already rehearsed the argument for Cowperwood and Witla and indeed for himself. "He would become a quiet, reserved, forceful man, weary of the silly women who were buzzing around him solely because he was a musician and talented and good-looking. . . . [Marjorie] knew what they wanted, these nasty women. . . .

Well, they wouldn't get him. . . . She had him. He had married her. And she was going to keep him. So there!"[21]

"Free" picks up the middle-class marriage at its close, when the wife of a sixty-year-old architect is dying. Rufus Haymaker, whose conventionality has been rewarded with all the signs of a successful career, including an apartment on Central Park, has led a wretched life personally. The problem is reviewed several times in the story, which is largely told as an interior monologue to capture the emotional exhaustion of the protagonist. Although it is Dreiser's most frequently anthologized today, it is not one of his best stories, perhaps because he had not experienced that segment of married life. He was not a writer who began with a blank sheet; his imagination required known facts that had been lived through, not simply acquired through research. In cases where both experience and research deserted him, he was lost. Rufus's wife is dying of several ailments, including leaky heart valves, for which she is given horse blood because Dreiser thought that it was thicker. "Who in hell was your medical consultant in 'Free'?" Mencken asked. "Some 3rd ave. abortionist, I do suspect. Know ye that blood transfusion is not done for leaky heart valves . . . that horse blood is not thicker than human blood, that horse blood would poison the patient, etc., etc. Come to the old reliable Dr. Mencken when you want pathology."[22]

———

Boni & Liveright published *Free and Other Stories* in the summer of 1918. It contained, along with the marriage stories, those written on the Maumee, one based on Dreiser's railroad experience ("The Cruise of the 'Idlewild'"), and a few more recently penned tales, including one calling on another episode from the working manuscript of *Newspaper Days* ("A Story of Stories"). The collection of eleven short stories (many not so short, one running to almost eighty pages) sold 2,742 copies during the first four months, but the critics weren't so sure this was Dreiser's strongest genre. Even the classic "Nigger Jeff" was dismissed by the *New York Sun* as simply "a morbid report of a lynching."[23] Unlike the early pieces, the later ones strained to tell their tales in the space of a short story. Dreiser himself had confessed to an interviewer in 1912 that he probably needed "a large canvas." The reviews were mixed. One couldn't ignore the diversity of the stories, since they had originated over a time span of twenty years. The Zolaesque realism was deplored, of course, but several reviewers also noted a Hollywood quality, or "moving-picture touch," about the latest stories such as "Married." A young Virginia Woolf, with only one novel to her credit, thought that he "lacked all the necessary qualities for a writer of short stories." Yet she had nevertheless enjoyed "the book considerably" because of the vitality with which the author presented his American characters. Others thought Dreiser was trying too hard to write "popular stuff" in the newer stories.[24] Actually, he was trying too hard to stay alive as a writer and so was experimenting with genres other than the novel. The ongoing trouble over *The "Genius"* had temporarily stifled his creative instincts. *Free* itself had been largely a recycling of earlier work, and *The Hand of the Potter* had come almost as a dare in response to Sumner's attack on his novel.

His next book to be published by Boni & Liveright was *Twelve Men* (1919), a collection of mainly turn-of-the-century narratives, which is considered by many as Dreiser's finest book after *Sister Carrie* and *An American Tragedy*. While it was not a bestseller, it sold better than *Free* and gradually grew in popularity, being reprinted several times over the next decade. The twelve sketches, including "My Brother Paul," consisted of character analyses and autobiography. Mencken came back into the fold one last time to find the same "high swing" in the book as could be found in *Sister Carrie* and *A Hoosier Holiday:* "It shows, with a few unimportant breaks, a deliberate return to his first manner—the manner of pure representation, of searching understanding, of unfailing gusto and contagious wonderment." Mencken afterward urged Dreiser to write a full-length biography of his brother Paul, but Dreiser had already put most of the known facts into "My Brother Paul" as well as the yet-to-be-published *Newspaper Days*.[25]

This homecoming of twelve men who had either influenced Dreiser significantly or whetted his curiosity ranged from Peter McCord ("Peter") to William Louis Sonntag ("W.L.S."), both graphic artists who had taught Dreiser about the "color" of the city. Charlie Potter in "A Doer of the Word" was to Dreiser one of those mystery men, like the Captain in *Sister Carrie,* who did not exclusively follow their animal instincts for survival but who dedicated their efforts to others. "My Brother Paul," of course, was the jewel of the collection. Paul by this time had been reburied in Chicago with his parents, but his brother still thought of him "as not there or anywhere in the realm of space, but on Broadway between Twenty-ninth and Forty-second Streets. . . . Ah, Broadway! Broadway! And you, my good brother! Here is the story that you wanted me to write, this little testimony to your memory, a pale, pale symbol of all I think and feel." "The Country Doctor" is a conflation of both his family doctor and Jug's in Danville, Missouri. "Culhane, The Solid Man" celebrated William Muldoon, the boxing and wrestling coach who had harassed Dreiser back into good health at his sanitarium in White Plains, New York, in 1903. "A True Patriarch" was based on Dreiser's father-in-law, Archibald White, who like the author was one of thirteen children. One wonders what White had thought of Dreiser after he married his daughter (Jug's niece was so angry with Dreiser that she refused to cooperate with the early biographer Robert H. Elias), but Dreiser remembered his father-in-law as the Whitmanesque democrat who looked out for "the sick, the poor, the widows, the orphans, the insane, and dependents of all kinds." As noted earlier, despite his own large family, White followed to the core the bard's advice in the 1855 Preface of *Leaves of Grass* to love the earth, to "give alms to every one that asks, stand up for the stupid and crazy, devote your income and labor to others, hate tyrants" and so make one's life so that "your very flesh shall be a great poem."[26] The similarity with the Good Gray Poet was also physical, for Arch White also possessed a high forehead and flowing, white hair.

Recently, Dreiser himself had again been compared to Whitman. John Cowper Powys had seen the similarity in *The "Genius,"* and now William Marion Reedy in St. Louis remarked of *Free:* "I don't think Walt Whitman was a whit more American than Theodore Dreiser." (Reedy said he had known the poet's favorite brother, Thomas Jefferson Whitman, who had been a water commissioner in St. Louis before his death in 1890.) "Theodore was a serious boy," Reedy wrote, "bent on doing something big in letters. Well, he has done it in his novels. He does it something as Walt did his big things, by putting everything in."[27]

The other sketches in *Twelve Men* included the remembrance of the late Harris Merton Lyon ("De Maupassant, Jr."), whom Dreiser had met in 1906; a factually toned sketch of Elihu H. Potter ("The Village Feudists"), an eccentric Good Samaritan he had interviewed in Noank while staying with Arthur Henry in his "Island Cabin" off the coast of Connecticut; the story of Joseph G. Robin ("'Vanity, Vanity,' Saith the Preacher"), a New York financier Dreiser had met while editing the *Delineator,* who rose out of poverty and a murky past; yet another version of his epitaph for Mike Burke ("The Mighty Rourke"), the New York Central Railroad foreman of the masonry crew Dreiser worked for in 1903; and a reworking of his earlier piece on Thomas P. Taylor ("A Mayor and His People"), the quasi-socialist who had tried unsuccessfully to reform the city of Bridgeport, Connecticut. One common thread runs through the sketches: these men were dreamers who woke up to act out their romantic impulses. Though lovable, many are also self-destructive. The sketch of Joseph G. Robin, for example, may have influenced F. Scott Fitzgerald in the creation of Jay Gatsby.[28]

Underscoring the biographies is the implication that each man could not help becoming what he became. By the time Dreiser prepared *Twelve Men* for the press, he was working up many of the essays in *Hey Rub-a-Dub-Dub: A Book of the Mystery and the Wonder and Terror of Life* (1920). Several of these essays reflect the influence of the behaviorist Jacques Loeb's *The Mechanistic Conception of Life* (1912), which explained existence or nature as a series of tropisms, or predetermined and interrelated responses to physical stimuli. Earlier naturalists had attributed most activity to the instinct of self-preservation, but Loeb argued, for example, that the caterpillar does not climb to the topmost branch, where food is available in the first buds of spring, with any conscious purpose of feeding itself. Rather, the larva responds to light—as any plant turns toward the sun in a heliotropism. Man, as Dreiser wrote in "The Essential Tragedy of Life," was merely "an evolved arrangement of attractions and repulsions." This was the "equation inevitable," as he called it in an essay of the same name in *Hey Rub-a-Dub-Dub*: "due to an accidental arrangement of chemicals, his every move and aspiration [is anticipated] and accounted for by a formula."[29]

That was both the terror and wonder of life. Man is drawn to beauty the way the plant is drawn to the sun. Yet this mystery was undercut by religionists who insisted that man was "free" to choose from right and wrong in his pursuit of beauty. In the first place, such terms were merely relative to the situation. "You are mixing up religious balderdash with chemical and physical facts or laws," Dreiser told James Bann, a vitalist who insisted on the ultimate independence of living things from natural or chemical laws. "What is good in one climate, for instance, is not good in another." Furthermore, what was evil was not always wrong: "Murder among the Mpongwe is not wrong, although unquestionably it is an evil to the individual. . . . All we have, as any scientific chemist or physicist will quickly prove to you, is a neuro-plasmically developed sense of balance or proportion between all those things which relate to our material existence here— not elsewhere, get that!" Yet the superstitious and latently religious Dreiser didn't always completely believe everything he preached. He was both a mechanist and a vitalist who believed that man simply hadn't learned enough about the laws which governed him. This conviction would turn into an obsession in the 1930s as he researched and wrote the various parts of his unfinished *Notes on Life*.[30]

On May 11, 1919, at 1:45 in the afternoon Dreiser was hit by a car while crossing Columbus Circle. The police report states that he was treated at Roosevelt Hospital for lacerations of the scalp, which required three stitches, and of the right hand as well as a bruised right hand and right side. Upon hearing of the obviously minor mishap, Mencken recommended an attorney who "takes only 50% and expenses." Dreiser refused to press charges against the twenty-seven-year-old driver. He did, however, exaggerate his injuries to May Calvert Baker, describing his condition as "two ribs broken and my scalp cut & my left arm nearly broken." The teacher and her former student had maintained a correspondence since their epistolary reunion in 1917. When he had sent her a copy of "Married," she replied on March 29, 1918, that it was "a very true picture of many a married life," including her own early marriage, which had ended even before she had become Dreiser's teacher. "I freed myself from a loveless marriage which I had no business to make. The result—a life of hardship and aloneness."[31] It is not surprising that she had been so affectionate then toward Dreiser the student. She was now as well.

That September he was planning a cruise down the Mississippi River from St. Paul. He planned to visit her on the way out (perhaps making a visit to Murrel Cain in Carmel as well), but the trip was canceled because his two traveling companions were compelled to remain in New York to await the military draft.[32] Baker was "so disappointed" and urged him to make his visit the following spring, telling him that with time away from "hard, merciless New York" life would not "seem quite so tragic." She had earlier tried to get him to lighten up, to write more idealistically about life. But as he told her, "New York doesn't make me any sadder or more cynical than any other place in America or elsewhere. Life makes me sad."[33]

When Dreiser finally made his visit to her in June 1919, they apparently enjoyed an ecstatic reunion. The now retired teacher and her brightest student motored to several Indiana towns, including Warsaw, where Dreiser was not exactly welcome because of his descriptions of the "elite" in *A Hoosier Holiday*. When he left her on June 24 to take the Interurban train to Indianapolis, where he would be reunited with Maxwell, she was "greatly grieved" at his going, adding that she must have "made an awful fool of myself last week. . . . I miss you dreadfully and to think of you going back to New York without another glimpse of you gives me the horrors." She begged him to return to Huntington on his way back east. "I won't tell a soul you are here and you can spend the night, . . . and no one need know. . . . Please say you are coming for the 'Fourth' [of July], and I'll love you forever and a day." Dreiser didn't make the detour. He promised to send her more of his books, but mainly in the hope that she would canvass Indiana bookstores to promote them. As to his coming back any time soon, he told her idly, "If the state of Indiana will make me a present of a small house & garden on the Wabash I'll come back there and live."[34] Their extant correspondence breaks off here for the next eleven years.

Soon after his return, he and Estelle spent two days at the New Jersey shore resorts of Ocean Grove and Asbury Park, where they were joined the second night by Marion and "Menck." Dreiser's short diary entries for July 12–14 don't express much enthusiasm for the outing. He passively describes the scenes, refers rather distantly to Mencken, and gives no descriptions of any "fierce rounds" with Estelle. He also exaggerated the pain of a sprained ankle to avoid much socializing.[35] He would keep up his relationship with Mencken, but it would continue to cool over the next few years. Estelle, too, would continue as his typist for *Newspaper Days,* but their intimacy was now coming to an end. For Dreiser was about to fall in love again, the way he had fallen for Kirah in 1913.

———

Her name was Helen Patges Richardson, and she was his second cousin— her grandmother, Esther Schänäb Parks, and Dreiser's mother had been sisters. Helen, a tall beauty with gold-chestnut hair and a sensuous body, was twenty-five but looked younger. She had been raised in a "matriarchy" in Portland, Oregon, where her grandmother and mother operated a hotel that backed up on a vaudeville theater. Her mother had married a Danish musician named George Christian Patges, but the marriage failed when Helen and her sisters, Myrtle and Hazel, were children. At sixteen the stage-struck Helen fell in love with the actor Frank Richardson. She married him, and the couple tried their luck at theaters and clubs in Oregon, Washington, and finally the romantic city of San Francisco. But the romance soon stalled when booking agents, according to Helen's memoir, preferred assigning her as a single. Eventually, the couple relocated to Richardson's hometown of Charleston, South Carolina. Here, bored with her marriage, Helen met a family friend, W. E. Woodward, an executive with the Industrial Finance Corporation in New York, who eventually hired her as a secretary.

Woodward happened to be a fan of Dreiser's writing and at the time was much taken by the just published *Twelve Men.* When Helen mentioned that she was related to the author, Woodward urged her to meet him.[36] Apparently, she did not know his address but had Ed's out in Far Rockaway. She approached Dreiser's youngest brother, who, fearing this attractive woman was a gold digger, took an instant and lifelong dislike to her. Nonetheless, he gave her his brother's address in the Village. "This day I met Helen," Dreiser wrote in his diary for September 13, 1919; otherwise, he remembered little about that Saturday morning. He was stunned by her beauty, the sound of her voice which was "emotional and moving," the way her hair turned in the light between gold and brown, her beautiful hands and figure. She reminded him of his sister Theresa, who had been killed by a train in 1897. Dreiser records that Helen's first question was about Ed's address, which may in fact have been an accurate account. Determined to meet her famous cousin, Helen may have used her interest in Ed as a pretense. Whatever the case, Dreiser and his cousin were immediately and intensely interested in each other. "Give her Ed's address," Dreiser recorded in his diary for that day. "Then ask her for hers. She trembles as she writes. . . . I am tempted to take her in my arms & kiss her."[37] Instead, he gave her a copy of *The Hand of the Potter,* autographed to "My little Oregon cousin."

Dreiser had to have this enticing woman, whose body, Ed's daughter Vera later recalled in echo of her parents' view of Helen as an interloper, "reeked of sex appeal." The preliminaries were quick. Helen, too, was looking for love as well as a new adventure in life. She and Woodward had trysted briefly, but their sexual relationship wasn't going anywhere.[38] She had saved just enough from her secretary's job to try her luck as an actress and was planning to embark for Hollywood within weeks. Dreiser had the coincidental excuse of investigating an offer from a motion picture company now that the movie industry was rebounding from the national flu epidemic that had emptied out the movie theaters in 1918. After a meeting or two, frustrated encounters for Dreiser in which he told her "there can be no simple friendship between us," Dreiser victoriously announced in his journal for September 20, "Sex satisfaction & agreement have brought us close together. . . . Feel that I am due for a long period with her, maybe years."[39] Almost a month before, he had celebrated his forty-eighth birthday.

By this time, Dreiser had reneged on his commitment to John Lane and agreed to give Boni & Liveright the finished manuscript of *The Bulwark.* The firm in turn agreed to pay him an advance of $4,000 in the form of twelve monthly payments of $333.33. The advance was also to be applied to the other books the firm had either published or had in press, but it was clear that Dreiser received the advance for mainly one reason. "We are to have and have the sole right to publish in book form the novel you are now writing." The contract refers specifically to "The Bulwark" and also describes it as the book listed in the John Lane catalog for "1917 or 1918." Given Dreiser's growing capriciousness with publishers because of the mistrust built up over the years, it was probably important that Liveright laid claim to the next "novel you are now writing." Perhaps the publisher should have been clearer on the length, but he merely urged the wordy Dreiser to keep it "well within 175,000 words."[40]

Dreiser sublet his Greenwich Village flat for $50 a month, and he and Helen sailed on the *Momus* for New Orleans on October 8, the first stop on their journey to Los Angeles. The suddenness of their departure was probably due to the pressures of Dreiser's other female commitments. Even though the emotional Estelle wasn't with him that steadily any longer, it would have been difficult for him to explain Helen. At the same time Louise, fearing that he was breaking with her, wrote a letter begging to see him before he left. And Lillian, whose tenacity had already outlasted several others, came to the boat to kiss him goodbye once Helen had gone below to their berth. Even though it was October, New Orleans was "sweltering," and Dreiser got mysteriously sick—so ill that they considered returning to New York. As a tentative step, they took a train to St. Louis, where by the time of their arrival he had recovered. Apparently, he had developed a chill from lying on the grass at an old Spanish fort they had visited near the Crescent City.[41]

Seeing St. Louis again after so many years, the city where he had become a full-fledged journalist, no doubt speeded up his recovery. The magnificent train station with its gilded arches that greeted them had still been under construction when he left the city in 1894. He walked downtown past the buildings that housed the *Globe-Democrat* and the *Republic,* but he apparently didn't visit either establishment. He and Helen were soon on their way again by train, reaching Los Angeles during the first few days of November 1919. They found oil wells scattered all over the sprawling city and, it seemed, almost as many movie studios. Hollywood and its immediate environs had become the home of more than fifty studios by 1920, employing some twenty-five thousand people. And there were many more, like Helen, who were there looking for work in the "moving pictures." It had all started with Edison's "studio" in New Jersey; by the time World War I had ended, the American film industry had surpassed even the French and the Italian moviemakers. Southern California emerged as its capital because of its diverse geography and clement weather. And, in addition to the adjacent deserts, mountains, and forests, the studios could keep costs lower than in the East because Los Angeles was a non-union city.[42]

This was still the era of silent film; the talkies were almost a decade away. It was also the beginning of the Hollywood star system, and some of the biggest names in the motion picture business in 1920, both actors and directors, were D. W. Griffith, Mary Pickford, Charlie Chaplin, Douglas Fairbanks, and William S. Hart—all making astronomical salaries for that day, or even this one. Only a year before these people had banded together to form United Artists, their own distribution company through which they could earn even more money from their unique talents. Also, as independent producers instead of contract players for such directors as Jesse L. Lasky, William Fox, Cecil B. DeMille, Adolph Zukor, Louis B. Mayer, or Samuel Goldfish (soon to be changed to "Goldwyn"), they could better control the aesthetic quality of their productions. The industry was otherwise monopolized by sentimental or (in the case of DeMille) oversexed scenarios. One of the first movies United Artists produced was Griffith's *Broken Blossoms* (1919) starring Miss Pickford. Her success in this film and earlier ones or the performance of Gloria Swanson in *Male and Female,* released the same year, emboldened thousands of young women who imagined they were as talented and beautiful to flock to Hollywood in search of movie stardom. Most were sent home broke and demoralized after a few weeks or months. Those that were luckier, like Helen, landed bit parts in movies that paid between $7.50 and $10 a day.

After spending a week at the Stillwell Hotel at Ninth and Grand, on November 8 they rented a room with a modest balcony on Alvarado near Westlake (now MacArthur) Park for thirty dollars a month. Even though Dreiser was under contract to finish *The Bulwark,* he tried writing screenplays that he offered, without success, to the Lasky Studio and elsewhere. One was "The Long, Long Trail," which had a "fugitive" plot. Another was a South Sea scenario. A third was called "Lady Bountiful, Jr.," which he tried to pitch to United Artists. He admitted to himself, however, that he was writing sentimental claptrap and scoffed in his journal that "The agent thought it was so good." It is worth noting that the plot of "Lady Bountiful, Jr.," involving a young woman who is rescued by a father she had never known, generally resembles the story in Augustin Daly's *Under the Gaslight*—the play that makes a "star" of Carrie in the eyes of Hurstwood and Drouet.[43]

Dreiser kept his street addresses a secret throughout his stay in Los Angeles, mainly because Jug was seeking alimony and would presently appeal to Liveright for his whereabouts.[44] "P. O. Box 181" was all that anyone got. When friends came to town, he met them in either a restaurant or their hotel lobby. The postal box also allowed him to receive mail from female admirers without Helen's knowledge. He apparently left New York without telling anybody, including Mencken, who didn't think any more of Southern California than he had of Greenwich Village. "What in hell are you doing in Los [Angeles], among all the New Thoughters, swamis and other such vermin?" he inquired in his characteristic blend of mockery and humor. "I hear that all the old maids west of the Mississippi flock to town in the hope of being debauched. I surely hope you don't risk your old fowling-piece on any such game." It was true that many a young actress hopeful of working in the movies was more often than not invited to become the mistress of a director, assistant director, casting director, or even camera man. Such repeated overtures to Helen almost turned "the Hollywood Fornicator" (as Mencken privately described Dreiser to Estelle) into the very puritan he so despised. Dreiser was so irritated that he tried to expose the practice in a four-part magazine series entitled "Hollywood: Its Morals and Manners." One of Helen's aspiring suitors was Rex Ingram, an imposing actor who had played a bit part in *Tarzan of the Apes* (1918) and then became director of *The Four Horsemen of the Apocalypse* (1921), Rudolph Valentino's first film and Helen's biggest opportunity.[45]

At the end of November 1919, they moved again, to the front suite of a large white stucco house on the southeast corner of North Larchmont and Clinton streets. The move put them closer to Hollywood, within easy walking distance of many film studios. They often walked as far as West Hollywood, past enormous eucalyptus trees with their bark stripped off and lying about. The sidewalks were "literally carpeted" with red peppers, which had fallen "from overhanging pepper trees." The aspiring actress and the would-be screenwriter remained at this address for about nine months, then moved at the end of August 1920 to a community called Highland Park, populated, as it turned out to their surprise, with demonstratively religious people. These included their landlord, who lived upstairs and who loudly greeted Dreiser each morning with "Praise the Lord . . . Praised Be His Name!" This small, intensely devoted religionist no doubt reminded Dreiser of his own father. The landlord's wife was "a large, bony, physically hardened and angular woman," Helen recalled, "who had probably worked hard all her life, trying to keep the family going." Obviously, she was the more practical one. There was also a fifteen-year-old daughter living in this two-story house at 1553 Curran Street, to whom Dreiser was mildly attracted. But more than that, he saw in her the burning desire to somehow extricate herself from her parents' near poverty as well as their religious fanaticism.[46]

It was at this Southern California address, just east of Hollywood with its rank melodrama and frivolous comedies, that the idea for *An American Tragedy* was fully born. Not all in Hollywood was lightweight, of course. There were serious films too, if very much in the minority, and one wonders whether Clyde Griffiths's last name does not owe something to the omnipresence of D. W. Griffith in the filming community. There were also real-life people and events that might have suggested more serious themes. The Fatty Arbuckle scandal, in which the popular film comedian was accused of raping and murdering a Hollywood actress, broke in September of 1920.[47] By that time Dreiser had abandoned work on *The Bulwark*. On April 9, as he completed chapter 13 of the latest version, he expressed his discouragement over the story. By July 7, he was "greatly wrought up" over the "fruitless results of my efforts to write." Instead, he began work on *An American Tragedy*, of which he completed twenty-one chapters, or just a little beyond the first of the three "books" in the novel, while in California. The final version, less biographical than the earliest draft of Book I, begins with a street scene in which Asa Griffiths and his wife run a mission for the down and out in Kansas City. Asa, in a trait reminiscent of the Curran Street landlord, is known as "Praise-the-Lord Griffiths" because of his inevitable greeting. He is also, as noted earlier, partly rooted in the impractical Andrew Conklin ("Asa" in *Dawn*), who ran the real estate company Dreiser worked for in Chicago in the 1890s. Asa Griffiths's wife resembles Helen's description of the landlord's spouse: "perhaps five years his junior, taller, not so broad, but solid of frame and vigorous, very plain in face and dress, and yet not homely." Besides twelve-year-old Clyde and the other Griffiths children, there is "Esta" (for Hester; as with *Sister Carrie* Hawthorne's magnum opus somehow imposed itself on Dreiser's second classic), who at fifteen sings hymns accompanied by a street organ and who may be modeled on the teenaged female living at 1553 Curran Street. Esta eventually runs away with an actor who will abandon her in pregnancy, but for now she does not seem to mind the stares of male onlookers. "Physically," Dreiser writes in chapter 1 of his great novel, "she was of a pale, emasculate and unimportant structure, with no real mental force or depth, and was easily made to feel that this was an excellent field in which to distinguish herself and attract a little attention."[48]

Just why Dreiser and Helen moved *away* from Hollywood is not known. Dreiser may have wanted to get away from its immediate influences, so that he could work in earnest on his new novel. Curran Street was in the hills, and they had a "beautiful view." Once away from the neighborhood on North Larchmont with its noisy Hollywood traffic and tourists (even then), he wrote in his diary for Labor Day: "I work on 'An American Tragedy' till 4 P.M." Five weeks later he visited the Los Angeles Bible Institute, "looking for someone who knows of little cheap missions." Indeed, it seems likely he may have actually begun the book, or at least conceived its outline, while still on North Larchmont in the summer of 1920, when he told Will Lengel that he didn't know when *The Bulwark* would be finished and he was working on another novel.[49]

After the first twenty-one chapters, Dreiser made relatively little progress on his great novel during the rest of his stay in Southern California. Worried more than usual about money, he not only worked on screenplays and short stories, but began the sketches for *A Gallery of Women* (originally, "Twelve Women"). He tried to sell them individually to *Hearst's International-Cosmopolitan,* where Will Lengel had become managing editor. Many of these were based on female acquaintances (not lovers in most cases) whom he had known in Greenwich Village. In fact, the series may have been initiated by his meeting with Florence Deshon in Hollywood. Her life in New York and California became the basis of "Ernestine" in *A Gallery of Women.* Deshon had been the mistress of Max Eastman while living in Greenwich Village and working for the "legitimate stage." When the film industry beckoned in 1919, she went to Hollywood and became the mistress of Charlie Chaplin. Dreiser recorded in his diary for November 29, 1920, that he met with her for lunch at the Come-On-Inn on Gower Street in Hollywood. Florence told him about her life with Eastman (how he could always get money from the rich for his socialistic causes) and Chaplin (who was the victim of his first wife's paternity suit after she had failed to snag D. W. Griffith, whose name Dreiser rather significantly misspells with an "s"). Florence offered to introduce him to Chaplin if he came back, but Dreiser did not "promise" because he was too busy with *An American Tragedy.* He also thought she had her eye on him. ("Tells me of [Chaplin's] peculiarities. Likes him but . . . craves, as I can see, another literary celebrity.") Deshon committed suicide in 1922.[50]

The first sketch he actually completed concerns an equally sad case of American womanhood in the teens and twenties. "Olive Brand" was modeled on Edith De Long Jarmuth, who had married and divorced a wealthy man in the West. In 1918 she married Edward H. Smith, a journalist at the *New York World* who was one of Dreiser's most loyal friends. Before she was able to develop her newfound talents as a writer and social activist (having been broadened by creative writing courses at Columbia University and life in the Village), she died in the influenza epidemic of 1918. Dreiser kept in touch with Smith while he was in California, and it was Smith who kept him abreast of the New York productions of "The Girl in the Coffin" and *The Hand of the Potter* in the fall of 1920. The following winter Smith published an article on Dreiser's literary status twenty years after *Sister Carrie,* comparing him to other greats, such as Poe and Whitman, who were also scorned by establishment critics. He also pointed to other, lesser writers of the past who "succeeded in writing but one book before the iron hand of convention took hold of them." Smith concluded that Dreiser "keeps steadfastly on his way in the teeth of organized, commercialized, capitalized Philistinism."[51]

Interestingly, Dreiser started reading Poe again at this time. He also dipped into John W. Robertson's psychological study and in perhaps an ironic twist of Poe's concept of the doppelgänger made Clyde Griffiths's cousin Gilbert almost a twin. He had already read several biographies and studies of Poe, he told the bookseller who had sent him Robertson's book, but this was the first, he thought, to condemn Poe's "Iago-like" literary executor, Rufus Wilmot Griswold, and to clear Poe's name of many of his assertions and accusations. Poe's main attraction for Dreiser, however, had been clearly visible all along. "I accept wholly [Robertson's] theory of morbid heredity in the case of Poe with its corollary that, 'he was not always to be held responsible either for his acts or words.'"[52]

With that other Baltimore writer alternately amusing and annoying him (Mencken was currently reading the typescript of *Newspaper Days*), Dreiser made two new friends, George Douglas and George Sterling. Douglas was at the time a literary editor and columnist for the *San Francisco Bulletin*. Sterling, also then living in San Francisco, was an exotically romantic poet and bohemian who had begun as a protégé of Ambrose Bierce. During the week of October 18, 1920, Dreiser traveled by himself to San Francisco at the invitation of Paul Elder, an art dealer who proposed a reception for him at his gallery. The week consisted of several gala events and late-night bouts of hard drinking with the two Georges, who had already been tested by Mencken in an earlier visit to the city. Dreiser was happy to take a vacation from Helen, whose novelty at the moment seemed to be wearing a bit thin. Conveniently, Lillian Rosenthal, who was in the cast of a play appearing in San Francisco that week, secretly waited in his hotel room for him one night. Meanwhile, Helen, who had quarreled with her "Teddie," sent him frantic telegrams in response to at least one of his own. "Your telegram final blow," she exclaimed on October 18. "Good God. If you knew the agony of this loneliness. Fear breakdown."[53] His sexual varietism was beginning to resurface, and there may also have been a woman or two he was seeing in Los Angeles.

On or about January 25, 1921, Teddie and Helen moved back into Hollywood proper and rented rooms in the home of Mr. and Mrs. D. H. McDonald at 6309 Sunset Drive. Helen was working at the Morosco Studio in a Bebe Daniels picture. Dreiser glumly noted that "her new director, an ex-army colonel, struck on her,—her usual experience." On March 8 they moved down Sunset only a few intersections to 1515 Detroit. At this point, the working title for *An American Tragedy* was "Mirage"—which Dreiser also used as the title of a poem. By that summer, he told a friend that he had "a box full of poems, unpublished," perhaps including "Mirage" the poem.[54] Dreiser's poetry is often about nature, not brute nature, but the nature of romantic illusions and mysteries in the vein of Thoreau's spiritual quests. In "Mirage," which first appeared in *Moods: Cadenced and Declaimed* (1926), the elusive "you" is not found in the "dark days" of the present but in the writer's childhood past—"in the depths of a green wood in spring." Aside from its title, which otherwise suggests life as a complete illusion or mirage, the poem seems to have little to do with the tragic theme of *An American Tragedy*.

That spring Dreiser and Helen visited her mother in Portland. On the way, the couple stopped in San Francisco, where this time Helen got to enjoy the festive company of Sterling and Douglas, the former openly flirting with her, apparently with Dreiser's tacit permission. On a subsequent visit, in August of 1922, late one night or early in the morning as they drove through Golden Gate Park, Sterling plunged into a lily pond to retrieve a flower for Helen. She later fondly recalled the incident in her memoir, remembering Sterling as "a tall beautiful person with gray hair carefully arranged over his forehead to cover some imaginary defect." During the 1921 trip, they also spent time with Powys and his brother Llewelyn, who were also in San Francisco.[55]

All the while Horace Liveright was waiting impatiently, pleading for that next "Dreiser novel," but he had to settle instead for a part of Dreiser's autobiography that would eventually become known as *Newspaper Days*, but was originally published as *A Book about Myself* in 1922. There was also the problem of the John Lane Company's trying to hold onto *The Bulwark* at the same time that Liveright was doling out a $4,000 a year for it in monthly payments, now extended and modified with a $1,000 advance for the forthcoming autobiography. Lane had also advanced money for *The Bulwark* and still retained the legal rights to *The "Genius,"* and it not only refused to sell the novel itself but also declined to sell Dreiser copies so that he might resell them on the lucrative black market. The question of what publisher legally owned *The Bulwark* was further complicated when John Lane closed its New York office and assigned its American titles to Dodd, Mead, & Company. Mencken, who didn't think that highly of Liveright, advised his friend to turn what books he could over to Dodd, Mead. Dreiser, however, didn't trust the company to support him in the event another of his books fell under the gun of the censor. On *The Bulwark,* he owed John Lane around $1,600 and Liveright another $1,400, and he even considered asking Dodd, Mead for a $3,000 advance to pay off both. Ultimately, however, Dodd, Mead, which had taken over Dreiser's debt to Lane, decided against reissuing *The "Genius."* In exchange for the cost of the plates, bound copies, and copyright as well as the money owed to Lane, the company—perhaps unwilling to be the next publisher of Dreiser's most controversial book— turned *The "Genius"* over to Liveright. It would be republished without any of the recommended expurgations.[56]

The "Genius" would become Dreiser's second most profitable book, but it didn't reappear until the spring of 1923. In the spring and summer of 1921, Dreiser was still scraping about to make a living. Helen's sister Myrtle arrived in June, apparently separated from her husband and eventually in the company of a man named Grell, who simply disappeared one day. (Myrtle would become the general basis for the hedonistic sister-in-law in "Reina," the opening sketch in *A Gallery of Women*.) Helen bought a car, then another after the first broke down, and they toured even more of California, especially around Los Angeles. But Dreiser couldn't relax, especially when working on a novel. As 1921 began to fade and he had made so little headway on *An American Tragedy*, he began to fret over his place in the American literary pantheon. A new novel was needed to restore what some perceived as his waning reputation. "Mr. Dreiser died without visible means of support of any kind," he wrote not altogether in jest to Mencken in September. "His body now lies in row eight, grave number seventeen of the present L. A. Gas Works extension of what was recently the old St. Ignatz cemetery." Whether Mencken could read between the lines, he responded with his usual wit and hilarity. The man who boasted of occasionally urinating on Poe's grave in Baltimore after a night of beer drinking told Dreiser: "You will recall the case of the late Walt Whitman, another literary man. For years he practised the following last words: 'My one regret is that I could not die on the field of honor, fighting for democracy.' But his actual last words were: 'Lift me up, Horace; I want to shit.'"[57]

By this time, Dreiser and Helen had moved again, their seventh address in Southern California in less than two years. In August, they had rented a place at 652 North Columbus Street in Glendale, a community a few miles northeast of Hollywood. Together they built flower boxes for the windows of the little house, and Dreiser cultivated a small garden, something he apparently did wherever he could. Once again he felt he had to put some space between himself and Hollywood, and he tried another criticism of the movie industry. "An Overcrowded Entryway," which was never published, essentially recycles the same material he had put into "Hollywood: Its Morals and Manners" and "Hollywood Now."[58] Apparently not making any progress on his new novel, he tried at this time to sell the portraits that would make up *A Gallery of Women* to *Hearst's International-Cosmopolitan*, but they were simply too complicated and undersexed for that magazine. He even thought to sell the manuscript of *Sister Carrie*, for which he believed he could get $2,000. He had given it to Mencken and now offered to split the profits. Mencken refused to reap any personal profit from a private sale and offered to return the manuscript to Dreiser.[59] He was eventually allowed to donate it to the New York Public Library, where it is preserved today.

Just why Dreiser returned to New York is not altogether clear, though he had indicated to correspondents that his return was imminent. (One of them was Estelle, who had urged him to return to finish *The Bulwark*, "then the 'American Tragedy.'") No doubt Helen finally became discouraged by the younger competition in Hollywood, where her movie career had amounted to not much more than the status of an extra. When Roberta Alden in *An American Tragedy* applies for a job in the Griffiths collar factory, Dreiser describes her as one of "the extras or try-outs."[60] Like her lover, Clyde, who is driven into her arms out of a sense of not belonging to his rich uncle's society, Dreiser had also been an outsider in Hollywood, unable to sell any screenplays and having to hear of its doings through Helen. In his last diary entry before returning to New York that fall he laments a rejection by *Hearst's International-Cosmopolitan.* Now he was spending a good part of his time either gardening or watering his lawn in the great California desert. "Personally feel very much depressed and soon go to bed. At the moment see no very clear way out of money troubles or that I am making any real artistic headway with work. The relentless push against the individual on and away into dissolution hangs heavy on me." In 1922 *Shadowland* magazine, which had published his four-part series of Hollywood articles, ranked Dreiser fourteenth out of "America's Top Favored Forty" writers, well behind fellow Hoosier Booth Tarkington and Edith Wharton, who occupied first and second place. Edgar Lee Masters ranked eighth, five places in front of Robert Frost. Sinclair Lewis was tenth. Mencken was twenty-fourth on this dubious list.[61]

THIRTEEN

An American Tragedy

I feel it an honor to be permitted to even
tell such a tale & on that basis I am working on.

DREISER TO HELEN RICHARDSON, JUNE 18, 1924

IN THE SUMMER OF 1906, Grace ("Billy") Brown drowned on Big Moose Lake in Herkimer County, New York. Less than two years later Chester E. Gillette was electrocuted for her murder in Auburn Prison, following a sensational trial that was graphically reported in the *New York World* and elsewhere. This was the basis for the story of Clyde Griffiths and Roberta Alden that Dreiser, the failed screenwriter, brought back from Hollywood, the tale he would struggle with, sometimes desperately, for the next three years, trying to breathe life and meaning back into these grim facts of death. Dreiser later claimed that this particular case hadn't influenced him until after he returned from California, but this statement is clearly contradicted by others. In 1926, for example, he told Thomas P. Beyer of Hamline University in St. Paul that he "had thought and brooded upon the Chester Gillette murder case for many years" before ever setting pen to paper. A year later he told another enthusiast that he "had long brooded" on the case and his purpose in writing the novel had been "to give, if possible, a background and a psychology of reality which would somehow explain, if not condone, how such murders could happen." Moreover, we already know that he had investigated a street mission before leaving Los Angeles. Chester Gillette had not only the same initials as Clyde Griffiths, but also parents who were street preachers. Indeed, the facts of the case and the novel are so parallel that a few critics have tended to discount *An American Tragedy* as art.[1]

Like Clyde, Chester Gillette had lived in various cities in the West, where his parents worked for the Salvation Army. Chester's family wasn't as poor as Dreiser makes the Griffithses, but after Frank Gillette gave up his engineer's job in 1892—when his son was ten—to follow his religious calling, the family income was significantly reduced. The boy attended Oberlin, as has also been pointed out in source studies for the novel, but it was the preparatory school, not the college, and the tuition was paid by a distant relative. Unlike Clyde, who can hardly keep up with his rich cousins' social set when the conversation turns to colleges, Chester never disabused his friends of the fiction that he had studied at the college level. His uncle, Noah H. Gillette, the owner of a skirt factory in Cortland, New York, first gave Chester a job in his plant in the summer of 1901 while he was still a student at Oberlin. Afterward, Chester dropped out of school because of failing grades, drifted around the country, and became a brakeman for the Chicago, Milwaukee and St. Paul Railroad. In 1905 he went to work full-time for his uncle.[2]

Clyde, who also comes east from Kansas City and Chicago to seek his fortune, is given similar duties in his uncle's collar factory in Lycurgus, where he becomes involved with Roberta ("Bert") Alden, one of several factory hands under his supervision. There he is warned by his look-alike cousin Gilbert not to socialize with the female employees, while also not immediately invited to join his uncle's social class. There were no such caveats issued to Chester, who was free to flirt openly with the factory girls, including Grace Brown, while also moving in the higher social circles of his uncle. He led a double life in Cortland: the ex-brakeman was rough enough for one set, while the ex–prep school student was polished enough for the other. The only warning he received, also from a cousin who supervised his work, was that socializing with fellow employees (Chester wasn't an overseer of Grace Brown the way Clyde is placed over Roberta Alden) might decrease their efficiency as factory workers. This difference is probably important in appreciating how Dreiser turned fact into fiction. For just as he may have exaggerated in *Newspaper Days* the chasm between the rich and poor, he raises these barriers at least a little higher in *An American Tragedy* than they actually were in supposedly democratic America. Leaning more and more toward the socialist idea in the 1920s, Dreiser sought to see Clyde as a victim of social and economic forces beyond his control. To do so, he induces an Aladdin-like dream in which the vain and beautiful Sondra Finchley falls in love with Clyde and sweeps him up to her social level briefly, whereas in

Chester's case the young man never fully succeeded in securing the attentions of any one particular female among Cortland's leisure class.

Although he was moving up socially, Chester was still only on the periphery of the circle that included such privileged young ladies as Harriet Benedict and Josephine Patrick when he got "Billy" Brown in trouble. By the summer of 1905 he and Grace had become a "couple"—seen together mainly at the factory during lunch breaks. Chester also visited her regularly, first in her sister's parlor and later in a room Grace rented by herself (paralleled by Roberta's move away from Grace Marr in a home with social supervision to a rented room with a private entrance), but he seldom took her out in public. She wasn't, however, the simple farmer's daughter the newspapers made her out to be, but someone who sought to better herself through reading (to become Chester's "equal"); once she became pregnant, though, she fell apart. She subsequently wrote Chester a series of pathetic—indeed, masochistic—letters, some of which were used nearly verbatim by Dreiser in his novel. By May, fearing that her pregnancy was beginning to show, she quit her factory job and returned to her parents' home just outside South Otselic ("Biltz" in the novel).

From her parents' shabby farmhouse, she pleaded with Chester to come to her, apparently under the impression that he had indicated a willingness to marry. But Chester continued to socialize in Cortland as before. When this news got back to her through friends, Grace became angry and jealous and threatened to expose him to the community and no doubt to his uncle. Like Clyde, he delayed action as long as he could, but there is little or no evidence that the couple considered abortion as they do in the novel. Chester may have been interested in this option, but Grace insisted that he marry her. It was a time in America when both abortions and the publication of birth control information were criminal offenses. Dreiser, as we have noted, supported Margaret Sanger's position on birth control and may have seen the moral and social aspects of Clyde's dilemma as important subissues to the theme of the young man's helplessness as a pawn of nature and society. Had Clyde been part of a more powerful class, he could have found an abortionist as one of his defense lawyers had done in his more privileged youth. Gillette "merely wished to divest himself of the poorer relationship in order to achieve the richer one," Dreiser later wrote of the case. "And you may depend upon it that if he had had money and more experience in the ways of immorality, he would have known ways and means of indulging himself in the relationship with Billy Brown without bringing upon himself the morally compulsive relation of prospective fatherhood."[3] As Dreiser saw it, Clyde was merely acting according to social norm by wanting to better himself by marrying a rich girl. Because of chance (and a lack of birth control information), Roberta had become an obstacle to the fulfillment of this American Dream, the same fantasy of marrying into a rich family that Dreiser himself admitted in his autobiography to sharing as a young man.

Once Chester had returned to Cortland from a Fourth of July weekend at Lake Skaneateles with Harriet Benedict and her friends, Grace told him: "I am writing to tell you I am coming back to Cortland. I simply can't stay here any longer. Mama worries and wonders why I cry so much, and I am just about sick. Please come and take me away some place, dear." Dreiser has Roberta write almost the same words.[4] Not wanting to expose himself to her parents in South Otselic or his connection to Grace in Cortland, Chester met her in DeRuyter, where the fated couple took a train to Utica. They left the Tabor Hotel the next day without paying and took another train north to the Adirondacks and Tupper Lake, where they spent their second night together. They found this resort not to their liking, however, and retraced their journey back down to the then relatively secluded Big Moose Lake. Here, at the Glenmore Hotel, Chester registered as Carl Graham of Albany. Clyde takes the same name when he and Roberta register at a similar hotel at Big Bittern. That afternoon Chester and Grace rented a boat, indicating that they planned to return for dinner around six and then take the train south for home. They left Grace's suitcase at the hotel, while taking Chester's because it allegedly contained their packed lunch. Chester also took along, strapped to the side of his valise with the initials "CG," the tennis racket which he was accused of using to strike Grace unconscious before she fell into the water and drowned.

Chester maintained his innocence at his murder trial, claiming that Grace committed suicide by throwing herself in the water when he announced that they would have to tell her parents about the pregnancy. He maintained that his alias at the Glenmore had been designed to protect Grace in her shameful state. But he had already given three different and conflicting stories upon his arrest at a nearby lake where he had gone to meet his society friends immediately following the drowning, and the fact that he hadn't saved her from drowning (not a crime in itself before Good Samaritan laws) reinforced the jury's notion of his guilt. There were a number of incidental witnesses who remembered seeing the two traveling together, but the most damaging witness against him was Grace Brown herself. The

Herkimer County District Attorney, George W. Ward, whipped up sentiment by reading fourteen of her pleading letters in court and afterward allowing them to be published in the *New York World.* The prosecutor was then running for county judge and hoped a victory in such a widely reported trial would guarantee his political victory. There was also the testimony of five physicians (later denounced by the defense as conspirators for the prosecution) that a blow on the head had rendered her unconscious before she went into the water. Chester was found guilty of first-degree murder by the jury after four hours' deliberation in which only one juror had held out for acquittal. He was convicted solely on circumstantial evidence, but Grace's letters overwhelmed the case and rendered the accused *ipso facto* guilty not only of murder but of the moral crimes of fornication and seduction. Gillette, whose court-appointed counsel was assigned late in the indictment process, was executed on March 30, 1908.[5]

The circus atmosphere of the trial must have reminded Dreiser of the festive nature of the black lynchings he had seen and read about while working as a reporter in St. Louis. Clyde, as he envisioned him, was simply a white "nigger," not too different from his brother Rome, who had also worked for the railroad and drifted around the country. Dreiser may have followed the Gillette-Brown case as it unfolded in the newspapers in the fall of 1906. For it suggested not only the tragic reverse of the American Dream, but the emergence of a social category noted for its "conspicuous consumption" in Thorstein Veblen's *Theory of the Leisure Class* (1899), with which Dreiser was obviously familiar.[6] Clyde's Lycurgus cousins and their set, including Sondra, have few responsibilities and unlimited time on their hands for boating, dancing, driving, and late-night parties and dinners at their parents' richly appointed residences in the city and vacation homes on lakes in the North Woods. Because it is somewhat unrealistic that such a Rome-like figure gains unqualified entry into this world, Dreiser carefully established that Sondra's initial interest in Clyde is based on her frustration that his look-alike cousin Gilbert was ignoring her.

Dreiser seems to alternate the setting of this crime story between the post-Victorian era of 1906 and the liberated 1920s, when the crass consumerism noted in Veblen had reached its pinnacle in the wake of the Great War and the era of Prohibition, ushered in on January 1, 1920. There is the omnipresence of the automobile (killing the child in Kansas City and setting Clyde on his tragic odyssey), which makes it clear that this is a highly mobile society, no longer dependent on the train. Yet Clyde and Roberta, being poor, do still depend upon it. Dreiser, the author of *The*

Financier and *The Titan,* certainly knew how to write a documentary novel. But in *An American Tragedy,* while depending on the facts of an actual crime, he deliberately blurred the historical moment. For the problem dramatized in his novel did not belong exclusively to the twenties, but to the preceding thirty or so years, in which he had first become conscious of the painful contrast between wealth and poverty in America set in motion after the Civil War by the economic plundering of the Robber Barons. "It was in 1892, at a time I began work as a newspaper man," Dreiser wrote in 1934, "that I first began to observe a certain type of crime in the United States. It seemed to spring from the fact that almost every young person was possessed of an ingrowing ambition to be somebody financially and socially. . . . I was witnessing the upbuilding of the great American fortunes. And once these fortunes and the families which controlled them were established, there began to develop our 'leisure class,' the Four Hundred [families] of New York . . . , plus their imitators in the remainder of the states."[7]

In an early draft of *An American Tragedy,* Clyde arrives in Lycurgus in 1919. Yet there is no direct indication of World War I and its devastating effects on the morals of the nation as there is in F. Scott Fitzgerald's *The Great Gatsby,* though the two novels were published in the same year. (Dreiser, incidentally, met and snubbed Fitzgerald in the winter of 1923 at a party at the St. Luke's Place apartment he had taken on his return to New York.)[8] Today's readers are surprised to hear that the two appeared in the same year, that Dreiser's novel wasn't published earlier. Both Nick Carraway and Jay Gatsby in Fitzgerald's novel have served in the war (while Tom Buchanan apparently has not), but nobody in *An American Tragedy* seems to have ever heard of either the Great War or Prohibition. Yet they have heard the song "Brown Eyes, Why Are You Blue?" (released in 1925), and the young women wear flapper-like rhinestone bands around their foreheads.

But, again, Dreiser's themes spanned a larger time frame. One of the quickest and easiest ways to get rich in America, according to the pulp fiction at the turn of the century, was to marry money. Often, however, there was a poorer girl whose pregnancy already laid claim to the ambitious suitor. "What produced this particular type of crime about which I am talking," Dreiser wrote, "was the fact that it was not always possible to drop the first girl." The only way out was often murder, since the pregnant girl could not deal with her shame and demanded marriage, while the rich girl would have vanished at the first whiff of scandal. It probably impressed Gillette in the middle of New York's lake country where there were frequent boating mishaps—as it no doubt did Dreiser in writing his novel, since he had grown up in a lake district around Warsaw—that such a crime could plausibly be staged as an accident. In fact, Dreiser had studied at least fifteen such cases before he finally decided to base his novel on the Gillette-Brown case, mainly because of the availability of the stories in the files of the *World* and other newspapers.[9]

In the early 1890s, while still in St. Louis, Dreiser took note of a case in which a young perfume dealer had poisoned his girlfriend so that he could marry into one of the old French families of St. Louis. One of the "most tragic" of the cases Dreiser encountered, when he first came to New York in 1894, is remarkably similar in the choice of murder weapons. Carlyle Harris, a young medical student, also poisoned a poor girlfriend to be with a rich one and was tried, convicted, and executed for murder.[10] It was the Roland Molineaux case of 1898–1902, however, that Dreiser first studied seriously and tried to adapt as a novel during the winter of 1915, what was in effect the first version of *An American Tragedy* . Curiously, this was yet another poisoning case: Molineaux, a chemist, had sent poison to a fellow club member following a quarrel.

In fact, Molineaux was convicted of poisoning the rival member's aunt, who accidentally consumed the poison intended for her nephew on December 28, 1898. He was granted a second trial, however, mainly because of his influential family connections, and was then acquitted. Earlier, after he had quarreled with another club member over the hand of a wealthy woman, this man too had died of a mysterious poisoning. It was one of the most sensational crime stories of its era. Molineaux, who spent twenty months on death row at Sing Sing before his second trial, went on to write and produce a play before going insane and being committed to a mental hospital, where he died in 1913. (Coincidentally, before going completely mad, he had been a patient at Muldoon's Sanitarium.) Dreiser's story was originally called *The Rake* (not to be confused with Dreiser's earlier unfinished book, following *Sister Carrie,* "The Rake," which was essentially the earliest draft of *The "Genius"*), but extant drafts of the first six chapters show that he couldn't extract from the case the story he had really wanted to tell: that of the ambitious lover who is also poor.[11]

Dreiser also began a novel based on the 1911 Clarence Richeson case in which a New England minister poisoned his sweetheart in order to wed a rich parishioner; this manuscript is now lost.[12] Other cases to come under consideration were, along with the Gillette-Brown case, the William Orpet case of 1916 (yet another poisoning case), and the Harry New, Jr., murder trial of 1919, in which the accused was the son of a powerful and wealthy Indiana ex-Senator and postmaster general. In "Neurotic America and the Sex Impulse," written after his visit to Savannah in 1916 and appearing in *Hey Rub-A-Dub-Dub,* Dreiser mentions all these cases, including Gillette-Brown, and others as well.

———

By 1920, however, it had become abundantly clear that Chester Gillette's case best matched the kind of crime required as the historical basis for *An American Tragedy.* During its composition, Dreiser was briefly distracted by the sensational 1924 trial of Nathan Leopold and Richard Loeb for kidnapping and murder. They were defended by Clarence Darrow, whom Dreiser probably knew through his Chicago connections. He told Helen: "It's one of those fantastic things that seems to hold so much more than is on the surface. Just the desire to kill doesn't seem to explain it. . . . A great novel there somewhere."[13] (There was, but it would not be written until Meyer Levin's *Compulsion* in 1956.) Leopold and Loeb were two brilliant but spoiled rich college boys in Chicago who had tried to commit the perfect crime, mainly for its own sake. Yet as in the Molineaux case Dreiser needed a youth who, incidentally like himself, had grown up in relative poverty and come east to seek his fortune under the compulsions of the American Dream of getting rich almost overnight.

Once back in New York, Dreiser renewed research on his novel. As the seventeenth anniversary of the drowning of Grace Brown approached, he and Helen motored to the crime scenes. They left the city on June 30, 1923, stopping the first night in Monticello and reaching Cortland on July 1. There they drove around, as Helen remembered, "to get a general impression of the city as a whole—the best residential section, the factory section and the poor streets of the town." Dreiser noted the same pattern of wealth and poverty he had observed when he had initially explored the cities he passed through on his journey east in the early 1890s. The next day they drove east to the Brown homestead outside South Otselic and met a farmer who had known Grace's father, who had died in the interim. Dreiser described the same lonely country road leading to the house in his novel, according to Helen. From there they went up to De Ruyter, which marked the entrance to the lake country as well as the beginning of Grace's fateful journey, and traced the couple's steps to Big Moose Lake (Big Bittern in the novel). It was July 3 when he and Helen registered at the same Glenmore Hotel. On the Fourth Dreiser spoke to the guide who claimed to have found Grace Brown's body. Afterward, he rowed out on the lake with Helen to the secluded South Bay, where the girl had died. In the boat, Dreiser's concentration on the scene was so intense that it appeared to Helen as if he was about to fall into the same catatonic state that envelops Clyde before he accidentally hits Roberta with the camera, sending her to her death. Finding themselves drifting over the "deathlike stillness" that was once Grace Brown's grave, Helen recalled that she became a little frightened. "Maybe Teddie will become completely hypnotized by this idea," she fantasized, "and even repeat it, here and now."[14]

We don't have a record of what the guide told him, except for what was absorbed into *An American Tragedy,* but one of the search party left a brief record of his impressions. Roy C. Higby was thirteen at the time of the incident and was on the scene because his uncle owned the Big Moose Transportation Company. It was he who first spotted Grace's body from the deck of the craft coordinating the rowboats that had set out in search of the missing couple. "I can remember exactly my first sight of the body," Higby wrote in recalling that day Grace was brought to the surface by either a pole or a hooked line.

> Her forehead was badly cut from the hairline of her left forehead across the right eyebrow and looked as though it had been struck by a fairly sharp or medium blunt instrument, heavily enough to lay the scalp wide open. She was dressed in a white shirt-waist, green (light green) skirt and button shoes and stockings. . . . I do not remember too much about what was done with the remains after being taken to the hotel, but I do recall that the men searched about an hour for the body of her companion and after hearing about his having taken his suitcase, etc., with him in the boat, their native shrewdness told them there was more to this than an accidental drowning.

Here is how Dreiser described the scene in his novel:

> But what created far more excitement after a very little time was the fact that at high noon one of the men who trolled—John Pole—a woodsman, was at last successful in bringing to the surface Roberta herself, drawn upward by the skirt of her dress, obviously bruised about the face—the lips and nose and above and below the right eye. . . . John Pole, who with Joe Rainer at the oars was the one who had succeeded in bringing her to the surface, had exclaimed at once on seeing her: 'Why, the pore little thing!

She don't seem to weigh more'n nothin' at all. It's a wonder tuh me she coulda sunk.' [Grace Brown stood 5' 2" and weighed 100 pounds.] And then reaching over and gathering her in his strong arms, he drew her in, dripping and lifeless, while his companions signaled to the other searchers, who came swiftly. And putting back from her face the long, brown, thick hair which the action of the water had swirled concealingly across it, he had added: 'I do declare, Joe! Looka here. It does look like the child mighta been hit by somethin! Looka here, Joe!' And soon the group of woodsmen and inn guests in their boats were looking at the brownish-blue marks on Roberta's face.

Dreiser not only deepens the drama of the discovery of the dead girl's body, but reflects the emotion of the woodsmen, who in actuality planned to lynch Gillette, had they found him before the police.[15]

Dreiser's last stop before returning to New York was Herkimer, the county seat where Chester had been tried for murder, the Bridgeburg of *An American Tragedy.* He visited both the courthouse and the county jail in which Chester had been incarcerated until his trial began. Here Dreiser may have hoped to examine the court record, but by this time, so many years after the 1906 trial, its 2,129-page "abstract" was obtainable only in large New York State law libraries. As a result, his major sources were the newspaper accounts, especially those in the *World* and the *New York Sun,* and a 1906 pamphlet entitled *Grace Brown's Love Letters,* which Dreiser may have picked up in Herkimer.[16] His biggest source was his imagination, which had been recently tested in the writing of *Newspaper Days.* Some reviewers complained that the autobiographical volume was too long at more than five hundred pages, but what impresses the reader today is Dreiser's imaginative reading of his past, for he surely could not have remembered all the conversations and extended minutiae that buttress the narrative. It was this same big silver screen that would fictionalize the biography of Chester Gillette.

Upon his return from California in the fall of 1922, Dreiser had established his New York residence at 16 St. Luke's Place in the Village, where one of his neighbors was Sherwood Anderson, and another was A. A. Brill, the Freud translator and psychiatrist, whom Dreiser had known since 1917. In 1923 Boni & Liveright issued *The Color of a Great City,* a collection of sketches and stories about New York, mostly old, some done around the turn of the century. The firm also finally reissued *The "Genius"*—in its original and completely uncut form, in spite of the complaints by Sherman and others and the censoring efforts of Mencken made in hopes of salvaging the book. It brought Dreiser the highest royalties of any book to date, indeed significantly more than he had earned from a number of the earlier ones. When *The "Genius"* was first issued by John Lane, it had sold 7,982 copies and earned Dreiser royalties in the amount of $2,394.60 before it was withdrawn the next year in the face of Sherman's threats of prosecution. When Liveright reissued it, it sold over 48,000 copies between 1923 and 1933 and earned Dreiser more than $25,000. He also continued to receive $4,000 a year from Boni & Liveright in the form of advances while he worked on *An American Tragedy*. By that fall, he told several correspondents that the new novel was "1/2 done" and that he expected to complete it by the following August.[17]

By this time Dreiser and Helen were quarreling frequently. It is not altogether clear whether Helen ever made St. Luke's Place her primary address, but she had taken her own apartment at 35 West 50th Street soon after their return east. Their relationship had suffered somewhat in California, possibly because of the attention Helen was receiving from randy producers and directors. There, amid the glamour of fast fortunes and the possibility of overnight stardom for beautiful young women, Dreiser's sagging literary fame was no match for the allure of the Hollywood moguls. Back in New York, he started seeing other women—those with whom he had already trysted, Louise Campbell and the others, but also a new one, named Sallie Kussell, an aspiring if neurotic writer from Chicago who would become one of the typists and editorial advisors of *An American Tragedy*. "The trouble with you," Dreiser told her at the height of their attraction to each other in the summer of 1923, "is that you have a gripping sex appeal for me." With this rivalry, Helen's relations with Dreiser had reached the same level of frustration over his philandering as Estelle had felt shortly before he met Helen in 1919. Both women complained bitterly at their neglect, and Estelle often whined, which, given her nickname of "Bert," may have suggested the character of the distressed Roberta Alden once she finds herself pregnant and unloved by Clyde. (Another model, of course, was Jug, whose seniority to Dreiser may have prompted the idea of making Roberta two years older than Clyde. The only legitimate Mrs. Dreiser had, of course, already served as the basis for Angela in *The "Genius"* and inspired the marriage stories in *Free*.) In March of 1924 Helen left New York for Portland to visit her mother and sister, with the intention of eventually making her way back to Hollywood to revive her career, this time as a singer. Dreiser, while persisting in his "varietism," missed her dearly. And it is because of their separation that we have an epistolary record of his emotional ups and downs as he struggled to complete *An American Tragedy*, "harder," as he told Helen on March 30, "than any I ever wrote." Later in 1924, Louise Campbell returned from a year in Europe, and started typing and editing the manuscript. The transcript in turn was being sent in sections to his publisher, who immediately set it up in type in the hope of getting a running start on its eventual publication.[18]

Dreiser did little else but work on the book, but by June he had only reached the point "where the factory girl & the rich girl in Clyde's life are enlarging & by degrees destroying him." He found himself in a similar quandary, because he had set himself between Helen and other women. Fearing that she was possibly seeing someone else, he told her on one day that he wasn't "sleeping with anyone." On the very next he recorded in his diary a sexual encounter on the beach with one Magdalene Davis, an actress by night and secretary by day who came from the grimy coal town of Ebensburg, Pennsylvania. He was now drinking bathtub gin and occasionally even smoking cigarettes, something very unusual for Dreiser because of his bronchial history. One night he stumbled into Mame's apartment and sobbed bitterly that he couldn't finish his novel. It was around this time that Esther McCoy entered his life, after writing him the usual fan letter. She was then an undergraduate at the University of Michigan, and her leftist political leanings would encourage Dreiser's commitment to communism in the 1930s. One night in May, perhaps in search of further romance, he attended a party at the Long Island Sound mansion of W. C. Fields. He was running himself down and even thought "of going to the country for a few days—to a work-farm like Muldoon's used to be to see if I can be pulled into shape."[19]

By the fall of 1924 Dreiser had moved to a street-level flat at 118 West 11th Street near Washington Square, one of the Rhinelander apartments, where Mame and Austin also lived as managers. He worked every day on the novel, even Sundays, sometimes from eleven in the morning until ten at night. By the end of the year he had Books I and II written, typed, and sent to his publisher. Thomas R. Smith, the editor-in-chief at Boni & Liveright, told Dreiser the following spring that he had read the last five or six chapters of Book II "with real agony. The slow, fatal working-up to the death of Roberta is one of the grimmest and most gripping tragedies that I have read in years." It was so moving, he said, that he had difficulty in copyediting it. In fact, Smith, described as "cherubic and acidulous, and a remarkable drinker," quarreled with Dreiser several times during the summer of 1925 over material the editor had wanted excised from the manuscript.[20] Meanwhile, Helen had finally relented and returned to New York in the late fall, and in January of 1925 the couple took a flat at 1799 Bedford Avenue in Brooklyn for a year. Through the help of Joseph Jay Robin, the Gatsby-like friend of *Twelve Men,* Dreiser also rented an office in which to work, in the Guardian Life Building near Union Square. Robin, who had recently acquired a law degree, had an office in the same building. Together with Arthur Carter Hume, another friend and attorney, he advised Dreiser on the legal aspects of Book III, which covers the trial and execution of Clyde Griffiths.[21]

To help himself imagine a death house similar to the one where Clyde is sent, Dreiser asked Mencken, who had recently accepted Dreiser's short story, "Convention," for the newly established *American Mercury,* to use his influence to get him onto death row at nearby Sing Sing. Curiously, he wanted only to visit the death house, not the actual execution chamber. He had applied himself to the warden, but had been summarily refused. Mencken got the *World* to send Dreiser to Sing Sing as a reporter to cover the anticipated confession of a convicted murderer, Anthony Pantano, who had been sent back to the "big coffin" to die after having been free for a retrial. On November 27, 1925, two days after he had allegedly written the last words of *An American Tragedy,* Dreiser sat for three hours in a wire cage and spoke with the chain-smoking murderer, whose three accomplices had already been executed. There were at the time fifty-two men and women at Sing Sing waiting to die, and the four wings of the X-shaped death house may have reminded Dreiser somewhat of the prison that served as the basis for Cowperwood's incarceration in Philadelphia. This time, however, his literary subject was no Nietzschean superman and wasn't getting out, and neither were the other inmates, whose bleak situation caused him to lower his voice to a whisper. He noticed that the guards wore felt-soled shoes, and the condemned prisoners themselves were also silent. "One opened an unwinking eye and regarded me stilly," he later told Dudley Nichols of the *World,* "as if he were in another medium beyond communication, like a fish in an aquarium."[22]

Like Clyde's (and Chester's) guilt, there was some doubt about Pantano's— based at least on the condemned man's argument that he had been involuntarily and forcibly drawn into the deadly crime in which a bank robbery had turned into murder. Like Clyde at the end, he also subscribed vaguely to the precepts of organized religion. The visit was like a dream, or a nightmare, to Dreiser, who said he couldn't imagine how Pantano ever "got mixed up in this crime as you are supposed to have been." In *An American Tragedy* while Clyde is on death row, there is the execution of Pasquale Cutrone of Brooklyn, "an Italian, convicted of the slaying of his brother for attempting to seduce his wife." Possibly Dreiser may have amended the details of his death row scenes slightly after his visit to Sing Sing. The execution of Cutrone, who doesn't even speak English, throws Clyde back into the full misery of his situation, which had been somewhat alleviated by the erudite and eloquent musings of fellow inmate Miller Nicholson, a lawyer from Buffalo who—like the murderers in several of the cases Dreiser considered for his novel—has poisoned his victim.[23]

We never see the execution chamber in *An American Tragedy*, only the door to it as it shuts after the prayerful Italian immigrant passes through. "There—sure—that's the end now," says one guard. "Yes. He knows what's on the other side now," answers another. The execution is the first one to take place since Clyde's confinement on death row, and it absolutely terrorizes him, but Nicholson, who is next, quietly destroys personal papers in his cell and promises Clyde that he is sending him "something to remember me by." He leaves him two books, *Robinson Crusoe* and *The Arabian Nights*, both romances about survival. But unlike Defoe's protagonist, who finds a tolerable existence in raw nature, or the boy in "The History of Aladdin," who discovers that magic lamp which releases him from his uncle's prison and fulfills every desire, Clyde now no longer fantasizes that he can rise above the limits of his situation. As a bellhop at the Green-Davidson in Kansas City, he may have found splendor in its garish lobby (the same kind of wonderland where Hurstwood takes temporary refuge in his American tragedy), but in Dreiser's account there is no fantasy left now but religion—belief in "a literal Heaven and Hell" upheld by Pantano before Dreiser had said his good-bye. Even here the Rev. Duncan McMillan, the itinerant clergyman who is overwhelmed by the sordid aspects of Clyde's confession to him (that "the unintentional blow [upon Roberta] still had had anger in it"), concludes erroneously that Clyde was guilty both "before God and the law."[24] Yet technically Clyde was no more guilty of purposely striking Roberta than Hurstwood was in shutting the safe at Fitzgerald and Moy's. In both cases, they "didn't do it."

What both did do was to participate in circumstances surely leading up to each climactic and tragic scene. Clyde is driven onward by both chemic forces and circumstances beyond his control. Since the story was conceived after Dreiser had read Freud, it is thought to be heavily psychological in this modern sense. But in the many interior monologues in which Clyde argues with himself and tries to figure his way out of the chaos surely promised by Roberta's condition, we also find traces of that earlier, nineteenth-century psychologist, Edgar Allan Poe. Like the narrator of Poe's "The Imp of the Perverse," Clyde cannot help himself. This narrator, like Nicholson, is interestingly enough another poisoner. After Dreiser left Sing Sing that day, he told Mencken, "My imagination was better—(more true to fact)—than what I saw."[25] Perhaps, but the more immediate point here is that in *An American Tragedy* it was an imagination born in the century of Poe and honed in the age of Freud.

Shortly before or right after Dreiser's scheduled visit to Sing Sing, the judge granting the *World* permission to send in a reporter became suspicious—when the reporter turned out to be Dreiser and the judge heard rumors of his novel-in-progress. This led to a brief quarrel between Dreiser and Mencken when, to cover its tracks, the *World* asked Dreiser to write up his Sing Sing visit in exchange for getting him into the prison—that is, without any payment—and he refused. "World complains that after getting you permit with great difficulty by saying you represented it," wired Mencken, still piqued because Dreiser had republished The *"Genius"* without incorporating any of Mencken's efforts to save it in a more sanitized form, "you now demand money. This puts me in a nice hole indeed." Dreiser shot back, "The World lies. Your telegram is an insult." A little more calmly the following week, Dreiser—who never forgot his shabby treatment at the *World* in 1894—pointed out that it was unfair of the newspaper to expect a five-thousand-word article free of charge, which it could then syndicate. After Dreiser agreed to be interviewed by the *World* for an article on his visit to Pantano, Mencken quickly agreed that it was all an innocent misunderstanding and lapsed into his characteristic humor.[26]

But as we shall see, Mencken did not forget.

The plot of *An American Tragedy* is by now familiar even to those readers of this biography who have not yet read the novel, or have not read it in many years, for it follows the Gillette-Brown case almost exactly. Both the novel and the real-life story feature two post-adolescents from the ranks of poverty. While they cannot enjoy the freedoms of their crassly rich counterparts in Lycurgus and Cortland, they are in no way free from the influence of the American Dream. In fact, their poverty makes them more vulnerable to this great fiction than the New York Griffithses or Gillettes, who at least realize that their success depends on the existence of the poor. Moreover, Dreiser realized from the other cases he had studied, which had involved rich murderers rather than poor ones, that the Dream hounded all Americans into improving their status, no matter how high it already was. Just as Roberta looks to Clyde to lift her up socially, Sondra looks to Gilbert to improve her status, and he in turn resists it because the Griffiths Collar Factory is superior in wealth and status to her family's Finchley Electric Sweeper Company.[27] Dreiser, because of his own background, could draw Roberta much better than Sondra. Not only could he not empathize with rich people, but the depiction of Sondra was probably an extension of one of the many mental sketches he made of the starlets competing with Helen for movie stardom.

Dreiser followed his instincts and the script of the actual murder, but the greatest pathos of the novel also came out of his past, for the protagonist is in part Theodore Dreiser, the kid who grew up in Indiana and came east; the youngster whose family knew Jimmie Bulger, who had gone to the gallows at Sing Sing under the name of "Whitey Sullivan"; and the young man in Chicago who stole twenty-five dollars for an overcoat. Any one of his friends or brothers could have taken the tragic turn that Clyde follows—Paul, Rome, even Al, who was out of contact with most family members after 1906.[28] As Dreiser wrote his novel, he was reminded of the potential closeness at one time in his family life to Clyde's fate. His sixty-one-year-old sibling Emma, the prototype "sister" for *Sister Carrie* who had gone off with the thief Hopkins, now lived nearby in Greenwich Village in rather depressed and depressing circumstances. Her daughter Gertrude, now a woman in her early thirties, had been seriously ill for a time and was still single. Both Mame and Sylvia had become pregnant out of wedlock. There were any number of Robertas "trifling with fire and perhaps social disgrace" in Dreiser's foreground to both *Sister Carrie* and *An American Tragedy*.[29]

Since the newspaper reports did not give him much information about Gillette's early background, Dreiser—as he had with Cowperwood—turned to his own life to fill in the details. He relied upon the memory of his own fanatically religious father, who like Asa Griffiths was otherwise helpless to take care of his family. He placed the Griffiths family first in Kansas City—one of the few major American metropolises Dreiser had never visited, for the last impression he wanted to give in his novel based so securely on fact was a definite sense of place. Clyde could and did come from any place in America. "Dusk— of a summer night," the now famous opening reads. It is a dreamlike entry into a tragedy that was peculiarly American. No one falls from a high place as in the classical definition of tragedy; instead he falls from or out of a dream, the American one based upon Benjamin Franklin's rags-to-riches story in his *Autobiography*. In spite of Emerson's effort to realign that dream with the higher reality of spiritual fulfillment, it is no wonder that by the hedonistic 1920s not only Dreiser but Fitzgerald inverted this dream into the tragedy that was too often inevitable.

More specifically, Clyde Griffiths of Book I is also a clear reflection of Theodore Dreiser in *Dawn*. Both are daydreamers who have "an abnormal interest in girls" and at the same time are exceedingly shy with them. They both have mothers who are stronger than the boys' fathers. Indeed, Dreiser introduces his obsession with mother love through phraseology reminiscent of Paul Dresser's nostalgic songs. On the windows of the "Door of Hope" that fronts the Griffithses' mission in Kansas City, its congregants are asked, "How Long Since You Wrote to Mother?" Esta's running away with a man and returning alone pregnant, as noted, found several examples in Dreiser's family. In fact, Clyde's insensitivity to his sister's plight reflects Dreiser's own shame and attempts to distance himself from such family crises. In both cases, these pregnancies threaten their dreams of success and wealth. And Dreiser's own insensitivity to the demands of the women in his current life suggests Clyde's stubborn resistance of Roberta after he becomes involved with Sondra.

At the time he first undertook *An American Tragedy,* Dreiser was also working on—indeed almost finishing—the fifteen sketches for *A Gallery of Women*.[30] Here the female protagonist is not the dependent lover or long-suffering mother, but the American woman of the early twentieth century who dares to ignore the conventions of marriage and motherhood in order to realize her personal or professional ambitions. Most fail because of their defiant or proto-feminist lifestyles. He was then also corresponding with Marion Bloom, another female aspirant in a male world who would, as already noted, appear in one of the *Gallery* sketches as a minor character. She was now living in Washington and married to Lou Maritzer, who later abandoned her as abruptly as Hans Kubitz had deserted her sister Estelle.

Curiously, as Mencken became Estelle's personal correspondent, Marion tried to become Dreiser's. Although he was not taken in by Marion's chatty letters, which exuded the same pagan sensuality that had once charmed

Mencken, he did visit her and Lou in the fall of 1923. Her flirtations may have suggested the character of Hortense Briggs in Book I of the novel, the "crude shop girl" who tries to seduce Clyde into buying her an expensive coat. Her depiction—a near caricature of the femme fatale—is one of the gems of character portraiture in the novel and also reflects the posing and primping of Dreiser's sisters. When Clyde as a bellhop at the Green-David-son becomes intoxicated with Hortense and tells her that he could spend more money on her than could another suitor, she "was not a little intrigued by this cash offer . . . and not a little set up in her mood by the fact that she could thus inflame nearly all youths in this way. She was really a little silly, very lightheaded . . . [and] infatuated by her own charms and looked in every mirror." In fact, Dreiser satirizes both Clyde and Hortense. Clyde refuses to have a girlfriend who is not pretty, but for Hortense, "it was her own appearance, not his, that interested her."[31]

Clyde is Dreiser only up to a point, however. Then he is Rome or "Whitey Sullivan," fully swept away by the promised delights of a hedonistic world. In 1920 Dreiser had tried to tell Sullivan's (or Bulger's) story in "Her Boy," a manuscript he never completed. As he relates near the beginning of Book II of *An American Tragedy,* where the action shifts to New York, "Clyde had a soul that was not destined to grow up. He lacked decidedly that mental clarity and inner directing application that in so many permits them to sort out from the facts and avenues of life the particular thing or things that make for their direct advancement."[32] Like Carrie Meeber and George Hurstwood, Clyde is helpless in the face of the possibility of sexual ecstasy and the opulence it symbolizes. Other Dreiser protagonists like Frank Cowperwood, Eugene Witla, and even Jennie Gerhardt have something of a mind of their own in spite of the dictates of their "chemism."

Of course, Clyde is formally based on Chester Gillette, who Dreiser later maintained was anything but antisocial in the murder of Grace Brown. (Gillette allegedly confessed right before his execution.) If Gillette's case "proved anything," Dreiser concluded, "it proved that he desired to reach a social state in which no such evil thing as murder could possibly have been contemplated. In short, as I said to myself at the time, it cannot be true that this boy is unsocial in his mood or tendencies. It is just the re-verse. He is pro-social. The fact that he aspired to a better social state with this other girl proved, if anything, that he had no desire to go against the organized standards of the society of his day."[33] In other words, the state put Chester up to murder by first denying him birth control information and then demanding, through the pressure of Grace's threats to expose him to his uncle, that he surrender his dreams. This was not the Clyde, of course, that was ever allowed in the movie versions of the novel, but it was the one championed by the winner of an essay contest ("Was Clyde Griffiths guilty of murder in the first degree?") sponsored by Boni & Liveright to keep what immediately became a best-seller in the public eye. The winner, a young liberal law professor, Albert H. Lévitt of Washington and Lee University, held that Clyde was morally guilty of Roberta's death but legally and socially innocent.[34]

As if to induce the dreamlike mood of the beginning of the book, Dreiser's epilogue, entitled "Souvenir," opens with the same phrase, "Dusk, of a summer night." He returns to the itinerant street preachers, Clyde's parents, now in San Francisco. It follows the scene in which Clyde, dressed for death in black trousers, a white shirt without a collar, and new felt slippers, walks with a clergyman on either side to the electric chair. (One reviewer of the novel pronounced the death row scenes "something that every believer in capital punishment ought to read.") His parents and their grandson, Esta's illegitimate son of eight years named Russell, set up the portable organ on a busy street corner and sing hymns to passers-by who are critical of the activity because it involves one so young: "That gray and flabby and ineffectual old man, in his worn and baggy blue suit. This robust and yet uncouth and weary and white-haired woman; this fresh and unsoiled and unspoiled and uncomprehending boy. What was he doing here?" Dreiser, who habitually hummed camp meeting hymns to himself, often as he sat dreamlike in a rocking chair, was thinking not only of his own preadolescent youth but of young America in the same grand illusion that seduces Clyde. Here, he is saying, is the perpetual recycling of another who, like the sex-driven murderer in *The Hand of the Potter,* didn't make himself. In the final lines of this story of crime and punishment almost as haunting as Dostoyevsky's great novel, which Dreiser may have reread shortly before writing *An American Tragedy,* Mrs. Griffiths decides that she must be kinder to her grandson, "more liberal with him, not restrain him too much, as maybe, she had———. . . . For *his* sake."[35]

Almost immediately upon finishing his novel, Dreiser got out of town to wait for the reviews. Nine days before the official publication on December 17, 1925, he and Helen left by car for Florida. He gave up both his apartment in Brooklyn and the office in the Guardian building, directing his mail to the offices of Boni & Liveright at 61 West Forty-Eighth Street. They first went to Philadelphia, and from there Helen went ahead to Paoli, the studio home of the artist Wharton Esherick, who worked in wood and stone. On his extra day in Philadelphia, Dreiser enjoyed a rendezvous with Louise Campbell.[36] From Paoli, their next layover was Washington, but they stopped on their way through Baltimore to see Mencken at 1524 Hollins Street. It was, however, bad timing for a reunion. Mencken's mother was in the hospital, near death after an operation. Her son was sorely irked when Dreiser failed to ask about her health. Then Mencken discovered that Dreiser had left Helen out in the cold car while he first knocked to see whether his friend was at home and in the ensuing conversation apparently forgot about her. Finally, when Dreiser asked for a bottle of his bootleg scotch and Mencken willingly provided it, Dreiser further offended him by insisting on paying for it.

In fairness to Dreiser, he was wrought up and exhausted after the completion of his novel. Later, after Dreiser's death, Mencken reminded Helen of the incident ("how I resented . . . his aloof indifference to my mother's illness"), saying while it was a long while afterward before he ever felt close to Dreiser again, he should "have known him better. There was a curiously inarticulate side to him, and it often showed up when he was most moved." Dreiser had merely forgotten to offer his condolences, but he recorded the fact of Anna Mencken's illness in his diary for that day. A few weeks later he asked Mencken the neglected question and was informed without any word of forgiveness that she had died the day after his visit.[37] The iron had entered Mencken's soul.

By then Dreiser was already ecstatic about the sales of his book, whose two volumes at the expensive price of five dollars did nothing to limit its commercial success. "The reviews are amazing, enthusiastic and dignified," wired T. R. Smith to him in Fort Lauderdale, Florida. "Your position is recognized. The sales are excellent."[38] One of the most surprising was written by Dreiser's old nemesis, Stuart P. Sherman, who was now reviewing full time for the *New York Herald Tribune* and whom Dreiser and Liveright had expected to "hand out *the* grand slam of his life" against *An American Tragedy.* Actually, they shouldn't have been so surprised. Since meting out "The Naturalism of Mr. Dreiser" in 1915 (reprinted as "The Barbaric Naturalism of Theodore Dreiser"), in which he had summed up Dreiser's books from *Sister Carrie* to *The "Genius"* as arguments for a crude "jungle" philosophy, Sherman—whom Mencken had long ago designated as the most intelligent of Dreiser's detractors—had moved away from the Arnoldian idea of literature embraced by his mentors, Irving Babbitt and Paul Elmer More. In his review of *An American Tragedy*, he first qualified his new opinion by stating that Dreiser "has either renounced or effectually suppressed the naïve naturalism of his previous novels." There were "no interspersed philosophical dissertations here . . . no special pleading, no coloring of the news" he had found especially in the Cowperwood books and *The "Genius."* But after covering his old tracks, Sherman applauded almost the same Dreiserian picture of man as relatively helpless against the forces of (his) nature. Now Sherman encountered only "detachment," "impartiality," and "objectivity" in *An American Tragedy*. Possibly, changes in Sherman's personal life had helped him in this conversion about Dreiser as well as in his newfound philosophy. Ironically, he drowned that summer in a boating accident reminiscent of the one in *An American Tragedy*.[39]

On the matter of Dreiser's style, however, Sherman did not convert but followed the line of other reviewers, whose complaints on this issue had become commonplace and indeed almost de rigueur in the assessment of any Dreiser novel since *Sister Carrie*. Admittedly, Dreiser's style is crude, but there is no getting around the fact that at his best he tells an irresistible story. Joseph Wood Krutch, who considered *An American Tragedy* "the greatest novel of our generation," noted that its 840 pages were "continuously interesting and continuously terrible, [marching] forward with a resistless energy."[40] Dreiser's sentence structure is often contorted and his content occasionally redundant (though his repetitions serve to underscore the drama he is building detail by detail), but some of what Sherman and others credit as slovenly style seems unexceptionable today. Much of what was in Dreiser's prose then considered slang has become part of what we now call standard English. Dreiser had learned to write as a newspaper reporter and magazinist for whom triteness was—and is—not a sin. Moreover, this realist knew best the common man and woman—for whom the spoken word was both spontaneous and visceral. The most outspoken critic on the matter of style was T. K. Whipple in the *New Republic*. He wrote that Dreiser violated not only English but American idiom. "This is all very true when the thing to be communicated is an abstract idea or philosophy," answered Henry Miller, who would extend the master's realism in his own works. "The novel, however, is effective because of images and emotions and not because of its abstract ideas." Comparing Dreiser to James Joyce, Miller argued that Dreiser's novels succeed not in spite of but because of his style which enabled him "to present a world which a more elegant and precise style could only hint at. . . . He identifies his language with the consciousness of his characters."[41]

Dreiser, who claimed over and again that he never paid attention to reviews, obviously gave no heed to them when they touched on style. Otherwise, he was no doubt paying attention now, for they were radiant with praise. Heywood Broun in the *New York World* called *An American Tragedy* "the Mount Everest of American fiction." Clarence Darrow, the "Attorney for the Damned," thought it seemed more real than fiction: "the feeling is rather that of a series of terrible physical impacts that have relentlessly shocked every sensitive nerve in the body." Carl Van Doren in *Century* admired its steady massing of detail leading up to the climax and beyond. "Only 'Moby Dick' among American novels with the same fateful tread, carrying all its documents on its back, and yet never seriously delaying" could be compared to it. Its "measured, implacable tracing of a disintegrating personality" was compared to Hurstwood's decline in *Sister Carrie*. Another critic refused to say which was the superior novel. But the reading public had no doubt, helped along this time, of course, by favorable publicity and a publisher friendlier than Doubleday. By the end of December, only two weeks after the date of publication, the two-volume set had sold 13,914 copies and earned its author $11,872.02. By the end of 1926 it had sold over fifty thousand copies and earned Dreiser a total $45,887.54 in direct royalties.[42]

The dust jacket carried a blurb from Mencken that spoke only generally of Dreiser as one of America's great novelists. He had promised to review his friend's "vasty double-header" in "a höflich [polite] and able manner," but this was before their December reunion. Still simmering in the juices of Dreiser's imagined slight to his dying mother, their "misunderstanding" over the arrangement with the *World,* and the republication of *The "Genius"* uncut in 1923, he wrote a doubleheader of his own in which he first excoriated the novel, then praised it. "As a work of art," he said, it was "a colossal botch, but as a human document it is searching and full of a solemn dignity. . . . The first volume heaves and pitches, and the second, until the actual murder, is full of psychologizing that usually fails to come off." It was only in Book III that the old Dreiserian genius fully comes to life. What he particularly admired was the disintegration of Clyde, which he, too, compared with the fall of Hurstwood. It was clearly less than even a mixed review, with positive comments cast only in terms of Dreiser's general strengths as a novelist, and not for his particular achievement in *An American Tragedy.*

"I have taken a dreadful hack at the book in the Merkur for March," Mencken had warned him, "but there is also some very sweet stuff in the notice." Yet no amount of sweetness could erase or mitigate the insults that laced the review. Dreiser was "wholly devoid of what may be called literary tact." He was a maudlin moralizer, deaf to his "dreadful cacophony," who seemingly taunted his well-meaning critics by throwing out "the present and forbidding monster—a heaping cartload of raw materials for a novel, with rubbish of all sorts intermixed—a vast, sloppy, chaotic thing of 385,000 words—at least 250,000 of them unnecessary!" Dreiser may have sensed this coming when he and Helen left Hollins Street that December afternoon. "It doesn't matter what he ever says about me or does to me," he told her, "he is a great guy and a great friend and I will always love him." Perhaps the inscribed copy of *An American Tragedy* he sent Mencken in January was intended to soften any bad feeling that might bleed into his review for the *American Mercury*. More than likely, it was a true act of friendship and perhaps a way of apologizing for his failure to ask about Mencken's mother. Perhaps in a small way, Mencken retaliated against Dreiser's presumed insensitivity when he referred to Elvira Griffiths, Clyde's mother so obviously based on Dreiser's own, as a "pathetic, drab wife" in spite of her valiant and touching efforts to save her son from the electric chair. When Dreiser finally read an advance copy of Mencken's review sent to Boni & Liveright, he was outraged. "As for your critical predilections, animosities, inhibitions,—et. cet. Tush," he told Mencken on February 8, 1926, "Who reads you? Bums and loafers. No goods. We were friends before ever you were a critic of mine, if I recall."[43]

Dreiser and Helen shipped their car back by rail and returned to New York that winter on the *Kroonland,* the same ship that had brought him back from Europe in 1912 instead of the *Titanic* and now on one of its final voyages itself. Florida was in the midst of a real estate boom, which may have been the reason for their trip there. Dreiser lost $4,000 on beachfront property in Fort Lauderdale when it later washed into the sea during a hurricane. No doubt, the investment came from the royalties of The *"Genius."* "Millions of realtors and all hick-dom from Wyoming & Texas to Maine— moving in," he told Louise Campbell. He had already witnessed one such "real-estate madhouse" in Los Angeles when he had had no money to invest and now probably thought it foolish to pass up the same opportunity in Florida, where the entire state was swarming with realtors "shouting about their subdivisions."[44] Back in New York, he and Helen rented a suite in the Pasadena Hotel on Sixty-Eighth Street, just west of Broadway.

Dreiser could afford to live in swankier accommodations now. In March, to expand the profits of *An American Tragedy*, Liveright arranged to have the novel dramatized for the stage. The play ran successfully at the Longacre Theater on Broadway for 216 performances that year and the next, grossing over $30,000 a week. The book was adapted by Patrick Kearney, a former actor who had written the successful *A Man's Man*. He agreed to only 45 percent (instead of the usual 50 percent) of the royalties and to give Dreiser an advance on the production of $1,500.[45] That same month a bigger avalanche of cash came his way—$80,000, the most money then ever paid by Hollywood for film rights to a novel—but it also cost Dreiser something in terms of his personal reputation, even to this day.

On March 19, 1926, during lunch at the Ritz, Dreiser hurled a cup of coffee ("The coffee wasn't cold," one witness recalled) into the face of his publisher Horace Liveright.[46] The events leading up to this spectacle are not altogether clear, but the following picture emerges. Once the idea of the play version became a contractual reality in March, Dreiser became interested in selling the novel, born in Hollywood, to the movies. Jesse Lasky, president of the Famous Players–Lasky Corporation (later Paramount), was one obvious buyer since Dreiser had had brief dealings with him in California. Liveright, however, told Dreiser he did not think that a story about unwed pregnancy would pass the Hays Code of voluntary censorship. While Dreiser had been in Hollywood, the film industry came under severe criticism from politicians and the public for its raciness. Will Hays (interestingly born in Sullivan, Indiana, where Dreiser had spent some of his formative years) left his job as postmaster general to become the president of the self-censoring organization that resulted, the Motion Picture Producers and Distributors of America. In fact, in writing the novel, Dreiser himself had engaged in a certain amount of self-cleansing, especially in the much-revised scenes in which Clyde seeks to be alone with Roberta in her newly rented room.[47]

Liveright, whose cash flow was worrying him, may not have been altogether candid with Dreiser, perhaps hoping to get as high as 30 percent of the movie royalties since he had commissioned the play on which he thought the movie would most likely be based. It was true, as Liveright possibly hinted to Dreiser, that Lasky had already considered *An American Tragedy* for the screen and rejected it because of the Hays restrictions. Yet Lasky and his assistant, Walter Wanger, had apparently changed their minds after reading Quinn Martin's article in the *New York World* of March 7, which argued that the book could be made into "the greatest film yet produced" without violating the decency code. Almost overnight, the view in Hollywood changed from negative to positive. Lasky tried in vain to get in touch with Dreiser directly, thinking (as Dreiser was already thinking) that the stage play was no necessary part of a movie deal, but Liveright apparently tried to delay the contact until he could secure his own agreement with Dreiser about his share.[48] According to the general contract with Liveright that Dreiser had signed in 1923, the publisher was entitled to only 10 percent of any movie rights.

On the day of the incident, Dreiser met with Liveright in his office to sign the Kearney contract. It stipulated that Liveright got nothing more than his 10 percent from the picture rights if the novel was sold for $30,000 or more *before* the play was produced.[49] If the film deal went through after the beginning of the Broadway production, Liveright felt that he had a right to a percentage of the sale higher than the contractual 10 percent because the play of which he was the contractual "manager" would have led to the movie contract. The figure of $30,000 reflected Liveright's earlier estimate of the most he had thought Hollywood would pay for the novel before Martin's article appeared. Dreiser may have believed that he was being set up by Liveright. Always suspicious of publishers since his dealings with Doubleday in 1900 and never fully trusting of Liveright because he moved in such fast company, producing plays and mingling with movie moguls, he may have concluded that his publisher-agent was conspiring with Lasky to keep the price artificially low so that Liveright could take a commission under the table.

During their meeting that morning, Liveright admitted that Lasky was now interested in buying the novel and asked Dreiser how much he wanted for it. The reply was $100,000. Liveright, now upping his estimate, thought $60,000 a more reasonable asking price. But he also suggested that Dreiser join him to meet with Lasky for lunch, which he would arrange that very afternoon at the Ritz-Carlton Hotel. Lasky in his memoir suggests that Liveright planned all along to bring Dreiser to what was a prearranged date, even though he appeared to invite him at the last minute. On the way to the hotel just around the corner from Liveright's office, after a few drinks together in the office, Liveright asked Dreiser if he would "take care" of him in the sale. "You were sure I would," Dreiser told his publisher in a tongue-lashing letter a week later. "But just how you did not say. And only when I finally inquired what you meant by 'take care of you,' you announced that I should take 70 percent of whatever was paid and you 30." At the time Dreiser only smiled, he remembered. When Liveright asked the question a second time, Dreiser recalled, "I merely replied that I would do so," meaning the 10 percent in the original book contract.

The best account of this matter is contained in Dreiser's letter, which Liveright did not challenge in his subsequent responses except to say that it had all been one big misunderstanding. "I may have had too much to drink—you may have had too much to drink," he wrote in his own defense. "I don't know . . . , but at any rate my memory is that you told me all over $60,000 was mine. When I asked $100,000, $70,000 for you and $30,000 for me, I thought you were pleased; at least you made no comments to the contrary." The actual conversation leading up to the coffee incident is obscured by conflicting accounts. Apparently, when Lasky asked how much Dreiser wanted, Liveright excused himself so that Dreiser might speak with Lasky "unconstrainedly." When a contract had been tentatively agreed upon at $90,000 and Liveright returned to the table, he asked for everything over $60,000, claiming that Dreiser had agreed to such a split. At this point Dreiser, already beginning to fume, said, "You will get your ten percent." Liveright reminded Dreiser that he had promised to "take care" of him, at which Dreiser countered he had intended only 10 percent. Then Liveright called his leading author a liar, and Dreiser soaked him with coffee. Dreiser left immediately, but in a few days the contract was signed, and Liveright got slightly more than his 10 percent: $80,000 was to be paid directly to Dreiser and $10,000 to Liveright.[50]

As this incident must have suggested, Dreiser now found himself rich but also painfully vulnerable. It may not have been a coincidence that Rome, already dead and buried in *A Hoosier Holiday,* resurfaced in need of a handout that year. He had been living in a low-budget residential hotel in Chicago "a long time," the manager told Louise Campbell, who was serving as Dreiser's secretary, "and would be very glad to hear from his brother." Now Rome, along with Mame and no doubt Emma, was on the Theodore Dreiser family dole. Worse yet for the man who never shed his poverty complex, Jug—as if she were Roberta risen from the grave—reapplied for assistance. "Dear Theo," she wrote on March 31, "I have just heard of your wonderful good fortune & congratulate you." She wasn't referring to the publication of the novel, which had happened almost six months previous, but to the movie contract. Liveright had publicized the sales figure to further advertise the novel. Jug wrote a week later that she hadn't had any "idea that such an enormous sum had been paid you" and wondered whether he "wouldn't be willing to give me something, now that you are able to do so." Dreiser brooded on these letters for almost a month before venting his suspicions about her "purely financial interest in my career." He had written "eight or nine books" over the last twelve years, he told Jug, and hadn't heard one word of congratulations from her.[51]

This biting rebuke brought forth a response that Dreiser probably should have burned to keep out of the hands of future biographers, but there is no evidence that he ever purposely destroyed papers, as many writers and other famous people invariably do. Jug, now fifty-seven, with sore feet and varicose veins due, she said, "to my almost constant standing at my work," told him that she hadn't known of these "8 or 9 books." "I read nothing— I have no time for reading. I know of 3 books only that you have written during that time. Your trip to Indiana with—— Booth, which I have never seen, Twelve Men, which I stood in the book Dept. in Wanamakers to run hurriedly [through] the stories of Peter and Mr. Paul to see if you were able to write of them as strongly as you felt & as you did of my father, & the 3rd was Hey Rub a dub dub. . . . I have not seen your last book except thro' the window of a store here in the Village."

What stung Jug more than Dreiser's cynical response to her "congratulations" was the outrageous notion that she might now value him as a great writer simply because one of his books had finally made money. In his letter he had noted all his books "seemed to me at least to be worthy of some form of congratulation, however little the financial return." "Your success as far as fame goes," she told him poignantly, "was just as great at the time Jennie Gerhardt was published as it is today. . . . As for me you well know it was just as great when Sister Carrie was written—not even published . . . I suppose tho' it is useless to try to defend myself. I only throw myself on your mercy & ask you to please make life a little easier for me now that you can do so without limiting yourself." She desired to return to Missouri to adopt her niece, the orphaned daughter of her late sister Rose. Jug reminded him of her earlier contribution to his literary career, specifically the editing (or cutting) of Jennie when they were together in Virginia in 1902, and closed by asking him for "an answer one way or the other."[52]

When he did not respond in May, Jug hired the law firm of House, Grossman, and Vorhaus. In the ensuing negotiations, Dreiser told his lawyer that he felt he had already given her enough, supporting her in their marriage until 1910 and then with alimony payments of $100 a month through 1915.

Additionally, he had given up their furniture when they separated, the two lots on Grandview Avenue (now worth at least $2,000, he guessed), the ten-acre apple orchard in Washington (for which he had paid $3,000 and which was now worth $30,000, he supposed), and contributed $600 to her trip to England in 1910 (where Jug, he failed to mention, was sent to look after his literary interests). Dreiser ultimately agreed to pay her $200 a month for the rest of her life as long as she remained unmarried.[53] Jug couldn't have remarried, of course, without giving Dreiser a divorce, but there was no mention of it. Earlier, in order to placate Helen, he had tried (not too seriously) to get a divorce. His "married" state had ironically kept him "free" for many years. Now his old tie to Jug also kept him just out of matrimonial reach of every other woman, including Helen.

The fame from *An American Tragedy* would not come without its aesthetic costs either—as it cast Dreiser into a kind of literary never-never land, a blur of his creative aims from which the muse would soon decamp.

FOURTEEN

Celebrity

*Before he had talked more than five minutes
I realized that his trip to Russia had converted him to Communism.*

W. E. WOODWARD

DREISER HAD BEEN WRITING POEMS and publishing them occasionally in magazines since the 1890s, when he supposedly had a book of them in press somewhere. In 1926 Boni & Liveright brought out *Moods: Cadenced and Declaimed.* The idea behind the title came, indirectly at least, from Dreiser's early reading of Emerson. "Life is a train of moods like a string of beads," the transcendentalist wrote in the essay "Experience," "and as we pass through them they prove to be many-colored lenses which paint the world their own hue, and each shows only what lies in its focus." In other words, one's view of the world, or nature in all its harmony as an emblem of God, depended on temperament. Like Emerson, Dreiser also saw more than nature in nature, but up to this point he couldn't say that it revealed the *benign* emanation of God. For him the isolated and often contrary moods, the beads on that iron wire, too often compelled bewilderment along with wonderment. Moreover, such mood swings were the consequence of the moodiness of God. In "The Little God"—reflecting the idea expressed in *Hey Rub-A-Dub-Dub* that God Himself may be a victim of a higher god— Dreiser compares man's treatment of lower nature to the capricious way God deals with man.[1]

Ultimately, Dreiser was of two minds when it came to naturalism and transcendentalism. It is his naturalism that most readily meets the eye, but the other is always somewhere in the background. In his poems the mysticism is more apparent—there he seems to ride the horses of naturalism and transcendentalism in tandem. Yet this ambivalence is also found in his fiction, and it is what makes him so much more interesting than a pure naturalist like Norris or even Zola. Even the skeptical Mencken conceded that Dreiser, though he describes life minutely, "never forgets the dream that is behind it." And as early as 1909 he had insisted to Mencken that even scientific inquiry is a "form of prayer."[2] He may have spent his life denying his father's Catholicism, but he never dismissed the Emersonian conviction that nature's beauty had a spiritual element. Carrie rocks in her chair and wonders what is missing from her new life of opulence and fame. The Italian on death row who precedes Clyde in the electric chair soon finds out what's on the other side. In "The Hidden God," Dreiser sounds the same note of frustration if not anger that we find in Stephen Crane's poetry. He finds it necessary to pray, but he knows not to whom:

> I have known many gods
> . . . .
> They have dreamed
> Or beamed
> Upon me,—
> Been threatening
> Or indifferent.
> But they have all gone,—
> All.

Yet in "The Great Blossom," he reminds us of Thoreau sitting in the entrance to his cabin at Walden Pond, utterly transfixed by the beauty of nature. Dreiser is also mesmerized before its charms:

> I sit in my doorway
> From dawn until sunrise,
> From sunrise until noon,
> From noon until night,
> The bloom of the present moment,
> The gorgeous life-bloom itself,
> Forever before me.

The "great blossom" is nature itself, forever recycling death back into life in the beauty of the natural landscape.

When exercising his mystic tendencies in verse, however, he is often overly abstract—or even banal as in "The Little Flowers of Love and Wonder," which "peep and dream, / and quickly die."[3] Generally, many of the poems are fragments or random thoughts, not only about nature but society. Because the first *Moods* appeared in a limited edition of only 550 copies, the book was not widely reviewed until its second, more commercial edition of 1928. This reprint had fifty-eight additional pages featuring twenty-nine new poems, including one of his best, "The Road I Came." Masters, who wrote a biography of Whitman, had called Dreiser "Theodore the Poet" in his *Spoon River Anthology,* but Dreiser's free-verse style wasn't even as forceful as Masters's. Nevertheless, the *Brooklyn Eagle,* once edited by Whitman, said it was constrained to deal gently with Dreiser's "work upon the lyre"— even though his first two editions often dropped fugitive thoughts in the reader's lap without explanation.[4]

Dreiser might not have had these publications without the success of *An American Tragedy.* Liveright even published *The Songs of Paul Dresser* that year with an introduction by Dreiser, which essentially reworked parts of "My Brother Paul." It was a rushed production job as well: "My Gal Sal" is listed in the table of contents as beginning on page 271, but it is found on page 263, and its musical score is completely missing. The collection, which wasn't complete, has nevertheless helped to keep Paul's memory alive. By the 1920s his reputation had faded and was yet to be revived, even in Indiana, where today he is better known (and liked) than his little brother because he didn't write the truth about Hoosiers he knew.

Dreiser and Helen left New York for Europe on June 22, 1926, for a tour of what turned out to be nine countries. The ostensible reason was to conduct business with his European publishers and to continue his research on Yerkes for the last volume of his trilogy of desire. (With the federal income tax now in place and the mounting wealth from *An American Tragedy,* Dreiser was becoming almost as financially conscious as Cowperwood, even forming his own corporation.) The real reason was to reward himself for his success, which continued to yield opportunities as well as royalties and advances. It may also have been to stir the waters for the Nobel Prize. They first sailed to Scandinavia, visiting Oslo, Stockholm, and Copenhagen. From Oslo, they sailed along Norway's rugged coast in mail boats instead of liners, and toured the famous and seemingly endless fjords. "We cruised for miles," Helen later recorded, "through deep and narrow waterways bordered on both sides by high mountainous slopes, so steep and dangerous that one would think only a mountain goat could venture there." In Stockholm they spent an afternoon with one of Dreiser's publishers, Norstedt and Soner. In Copenhagen they were charmed by the autoless streets filled instead with thousands of bicycles. It was restful after the New York of the Roaring Twenties. Here they met the critic Georg Brandes, who had known Ibsen and Strindberg. Brandes had visited the United States in 1914 and wondered whether there was anything such as sex in American literature. Dreiser and Helen were amused to hear that he had been advised to read Dreiser.[5]

They visited Germany, especially the smaller towns, but Dreiser probably didn't go to Mayen again.[6] The villages soothed him, but in Berlin he felt an old uneasiness. Just as in 1912 he had sensed the militarism of the Germans before World War I, he now complained about the Prussian temperament. "The Prussians are too drastic," he told Helen. "They should mix and mingle with the milder Germans." They visited Hamburg, Prague, Vienna, Budapest, Munich, Salzburg, Paris, and finally London, where Dreiser met another of his foreign publishers, Otto Kyllmann of Constable and Company. He had failed to meet Freud in Vienna, but he had a brief reunion with Emma Goldman in Paris. Having left the United States for Russia during the mass deportation of anarchists in 1919, she was now in exile from the Soviet Union, where she had even disagreed with the Bolsheviks. In London he lunched with George Bernard Shaw, whose quick wit reminded him of his old and almost ex-friend Mencken. Helen missed this opportunity because of illness, but Dreiser told her that the seventy-year-old playwright had demonstrated the value of his vegetarian diet by suspending himself between two chairs with "his legs out horizontally some distance from the floor."[7]

Just before he returned to New York on October 22, he was accused of plagiarizing from Sherwood Anderson's *Winesburg, Ohio.* Probably because *Moods* was initially a limited and signed edition, Dreiser had felt he could publish some of the poems elsewhere. Thirteen of them were printed in *Vanity Fair,* including "The Beautiful."[8] Writing in the *New York World* of September 7, Franklin P. Adams juxtaposed the poem with a passage from Anderson's "Tandy," a sketch about a neurotic man (typical of the characters in *Winesburg, Ohio*) who has "not found my thing to love" until he discovers potential love in a child named "Tandy." Although Adams had to misquote at least two of the lines from Dreiser's poem to make it more fully parrot Anderson's thought ("perhaps of all men I alone understand" is not in Dreiser's poem), parts of "Tandy" and "The Beautiful" are in fact similar, indeed almost identical. Both address the challenge of womanhood in the age of Freud.

It makes no sense that Dreiser on the crest of his biggest literary coup felt the need to steal lines from another writer. When *Winesburg, Ohio* appeared in 1919, Dreiser was beginning to get interested in Freud. He may have written "The Beautiful" about that time. He was never at a loss for words or details, having, as many suspect, a photographic memory. He had, of course, been accused of stealing from George Ade's "Fable of Two Mandolin Players" in *Sister Carrie,* but this, too, may have been the unconscious borrowing of a photographic mind. At any rate, Anderson, whose career Dreiser had long ago sought to assist, wasn't troubled by the parallels, though he did hint at the possibility of unintentional plagiarism, saying "It is one of the accidents that occur."[9] This was the price of celebrity—that even a poem by the author of *An American Tragedy* would be so scrutinized by the hungry press. Nor was this the last time Dreiser would face the charge of plagiarism.

Also that October, the play based on *An American Tragedy* began its successful run on Broadway. Dreiser wept when the curtain came down on Clyde's death-cell scene. The handkerchief which he habitually folded and unfolded was, according to one witness, "a limp and twisted thing" at the end of the play. During the intermissions, the author remained in his seat and spoke to no one. "The poor boy," he finally said at the close of the performance, "The poor bastard! What a shame!"[10] One of the reasons that the composition of the novel had drained him both artistically and emotionally was his empathy and identification with Clyde as a kind of economic Everyman. Like Whitey Sullivan, Clyde—or Chester Gillette—had gone to the chair partly because he had been poor. Dreiser was now divided about his story. Up until now he had bemoaned social conditions for the laboring classes but insisted that man was chemically and cosmically programmed. Now he began to think more like a sociologist.

The next month—on November 17—Dreiser lost another name out of a more recent past. George Sterling committed suicide in San Francisco.

———

Upon their return to New York, he and Helen had taken up their suite in the Pasadena Hotel, and Dreiser rented an office in which to write in the Manufacturers Trust Building on Columbus Circle. They soon signed a lease for a two-story corner apartment—on the thirteenth and fourteenth floors—in Rodin Studios at 200 West Fifty-Seventh Street, next to Carnegie Hall. (This was Helen's idea. She was surviving what amounted to an open marriage, though open only for Dreiser, and sought fulfillment as the "wife" of a literary celebrity.) The lower floor had a large reception hall that led to Dreiser's study, or studio, an enormous room with cathedral windows looking north across Fifty-Seventh Street. Its high ceiling extended to both floors in places. There was also on this level, along with a bathroom and the dining room and kitchen, a maid's room, soon occupied by a black woman named Pearl. The second floor featured two large bedrooms separated by a second bathroom. The living and reception rooms were generously lined with bookcases, and for the first time Dreiser had room for all his books. (His personal library at the time of his death contained almost two thousand volumes).[11] Like his fictional Carrie twenty-five years earlier, Dreiser had now arrived. The place was decorated with new furniture, a Steinway piano, pictures of primitive types including a large canvas of a naked woman, and a Russian wolfhound named Nicholas Romanoff, a gift from one of Helen's sisters. Not long after they occupied their new home in February 1927, he and Helen began the practice of holding an open house every Thursday evening between six and nine.

Ensconced in his success that winter, Dreiser recommended a collection of short stories by Arthur Henry to Boni & Liveright. This probably wasn't the only friendly interlude to their estrangement after the publication of *An Island Cabin* in 1902. Henry and his daughter Dorothy from his first marriage were occasional guests at Dreiser's Thursday night soirees. Also, Henry owed Dreiser a debt for helping him with *The Unwritten Law,* a 1905 novel that includes a dishonest financier as well as an Old School German named Karl Fischer, the father of two daughters. (The real "Carl" Fischer and Dreiser's father had fled the German draft together in the 1840s.) Liveright's chief editor, T. R. Smith, declined the opportunity of publishing Henry's manuscript, telling Dreiser that while his latest stories were "pleasantly readable," they had "no variation to speak of" and were in fact "fairly monotonous throughout."[12]

Between March 25 and April 11, 1927, Dreiser embarked on a solitary walking tour from Elizabeth, New Jersey, through Pennsylvania, Maryland, West Virginia, and Virginia. Years before, back in 1902, he had hit the trail for his health following the *Sister Carrie* debacle, and now at age fifty-five he sought to get back some of that health he might have squandered on the struggle with his other masterpiece. Meanwhile, that spring his publishers issued his second collection of short stories, *Chains*. Unfortunately, it was subtitled *Lesser Stories and Novels*. Some critics thought the pieces were "less" in terms of quality, and they found no "novels" in the book, only very long stories. All but two of the fifteen stories had been previously published in magazines and newspapers, though many of them had first been rejected multiple times. Reviewers naturally compared *Chains* unfavorably to *An American Tragedy*, though more than a few of the situations or plots of his latest batch of stories could have been the seed for such a novel.

Chains consisted of more of Dreiser's marriage stories. In *Free*, his first collection, the theme had been the male quest to be free from the "chains" of matrimony and monogamous sexual relationships. The marriage stories in *Chains*, however, describe these eternal conflicts from the other side of the bed, or at least allow the woman more say than she has in *Free*. The strongest tale is "Typhoon," originally published in *Hearst's International-Cosmopolitan* the previous October under the title of "The Wages of Sin." With the plot and the zest of "Butcher Rogaum's Door" and *Jennie Gerhardt*, Dreiser tells the familiar tale of the daughter of the morally rigid immigrant German father. It also borrows from *An American Tragedy* in dramatizing the shame of the daughter, who is swiftly impregnated and abandoned by the first boy her father allows her to date. But this unwed mother-to-be strikes back. After a period of Roberta-like whining and pleading, Ida Zobel fatally shoots her seducer and is acquitted by a sympathetic jury. She has the child, which, like Old Gerhardt, her father comes to love, but Ida ultimately commits suicide because of her love for the boy she killed. The impact of the story is strengthened by Dreiser's putting the reader in the place of such unfortunate young women before the advent of legal birth control.

In "The Old Neighborhood," published as early as 1918 in the *Metropolitan*, the unnamed protagonist is a married man who wishes his children dead in a moment of carefree fantasy reminiscent of Sarah Dreiser's death-wish for her children. As already noted, Dreiser relates in chapter 1 of *Dawn* how his mother saw three lights bobbing in the woods after making the wish to be free of her husband and first three sons. He may have been writing this section of his autobiography about the same time he was working on this story, for in "The Old Neighborhood" the narrator of this melancholy interior monologue sees two such lights "dancing down the hill." In both cases, the mysterious lights signal the coming deaths of the children. Soon after the death of his boys, the narrator abandons his wife and becomes a wealthy engineer and inventor. When he returns to his "old neighborhood" twenty years later, now remarried with more children, he is deeply remorseful about his past.

"St. Columba and the River," developed into fiction from a newspaper piece of 1904, ranks with the two just described as the best of the lot in *Chains*. It was an old story in 1927, having been accepted and then returned by the *Saturday Evening Post* ten years earlier because it favors the mechanistic over the religious view of life. Based possibly on one of Dreiser's "amateur labors" at the turn of the century when he may have been a worker on the construction of the Holland Tunnel, the story concerns an Irish-Catholic laborer who credits his continued survival from close calls to the protection of St. Columba, the patron saint of those who work near water.[13] Dreiser on the other hand clearly implies that Dennis McGlathery is in the clutches of an indifferent river as well as an apathetic God: his survival from repeated disasters in the dangerous tunnels is merely accidental. "St. Columba and the River" was probably not completely representative of Dreiser's point of view in 1927. He was already beginning to drift toward the mysticism and religiosity of his final novels. He was also on the verge of a political conversion that would ultimately become a religious quest of its own.

The title story "Chains" was originally called "Love" when it first appeared in the *Pictorial Review* in 1919 after being rejected by ten other magazines, including *The Smart Set*. And deservedly so. Its only interesting aspect, and that only in light of Dreiser's history, is that it is about a cuckold instead of an unfaithful husband. The story also mocks the narrator for marrying a woman half his age. He seems to deserve the neglect of the hedonist who sleeps with younger men at every opportunity. In "Fulfillment," the woman is a faithful wife, but one who does not love her husband. In "Marriage—for One" it is the unfaithful wife who does not love her husband. The wife in "The Shadow" also dwells in a loveless marriage, but she ends her affair because she fears she will lose custody of her son. "Convention" mixes one of the poisoning cases Dreiser studied for *An American Tragedy* with scenes from his St. Louis days as a reporter. When the wife of a journalist tries to frame her husband's mistress with trying to kill her, the force of convention is so strong that the grand jury refuses to indict the wife. And the straying husband, now fearful of being exposed for his infidelity, promptly returns to his (homely) wife and falsely denounces his girlfriend as a prostitute.

It is difficult to pin down a consistent or overarching theme in *Chains*, but obviously Dreiser was still objecting to the institution of marriage and perhaps trying to justify his continued flight from it with Helen. For Dreiser, as for many novelists, this smaller canvas was his sketch book in which he experimented with different methods of narration and tried to answer recurring questions that nagged at him. "Sanctuary," the lead story, is another of Dreiser's take-offs on the work of Stephen Crane. Like Crane's Maggie, who "blossoms" in a mud puddle, Dreiser's Madeleine flowers in a "dung-heap." (Interestingly for Dreiser, it presents Catholic nuns, who eventually take the wayward Madeleine off the streets, in a positive light.) "The Hand" is a mere ghost story. Two of the weakest, "Khat" and "The Prince Who Was a Thief," borrow from exotics of *The Arabian Nights* and perhaps Mark Twain. "Phantom Gold" is about a Rip Van Winkle who wakes up to find his previously worthless land full of valuable zinc. But in trying to cheat his irascible wife and indolent children out of the profits from its sale, he accidentally sells the property for far less than it is worth. (Dreiser told Mencken in 1916 that he was once "dippy over Washington Irving.")[14] In "The Victor" the protagonist is likewise a hard-boiled financier who before his death sought to disenfranchise his family and will his fortune to orphans' homes. Heartless to all throughout his career, he had a weak spot for dispossessed children only because he was born an orphan himself. But like the old man in "Phantom Gold," age takes him out of action before he can change his will.

By far the most interesting story in *Chains* in terms of Dreiser's worldview in the mid-twenties is "The 'Mercy' of God," first published in Mencken's newly founded *American Mercury* in 1924.[15] Like a Poe short story, it opens with an epigraph that doesn't immediately shed light on the meaning of the story and a discussion of the problem, which is then dramatized with an anecdote. In the opening dialogue between a celebrated "interpreter of Freud" and a mechanist in the style of Jacques Loeb, the psychologist suggests that there is something else in nature, or behind it, "some not as yet understood impulse, which seeks to arrange and right and balance things at times." The mechanist, something of a Hindu, who is indifferent to action because the world is not responsive to human desires, believes that the beauty of nature, like everything else in life, is merely the result of a cosmic accident. The psychologist counters that man's love for beauty and goodness is proof of a plan, that man is a conduit of God's benevolent will.

He gives an example of nature's attempt to relieve human suffering in the story of Marguerite, the daughter of another of those staunchly religious fathers in the fiction of Theodore Dreiser. Marguerite is a homely girl who misses out on the social opportunities enjoyed by her more attractive siblings. She becomes bookish because of her plainness and eventually falls in love with a teacher who does not marry her. She finally goes insane and comes to believe that she is a beauty men cannot resist. This is nature's way of protecting the woman from her loneliness. The story concludes with the narrator speaking from the point of view of the mechanist and wishing he could believe in the intervention of God in human affairs. Part of the epigraph is used to close the tale—to the effect that in order to believe, one must want that conversion as much as a drowning person desires air. As Dreiser admitted in his poem "The Hidden God," he had arrived at "the place in my life / Where I must pray." The story, with its backdrop of the scientist "connected with one of the great experimental laboratories of the world" devoted to explaining the nature of man, also prefigures Dreiser's formalized interest in science and his visit to Woods Hole in 1928.[16]

Liveright, still eager because of the firm's declining revenue to squeeze all the money he could out of the success of *An American Tragedy,* published two other books by Dreiser in 1927, both revised editions of earlier works. One was the controversial play *The Hand of the Potter,* for which Dreiser chopped off three or four pages from the last act dealing with the reporters' exchange over the abnormal psychology of a child molester.[17] The second was *The Financier,* now cut down, mainly by Louise Campbell, from its 780 pages of 1912 to just over 500; the revised version was also issued in London in 1927 by Constable & Company. Even though Mencken was now a stranger, Dreiser didn't hesitate to allow his publisher to recycle the influential critic's remark about Dreiser's standing isolated today but still more likely to endure than other writers. Boni & Liveright also claimed in advertisements that the new version of *The Financier* was "completely revised," even stating, not altogether falsely, that Dreiser had originally been "unable to give his manuscript the close revision that he gives all his books."

One of the blurbs used in the promotion—from the *Cincinnati Enquirer*—claimed rightly that the tempo had been increased, but wrongly that the characterization had been clarified. The character of Cowperwood's father, for example, is altered to make him less plodding in his rise from bank teller at the beginning of the novel and a little more like the financier his son will become. Aileen Butler's character also becomes more forceful than the merely headstrong girl of the 1912 edition. Dreiser streamlined the novel by collapsing much of its early dialogue into the narrative and by cutting down his characteristic repetition. The determinism, while still in place, becomes less explicit.[18] With the bullish market on Wall Street that year, the sky seemed the limit to human endeavor. That year Babe Ruth hit sixty home runs, and Lindbergh crossed the Atlantic.

But the story remained more relevant for 1912 than for 1927. Then the moguls of the 1890s had still commanded interest; now everybody seemed to be getting rich. Yet even though *The Financier* of 1927 went unreviewed by most major newspapers and magazines, it sold a reasonable number of copies (more than its predecessor), probably because of the drawing power of the name of the author of *An American Tragedy*.[19] That fame was also helped when Sinclair Lewis's *Elmer Gantry* (1927) was banned in Boston in April under a previously untested obscenity law against "Literature manifestly tending to corrupt the morals of youth." Donald Friede, who had joined Boni & Liveright as an assistant editor and was now a senior vice president, decided to test the ban by offering to sell a Boston police lieutenant a copy of *An American Tragedy*, for which he was promptly arrested. Friede was a figure as colorful as Liveright. The son of a Russian immigrant who had represented the Ford Motor Company in Czarist Russia, he grew up rich, got himself expelled from Harvard, Yale, and Princeton, and married six times during a successful career as a publishing insider who represented not only Dreiser but Ernest Hemingway, MacKinlay Kantor, and others. But even though Friede had the counsel of Clarence Darrow, he lost the obscenity case and was fined a hundred dollars. The main charge against the novel was that it invited young people to learn birth control methods.[20]

An American Tragedy was effectively banned from the New England capital for the next two years (until a successful legal appeal), but that only served to stimulate sales. In fact, the book had not even been targeted by the Boston Watch and Ward Society until Friede became its "self-appointed scapegoat." In May, as the money kept coming in, Dreiser bought himself a country seat in Westchester County, New York, where his longtime friend Joseph G. Robin had an estate.[21] He called the thirty-six acre property overlooking Croton Lake "Iroki," a variation of the Japanese word "iroke," meaning "beauty." It was about three miles from Mt. Kisco, New York, which could be reached from Manhattan by automobile in about an hour and fifteen minutes as well as by train. The property had been a hunting lodge, but Dreiser soon poured money into its expansion, though he eventually came to regret it. He enlarged the cabin into a main house that had comfortable living areas and a large workroom downstairs. He also erected a small guest house. Both had modern plumbing and were constructed of bark shingle siding and roofing. Some remarked that the two structures looked like something out of "Hansel and Gretel" with its gingerbread décor. Additionally, there were two smaller cottages without indoor facilities.[22]

That summer Rome resurfaced. As noted earlier, Dreiser learned that his second-eldest brother was living quietly in a residential hotel on South Peoria Street in Chicago. At sixty-seven and in delicate health after a lifetime of drinking and kicking about the country, Rome was now content to smoke (cigarettes, cigars, and a pipe) in his forty-cent-a-day room and live on a small expense account, which Dreiser soon provided. His expenses for September 1927 totaled $46.10, including $5.50 for two tickets to see *An American Tragedy* at the Garrick Theater and sixty cents for half a dozen handkerchiefs (for all we know, the handkerchief rolling may have been a family tradition). He would later rejoin Theo and his sister Mame on a visit to Iroki, but not before he broke his arm in two places after being run over by an indigent truck driver in 1929.[23] Although Rome may have remained in Chicago, most of the surviving Dreiser siblings had become New Yorkers.

New York City was now, and had been for a long time past, home for the American writer who had recorded the swarm of immigrants into the great metropolis. No longer a Hoosier and a Catholic, Dreiser found America's identity along with his own in this city, "My City," as he would call it in a future publication. Although always a critic of American society, he identified himself as an American first and last. His father had come from Germany, not Dreiser, who felt himself a stranger in the Fatherland. What he most valued about America was the freedom it offered to the talented individual to develop to the benefit not only of himself but of the society at large. He took pride in the unselfish work of scientists and even American financiers who had built up American industry (and America) and now, he guessed, paid up to 50 percent of their earnings in federal income tax.[24] So it was as an individualist with a social conscience that Dreiser in the fall of 1927 accepted an invitation to visit the Soviet Union on the tenth anniversary of its Bolshevik Revolution.

Dreiser was one of hundreds of famous intellectuals around the world to be invited to Moscow for the week-long celebration of the start of the Revolution of November 7, 1917, but perhaps the only one offered an extended stay at Soviet expense in order to tour some of the provinces of the new Russia. At the time, the United States had not yet recognized the Soviet Union diplomatically. Moreover, many prewar leftists who had preached rebellion at home were now disenchanted with the Leninist experiment, which though still in its own idealistic, pre-Stalinist state of producing a workers' utopia, insisted on exporting the socialist overthrow of governments around the world. Two prominent American dissenters were Emma Goldman (as mentioned above) and Max Eastman, who vented his disappointment in the Socialist experiment in a book entitled *Since Lenin Died* (1925).[25] Anyone who came to approve of that experiment by 1927, when Stalin had already forced Trotsky into exile in Siberia, had to see the economic upheaval as, ironically, religious. In spite of its materialistic rule over the churches, the Soviet Union, as John Dewey noted during his visit to the celebration, presented "a widespread and moving religious reality. . . . I [had] associated the idea of Soviet Communism, as a religion, too much with intellectual theology, the body of Marxian dogmas, with its professed economic materialism, and too little with a moving aspiration and devotion." He was convinced following his visit to Russia that its new direction was possessed of "the moving spirit and force of primitive Christianity."[26] In a manner of speaking, so was Dreiser. His seventy-seven-day "look" at Russia would change his life.

It all began on October 3, when Arthur Pell, the attorney and treasurer for Boni & Liveright, told him that "some representative of the Soviet Russian government" was seeking to offer him a free trip to Russia in order that he might see what good had been achieved by the Soviets in the decade since the October Revolution. A week later he met with F. G. Biedenkapp, executive secretary of the International Workers' Aid, "after its fashion," Dreiser noted in his diary, "a Russian Red Cross" to aid workers politically in foreign countries. Although he would have to badger the Soviets at the end of his visit, all his expenses were ultimately paid. And even though he was, as he announced himself in the book about his trip, "an incorrigible individualist," he was free to choose his own itinerary, ask any questions he desired, have an interpreter wherever he went, and write—if he liked—an unfavorable book about the country, or simply no book at all.[27]

Helen wanted to accompany him (so that he might not "fall in love with one of those Russian girls and get yourself all tangled up again"), but Dreiser insisted on going alone. He was already tangled up with several women at home. One of them, identified only as "B——" in Dreiser's Russian diary, wrote him a series of sexually suggestive letters "one of which I am to read on ship board each day." Other current flames were Esther McCoy, the University of Michigan graduate who had relocated to New York to become another of his researchers and typists; Louise Campbell, whom he had known for years now, and another unidentified woman listed only as "Ch——" in the diary. He spent one of his last evenings with Esther, who wanted to know "if she can't come to London and return with me!"[28] B—— also wanted to meet Dreiser in Europe on his way home from Russia. Helen, he probably noted with a smile, was kept busy and "all agog" with the financial responsibilities she would have to shoulder in Dreiser's absence.

On October 19, Dreiser sailed on the *Mauretania,* the sister ship of the ill-fated *Lusitania* and the same one he had taken to Europe in 1912. He was armed with letters of introduction to, among many others, the Russian filmmaker Sergei Eisenstein, Trotsky's sister Olga Davidovna Kameneva, the Russian critic Sergei Dinamov, who was already familiar with Dreiser's work, and Big Bill Haywood, the labor leader on whom Dreiser had based the character of John Ferguson in "The Girl in the Coffin." Haywood had fled the United States in 1920 while awaiting retrial for violating the Sedition Act and was now dying in Moscow. There was a send-off dinner for Dreiser at a restaurant in the Village attended by many of his friends, including T. R. Smith, Ernest Boyd, and Floyd Dell. One of the guests was Diego Rivera, the Mexican muralist, who was on his way to Russia in the hope of devoting his art to the cause of Soviet propaganda. Like a good socialist, he went third-class on the same ship on which Dreiser was billeted in first. It didn't keep them apart; nor did their lack of a common language, thanks to an interpreter who was traveling with Dreiser's party. Dreiser was enormously impressed with this artist and the story of his "artistic history." After seeing samples of his paintings one evening, he took a bottle of whiskey and his interpreter down to third class and talked through half the night with Rivera.[29]

Their ship docked in Cherbourg on October 25, and Dreiser, traveling with the publisher Ben Huebsch and another companion, took the train down to Paris, where they spent the night at the Hotel Terminus near Gare de l'Est. On the train he fell for the smile of a beggar girl around thirteen. All the rest of the next day he found it impossible to shake off the image of her "natural beauty and a most moving smile." France, he thought, had fairly well recovered from the Great War. They saw the usual Parisian sights, the Palais de Justice, the shops along Boulevard St. Michel, the book stalls on the Seine, the Jardin de Luxembourg. He encountered Victor Llona, the French translator of *An American Tragedy,* and a young writer named Ernest Hemingway. Dreiser noted in his diary that he was the author of *The Sun Also Rises* (1926), but he had nothing else to record about this rising star. They sat at a sidewalk cafe, as the "talk, talk, talk" finally turned to James Joyce.[30]

The next day, October 27, Dreiser and his party caught the overnight train to Berlin. As the train crossed Germany the following morning, he admired its cleanliness—"the lovely, carefully gardened fields." In Berlin he came down with bronchitis "worse than ever." He was subsequently warned by several doctors that his illness was too serious to chance a trip into sub-freezing Russia. An X-ray falsely revealed a heart problem, but Dreiser boldly pushed ahead, telling two of the physicians, "I do not happen to be afraid of death." This rings true when we consider how severely his bronchitis, a life-long malady, had flared up this time. Dorothy Thompson, a foreign correspondent for the *Philadelphia Public Ledger* and the *New York Evening Post* living in Berlin, was planning to cover the tenth anniversary in Russia. She tried to minister to Dreiser's health problems, to "mother" him, as she put it. Her fiancé of only a few weeks, Sinclair Lewis, was also in Berlin. Lewis, whose fame from *Main Street* (1920), *Babbitt* (1922), and other successful novels overshadowed Dreiser's (even after *An American Tragedy*), thought Dreiser liked him. But Dreiser's diary for that evening tells another story. Lewis had failed to review *An American Tragedy.* "I never could like the man," Dreiser recorded. "He proceeds—and at once, to explain why he did not review." He suspected that Lewis himself was concealing his own dislike, "but some how feels it his duty to pay attention to me."[31] It was Dorothy that Dreiser liked—too much, of course.

The train for Moscow departed on November 2. Crossing the plains of Poland, he noted that they resembled those of Kansas. Once at the Russian border and across it, he felt "a change at once. Something softer—more emotional, less iron." Thompson, traveling on the same train, told Lewis, who had delayed his visit to Moscow to work on a new book, that there loomed over the tracks at the border "a huge, glowing red star."[32] As they changed trains, the guests were treated to a reception at the depot. Once in Moscow Dreiser and the other visitors invited to the celebration of the October Revolution were put up at the Grand Hotel in view of the Kremlin. At the hotel Thompson was still trying to "mother" Dreiser, even after he had transformed himself into "quite a gay dog" in Moscow as his bronchitis improved. Dreiser imagined she was flirting with him, and on the evening of the big day, November 7, following an endless parade past the Kremlin, he made his move. "After a supper with the American delegation," he noted in his diary, "she comes to my room with me to discuss communism & we find we agree on many of its present lacks as well as its hopeful possibilities. I ask her to stay but she will not—tonight."[33]

Dreiser was apparently unruffled by the rejection, thinking it a mere prelude. At any rate, he had already realized Helen's fears and become entangled with "one of those Russian girls." Actually, she was an American expatriate by the name of Ruth Kennell, who after their first sexual encounter complained that he had worn no "protection." A native of Hobart, Oklahoma, she was the thirty-two-year-old divorced mother of one son, who was now living with his father in England. The couple had become involved with I.W.W. politics in Berkeley, California. They left the United States for Siberia in 1922 with an American engineering group that had been contracted by the Soviets to run mining and manufacturing projects there. Kennell eventually took a Russian lover and later came to Moscow, where she worked as a librarian. She was enthusiastic about the Soviet program, and it seems she was ultimately instrumental in converting Dreiser to believe in the New Russia—though they quarreled repeatedly over these issues while together there. Kennell was the basis for "Ernita" in *A Gallery of Women* and one of possibly two characters in the book with whom Dreiser actually had an affair.

Like Dreiser, her radicalism had its origins in an impoverished background. Ernita (or Ruth) in *Gallery* tells the narrator, "Long before Communism flashed into being in Russia, I felt there should be some change somewhere—a new social order in which war would be obviated by social justice—some world union of the workers or the oppressed." In 1969, without revealing the full extent of her relationship with Dreiser, Kennell published her own account of his travels there. Twenty-two years and the Cold War had not changed her mind. She gladly quoted Dreiser's prediction that the United States would "eventually be sovietized." Since coming to Moscow she had been living in a small room in the Lux, described in "Ernita," as "a large rambling hotelly sort of an affair with communal kitchens and baths on every floor—the Communist International Headquarters."[34] Without Kennell, Dreiser might have cut short his visit to Russia and returned home with most of the other invited dignitaries after November 10. He had taken to drinking vodka and brooding in his hotel suite because he wasn't being given enough attention or freedom to see what he wanted. Scott Nearing, another American expatriate working for VOKS, the Soviet agency for Cultural Relations with Foreigners, arranged for Kennell to become his personal secretary and to accompany Dreiser on his inspection of some of the Russian provinces.[35]

Evidently, Dreiser soon afterward decided definitely to write another travel book, for he began gathering notes and having Kennell type up his daily diary entries. They show him trying to fathom the Russian mind. After the Revolution, it might be true that Russian waiters served food, not people, but the Russian people were also sluggish and slovenly before the Revolution. The German in him couldn't ever understand why this nation of peasants found itself so at home in dirt and grime. And then Dreiser the individualist worried about the loss of creative freedom and the rights of the "big brain" over the "little brain" in this utopian quest. He compared the Soviet propaganda programs with what he considered the brainwashing efforts of the Catholic Church. He joked to himself about the ubiquity of icons of Lenin as the new Christ of the land. "In Moscow alone," he wrote in what would become a long tradition of Lenin bashing by the Russian intelligentsia, "there are so many busts & statues of him that they seem to constitute an addition to the population. Thus: Population of Moscow— without statues of Lenin—2,000,000, with statues of Lenin—3,000,000." His faith in Russian communism, however, grew during his visit to the Soviet Union. While in Moscow he wrote a foreword to the English translation of *The Road to Buenos Ayres* (1928), an exposé of "White Slavery," or world-wide prostitution rings, by Albert Londres, who blamed not kidnapping but poverty as the culprit and impetus. If there was any chance to eradicate the "world's oldest profession," Dreiser thought it was to happen in the new Russia. The realist was becoming something of a romantic when it came to reform.[36]

———

With Ruth Kennell he visited schools and factories around Moscow. He felt that the students and workers were "seized with all the doctrines of Marxism—as much as any Catholic with the doctrines of Catholicism." Their religion was, of course, communism, in a state run by the party instead of, as was falsely advertised, the proletariat. In the book he wrote on his experiences after his return to the United States, *Dreiser Looks at Russia* (1928), he recognized that the idea of a "Dictatorship of the Proletariat" was a misnomer. Rather it was a dictatorship of "the Communist Party in the interests of the Proletariat," with the party consisting of "1,200,000 members who rule the rest of Russia." He worried, therefore, about intellectual and creative freedom, while at the same time admiring the apparently unselfish nature in this stage of the development of communism in the Soviet Union. It was still an idealistic period, before the Stalinist campaign of terror got fully underway in the 1930s. Stalin made only 225 rubles a month, Dreiser happily recorded in his book, 25 rubles less than a mine worker. He hoped in vain to meet this great man of the people.[37]

In Moscow he did meet several of the people for whom he had letters of introduction. Sergei Dinamov lived in a crude tenement with "no sanitary toilet and no bath in the house." With the November snow yet to fall, the newer buildings in the neighborhood he visited with the critic could be reached only by stepping from plank to scattered plank laid across a sea of mud and slush. The individual apartments had to accommodate ten to fifteen people, two to seven to a room, providing "no privacy of any kind." It gave one, he recorded, "the mood of a slum—or a Pennsylvania mining village under the rankest tyranny of capitalism." Their clubrooms and "Lenin Corners" were covered with red banners and slogans as well as with civil defense instructions. "All are led to believe that Europe is ready to pounce on them." Later he complained that this national paranoia made any foreigner cling to his passport, for without it he could not leave the country or even get his hotel mail.[38]

When the Soviets again dragged their feet on his promised tour of the provinces, Dreiser threatened to go home, saying literally that the government and the head of VOKS could go to hell. Once he got their attention again, plans for his trip began to move along. In the interim, he met Eisenstein, Russia's most famous movie director and the creator of *Battleship Potemkin* (1925) and other cinematic classics of Soviet propaganda. The future author of the first screenplay of *An American Tragedy* lived slightly better off than Dinamov in a one-room apartment. The twenty-something Soviet cinema king, whom Dreiser described as having a boyish face and "a mass of thick, curly hair," defended his country's political censorship by saying that America had the same restrictions, only they were moral instead of political. Before he left Russia, Dreiser found that the sting of political censorship wasn't that different from the moral brand that had threatened *Sister Carrie* in America. Soviet censors rejected the play *An American Tragedy* because of the plot's opening "religious section" and the improper relationship between employer and worker.[39] Free love along with divorce might be tolerated in the new society free of religious superstition, but never in the sanctum sanctorum of the Soviet workplace.

On November 21, he visited Tolstoy's home at Yasnaya Polyana, a hundred miles south of Moscow; it was the seventeenth anniversary of the Russian novelist's death. Dreiser met Tolstoy's youngest daughter, Olga, and attended memorial services. As Kennell remembered, a "ragged Tolstoyan peasant" recited poems at the grave.[40] Still waiting for his tour to begin, Dreiser decided to visit Leningrad, formerly (and again today) St. Petersburg, the Czar Peter's famous "window to the West." Hardly out of the train station, Dreiser thought that he had never seen a more beautiful city, the "Venice of the north" with its numerous bridges and canals that crisscross the city, elegant architecture, and—Dreiser could not have forgotten—the home of Dostoyevsky and the Peter and Paul fortress, where the great Russian novelist had stood before a firing squad.

He stayed at the Europa, Leningrad's grandest hotel on Nevsky Prospect, the city's Fifth Avenue. He visited both the czar's summer palace some fifteen miles out of town and the winter palace in the center of the city overlooking the Neva River. The latter had already been partly transformed into the museum that is famous today throughout the art world as the Hermitage. Then its "art" also included a part of the palace "kept as the last czar left it suddenly on Monday, July 30, 1917." Almost incredulous at the thought that the Russian royalty treated themselves to such opulence and still considered themselves human, he "could understand quite clearly why it was necessary to get rid of these people." He spent one evening at the State Circus, a one-ring affair about the size, he said, of the old Madison Square on the east side of Manhattan. As he toured Leningrad, visiting homes, schools, and factories as he had in Moscow, he ironically found himself defending capitalism for at least its affording Americans superior living conditions. Regarding social justice, he was willing to make concessions to the Soviets. Yet for some reason the author of *An American Tragedy* was less than cooperative in condemning America in the case of Sacco and Vanzetti. Shortly before their execution on August 23, 1927, he had told Patrick Kearney that he thought the two immigrants were guilty of the charge of murdering a Massachusetts paymaster and his guard.[41]

Dreiser spent another week in Moscow before finally beginning his tour of the Russian provinces. Between December 8 and January 13, he followed a line southeast to Baku on the Caspian Sea and then northwest to Batum and across the northern coast of the Black Sea to Odessa. More often than not it was an uncomfortable journey featuring overcrowded trains and "one-sheet" and "no-sheets" hotels. His bronchitis continued to plague him. To lift his spirits, he took to spicing up his tea with vodka, which Ruth quietly administered. This may be the point at which he started nipping in the mornings. Yet Dreiser was remarkable in his ability and resolve to push on to see as much as possible. When Helen toured the Netherlands with him in 1926, she had begun "to realize what traveling with a man of Dreiser's caliber meant: [a] vigorous and rigorous program every hour of every day."[42]

Dreiser was supposed to meet Helen in Constantinople, but when he reached the end of his tour in Odessa there was no boat to Constantinople for another week. He decided to go through Poland straight to Paris to meet her there, but he ran into Russian red tape regarding not only the acquisition of a Polish visa but Soviet restrictions on how much money he could take out of the country. He also needed special permission to leave with his journal notes for his book. When he cleared up these difficulties after four days of waiting and was ready to leave Russia, he wrote in his diary: "At last I was going to leave, yes, literally crawl across the border. I'd rather die in the United States than live here." He left Russia on January 13 in a foul mood, but the departure was otherwise poignant because he and Ruth had finally to say goodbye. As they boarded their separate trains, hers bound for Moscow, she recorded in a letter to him the following day, "it seemed as if [the uncoupling of their railroad cars] were a physical separation of just us two, as if you were cut away from me, or worse, that only a part of me had been cut away from you and the rest had gone on with you in the darkness in that other coach." She sat in her coach feeling desolate, not wanting to "pick up the threads" of her individual life after having merged so completely with him for the seventy-some days. His overpowering personality still enveloped her spirit.[43] They would keep in touch, as she edited things of his, including the Russian book. In their subsequent correspondence, which lasted until Dreiser's death, Ruth's enthusiasm for the Soviet Union and worldwide communism never flagged. Nor did its effect on Dreiser, eventually leading to his membership in the Communist Party.

These mixed impressions were detailed not only in *Dreiser Looks at Russia* and a series of articles under the same awkward title in the *New York World,* but also in a special statement taken by Kennell and released to the western press in February (the Soviets refused to publish it). "Personally I am an individualist, and shall die one." He had seen nothing, he said, in Russia to dissuade him from his "earliest perceptions of the necessities of man." Yet he could understand the Russian people's wanting to try this experiment after "the crushing weight of czardom." It severely annoyed him that Winston Churchill, whom he interviewed for a magazine article that was apparently never published, gave the Soviet experiment a life expectancy of only seven more years. Dreiser praised the Soviets for sweeping away from their midst "dogmatic and stultifying religion," yet he also worried about their horrid living conditions, homeless children, and general uncleanliness. "They live too many in one room," he remarked, "and are even lunatic enough to identify it with a communistic spirit."[44] Though he wasn't ready to have the communist system in the United States, he thought it would succeed in Russia, given the availability of modern technology. Within three months of his return, this notion had been transformed into the prediction, largely correct as it turned out, that in twenty years the Soviet Union would be one of the great industrial nations of the world. Forgotten were the dirty and crowded trains. They had been very pleasant with spacious compartments, he later told W. E. Woodward, Helen's old boss, who had in 1919 prompted her to meet her famous cousin. For whatever reason, perhaps simply willed optimism with regard to the Russian people, whose romantic spirit any long-term visitor to Russia will testify is infectious, Dreiser became a convert to communism and a cheerleader for the Soviet Union.[45]

Once back home in February 1928, Dreiser put Louise Campbell to work on the Russia book as well as *A Gallery of Women,* which had originally sixteen or seventeen sketches instead of fifteen. That summer he visited Woods Hole Marine Biological Laboratory on Cape Cod at the personal invitation of the Nobel Laureate Calvin Bridges. This was the beginning of his scientific quest to probe the riddle of the universe through a microscopic look at nature. He told Marguerite Tjader Harris, whom he had recently met at one of his parties, "I've written novels; now I want to do something else."[46] At this point Dreiser essentially gave up fiction except for sketches, which he published in *A Gallery of Women* and elsewhere, but most of these too were not new work. His trip to Russia had not only made him a convert to communism (in Russia, not America yet) but turned his energies to social activism, a pattern that would develop fully in the Depression.

In a distant anticipation of the National Endowment for the Arts, he advocated that Congress establish a Secretary of the Arts to oversee among other activities the display of paintings and murals in subway stations and other public places (art, he said, makes "up for the absence, at times, of sunlight, flowers, soothing breezes or views"). He tried unsuccessfully to bring the Moscow Grand Opera's Ballet to New York, proposing a complex scheme of issuing $150,000 worth of stock to be purchased by "a small group of patrons" to underwrite the project at $25,000 apiece. It was in a way a veiled attempt to help the Soviet Union achieve official recognition from the United States, which would not come about until 1933. The financier Otto Kahn, chairman of the board of the New York Metropolitan Opera, gave the first (and apparently the last) $25,000. Yet he noted cautiously in his letter of support that the project, "it is clearly understood, has not the remotest relationship to propaganda, and no aim other than an artistic one" The Soviet government also feared that these artists might defect.[47]

In spite of his carping about living conditions and caps on individual talent, which may have fueled Soviet fears about dancers' defecting, in his Russia book Dreiser celebrated the Soviet experiment as having the greatest potential to produce an egalitarian state free of the humiliating poverty he had known as a child. Even though it was put together by Kennell and Campbell as well as the nominal author, *Dreiser Looks at Russia* retained much of his magic as a travel writer. For at its heart it is more about his impressions of Russia, his acute observations about people in general, than it is about Russia itself. Dorothy Thompson's *The New Russia*, published the same year, was by comparison pedestrian in its journalistic treatment. There were, however, "deadly parallels" between the two books, and in a letter to Horace Liveright, Inc. (the publishing house's new name in 1929), Thompson's lawyer threatened suit unless the publisher withdrew the book from sale at once and turned over all profits to Miss Thompson. She by this time was the new Mrs. Sinclair Lewis. Her famous husband was the one most outraged by the apparent plagiarism, which actually involved the articles Thompson had published in the *New York Evening Post* that were the basis of her book. Part of his rage probably came from his alcoholism, which grew more severe once he had remarried and returned to the United States.[48]

Dreiser, however, dismissed the charge as if it were baseless, even suggesting that Thompson had taken material for her book from conversations the two had had in Moscow. The similarity between the two books should not have been surprising, one student of the controversy has remarked, because they relied on the same interpreters, official news releases, and newspaper accounts. In her book Thompson even confessed that it was "inevitable" that much of her information was "second hand." But unfortunately the parallels went beyond even this point, and it is baffling as to how Dreiser got himself into this predicament. The many resemblances certainly cannot be dismissed as another consequence of his photographic memory. Dreiser may not have even proofread the book, either carefully or at all; Campbell and Kennell apparently did most of the final work. His characterization of the affair in letters and responses to friends as trivial may have been a form of denial. This feeble defense, or the lack of any real defense, however, may have cost him the Nobel Prize, for his reputation took a beating from the scandal, even though it never materialized into a lawsuit. Also brought up during the controversy was the reminder that Dreiser had been accused of plagiarizing in *Sister Carrie* as well as in the poem in *Moods* that resembled a sketch in *Winesburg, Ohio.*[49]

If Liveright didn't have enough on his plate with regard to his star writer, Dreiser made noises about breaking his contract, not due to expire until 1932. The company had yet to fulfill its promise of publishing a uniform or collected edition of his works and had not lived up to the letter of its promise to promote his books weekly in the newspapers. Dreiser was also becoming aware that Liveright, Inc. was living beyond its means and was being operated not as a corporation but "as the property of one man." This latest tiff between them was settled after Liveright put Dreiser on the payroll, not only as a "director," which he had already been, but as an acquisitions editor. His appointment kept T. R. Smith busy turning down book manuscripts written by Dreiser's friends and, in at least one case, a girlfriend. He dismissed Ruth Kennell's *Vanya of the Streets* as "a Russian story of the third class." (A children's book, it was published elsewhere in 1931 and became the first of a successful series of such books by Kennell.) Anything with Dreiser's name on it, of course, was automatically published by Liveright, including *My City,* a twenty-page prose and poetry celebration of New York's rich and poor—in the words of Robert H. Elias, "of tall towers and lowly slums, of riches and poverty-stricken tenements, of the hoping and despairing as though each were an element in a glorious symphony."[50]

In February 1929, the glossy *Hearst's International-Cosmopolitan* began the publication of three stories spread over six monthly installments under the general title of "This Madness." "You people may not realize it, but in 'This Madness' you are publishing the most intimate and important work so far achieved by me," Dreiser was quoted as saying at the beginning of the third story in the series, "Sidonie," which was based on his love affair with Kirah Markham. They weren't any more intimate than the stories based on old romances he had published in *Free* and *Chains,* but they were otherwise fairly accurate as to the facts. In literary quality, however, they fell below those earlier sketches. Today such stories as "This Madness" would be relegated to the tabloids found at the checkout counters of supermarkets, and in the *International-Cosmopolitan* the latest art from the pen of the author of *Sister Carrie* and *An American Tragedy* squeezed itself down narrow columns of pages advertising Kotex, toilet bowl cleaners, and mints for the relief of constipation. The other two stories in the series were drawn from two very long-term relationships. "Aglaia" was based on Lillian Rosenthal, and "Elizabeth" on Anna Tatum—two women he had met around the time he left Jug. Dreiser's old concerns about the lack of free will were still apparent, but the sketches were otherwise lugubrious in their sentimental descriptions of "romance" gone awry.

At the same time he was finalizing for the press the sketches for *A Gallery of Women,* which would appear that fall in two volumes. One of its initial promotional problems, Dreiser feared, might be the public's confusing the "This Madness" stories with those from *A Gallery.* For they were indeed similar. Their main interest lay in the fact that the women portrayed were ultimately defeated after trying to defy convention and follow the example of the New Woman. And "Sidonie" was also originally intended for *A Gallery.* The Bloom sisters, or at least Estelle, could have fit into "This Madness." Instead, they went into *A Gallery,* but only as minor characters, the Redmond sisters, in "Regina C———." Dreiser also wrote a sketch called "Gloom," but this portrait of Estelle Kubitz does not appear in either *Gallery* or "Madness." In fact, Dreiser had begun many of these sketches when he was still with Estelle. Although the idea for such a book probably solidified after the critical success of *Twelve Men,* he told Mencken in 1919 that he had planned such a book "for years." He added: "God what a work! if I could do it truly—The ghosts of Puritans would rise and gibber in the streets."[51]

When the book finally materialized in fall of 1929, nobody gibbered, for by now—certainly after *Hey Rub-A-Dub-Dub,* if not *An American Tragedy*—there was no longer anything shocking about Dreiser's "philosophy of atomic purposelessness." Moreover, critics who had admired *Twelve Men* were disappointed. Generally, Mencken, who had loved that book and who was troubled over neither the question of free will nor—for that matter—the status of women, wrote that *A Gallery* wasn't as interesting as *Twelve Men* "because women themselves are considerably less interesting than men."[52] To Dreiser, however, women were at least equally interesting, and not just for their sexuality. The identities of most of the female characters are now either known for sure or suspected; only two remain unidentified. "Reina" was based on Helen's sister, Myrtle Patges. In an almost Lardneresque tone, Dreiser describes her descent on them in Hollywood in the early twenties. The woman in "Olive Brand," as already noted, is Edith DeLong Jarmuth, who married Edward H. Smith, Dreiser's friend at the *New York World*. Dreiser probably first drafted these two stories while in California. Another initially drafted there was "Ernestine," based on the Hollywood actress Florence Deshon, the mistress of Max Eastman and Charlie Chaplin, both of whom appear in the story under pseudonyms. It was initially published as "Portrait of a Woman" in *Bookman*.[53] "Giff" is based on Jessie Spafford, a fortune-teller Dreiser, Mencken, and the Bloom sisters consulted, generally for laughs.

In "Ernita" Dreiser may have been thinking vaguely of the American revolutionary Emma Goldman, whom he had recently seen in a low state in Paris, but this story, as already noted, is specifically based on the life of Ruth Kennell. It was one of the last written, suggesting the lingering impact of his time in Russia. Ruth "edited" the story for facts, and lamented that the tale didn't extend to her having "met a certain great man and [come] to know him very intimately and with deep, almost maternal, affection." Otherwise, she asked him, "Does Ernita get anywhere with her life? I'm afraid that is the reason you like the story—it just proves your philosophy, that puny man always is defeated."[54] "Regina C——" refers to Miriam Taylor, a friend of the Bloom ("Redmond") sisters and a nurse who became a morphine addict. Dreiser had used his father-in-law, Arch White, in *Twelve Men*. In *A Gallery* he returned to Jug's family in "Rella" to write about sister Rose and his attraction to her. "Rona Murtha" stems from Anna Mallon, Arthur Henry's second wife. "Emanuela" is either about Thelma Cudlipp (whose affair with Dreiser was never sexually consummated) or a literary agent named Ann Watkins. Since the narrator is frustrated in never bedding down Emanuela because of her repressed sexuality, it is more likely about Thelma—who was now on her second marriage. "Esther Norn" is Mary Pyne, a young artist who became first the wife of Harry Kemp, a Greenwich Village poet and ne'er-do-well, and then the lover of the writer Hutchins Hapgood. Dreiser writes somewhat disparagingly about both men, but he is particularly hard on Hapgood, who allegedly abandoned Pyne as she was dying at twenty-five from tuberculosis. Hapgood got revenge a couple of years later, leading to Dreiser's dubious reputation today as an anti-Semite.

"Ellen Adams Wrynn" is based on the artist Anne Estelle Rice, whom Dreiser first met in 1912 in Paris.[55] Wrynn divorces her rich husband from the West, who had underwritten her art studies at Columbia University, for a Scottish artist who ultimately leaves her. The story's main strength is to suggest the moral ambivalence of the art world in the postwar years in New York and Paris, when the impressionists were giving way to the post-impressionists. Dreiser had already written about this world in its earlier manifestation in The "Genius," where the Ashcan School of realistic art grew out of the work of magazine illustrators in New York. Now, on the international level, such impressionists as Monet, Manet, Degas, and Renoir were being challenged by Matisse, Picasso, and others. "Lucia" is possibly based on Marguerite Tjader Harris, whose European background may have been changed in the story. Dreiser had met her as he was finishing the Gallery sketches.[56] This one focuses on a painter who never becomes fully aware of her limited talent as an artist. (Dreiser had felt, for example, that Kirah Markham of "Sidonie" lacked the necessary artistic acuteness to succeed as an actress.) The story is also interesting as a gauge or marker to Dreiser's growing hatred of the British and love of the Russians, for Lucia is the product of an English mother (cold and conventional) and a Russian father (warm, the one love of Lucia's life).

In addition to the unpublished "Gloom," "Albertine" may also be based on Estelle Kubitz. The story is about the wife of an art importer who ignores her for his career. After Estelle broke up with Dreiser in 1919, she married Arthur Williams, a wealthy wine importer. The name "Albertine," of course, contains "Bert," one of Estelle's nicknames with Dreiser. In the story she is seduced by the narrator and has a child whom he thinks is his, pure fantasy on Dreiser's part since, as we have seen, he was probably sterile. An architect then enters the picture to have an affair with her. The narrator, for whom work as a writer always came first (like Dreiser), is nevertheless jealous (like Dreiser) of the woman's having a lover other than himself. It may not be a coincidence that the melodrama here—seemingly unconscious in Dreiser's story—reminds one of Eugene O'Neill's Strange Interlude (1928).

The sources for the remaining two stories are unknown. "Bridget Mullanphy" (perhaps her real name) is based on an Irish charwoman whom Dreiser obviously knew when he lived at 165 W. Tenth Street. "Ida Hauchawout" is an insignificant sketch about a country daughter who is victimized by her father and husband. Following the father's death, Ida inherits part of his farm, but after she marries a man as insensitive as her father, he gets the property when she dies in childbirth.

Sometime during 1929 Dreiser began a new affair. Yvette Székely, who, like Thelma Cudlipp almost twenty years earlier, was still in her teens. She was the daughter (actually, stepdaughter) of a female acquaintance, a freelance journalist from Hungary who frequented Dreiser's weekly soirees. The result of her father's tryst with a French prostitute, who relinquished custody of the child, Yvette became the ward of her father and his wife in Budapest. The couple soon divorced, with the court giving custody of Yvette to her father. But Margaret Székely wasn't one to hesitate when it came to getting on with her life. She soon fell in love with an American colonel who left her to go back to his wife, but the affair gave her the idea of going to America anyway. She stole Yvette away from her father and, along with their younger daughter, Suzanne, left for America. Five months later in New York she met and married Roy Phelps Monahan. That marriage lasted only weeks, and the new Mrs. Monahan took her daughters to a hotel room to live. The year was 1922, when Yvette was about nine years old. It was at this time that she was first sexually molested by a neighbor Margaret Monahan had casually employed to watch her children when she was out.

As Yvette wrote in her memoir, Margaret Monahan "had a way of being where the action was, more especially if the situation held people of fame and importance," such as the now celebrated Dreiser. There is even the possibility that Margaret herself had an affair with Dreiser. (Assertions that Suzanne did also are improbable, however).[57] By the time they met him, Margaret and her two daughters were living on the Upper West Side, not too far from Dreiser's midtown apartment at Rodin Studios. After she took her two daughters to a number of the Dreiser gatherings, Yvette and her sister came to view the author as a father figure and to call him "TD" instead of "Mr. Dreiser." At one of his Thursday night receptions, possibly just after Margaret had interviewed Dreiser for a Budapest newspaper, he slipped the seventeen-year-old Yvette a note to meet him the following Tuesday at the Fifty-Seventh Street Schrafft's Restaurant near his studio apartment. Fatherless and starstruck by Dreiser's literary fame, Yvettte was already prepared to endure his advances to win his friendship and attention.[58]

As they sat in the restaurant, Dreiser continued to regard her in an avuncular way, but it became clearer and clearer after a number of similar meetings that he wanted her sexually. Eventually the two retreated to the Mt. Kisco house, which Yvette along with her mother and sister had visited before Dreiser began his overt efforts at seduction. Yvette remembered his taking out a rubber sheet from a black leather satchel and spreading it out on the bed upstairs. "I lay down on the sheet," she recalled, "hoping this part of the 'business' would soon be over with. Then a mountain lowered down on me, propping part of its weight on elbows." After that they met a few times in the Hotel Wellington, conveniently near his residence, and finally in a basement room he had her rent on Eighty-Eighth Street. This time Dreiser was not merely crossing the line of conventional morality. Yvette was legally a minor at seventeen, and he was breaking the law. Her mother, of course, through her long-standing lack of supervision and perhaps her eagerness to use her daughters socially to maintain her own professional relationship with a famous man, had practically hand-delivered the girl to Dreiser. (A year or so later, Margaret Monahan sent her daughter to the apartment of Max Eastman to return a fountain pen he had left in Yvette's bedroom during a party at their house, possibly as "bait." Eastman was waiting for Yvette in his pajamas, explaining that he was recovering from surgery on his inner thigh. As it had been raining, he urged the "lithe and dark-haired" girl with upward curled lashes to remove her wet shoes. "When I did," she recalled, "he rose, peeled off the rest of my clothes, and led me to bed with him.") For his part, Dreiser expressed concern if not fear about the consequences of his actions, asking Yvette over the next year when she would turn eighteen. Whether he realized it, he had committed rape in the second degree according to New York state laws in 1929. This carried a maximum imprisonment of ten years, though a conviction would have required more than the victim's uncorroborated testimony. Their relationship, however, was not exclusively sexual. Dreiser often had Yvette read poetry to him. As with the other women, he listened to her and shared his moods and thoughts. Yvette joined his army of "secretaries" (at six dollars a week) and was put to work on his scientific essays. Long after their sexual relationship had ended, Yvette remained his friend, and they corresponded until Dreiser's death. In the 1950s, she married the widowed Eastman, whom she had first met at Dreiser's West Fifty-Seventh Street apartment so many years before.[59]

While Dreiser may have been waiting for the other shoe to drop on this latest sexual exploit, one fell instead on his fortune. The stock market crash of October 1929, "Black Tuesday," wiped out approximately half his financial worth. The country would soon be deep in poverty that spread now from the traditional poor to men in suits and ties who sold apples on the streets as a respectable way of getting a few cents without actually begging. To Dreiser the economic and social catastrophe, as we shall see, only reinforced his belief in communism and drove him further down the path toward social activism, if not civil disobedience.

FIFTEEN

Tragic America

Do I seem to you to go through the world making bellicose noises?

DREISER TO E. S. MARTIN, SEPTEMBER 4, 1934

IN 1930, AT THE START of the nation's long economic ordeal, Dreiser looked every day of his fifty-eight years. His slightly jowly face and graying hair in faint retreat from the top of his head suggested a certain fatigue, while the steely gray eyes revealed, in spite of his cast, the same old alertness to his surroundings. In most pictures of the time, his smile is nothing more than a broken grin, as if to suggest wariness but not trepidation. His shoulders had become somewhat rounded as his original height of six feet, one and a quarter inches shrank almost an inch with increasing age. Although Dreiser had taken at least two major walking tours in his life, he never exercised on a regular schedule. The degree of health he still enjoyed he probably owed to all the walking he was forced to do as a youth in Indiana. Since Russia, he had taken to drinking during the day, and even in the morning. With age, he also had more frequent bronchial attacks, which would not respond well to the wet Northeast winters any longer. His weight hovered around two hundred pounds.

That spring the stock market recovered about 20 percent of its losses, and President Herbert Hoover, the Great Engineer who had fed the starving Belgians during the First World War and overseen the recovery of the shattered European economy, still hoped that his organizational skills would lead America out of its own financial woes. Historians have long maintained that Hoover was the scapegoat for the Depression. Even though he had never held elected office before, he was probably one of our more qualified presidents, in theory if not practice. Franklin Roosevelt, his successor in 1932, would fly largely by the seat of his pants into the chaos of the coming decade, accomplishing with a smile and a handshake what Hoover could not. Compared with Roosevelt, as one historian has hinted, Hoover was "a peculiarly artless politician." He kept hoping that the Depression was merely a rather longish downturn in the business cycle, while Roosevelt sensed that the American people needed some sort of immediate uplift, both psychological and economic. Ultimately, there was the fear that America would see its hard times as permanent. More than thirteen hundred banks closed in 1930, half of them in the last two months of the year. By the same time, an unprecedented 26,355 business failures had been recorded.[1]

The tough times, exacerbated for Dreiser by a grass fire the following year at Mt. Kisco that consumed one of his Iroki cabins, merely hardened his growing antagonism for capitalism. He suspected corporations of stealing from the people while noncommunist labor organizations stood passively by. In an open letter to the John Reed Club, he stated his belief that the current economic system in America was "changing into an oligarchical over-lordship," comparable to the British aristocracy. Dreiser wasn't alone in seeing capitalism in the Depression as a corrupt and worn-out system. Other artists and intellectuals who supported the communist view of American society included Sherwood Anderson, John Dos Passos, Sidney Hook, Langston Hughes, and Edmund Wilson.[2] Indeed, there was a latent feeling among the general population that the Depression had revealed capitalism to be a failed economic system.

Since 1928 Dreiser had been involved, initially because of Ruth Kennell, with the case of Thomas J. Mooney, a labor agitator imprisoned since 1917 on fraudulent evidence for bombings in San Francisco. In May, while vacationing in the West for his health, he visited Mooney in San Quentin. Interestingly, he privately considered the embattled Mooney more valuable in jail as a symbol of injustice, though he wrote to California Governor C. C. Young demanding his release. He was even reported in the *San Francisco Chronicle* to have opined that Mooney should, if he was not released, be forcibly freed by vigilantes.[3] By now he was becoming fed up with America, leading him to make intemperate remarks to reporters in interviews and in *Tragic America* (1931), a cobbled-together screed against capitalism in all its forms, as well as against the Catholic Church. The country's economic problems, he argued, could be remedied only through the dominance of labor and communism. The monograph was eventually banned from many U.S. libraries, including one of the Carnegie libraries in Dreiser's home state, where *all* his books were not simply banned, but supposedly burned. Its economic "facts" were roundly challenged by reviewers. When Dreiser indignantly asked Stuart Chase to elaborate on the "eighteen errors of fact" he had found in the chapter on "Our Banks and Corporations as Government," Chase, a popular leftist himself on economic matters, replied almost apologetically that he had actually found "more than forty." He hastened to express his admiration for Dreiser's "other work" and the conviction that in *Tragic America* the great novelist "had entered a strange field."[4] Dreiser's lifelong pessimism about the human condition and its social ramifications had animated all his books since *Sister Carrie,* but the trip to Russia had indeed taken his literary gifts into a strange field.

In the fall of 1930, he was known to be one of two American finalists for the Nobel Prize in literature, but the award—the first to an American writer—went (along with a check for $46,000) to his longtime nemesis, Sinclair Lewis. The bad publicity Dreiser had received over Dorothy Thompson's plagiarism charges probably hadn't helped his cause. Furthermore, Lewis had long cultivated his image with the Swedes, where he was a best seller (because he satirized America, many thought), while Dreiser's only book in translation there, *An American Tragedy,* had sold but a pitiful 197 copies by 1927. Later, because of arrangements he had made with publishers while touring Scandinavian countries, there were translations of some of his other books, but nothing compared to the coverage achieved by Lewis. When Ernest Boyd's wife, Madeleine, a literary agent, told Dreiser that giving the prize to Lewis proved that the Nobel Committee was more interested in politics than achievement, he waved her off by saying that he could not "imagine the prize lessening or improving the mental standing of any serious writer— writing is, after all, his or her main business." Generally, Dreiser was stoical about the decision, though eight years later he expressed his disappointment at not having won to his Swedish publisher.[5]

Dreiser, not Lewis, after all, was the "Father of American Realism." To his everlasting credit, Lewis acknowledged this fact. In his Nobel Prize acceptance speech, he singled out Dreiser as the American who had most advanced the cause of modern letters in the United States: "He has cleared the trail from Victorian, Howellsian timidity and gentility. . . . Without his pioneering I doubt that any of us could, unless we liked to be sent to jail, express life, beauty and terror." Lewis himself soon began to think Dreiser had better deserved the Prize and as a Prize holder, beginning in 1931, even nominated him year after year to the Nobel Committee.[6]

Dreiser suffered another setback in the winter and spring of 1931. Jesse Lasky, after four years of letting the film version of *An American Tragedy* lie fallow, produced a movie in which Clyde was reduced to "a more or less over-sexed and worthless boy." In other words, Clyde and not society was to blame for the tragedy. Initially, Paramount—which because of the transition to "talkies" now paid Dreiser an additional $55,000 for the sound rights—had brought Sergei Eisenstein to America to oversee a script, but the result was too long and too reductively Marxist in its depictions of capitalistic America for Hollywood. (As one film critic has remarked, "Dreiser could not have asked for a more respectful, or understanding director" than Eisenstein.)[7] Instead Lasky turned over the project to the renowned film director Joseph von Sternberg, who had on occasion "expressed his contempt and dislike" for Dreiser—these are the words of Arthur Hays, who wrote the letter of complaint on Dreiser's behalf to Paramount.

On June 26 Hays threatened an injunction unless the picture was changed to "represent Mr. Dreiser's work"—which "presented the situation of an ordinary but weak youngster who, through the vicissitudes of life, over which he had little or no control, was gradually forced to one position after another, until he became involved in a great tragedy."[8] Dreiser may have believed that *An American Tragedy* was more of an indictment of capitalistic America after visiting Russia, when in fact it was—like *Sister Carrie*—as much of a cosmic complaint as a social one. Rather than showing Clyde as a victim of cosmic forces, not to mention the social ones, the movie script focused mainly on the courtroom scenes to the detriment of the material in Book I of the novel, which narrates Clyde's initial impressionable life and its deprivations, which led to his distorted view of the American Dream. It also excluded the death house scene as "too gruesome to show the American public"—a scene that had proved to be the most riveting in the play version of *An American Tragedy*. Lasky claimed that it was too late to make changes and that his corporation had been unable to locate Dreiser at the appropriate time.[9]

Dreiser sued and lost a year later. He had tried to reason with "Hooeyland," as he came to refer to Hollywood, even going out there on one of the earliest transcontinental flights, at Paramount's expense. The studio yielded to the extent of adding a few shots of Clyde's early life. When the completed film was previewed in New York to a number of Dreiser's cronies on June 15, however, it was deemed unworthy, though at least one of them,

Ernest Boyd, agreed beforehand to condemn the film.[10] In deciding against Dreiser, the judge in the case stated that Paramount "must give consideration to the fact that the great majority of people composing the audience . . . will be more interested that justice prevail over wrongdoing than that the inevitability of Clyde's end clearly appear." Hollywood, of course, wasn't particularly interested in conveying even this social lesson over Dreiser's deterministic argument. When Hollywood was compared unfavorably to the achievements of foreign filmmakers, Samuel Goldwyn retorted: "There's too much education in the foreign celluloids. Americans don't want to go to the theater to be educated. When they want that they go to schools."[11] The stakes were high here, as approximately four-fifths of the American people in the early 1930s went to a movie theater once a week.

Dawn, the first volume of his autobiography written so many years earlier and then held back for fear it would be too embarrassing to family members, finally appeared in 1931—almost a decade after the appearance of the "second" volume, *A Book About Myself.* In a way, the appearance of this early part of Dreiser's history may have made up for the absence of Clyde's youth in the Paramount film. If Dreiser's readers in the 1930s had begun to wonder at the author's increasing activity as a social radical, *Dawn* told them of the early, Clyde-like poverty that had first fired these passions, especially when it came to his endorsement of communism. That March he told another Mooney—James D., president of the Export Division of General Motors whose *Onward Industry!* (1931) he curiously admired—that the "solution for the difficulties of the world, and particularly those in America, is Communism."[12] His losses from the stock market crash, of course, hadn't done anything to maintain his tolerance for capitalism.

Five days later, on March 19, the irascible author slapped Sinclair Lewis (twice) for accusing him, once again, of having plagiarized Dorothy Thompson's book on Russia. Lewis made the accusation publicly at a dinner in honor of a Russian writer at the Metropolitan Club when he pointedly refused to take the podium in the presence of the plagiarist as well as "two sage critics" (Heywood Broun and Arthur Brisbane) who had objected to his receiving the Nobel Prize. According to one eyewitness, "later in the evening while Lewis and Dreiser were sitting together talking privately, Dreiser suddenly slapped Lewis's face. It was a dinner attended by thirty or forty people and there were long stories about it in the papers the following day." One report mirthfully declared that Lewis's cheek had been buffeted by the "hand of the potter." Dreiser was "big, heavy, quite strong," Wharton Esherick later remembered. "You wouldn't want to fuss with him."

Lewis, who had been drinking that evening, may have called Dreiser a plagiarist more in response to a lingering rumor that Dreiser and Dorothy
Thompson had slept together while in Russia than the idea that he had
stolen her words.[13]

Dreiser was an obstinate man. Once he set his mind to something, nothing could change it. As an adult, he also seems never to have admitted either
regret or embarrassment over his actions, no matter how ridiculous or
wrong-headed some of them might seem today. As he had told Marguerite
Tjader Harris, now another of his intimate companions, he wanted to do
something other than write novels.[14] His energy would go strictly to social
causes, no matter how far afield they would take him from his life in literature or how unflatteringly they might cast him in the public eye. One of
the first was the notorious case of the Scottsboro Boys. Nine black youths
accused of raping two women, later regarded as prostitutes, were convicted
in Alabama that spring. After a short trial, eight were sentenced to death
and the ninth, only thirteen years old, was given life imprisonment. Dreiser,
along with Lincoln Steffens, publicized the outrage. Other protesters included the NAACP, the American Communist Party in the form of the
National Committee for the Defense of Political Prisoners, Clarence Darrow, Burton Rascoe, and John Dos Passos.

"The State of Alabama has now set July 10th as the date for the judicial
massacre of eight children," Dreiser wrote in an open letter in May. He was
appealing for funds for a new trial, which was finally granted after several
delays in the sentencing. Ultimately, the Scottsboro defendants were tried
four times in all, the last trial in 1936 resulting in the acquittal of four of
the accused. Dreiser may have helped here. In a pamphlet entitled *Mr. President: Free the Scottsboro Boys,* sponsored by the Communist Party in 1934,
he appealed directly to President Roosevelt. The case was in its fourth year,
and two electrocutions were still scheduled. Dreiser was following an
American literary tradition, going back at least to Ralph Waldo Emerson,
who in 1838 protested to President Martin Van Buren about the involuntary removal of the Cherokee Indians from their gold-rich lands in Georgia to the territory of Oklahoma, resulting in the infamous "Trail of Tears."
The Scottsboro case has taken a similar place in American history and lore.
Dreiser likened the planned executions to "judicial lynchings," and was no

doubt reminded again of the lynching he had witnessed outside St. Louis. In a letter to the Association of Southern Women for the Prevention of Lynching, he wrote: "The whole Southern attitude toward the Negro has become a national ill."[15]

That summer he went to Pittsburgh with William Z. Foster, the Communist Party's candidate for president in 1932, and Joseph Pass, who had been active in the party's activities in the South. The Communist-backed National Mine Workers had challenged the United Mine Workers, an affiliate of the American Federation of Labor, in organizing attempts in Pennsylvania. Violence followed in one of the nearby mining towns. At first Dreiser tried to remain neutral between these two labor groups, but after visiting, by his own count, fifteen mines where he interviewed miners and their wives and returning to New York, he publicly sided with the NMW, saying the AF of L was in cahoots with the big corporations and discriminated against minorities and immigrants.[16] The Pittsburgh venture, however, was merely a dress rehearsal for Dreiser's much more publicized and ultimately embarrassing encounter with the coal miners' strikes in Harlan County, Kentucky, in November. Here Dreiser fell into what became known in the national press as the "toothpick trap."

All during the 1920s coal miners in Harlan, Bell, and Knox counties had been fighting for higher wages and safer working conditions. A "mine war" broke out in the fall of 1931 in Harlan County in which miners were shot or roughed up for holding "free speech" meetings and trying to become members of the National Mine Workers. In New York the International Labor Defense, later dubbed a "Communist Front" by the FBI and the press, asked Dreiser, as a prominent American friendly to the Communist cause, if he would organize a committee and look into the matter. Just coming off the Pittsburgh strike, he might have declined. It was clearly dangerous ground, especially for pro-labor outsiders. But he had seen such labor atrocities since his newspaper days in Pittsburgh. Neither his sympathies nor his nerve ever flagged when it came to the average laborer beaten down by the system. "I was early drawn into this sort of thing," he later wrote, "and as early, of course, witnessed the immense injustice which property in America has not only sought to but has succeeded in inflicting on labor."[17] Dreiser originally sought to gather together a blue-ribbon committee of prominent Americans, but no doubt because of his Communist Party affiliations his invitations were unanimously declined by newspaper editors, college presidents, and even the future Supreme Court Justice Felix Frankfurter, then on the Harvard Law School Faculty.

"Having thus failed to interest the representative Americans," Dreiser told Lester Cohen, a Liveright author whom he had known for over twenty years and who accompanied him to Kentucky, "we are now reduced to writers." Of the twenty he asked, six accepted, including Dos Passos, whose labor chronicles in the trilogy *U.S.A.* (1938) were no doubt influenced by the experience. The group registered in the Continental Hotel in Pineville. Dreiser gave interviews to the press and called the attention of local authorities under the control of the mine owners to his bold errand into the Kentucky wilderness. He did not go out of his way, however, to advertise the fact that he had brought along a young woman, Marie Pergaine, whom Cohen had never seen among the various secretaries Dreiser employed in his latest office at the Hotel Ansonia at Broadway and Seventy-Third Street.[18]

The next day the "Dreiser Committee" set up court in the Lewallen Hotel to hear out the miners. Transcripts of these proceedings, edited by Dos Passos with an introduction by Dreiser, were eventually published in *Harlan Miners Speak* (1932), a collection of essays by the Harlan pilgrims for the National Committee for the Defense of Political Prisoners. The colorful "Aunt Molly" Jackson, a midwife and nurse for the settlement, testified to the general destitution of the miners and their families, especially their small children, many of whom suffered from cholera, famine, flux, and "stomach trouble." Their food, procured from the company stores, consisted of "beans and harsh foods" fried in lard. Such fare was the best the Red Cross could or would supply, she said And it did not give to everyone, clearly not to members of the National Mine Workers. "The Red Cross is against a man who is trying to better himself," she charged. "They are for the operators, and they want the mines to be going so they won't give anything to a man unless he does what the operators want him to."[19] Story after story infuriated and saddened the man who had come from so little himself.

More than two thousand miners were then on strike, and many of them crowded around and into the hotel to witness the hearings. The local press was unsympathetic or apathetic, but there were reporters on hand from the Associated Press and United Press. The grim stories of the Harlan mine workers went out over the syndicate wires, tales of soup kitchens being dynamited and miners being arrested for criminal syndicalism, an old law passed in the wake of the Great War and generally no longer enforced because of its constitutional ambiguity. Locals sympathetic to the coal companies fairly seethed until Herndon Evans, editor of the *Pineville Sun,* started asking questions of the interrogator himself. Evans was also head of the local Red Cross.

"You are a very famous novelist and have written several books," Evans noted of the writer, who sat at the end of a long table dressed in a crumpled blue suit and bow tie. "Would you kindly tell us what your royalties amount to?" Also, how much did he earn last year? Dreiser set his lifetime royalties at $200,000 and his 1931 "salary" at $35,000. How much did he contribute to charity, Evans asked, perhaps somehow knowing of the writer's parsimonious ways. When Dreiser admitted he had contributed nothing, Evans simply said, "That is all."[20]

While the miners present were in awe of Dreiser's stature and certainly his earning power, they were apparently not surprised or shocked at his poor record of giving. Dreiser defended it by comparing individual contributions to "a patch on a rotten pair of pants that ought to be thrown out. I believe in a whole new suit." "Hell," remarked one miner in an apparent attempt to translate, "I don't keer for charity myself. I only want what's coming to me." The Dreiser committee then visited mining camps in the area to get a clearer picture of the horror of life in the Kentucky hills. They heard the same sad story again and again. "Dreiser," Cohen remembered, "listened with grave intensity. . . . Our party had toured the mine camps all day; some of us were hungry, tired, cold, wanted to go. Not Mr. Dreiser; he stayed to the last. And when he left, with a hundred or more men and women crowding around him, wanting to shake his hand, he seemed to have a soft, warm, giving quality."[21]

Things were going nicely in the propaganda war by this time, but the folks in Pineville were not finished with their "outside agitator." The mysterious Marie Pergaine was waiting for Dreiser upon his return to his hotel. When she accompanied him to his room, local busybodies, tipped off by either the hotel clerk or manager, laid toothpicks against the door to determine whether Miss Pergaine remained the night. After the toothpicks were still standing the next morning, Dreiser was formally charged with adultery. By this time he had already left for New York, the "crime" only a misdemeanor he could safely ignore outside Kentucky. But had his reputation, or his mission, been tarnished by the scandal? While still en route on the train, he issued a statement to the AP that he could not possibly be guilty of the charge because he was impotent—"so much so that the fact that I may be seen here or there . . . with an attractive girl or woman means nothing more than that a friendly and quite moral conversation is being indulged in."[22]

This tongue-in-cheek defense (Helen later vigorously insisted that Dreiser had been potent until the day he died) had been a feeble attempt to shift the focus. "Now, if I have really succeeded in getting the American mind off sex for a moment," he continued, "I would like to discuss the Harlan situation and other matters."[23] Once back in New York, Dreiser learned that he as well as his "committee" had also, like the miners they tried to help, been indicted on the same flimsy charge of criminal syndicalism. Unlike the adultery charge, this was an extraditable offense. All charges, however, stemming from the Harlan adventure were eventually dropped or ignored. But just as Russia had converted Dreiser to communism, Harlan turned the writer into a committed foe of the capitalistic establishment.

Dreiser was no conventional communist, of course. His inexorable sense of individuality kept him from official party membership for many years. He told a correspondent a year later: "The Party would not accept me as a member. . . . while I have found Communism functioning admirably in the U.S.S.R., I am not at all convinced that its exact method there could be effectively transferred to the self-government of the people in the United States." He had often used the party, asked its advice, but he had not always followed it. Communist Party member or not, Dreiser was by now considered a Red by the FBI, which opened a file on him in the early thirties. The Soviets had quoted and misquoted him in *Izvestia*. He had been marked for endorsing in the late twenties the Workers' International Relief (another "Communist Front") and joining the International Committee for Sacco and Vanzetti (interestingly, in spite of his belief that they were guilty). "Dreiser is intellectual," a later FBI report noted in its bureaucratic shorthand as the New Deal got under way, "Communist and member of numerous Communist subsidiaries and recognizes fact that President Roosevelt has done, as Democrat, what Reds have failed to do under their own party line-ups, that is, converted U.S. to Socialism."[24]

Sometime before the end of 1931, Dreiser began a relationship with yet another young woman who had fallen for him because of his books and who shortly afterward joined the ranks of his secretaries. Clara Clark, the twenty-four-year-old daughter of a prominent Quaker family in Philadelphia, found Dreiser physically shocking at first, but was drawn by "the rough, massive force" of his face, "with its dark, leathery skin and the thick lips continually parted over large, yellowy teeth." Bored that summer with upper-middle-class life in the Germantown section of the city, Clara, who hoped to become a novelist, picked up a copy of the recently published *Dawn* and found a "kindred spirit" in the author's way of talking frankly about the experiences that had pained him. She turned next to a cheap edition of *An American Tragedy,* which totally absorbed her. She read it in days. "When I finished it," she later wrote, "I slipped on my knees beside my bed, and wept." Clara wrote the author a letter in care of his publisher, but didn't mail it until September or October. Soon she received an answer, calling her intense, poetic, and aesthetic—the last one of Dreiser's favorite adjectives at the time—and suggesting she pay him a visit in New York.[25]

Having heard of Dreiser's reputation as a womanizer—it was more than locally known by 1931, really ever since his fame from *An American Tragedy*—she didn't tell her parents at first. More letters arrived, along with copies of *Sister Carrie* and *Jennie Gerhardt,* until she finally agreed to meet their author. As if leaving home for the first time, she finally told her parents and kissed them good-bye. Dressed in a new black fur jacket over a black dress trimmed with red and a hat with a red feather, Clara boarded the train to New York. She took a room at the Ansonia (having never entered a hotel lobby alone before) and called Dreiser, who came right down from his office quarters on the fourteenth floor. At dinner in a nearby French restaurant—seven courses and a bottle of red wine—he lied about having met Stalin while in Russia. He spoke of the hard times she had read about in *Dawn,* the love he still felt for his mother and his brother Paul. When they returned to the Ansonia and boarded the elevator, he got off at her floor. As she recalled the evening, she unlocked her door and held out her hand to say good night. She soon learned, however, that he had no intention of leaving.[26]

Clara eventually moved to New York and received a salary of twenty-five dollars a week to edit chapters of *The Stoic,* which had been in process for almost thirty years in one form or another. By this time, Dreiser was living in the city, while Helen spent most of her time at Iroki in Mt. Kisco. An acquaintance at the time described her as often looking "sad," and Ellen Copenhaver, Sherwood Anderson's last wife, wrote of Helen: "Rumor has it that she has lost Dreiser." Between April and August of 1932, he wrote about two-thirds of the final volume of his Cowperwood trilogy. Clara dined out with him regularly during this time and observed his habits and friends. He drank a lot, she remembered, but she never saw him intoxicated. A friend in upstate New York sent him applejack, which they both drank liberally, dropping a piece of charcoal into the brew to filter out any impurities common (and sometimes dangerous) in Prohibition-era intoxicants. Clara, already a chain-smoker, soon became dependent on alcohol as well. One night while they dined out, "a tall, thin, red-faced man with sandy hair" walked into the restaurant and headed straight for the bar. "That was Red Lewis," Dreiser told Clara, after the man had gulped down his drink and quickly departed. He spoke of their quarrel and how the Nobel Prize should not have been awarded to Lewis. On another occasion she met George Jean Nathan, "a rather small, slender man, with gray hair, dark, wise eyes, a small nose and wide, loose-lipped mouth." He and Dreiser were discussing the possibility of beginning a new magazine, which would be called the *American Spectator,* and Dreiser wondered whether Mencken, from whom he was still estranged, might be interested in the enterprise.[27]

Clara accompanied Dreiser on a trip to San Antonio in the spring of 1932. He was traveling again for his health, this time under the assumed name of T. H. Dryer, perhaps to avoid a hostile press after the publication of *Tragic America.* Eventually he went west to El Paso before returning to New York. The trip had also been initiated, as had others, by a quarrel with Helen. He was striving to work on *The Stoic* in peace somewhere. Clara, who met none of Dreiser's other women except Helen at Mt. Kisco, left the writer's service after three years and returned to Philadelphia, her departure hastened by an auto accident that occurred while she was chauffeuring Teddie and Helen.[28] She eventually married and moved to England, where she became involved with the Oxford Group, later known as the Moral Rearmament Movement, in the 1940s.

That summer Liveright, Inc., filed for bankruptcy, with thousands of copies of Dreiser's various books on hand. The unsold stock included more than 3,000 copies of *An American Tragedy,* more than 4,000 copies of the recently issued *Dawn,* 4,000 copies of *A Gallery of Women,* and 1,408 copies of the controversial *Tragic America.*[29] Liveright himself went out almost as quickly. A heavy drinker, he died broke of pneumonia at age forty-six on September 24, 1933. Dreiser owed this publisher much, but he had never trusted him. Later, in the hands of another who eventually remaindered his books, he thought that he had never had a truer publisher than Liveright.

Meanwhile, the *American Spectator* had already been incorporated and was to be jointly edited by Dreiser, Nathan, Ernest Boyd, Sherwood Anderson, James Branch Cabell, and Eugene O'Neill. According to its prospectus, this "Literary Newspaper" sought to publish writers who ignore "the conventionalist, the moralist, and the religionist." It would be published every month at first and then weekly. No one contributing author could accept an article by himself, a rule that kept Dreiser busy trying to recruit material suitable to Nathan and the others, but his preference for anticapitalist and procommunist material often failed the test. When Dreiser sent him an invitation to submit, Upton Sinclair commented that the editorial board was "an oddly assorted bunch, and it will be interesting to see what you are all able to agree upon." Dreiser apparently had less trouble publishing his own work, which was mostly written on whim when he remembered that he was more comfortable as a writer instead of an editor. During the period of the *Spectator* years he published two sketches that were reminiscent of the ones in *Twelve Men,* "Townsend" and "Winterton." The first focused on a clerk who aspires to the riches of a Vanderbilt or a Rockefeller, but wastes away—like Hurstwood in the hard economic times of the 1890s—in that earlier "Great Depression." The other portrait reached back to his newspaper days. Winterton, an editor of the *New York Express,* modeled no doubt on one of the *New York World* editors Dreiser had failed to win over, is eventually ruined by Anthony Comstock, whose men raid Winterton's private collection of nude photographs and French posters.[30]

A similar piece came out in one of the earliest issues of *Esquire,* where Dreiser once again had a magazine connection through Will Lengel. "Mathewson," one of his best sketches since those of *Twelve Men,* is based on the decline of a talented journalist, the son of a wealthy printer who because of his alcoholism works only intermittently for the various St. Louis newspapers. These include the *Globe-Democrat* and the *Republic,* where Dreiser had once worked. Like Dreiser's friend at the *Globe-Democrat* Dick Wood, who wrote a novel in the naturalistic mode of the French, Wilson Mathewson admires Zola and writes an article about him that fascinates the narrator, who is fashioned after Dreiser as a St. Louis reporter. He subsequently reads "of this man Zola with intense interest." (This detail in the plot gives us pause as to Dreiser's denial that he *ever* read Zola and certainly not before writing *Sister Carrie.*) Zola's "Paris, his people," Dreiser writes, "the kind of people who appeared to be not so much different from what was all about me here in St. Louis!" The story also shows in the narrator's fascination for Wilson Mathewson shades of Poe's "William Wilson." And the young reporter's visit to the mother of the Jeff Ingalls in "Nigger Jeff" is essentially redone when the narrator in "Mathewson" visits the widow of an engineer horribly killed in a railroad accident. He had been sent there by Mathewson, who was a temporary city editor one night at the *Globe-Democrat.* Mathewson, who later dies of a drug overdose, admired the young reporter because he hadn't bothered the sobbing woman with a reporter's needless questions. Marguerite Tjader, who typed out the story for Dreiser, noted later that it was a refreshing change from the combative political writing of recent years. She found the character of Mathewson "as eerie as a character out of Poe or Baudelaire." The story is not, of course, unpolitical, for Mathewson reflects Dreiser's anger over poverty in America—both in 1894 and in 1934. "Do I seem to rave?" the narrator asks. "Life, in the main, is a cause for raving."[31]

Unfortunately for Dreiser that year, this sympathy for the disadvantaged did not always extend to the Jewish people, many of whom were already trying to get out of Hitler's Germany. Unlike the work of Wharton or Hemingway, there is no memorable Jewish stereotype in Dreiser's fiction, yet he was personally capable of occasional anti-Semitic slurs. He may have distrusted Liveright primarily because he was Jewish. He shared the bias commonly directed at Jews before the 1930s that labeled them as shrewd, money-minded lawyers, bankers, and merchants. But Dreiser was always of two minds concerning Jews, for he also accepted the other stereotype of the Jew as somehow smarter than the average Gentile. And the superstitious Dreiser, as he had written in *A Hoosier Holiday,* once stated that "for a period of over fifteen years in my life, at the approach of every marked change . . . I have met a certain smug, kindly Jew, always the same Jew, who has greeted me most warmly."[32]

In the September 1933 issue of the *Spectator,* the editors ran the proceedings of "A Jewish Symposium," reprinted perhaps somewhat apologetically as "Editorial Conference (With Wine)" in 1934. This was one of several such conferences, or editorial bull sessions, in which the usually half-hour remarks by the editors were recorded by Evelyn Light, Dreiser's current secretary. Some were never published, and this one certainly shouldn't have been. Dreiser is heard to say that "the world's quarrel with the Jew is not that he is inferior, but that he is superior." After some disagreement from Nathan and Boyd, Dreiser responds that Jews have been not only dispersed but suppressed for nearly two thousand years. His "real quarrel" with them, he said, was that they were actually "too clever and too dynamic" for their own good—certainly for the good of the societies they invaded in what he deemed an almost parasitic fashion. "In other words, temperamentally they are inclined to drift to whatever nation is of promise in their time." He recommended a separate Jewish state rather than their integration of other countries. Cabell chimed in facetiously at the close of the "conference" to propose that Jews be given the state of Kansas. "Thereby, in the first place, we might rid ourselves of Kansas; in the second place, of the Jews."[33]

Hutchins Hapgood, who had known Dreiser since his Village days and who was partly responsible for the Provincetown Players production of *The Hand of the Potter* in 1921, found the piece unsettling and asked the editors to print his response. He was the author of seven books, including *The Spirit of the Ghetto* in 1902, which had sought to challenge the image of the Jewish ghetto as a place only of poverty, immorality, and ignorance, a stereotype first brought to the attention of middle-class New York by Jacob Riis in *How the Other Half Lives*.[34] Hapgood had become interested in the Jewish people while working under Lincoln Steffens at the *New York Commercial Advertiser* in the late 1890s. His depictions of Jewish people, especially on the lower East Side, attempted to stave off turn-of-the-century anti-Semitism by opening cultural channels between Jews and Gentiles in New York.

The handsome writer, who came from a wealthy family with a considerable estate at Hastings on the Hudson, lived in nearby Dobbs Ferry, New York, with a wife and four children, but he had spent much of his time in Greenwich Village mingling with other writers. As we have seen, in "Esther Norn" of *A Gallery of Women,* Dreiser tells the thinly veiled story of the artist Mary Pyne, the estranged wife of the poet Harry Kemp and asserts that she and Hapgood, as "JJ" in the story, had had an affair. Pyne died in poverty at age twenty-five, a victim of crippling health problems that culminated in tuberculosis. According to Dreiser's scenario, "JJ" did nothing to help her except to pay her funeral expenses. Like "Rona Murtha," the sketch that depicted Arthur Henry in an unfavorable light, this one may have followed basic facts (though Hapgood later denied the affair), but it gave "JJ" no benefit of the doubt. In the twenties, Hapgood apparently disappeared into alcoholism until resurfacing in Dreiser's life in 1932 to ask for his help in placing a thirty-thousand-word memoir entitled "My Forty Years of Drink," already rejected by several publishers. Hapgood had apparently not yet become aware of how he had been used in *A Gallery.* At first, Dreiser seemed to brush off the request, then had the ever discreet Evelyn Light apologize, saying that her boss had been busy working on *The Stoic.* He eventually read Hapgood's manuscript, praised it, and promised to recommend parts of it to the *Spectator,* where nothing ever appeared.[35]

When Hapgood challenged the editors of the *Spectator,* they ducked the issue of anti-Semitism by ignoring his request and passing his letter onto Dreiser, hoping the two would somehow resolve the matter as between friends. Hapgood had sought to remind the editors of their obligations to liberalism, a more broadened concept of democracy then being cultivated by FDR in his Fireside Chats on the radio. Instead of somehow trying to placate Hapgood, however, Dreiser walked into a self-constructed firestorm. He suggested that liberalism was foolish in a society already threatened with being overrun with too many "types," whether they be Arabs, Catholics, Jews, or blacks. Then he singled out Jews as possibly the most threatening "type," insisting that they preferred to be white-collar workers rather than farmers or mechanics (thereby not helping to carry the national workload). He also quoted unnamed Jews on Jews about their "sharp" practices when it came to money. And, to buttress his point, he mentioned that several states were considering a quota on the number of Jewish lawyers. "The Jews lack, if I read the Pennsylvania Bar Association correctly," he told Hapgood, "the fine integrity which at least is endorsed and, to a degree, followed by the lawyers of other nationalities. At least, that is the charge. Left to sheer liberalism as you interpret it, they could possess America by sheer numbers, their cohesion, their race tastes and, as in the case of the Negro in South Africa, really overrun the land."[36]

This was the very same person—the author of "Nigger Jeff"—who had gone to bat for the Scottsboro boys and condemned racial prejudice in the American South. Hy Kraft, a Jewish Broadway producer and close associate of Dreiser's at the time, later characterized the incident as "his anti-Semitic aberration." In the *Jewish Advocate* fifteen years earlier, Dreiser had boldly gone on record to hail the Jewish people of the Lower East Side as "essentially artists, transfiguring the commonplace with a glow of hope, and seeing in the humdrum everyday the stepping-stone to a larger and more vigorous life." Indeed, as late as 1925 he had told another journalist almost the opposite of what he was now telling Hapgood: "I believe, although many people won't agree, that the Jews understand and love this country better than the so-called Anglo-Saxon stock. They sink deep roots here, they appreciate the material opportunities and try to give something in return." In spite of his very early anti-Semitism in Chicago (which he acknowledges in *Dawn*), he had held the Jews in high regard, especially as artists. The turning point came after he visited the Soviet Union, fell in love with socialism, and concluded (as the Soviets did) that "Jews are natural-born traders" who cannot be made amenable to socialism. "Now I do not assert," he told an interviewer in 1929, "that the Jew cannot be happy in Russia. . . . But just the same while I was in Russia the thought frequently came to me that because of their rather general instinct for trading and because of Communism's fatal opposition to that instinct, the Jews must needs be unpleasantly affected by it." Now some five years later, as he had become completely enamored of the Soviet experiment, Dreiser apparently had no idea how irrevocably he was branding himself as a racial conservative, if not a racist. "In this particular symposium," he coolly told the now heated Hapgood, "I did not say anything which should cause an intelligent Jew to quarrel with my position."[37] Yet as Hitler's anti-Semitism campaign got underway in 1933, soon after his installation as chancellor, the climate for speaking critically or abusively about Jews in the United States as a separate entity was changing almost overnight. It easily set the stage for Hapgood's response to the effect that if Dreiser hadn't signed the letter, he might have thought it was "written by a member of the Ku Klux Klan or a representative of Hitler." Yet Dreiser had many Jewish friends and was accustomed to speaking frankly to them about their culture without offense because those he knew were writers more interested in assimilation.

With his second letter Dreiser merely got himself deeper into the morass. He insisted on a higher number of Jews in America than Hapgood would allow, including "half-Jews" and "quarter-Jews" that any census might miss. Calling now for an international conference to decide whether Jews ought to establish their own state or blend in with the populations through intermarriage, he ignored the contradiction of his earlier statement against assimilation by saying: "As Shaw urged only recently, why not every Jewish male forced to marry a Gentile female, and every Jewish female a Gentile male? Would not that solve this very vexing question of how the Jew is to be disposed of among the various races and nations of the world?"[38]

When Hapgood published this exchange—with Dreiser's permission, no less—in the Nation in 1935, it caused immeasurable damage to the novelist's personal reputation, opprobrium that lasts to this day. By this time Germany had openly stripped its Jews of their citizenship, barred them from teaching in the universities, and forbidden their intermarriage with Gentiles, or "Aryans." A reader who had long admired Dreiser's work and recently met him wrote that she had learned of his statements to Hapgood with something more than profound regret: "They say blood ties are strong and apparently the ideas inculcated probably by your German parents have proven stronger than your American education." Now in spite of his literary talent, she found him personally despicable: "the meanest Jew in this country who has at heart the American traditions and ideals of freedom and toleration . . . has more right in this country than you."[39] Realizing by now that he had stepped into more than he expected, Dreiser tried to backpedal, but his stubbornness doomed the effort. In "Dreiser Denies He Is Anti-Semitic" in the *New Masses,* where he had long been a favorite contributor and topic, the editors were forced to admit that they were "far from satisfied as to the adequacy of his final statement." Dreiser disavowed any hatred for Jews or admiration for Hitler. (Ironically, the Nazis banned all his books that year, thinking that "Dreiser" was a Jewish name.) As a communist sympathizer, he insisted that he favored the Jewish worker against the Jewish exploiter as vigorously as he defended Gentile workers against Gentile exploiters. This statement did little to mollify his critics, especially the American Communist Party, which feared it would lose Jewish members since it had frequently cited or quoted Dreiser in support of its ideology. In a subsequent issue of the *New Masses,* party member Mike Gold's response to Dreiser's "retraction" was that only "years of devoted battle against anti-Semitism and fascism" could get him off the hook.[40]

By the end of this latest imbroglio, the *Spectator* had quietly gone out of business. Dreiser himself had cut his ties to it at the beginning of 1934, disgusted with his inability to publish writers he alone favored. Even O'Neill, who viewed Dreiser as a major literary influence, had sided against him on an article submitted by Powys. "Fundamentally," Dreiser had told Nathan in the summer of 1933, "Mencken stated the case to me in regard to you in 1926, . . . that all you could contemplate was the frothy intellectual and social interest of the stage."[41] Actually, Dreiser had other competing interests. After his bruising battle with Paramount over *An American Tragedy,* he quietly and without any strings attached sold the film rights to *Jennie Gerhardt* to the same studio, which produced the movie in 1933. Then, after collecting $25,000 plus 7 percent interest in the film profits, Dreiser gave the film only lukewarm praise, mainly because Jennie's character, played by Sylvia Sidney, loses what one film critic calls her "almost pathologically giving nature." In fact, as Dreiser later told Eisenstein with particular reference to the film of *Jennie Gerhardt,* "All in all I am thoroughly disgusted with the moving picture industry over here, not only because of the results of my work, but in general, as you very well know, because of their cheap commercialism and toadying to the lowest and most insignificant tastes."[42] Such crassitude, which went hand in hand with capitalism anyway, would not, however, keep him from selling to Hollywood again.

The next year he endorsed Upton Sinclair, who had won the Democratic primary for governor of California. In a pamphlet entitled *I, Governor of California and How I Ended Poverty* (followed after the election by *I, Candidate for Governor: And How I Got Licked*), the muckraking novelist promised to eradicate poverty in California by turning private property and land over to cooperatives for workers and farmers. In the December issue of *Esquire,* Dreiser published "The Epic Sinclair." The biographical article, whose title contained the acronym for Sinclair's slogan, "END POVERTY IN CALIFORNIA," didn't appear until the eve of the election. This was probably fortunate for Sinclair, even though he lost. For Dreiser, who alleged that he had read ten of the candidate's books, including *The Jungle,* merely reminded his readers of Sinclair's rejection among capitalists as a crank (one of whose books had to be published by the same "almost shady company, which had also ventured to republish my 'Sister Carrie'") and celebrated his socialistic programs for America. Moreover, he opined, Sinclair had "done a more brilliant job than either Mussolini or Hitler." Still seeing Hitler as a German New Dealer in 1934, Dreiser saluted Sinclair by alluding once more to the fascist. "I can't say, Heil Hitler, he concluded, "But I will say, 'Hey, Sinclair, more power to you!!!'"[43]

Dreiser seemed besieged and obsessed by such political projects. One, in collaboration with Hy Kraft, turned into a movie script, which he called in succession "Tobacco and Men," "Tobacco," and then simply "Revolt." It wasn't to be confused, he told one prospective producer, with Erskine Caldwell's *Tobacco Road* (1932), now a successful play about poor whites, particularly appealing in the Depression; this was about the bloody tobacco wars of 1907 in North Carolina between farmers and the Duke Tobacco Trust—an uprising similar to a later one that became the basis for Robert Penn Warren's *Night Rider* (1939). Dreiser's plot would, according to one proposal, cover several generations, beginning briefly like *The Financier* in antebellum America. It would also feature a family named Barnes, a surname that reappears in *The Bulwark.* Cumbersome in its plot if also compassionate toward the exploited tobacco farmers, the script was never produced, mainly because Dreiser suspected Kraft of trying to steal the screenplay for himself and sell it to Hollywood.[44]

In the fall of 1934 Dreiser found a new publisher in the firm of Simon and Schuster. The publishers gave him a cash advance of $5,000 plus another $2,000 to pay off the debt to the creditors of Liveright for the plates to his other books and an additional $3,000 to buy up the stock of his old books. In return, they expected to get *The Stoic,* another volume of short stories, and the third volume of his autobiography. Instead, Dreiser gave them an expanded edition of *Moods,* which Simon and Schuster, perhaps as a result of their disappointment, put into a cheap binding, their first mistake—as they would later discover—with their famous but irritable writer. "The Works of Theodore Dreiser, past and present," the firm proudly announced following the signatures on the contract, "will henceforth be published by Simon & Schuster. . . . The fame of Theodore Dreiser is an unshakable bulwark. He symbolizes the heroic mind and comprehending heart." To seal their bargain, they stood the expense of a lavish reception at Iroki. In the introduction to the new *Moods,* Sulamith Ish-Kishor, whose biography of the Roman emperor Hadrian Dreiser was promoting, continued the hyperbole by suggesting that if Dreiser hadn't already been known as a realist he would "without question be hailed as a 'new Walt Whitman.'"[45]

Instead of continuing to work steadily on *The Stoic,* Dreiser was "eating and sleeping *science.*" It was for a book on philosophy, as he told George Douglas, the San Francisco journalist and friend from the early 1920s, who was now living and working in Los Angeles. Dreiser, always generous with unknown artists, tended to support second-rate talents, including Charles Fort, Ralph Fabri, the Hungarian sculptor whom Helen liked so much, and the artist Hubert Davis. Douglas was another. Dreiser thought he belonged in the New York literary scene and even published several left-wing pieces by him in the *American Spectator*—anonymously, so Douglas wouldn't get in trouble with his newspaper. Douglas also served Dreiser as a foil to Mencken, whom Douglas criticized as a reactionary (true enough by the mid-thirties, but Douglas may also have been jealous of the fellow journalist's success as a cultural and political critic).[46]

Douglas encouraged Dreiser's random scientific inquiries and the sometimes fuzzy speculations on how this or that phenomenon was a microcosmic clue to the secret of the universe. "You are most lucid when most philosophical," the California journalist and essayist told Dreiser, apparently never having read *Hey Rub-A-Dub-Dub.* Like most literary men going back to Whitman if not Emerson, Dreiser was not always lucid outside the magical realm of literature. There are parts of the posthumously published *Notes on Life* that sink to near gibberish.[47] Overall, he probably succeeded in providing a coherent summary of the mechanistic theory at work in his time. Whatever literary energy and imagination he now had left was almost totally devoted to these speculations. He thrived on Douglas's flattery and readily accepted an invitation to visit southern California for his health in February 1935—he attributed a recent illness to "some mysterious change which robbed me of 22 pounds."[48] After giving up his Ansonia suite and recuperating at Iroki, Dreiser spent the spring and most of the summer at Douglas's house in Los Angeles on South Westmoreland Avenue. The two were like lay brothers in an almost mystical pursuit, Douglas fully enlisted in Dreiser's open-ended exploration of science. In August Helen came out, and the couple took up temporary residence on Rosewood Avenue until the fall.

Once back in New York and at Iroki, he published an essay entitled "Mark the Double Twain" in an academic journal. It opposed Van Wyck Brooks's thesis that puritan America had stifled Mark Twain and tried to split him in two, the humorist who was forced always to stay within the confines of convention and the powerful pessimist who could only speak freely from the grave in such posthumous writings as *The Mysterious Stranger* (1916), *What Is Man?* (1917), and the *Autobiography* (1924). "The truth is," he concluded, "that Twain was *not* two people, but one—a gifted but partially dissuaded Genius who, in time, and by degrees changed into his natural self."[49] That November he hired the bright and breezy Harriet Bissell. Just out of Smith College, a petite blond, she answered his anonymous newspaper advertisement for a secretary at twenty-five dollars a week. It was the depth of the Depression in 1935, and she won out over dozens of other applicants, shortly after she was interviewed at Mt. Kisco. Harriet worked mainly at Iroki alongside Helen, who in the face of her Teddie's relentless philandering had begun to seek peace of mind in Buddhism and Christian Science, later suggesting the dénouement for Berenice's love affair with Cowperwood in *The Stoic*.

Dreiser was grief-stricken when he learned the following February of Douglas's sudden death by heart attack; he sent four dozen roses to the funeral. About the same time, however, another friend returned from a decade-long estrangement. Just as he had first appeared at the end of Dreiser's close friendship with Arthur Henry, H. L. Mencken now re-established himself in Dreiser's volatile life. Actually, their correspondence had resumed in the fall of 1934, when Dreiser wrote to Mencken to deny a rumor attributed to him on why the two had had their falling out. They had already spent an evening drinking together, and in 1935 Mencken had dissuaded Dreiser from being drafted into the National Institute of Arts and Letters by reminding him that his old nemesis Hamlin Garland was one of its "most eminent members."[50] In 1930 Mencken had married Sara Haardt, eighteen years his junior, but she was in poor health and died in 1935. By then Mencken was well adrift from the literary world, having given up the *American Mercury,* and was flourishing as a political correspondent. He had also drifted further to the right, or as far in that direction as Dreiser had strayed to the left. The Republican and the Communist now had little more in common than their past together, but that was apparently stronger than either of their current political leanings. As with the First World War, the returning storm clouds from Germany provided another basis for their renewed relationship, though the two writers would never be as close as they had been in the heyday of their dinners at Lüchow's.

In April of 1937, a twenty-two-year-old graduate student in English at Columbia University wrote to ask Dreiser to reconcile his recent activity as a reformer with his literary reputation as a determinist. Robert H. Elias had written his master's thesis on Dreiser and would eventually become his biographer. The answer he got might have easily discouraged Elias from choosing Dreiser as a topic for his Ph.D. dissertation at the University of Pennsylvania. While he sympathized with the weak whose suffering seemed undeserved, Dreiser told the graduate student: "I am forced to realize that the strong do rule 'the weak.' . . . When I take part in Communist activities and write *Tragic America,* I am still a determinist and still a helpless victim of my own feelings and sympathies."[51] Whether Dreiser realized it, he had effectively dodged the question. He never explains how one can honestly believe in reform and remain a determinist, only that as a determinist he also feels sorry for the weak. But then this is not an uncommon phenomenon in social thought. From Marx to Lenin and beyond, we have the belief in historical determinism alongside the contradictory idea that history can be directed.

Like many supporters of communism then and idealists in general, he held onto the Soviet dream even after it became evident that Stalin was killing his own people in a maniacal effort to make that dream come true. Four years earlier, Dreiser had rebuffed Max Eastman's request to voice public support for imprisoned Bolsheviks loyal to Trotsky. Dreiser was so interested "in the present difficulties in Russia and in Russia's general fate," he said, "that I am not prepared, without very serious consideration, to throw a monkey wrench such as this could prove to be, into their machinery." This allegiance to the socialist ideal had been set in stone with him almost since his visit to Russia. He told Kennell, shortly after returning, "while I am going to stick [in *Dreiser Looks at Russia*] to what I saw favorable and unfavorable I'm going to contrast it with the waste and extravagance and social indifference here."[52] When that waste and indifference changed to poverty in the Depression, he changed irrevocably into a communist.

———

With most of his books out of print, Dreiser had already begun his descent into literary oblivion. The joining of his name with that of the Communist Party of the United States plus his support of the Soviet Union hadn't helped his image much abroad or at home. It was one thing to be vaguely socialist—most writers of the era were—quite another to endorse the outcome of the Revolution in the Stalinist 1930s. The next American to win the Nobel Prize was Eugene O'Neill in 1936, who felt he had stolen the award from his friend and former associate at the *Spectator*. He said as much in the press, reflecting the American bitterness over the 1930 decision. Privately, O'Neill told Dreiser: "I can say to you with entire sincerity and truth . . . that I would take a great deal more satisfaction in this prize if you were among those who had had it before me." Upon receiving the award in 1950, William Faulkner was even more emphatic, initially refusing to go to Stockholm in part because the judges had "passed over Dreiser and Sherwood Anderson to reward a writer like Sinclair Lewis and Old China Hand Buck."[53] Faulkner might have added that the Swedes had earlier ignored Mark Twain and Henry James.

No Pulitzer Prizes had ever come Dreiser's way either, but this couldn't have surprised anyone, since it was then given "for the American novel . . . which shall present the wholesome atmosphere of American life, and the highest standards of American manners and manhood." Sinclair Lewis had declined it in 1926, stating that such standards allowed censorship of great literature (but mainly because the Pulitzer judges had ignored their committee's selection of *Main Street* in 1921).[54] Dreiser was becoming almost exclusively a political commodity. Yet early in 1938 Longmans, Green, and Company offered him $500 to present Thoreau in its Living Thoughts series. He needed the money, but it was also an honor—one of the last the novelist received in recognition of his work—since others who agreed to do such books were André Gide (Montaigne), Julian Huxley (Darwin), John Dewey (Jefferson) and Edgar Lee Masters (Emerson). Dreiser spent the money before doing any work on the project.

Before he could get down to work, he was invited to attend a peace conference in Paris that summer with all expenses paid. It was hosted by the League of American Writers and was to focus on the current problems in Spain. The League was also taking part that week in the World Conference for Peace Actions and Against Bombing Open Towns. The previous summer General Franco had further seeded the developing European storm clouds by casting Spain into a civil war between Fascists and Loyalists. Franco received the support of Germany and Italy, while the socialist-minded Loyalists were backed by France's Popular Front government of Léon Blum and the Soviet Union. The Soviet interest might have been argument enough for Dreiser to attend. He crossed on the *Normandie,* where he met the sister of Jack Powys, Marian, on the boat. She and her son were on their way to visit Jack in his new home in Wales and urged Dreiser to visit there on his way back to the United States.

"Here is the first result to the trip 4 addresses so far. Plenty of publicity for the Loyalists," he told Marguerite Tjader, with whom he had been staying that summer in Noroton, Connecticut. (For the last two years, he and Helen had been living apart for long stretches. Marguerite had divorced her husband, Overton Harris, in 1933.) He added that his speech in Paris, to the more than one thousand delegates at the World Conference for Peace, had been a success and that Marguerite should print it in her little magazine called *Direction.* Actually, his speech had been moved to last on the program after he voiced his objections publicly that the conference, far from being a progressive attempt to aid Spain and end the bombing of open towns, was in fact a move to win popular support for England's position of neutrality in the face of Hitler's saber rattling. As it turned out, the French socialist government ultimately gave in to British pressure and abandoned Spain, and Russia was too far away to effectively aid the Loyalists. By 1939 Spain belonged to Franco and the Fascists.[55]

Dreiser's speech was given full space in the Paris newspapers, but it received no notice whatever from the heads of the World Conference, who did not ask him to speak again. Undaunted, Dreiser headed to Spain to see things for himself. He was anxious to get out of Paris anyway. "It's not that Paris isn't interesting but I've seen it before & it hasn't changed very much," he told Harriet Bissell. He was also suffering from insomnia, and his morning depressions were "stupendous." (Dreiser's pessimistic moods usually cleared by noon.) When he reached Barcelona in early August he told her: "I am here in a dangerous atmosphere. They are expecting a big push from Franco & more intense bombings every hour." He dined with the heads of the Loyalists and took away from them a proposition for President Roosevelt. A few days later he was in London, seeking out government officials who might be sympathetic to Spain, but he found the British bureaucracy overwhelming. He told Harriet that he was "going [to] run up to Corwen, in Wales to see Jack & his brother Theodore," who was also a novelist.[56]

No writer was more devoted to Dreiser than John Cowper Powys, who after many years of living in America had returned to England and finally settled back into what he considered his ancestral home in Wales. He had even praised *Tragic America,* while at the same time admitting that he paid little attention to politics. Dreiser felt the same toward Jack. When Dreiser first came to visit Marguerite Tjader in 1928, she pulled from her bookshelves a recently published volume of poetry by Powys, which she praised, assuming that Dreiser had never heard of its author. "It was then," she later wrote, "that Dreiser uttered the word *Jack* in such a tone that I could sense his affection even before he began to tell me about their deep friendship." Powys was "living as simply as any retired Welsh farmer," Marguerite learned from Dreiser following his visit to Corwen. "His luxury was the long walk which he took each day. . . . Usually wrapped in a rough greatcoat or tweed cape, Powys was the unforgettable figure he had always been to Dreiser. Their walks together, at various times in the past, as now, partook of the nature of some earthy, pagan or mystic rite."[57]

Before leaving England to return to the States in mid-August, Dreiser visited Reading Gaol, where Oscar Wilde had been imprisoned for two years for the crime of sodomy. Inside cell C.3.3, he wrote a poem, which he sent to Marguerite:

> Tie your spirit to a sail
> Call for sky and wind
> Fly in mood to Reading Gaol
> To a cell bound mind
>
> Write a message on a wall
> To a heart that died:
> "Yet this day shalt thou with me
> In Paradise abide."

For years he had been interested in homosexuality as yet another example of the belief that man did not make himself. Before long he would become something of an activist on the issue, writing on behalf of a man sentenced to fifteen years in San Quentin for a homosexual offense. "As I understand it," he told the California Board of Prison Terms and Pardons in 1940, "[X] is a creative artist of considerable ability. . . . The failure to cure a man of an abnormality with which he was born was proved beyond a doubt in the case of Oscar Wilde,—and to destroy the man is to destroy the artist. . . . Even conservative England only gave Wilde 2 years."[58]

Once back in New York, Dreiser turned to the Thoreau project, over which he had both procrastinated and worried aloud in letters back to Harriet. Scanning a volume a day of the complete works of Thoreau, she provided the basis for Dreiser's thirty-two-page introduction. Dreiser himself had read *Walden* years before, and indeed its ant scene may have inspired the short story of the pre–*Sister Carrie* era, "The Shining Slave Makers." Claiming to have read some 2.4 million words of Thoreau for the introduction and selection, he singled out Thoreau of all the New England transcendentalists, including Emerson, as being at least partially redeemed from their heady optimism because of his healthy skepticism and insistence on sticking with natural facts for their own sake as well as possible emblems of the Oversoul. Thoreau, he said, speaking for himself as well, was "forever knocking at the door of the mystery." He seems to have sensed some of the faint pessimism in *Walden* without having read of Thoreau's doubts expressed in *The Maine Woods* about nature's harsh or fickle treatment of man. Dreiser was still eating and sleeping nature, or science, himself, and this interest dovetailed nicely with Thoreau's activity as naturalist as well as transcendentalist. He concluded that any inconsistencies in Thoreau's thought counted "for nothing, because, as I see it, his *source* [nature] is inconsistent."[59]

Apparently, President Roosevelt saw no political contradictions in Dreiser's anticapitalistic stance (earlier he had advised FDR to close Henry Ford's factories if the auto maker did not allow collective bargaining) and his request for a personal interview on the matter of the Loyalists in Spain, whose proposal he had brought back with him. Dreiser conveyed their plan for Roosevelt to help them as quietly as he was assisting Great Britain, despite the restraints of the Neutrality Act of 1937. As he told Helen, the Spaniards wanted the president "to do certain things for women & children . . . which he can do without publicity of any kind." After some initial confusion—or procrastination by reluctant staff members in the office of the Assistant Secretary of State—Dreiser, whose FBI file thickened by the year, was invited to dine with the president on September 7 aboard his yacht on the Hudson River. There it was decided that Dreiser would attempt to form a committee of prominent citizens to organize donations of food and medicine to the Loyalists, thereby circumventing the restrictions of the law against the U.S. government's active involvement in the growing crisis in Europe. As he had with the committee of prominent citizens for the Harlan coal miners, however, to his great disappointment he failed here, too, no doubt because of his growing reputation as a communist as well as—it now appeared—a political crank. Roosevelt, who had probably read either *Sister Carrie* or *An American Tragedy* and was therefore impressed and somewhat softened politically toward Dreiser because of his literary achievements, subsequently formed the committee himself and sent flour to Spain.[60]

Strange bedfellows these two—Roosevelt and Dreiser. One, who followed his second cousin to the White House, was considered a "second-rate intellect" but a world-class political strategist, while the other was the son of poverty and heir to nothing more than his own genius, a light now largely gone out. TD, as many of his lovers called him, was closer in temperament and intellect to TR than FDR; in fact, he had twice visited that earlier White House as chief editor of the *Delineator*. With TR in 1908, the subject had been the Child Rescue Program; thirty years later with FDR, it was a rescue of a different order. One wonders whether TR, one of America's best-read presidents, ever perused *Sister Carrie* the way he read Edwin Arlington Robinson's poems. This had led him to give Robinson a government sinecure in the New York Custom House in 1902, the same year Dreiser had wandered the streets of Philadelphia. Now the author of *Sister Carrie* found himself wandering once again.

"One comes into life a driven mechanism," he had once told an admirer of *The "Genius."* By this time his relationship with Simon and Schuster was going definitely sour. For one thing, the firm had remaindered the books purchased from the bankrupt Liveright, Inc. For another, Dreiser had not finished *The Stoic*. Since 1936 he had been renting out Iroki at various times and seeking to sell the cabins and their thirty-six acres for $65,000, more than twice what he had paid for it. He soon had a buyer on time for a lower price, perhaps $40,000, but the deal fell through because of the coming war. He had been "a dunce" to buy it in the first place, he now thought. "I soon found I didn't like the climate," he told his last lover, Hazel Mack Godwin, three years later. "Also being a rich man's region every form of service was high."[61]

With Iroki still unsold and the continued financial burden of its upkeep, Dreiser thought of returning to California. In the end, he rather backed into moving there permanently at the end of 1938. Because of his continued emotional involvements with other women, Helen was on another extended visit to her mother in Portland. He left New York for Portland in a Thanksgiving blizzard and eventually wound up with Helen in Glendale, California, where he established the first of his final residences in that state. There, he told Louise Campbell, the sun blazed up to ninety-two degrees and the "gold-leaved trees in tiger-tan mountain canyons greeted my eyes!"[62]

SIXTEEN

Facing West

*For the first two years or more it did not make any difference
to me that there was very little doing intellectually in Los Angeles—
or I might say in Southern California. I was lost in contemplating
the velvety brown mountains, the amazing flowers and the relaxed mood
in which every one took the perpetual and to me stimulating and
restoring sunshine. As a matter of fact, I owe Southern California
a debt—a romantic one to be sure, but nevertheless
one that I shall never be able to pay.*

DREISER TO GEORGE DOUGLAS, AUGUST 14, 1929

AS AMERICA INCHED CLOSER TO WAR, Dreiser warmed himself once again in the California sun. Instead of working on *The Bulwark,* now a couple of years overdue at Simon and Schuster, he dived back into his scientific studies, embarking this time on a quest that was decidedly religious. Perhaps like Melville at the end of his life in *Billy Budd,* this last American titan struggled to reconcile good and evil in the world. For Dreiser was the last great American writer of Melvillean dimensions who had been born in an essentialist world and grown up with the crosscurrents of Darwinism. Dreiser's ultimate testament of acceptance, lately quickened by his conversion to communism, would be found in Quakerism (which he would celebrate in *The Bulwark* as possibly a substitute for his father's Catholicism). Writing to an admirer who had heard him speak at Whittier College in January 1939 and asked rhetorically whether it wasn't "a tremendous thrill to know God occasionally," he reminded her that man's vision of God was severely limited and obscure. His entire talk, he said, "had been intended to convey the idea that the enormous revelations of Science in regard to nature indicate a necessary balancing of forces that at one point of man's limited grasp appear evil and at another point good." Life, he continued, required both. Ultimately, though, "no intentional evil or cruelty can be attributed to *the creative force* or God."[1]

In a way, Dreiser was becoming something of a latter-day transcendentalist. In a 1938 essay, he had argued as well that all nature was both good and evil. Man needed evil in this balancing act called life the way doctors needed disease; therefore, the distinction between good and evil was meaningless. "You might even say," he concluded, "that evil is that which makes good possible." Or as Emerson once stated, evil was merely "privative" or relative. Yet the determinist had the last word. "Be glad," Dreiser wrote, "if for the present you are not [evil's] victim."[2] Even though God's plan was all beauty in its grand scope, man's specific welfare in this creation was entirely expendable.

In February of 1939 he gave more lectures on the same general subject, mainly to women's clubs in Oakland, San Francisco, Portland, Salt Lake City, and elsewhere, earning almost $1,500 after commissions and travel expenses. In an interview he gave the evening before speaking at the San Francisco Town Hall Forum, he named John Steinbeck, Erskine Caldwell, and William Faulkner as the younger American writers he most admired because they "reported" the world "directly and forcefully and sensitively."[3] As fatigued as he might have been after relocating his residence across a continent, he pushed himself into lecture after lecture because he felt he needed the money. He may have, for he was $2,000 in arrears in alimony payments to Jug, who was still living in the Village in New York. It wasn't long, however, before he sold to Hollywood through his agents Will Lengel and Donald Friede screenplays based on *Sister Carrie* and "My Brother Paul" of *Twelve Men.* These became *Carrie,* featuring Laurence Olivier in his first important role as Hurstwood, and *My Gal Sal,* starring another rising actor, Victor Mature, as Paul Dresser.

Dreiser's first apartment on his return to California was located at 253A West Loraine Street in Glendale, but it was not only too small but too far from the studios. In May he and Helen moved to another apartment at 1426 North Hayworth Avenue in West Hollywood, just north of Sunset Boulevard. He told Edgar Lee Masters that he was now "within ten or fifteen minutes (by car) of the big barns." As in the early twenties, when they had occupied seven different residences in Southern California, the magnet was Hollywood. This time the novelist turned out to be a successful "screenwriter," selling his two literary properties for almost $100,000. Dreiser would sell one more novel, posthumously. *An American Tragedy* made a second film comeback as *A Place in the Sun* in 1951. Sometime in the early forties he met Elizabeth Taylor, whose family had relocated from London to escape the war. "Wouldn't it be wonderful," he told the child actress, who would star in *A Place in the Sun* opposite Montgomery Clift, "if you would act in one of my pictures some day?" Earlier, he had beseeched an ailing John Barrymore to act in what would become *Carrie*. "Don't die. Live to present Hurstwood for me. I have, for so long, thought of *you* treading—in . . . his sorrowful way."[4] But Barrymore was making his last stage appearance in Chicago and would die in 1942.

Dreiser was still in the Glendale house when the columnist Arthur Millier interviewed him for the *Los Angeles Times* of March 12, 1939. During most of the interview, Dreiser stewed over the way Hollywood mangled literary works, even as he profited from their desecrations. Millier described Dreiser as "white-haired, tall, erect, rangy, discreetly paunched." Dreiser offered his guest a chair and then retreated to "a small rocker for himself and rocked, rocked, rocked." As he did so, he "picked from a neat pile on the table the first of some 20 paper handkerchiefs which, throughout the interview, he twisted, untwisted, and folded." Millier described Dreiser's accent as "pungent city editor's American." He was wearing his trademark small bow tie—"of the sort college boys and drummers wore about 1912." By now Dreiser was almost forgotten as a writer. Even though his works were being made into movies, he complained that the producers' and directors' names were plastered all over the films, while the credits featuring the author's name in much smaller letters rolled by in an instant. Bucking the popular view, the interviewer predicted that Dreiser's "novels will be read when most 20th century American fiction is forgotten."

In December 1940 he used part of the profits from the movie to be based on *Sister Carrie* to purchase a Spanish-style home at 1015 North Kings Road (today replaced by a Spanish-style apartment building). Southern California in those days was still a reasonably priced place to live, but even so Dreiser had to pay $20,000 for the modest six-room house on a spacious lot. His first novel and masterpiece, which had once rendered him almost homeless, now provided for his last sanctuary. He furnished the new house, only seven blocks west of his previous residence, with items that had been stored at Mt. Kisco, including his writing desk made out of Paul's rosewood piano. (That year Dreiser lost another brother with the passing of Rome, who managed in spite of his bad living habits to reach the age of eighty.) After Iroki's strange shapes, this house—only the second he ever owned—seemed more conventionally appointed. Its white stucco was offset with awnings of deep orange and its banana palms were encircled with neat flower beds. As Marguerite Tjader remembered it, the house "was one-storied, except for a square tower-room which rose beside a Moorish-style archway, leading to a matching stucco garage." In the back there was a small pond shadowed by two avocado trees.[5]

By now Germany and Russia had signed a nonaggression treaty. This kept Dreiser's sentiments vaguely on the side of Germany and against Great Britain, which he blamed for getting the Americans to fight the Germans in the last war; it also made him an ally of the America First movement, spearheaded by Charles Lindbergh. Americans in general had no appetite for another European war. The first one had been a great disappointment; certainly it had not been the war—in the words of President Woodrow Wilson—"to make the world safe for democracy." High-profile novels such as Hemingway's *A Farewell to Arms* (1929) and Remarque's *All Quiet on the Western Front* (1929) were decidedly antiwar. What was not addressed, however, was the fact that the First World War had been left largely unfinished, with Germany again poised for combat. Yet as long as Germany did not attack his cherished Soviet Union, Dreiser wanted the United States to continue its isolationist policies. He resented Roosevelt's "personal animosity toward Hitler," and told Mencken, who detested FDR for his New Deal policies: "I begin to suspect that Hitler is correct. The President may be part Jewish." While visiting Washington, D.C., that November he delivered a radio address on behalf of the American Peace Mobilization in which he accused England of conspiring to get Hitler to attack Russia.[6]

As Roosevelt tried to prepare the American people for the possibility of intervention in the war that fall, Dreiser threw together another political screed swelling with statistics and half-truths (about British atrocities and the success of the Soviet state). Published in January 1941, *America Is Worth Saving* (changed at the last minute from "Is America Worth Saving?" and partially ghost-written) mainly unleashed all of Dreiser's pent-up hatred for the British. As German bombs fell on England, he claimed to see no difference between the two countries ("Hitlerdum and Hitlerdee") and urged that the United States pay more attention to its own social problems at home. Like *Tragic America,* this book was another "long soap-box speech" mainly inspired by the author's conversion to communism. Its thesis is best summed up by the review in the *New York Herald Tribune* of February 2, 1941. Modern technology has brought the fruits of democracy closer to the common man than ever before. (This was the "Technocracy" message of Howard Scott, whose economic theories had fascinated Dreiser since his days among what Mencken called the "Red ink" fraternity in Greenwich

Village.) England with "a branch office" in America, however, had prevented this economic revolution by artificially restricting production except in times of war. "Then, production zooms, war profits pile up, and the innocent millions go to the slaughter. The present war in Europe is primarily a repetition of the last one except that this time the British bungled things badly at the start when the hoped-for Russo-German conflict failed to materialize." The *New York Times* lamented the "death" of the author of *Sister Carrie* and suggested that his latest book offered aid and comfort to the enemy.[7]

Dreiser's heart was in the right place, but not his head. Ever since Winston Churchill, whom Dreiser met in England on his way back from Russia, had predicted that Soviet Communism would inevitably fail, he had been down on the British as natural enemies of the new Russia. He wanted social justice worldwide, on the scale he imagined the Soviet utopia was already attaining, and he sincerely came to believe that capitalism (at least in its current application) was the enemy of democracy. But as the leftist critic Granville Hicks pointed out in a review that tried its best to be sympathetic, Dreiser's position was "simply that British imperialism is even worse than Hitler fascism and therefore we must not take sides."[8] Behind this America First campaign, for which the book was only the latest American argument, lay of course a pro-German but not pro-Hitler attitude. Millions of German-Americans had not forgotten how they had been discriminated against during the First World War and how afterward Germany had suffered so under the weight of war reparations demanded by the British and their allies.

It was this visceral if also subliminal need to avenge the German people as well as his new-found love of the Soviet Union that led Dreiser to pile on the insults to Great Britain, so much so that the FBI secretly recommended him for "custodial detention in the event of a national emergency."[9] He lost friends over the book as well. Otto Kyllmann, an old acquaintance and the head of Constable and Company, Dreiser's British publisher, was so aghast at the attack on his country that he wrote two letters of protest in the summer of 1941. In the first he said he had not read *America Is Worth Saving* through, but he had read enough "to horrify me." "That you of all people my dear Dreiser," he continued in the second, "could feel & write and publish at this time such heartless & callous words about us was just more than I could bear."

Dreiser was obviously pained by Kyllmann's response but not penitent about his book. He was touched, he said, from "the personal viewpoint," but confessed that he was now politically a Bolshevik—a "'Fifth Columnist' or 'Red,' or what you will, for I believe heart and soul in the value and probable successful outcome of the great Soviet or Communistic system or experiment." He was not against the English people, "the English rank and file," but only its "Lords and Ladies and financiers" who had brought on the First World War in order to get Germany to crush the Soviet Union and its worldwide crusade for communism. Ludicrously, he closed by telling his ex-friend: "You need not publish any more of my books." Earlier, Will Lengel, who was acting as Dreiser's agent for *America Is Worth Saving*, wondered whether "it is really necessary for you to be so hard on the English so as to injure your own publishing relations in Great Britain." Dreiser replied, "Don't worry about my English publishers. The war seems to have finished them."[10]

By the time of Kyllmann's letters, however, the thesis of the book was already moot, for on June 22 the Germans broke their pact by invading Russia. Dreiser continued to hate the British aristocrats, telling a correspondent: "I mistrust England as much as I mistrust Hitler." But he loved the Russians more and now stood up for the American intervention in Europe.[11] Yet Dreiser's shelf life as a political radical wouldn't last much longer, at least not at the same level it had between the bookends of *Tragic America* and *America Is Worth Saving*. In fact, one more incident would pretty much bring about his retirement. He had been dedicated to this public life since Russia, even more intensely once he had lost the Nobel Prize and perhaps given up literature because of it. There was nothing an old friend like Kyllmann could say to dissuade him. Neither could the pleading of another old friend and writer to return to storytelling affect him. Sherwood Anderson had died trying on March 8, 1941. Dreiser sent his tribute, which was read at the memorial in Marion, Ohio. "Anderson, his life and his writings, epitomize for me," he wrote, "the pilgrimage of a poet and dreamer across this limited stage called Life."[12] Just as Dreiser had thought the short story or sketch was Anderson's strong suit over the novel, Anderson had thought writing about life instead of living it was Dreiser's.

———

That fall he used more of his movie profits to buy himself out of the contract with Simon and Schuster. He had been unhappy with the firm, even thinking that the Jewish publishers may have thought him anti-Semitic and now wished to quietly suppress his books. "This constant undercover talk about my anti-Judaism," which he characterized in a 1939 letter to Lengel as the result of "the mild correspondence" he had had with Hapgood, "has caused all sorts of people who are inimical to me—writers and what not—to not only play this up but exaggerate it in every quarter." For $8,500, he was now free to accept an offer from Putnam's, where once again the possibility of publishing a uniform edition of his books was dangled before him. *The Bulwark* was promised by June 1, 1942. That Christmas, Mencken hoped that Dreiser had got through the holiday "without too much misery." The Japanese attack on Pearl Harbor on December 7 hadn't helped. A week later Dreiser told Louise Campbell, "Everybody seems to be expecting the sudden arrival of a thousand Jap planes that will level L.A., San Francisco, Portland, Seattle & points North. Helen is stewing about her poor mother in case they blow up her house." Yet he closed on a lighter note, saying he had "defense work here on my own desk . . . to defend myself against rising taxes by turning out more so-called literature."[13]

Americans were now fully committed to war, both in Europe and the Pacific. Dreiser was primarily interested in the Pacific front as well as aid to Russia, not the "'hands across the sea' stuff" that brought supplies to England. This was unfortunately still his state of mind when he accepted an invitation to speak at another town forum—this time in Toronto on September 21, 1942. Since March Dreiser had been conducting a personal correspondence with Hazel Mack Godwin, an American living in Toronto who had first written him a fan letter back in 1936. Between 1942 and 1945 he wrote this fortyish housewife over two hundred letters in which he frequently fantasized about their lovemaking. She had paid him a visit at his expense in Los Angeles that summer. Leaving Helen alone at the North Kings place, he stayed with Hazel in the Hotel Mayfair at Seventh and Witmar in Los Angeles for at least two nights, possibly longer.[14]

The speech Dreiser was supposed to make in Toronto on September 21 was entitled "Democracy on the Offensive," but he never gave it because of remarks about the British he casually made to the press the day before. "Should Russia go down to defeat," he told a reporter from the *Toronto Evening Telegram,* perhaps thinking it was off the record, "I hope the Germans invade England. I would rather see Germans in England than those damn, aristocratic, horse-riding snobs there now." He went on to accuse the British of failing to open a second front in the war to aid Russia. Instead, Churchill "does nothing except send thousands of Canadians to be slaughtered."[15] When these provocative statements were published the next day, the lecture was immediately canceled, and Canadian authorities even considered detaining Dreiser, if only "for his own protection." One Toronto politico suggested that he should "be thrown into the North Sea."

Dreiser and Hazel quickly boarded a train for the United States, where their first stop was Port Huron, Michigan. Following the blowout in Toronto, he had refused to give further statements to the press. But here reporters caught up with him and "Mrs. Dreiser"—even staking out his hotel room, where Dreiser had registered as "T. H. Dresser." Unlike the vigil of strike opponents in Harlan, Kentucky, the interest here was not with the woman in his room (incredibly, never assumed by the press to be anybody but Dreiser's wife), but with his political statements. After a telephone interview failed (Hazel responding, "Is Mr. Dreiser in town? . . . I'd certainly like to meet him"), reporters for the *Port Huron Times Herald* interviewed the elusive author on a street corner. The result in the next day's newspaper was a front-page photograph of a sullen Dreiser under the heading "Second American Tragedy." His hands were thrust into his suit coat pockets as he posed defiantly. Although he later made a weak attempt to backpedal, he now essentially repeated his statements about the British and America's Lend-Lease program, saying additionally that the "English have done nothing in this war thus far except borrow money, planes and men from the United States. They stay home and do nothing. They are lousy."[16]

Since it was wartime, no one seemed to mind that Dreiser had been denied his freedom of speech in Toronto. In New York, the Writer's War Board, consisting of such authors and critics as Rex Stout, Pearl Buck (who won the Nobel Prize in 1938), Franklin P. Adams (an old foe of Dreiser's who had accused him of plagiarism), and Clifton Fadiman (whom Dreiser had known at Simon and Schuster), issued a statement expressing regret that "an American writer of Mr. Dreiser's eminence should thus insult and offend our Allies. . . . Certainly our enemies would pay him well for his disservice to our country's cause." Many newspapers seconded this opinion. Even Dreiser's old employer, the *St. Louis Globe-Democrat,* piled on with an editorial entitled "Dunder-Headed Talk." While the forty-three-year-old former antiwar novelist Ernest Hemingway bathed in the limelight of the press for announcing his plans to somehow get himself into the war in Europe, the seventy-one-year-old writer who had broken the ground for Hemingway's realism was described as that "hulking U.S. Novelist" who had once again given aid and comfort to the enemy. Only George Bernard Shaw came to his support: "Although the English do not know their own history, . . .

Dreiser evidently knows it and reacts explosively when we pose as Herren-volk exactly as Hitler does." There was nothing to fuss about as long as Dreiser was "soundly determined to see Adolf Hitler damned first." Dreiser promptly thanked the Irishman "for the kindly life-line to the presumably drowning critic of dear old England."[17]

Dreiser's return to California involved a stayover in Chicago, where he re-covered from another bout of bronchitis. By the time he got back home, Jug had died—on October 1—at the age of seventy-three in St. Louis. There is no record of Dreiser's reaction, though it is known that he was paid up on her alimony at the time. Once, more than twenty years earlier, she had asked a friend whom she hadn't seen in years: "Are you married! Or are you like me—Never Again!" This fairly sums up her life after her twelve years with the author of *Sister Carrie* and *Jennie Gerhardt,* two books she had helped to edit. She had endured the early death of her sister Rose, and her brother Dick had been badly injured on a naval exercise. Although she had become "Aunt Jug" to Ed Dreiser's family, she probably went to her grave somewhat embittered about her only husband. When the biographer Robert H. Elias asked her for information in 1939, she wrote: "I am sorry, but I can not oblige you by talking about my life with Mr. Dreiser. Altho I've been asked by many others, I have talked to no one." For Dreiser's part, he felt he had treated her fairly, paying her alimony off and on for more than thirty years.[18]

Upon Teddie's return, Helen observed that he was "noticeably quiet. The trip east with its accompanying notoriety [though she apparently never read the report that he had been accompanied by 'Mrs. Dreiser'] had taken its toll in spite of his well developed immunity to criticism." With American involvement in the war getting into full swing and his bank account re-plenished by Hollywood, Dreiser eventually turned back to literature—to two projects that had been gestating for more than a quarter of a century. He turned first to *The Bulwark,* and by March of 1943 had completed or revised thirty-four chapters. At the same time he described *The Stoic* as "half done." He also planned to write a third volume of his memoirs, to be called "A Literary Apprenticeship," which was to have carried his autobiography through the first decade of the twentieth century. One problem, however, was that he was soon in need of another publisher. He had decided to bolt from Putnam's because the firm, waiting in vain for *The Bulwark,* had failed to even begin to publish a uniform edition of his books. He told Mencken he was looking for another publisher who would cover Putnam's $2,000 advance on the "complete works" as well as another $1,000 advance on *The Bulwark.*[19] Ironically, the search led him full circle back to Doubleday, the publishing house that had first started him down his rocky road to literary fame.

The Bulwark ultimately shows faint signs of the old Dreiser magic at telling a story, but the plot in the first forty-two chapters, or half the book, is too linear and rushed in its unfolding—ultimately the result of the work of Doubleday's editor, Donald Elder.[20] Instead of developing the root causes of this Quaker Tragedy, the chapters merely flesh out the plot as prelude to the tragic denouement in which a Quaker family's spirituality is finally crushed by materialism and the modern age. Its patriarch, Solon Barnes, is partially an incarnation of John Paul Dreiser, in that he sees everything in terms of divine order and tries unsuccessfully to insulate his five children from the temptations of a material world. Isobel, homely like Marguerite in "The 'Mercy' of God," becomes disillusioned in her spinsterhood. Orville and Dorothea grow up like Clyde's cousins to become greedy consumers who value society over individual merit. In other shades of *An American Tragedy,* Stewart gets into trouble while joyriding in an automobile. Etta goes the way of so many of Dreiser's devotees of beauty and romance in *A Gallery of Women.*

Originally, Dreiser had planned to present Barnes as the disillusioned re-ligionist: "The good man," as Edgar Lee Masters recalled upon first hear-ing of the book upon meeting Dreiser in 1913, "who loved God and kept his commandments, and for a time prospered and then went into disaster." But by the time Dreiser turned back to the project in the early forties, he had—in the words of a close friend—"no interest in novels" and had also undergone something of a religious conversion himself.[21] Indeed, the rea-son for his return to fiction after more than fifteen years was not artistic at all. He did so in order to enshrine his newly awakened religious sentiment. He endowed his latest fictional creations with the transcendentalist belief that in spite of all the adversity life had to offer there lay behind it a struc-ture and divine plan if one could only see it. This was not altogether a new idea in Dreiser's thinking, of course. He had allowed the existence of such religious figures in *Jennie Gerhardt* and *An American Tragedy* (in the case of the Rev. McMillan). Furthermore, as an inoculated Catholic, he was always alert to the duality of life in which man was an insignificant part until he surrendered himself to the mystery of a universe and envisioned its ultimate order and purpose.

What was now "new" was Dreiser's affirmation, not only in *The Bulwark* but in *The Stoic,* of the unity and plan of "the Creative Force" that was working through us. In the big picture of Dreiser's literary career, it wasn't a radical change but (to quote Richard Lehan) a shifting of "the magnifying glass . . . showing Spencer's realm of antithetical forces being absorbed—contradictions and all—within Thoreau's oversoul—that is, on a transcendental level of beauty and order."[22] That little editing job for which Harriet Bissell had done most of the reading probably turned out to be a catalyst in Dreiser's final development as a writer and a thinker.

There is something of a parallel, of course, between transcendentalism and the Inner Light of Quakerism. Emerson was one of Dreiser's heroes, and Elias Hicks was another. "The religion that appeals to me as the most reasonable of all religions," he had told an interviewer in 1927, "is that interpreted and taught by Elias Hicks, a Quaker. Hicks believed [like Emerson] that every individual must have his own revelation of the truth. He believed there was a divine instinct in every man, something that told him to sit still and listen." About the time that Dreiser was writing his introduction to the Thoreau selection, he discovered or perhaps became more acquainted with the life and writings of the Quaker John Woolman through a meeting with Rufus Jones. Dreiser had consulted Jones, who was then chair of the American Friends Service Committee, in his doomed efforts following his return from Spain and his meeting with President Roosevelt to form a committee of distinguished citizens to provide American relief for the Loyalists. After visiting Jones at his home on the Haverford College campus outside Philadelphia, Dreiser read at least one of his books on the history of the Friends as well as the Quaker's autobiographical writings. In December 1938, he told Jones (whose first name became that of the father of Solon Barnes in *The Bulwark*): "As you know I am very much interested in the Quaker ideal. Like yourself I rather feel that it is the direct road to— not so much a world religion as a world appreciation of the force that provides us all with this amazing experience called life."[23] In other words, the "Creative Force," a term Dreiser preferred to God because of the latter's association with the old ideology of sin and redemption he had initially absorbed as a Roman Catholic.

As noted earlier, the original story of *The Bulwark* had come from Anna

Tatum, his live-in lover following his return from Europe in 1912 (later a somewhat pathetic figure who had to hock her typewriter during the Depression). But the early life of Solon Barnes, which makes up Part I of the three-part novel, was based largely on the life of Rufus Jones himself. Part II consisted of a merging of three various drafts written over the years, and the last part was written in 1944 and 1945 with the help of Marguerite Tjader. Just as Ruth Kennell may have been Dreiser's conscience on Russia, Marguerite became his muse on religion as they edited *The Bulwark*. A pacifist, she had converted to Roman Catholicism in the 1930s.[24]

As finally published in 1946, *The Bulwark*, after racing rather woodenly over years and events, settles down to focus on Solon Barnes and his two youngest children, Stewart and Etta. Stewart is another Clyde, eager for the fruits of life, but also endowed with a conscience, which leads him to suicide when he is accused with other boys of causing the death of a young woman through the administration of a drug intended as an aphrodisiac. Etta, based on Anna Tatum (who had initially forbidden Dreiser from writing her story until her mother died),[25] leaves her Quaker home outside of Philadelphia to attend the University of Wisconsin. There she falls in with a liberated woman who had drawn her there and whose affection for Etta may be homosexual. This possibility, however, is not developed. Rather, Dreiser sends Etta on to New York, where she falls in love with an artist resembling himself in his early Greenwich Village days.

Ultimately cast off by this painter, Etta is ashamed to return home for Stewart's funeral. Fearful that her presence would only add to her parents' grief, she remains in the shadow of her past, much like the harlot in Paul Dresser's "Just Tell Them That You Saw Me." She finally comes home when her mother is dying and remains there to console her father. Barnes by now is a broken, disillusioned man. The diametric opposite of Frank Cowperwood, whom Dreiser would soon finish off, Solon cannot abide the dishonesty of the banking business to which he has devoted his professional life. Generally, he sees Quakers all around him giving in to American materialism. With the bulwark of his old morality gone, Solon eventually comes to see a larger truth in which the world's ills can be explained as part of a divine plan. One day he comes upon an insect "industriously nourishing itself" on a flower. "Why was this beautiful creature . . . compelled to feed upon another living creature, a beautiful flower?" he asks himself. The answer is that behind everything in nature both good and evil "there must be a Creative Divinity, and so a purpose, behind all of this variety and beauty and tragedy of life." Etta, too, shares in this conversion and at her father's funeral declares: "Oh, I am not crying for myself, or for Father—I am crying for *life*."[26]

Dreiser would apply a similar romantic paradigm to *The Stoic* (1947), which follows Cowperwood to London, where he tries and ultimately fails to control the finances of the city's Underground. This time, however, it was Helen who made her religious interests felt in a Dreiser novel. Indeed, one of Cowperwood's passing lovers in the final volume, Lorna Maris, is related to Frank the way Dreiser was to Helen. In Frank and Lorna's case, it was Frank's father and Lorna's grandfather who were siblings. (Dreiser's mother and Helen's grandmother, of course, were sisters.) But Helen also influenced Dreiser's sending Berenice Fleming, who is the final threat to Aileen Cowperwood, to India after Frank's death at sixty from Bright's Disease. There she studies the *Bhagavad Gita* and gives up the material world, ultimately returning to America to found a hospital for the indigent with money and valuables left to her by Cowperwood. Dreiser owned a copy of the Hindu Scripture, but he apparently didn't read in it deeply. Rather, it was Helen's interest in the subject, perhaps as a final attempt to live with Dreiser's infidelities, which went on almost to his death, that led to this particular denouement in the novel. Berenice can also now accept the fact of Cowperwood's sexual infidelities as part of the Divine Plan, something the *Bhagavad Gita,* which celebrates duty (including marital fidelity) along with other principles of self-control and the ultimate transcendence of material and sexual desires, wouldn't have sanctioned.[27]

And there was another woman who not only influenced one of Dreiser's texts but also inserted her own material into his oeuvre. In late December of 1943, he told Louise Campbell that he had a contract with *Esquire* to write six sketches about "Unworthy Characters." It turned out to be his "Black Sheep" series, which ran between October 1944 and March 1945— "amusing pictures of people who just weren't able to conform to social theories." He told Louise that the first, "Black Sheep No. One: Johnny" would be based on Rome, who "was a scream!" "And in that connection I've been thinking that you might have some character—male or female—who . . . might fit into the series." In other words, her writing would be published under Dreiser's name. The sketch would, like the others, earn $300, out of which he promised to pay Louise one third. As it turned out, she got only $50 for "Black Sheep No. Four: Ethelda," concerning a woman who uses up well-meaning beaux until her chances in life fade away with her looks. It is obvious that Dreiser touched up the portrait, for its style bears a resemblance to the sketches in *A Gallery of Women,* but *Esquire* no doubt would have published it untouched because it was in actuality buying Dreiser's name, not these generally banal stories.[28]

———

On January 4, 1944, Walter Damrosch, president of the American Academy of Arts and Letters, informed Dreiser that he was to receive its Award of Merit, given every five years. It was "not only for the distinction of such books as THE [*sic*] AMERICAN TRAGEDY, SISTER CARRIE, TWELVE MEN, and a long line of other volumes, but also for your courage and integrity in breaking trail as a pioneer in the presentation in fiction of real human beings and a real America." Evidently, Dreiser's literary oblivion was not complete, perhaps held off by Sinclair Lewis's repeated efforts to renominate him for the Nobel Prize. The award carried a $1,000 prize and travel expenses to New York in May for the ceremony, which would also honor S. S. McClure, Willa Cather, and the actor Paul Robeson. Mencken disapproved. "I hear that you are going to New York to be crowned with a laurel wreath by the American Academy of Arts and Letters. If this is true," he told Dreiser in March, "I can only deplore the fact that you are having any truck with that gang of quacks. Its members for many years were your principal defamers." He advised Dreiser to tell the Academy to stick the award "up their rainspouts."[29]

This time Dreiser did not take his old friend's advice, as he had almost a decade earlier in refusing membership in the National Institute of Arts and Letters, several of whose members had opposed *The "Genius."* Struggling off and on with *The Bulwark,* he needed some palpable recognition of his literary gifts, something to suggest that he could still write—and finish both *The Bulwark* and *The Stoic.* The honor also reactivated his lifelong plan for an edition of his collected works, now to carry an introduction by Richard Duffy. When he arrived in New York in May, Marguerite Tjader was shocked at his altered appearance. He seemed thinner and older. Once in his room at the Commodore Hotel, however, he pulled her to his side "with his old vibrant quality." At the same time, he was also full of the religious sentiment that had gone into *The Bulwark.* "Well, I believe in God, now—a Creative Force," he told her that afternoon in New York. He spoke of the summer of 1937 when he had visited Calvin Bridges at the Carnegie

Biological Laboratory in Cold Spring Harbor, New York. One afternoon after hours in a laboratory, he came into the sunshine and stooped over some yellow flowers to find the "same exquisite detail [he] had been seeing all day in the tiny organisms under the microscope."[30]

On this last visit to the city in which he had spent more than half his life, he met other old friends and family. Duffy, who had supported him in the days both before and after the publication of *Sister Carrie,* saw him. Dreiser also enjoyed a reunion with Edgar Lee Masters, who accompanied him to the awards ceremony. He spent time with his niece, Ed's daughter Vera. He greeted a number of other old friends in his hotel suite, including his second biographer, Robert H. Elias, but his planned reunion with Mencken, who was the first to tell Dreiser's life from the standpoint of his works, never came off because of the latter's illness. In another, more devastating disappointment, he said good-bye to Mame, his eldest sister, who was dying at age eighty-four. Austin Brennan had already preceded her. A Christian Scientist for many years, she told her brother at one of their last meetings: "Just think, Theodore. We can't even make a little blade of grass grow, without God." At Mame's funeral, he saw his brother Ed, who though only two years his junior now looked much younger than Dreiser.[31]

Before Dreiser boarded his train to Chicago and the West on June 5, he recorded two radio broadcasts for the Office of War Information, located just down the street from his old Fifty-Seventh Street apartment. He didn't know it, of course, but the occasion was just days before the D-Day invasion of France by Allied Forces. In spite of his FBI record or perhaps because of it, the OWI considered Dreiser somebody who could influence the German people. On one of the recordings he reminisced about his father who had left Mayen to avoid the militarism under Bismarck. He closed by saying, "Just as a try-out, let's have a few hundred years of the brotherhood of man!"[32] He also visited the Mt. Kisco house one last time; it had finally found a buyer.

He returned, not to Los Angeles, but to Portland. Helen had not accompanied him to New York because she had to visit her sick mother in the Northwest. Dreiser, fearing that Helen might not have full legal claim to his estate, had finally decided to marry her in a secret ceremony planned in Stevenson, fifty miles east of Portland. Yet on the way to the altar, he had conflicting thoughts. "I miss you so intensely!" he wrote Marguerite from Stevenson the day before the ceremony. "In fact the long slow trip— that 15-car train crowded with soldiers, their wives or girls, their noise and [blather] & drinking, was enough to drive me mad. For mentally and emotionally I was seeking to be back with you in the Commodore." When he married Helen on June 13, 1944, it was under the name of Herman Dreiser instead of his full name. Helen thought it was to avoid publicity.[33] It was.

Before he left New York, he had asked Marguerite to come out to California to help him finish *The Bulwark*. Helen had been acting as his latest secretary, but she reluctantly agreed to the idea once Marguerite had cautiously asked for her approval. She and her young son Hilary reached Hollywood in August 1944 just in time for Dreiser's seventy-third birthday. The guest list reached sixty persons and included two other old girlfriends, Lillian Rosenthal Goodman and Esther McCoy (now Mrs. Berkeley Tobey), both by then California residents. Clare Kummer, Arthur Henry's third wife, and her daughter from an earlier marriage, who were living in Northern California, also came to the celebration; Arthur had died in 1934.

Marguerite and her son took a small bungalow near the Dreiser residence. Dreiser spent most of the day there dictating the rest of the novel to her. Work was completed the following May, but the manuscript then underwent several changes. First it went to Louise Campbell back in Philadelphia, who thought it was a disaster as a literary work and also didn't like the heavy religious theme and so cut it severely. Elder at Doubleday (who had advanced Dreiser $4,000 on the novel) put back about half the material Campbell had excised.

The work left Dreiser physically exhausted until the summer when he took up *The Stoic* with Helen's assistance. *The Bulwark* had also left him emotionally exhausted. Helen noticed that whenever he spoke of Solon Barnes, his eyes filled up with tears. He was thinking not only of his father, she added dubiously, but "what he considered his own shortcomings." It was in this state of mind that he decided to become a member of the Communist Party. Most of those close to Dreiser went into denial over the decision, saying that it wasn't a political choice but a quasi-religious one in which he could somehow enter the realm of acceptance along with Solon Barnes. "Knowing that the final chapter of his life was approaching, and soon he would no longer be able to speak out against Fascism and inequity in the world," Helen recalled, "he felt that joining the Communist Party would safeguard his position on the side of the common man. But to say he was informed as to the political workings of the Party in this country would be a false statement." Mencken later branded Dreiser's membership in the Party as "an unimportant detail in his life."[34] Yet Dreiser considered himself a full-fledged communist and a "Bolshevik." His political activities since the early 1930s had clearly been in concert with ostensible communist aims with regard to the working class. And not long before he took up formal membership, he had received a check from the Soviet Union for the equivalent of $34,600 in back royalties.

In a letter to the recently installed head of the American Communist Party, William Z. Foster, which Dreiser approved if in fact he didn't altogether compose, he cited his reasons for joining the party. As Helen noted, besides his link with the common man, he thought that communists around the world had stood up to the evils of fascism. He also felt that as an artist he wasn't alone, citing the party memberships of Pablo Picasso of Spain, Louis Aragon of France, Martin Andersen Nexo of Denmark, and Sean O'Casey of Ireland. "Belief in the greatness and dignity of Man has been the guiding principle of my life and work. The logic of my life and work leads me therefore to apply for membership in the Communist Party."[35]

Dreiser may have also chosen to become a formal member of the party because of the harassment he had received from the FBI and what was to become the Congressional Committee for Un-American Activities. The latter was already looking askance at the movie industry for its alleged sympathies with communism. In Dreiser's day the Congressional committee was initially called the Dies Committee, after its chairman, Texas Congressman Martin Dies—who, oddly enough, was a distant relative of both Theodore's and Helen's (they of course being second cousins). In a further irony, the man who ultimately became Dreiser's literary executor following the deaths of Helen and her sister, Myrtle, was Harold Dies, a cousin of the Congressman's as well as Helen's. He and Helen had reestablished their relationship after Helen encountered him in Oregon when she was visiting her mother in the late 1930s. Harold Dies was a commissioned army officer during the Second World War and was stationed in Los Angeles. One day during a visit to the North Kings Road house, he was asked by Dreiser whether he went "along with that cousin of yours, Martin Dies." Harold assured Dreiser that he didn't, but he undercut some of that assurance when he cast doubt on the viability of democracy in the

Soviet Union. Indeed, Dies later remembered that his remarks provoked Dreiser "almost to the point of rage. He denied that there was any such condition and was so upset that Helen was afraid he might have a heart attack."[36]

There was nothing else left to do now but to finish off Cowperwood, whose capitalistic plundering Dreiser no longer admired. Since the financial empire of the real-life Yerkes had crumbled soon after his death, the task of showing how the equation of life cancels out Cowperwood's achievements was relatively easy. Actually, he hadn't really changed his mind about Cowperwood, for he had hinted at the end of *The Financier* (as well as *The Titan*) of his antihero's inevitable demise. Cowperwood was as much a pawn of fate—or now the Creative Force—as the commonest of men. Dreiser (and Helen) finished *The Stoic* by the middle of October 1945. Like some other early readers of the manuscript ultimately published in 1946, the novelist James T. Farrell, who had written his own trilogy about Studs Lonigan, thought that Dreiser's trilogy shouldn't end with Berenice's pilgrimage to India. He had other complaints while lavishing praise on the book in general. Dreiser was grateful and accepted most of his ideas for revision. He thanked the younger writer and poignantly confessed that he had "simply stopped writing at the end because I was tired."[37]

Dreiser died four days after writing to Farrell, on December 28, 1945, the delayed result of a heart attack the night before. It was exactly forty-seven years to the day of his marriage to Jug and forty years to the day after the death of the model for the man he had just killed off in *The Stoic,* Charles Tyson Yerkes. He was seventy-four years old and had complained of acute pain in his kidney the night before. During the afternoon of the 27th he had started to work on the final new chapter of *The Stoic.* Around five he and Helen drove down to the beach at the end of Washington Boulevard to watch the sunset. Strolling along the boardwalk, they came upon a hot dog stand run by a cheerful man who told them proudly of his five children. Dreiser remarked that he seemed grateful for so little. Upon their return to the North Kings Road house, he looked pale but insisted that Helen read him the penultimate chapter of *The Stoic,* which they had revised earlier in the day.

He complained of the kidney pain shortly before they retired. Helen was awakened in the middle of the night by Dreiser standing in the center of her bedroom in his nightgown. As she approached him, he collapsed to the floor in pain. A physician was summoned, and Dreiser was stabilized for the night. The next day he felt revived after receiving oxygen, but by late afternoon he was clearly dying, his semiconscious state cadenced by shallower and shallower breathing and his extremities turning blue. The physician returned to pronounce him dead at 6:50 P.M. Dreiser was buried in the Whispering Pines section of the sprawling Forest Lawn Memorial Park, northeast of his residence. In a final irony for the writer whose social protests were sounded from both within and without his literary works, his burial in this upscale cemetery was delayed until January 3 because of a grave diggers' strike.[38]

The funeral service at the Church of the Recessional, the cemetery chapel, mirrored the conflicted philosophy of Theodore Dreiser. It was jointly conducted by Dr. Allan Hunter of the Mt. Hollywood Congregational Church, where Teddie and Helen had occasionally attended services, and the playwright John Howard Lawson, who had once been hired to dramatize *Sister Carrie*. The Rev. Hunter spoke of Dreiser's fascination with the journal of John Woolman, while the progressive Lawson—soon to become one of the "Hollywood Ten" during the McCarthy hearings—reminded mourners that Dreiser had recently joined the Communist Party. All the while Dreiser lay serenely in his open coffin, with a countenance, Helen remembered, that seemed to comfort supporters on both sides of the debate. Perhaps like Pasquale Cutrone, the Italian immigrant in *An American Tragedy* who is the first man to precede Clyde on death row, Dreiser now knew "what's on the other side."[39]

Just before the coffin was closed, Helen, whose marriage to the deceased had been kept a secret until now, put in "To a Poet," her sonnet which spoke hopefully of having touched "the margin of your soul." It was inscribed on her gravestone ten years later when she was buried beside Dreiser. (Helen died of a stroke at age sixty, having spent the last three years of her life paralyzed from an earlier stroke.)[40] Charlie Chaplin, whom Dreiser had known since the twenties and had come to know more closely in the forties, read from Dreiser's poem "The Road I Came" and served as a pallbearer. In his autobiography, the famous comedian, who spoke in silence for the little man, described Dreiser as "a kindly soul" with "a burning indignation." The newspapers remembered him in their obituaries as the "great writer who didn't know how to write." "Between 1900 and the time of his death," the *New York Herald Tribune* observed, "he turned out more than a score of well-known novels and other books and, after each was published, critics agreed, in general, that the work was poorly written—but, still a good book, and, sometimes, a great book." The *New York Times* was more upbeat about the novelist who wrote "ungainly" prose. It quoted Mencken's earlier assessment as he "gazed from his Baltimore study across the country's literary wasteland" that Dreiser "stands isolated today, a figure weather-beaten and lonely, yet I can think of no other American novelist who seems so secure or so likely to endure."[41] Mencken, of course, had been a mixed blessing in Dreiser's literary life and—ultimately—in the making of his reputation today.

SELECTED WORKS OF THEODORE DREISER

NOVELS

Sister Carrie. New York: Doubleday, Page & Co., 1900.

Jennie Gerhardt. New York: Harper & Brothers, 1911.

The Financier. New York: Harper & Brothers, 1912; revised edition, New York: Boni & Liveright, 1927.

The Titan. New York: John Lane Company, 1914.

The "Genius." New York: John Lane Company, 1915; reissued, New York: Boni & Liveright, 1923.

An American Tragedy. New York: Boni & Liveright, 1925.

The Bulwark. New York: Doubleday & Company, 1946.

The Stoic. New York: Doubleday & Company, 1947.

SHORT STORIES AND SKETCHES

Free and Other Stories. New York: Boni & Liveright, 1918.

Twelve Men. New York: Boni & Liveright, 1919.

The Color of a Great City. New York: Boni & Liveright, 1923.

Chains. New York: Boni & Liveright, 1927.

A Gallery of Women. New York: Horace Liveright, 1929; 2 volumes.

POEMS

Moods: Cadenced and Declaimed. New York: Boni & Liveright, 1926 (limited edition of 550 signed copies).
Moods: Cadenced and Declaimed. New York: Boni & Liveright, 1928.
Moods: Philosophic and Emotional, Cadenced and Declaimed. New York: Simon and Schuster, 1935.

PLAYS

Plays of the Natural and the Supernatural. New York: John Lane Company, 1916.
The Hand of the Potter. New York: Boni & Liveright, 1919; revised edition, New York: Boni & Liveright, 1927.

TRAVEL BOOKS

A Traveler at Forty. New York: The Century Company, 1913.
A Hoosier Holiday. New York: John Lane Company, 1916.
Dreiser Looks at Russia. New York: Horace Liveright, 1928.

AUTOBIOGRAPHIES

A Book About Myself. New York: Boni & Liveright, 1922; reissued as *Newspaper Days,* New York: Horace Liveright, 1931.
Dawn. New York: Horace Liveright, 1931.
An Amateur Laborer, ed. Richard W. Dowell. Philadelphia: University of Pennsylvania Press, 1983.

POLITICAL AND PHILOSOPHICAL WRITINGS

Hey Rub-A-Dub-Dub: A Book of the Mystery and Wonder and Terror of Life. New York: Boni & Liveright, 1920.
Tragic America. New York: Horace Liveright, 1931.
America Is Worth Saving. New York: Modern Age Books, 1941.
Notes on Life, ed. Marguerite Tjader and John J. McAleer. University: University of Alabama Press, 1974.

Theodore Dreiser: A Selection of Uncollected Prose, ed. Donald Pizer. Detroit: Wayne State University Press, 1977.

Selected Magazine Articles of Theodore Dreiser: Life and Art in the American 1890s, ed. Yoshinobu Hakutani. Rutherford, N.J.: Fairleigh Dickinson University Press, 1985, 1987, 2 volumes.

Theodore Dreiser: Sister Carrie, Jennie Gerhardt, Twelve Men, ed. Richard Lehan. New York: Library of America, 1987.

Theodore Dreiser: Journalism; Newspaper Writings. 1892–1895, ed. T. D. Nostwich. Philadelphia: University of Pennsylvania Press, 1988.

Theodore Dreiser's Ev'ry Month, ed. Nancy Warner Barrineau. Athens: University of Georgia Press, 1996.

Collected Plays of Theodore Dreiser, ed. Keith Newlin and Frederic E. Rusch. Albany, N.Y.: Whitston Publishing Company, 2000.

Art, Music, and Literature, 1897–1902: Theodore Dreiser, ed. Yoshinobu Hakutani. Urbana: University of Illlinois Press, 2001.

Theodore Dreiser's Uncollected Magazine Articles, 1897–1902, ed. Yoshinobu Hakutani. Newark: University of Delaware Press, 2003.

LETTERS AND DIARIES

Letters of Theodore Dreiser, ed. Robert H. Elias. Philadelphia: University of Pennsylvania Press, 1959, 3 volumes.

Theodore Dreiser: American Diaries 1902–1926, ed. Thomas P. Riggio. Philadelphia: University of Pennsylvania Press, 1983.

Dreiser-Mencken Letters: The Correspondence of Theodore Dreiser and H. L. Mencken, ed. Thomas P. Riggio. Philadelphia: University of Pennsylvania Press, 1986, 2 volumes.

Dreiser's Russian Diary, ed. Thomas P. Riggio and James L. W. West III. Philadelphia: University of Pennsylvania Press, 1996.

ABBREVIATIONS

AD   *Theodore Dreiser: American Diaries 1902–1926,* ed. Thomas P. Riggio. Philadelphia: University of Pennsylvania Press, 1983.

AL   *An Amateur Laborer,* ed. Richard W. Dowell. Philadelphia: University of Pennsylvania Press, 1983.

AT   *An American Tragedy.* New York: Boni & Liveright, 1925.

CGC   *The Color of a Great City.* New York: Boni & Liveright, 1923.

Cornell   Carl A. Kroch Library, Cornell University.

CP   *Collected Plays of Theodore Dreiser,* ed. Keith Newlin and Frederic E. Rusch. Albany, N.Y.: Whitston Publishing Company, 2000.

D   *Dawn: An Autobiography of Early Youth,* ed. T. D. Nostwich. Santa Rosa, Calif.: Black Sparrow Press, 1998; originally published 1931.

DML   *Dreiser-Mencken Letters: The Correspondence of Theodore Dreiser and H. L. Mencken,* ed. Thomas P. Riggio. Philadelphia: University of Pennsylvania Press, 1986, 2 volumes.

DN   *Dreiser Newsletter.*

DRD   *Dreiser's Russian Diary,* ed. Thomas P. Riggio and James L. W. West III. Philadelphia: University of Pennsylvania Press, 1996.

DS   *Dreiser Studies.*

FF   Dorothy Dudley, *Forgotten Frontiers: Dreiser and the Land of the Free.* New York: Harrison Smith, 1932. Reprinted as *Dreiser and the*

	Land of the Free. New York: Beechhurst, 1946. Citations are to the 1932 edition.
Free	*Free and Other Stories.* New York: Boni & Liveright, 1918.
GW	*A Gallery of Women,* New York: Horace Liveright, 1929, 2 volumes.
Hey	*Hey Rub-A-Dub-Dub.* New York: Boni & Liveright, 1920.
HH	*A Hoosier Holiday.* New York: John Lane Company, 1916.
Indiana	Dreiser Papers, Lilly Library, Indiana University.
JG	*Jennie Gerhardt: The Pennsylvania Edition,* ed. James L. W. West III. Philadelphia: University of Pennsylvania Press, 1992; originally published 1911.
L	*Letters of Theodore Dreiser,* ed. Robert H. Elias. Philadelphia: University of Pennsylvania Press, 1959, 3 volumes.
ML	Helen [Richardson] Dreiser, *My Life with Dreiser.* Cleveland and New York: World Publishing Co., 1951.
ND	*Newspaper Days,* ed. T. D. Nostwich. Philadelphia: University of Pennsylvania Press, 1991; unabridged edition of the work originally published as *A Book About Myself,* 1922, and reissued as *Newspaper Days,* 1931.
Penn	Van Pelt-Dietrich Library, University of Pennsylvania.
SC	*Sister Carrie,* ed. Donald Pizer. New York: W. W. Norton, 1991; originally published, 1900.
SCP	*Sister Carrie: The Pennsylvania Edition*, ed. John C. Berkey and Alice M. Winters. Philadelphia: University of Pennsylvania Press, 1981.
SMA	*Selected Magazine Articles of Theodore Dreiser: Life and Art in the American 1890s,* ed. Yoshinobu Hakutani. Rutherford, N.J.: Fairleigh Dickinson University Press, 1985, 1987, 2 volumes.
TD	Theodore Dreiser.
TDCR	*Theodore Dreiser: The Critical Reception,* ed. Jack Salzman. New York: David Lewis, 1972.
TDEM	*Theodore Dreiser's "Ev'ry Month,"* ed. Nancy Warner Barrineau. Athens: University of Georgia Press, 1996.
TDJ	*Theodore Dreiser: Journalism; Newspaper Writings, 1892–1895,* ed. T. D. Nostwich. Philadelphia: University of Pennsylvania Press, 1988.
TDS	*Theodore Dreiser: A Selection of Uncollected Prose*, ed. Donald Pizer. Detroit: Wayne State University Press, 1977.
TDU	*Theodore Dreiser's Uncollected Magazine Articles, 1897–1902,* ed. Yoshinobu Hakutani. Newark: University of Delaware Press, 2003.

Texas	Harry Ransom Humanities Research Center, University of Texas.
TF	*A Traveler at Forty.* New York: The Century Company, 1913.
TM	*Twelve Men,* ed. Robert Coltrane. Philadelphia: University of Pennsylvania Press, 1998; originally published 1919.
Virginia	Alderman Library, University of Virginia.

NOTES

ONE. HOOSIER HARD TIMES

1. *D*, 6–7. There is also a bobbing light in "Phantom Dunkard," an unpublished ghost story Dreiser wrote about his maternal uncle (Virginia).

Dreiser the realist seldom concealed his flaws, and those included errors in orthography and punctuation. Following the example of Robert H. Elias in his three-volume edition of Dreiser's letters (*L*), I have silently corrected Dreiser's misspellings in his holograph letters and manuscripts. Typical examples of his regular mistakes include *accross, allready, alright, distroy, forrest, grammer, opourtinity, priviledge, rediculous, seperate, thousend, your* (for "you're"), and *its* (for "it's"). He also failed to follow the rule of *i* before *e* except after *c* and often concluded interrogatory statements with a period instead of a question mark.

2. *D* holograph, material Dreiser deleted from chap. II (Indiana); Renate Schmidt-von Bardeleben, "Dreiser on the European Continent. Part One: Theodore Dreiser, the German Dreisers and Germany," *DN* 2 (Fall 1971): 4–10; Dreiser family genealogy (Indiana), where the year of Paul Dresser's birth is given as 1858; and Dreiser family Bible (Penn). See also Mary Francis ("Mame") Brennan, "Pudley: A Memory of Paul Dresser," [1906] (Penn).

3. *D*, 8.

4. *D*, 81; and *D* holograph, material deleted from chap. III.

5. *D*, 10; Vera Dreiser, *My Uncle Theodore* (New York: Nash Publishing Co., 1976), 32; Tedi Dreiser Godard to Jerome Loving, March 21, 2000; and *SC*, 369.

6. *D* holograph, material deleted from chap. III; and *D*, 19.

7. *D,* 150–51, 49–50; see also *ML,* 28–29.

8. *TF,* 431, 433, 441; and Schmidt-von Bardeleben, "Dreiser on the European Continent. Part One," 4–10.

9. Thomas P. Riggio, "The Dreisers in Sullivan: A Biographical Revision," *DN* 10 (Fall 1979): 1–12; Richard Lingeman, *Theodore Dreiser* (New York: G. P. Putnam's Sons, 1986), 1: 23; and *HH,* 392. For a slightly different account of John Paul Dreiser's fortunes before the birth of Theodore, see Clayton W. Henderson, *On the Banks of the Wabash: The Life and Music of Paul Dresser* (Indianapolis: Indiana Historical Society Press, 2003), 14–22.

10. As an adult Dreiser possessed "a sketchy knowledge of German." *Letters to Louise,* ed. Louise Campbell (Philadelphia: University of Pennsylvania Press, 1959), 21.

11. *D,* 21; and Dreiser family Bible.

12. *D,* 26; and *HH,* 403.

13. *TF,* 208, 365; and *D,* 26.

14. *D,* 110; Lingeman, *Dreiser,* 1: 35–36; and Brennan, "Pudley."

15. Marguerite Tjader [Harris], *Theodore Dreiser: A New Dimension* (Norwalk, Conn.: Silvermine Publishers, 1965), 139.

16. *D,* 22–23; and *D* holograph, material deleted from chap. V.

17. *D,* 30, 34–35.

18. *D,* 70, 93.

19. *D,* 40–42; and see *New York Times,* March 10 and 25, 1903. "'Whitey' Sullivan," the alias under which Bulger was officially executed on March 24, 1903, was changed to "'Red' Sullivan" in the printed version of *D,* and "Bulger," Sullivan's actual name was changed to "Dooney." In a letter to TD, November 2, 1901 (Penn), Austin Brennan, Mame's husband, asked him: "Do you remember Jimmy Bulger of Sullivan, Indiana? Paul writes that he is to be electrocuted for murder [December] 8 under the name of James Sullivan. A case of wandering down the wrong path of life."

20. *D,* 60.

21. *D,* 104–6.

22. Thomas E. Hill, *Hill's Manual of Social and Business Forms: Guide to Correct Writing* (Chicago: Moses Warren & Co., 1880), 112, 119, 162.

23. *D* holograph, material deleted from chap. XV.

24. *D,* 112–17.

25. *D,* 130.

26. *D* holograph, material deleted from chap. XXVII.

27. Clara [Clark] Jaeger, *Philadelphia Rebel: The Education of a Bourgeoise* (London: Grosvenor, 1988), 82; and Jean West Maury, "A Neighborly Call on Theodore Dreiser," *Boston Evening Transcript,* January 29, 1927.

28. *D,* 167–70.

29. *Biographical and Historical Record of Kosciusko County, Indiana* (Chicago: Lewis Publishing Co., 1887), 676; and *D,* 185.

30. *D,* 194. Howells's name appears on Dreiser's reading list in the holograph but not the published version of *D.*

31. West Ward Public Schools No. 2 and No. 4, Kosciusko County Old Jail Museum and Library, Warsaw, Indiana, where the year for Dreiser's first semester is clearly 1883, not 1884 as is usually claimed for the family's first year in Warsaw. Claire Dreiser's records were not found at this source.

32. *D,* 198.

33. *D,* 168.

34. *HH,* 317–18.

35. *D,* 192–95; *D* holograph, material deleted from chap. XXXIII. For "Carrie," see also Thomas P. Riggio, "Notes on the Origins of 'Sister Carrie,'" *Library Chronicle* 44 (Spring 1979): 7–26.

36. I am indebted to Stephen C. Brennan for first calling this discrepancy to my attention.

37. *D,* 247–49.

38. Newspaper articles on the Hopkins incident are reprinted *SC,* 387–93.

39. *D* holograph, material deleted from chap. XL.

40. *D,* 254–63.

41. *D* holograph, material deleted from chap. XLIII.

42. *D,* 273–75.

43. *D,* 277–79.

TWO. A VERY BARD OF A CITY

1. TD, "Biographical Sketch," written for *Household Magazine* (1929; Penn).

2. Donald L. Miller, *City of the Century: The Epic of Chicago and the Making of America* (New York: Simon & Schuster, 1996), 176–97.

3. *D,* 296, 298.

4. *D,* 302–3, 299.

5. *D,* 314.

6. *D,* 317–21, 325–26; and TD to Richard Duffy, February 2, 1902 (Penn).

7. *D,* 327–28.

8. *D,* 330.

9. *D,* 335–37, 341–44.

10. *D,* 347–49.

11. William J. Heim, "Letters from Young Dreiser," *American Literary Realism* 8 (Spring 1975): 158–63. In the late 1920s, an examination at the Mayo Clinic revealed a trace of scar tissue from "a serious condition which developed when

[Dreiser] was only seventeen years old, while working in the basement of Hibbard, Spencer, Bartlett and Company in Chicago" (*ML,* 55).

12. *D,* 368–70. See TD to Richard Duffy, November 18, 1901 (Indiana).

13. *D,* 410; *The Department of English at Indiana University* (Bloomington: privately published, n.d.), 38; and Thomas D. Clark, *Indiana University: Midwestern Pioneer* (Bloomington: Indiana University Press, 1970), 1: 233–64.

14. *D,* 410–12.

15. *D,* 412–13; Joseph Katz, "Theodore Dreiser at Indiana University," *Notes and Queries* 13 (March 1966): 101; and *Department of English,* 206.

16. *D,* 415.

17. *D,* 381–82.

18. *HH,* 492–93.

19. *D* holograph, material deleted from chap. XLVII (Indiana); Robert H. Elias, *Theodore Dreiser: Apostle of Nature* (Ithaca: Cornell University Press, 1970; orig. pub. 1948), 27; and Richard W. Dowell, "'You Will Not Like Me, Im Sure': Dreiser to Miss Emma Rector, November 28, 1893, to April 4, 1894," *American Literary Realism* 3 (Summer 1970): 259–70.

20. *HH,* 493–95.

21. *D,* 391–92.

22. For the argument that Dreiser's pity for the poor was essentially self-pity, see Lionel Trilling, *The Liberal Imagination* (New York: Viking Press, 1950), 7–21; reprinted in Donald Pizer, ed., *Critical Essays on Theodore Dreiser* (Boston: G. K. Hall, 1981), 38–46.

23. Richard Lehan, *Theodore Dreiser: His World and His Novels* (Carbondale: Southern Illinois University Press, 1969), 46–47; and *D,* 393–96.

24. *D,* 401.

25. *D,* 402–8. See also Thomas P. Riggio, "Mark Twain and Theodore Dreiser," *Mark Twain Journal* 19 (Summer 1978): 20–25.

26. *D,* 432–39. In chap. 60 of *HH* Willy is named simply as W——.

27. *D,* 441, 448.

28. *D,* 376; Katz, "Dreiser at Indiana University," 100–101; and *D* holograph, material deleted from chap. LXXVI. In his November 18, 1901, letter to Duffy (see n. 12), Dreiser spoke of his dislike of academe, "its cut and dried methods of imparting information," but added quickly about his time at Indiana University: "this is not wholly true, however, for the beauty—natural and architectural—which invested the scene carried me to mental heights not previously attained."

29. *D* holograph, material deleted from chap. LXXIX; and *D,* 469–73.

30. *D,* 488.

31. *D,* 491, 495.

32. *D,* 513.

33. *D,* 506, 512.

34. *D,* 516–19.

35. *D,* 523–24.

36. *D,* 527–28.

37. *D* holograph, material deleted from chap. LXXXVI; and *D,* 535–38.

38. *D,* 557–64.

39. *D,* 567.

40. *D,* 582–85.

41. *D* holograph, material deleted from chap. XXVI.

42. *ND,* 31–37. This second and final volume of a planned four-volume autobiography was first published as *A Book About Myself* by Boni & Liveright in 1922; it was reissued as *Newspaper Days* by the same publisher in 1931.

THREE. THIS MATTER OF REPORTING

1. *ND,* 38, 691.

2. *ND,* 6–8, 42; and *DML,* 1: 196–97.

3. *ND,* 45–54.

4. *ND,* 63, 57.

5. *ND,* 59.

6. "Cheyenne, Haunt of Misery and Crime," in *TDJ,* 4–7.

7. *ND,* 127.

8. *TDJ,* 7; and *ND,* 81–82.

9. *ND,* 91–94.

10. *ND,* 86–87.

11. See chapter 1 and *ND,* 128.

12. *ND,* 102–3, 128. In an interview with W. A. Swanberg on May 22, 1964, Dreiser's niece Vera Dreiser said: "I believe that all his life TD confused impotence with premature ejaculation" (Penn).

13. *ND,* 84; and "The Return of Genius," *TDJ,* 16–17; also reprinted in *TDS,* 33–35.

14. Robert H. Elias, *Theodore Dreiser: Apostle of Nature* (Ithaca: Cornell University Press, 1979; orig. pub. 1948), 42–43; and W. A. Swanberg, *Dreiser* (New York: Charles Scribner's Sons, 1965), 39.

15. James Neal Primm, *Lion of the Valley: St. Louis, Missouri, 1764–1980* (St. Louis: Missouri Historical Society Press, 1981), 1: 32–33.

16. Eugene Field, *A Little Book of Western Verse* (1889; repr. Great Neck, N.Y.: Cora Collection Books, Inc., 1979), 36.

17. *ND,* 107; Jim Allee Hart, *A History of the St. Louis Globe-Democrat* (Columbia: University of Missouri Press, 1961), 136–60; and Charles C. Clayton, *Little Mack: Joseph B. McCullagh* (Carbondale: Southern Illinois University Press, 1969), 216–23, and *passim.*

18. "The Animal in Us," *St. Louis Globe-Democrat,* January 8, 1893.

19. "Tortured and Burned," *St. Louis Globe-Democrat,* February 2, 1893; "Vengeance Again in Repose," *St. Louis Globe-Democrat,* February 3, 1893; and "Race Troubles in Texas," *St. Louis Globe-Democrat,* February 6, 1893. See also T. D. Nostwich, "The Source of Dreiser's 'Nigger Jeff,'" *Resources for American Literary Study* 8 (Autumn 1978): 174–87; and *TDJ,* 251–58. Nostwich prints in both of these sources an article from the *St. Louis Republic* of January 18, 1894, entitled "Ten-Foot Drop," which much more closely parallels the plot of "Nigger Jeff" and is discussed in chapter 6.

20. *ND,* 108.

21. *ND,* 148–49.

22. *ND,* 200–206.

23. *TDJ,* 38–55.

24. *ND,* 208, 211.

25. Arch T. Edmonston to TD, September 27, 1929 (Penn).

26. See the chapters on Whitman and Twain in Shelley Fisher Fishkin, *From Fact to Fiction: Journalism and Imaginative Writing in America* (New York: Oxford University Press, 1985).

27. Despite the unlikelihood that TD wrote the piece, "John L. Out for a Lark" is included in *TDJ,* 90–91. See also *ND,* 184, where TD writes of Sullivan: "I adored him. I would have written anything he asked, and I got up the very best interview I could and published it."

28. *Theodore Dreiser's "Heard in the Corridors" Articles and Related Writings,* ed. T. D. Nostwich (Ames: Iowa State University Press, 1988), 141–42.

29. Clarence Gohdes, "Amusements on the Stage," in *Literature of the American People,* ed. Arthur Hobson Quinn (New York: Appleton-Century, Inc., 1951), 790.

30. Arthur Hobson Quinn, *A History of the American Drama from the Civil War to the Present Day* (New York: Appleton-Century-Crofts, Inc., 1936), 1–38; and *ND,* 219, 712.

31. *ND,* 215–16; *TDJ,* 91; and *ND,* 225–26.

32. *TDJ,* 94; and *ND,* 716–17.

33. See "An Able Dramatic Critic" in the *St. Louis Post-Dispatch* and "Imaginative Journalism" in the *St. Louis Chronicle* of May 1, 1893, both afternoon papers.

34. *ND,* 255–56.

35. H. B. Wandell to Boni & Liveright, December 29, 1922 (Penn); and *ND,* 126.

36. See *TDJ,* 99–265; and T. D. Nostwich, "Dreiser's 'Poet of Potter's Field,'" *DS* 18 (Fall 1987): 3.

37. *ND,* 339–45.

38. *ND,* 190–99, 282–84.

39. *TDJ*, 127.

40. *ND*, 308.

41. Donald L. Miller, *City of the Century: The Epic of Chicago and the Making of America* (New York: Simon and Schuster, 1996), 488–91; and Gary Szuberla, "Dreiser at the World's Fair," *Modern Fiction Studies* 23 (Autumn 1977): 369–79.

42. *ND*, 306.

43. *ND*, 385; and Alphonse Dreiser to TD, February 23, 1897 (Penn).

44. *ND*, 394.

45. *ND*, 425, 434, 439.

46. *HH*, 248, where Hutchinson is unmarried. In *ND* (453) he is married.

FOUR. SURVIVAL OF THE FITTEST

1. *ND*, 440; and Richard W. Dowell, "'You Will Not Like Me, Im Sure': Dreiser to Miss Emma Rector, November 28, 1893, to April 4, 1894," *American Literary Realism* 3 (Summer 1970): 259–70.

2. *ND*, 447, 485, 491.

3. *HH*, 248; and *ND*, 451.

4. *HH*, 250–51.

5. *HH*, 253; and Maude Wood Henry to Robert H. Elias, March 12, 1945 (Cornell). In this letter, Henry's first wife maintains that Dreiser and Henry did not meet until 1895, when Dreiser was editor of *Ev'ry Month*, while Henry is quoted in *FF* (104) as saying he met Dreiser in Toledo while he was city editor of the *Blade*. See Maude Wood Henry to Elias, April 2, 1945 (Cornell), for her husband's alleged relation to Patrick Henry.

6. Arthur Henry, *Nicholas Blood, Candidate; A Prophecy* (New York: Oliver Dodd, 1890), 32, 39, 200. There is a copy of *Nicholas Blood, Candidate* at Texas that was thought to have markings in Dreiser's hand, but it has now been established that this is the handwriting of another who apparently approves of the novel's racist views and, further, offers advice in punctuation and diction. Dreiser, who is notorious for his disdain for spelling and grammar, would not be giving Arthur Henry (who helped edit *Sister Carrie*) such advice. See D. Gene England, "A Further Note on the 'Dreiser' Annotation," *DN* 4 (Fall 1973): 9–10.

7. Ellen Moers, "A 'New' First Novel by Arthur Henry," *DN* 4 (Fall 1973): 7–9; and James L. W. West III, "*Nicholas Blood* and *Sister Carrie*," *Library Chronicle* 44 (Spring 1979): 32–42.

8. Maude Henry Wood to Robert H. Elias, May 2, 1945 (Cornell).

9. *FF*, 104.

10. *TDJ*, 269–73; and the *New York World*, January 15–16, 1894. In the letter to Elias of March 12, 1945, in which she states she did not remember Dreiser ever

reporting for the *Blade* (and so meeting Henry at that time), Maude Wood Henry insists that she wrote the articles on the streetcar strike. She also asserts in this letter that Dreiser began *Sister Carrie* in 1897, which is highly improbable.

11. *ND*, 470–71.

12. *ND*, 474–75.

13. *ND*, 478–80.

14. *ND*, 486–87.

15. Thomas A. Bailey, *The American Pageant: A History of the Republic* (Lexington, Mass.: D. C. Heath Company, 1975), 631–35.

16. *ND*, 487.

17. *ND*, 489.

18. *ND*, 501.

19. *ND*, 503–4.

20. *ND*, 496–97; and "The Shining Slave Makers," *Ainslee's* 7 (June 1901): 445–50.

21. *ND*, 508; and the *Pittsburgh Dispatch*, April 5–6, 1894.

22. *ND*, 510–11; *TDJ*, 285–86; and "Thomas Brackett Reed: The Story of a Great Career," *Success* 3 (June 1900): 215–16; reprinted in *TDU*, 78–85. See also Yoshinobu Hakutani, "The Crucible of an American Writer: Dreiser in Pittsburgh," in *Studies in English Language and Literature in Honor of Professor Michio Masui's Retirement* (Tokyo: Kenkyusha-Shuppan, 1983), 513–22.

23. *ND*, 515; and Thomas P. Riggio, "Notes on the Origins of 'Sister Carrie,'" *Library Chronicle* 44 (Spring 1979): 7–26. See also Philip Gerber, "Dreiser Meets Balzac at the 'Allegheny Carnegie,'" *Carnegie Magazine* 46 (April 1972): 137–39, where it is noted that the Allegheny Library at the time contained twenty-eight titles by Balzac.

24. *ND*, 487; and *DML*, 1: 231–32. See chapter 5 for Dreiser's experiment in comic drama.

25. *TDJ*, 286–88. Crane's "An Experiment in Misery" appeared in the *New York Press* for April 24, 1894.

26. *TDJ*, 301.

27. Quoted in Lars Ahnebrink, "Garland and Dreiser: An Abortive Friendship," *Midwest Journal* 7 (Winter 1955–56): 285–92; Dreiser's letter to Garland, dated January 8, 1903, is at the University of Southern California Library.

28. *ND*, 518; *TDJ*, 314–16; and T. D. Nostwich, "Dreiser's Apocryphal Fly Story," *DS* 17 (Spring 1986): 1–8.

29. *ND*, 537–38.

30. *ND*, 538–40.

31. *ND*, 531–32; *TDJ*, 323; and "A Monarch of Metal Workers," *Success* 2 (June 3, 1899): 453–54 (in *SMA*, 1: 158–69), which was reprinted as "Carnegie as Metal Worker" in *How They Succeeded*, ed. Orison Swett Marden (Boston: Lothrop, 1901), 253–75, and as "A Poor Boy Who Once Borrowed Books Now Gives Away

Libraries—Andrew Carnegie," in *Little Visits with Great Americans,* ed. Marden (New York: The Success Company, 1903), 51–70.

32. *TM,* 187–89; *Walt Whitman: Leaves of Grass,* ed. Jerome Loving (New York: Oxford University Press, 1990), 446; and *ND,* 551–52.

33. *ND,* 558.

34. Dreiser Papers, Box 405, Folder 13816 (Penn).

35. *ND,* 573–74.

36. *TDEM,* 46–47; *ND,* 571; and *SC,* 226–27.

37. *ND,* 576–79.

38. *TM,* 82–86.

39. *ND,* 589–93.

40. *ND,* 610.

41. Donald Pizer, *The Novels of Theodore Dreiser: A Critical Study* (Minneapolis: University of Minnesota Press, 1976), 12; Richard Lehan, *Theodore Dreiser: His World and His Novels* (Carbondale: Southern Illinois University Press, 1969), 45–47; and *SC,* 56–57.

42. *ND,* 610.

43. *ND,* 615.

44. *ND,* 620.

45. *ND,* 623.

46. Richard Lingeman, *Theodore Dreiser* (New York: G. P. Putnam's Sons, 1986), 1: 151.

47. *ND,* 640.

48. *TDJ,* 331–33.

49. Robert Penn Warren, *Homage to Theodore Dreiser* (New York: Random House, 1971), 35.

50. *FF,* 197.

51. *D* holograph, material deleted from chaps. XXXII and XLIV.

52. *ND,* 651; and *SC,* 336. In chap. XXXIX of the *D* holograph, Dreiser wrote: "Some phases of this tragedy [of Emma and Hopkins] are the bases of *Sister Carrie* but not all. . . . Her paramour never died of want in the way described [in Dreiser's novel], though he fell rather low, socially."

FIVE. EDITORIAL DAYS

1. "A Literary Apprenticeship" (Penn).

2. *ND,* 665.

3. Dreiser also claimed to have encountered Twain on two other occasions: when he was writing the *Success* articles in the late 1890s and just before he was editor of the *Delineator* in the first decade of the twentieth century; see his "Mark Twain: Three Contacts," *Esquire* 4 (October 1935): 22, 162, and his "Mark the

Double Twain," *English Journal* 24 (October 1935): 626. See also Richard Lehan, *Theodore Dreiser: His World and His Novels* (Carbondale: Southern Illinois University Press, 1969), 248. In 1920 Dreiser told Mencken that he had encountered Twain drunk in a New York saloon "back in—well—roughly—1905-6-or 7. . . . [H]e took up the American notion that all marriages were made in heaven. . . . It was then that he referred to his wife . . . [saying] [s]he is a good enough woman [but] . . . that he was damned unhappy—just like most other men—but that for her sake—or the children's—or his standing or something he had to keep up appearances." These attitudes appear to better suit Dreiser himself in 1920 when, under pressure from his future second wife to marry, he was angry with Jug for refusing to grant him a divorce. It is also strange that Dreiser used the present tense to describe Twain's alleged feeling toward his wife and refer to his offspring as children in "roughly—1905–6-or-7," when Olivia Langdon Clemens had died in 1904 after a long illness, and his living children, Clara and Jean, were already adults (*L*, 1: 305–7).

4. *FF,* 135.

5. *FF,* 139; Richard Lingeman, "Dreiser's 'Jeremiah I': Found at Last," *DS* 20 (Fall 1989): 2–8; and Donald Pizer, "'Along the Wabash': A 'Comedy Drama' by Theodore Dreiser," *DN* 5 (Fall 1974): 1–4.

6. Robert H. Elias, *Theodore Dreiser: Apostle of Nature* (Ithaca: Cornell University Press, 1970; orig. pub. 1948), 88.

7. TD, ed., *The Songs of Paul Dresser* (New York: Boni & Liveright, 1927), 1–3. For the most recent information on Dresser, see Clayton W. Henderson, *On the Banks of the Wabash: The Life and Music of Paul Dresser* (Indianapolis: Indiana State Historical Society Press, 2003).

8. Paul Dresser, "Making Songs for the Millions: An Unconventional Chapter from the Biography of the Man Whose Songs Have Sold to the Extent of Five Million Copies," *Metropolitan* 12 (November 1900): 701–3.

9. The actual basis of "Just Tell Them" was apparently the suicide of a friend from Terre Haute who had failed to become a success as an actor in New York; see Henderson, *On the Banks,* 385–86.

10. Arthur Henry, *Lodgings in Town* (New York: A. S. Barnes, 1905), 80–83.

11. Joseph Katz, "Theodore Dreiser and Stephen Crane: Studies in a Literary Relationship," in *Stephen Crane in Transition: Centenary Essays,* ed. Joseph Katz (Dekalb: Northern Illinois University Press, 1972), 174–204. For Jenks, see Albert Johannsen, *The House of the Beadle and Adams* (Norman: University of Oklahoma Press, 1950), 2: 164–65; Ellen Moers, *Two Dreisers* (New York: Viking Press, 1969), 37–38; and Lydia Cushman Schurman, "Richard Lingeman's Myth Making: Theodore Dreiser's Editing of the Jack Harkaway Stories," *Dime Novel Roundup* 64 (1995): 151–65.

12. See, for example, Yoshinobu Hakutani, "Theodore Dreiser's Editorial and Free-Lance Writing," *Library Chronicle* 37 (Winter 1971): 70–85.

13. *Songs of Paul Dresser,* 42.

14. *TDEM,* 24–25.

15. *TDEM,* 27–28.

16. *TDEM,* 26–27, 34.

17. *Ev'ry Month,* December 1895, 3–4.

18. *Ev'ry Month,* December 1895, 7–8; and *Letters of Ralph Waldo Emerson,* ed. Ralph L. Rusk (New York: Columbia University Press, 1939), 3: 9.

19. *TDEM,* 46.

20. *Walt Whitman: Leaves of Grass,* ed. Jerome Loving (New York: Oxford University Press, 1990), 82–83; and *TDS,* 60.

21. *TDS,* 61.

22. *TDEM,* 92–93, 98.

23. TD to Sara Osborne White (Jug), May 1 and May 2, 1896 (Indiana).

24. TD to Jug, June 12 and July 10, 1896 (Indiana).

25. TD to Jug, May 2 and October 4, 1896 (Indiana).

26. TD to Jug, October 11, 1896 (Indiana).

27. *TDEM,* 35, 168–70; and TD to Jug, November 4, 1896 (Indiana).

28. TD to Jug, January 24, 1898 (Indiana); and Louis Menand, *The Metaphysical Club* (New York: Farrar, Straus and Giroux, 2001), 351–58.

29. TD to Jug, n.d. and [March 24, 1897] (Indiana).

30. *TDEM,* 96–97; Katz, " Theodore Dreiser and Stephen Crane," 185; and TD to Max J. Herzberg, November 2, 1921 (Penn).

31. *TDEM,* 110–11. For Twain and Dreiser, see n. 3 above.

32. *TDEM,* 99, 108; and TD to Jug, [November 17, 1896] (Indiana).

33. *TDEM,* 95–96, 134–35. This is actually Elizabeth Stuart Phelps Ward, the daughter of the novelist Elizabeth Stuart Phelps (1815–52).

34. *TDEM,* 129–31; and TD to Jug, November 4, 1896 (Indiana).

35. *TDEM,* 143; "Forgotten," *Ev'ry Month,* August 1896, reprinted in *TDEM,* 152–57; and Moers, *Two Dreisers,* 95–96; *TDJ,* 286–88; and *TDEM,* 152–57, 322n, where the editor speculates that Dreiser also adapted material from his unsigned story "Where Sympathy Failed," *Pittsburgh Dispatch,* August 25, 1894.

36. "Each member of the firm is strongly opposed to my convictions but still bows to my judgment" (TD to Jug, November 4, 1896, [Indiana]). See also Arthur Henry's impression in *Lodgings in Town,* 82–83: "this was no commune. In the midst of [the offices of Howley and Haviland] a short, thin man [Fred Haviland] moved with quick gestures, short orders, and sharp glances from his restless eyes."

37. Arthur Henry, "It Is to Laugh: A Little Talk on How to Write a Comic Opera," *Ev'ry Month,* April 1897, 13–15; and *Lodgings in Town,* 80–81.

38. *TDEM,* 178–79.

39. *TDEM,* 192–94.

40. *TDEM,* 214.

41. *TDEM,* 223; TD to Jug, [December 26, 1896] (Indiana); and Vera Dreiser, *My Uncle Theodore* (New York: Nash Publishing Co., 1976), 75.

42. TD to Jug, [January 26, 1897] (Indiana).

43. *TDEM,* 264.

44. *TDEM,* 268.

SIX. THE WRITER

1. *FF,* 142.

2. Eric Sundquist, "Realism and Regionalism," in *Columbia Literary History of the United States,* ed. Emory Elliott (New York: Columbia University Press, 1988), 502.

3. Vera Dreiser, *My Uncle Theodore* (New York: Nash Publishing Co., 1976), 78.

4. TD, ed., *Songs of Paul Dresser* (New York: Boni & Liveright, 1927), 72.

5. TD to Sara Osborne White (Jug), May 15, 1898 (Indiana); Richard W. Dowell, "'On the Banks of the Wabash': A Musical Whodunit," *Indiana Magazine of History* 66 (June 1970): 95–109; and Dowell, "Dreiser's Contribution to 'On the Banks of the Wabash': A Fiction Writer's Fiction!" *Indiana English Journal* 6 (Fall 1971): 7–13.

6. TD, "Birth and Growth of a Popular Song," *Metropolitan* 8 (November 1898): 497–502 (reprinted in *SMA,* 2: 19–22); *HH,* 350; and *TM,* 100–101. Dreiser also stated through his secretary (Esther Van Dresser to Ellis D. Robb, May 15, 1929) that he was "responsible for the skeleton of the first verse and the chorus, while the credit for the music, the finished first verse and the second belongs to Paul Dresser" (Virginia). The claim was also made by Mencken in his seminal essay on Dreiser in *A Book of Prefaces* (New York: Alfred A. Knopf, 1917), 106. See also Carol S. Loranger and Dennis Loranger, "Collaborating on 'The Banks of the Wabash': A Brief History of an Interdisciplinary Debate," *DS* 30 (Spring 1999): 3–20.

7. TD to Lorna D. Smith, April 3, 1939 (Penn).

8. *L,* 1: 212; and Maude Wood Henry to Robert H. Elias, May 2, 1945 (Cornell).

9. Robert H. Elias, *Theodore Dreiser: Apostle of Nature* (Ithaca: Cornell University Press, 1970; orig. pub. 1948), 95.

10. "Rona Murtha," in *GW,* 2: 567; and Arthur Henry, *Lodgings in Town* (New York: A. S. Barnes, 1905), 83.

11. Theodore Dresser, "New York's Art Colony," *Metropolitan* 6 (November 1897): 321–26; reprinted in *TDU,* 183–87.

12. "On the Field of Brandywine," *Truth* 16 (November 1897): 7–10; reprinted in *TDU,* 188–91.

13. "The Haunts of Bayard Taylor," *Munsey's* 18 (January 1898): 594–601, reprinted in *SMA*, 1: 43–49.

14. For "The Homes of Longfellow," see Judith Kucharski, "Dreiser Looks at Longfellow," *DS* 26 (Fall 1995): 30–47. Dreiser also published an essay entitled "The Home of William Cullen Bryant" in *Munsey's* 21 (May 1899): 240–46; see *SMA*, 1: 92–99.

15. John F. Huth, Jr., "Theodore Dreiser, Success Monger," *Colophon* 3 (Winter 1938): 120–33; and *SMA*, 1: 30. There is a series of stock questions for the *Success* interviews at Virginia.

16. "A Photographic Talk with Edison," *Success* 1 (February 1898): 8–9, reprinted in *SMA*, 1: 111–19; "Life Stories of Successful Men—No. 10," *Success* 1 (October 1898): 3–4, reprinted in *SMA*, 1: 120–29; and TD to Jug, June 22, 1898 (Indiana).

17. *TDS*, 272–81.

18. TD to Jug, July 27, 1898 (Indiana).

19. See "Life Stories of Successful Men—No. 12 [Marshall Field]," *Success* 2 (December 8, 1898): 7–8, reprinted in *SMA*, 1: 130–38; and "The Town of Pullman," *Ainslee's* 3 (March 1899): 189–200; reprinted in *TDU*, 229–39.

20. TD to Jug, [January 24], February 1, and February 23, 1898 (Indiana).

21. TD to Jug, July 29, February 16, and September 2, 1898 (Indiana). In the first chapter of *Sister Carrie*, Dreiser borrowed heavily from Ade's "The Fable of the Two Mandolin Players and the Willing Performer"; see *SC*, 3n; and Jack Salzman, "Dreiser and a Note on the Text of *Sister Carrie*," *American Literature* 40 (January 1969): 544–48.

22. "The Making of Small Arms," *Ainslee's* 1 (July 1898): 540–49 (reprinted in *TDU*, 112–21); "Scenes in a Cartridge Factory," *Cosmopolitan* 25 (July 1898): 321–24 (reprinted in *TDU*, 122–26); and "Carrier Pigeons in War Time," *Demorest's Family Magazine* 34 (July 1898): 222–23 (reprinted in *TDU*, 273–80).

23. "Night Song," *Ainslee's* 2 (August 1898): 73.

24. "The Return," *Ainslee's* 2 (October 1898): 280; and *FF*, 147.

25. Grace Gupton Vogt to Robert H. Elias, July 12, 1945 (Cornell); and TD, "Bondage," *Ainslee's* 3 (April 1899): 293.

26. *D*, 397; Ellen Moers, *Two Dreisers* (New York: Viking, 1969), 48; and *FF*, 197.

27. "How He Climbed Fame's Ladder," *Success* 1 (April 1898): 5–6, reprinted in *American Literary Realism*, 6 (Fall 1973): 339–44 ; and "The Real Howells," *Ainslee's* 5 (March 1900): 137–42. The latter is reprinted in *TDS*, 141–46, as well as in *American Literary Realism* 6 (Fall 1973): 347–51. For the theory that Dreiser plagiarized his *Success* interview from *My Literary Passions*, see Ulrich Halfmann, "Dreiser and Howells: New Light on Their Relationship," *Amerikastudien* 20, 1 (1975): 73–85; and John Crowley, *The Dean of American Letters* (Amherst: Uni-

versity of Massachusetts Press, 1999), 72–73, 77–79. The rough notes on How-ells in Dreiser's hand are at Virginia.

28. "The Real Howells."

29. "Curious Shifts of the Poor," *Demorest's Family Magazine* 36 (November 1899): 22–26, reprinted in *SC*, 415–24.

30. According to Richard Lingeman, *Theodore Dreiser* (New York: G. P. Put-nam's Sons, 1986), 1: 213–14, 439, "A Cincinnati house had offered him an ad-vance of $500 [for such a book], but the firm went bankrupt" (214).

31. "Edmund Clarence Stedman at Home," *Munsey's* 20 (March 1899): 931–38; and Edward Mercur Williams, "Edmund Clarence Stedman at Home," *New England Quarterly* 25 (June 1952): 242–48.

32. In a letter to H. L. Mencken of May 13, 1916 (*DML*, 1: 231–34), Dreiser re-called only five stories: "The Shining Slave Makers," "Butcher Rogaum's Door," "When the Old Century Was New," "Nigger Jeff," and "The World and the Bub-ble," which was rejected by *Ainslee's* (*Ainslee's* to TD, January 9, 1905 [Penn]) but has otherwise never been fully identified. However, a letter from Arthur Henry to Dreiser dated in the summer, possibly August, of 1900, mentions "A Mayor and His People," generally thought to have been written shortly after *Sister Carrie,* along with "Nigger Jeff" as placeable in either *Ainslee's* or *Frank Leslie's* (typescript in Box 72 of the Elias collection at Cornell). It is possible, of course, that Dreiser wrote "A Mayor and His People" even before he went to Maumee. It was first pub-lished in the *Era* 11 (June 1903): 578–84 and later in an expanded edition in *TM.*

33. Maude Wood Henry to Robert H. Elias, March 12 and May 13, 1945 (Cornell).

34. Arthur Henry and Maude Wood Henry, *The Flight of a Pigeon and Other Stories* (Toledo: W. J. Squire, Publisher, 1894); Maude Wood Henry to Robert H. Elias, July 25, 1945 (Cornell); and *DML*, 1: 232.

35. *TM,* 364; see also n. 32, above.

36. See, for example, Donald Pizer, "A Summer at Maumee: Theodore Dreiser Writes Four Stories," in *Essays Mostly on Periodical Publishing in Amer-ica,* ed. James Woodress (Durham, N.C.: Duke University Press, 1973), 193–204.

37. *TM,* 340–41.

38. *D,* 325.

39. *DML,* 1: 232; and Henry M. Alden to TD, October 9, 1899 (Penn); cited in Don B. Graham, "Dreiser's Ant Tragedy: The Revision of 'The Shining Slave Makers,'" *Studies in Short Fiction* 14 (Winter 1977): 41–48.

40. "Electricity in the Household," *Demorest's* 35 (January 1899): 38–39 (reprinted in *SMA,* 2: 137–42); "Japanese Home Life," *Demorest's* 35 (April 1899): 123–25 (reprinted in *TDU,* 281–90); and *L,* 1: 45–47. For other possible sources for "The Shining Slave Makers," including Thoreau's passage on the ants in *Walden,* see Joseph Griffin, *The Small Canvas: An Introduction to Dreiser's Short Stories* (Rutherford, N.J.: Fairleigh Dickinson University Press, 1985), 29.

41. *Free*, 71.

42. Griffin, *Small Canvas*, 26; and Donald Pizer, *The Novels of Theodore Dreiser: A Critical Study* (Minneapolis: University of Minnesota Press, 1976), 17.

43. Griffin, *Small Canvas*, 37.

44. "Butcher Rogaum's Door," *Reedy's Mirror* 11 (December 12, 1901): 17.

45. See chapter 15; and W. A. Swanberg, *Dreiser* (New York: Charles Scribner's Sons, 1965), 527.

46. "Nigger Jeff," *Ainslee's* 8 (November 1901): 366–75. The manuscript of "A Victim of Justice" is at Virginia.

47. T. D. Nostwich, "The Source of Dreiser's 'Nigger Jeff,'" *Resources for American Literary Study* 8 (Autumn 1978): 174–87, where the two *Republic* articles are reprinted; both are also in *TDJ*, 249–58.

48. *TDJ*, 257; and "Nigger Jeff," 372–73.

49. See Maude Henry Wood to Robert H. Elias, May 2, 1945.

50. TD to Jug, May 20, 1898 (Indiana); "Haunts of Nathaniel Hawthorne," *Truth* 17 (September 21, 1898) 7–9, (September 28, 1898): 11–13; reprinted in *SMA*, 1: 57–66.

51. *DML*, 1: 232.

SEVEN. *SISTER CARRIE*

1. Allen F. Stein, "*Sister Carrie*: A Possible Source for the Title," *American Literary Realism* 7 (Spring 1974): 173–74.

2. Arthur Henry, *A Princess of Arcady* (New York: Doubleday, Page, & Co., 1900), 17.

3. Henry, *Princess of Arcady*, 170, 307.

4. *SC*, 1; see *SCP* for the uncut original version of *Sister Carrie*.

5. *FE*, 162, where Dreiser is paraphrased to say that he finished the book in May, but the completion date was definitely earlier, possibly as early as March. In an interview with the *St. Louis Post-Dispatch*, January 27, 1902, Dreiser gives March, but in "The Early Adventures of *Sister Carrie*," (*Colophon*, Part Five [March 1931, unpaginated, 4 pp.]) which is included as a preface to the first Modern Library edition of the novel in 1932, he states that he finished the book in May. The manuscript is dated as having been completed in March (see n. 18 below); the revisions by Jug and Arthur Henry, which included a different ending, no doubt took the process a little longer, but not into May, for by May 2, it had already been rejected by Harper's.

6. *DML*, 1: 233; see also Vrest Orton, *Dreiserana: A Book about His Books* (1929; repr. New York: Haskell House, 1973), 13.

7. Arthur Henry, *An Island Cabin* (New York: McClure, Phillips, & Co., 1902), 213; and *The House in the Woods* (New York: A. S. Barnes, 1904). Henry's

statement about Burroughs appears in an undated and unpublished preface intended for a reprinting of *An Island Cabin* in 1903 (Cornell).

8. Henry, *Princess of Arcady,* 10; and *SC,* 48. Maude Wood Henry told Robert H. Elias in a letter dated May 13, 1945, that when Henry announced he was leaving her, "Ann[a] was sitting cross-legged on the floor sewing" (Cornell).

9. See James L. W. West III, "John Paul Dreiser's Copy of *Sister Carrie,*" *Library Chronicle* 44 (Spring 1979): 85–93.

10. Dreiser had interviewed Field two years earlier; see "Life Stories of Successful Men—No. 12 ," *Success* 2 (December 1898): 78; reprinted in *SMA,* 130–38.

11. *SC,* 17, 49.

12. *SC,* 33–34.

13. *SC,* 72.

14. *SC,* 192–93.

15. *SC,* 84, 103.

16. *SC,* 276–321.

17. See *SC,* 327, 338–39; and *SCP,* 511–12, 538n. See also Ellen Moers, *Two Dreisers* (New York: Viking Press, 1969), 67n., for a slightly different view.

18. The manuscript of *Sister Carrie* is in the Manuscript Division of the New York Public Library.

19. *SCP,* 538n.

20. James L. W. West III, *A Sister Carrie Portfolio* (Charlottesville: University Press of Virginia, 1985), 42–45; and Philip Williams, "The Chapter Titles of *Sister Carrie,*" *American Literature* 36 (November 1964): 359–65. For parallels between Ames and Edison, see Lawrence E. Hussman, Jr., *Dreiser and His Fiction: A Twentieth-Century Quest* (Philadelphia: University of Pennsylvania Press, 1983), 30–32.

21. F. O. Matthiessen, *Theodore Dreiser* (New York: William Sloane Associates, 1951), 71.

22. *SCP,* 517; and *SC,* 369; see also Jerome M. Loving, "The Rocking Chair Structure of *Sister Carrie,*" *DN* 2 (Spring 1971): 7–11.

23. In a 1937 letter otherwise undated Dreiser told Louis Filler, "When I finished the book, I realized it was too long, . . . and marked what I thought should be cut out. Then I consulted with a friend, Arthur Henry, who suggested other cuts, and wherever I agreed with him I cut the book" (Penn).

24. *SCP,* 518.

25. Orton, *Dreiserana,* 13–14; and *L,* 1: 210n. Dreiser's railroad article was "The Railroad and the People," *Harper's Monthly* 100 (February 1900): 479–84.

26. *L,* 1: 210n.

27. *SCP,* 519–20; *DML,* 1: 231; and Orton, *Dreiserana,* 14.

28. *SCP,* 520–22; *DML,* 1: 231; and Richard Lingeman, *Theodore Dreiser* (New York: G. P. Putnam's Sons, 1986), 1: 281–82.

29. *DML,* 1: 231; and Frank Norris to TD, May 28, 1900 (Penn). Most of the

correspondence concerning *Sister Carrie* and Doubleday, Page, & Company is published in *L,* 1: 50–65, as well as in *SC.* See *FF,* 169, for Norris's location when he read Dreiser's book.

30. TD, "Early Adventures," 2; see also TD to Fremont Older, November 27, 1923, (*L,* 2: 417–21).

31. Jerome Loving, *Walt Whitman: The Song of Himself* (Berkeley: University of California Press, 1999), 451–53.

32. *SC,* 449; and *L,* 1: 55. See *FF* (170) for further suggestions, if not evidence, of Lanier's negative view towards *Sister Carrie.* There is in the Dreiser collection at Penn an unpublished typescript of an introduction to a later edition of the novel that credits Lanier for standing up for the book. But this introduction is also filled with factual errors and exaggerations.

33. Arthur Henry to TD, July 19, 1900 (Penn).

34. Frank Norris to Arthur Henry, July 18, [1900] (Penn).

35. Theodore Dreiser, "Biographical Sketch," written for *Household Magazine* (1929, Penn).

36. *L,* 1: 57.

37. Arthur Henry to TD, undated but received by Dreiser on July 31, 1900 (Penn); and *L,* 1: 59–60. The fact that Henry's letter is written on Doubleday, Page, & Company stationery suggests Henry's closeness to Norris, whose manuscript of *The Octopus* he had read.

38. *L,* 1: 54.

39. *L,* 1: 63–64; Memorandum of Agreement, August 20, 1900 (Penn); and *SCP,* 528–29.

40. Lingeman, *Theodore Dreiser,* 1: 294; and W. A. Swanberg, *Dreiser* (New York: Charles Scribner's Sons, 1965), 92.

41. *TDCR,* 6–7, 10. Concerning the *Mirror* review, William Marion Reedy told Dreiser on December 26, 1900, that he read *Sister Carrie* in one sitting and thought it was "damned good." Horton's puzzlement over Doubleday's actions was soon cleared up by Henry, whom he told on February 8, 1901: "I am not at all surprised at your version of the Doubleday-Dreiser story. I had fancied something of the kind" (Penn).

42. *L,* 1: 52–53; and Neda M. Westlake, "The Sister Carrie Scrapbook," *Library Chronicle* 44 (Spring 1979): 71–84.

43. "'Sister Carrie': Theodore Dreiser," *New York Herald,* July 7, 1907 (quoted from *SCP,* 584).

44. For TD's 1930 comments on Frank Norris, see *FF,* 168–69. Norris's autographed copy of *Sister Carrie* is in the University of California Library, Berkeley, Calif.; his response is published in the *Collected Letters: Frank Norris* (San Francisco: The Book Club of California, 1986), 144. For the pros and cons on whether Norris remained faithful to *Sister Carrie,* see Jack Salzman, "The Publication of *Sister Carrie:* Fact and Fiction," *Library Chronicle* 33 (Spring 1967):

19–33; Robert Morace, "Dreiser's Contract for *Sister Carrie:* More Fact and Fiction," *Journal of Modern Literature* 9 (May 1982): 305–11; and Joseph R. McElrath, Jr., "Norris's Attitude Toward *Sister Carrie,*" *DS* 18 (Fall 1987): 39–42.

45. *TDCR,* from which the review quotations that follow are taken.

46. George A. Brett to TD, September 21, 1901 (Penn). It is not altogether clear whether Dreiser was involved in the revision. See John C. Berkey and Alice M. Winters, "The Heinemann Edition of *Sister Carrie,*" *Library Chronicle* 44 (Spring 1979): 43–52; and *Sister Carrie: An Abridged Edition by Theodore Dreiser and Arthur Henry,* ed. Jack Salzman (New York: Johnson Reprint Corporation, 1969), v–x.

47. Doubleday, Page, and Company to TD, May 6, 1901 (Penn).

48. "When the Old Century Was New," *Pearson's Magazine* 11 (January 1901): 131–40; reprinted and slightly revised in *Free.*

EIGHT. DOWN HILL AND UP

1. TD to Richard Duffy, March 19, 1901 (Penn).

2. Arthur Henry, *The House in the Woods,* ed. Donald T. Oakes (Henson, N.Y.: Black Dome Press, 2000), 171–72.

3. "Rona Murtha," in *GW,* 2: 590; and Arthur Henry, *An Island Cabin* (New York: McClure, Phillips, and Company, 1902; repr. A. S. Barnes, 1904, 1906), 160.

4. Henry, *Island Cabin,* 162–63, 169.

5. Henry, *Island Cabin,* 193.

6. Typescript of unpublished Preface to *An Island Cabin* (Cornell).

7. Henry, *Island Cabin,* 167; and Arthur Henry to TD, February 17, 1904 (Cornell).

8. Arthur Henry to TD, February 17, 1904 (Cornell).

9. Henry, *House in the Woods,* 173, 182, 187–88; Maude Wood Henry to Robert H. Elias, April 2, 1945 (Cornell); and *GW,* 2: 613–24. Before Anna and Henry split, they had moved to Yakima, Washington, where she invested what money she had left from the sale of her typing agency in an apple orchard, becoming partners not only with Arthur (and Dreiser) but also Arthur's brother Alfred, a womanizing Methodist minister. Interestingly, Alfred wrote a sentimental novel about the Mormons that resembles his brother's *A Princess of Arcady*— it even features a parentless heroine brought up by a bachelor uncle and two male associates. He also pursued Anna after Arthur had abandoned her, but she was sorely distressed by his romantic advances. See Alfred Henry, *By Order of the Prophet* (New York: Fleming H. Revell Company, 1902).

10. "A Cripple Whose Energy Gives Inspiration," *Success* 5 (February 1902): 72–73. The others were "A True Patriarch: A Study from Life," *McClure's* 18 (De-

cember 1901): 136–44; "The Color of To-day," *Harper's Weekly* 45 (December 1901): 1272–73; "The New Knowledge of Weeds," *Ainslee's* 8 (January 1902): 533–38; "A Remarkable Art," *Great Round World* 19 (May 3, 1902): 430–34; "The Tenement Toilers," *Success* 5 (April 1902): 213–14, 232; "A Doer of the Word," *Ainslee's* 9 (June 1902): 453; and "Christmas in the Tenements," *Harper's Weekly* 46 (December 6, 1902): 52–53. "Curious Shifts of the Poor" became "A Touch of Human Brotherhood," *Success* 5 (March 1902): 140–41.

11. *FF,* 197.

12. TD to Richard Duffy, November 13, 1901; Duffy to TD, December 6, 1901; TD to Duffy, Dec. 10, 1901 (Penn); and *L,* 1: 66–69.

13. TD to Richard Duffy, December 23, 1901; Duffy to TD, January 30, 1902; TD to Duffy, February 2, 1902 (Penn); and William White, "Dreiser on Hardy, Henley, and Whitman," *English Language Notes* 6 (November 1968): 122–24.

14. Richard Duffy to TD, December 6, 1901, March 5, March 28, and July 31, 1902 (Penn).

15. *AD,* 70, 77; and TD to Richard Duffy, December 5, 1902, [December] 12, [1902] (Penn); and TD to Duffy, January 6, 1903 (Virginia).

16. *AD,* 55–113. See also *AL* for additional background on this period.

17. *L,* 2: 424; and "'Down Hill': A Chapter in Dreiser's Story about Himself," ed. Thomas P. Riggio, *DS* 19 (Fall 1988): 12.

18. Holograph manuscript of "Down Hill and Up," part I (Penn); and *DML,* 2: 688.

19. "Life Stories of Successful Men—No. 11, Chauncey Mitchell Depew," *Success* 1 (November 1898): 3–4; reprinted in *TDU,* 52–59. Twenty-seven years later, while writing the final chapter of *An American Tragedy,* Dreiser interviewed Depew, who at ninety-one was "still at his office every day of the week" ("Chauncey M. Depew," *Cosmopolitan* 79 [July 1925]: 86–87, 183–85).

20. "'Down Hill,'" 14–15; and Marguerite Tjader [Harris], *Theodore Dreiser: A New Dimension* (Norwalk, Conn.: Silvermine Publishers, 1965), 72–73, where a later mystical experience is discussed.

21. *AL,* 44.

22. Robert Van Gelder, "An Interview with Theodore Dreiser," *New York Times Book Review,* March 16, 1941.

23. *AL,* 52–54.

24. *CGC,* 171–81.

25. Austin Brennan to Paul Dresser, April 25, 1903 (Penn).

26. *AL,* 77.

27. "Culhane, the Solid Man," in *TM,* 142. Dreiser took his title from Ned Harrigan's song, "Muldoon, the Solid Man." The sketch included several inaccuracies, which Muldoon and his admirers resented.

28. Edward Van Every, *Muldoon, The Solid Man of Sport* (New York: Frederick A. Stokes Company, 1929), 4–7; and *Dictionary of American Biography,* 11,

Supplement One: 569. Van Every gives Muldoon's year of birth as 1845, but the *DAB*, which casts doubts on his Civil War participation, gives 1852.

29. *AL*, 90.

30. *AL*, 99–100; and Van Every, *Muldoon*, 3.

31. W. A. Swanberg, *Dreiser* (New York: Scribner's Sons, 1965), 107; and *AL*, 107.

32. *AL*, 111.

33. *AL*, 115.

34. "'Up Hill': A Chapter in Dreiser's Story about Himself," ed. Thomas P. Riggio, *DS* 20 (Spring 1989): 10–12.

35. *AL*, 120, 149.

36. "The Cruise of the 'Idlewild,'" *Bohemia* 17 (October 1909): 441–47, also in *Free;* Paul Dresser to TD, June 22, 1903 (Penn); and "The Mighty Burke," *McClure's* 37 (May 1911): 40–50, reprinted as "The Mighty Rourke" in *TM*, 289.

37. "The Irish Section Foreman Who Taught Me How to Live," *Hearst's International* 46 (August 1924): 20–21, 118–21. See Richard W. Dowell, "Will the Real Mike Burke Stand Up, Please!" *DN* 14 (Spring 1983), 1–9; and F. O. Matthiessen, *Theodore Dreiser* (New York: William Sloane Associates, 1951), 101–2. Dreiser expresses his frustration over the struggle to write Book I of *An American Tragedy* in a letter to Sallie Kussell, August 16, 1924 (Virginia).

38. *AL*, 176; "The Toil of the Laborer," *New York Call,* July 13, 1913; and "The Irish Section Foreman," 120.

39. Paul Dresser to TD, December 12, 1903; Dresser to TD, October 18, 1903 (Penn); and Richard Lingeman, *Theodore Dreiser* (New York: G. P. Putnam's Sons, 1986), 1: 381.

40. *Chains: Lesser Novels and Stories* (New York: Boni & Liveright, 1927), 98–132; and *CGC*, 104–7, 240, 269. See also Joseph Griffin, *The Small Canvas: An Introduction to Dreiser's Short Stories* (Rutherford, N.J.: Fairleigh Dickinson University Press, 1985), 94–96. Before "St. Columba and the River" appeared in *Chains,* it appeared as "Glory Be! McGlathery," in the *Pictorial Review* 26 (January 1925): 5–7, 51–52, 54, 71. For the possibility that the original newspaper version may have been based on Dreiser's experience as a laborer in the excavation of the tunnel under the North River, see Lester Cohen, "Theodore Dreiser: A Personal Memoir," *Discovery* 4 (September 1954): 99–126.

41. Lydia Cushman Schurman, "Theodore Dreiser and His Street and Smith Circle," *Dime Novel Round-Up* 65, no. 6 (1995): 183–95; *FF*, 205–6; Robert H. Elias, *Theodore Dreiser* (Ithaca: Cornell University Press, 1970; orig. pub. 1948), 133–34; and TD to Charles Fort, June 22, July 15, and August 11, 1905 (Penn).

42. "The Rivers of the Nameless Dead," *Tom Watson's Magazine* 1 (March 1905): 112–13; and "The Track Walker," *Tom Watson's Magazine* 1 (June 1905): 502–3; both reprinted in *CGC*, 284–87 and 104–7.

43. "The Silent Worker," *Tom Watson's Magazine* 2 (September 1905): 364, later reprinted as part of "Three Sketches of the Poor," *New York Call,* November 23, 1913, as "The Man Who Bakes Your Bread," *New York Call,* April 13, 1919, and as "The Men in the Snow" in *CGC,* 228–30; and "The Loneliness of the City," *Tom Watson's Magazine* 2 (October 1905): 474–75, reprinted in *TDS,* 157–58.

44. Paul Dresser to Austin Brennan, May 19, 1904 (Penn); Vera Dreiser, *My Uncle Theodore* (New York: Nash Publishing, 1976), 126; *New York Times,* January 31, 1906; and *D* holograph, chap. XXVII (Indiana).

45. Paul Dresser to Mary Francis (Mame) Brennan, December 10, 1905 (Penn); and *TM,* 105–6.

46. Vera Dreiser, *My Uncle Theodore,* 69, 125–128; Vera Dreiser to W. A. Swanberg, May 4, 1964 (Penn); Richard W. Dowell, "Dreiser vs. Terre Haute, or Paul Dresser's Body Lies A-Molderin' in the Grave," *DS* 20 (Fall 1989): 10; and Clayton W. Henderson, *On the Banks of the Wabash: The Life and Music of Paul Dresser* (Indianapolis: Indiana Historical Society Press, 2003), xxviii. Henderson questions whether the White Rats helped pay for the funeral (314), but also quotes from a letter by Ed Dreiser's wife, Mai, that "the White Rats society sent Mary [Mame] Brennan $250," which she spent in reburying Paul with his parents in Chicago (321).

47. Carl Dreiser to TD, May 28, 1901, November 10 and 28, 1907, October 16 and December 28, 1908 (Penn). Dreiser stated that Carl committed suicide at age sixteen (*D,* 599), but Vera Dreiser, Ed's daughter, more correctly remembered for biographer Richard Lingeman (*Theodore Dreiser,* 1: 212, 439) that Carl committed suicide, "barely out of his teens."

48. Lingeman, *Theodore Dreiser,* 1: 404; *FF,* 210; and *L,* 1: 75–79.

49. Quoted in Swanberg, *Dreiser,* 114.

50. "The Beauty of the Tree," *Broadway Magazine* 16 (June 1906): 130; "The Poet's Creed," *Broadway Magazine* 16 (August 1906): 353; and "Fruitage," *Broadway Magazine* 17 (February 1907): 566.

51. Elias, *Dreiser,* 136; *L,* 1: 84; *TM,* 214; and James L. W. West III, "Dreiser and the B. W. Dodge *Sister Carrie,*" *Studies in Bibliography* 35 (1982): 323–31.

52. See *TDCR,* 27–54, for the full texts of the 1907 edition reviews; Otis Notman's interview with Dreiser in the *New York Times Saturday Review of Books,* June 15, 1907, is reprinted in *TDS,* 163–64. For the alteration of the Ade passage in the 1907 edition, see Jack Salzman, "Dreiser and Ade: A Note on the Text of *Sister Carrie,*" *American Literature* 40 (January 1969): 544–48.

53. Elias, *Dreiser,* 137–38; TD to Professor L. S. Randolph, September 16, 1909 (Virginia); and *FF,* 219. Dreiser puts the figure for his highest salary at Butterick at $7,500; see the autobiographical account given to Grant Richards in 1911 (Virginia). In "The Irish Section Foreman" (121), however, Dreiser set his Butterick salary at $10,000.

54. Swanberg, *Dreiser,* 121; and William C. Lengel, "The 'Genius' Himself," *Esquire* 10 (September 1938): 55.

55. *Delineator,* September 1907, 284; and *L,* 1: 94–95.

56. Anonymous review reprinted in *TDCR,* 41–42.

57. *DML,* 1: 16–18; and Leonard Keen Hirshberg, B.A., M.D., *What You Ought to Know About Your Baby,* (New York: Butterick Publications, 1910), 21. Hirshberg told biographer Robert H. Elias on August 8, 1945, that Mencken "really wrote the articles by-lined by me in Dreiser's Delineator" (Cornell). In a copy of the collected articles, *What You Ought to Know About Your Baby,* Mencken inscribed to a friend: "I did this for the *Delineator,* then edited by Theodore Dreiser. Hirshberg drew up rough drafts and I wrote the articles" (Texas).

58. *DML,* 1: 10; and H. L. Mencken, *My Life As Author and Editor,* ed. Jonathan Yardley (New York: Alfred A. Knopf, 1993), 28.

59. "Henry L. Mencken and Myself," in Isaac Goldberg, *The Man Mencken: A Biographical and Critical Survey* (New York: Simon and Schuster, 1925), 378–81; reprinted in *DML,* 2: 738–40.

60. *TM,* 7.

NINE. RETURN OF THE NOVELIST

1. *TM,* 22, 377–78, 52–53.

2. Vera Dreiser to W. A. Swanberg, May 5, 1964 (Penn).

3. Robert H. Elias to W. A. Swanberg, May 10, 1962; and William C. Lengel to Swanberg, March 2, 1962, where Lengel, according to Swanberg's notes, told him: "Dreiser [while married to Jug] didn't know he was sterile" (Penn). Moreover, in spite of his long record of promiscuity, no offspring, legitimate or otherwise, have ever come forward to claim Dreiser as their biological father.

4. *The "Genius"* (New York: John Lane Company, 1915), 269.

5. *FF,* 233.

6. [H. L. Mencken], "In Defense of Profanity," *Bohemian* 17 (November 1909): 567–68.

7. [TD], "In the Days of Discovery" and "The Day of Special Privileges," *Bohemian* 17 (November 1909): 563–64 and 565–67.

8. [TD], "Empty the Cradle," *Delineator* 70 (October 1907): 491–92.

9. *Editor & Publisher,* November 2, 1907; and *Printing News,* December, 1907, both included in Dreiser's *Delineator* scrapbook at Penn; *New York Herald,* October 11, 1908; Theodore Roosevelt to TD, December 25, 1908; and James E. West to TD, January 11, 1909 (Indiana).

10. James B. Wasson to TD, January 23, 1909; and N. Lafayette-Savay to TD, April 24, 1909 (Indiana).

11. William C. Lengel to W. A. Swanberg, March 2, 1962; and Lengel, "The

'Genius' Himself," *Esquire* 10 (September 1938): 55, 120, 124, 126. Lengel told Dorothy Dudley in 1930: "Dreiser was big, ungainly, homely, but after [reading *Sister Carrie*] I would have done anything he asked of me" (*FF,* 221–23).

12. [TD] to Charles W. Taylor, Jr., December 11, 1908 (Indiana); and Louise Campbell to W. A. Swanberg, June 21, 1962 (Penn).

13. *DLM,* 1: 37–38. "The Decay of Churches" was never published in the *Bohemian.*

14. Mrs. Charles Seymour Whitman (formerly Thelma Cudlipp) to W. A. Swanberg, November 11, 1962 (Penn).

15. Mrs. Charles Seymour Whitman, "October's Child," unpublished manuscript; and Ann Watkins to W. A. Swanberg, November 12, 1962 (Penn).

16. Whitman to Swanberg, November 11, 1962.

17. Whitman to Swanberg, November 11, 1962; and TD to Whitman, February 23, 1943 (Penn).

18. *L,* 1: 104–9; TD to Annie Cudlipp, October 11, 1910; and Ann Watkins to Swanberg, November 12, 1962: "He threatened suicide with such frenzy that I was scared to death he'd do it right in my apartment" (Penn).

19. *DML,* 1: 52, 63–64.

20. Sinclair Lewis, "Editors Who Write," *Life,* October 10, 1907; quoted in Mark Schorer, *Sinclair Lewis: An American Life* (New York: McGraw-Hill, 1961), 179.

21. Schorer, *Sinclair Lewis,* 179; see also Martha Solomon, *Emma Goldman* (New York: Twayne Publishers, 1987), 1–28.

22. Thomas P. Riggio, "Dreiser's Song of Innocence and Experience: The Ur-Text of *Jennie Gerhardt,*" *DS* (Fall 2000): 22–38.

23. *D,* 599n. For an exhaustive and penetrating analysis of *Jennie Gerhardt* as well as the text before it was edited by Harper's, see *JG,* where it is also asserted on p. 422 of the "Historical Commentary" that Carl Dreiser lived with Mame at the turn of the century.

24. *JG,* 4, 108, 12–13.

25. Richard Lehan, *Theodore Dreiser: His World and His Novels* (Carbondale: Southern Illinois University Press, 1969), 80–81.

26. "A Literary Apprenticeship" (Penn); and Albert Mordell, "Theo. Dreiser—Radical," *Philadelphia Record,* December 13, 1913.

27. Lehan, *Dreiser,* 87; and *JG,* 321.

28. *JG,* 442 and 214. For examples of passages with redundancies, see 194–95, 298–99, and 304–5.

29. *DML,* 1: 81; *Letters of H. L. Mencken,* ed. Guy J. Forgue (New York: Alfred A. Knopf, 1961), 18–19; Lillian Rosenthal to TD, January 25, 1911; *L,* 1: 110; and Sara White Dreiser to TD, April 19, 1926 (Penn).

30. *FF,* 256.

31. H. L. Mencken, "A Novel of the First Rank," *The Smart Set* 35 (Novem-

ber 1911): 153–55; reprinted in *DML*, 2: 740–44. It is also reprinted in *TDCR*, where the other reviews of *Jennie Gerhardt* quoted are to be found (57–95).

32. Grant Richards, *Author Hunting: Memories of Years Spent Mainly in Publishing* (1934; repr. London: Unicorn Press, 1960), 138–43.

33. Lucia A. Kinsaul, "The Rudest American Author: Grant Richards' Assessment of Theodore Dreiser," *DS* 23 (Spring 1992): 27–28.

34. TD to Grant Richards, November 4, 1911 (Texas); reprinted in Richards, *Author Hunting,* 145–46.

35. Richards, *Author Hunting,* 148–49.

36. *DML*, 1: 82–84.

37. *DML*, 1: 126–27; Thomas P. Riggio, "Europe without Baedeker: The Omitted Hancha Jower Story—from *A Traveler at Forty,*" *Modern Fiction Studies* 23 (Autumn 1977): 423–40; and *TF,* 80. See also Renate von Bardeleben, "Dreiser's Diaristic Mode," *DS* 31 (Spring 2000): 26–42.

38. *TF,* 11, 32, 63.

39. *DML*, 1: 125; and *TF,* 113–27. A slightly truncated version of "Lilly: A Girl of the Streets" was also published in *The Smart Set* 50 (June 1913): 81–86, as "Lilly Edwards: An Episode."

40. Riggio, "Europe without Baedeker," 428n., 431–32.

41. Riggio, "Europe without Baedeker," 436.

42. *TF,* 146, 203.

43. *TF,* 208, 217, 247.

44. *L,* 1: 130–31.

45. *TF,* 271–72, 347–53.

46. TD to Floyd Dell, March 12, 1912 (Newberry Library); *DML*, 1: 93; and *TF,* 397, 447–48.

47. *TF,* 444, 453.

48. *TF,* 486; and *L,* 1: 137.

49. TD to Floyd Dell, May 1, 1912 (Newberry Library); and Richards, *Author Hunting,* 153.

50. Unedited typescript of *TF,* 1152–56 (Penn); and *TF,* 523.

51. *TF,* 523, 525.

TEN. LIFE AFTER THE *TITANIC*

1. *New York Times,* June 23, 1912 (reprinted in *TDS,* 192–95); *L,* 1: 143; and "Theodore Dreiser, Author of 'Jennie Gerhardt' . . . Woman the Centre of Interest in Contemporary Fiction," *New York Evening Post,* November 15, 1911.

2. W. A. Swanberg, *Dreiser* (New York: Charles Scribner's Sons, 1965), 162; and Anna Tatum to TD, November 7, 1911 (Penn). "The Mighty Burke" appeared as "The Mighty Rourke" in *TM*; see chapter 8.

3. Anna Tatum to TD, November 7, 11, 23, 1911, and April 12, 1913 (Penn).

4. *AD*, 207, where Dreiser also asserts Tatum's bisexuality.

5. *DML*, 1: 96–98.

6. *DML*, 1: 99.

7. Charles Shapiro, *Theodore Dreiser: Our Bitter Patriot* (Carbondale: Southern Illinois University Press, 1962), 44.

8. *ND*, 499.

9. "The Supremacy of the Modern Business Man" (Virginia).

10. Burton Rascoe, *Theodore Dreiser* (New York: Robert M. McBride & Co., 1925), 7–8.

11. "The Materials of a Great Novel," *New York World,* February 4, 1906; quoted in Philip L. Gerber, "Dreiser's Financier: A Genesis," *Journal of Modern Literature* 1 (March 1971): 354–74.

12. Charles Edward Russell, "Where Did You Get It, Gentlemen?" *Everybody's* 17 (September 1907): 348–60; *L,* 1: 208; Donald Pizer, *Novels of Theodore Dreiser: A Critical Study* (Minneapolis: University of Minnesota Press, 1976), 161–62; and Edwin LeFèvre, "What Availeth It?" *Everybody's* 24 (June 1911): 836–48. Dreiser consulted Henry Clews, *Fifty Years in Wall Street* (1887); Charles A. Conant, *Defense of Stock Exchange* (1903); John R. Dos Passos, *Treatise on the Law of Stock Brokers and Stock Exchanges* (1882); Francis L. Eames, *History of the New York Stock Exchange* (1894); Sereno S. Pratt, *The Work of Wall Street* (1903); S. A. Nelson, *The ABC of Wall Street* (1900), and *The Theory of Stock Speculation* (1903).

13. *The Financier* (New York: Harper & Brothers, 1912), 11–13; and "A Lesson from the Aquarium," *Tom Watson's Magazine* 3 (January 1906): 306–8, reprinted in *TDS,* 159–62.

14. See Richard Lehan, *Theodore Dreiser: His World and His Novels* (Carbondale: Southern Illinois University Press, 1969), 101–2; Philip L. Gerber, "The Financier Himself: Dreiser and C. T. Yerkes," *Publications of the Modern Language Association* 88 (January 1973): 117–18; and Robert Edwin Wilkinson, "A Study of Theodore Dreiser's *The Financier*" (Ph.D. diss., University of Pennsylvania, 1965), 12.

15. *The Financier* (1912), 127, 133; and *ND,* 132–36, 702n. In creating Butler and his daughter, Dreiser may have also drawn upon the plot of Henry M. Heyde's *The Buccanneers* (1904); see Philip L. Gerber, "Hyde's Tabbs and Dreiser's Butlers," *DN* 6 (Spring 1975): 9–11.

16. Joann Krieg, "Theodore Dreiser and the Penitentiary System," *DN* 8 (Fall 1977): 5–8; Krieg points out that Dreiser's otherwise meticulous description of the famous prison, which in its day was both an architectural and a penal model for prisons around the world, erred in stating that it opened in 1822 instead of 1829.

17. *The Financier* (1912), 575, 467, 470, 659–60.

18. *TDCR*, 101–4, 106, 114.

19. *TDCR*, 107, 126, 128; and *DML*, 1: 110–11.

20. Maurice Bassan, *Hawthorne's Son: The Life and Literary Career of Julian Hawthorne* (Columbus: Ohio State University Press, 1970), 212–20.

21. H. I. Brock, review of *The Reef, New York Times,* November 24, 1912.

22. Douglas Z. Doty to Grant Richards, undated, and William W. Ellsworth to Grant Richards, August 15, 1913 (Texas).

23. Grant Richards, *Author Hunting: Memories of Years Spent Mainly in Publishing* (London: Unicorn Press, 1934, 1960), 154; and TD to Grant Richards, July 12; Richards to TD, August 8; TD to Richards, December 16, 1912; and Douglas Z. Doty to Richards, October 19, 1913 (Texas).

24. TD to Grant Richards, July 24, 1912; Grant Richards to TD, August 8, 1912 (Texas); and Richards, *Author Hunting.*

25. Thomas P. Riggio, "Dreiser: Autobiographical Fragment, 1911," *DS* 18 (Spring 1987): 12–21; "An Author 'Personally Connected,'" *New York Times,* November 30, 1913; and Richards, *Author Hunting,* 167. When the initial sales for *The Financier* were less than expected, Richards wrote Dreiser on May 15, 1912, "I understand that you won't tie yourself up for any future book." Dreiser agreed that the sales had been disappointing, but he was intent on going through with the three-book deal on the trilogy with Harper's, telling Richards bluntly: "I have no particular quarrel with the house. They are civil & fairly decent as publishers" (*L,* 1: 143–44).

26. "The Lost Phoebe," *Century Magazine* 91 (April 1916): 885–96, reprinted in *Free* and *DML,* 1: 154. "The Father" was never published; it survives among Dreiser's papers at Penn.

27. *Hamlin Garland's Diaries,* ed. Donald Pizer (San Marino: Huntington Library, 1968), 123; Kim Townsend, *Sherwood Anderson* (Boston: Houghton Mifflin Company, 1987), 310; and *Sherwood Anderson's Memoirs: A Critical Edition,* ed. Ray Lewis White (Chapel Hill: University of North Carolina, 1969), 451. In 1964 Floyd Dell wrote that even though Anderson "began to tell people that it was Dreiser who got *Windy* published, . . . this wasn't true." See William A. Sutton, *The Road to Winesburg* (Metuchen, N.J.: Scarecrow Press, 1972), 609. Powys's description of first meeting Dreiser is quoted in "Table Talk," *Powys Society Newsletter* 44 (November 2001): 24.

28. Edgar Lee Masters to TD, November 27 and December 3, 1912 (Penn); and Masters, *Across Spoon River* (1936; repr. New York: Octagon Books, 1969), 329–30.

29. William C. Lengel to TD, July 1, [1912], and October 5, 1912 (Penn).

30. Floyd Dell, "A Great Novel," *Chicago Evening Post Literary Review,* November 3, 1911, reprinted in *TDCR,* 64–68; Dell, *Homecoming: An Autobiography* (New York: Farrar & Rinehart, 1933), 224; and TD, "This Madness. The

Book of Sidonie," *Hearst's International-Cosmopolitan* 86 (June 1929): 85. Markham was the basis for the fictional "Sidonie"; see chapter 14.

31. Maurice Browne, *Too Late to Lament: An Autobiography* (Bloomington: Indiana University Press, 1956), 133–34; and John Cowper Powys, *Autobiography* (1934; repr. London: Picador, 1967), 551, 648.

32. Kirah Markham [Elaine Hyman] to TD, February 4, 1916; and Markham to Helen Dreiser, December 27, 1952 (Penn).

33. "The Naturalism of Mr. Dreiser," *Nation* 101 (December 2, 1915): 648–50, reprinted in Stuart P. Sherman, *On Contemporary Literature* (New York: Henry Holt and Company, 1917) as "The Barbaric Naturalism of Theodore Dreiser." See also Donald Pizer, ed., *Critical Essays on Theodore Dreiser* (Boston: G. K. Hall & Co., 1981), 4–12. Ford's comment is quoted in *FF,* 302.

34. H. L. Mencken, "Adventures among the New Novels," *The Smart Set* 43 (August 1914): 153–57; and *Baltimore Evening Sun,* May 23, 1914; reprinted in *TDCR,* 172–73, 194–98.

35. Pizer, *Novels of Theodore Dreiser,* 184.

36. See Philip L. Gerber, "The Alabaster Protégé: Dreiser and Berenice Fleming," *American Literature* 43 (May 1971): 217–30; and his "Jolly Mrs. Yerkes Is Home from Abroad: Dreiser and the Celebrity Culture," in *Theodore Dreiser and American Culture: New Readings,* ed. Yoshinobu Hakutani (Newark: University of Delaware Press, 2000), 79–103.

37. See Kirah Markham to TD, May 9, 20, 21, 24, 1913, and May 1913 (Penn).

38. Floyd Dell to TD, March 31, 1913; and William C. Lengel to TD, March 31, 1913 (Penn).

39. *DML,* 1: 132, 135–36; and Anna Tatum to TD, March 16, 1914 (Penn).

40. J. Jefferson Jones to TD, April 20, 1914 (Penn).

41. *DML,* 1: 135, 63, 129.

42. *DML,* 1: 148, 144.

43. *CP,* ix.

44. *CP,* 11. Further quotes from the plays are to this edition.

45. *DML,* 1: 145; Terry Teachout, *The Skeptic: A Life of H. L. Mencken* (New York: Harper Collins, 2002), 26; and H. L. Mencken, *My Life as Author and Editor,* ed. Jonathan Yardley (New York: Alfred A. Knopf, 1993), 152.

46. *CP,* xvi.

47. Mencken, *My Life,* 152–53; and *Letters of John Cowper Powys to His Brother Llewelyn,* ed. Malcolm Elwin (London: Village Press, 1975), 1: 116.

48. *Washington Square Plays,* ed. Walter Prichard Eaton (New York: Doubleday, 1916), xii.

49. "The Girl in the Coffin," *The Smart Set* 41 (October 1913): 127–40; "The Blue Sphere," *The Smart Set* 44 (December 1914): 245–52; "In the Dark," *The Smart Set* 45 (January 1915): 419–25; and "Laughing Gas," *The Smart Set* 45 (Feb-

ruary 1915): 85–94. "The Spring Recital" appeared in *Little Review* 2 (December 1915): 28–35; and "The Light in the Window" in the *International* 10 (January 1916): 6–8, 32.

50. *DML*, 1: 146–47.

51. Kirah Markham to W. A. Swanberg, August 23, 1964 (Penn); quoted in *CP*, xv.

52. Keith Newlin, "Expressionism Takes the Stage: Dreiser's 'Laughing Gas,'" *Journal of American Drama* 4 (Winter 1992): 5–22; and Richard Goldstone, *Thornton Wilder: An Intimate Portrait* (New York: Saturday Review Press, 1975), 118–19.

53. "A Word Concerning Birth Control," *Birth Control Review* 5 (April 1921): 5; and Robert H. Elias, *Theodore Dreiser: Apostle of Nature* (Ithaca: Cornell University Press, 1970; orig. pub. 1948), 215. Later, in "The Right to Kill," *New York Call,* March 16, 1918, Dreiser argued that it was probably all right to kill the weak and defective infant because "Life is a grinding game" in which the weak are ground out anyway "after much suffering" (*TDS*, 224–29).

54. *D*, 43–47.

ELEVEN. THE GENIUS HIMSELF

1. Edgar Lee Masters, *Spoon River Anthology*, ed. John E. Hallwas (Urbana: University of Illinois Press, 1992), 127.

2. Diary notes for *A Hoosier Holiday*, alternately entitled "Back to Indiana," August 5–7, 1915 (Penn).

3. *HH*, 22, 24–25, 13.

4. *HH*, 46, 50. This was Louise Campbell. Another Pennsylvanian who later objected to Dreiser's slight of the Quaker State was Albert Mordell, a longtime acquaintance and literary admirer. See his "Talking About Pennsylvanians," *Philadelphia Record,* January 17, 1917; and his *My Relations with Theodore Dreiser* (Girard, Kansas: Haldeman-Julius Publications, 1951), 12.

5. *HH*, 68.

6. *HH*, 173; and Donald Pizer, Richard W. Dowell, and Frederic E. Rusch, eds., *Theodore Dreiser: A Primary Bibliography and Reference Guide* (Boston: G. K. Hall, 1991), 8. Although it is not indicated, the following edition, recently published, prints the altered passage instead of the original in what is purported to be a duplication of the first edition: *A Hoosier Holiday*, intro. Douglas Brinkley (Bloomington: Indiana University Press, 1997).

7. *HH*, 116.

8. *HH*, 78.

9. *HH*, 283, 311.

10. *HH*, 312, 322–23.

11. *HH*, 353, 371, 393; and *D*, 11.

12. *HH*, 397, 424.

13. *HH*, 440; and *D*, 34–35.

14. *HH*, 486, 503–4; and diary notes (Penn).

15. TD to Murrel Cain, February 8, 1916 (Virginia); and *HH*, 512.

16. [Alfred] Joyce Kilmer, "The Novel Is Doomed, Will Harben Thinks," *New York Times*, October 3, 1915.

17. Thomas A. Bailey, *The American Pageant: A History of the Republic* (Lexington, Mass.: D. C. Heath and Company, 1975), 749; *TDCR*, 242–44, 225–26, 232–33; and W. A. Swanberg, *Dreiser* (New York: Charles Scribner's Sons, 1965), 194.

18. "The Saddest Story," *The New Republic* 3 (June 12, 1915): 155–56, reprinted in *TDS*, 200–203; and *DML*, 1: 165, 187–88.

19. *DML*, 1: 164; *FF*, 327; and *TDCR*, 221, 225, 236, 243. Alternate titles are in the manuscript of *The "Genius"* (Penn).

20. *DML*, 1: 176, 149, 235.

21. *TDCR*, 218; and *L*, 3: 796–97. For Sonntag, see also TD, "The Color of To-day," *Harper's Weekly* 45 (December 14, 1901): 1272–73.

22. "A Master of Photography," *Success* 2 (June 10, 1899): 471; and "The Camera Club of New York," *Ainslee's* 4 (October 1899): 324–35. See also Joseph J. Kwiat, "Dreiser and the Graphic Artist," *American Quarterly* 3 (Summer 1951): 127–41; Kwiat, "Dreiser's *The 'Genius'* and Everett Shinn, The Ash-Can Painter," *Publications of the Modern Language Association* 67 (March 1952): 15–31; and *FF*, 328.

23. *DML*, 2: 684; and see note 47 to this chapter.

24. Richard Lehan, *Theodore Dreiser: His World and His Novels* (Carbondale: Southern Illinois University Press, 1969), 123–24; Louis J. Oldani, "A Study of Theodore Dreiser's *The 'Genius'*" (Ph.D. diss., University of Pennsylvania, 1973), 39; and Oldani, "Dreiser's 'Genius' in the Making: Composition and Revision," *Studies in Bibliography* 47 (1994): 230–52.

25. "Possible Insert" to William C. Lengel's "A Pregnant Night in American Literature," unpublished manuscript, 1960 (Penn); *ND*, 553; and Sara White Dreiser to TD, April 19, 1926 (Penn).

26. For the original (happy) ending, see chapter 104 of the manuscript and chapters 104–5 of the typescript; and *The "Genius"* (New York: John Lane Company, 1915), 733.

27. H. L. Mencken, "A Literary Behemoth," *The Smart Set* 47 (December 1915): 150–54; reprinted in *DML*, 2: 754–59.

28. John Cowper Powys, "Theodore Dreiser," *Little Review* 2 (November 1915): 7–13, reprinted in *TDCR*, 226–29; and *The "Genius*," 20.

29. Stuart Sherman, "The Naturalism of Mr. Dreiser," *Nation* 101 (December 2, 1915): 648–50, reprinted in *Critical Essays on Theodore Dreiser*, ed. Donald Pizer (Boston: G. K. Hall, 1981), 4–12.

30. H. L. Mencken, "The Dreiser Bugaboo," *Seven Arts* 2 (August 1917), 507–17; reprinted in *Critical Essays on Theodore Dreiser*, 19–26.

31. Sherman, "Naturalism."

32. *TDCR*, 234.

33. TD to Willard Dillman, February 7, 1916 (Virginia); *L*, 1: 206n.; H. L. Mencken, *My Life As Author and Editor*, ed. Jonathan Yardley (New York: Alfred A. Knopf, 1993), 153; *AD*, 132; *TDCR*, 281–83; and *DML*, 1: 241.

34. *DML*, 1: 245n.

35. *Cincinnati Enquirer*, September 14, 1916 (David Graham Phillips's posthumously published *Susan Lenox* was also targeted); "No More Free Ads for Racy Novels," *New York Tribune*, August 20, 1916; and *DML*, 1: 244.

36. *DML*, 1: 246, 245–46n; and Oldani, "A Study of *The 'Genius*,'" 179–85.

37. William C. Lengel, "The 'Genius' Himself," *Esquire* 10 (September 1938): 126; *DML*, 1: 271–73; and H. L. Mencken to Ernest Boyd, November 13, 1916, in *Letters of H. L. Mencken*, ed. Guy J. Forgue (New York: Alfred A. Knopf, 1961), 95–96.

38. *New York Times*, July 12, 1918.

39. *DML*, 1: 252–53; and *L*, 1: 152–54.

40. Quoted from ms. at Penn in Oldani, "A Study of *The 'Genius*,'" 222.

41. Lars Ahnebrink, "Garland and Dreiser: An Abortive Friendship," *Midwest Journal* 7 (Winter 1955–56): 285–92.

42. *L*, 1: 194.

43. Beach did not sign the preliminary list, but he added his name to the final protest (*DML*, 2: 802; and *L*, 2: 412n).

44. *DML*, 1: 279.

45. See, for example, Mencken's letter to TD on December 16, 1916 (*DML*, 1: 281–83).

46. *The Hand of the Potter* (New York: Boni & Liveright, 1918), reprinted in *CP*, 188–282; and *D*, 135.

47. *CP*, xx–xxii. See also Frederic E. Rusch, "Dreiser's Other Tragedy," *Modern Fiction Studies* 23 (Autumn 1977): 449–56. In the winter of 1915, Dreiser wrote six chapters of a novel to be called *The Rake* (not to be confused with "The Rake" of 1900; see chapter 7) based on the Roland Molineux case. The 1915 manuscript is discussed in conjunction with *An American Tragedy* in chapter 13.

48. H. V. Gormley to Emma Rector (Flanagan), June 27, 1918; and *D* holograph, chapter VI (Indiana).

49. Richard Lingeman, *Theodore Dreiser* (New York: G. P. Putnam's Sons, 1990), 2: 142.

50. Sigmund Freud, *Introduction to Psychoanalysis* (1920). See Walker Gilmer,

Horace Liveright: Publisher of the Twenties (New York: David Lewis, 1970), 25, 28; *CP,* xxix–xxx; Frederic E. Rusch, "Dreiser's Introduction to Freudianism," *DS* 18 (Fall 1987): 34–38; TD, "Olive Brand" in *GW,* 1: 81–82; and TD's "Remarks" on Freud's seventy-fifth birthday (1931) in *TDS,* 263–64. Dreiser was formally introduced to Freud's theories by Edith DeLong ("Olive Brand"), the future wife of Dreiser's longtime friend Edward H. Smith, in May 1918.

51. Wharton Esherick to W. A. Swanberg, June 25, 1962 (Penn). On the affair, see chapter 14.

52. *DML,* 1: 282–83; Ellen Moers, *Two Dreisers* (New York: Viking Press, 1969), 240–70; and *GW,* 2: 769.

53. *HH,* 378; and *The Hand of the Potter,* 170, 193.

54. Wharton Esherick to W. A. Swanberg, June 25, 1962.

55. *In Defense of Marion: The Love of Marion Bloom & H. L. Mencken,* ed. Edward A. Martin (Athens: University of Georgia Press, 1996); and *GW,* 2: 440. See also *AD,* 147–268. Information on the Bloom sisters is generally drawn from *Defense* and *AD,* as well as from Estelle Kubitz [Williams]'s letters at Penn.

56. Estelle Kubitz [Williams] to Marion Bloom, January 24, 1927 (Penn).

57. *AD,* 153.

58. Mencken later quoted two passages from the diary that present Dreiser in a depressed state over his literary fortunes in 1917 (*My Life,* 218). The typescript of the diary for 1917–18, now in the New York Public Library, was retained by Mencken until he wrote his memoir. On October 14, 1938, he wrote of it: "This curious document was handed to me in 1920 or thereabout by Dreiser's secretary. Whether she gave it to me because she was then on bad terms with Dreiser and eager to make him look foolish or because she thought that the diary would aid me in my writings about him I don't know. I put it aside and forgot it completely, and it was only the other day that I disinterred it" (*AD,* 147).

59. Estelle Kubitz Williams to Marion Bloom, September 12, 1916, and June 14, 1924 (Penn); also quoted in *In Defense of Marion,* 40–41, 204.

60. Estelle Kubitz Williams to Marion Bloom, September 12, no year given (Penn). "To this day," writes Edward A. Martin, a student of both sisters as thwarted women of this pre-Flapper era, "Marion and Estelle are remembered as 'the exotic Bloom sisters.'" Marion, who resembled her sister closely, though her eyes were more alluring and her countenance brighter, had fully realized by 1918 that Mencken would never marry her. As the United States entered World War I, she went to France as a nurse's aide on an American troop ship. On October 11 she wrote in her journal: "of how we are packed to overflowing with men bound for foreign soil to kill, of our going to nurse the remnants of humanity, a fearful epidemic [influenza] aboard, while all around are submarines bent on killing us. What is the meaning of it all ? . . . . It seems hard to connect disaster with the beauties of the evening, as if a fearful mistake was being made." She lived out her final decades in Washington, D.C., totally estranged for un-

known reasons from Estelle. Shortly before her death in 1975, she—like Estelle—shared her lover's intimate thoughts by selling her Mencken letters to the Enoch Pratt Library of Baltimore. See *In Defense of Marion,* xl, 90.

61. Louise Campbell to TD, February 24, 1917 (Penn). See *AD,* 157, for the fact that she was still married when she first wrote to Dreiser.

62. *Letters to Louise,* ed. Louise Campbell (Philadelphia: University of Pennsylvania Press, 1959), 10–11.

63. *AD,* 156–58.

64. *FF,* 363; and Swanberg, *Dreiser,* 210.

65. H. L. Mencken, "Theodore Dreiser," *A Book of Prefaces* (New York: Alfred A. Knopf, 1917), reprinted in *DML,* 2: 775–90; and *My Life,* 223.

TWELVE. BACK TO THE FUTURE

1. "Dreiser Favors Federal Control; Hits Financiers," *Huntington* [Indiana] *Press,* June 18, 1919; and *DML,* 1: 295–96.

2. Thomas A. Bailey, *The American Pageant: A History of the Republic* (Lexington, Mass.: D. C. Heath Company, 1975), 777.

3. "Life, Art and America," *Seven Arts* 1 (February 1917): 363–89, reprinted that year in pamphlet form and in *Hey,* 252–76.

4. "Mr. Bottom," *The Social War* 1 (April 1917): 2; "Our Greatest Writer Tells What's Wrong with our Newspapers," *Pep* 2 (July 1917): 8–9, reprinted as "Our Amazing Illusioned Press," *New York Call* 16 (December 16, 1971): 3.

5. Robert H. Elias, *Theodore Dreiser: Apostle of Nature* (Ithaca: Cornell University Press, 1970; orig. pub. 1948), 204.

6. TD to Waldo Frank, July 1, 1917; and Waldo Frank to TD, July 23, 1917 (Penn). Frank and Oppenheim's overture to Dreiser is quoted in the notes to the July 1 letter in Elias's transcript at Cornell.

7. H. L. Mencken, "The Dreiser Bugaboo," *Seven Arts* 1 (August 1917): 507–17, partly reprinted in *DML,* 2: 768–75.

8. *AD,* 181.

9. Walker Gilmer, *Horace Liveright: Publisher of the Twenties* (New York: David Lewis, 1970), 9.

10. Ben Huebsch to TD, March 6, 1918 (Library of Congress); *L,* 1: 250–51; and *DML,* 1: 312.

11. May Calvert Baker to TD, February 6, [1917]; and TD to Baker, February 15, 1917 (Penn).

12. Card at Penn.

13. *DML,* 1: 309; *AD,* 160n and 173n.

14. Gilmer, *Horace Liveright,* esp. 1–19.

15. Boni & Liveright to TD, August 8, 1917 (Penn).

16. *AD,* 191n; and Jug's 1914 agreement (Penn).

17. Dreiser states the amount for "Free" in *AD* as $750 (238). Elias estimates that "The Second Choice" earned around $600, possibly higher *(Theodore Dreiser,* 209). W. A. Swanberg claims that "Married" received $800, but he also errs in saying that "Free" earned only $500 (*Dreiser* [New York: Charles Scribner's Sons, 1965], 219). "Married" and "The Second Choice" appeared respectively in *Cosmopolitan* 63 (September 1917): 31–35, 112–15; and 64 (February 1918): 53–58, 104, 106–7. "Free" appeared in the *Saturday Evening Post* 190 (March 16, 1918): 13–15, 81–89. On Rose, see Sara White Dreiser to Fremont Rider, April 1, 1918 (Penn): "here am I whose death would make scarcely a ripple in the lives of men, & who would so gladly have gone in her stead. And she as wife & mother was so much needed."

18. *ND,* 103–5, 128; and *Free,* 139, 158, 162. See also chapter 3.

19. *ND,* 158.

20. See, for example, the first pages of Dreiser's notes for *HH* (Penn); and *L,* 1: 247–48.

21. *Free,* 324, 333.

22. *DML,* 1: 315.

23. "A Story of Stories" was based on the Red Galvin episode in chapters 48–50 of *ND.* In a pamphlet advertising *Free* (Virginia), Boni & Liveright used the *Sun's* dismissal of "Nigger Jeff" in juxtaposition with the *Cincinnati Enquirer's* assertion that the story was "powerful in its realism."

24. Joseph Griffin, *The Small Canvas: An Introduction to Dreiser's Short Stories* (Rutherford, N.J.: Fairleigh Dickinson University Press, 1985), 24, 16; *TDCR,* 306, 310; and [Virginia Woolf], "A Real American," *TLS,* August 21, 1919, reprinted in Ellen Moers, "Virginia Woolf on Dreiser," *DN* 7 (Fall 1976): 7–9.

25. *TM,* x; and *DML,* 2: 791, 399–400.

26. *TM,* 108, 188; and *Walt Whitman: Leaves of Grass,* ed. Jerome Loving (New York: Oxford University Press, 1990), 446.

27. *TDCR,* 314.

28. Dreiser first published his story on the mayor of Bridgeport in the June 1903 issue of *Era;* see chapter 6. For Burke see chapter 8, n. 36. Dreiser wrote the introduction to Robin's *Caius Gracchus* (1920), a verse tragedy published under the pseudonym of Odin Gregory.

29. Ellen Moers, *Two Dreisers* (New York: Viking Press, 1969), 246–50; and *Hey,* 243. The working title for *Hey* was "The King Is Naked."

30. *L,* 1: 284–87; and TD, *Notes on Life,* ed. Marguerite Tjader and John J. McAleer (University: University of Alabama Press, 1974).

31. Police Report in Dreiser's hand; *DML,* 2: 350; TD to May Calvert Baker, June 2, 1919; and Baker to TD, March 29, 1918 (Penn).

32. May Calvert Baker to TD, September 4, 1918; and TD to Baker, October 19, 1918 (Penn).

33. May Calvert Baker to TD, October 24, 1918; and TD to Baker, November 23, 1918 (Penn).

34. May Calvert Baker to TD, undated; *AD,* 257–68; Baker to TD, June 28, 1919; and TD to Baker, August 16, 1919 (Penn).

35. *AD,* 269–73.

36. *ML,* 12–23; *AD,* 318–19; and Vera Dreiser, *My Uncle Theodore* (New York: Nash Publishing Co., 1976), 141–42.

37. *AD,* 278–80.

38. *AD,* 339.

39. *AD,* 282; and TD, "Myself and the Movies," *Esquire* 20 (July 1943): 50, 159.

40. Boni & Liveright to TD, August 25, 1919 (Penn).

41. *AD,* 310, 283; and *ML,* 27–30.

42. Peter Cowie, *Eighty Years of Cinema* (New York: A. S. Barnes, 1977), 45; and Robert H. Stanley, *The Celluloid Empire: A History of the American Movie Industry* (New York: Hastings House, 1978), 43–44.

43. *ML,* 33; *AD,* 287–89, 294, 296, 307–8n; and Vera Dreiser, *My Uncle Theodore,* 143–44.

44. Horace Liveright to TD, September 18, 1920; Dreiser told Edward H. Smith on January 2, 1920, that he moved frequently "to escape the result of leaks" (Penn).

45. *DML,* 2: 360; *AD,* 338; Ephraim Katz, *The Film Encyclopedia* (New York: Harper & Row Publishers, 1979), 600–601; and TD, "Hollywood: Its Morals and Manners," *Shadowland* 5 (November 1921): 37, 61–63; (December 1921): 51, 61; (January 1922): 43, 67; and (February 1922): 53, 66. See also TD's "Hollywood Now," *McCall's* 48 (September 1921): 8, 18, 54. For Mencken's phrase, see his letter to Estelle Bloom Kubitz, May 26, [1922]; reprinted in *In Defense of Marion: The Love of Marion Bloom & H. L. Mencken,* ed. Edward A. Martin (Athens: University of Georgia Press, 1996), 174–75.

46. *ML,* 33, 35–36. The order and approximate beginning dates of their seven residences in Los Angeles between 1919 and 1922 are as follows: (1) November 1, 1919: Stillwell Hotel at 9th and Grand; (2) November 8: 338 Alvarado; (3) December 1: 558 North Larchmont and Clinton streets; (4) September 1, 1920: 1553 Curran Street in Highland Park; (5) around January 25, 1921: 6309 Sunset Drive; (6) March 8: 1515 Detroit Street near Sunset; and (7) August 1921 (until October, 1922): 652 North Columbus Avenue, Glendale, California.

47. Liveright later proposed that Clyde's last name would be easier to pronounce if spelled without an "s" (Horace Liveright to TD, April 23, 1924 [Penn]). As to Arbuckle, Dreiser initially thought of using this material somewhere, but a year later he recorded in his diary on September 21, 1921: "Working on cutting out all data relating to Arbuckle" (*AD,* 384).

48. *AD,* 310, 326; and *AT,* 1: 3, 6–7. It was originally thought that Dreiser

completed only twenty chapters in Los Angeles, but recently John Williams Reynolds discovered that there are two different chapters in the Dreiser collection at Penn marked VI ("The Genesis and Compositional History of Theodore Dreiser's *An American Tragedy* [Ph.D. diss., University of Connecticut, 1999]). For Conklin, see chapter 2.

49. *AD*, 336, 340. See also Horace Liveright to TD, April 22 and July 8, 1920 (Penn).

50. *L*, 2: 395; *GW*, 531, 562–63; and *AD*, 349–50.

51. *L*, 2: 396n; *L*, 1: 302; and Edward H. Smith, "Dreiser—After Twenty Years," *Bookman* 53 (March 1921): 27–39.

52. John W. Robertson, *Poe: A Study* (San Francisco: privately printed, 1921); see also *L*, 1: 369–71.

53. TD to George Douglas, September 27, 1920 (Penn); *AD*, 344n; and Helen Richardson to TD, October 18, 1920 (Penn).

54. *AD*, 350–51; and TD to Ethel Kelley, July 8, 1921 (Texas A&M University Library).

55. *ML*, 52–59. The dating of the lily pond incident has been somewhat confused because the illustration in *AD* featuring the newspaper clipping reporting Sterling's plunge is placed next to the visit in May of 1921 (367); whereas Dreiser records the incident in his diary for August 16, 1922 (391). In *AT*, Clyde Griffiths and Roberta Alden finally come together in a canoe on a lily pond.

56. *L*, 2: 390–98n.

57. *DML*, 2: 449–51.

58. TD to Helen Richardson, December 1, 1923 (Penn); and *AD*, 382–83n.

59. *DML*, 2: 480–81.

60. Estelle Kubitz to TD, January 22, 1921 (quoted in Reynolds, "Genesis and Compositional History," 47); and *AT*, 1: 246.

61. *AD*, 394; and Oliver M. Sayler, "Picking America's Premier Pen-Masters," *Shadowland* 5 (January 1922): 57, 63, 74.

THIRTEEN. *AN AMERICAN TRAGEDY*

1. See Jack Salzman, ed., "'I Find the Real American Tragedy' by Theodore Dreiser," *Resources for American Literary Study* 2 (Spring 1972): 3–75 [12]; reprinted from a series of essays by that title in *Mystery Magazine* 11 (February 1935): 9–11, 88–90; (March): 22–23, 77–79; (April): 24–26, 90–92; (May): 22–24, 83–86; and (June): 20–21, 68–73; partially reprinted in *TDS*, 291–99. For slightly different versions which led to "I Find the Real American Tragedy," see also "American Tragedies" (Penn); "Theodore Dreiser Describes 'An American Tragedy,'" *New York Post*, October 2–6, 1934; and the *Philadelphia Record* for approximately the same dates. Dreiser states in the early part of "I Find" that the Gillette case

did not come to his attention until two years before he completed the novel. But see Thomas P. Beyer to TD, December 2, 1926; TD to Beyer, December 16, 1926 (Penn); and *L,* 2: 458. For the idea that *An American Tragedy* was "mere journalism," see *FF,* 462; Oscar Cargill, *Intellectual America* (New York: Macmillan, 1941), 111; and H. L. Mencken, "Preface," *An American Tragedy* (Cleveland: World Publishing Company, 1947), i.

2. The most basic sources for the Gillette-Brown case and the genesis of the novel, aside from newspaper accounts, are the Herkimer County court records and abstract of the appeal; John F. Castle, "The Making of *An American Tragedy*" (Ph.D. diss., University of Michigan, 1952); John William Reynolds, "The Genesis and Compositional History of Theodore Dreiser's *An American Tragedy*" (Ph.D. diss., University of Connecticut, 1999); Joseph W. Brownell and Patricia A. Wawrzaszek, *Adirondack Tragedy: The Gillette Murder Case of 1906* (Interlaken, N.Y.: Heart of the Lake Publishing, 1986); and Craig Brandon, *Murder in the Adirondacks: An American Tragedy Revisited* (Utica, N.Y.: North Country Books, 1986). Brandon's information on the Gillette case is also used to advantage by Shelley Fisher Fishkin in "Dreiser and the Discourse of Gender," in *Theodore Dreiser: Beyond Realism,* ed. Miriam Gogol (New York: New York University Press, 1995), 6–7. One other source, now apparently lost because it appeared before dissertations were either kept by university libraries or microfilmed, is Emil Greenberg's master's thesis: "A Case Study in the Technique of Realism: Theodore Dreiser's *An American Tragedy*" (New York University, 1936).

3. "I Find the Real American Tragedy," 11; and Brandon, *Murder in the Adirondacks,* 60, 75–79.

4. Excerpts from both Grace's and Roberta's letters are juxtaposed in Castle, "The Making of *An American Tragedy,*" 36–44.

5. Brandon, *Murder in the Adirondacks,* 203, 236; and *New York World,* March 31, 1908.

6. In *Dreiser and Veblen: Saboteurs of the Status Quo* (Columbia: University of Missouri Press, 1998), Clare Virginia Eby adequately demonstrates that "Veblen's influence during Dreiser's lifetime was so pervasive that Dreiser could similarly have 'read' him without ever opening a single book" (8).

7. "I Find a Real American Tragedy," 5. For elucidating comments on the novel's setting, see Ellen Moers, *Two Dreisers* (New York: Viking Press, 1969), 278; Paul A. Orlov, *"An American Tragedy": Perils of the Self-Seeking "Success"* (Lewisburg, Pa.: Bucknell University Press, 1998), 66–67; and Donald Pizer, *The Novels of Theodore Dreiser: A Critical Study* (Minneapolis: University of Minnesota Press, 1976), 217.

8. See Richard W. Dowell, "Dreiser Meets Fitzgerald . . . Maybe," *DS* 22 (Fall 1991): 20–25; Thomas P. Riggio, "Dreiser, Fitzgerald, and the Question of

Influence," in *Theodore Dreiser and American Culture,* ed. Yoshinobu Hakutani (Newark: University of Delaware Press, 2000), 234–47; and TD to Ernest Boyd, January 15, 1923 (Virginia).

9. "I Find the Real American Tragedy," 6; *ML,* 76; and Robert H. Elias, *Theodore Dreiser: Apostle of Nature* (Ithaca: Cornell University Press, 1970; orig. pub. 1948), 220.

10. See "I Find the Real American Tragedy," 5–7, and "American Tragedies" (Penn),

11. Dreiser's extensive collection of clippings pertaining to the Molineaux trial, along with his handwritten copy of the coroner's jury verdict of February 27, 1899, and his trial chapters are in the Dreiser Collection at Penn. The chapters themselves have been edited by Kathryn M. Plank, "*The Rake,*" *Papers in Literature and Language* 27 (Spring 1991): 140–73.

12. Dreiser speaks of writing a novel based on the Richeson case in "American Tragedies."

13. TD to Helen Richardson, June 5, 1924 (Penn; partially quoted in *AD,* 412n).

14. *AD,* 400–401; and *ML,* 83–85.

15. Roy C. Higby, "Record of Gillett [*sic*]-Brown," [August 1973] (Cornell), reprinted in *A Man from the Past* (Big Moose Press, 1974); *AT,* 2: 86–87; and "Woodsmen Planned Lynching Gillette," *New York World,* July 21, 1906.

16. Brandon, *Murder in the Adirondacks,* 365; and Reynolds, "Genesis and Compositional History," 93, where it is noted that Dreiser admits in a deleted section of "I Find the Real American Tragedy" to using only newspaper sources, not court records, as the basis for his novel. See also TD to Randall Whitman, August 23, 1930 (Penn); and Pizer, *Novels of Dreiser,* 208, 215–17.

17. Burton Rascoe, "A Bookman's Day Book," *New York Tribune,* December 24, 1922; Boni & Liveright sales figures (Penn); TD to Marion Bloom, November 7, 1923, and TD to L. E. Pollinger, November 23, 1923 (Penn).

18. TD to Sallie Kussell, August 4, 1923 (Virginia); TD to Helen Richardson, March 30, 1924 (Penn); and *Letters to Louise: Theodore Dreiser's Letters to Louise Campbell,* ed. Louise Campbell (Philadelphia: University of Pennsylvania Press, 1959), 19–22.

19. TD to Helen Richardson, June 18 and June 2, 1924 (Penn); *AD,* 410n; *ML,* 105; *L,* 2: 430–31; and TD to Helen Richardson, May 26, 1924 (Penn).

20. Thomas R. Smith to TD, June 3, 1925 (Penn). Reviewers of the novel would concur: "Nothing that I have ever . . . read for thirty years affected me as those masterly pages where the crisis of the tragedy comes into sight" (*TDCR,* 458). For Smith's working relationship with Dreiser, see Donald Friede, *The Mechanical Angel* (New York: Alfred A. Knopf, 1948), 22.

21. *ML,* 106, where Helen Richardson errs in stating that the lease for the

Brooklyn apartment was signed on January 1, 1924, instead of 1925; see also 108–9.

22. *ML,* 113; and "Dreiser Interviews Pantano in Death House; Doomed Man Avows Faith in Hereafter," *New York World,* November 30, 1925.

23. *AT,* 2: 362–64.

24. *AT,* 2: 366, 369, 388, 398. See William L. Phillips, "The Imagery of Dreiser's Novels," *Publications of the Modern Language Association* 78 (December 1963): 572–85, reprinted in *Merrill Studies in "An American Tragedy,"* ed. Jack Salzman (Columbus, Ohio: Charles E. Merrill Publishing Company, 1971); and F. O. Matthiessen, *Theodore Dreiser* (New York: William Sloane Associates, 1951), 194.

25. *DML,* 2: 548; see also Moers, *Two Dreisers,* 266–85; Thomas P. Riggio, "American Gothic: Poe and *An American Tragedy,*" *American Literature* 49 (January 1978): 515–32, reprinted in *Essays on An American Tragedy,* ed. Harold Bloom (New York: Chelsea House, 1988); and Del G. Kehl, "An American Tragedy and Dreiser's Cousin, Mr. Poe," *Rocky Mountain Review of Language and Literature* 32 (Autumn 1978): 211–21.

26. *DML,* 2: 546–49; and *L,* 2: 435–36.

27. Matthiessen, *Dreiser,* 195.

28. For Bulger, See chapter 1. The last known address for Al Dreiser was in 1934, at 1235 Muirhead Street, Los Angeles; he had apparently written Dreiser about his share of the royalties from the publication of *The Songs of Paul Dresser.* See *L,* 2:, 667–69; and Evelyn Light (for TD) to Al Dreiser, March 29, 1934 (Penn).

29. TD to Helen Richardson, April 10, 1924 (Penn); and *AT,* 1: 294.

30. Thomas R. Smith to Horace Liveright, July 31, 1924 (Penn).

31. *AT,* 1: 77–78, 80.

32. Reynolds, "Genesis and Compositional History," 23; and *AT,* 1: 174.

33. "Admitting Guilt, Gillette Goes to Chair," *New York World,* March 31, 1908; and "I Find the Real American Tragedy," 10–11. There is some doubt cast on Gillette's confession since the press had already distorted other details of the case in order to sensationalize it. During his final visit with his mother, Chester hinted that he was guilty of murder, but he otherwise wanted to protect his family from having to bear that legacy. If he ever made a formal confession, there is no extant record of it. See Brandon, *Murder in the Adirondacks,* 248, 288–89, 292, 295.

34. Philip Gerber, ed., "'A Beautiful Legal Problem': Albert Lévitt on *An American Tragedy,*" *Papers on Language and Literature* 27 (Spring 1991): 214–42.

35. Robert L. Duffus, "Dreiser's Undisciplined Power," *New York Times,* January 10, 1926; *AT,* 2: 406–9; and William C. Lengel, "The 'Genius' Himself," *Esquire* 10 (September 1938): 55. In a magazine interview some months before publication, Dreiser referred to *Crime and Punishment* as "that supreme work"; see Walter Tittle, "Glimpses of Interesting Americans: Theodore Dreiser," *Century Magazine* 110 (August 1925): 441–47.

36. See TD to Helen Richardson, August 25, 1924 (Penn); *ML,* 110; and *AD,* 417–18.

37. *AD,* 419; and *DML,* 2: 727, 550–51.

38. Thomas R. Smith to TD, January 9, 1926 (Penn).

39. H. L. Mencken, "Theodore Dreiser," *A Book of Prefaces* (New York: Alfred A. Knopf, 1917), 134; *TDCR,* 442–43; *Dictionary of American Biography,* ed. Dumas Malone (New York: Charles Scribner's Sons, 1935), 9: 91–92; and "American Tragedies," 15–16.

40. *TDCR,* 469–71.

41. *TDCR,* 480–86.

42. *TDCR,* 473, 456, 495, 455, 475; and Dreiser's lifetime sales records (Penn).

43. *DML,* 2: 546, 554, 796–800; and *ML,* 117.

44. *ML,* 119; and *L,* 2: 439.

45. Horace Liveright to TD, March 11, 1926 (Penn).

46. Walter Wanger to W. A. Swanberg, January 14, 1963; quoted in W. A. Swanberg, *Dreiser* (New York: Charles Scribner's Sons, 1965), 307.

47. Horace Liveright to TD, March 8, 1926 (Penn); TD to Elmer Davis, January 15, 1926 (Library of Congress); and Reynolds, "Genesis and Compositional History," 245–49.

48. Jesse L. Lasky, *I Blow My Own Horn* (New York: Doubleday & Co., 1957), 222.

49. *L,* 2: 443.

50. *L,* 2: 443–46; Horace Liveright to TD, March 26, 1926 (Penn); and *ML,* 121–24. For a slightly different account of the coffee incident, see Bennett Cerf, *At Random: The Reminiscences of Bennett Cerf* (New York: Random House, 1977), 58–59.

51. John Hansen to Louise Campbell, October 27, 1926; Sara Osborne White Dreiser (Jug) to TD, March 31, 1926; Horace Liveright to TD, April 2, 1916; TD to Jug, April, 1926; and Jug to TD, April 7, 1926 (Penn).

52. Jug to TD, April 19, 1926 (Penn).

53. TD to Dudley Field Malone, [May 1926]; and Agreement of Support, June 21, 1926 (Penn).

FOURTEEN. CELEBRITY

1. Ralph Waldo Emerson, *Essays: Second Series* (1844; repr. Boston: Houghton Mifflin, 1891), 53–54; *Hey,* 117; and *Moods: Cadenced and Declaimed* (New York: Boni & Liveright, 1926), 290.

2. Roger Asselineau, *The Transcendentalist Constant in American Literature* (New York: New York University Press, 1980), 99; John J. McAleer, "Dreiser's Poetry," *DN* 2 (Spring 1971): 20; Richard W. Dowell, "The Poetry of Theodore

Dreiser," *Contemporary Education* 56 (Fall 1984): 55–59; and H. L. Mencken, *A Book of Prefaces* (New York: Alfred A. Knopf, 1917), 146. See chapter 9.

3. *Moods,* 177, 169, 182.

4. *TDCR,* 525–26; and see Edgar Lee Masters, *Whitman* (New York: Charles Scribner's Sons, 1937).

5. *ML,* 127–35.

6. It is asserted in Richard Lingeman, *Theodore Dreiser* (New York: G. P. Putnam's Sons, 1990), 2: 178, that Dreiser visited Mayen a second time in his life, but see Renate von Bardeleben, "Personal, Ethnic, and National Identity: Theodore Dreiser's Difficult Heritage," in *Interdisziplinarität Deutsche Sprache und Spannungsfeld der Kulteren,* ed. Martin Forster and Klaus von Schilling (Frankfurt and New York: Peter Lang, 1991), 335.

7. *ML,* 136–38; and *New York Herald Tribune,* October 23, 1926.

8. Donald Pizer, Richard W. Dowell, and Frederic E. Rusch, eds., *Theodore Dreiser: A Primary Bibliography and Reference Guide* (Boston: G. K. Hall, 1991), 12. "The Beautiful" appeared in "Recent Poems of Love and Sorrow," *Vanity Fair* 27 (September 1926): 54.

9. *New York Herald* (Paris Edition), undated, quoted in W. A. Swanberg, *Dreiser* (New York: Charles Scribner's Sons, 1965), 314.

10. Donald Friede, *The Mechanical Angel* (New York: Alfred A. Knopf, 1948), 42–43.

11. *ML,* 139–42, 159, 184; Claude Bowers, *My Life* (New York: Simon and Schuster, 1962), 163; and Roark Mulligan, "Dreiser's Private Library," *DS* 33 (Fall 2002): 40–67.

12. Maggie and Mark Walker to Jerome Loving, June 19, 2001; Office of War Information (OWI) Radio Broadcast, July 1944 (Texas); and T. R. Smith to TD, February 15, 1927 (Penn). In 1905, Henry had also published *Lodgings in Town* (New York: A. S. Barnes), an impressionistic study of his experiences in Manhattan at the turn of the century.

13. When Hamlin Garland first met Dreiser at a lunch on February 7, 1904, he spoke of Dreiser's afterward returning "to his work as [boss] of a gang of excavators" (*Hamlin Garland's Diaries,* ed. Donald Pizer [San Marino: Huntington Library, 1968], 123).

14. *DML,* 1: 231.

15. Published as "The Mercy of God," without the quotation marks around "Mercy," *American Mercury* 2 (August 1924): 457–64. For the citations for the original publications of the stories in *Chains* (excluding "Khat" and "The Prince Who Was a Thief," which had not been previously published), see Joseph Griffin, *The Small Canvas: An Introduction to Dreiser's Short Stories* (Rutherford, N.J.: Fairleigh Dickinson University Press, 1985).

16. *Chains: Lesser Novels and Stories* (New York: Boni & Liveright, 1927), 374, 383, 390–91; and *Moods,* 177.

17. For example: "If ye'd ever make a study ave the passion ave love in the sense that Freud an' some others have ye'd understand it well enough. It's a great force about which we know naathing as yet" (see *CP,* 330).

18. Robert Edwin Wilkinson, "A Study of Theodore Dreiser's *The Financier*" (Ph.D. diss., University of Pennsylvania, 1965), 40–113. See also James Hutchinson, "The Creation (and Reduction) of *The Financier,*" *Papers on Language and Literature* 27 (Spring 1991): 243–59; his "The Revision of Theodore Dreiser's *The Financier,*" *Journal of Modern Literature* 20 (Winter 1996): 199–213; and Kevin W. Jett, "Vision and Revision: Another Look at the 1912 and 1927 Editions of Dreiser's *The Financier,*" *DS* 29 (Spring and Fall 1998), 51–73.

19. In addition to the review in the *Cincinnati Enquirer,* other reviews of the revision of *The Financier* are to be found in the *New York World* of April 18, the *Washington Evening Star* of July 14, and the *Asheville Times* of August 7, 1927. For royalty figures, see Dreiser's summary records for June 30, 1933 (by which time the novel had sold 8,528 copies) at Penn.

20. Arthur Garfield Hays, *City Lawyer* (New York: Simon and Schuster, 1942), 315; and "Publisher Loses Boston Test Case," *New York Times,* April 23, 1927. Hays served as Friede's primary counsel.

21. Friede, *Mechanical Angel,* 135, 90; and "'Vanity, Vanity,' Saith the Preacher," *TM.*

22. Clara Clark Jaeger to Jerome Loving, February 8, 2001; and Marguerite Tjader [Harris], *Love That Will Not Let Me Go: My Time with Theodore Dreiser,* ed. Lawrence E. Hussman (New York: Peter Lang, 1998), 86n.

23. Louise Campbell to Dawes Hotel, October 27, 1926; John Hanson to Arthur Pell, July 20 and September 28, 1927; G. R. Bartels to TD, February 12 and March 26, 1929; TD to William A. Adams, June 19, 1929; and TD to John Hanson, February 11, 1930 (Penn).

24. *DRD,* 156, 158.

25. John P. Diggins, *The American Left in the Twentieth Century* (New York: Harcourt Brace Jovanovich, 1973), 94–106; see also Daniel Aaron, *Writers on the Left* (New York: Harcourt, Brace & World, 1961).

26. Quoted in Paul Hollander, *Political Pilgrims* (New York: Oxford University Press, 1981), 122.

27. *DRD,* 27–30; and *Dreiser Looks at Russia* (New York: Horace Liveright, 1928), 9.

28. *DRD,* 31–34.

29. TD to Helen Richardson, October 20, 1927 (Penn).

30. *DRD,* 40–42.

31. *DRD,* 49–50; and Vincent Sheean, *Dorothy and Red* (Boston: Houghton Mifflin Company, 1963), 79.

32. *DRD,* 56; and Sheean, *Dorothy and Red,* 59.

33. Sheean, *Dorothy and Red,* 59–60; and *DRD,* 71–72.

34. *DRD*, 65; Ruth Epperson Kennell, *Theodore Dreiser and the Soviet Union, 1927–1945* (New York: International Publishers, 1969), 94, 216; and *GW*, 1: 316, 349.

35. Kennell, *Dreiser and the Soviet Union*, 22–23.

36. *DRD*, 82; and James L. W. West III, "Dreiser and *The Road to Buenos Ayres*," *DS* 25 (Fall 1994): 3–22.

37. *DRD*, 88; and *Dreiser Looks at Russia*, 123, 16.

38. *DRD*, 90–91.

39. *DRD*, 98–101, 194.

40. Kennell, *Dreiser and the Soviet Union*, 69.

41. *DRD*, 143–46; and Horace Liveright to TD, August 24, 1927 (Penn): "Patrick Kearney tells me that he had dinner with you a few nights ago and that you believe Sacco & Vanzetti to be guilty."

42. *ML*, 133.

43. *DRD*, 269, 275–76, 281.

44. "Dreiser Looks at Russia," *New York World*, March 19–28, 1928; Ruth Kennell to TD, February 8, 1928; *Chicago Daily News*, February 6, 1928, reprinted in both Kennell, *Dreiser and the Soviet Union* and *DRD*. For Churchill, see Robert van Gelder, "An Interview with Theodore Dreiser," *New York Times Book Review*, March 16, 1941.

45. W. E. Woodward, *The Gift of Life* (New York: E. P. Dutton, 1947), 315–16.

46. *L*, 2: 468–71; and Foreword to TD, *Notes on Life*, ed. Marguerite Tjader and John J. McAleer (University: University of Alabama, 1974), vii.

47. MS. drafts on "A Secretary of Arts" and the "Russian Ballet Project" (Texas); and Otto H. Kahn to TD, February 25, 1929 (Virginia). See also Hy Kraft, *On My Way to the Theater* (New York: Macmillan, 1971), 70–73.

48. Ernst, Fox & Cane to Horace Liveright, Inc., November 14, 1928 (Penn); and Sheean, *Dorothy and Red*, 122–26.

49. Percy Winner, "Dorothy Thomas Demands Dreiser Explain Parallel," *New York Evening Post*, November 14, 1928; Sheean, *Dorothy and Red*, 148; Dorothy Thompson, *The New Russia* (New York: Henry Holt and Company, 1928), v.; and Percy Winner, "Dreiser's Book on Russia Parallels Miss Thompson's," *New York Evening Post*, November 13, 1928.

50. [Arthur Garfield Hays] to Horace Liveright, Inc., January 8, 1929; TD to Robert H. Rucker, February 20, 1929; T. R. Smith to TD, May 28, 1929 (Penn); and Robert H. Elias, *Theodore Dreiser: Apostle of Nature* (Ithaca: Cornell University Press, 1970; orig. pub. 1948), 238. The prose and poetry in *My City* had previously appeared in the *New York Herald Tribune* of December 23, 1928, and the *New York Evening Post Literary Review* of December 20, 1924, 8. The poetry also appears in the 1926 and 1928 editions of *Moods*.

51. Lingeman, *Dreiser*, 2: 327; Joseph P. Griffin, "Dreiser's Later Sketches,"

DN 16 (Fall 1985): 1–13; Yoshinobu Hakutani, "The Dream of Success in Dreiser's *A Gallery of Women*," *Zeitschrift für Anglistik und Amerikanistik* 27 (July 1979): 236–46; and *DML*, 2: 344.

52. *TDCR*, 565; and *DML*, 2: 800.

53. "Portrait of a Woman," *Bookman* 66 (September 1927): 2–14. Sallie Kussell did some work on "Reina" (TD to Sallie Kussell, August 7, 1923 [Virginia]).

54. Ruth Kennell to TD, June 9, 1928 (Penn).

55. Carol A. Nathanson, "Anne Estelle Rice: Theodore Dreiser's 'Ellen Adams Wrynn,'" *Woman's Art Journal* 13, no. 2 (1992–93): 1–11; see also her "Anne Estelle Rice and 'Ellen Adams Wrynn': Dreiser's Perspective on Gender and Gendered Perspectives on Art," *DS* 32 (Spring 2001): 3–35.

56. Thomas P. Riggio to Jerome Loving, October 16, 2001.

57. Yvette [Székely] Eastman, *Dearest Wilding: A Memoir* (Philadelphia: University of Pennsylvania Press, 1995), 6–13; and Miriam Gogol, "Interlocking, Intermeshing Fantasies: Dreiser and *Dearest Wilding*," in *Theodore Dreiser and American Culture*, ed. Yoshinobu Hakutani (Newark: University of Delaware Press, 2000), 187–96.

58. Jerome Loving, interview with Yvette Eastman, Philadelphia, Pa., November 9, 2000. Dreiser advised Margaret Székely Monahan on the publishing prospects for a manuscript; see TD to Margaret Monahan, January 9, 1929 (Virginia).

59. Yvette Eastman, *Dearest Wilding*, 42–58, 124; and Max Eastman, *Love and Revolution* (New York: Random House, 1964), 538.

FIFTEEN. TRAGIC AMERICA

1. David M. Kennedy, *Freedom from Fear: The American People in Depression and War* (New York: Oxford University Press, 1999), 40, 43, 45, 58, 65.

2. *L*, 2: 503n.; TD to the John Reed Club, March 30, 1930 (Texas); and Kennedy, *Freedom from Fear*, 22.

3. W. A. Swanberg, *Dreiser* (New York: Charles Scribner's Sons, 1965), 363; Raymond Dannenbaum, "Theodore Dreiser Discounts Intermarriage," *Jewish Journal*, June 4, 1930; James Flexner, "Dreiser Brings Pessimism Back from U.S. Tour," *New York Herald Tribune*, July 8, 1930; and *L*, 2: 500.

4. *L*, 2: 742; TD to Stuart Chase, January 29, 1932; and Stuart Chase to TD, February 12, 1932 (Library of Congress). Chase's review of *Tragic America* appeared in the *New York Herald Tribune Review of Books* for January 24, 1932, reprinted in *TDCR*, 631–33. See also John C. Hirsh, "*Tragic America*: Dreiser's American Communism and a General Motors Executive," *DN* 13 (Spring 1982): 10–16.

5. *L*, 2: 508; Rolf Lundén, "Theodore Dreiser and the Nobel Prize," *Amer-*

ican Literature 50 (May 1978): 216–29; and David D. Anderson, "Sinclair Lewis and the Nobel Prize," *Mid-America* 8 (1981): 9–21.

6. For Lewis's speech, *New York Times,* December 13, 1930; and George Seldes, "Encounters with Theodore Dreiser," in his *Witness to a Century: Encounters with the Noted, the Notorious, and Three SOB's* (New York: Ballantine, 1987), 284–88.

7. *L,* 2: 529; and Lawrence E. Hussman, "Squandered Possibilities: The Film Versions of Dreiser's Novels," in *Theodore Dreiser: Beyond Realism,* ed. Miriam Gogol (New York: New York University Press, 1995), 180. In "Myself and the Movies," *Esquire* 20 (July 1943), reprinted in *Esquire* 80 (October 1973): 156, 382, Dreiser credits his friend J. G. Robin with helping him secure the second payment from Paramount for the sound rights.

8. Arthur Garfield Hays to Paramount Publix Corporation, June 26, 1931 (Texas).

9. "'Hooeyland,' Says Dreiser, Back from Film Capital," *New York American,* April 12, 1931; and *L,* 2: 562n.

10. TD to Ernest Boyd, May 19 and June 10, 1931 (Virginia).

11. Thomas Strychacz, "Dreiser's Suit Against Paramount: Authorship, Professionalism, and the Hollywood Film Industry," *Prospects* 18 (1993): 187–203; and TD, "The Real Sins of Hollywood," *Liberty* 9 (June 11, 1932): 6–11, reprinted in *Authors on Film,* ed. Harry M. Geduld (Bloomington: Indiana University Press, 1972), 206–22.

12. *L,* 2: 513. Dreiser met James D. Mooney in January 1931 and agreed with him only generally about the solutions for America's economic ills. See John C. Hirsh, "Dreiser and a Financier: James D. Mooney," *DN* 14 (Spring 1983): 19–20.

13. J. Donald Adams (of the *New York Times*) to John Valentine, May 23, 1944 (Texas); Lester Cohen to W. A. Swanberg, October 3, 1962; "Lewis Is Slapped by Dreiser" and "An American Tragedy," *New York Times,* March 21, 1931; and Wharton Esherick to Swanberg, June 25, 1962 (Penn).

14. See Robert Coltrane, "'Dear Marguerite': A Early Dreiser Letter to Marguerite Tjader Harris," *DS* 19 (Fall: 1988): 22–26.

15. *Mr. President: Free the Scottsboro Boys* (New York: International Labor Defense, 1934), 30 pp.; and *L,* 2: 536.

16. *L,* 2: 537–61; and Statement to the Associated Press, June 25, 1931 (Penn).

17. John Dos Passos, ed., *Harlan Miners Speak: Report on Terrorism in the Kentucky Coal Fields* (New York: Harcourt, Brace, and Co., 1932), 4.

18. Lester Cohen, "Theodore Dreiser: A Personal Memoir," *Discovery* 4 (September 1954): 99–126; and Cohen to Swanberg, October 3, 1962 (Penn).

19. "Dreiser Investigating Interview with Miners," November 7, 1931 (Penn); *Harlan Miners Speak,* 280; and Townsend Ludington, *John Dos Passos: A Twentieth Century Odyssey* (New York: E. P. Dutton, 1980), 297–300.

20. Cohen, "Dreiser: A Personal Memoir," 112–13; and "Kentucky Editor Questions Dreiser," *New York Times,* November 7, 1931.

21. Cohen, "Dreiser: A Personal Memoir," 113–15, 117–18.

22. "Judge Jones, The Harlan Miners, and Myself," n.d. (Texas).

23. Cohen to Swanberg, October 3, 1962; and "Judge Jones, The Harlan Miners, and Myself."

24. *L*, 2: 586; and Federal Bureau of Investigation Freedom of Information Release of Censored Record for Theodore Dreiser, obtained April 9, 1999.

25. Clara [Clark] Jaeger, *Philadelphia Rebel: The Education of a Bourgeoise* (London: Grosvenor, 1988), 74, 66–69.

26. Jaeger, *Philadelphia Rebel,* 71–77.

27. Hilbert H. Campbell, "Dreiser in New York: A Diary Source," *DN* 13 (Fall 1982): 1–7; Clara Clark Jaeger to Jerome Loving, February 8, 2001; Donald Pizer, *The Novels of Theodore Dreiser: A Critical Study* (Minneapolis: University of Minnesota Press, 1976), 333–34; and Jaeger, *Philadelphia Rebel,* 89, 86–87.

28. *L*, 2: 589–90; TD to Helen Richardson, May 15, 1932; Jaeger, *Philadelphia Rebel,* 98–103; and "Report of Dreiser-Taggart Accident" (Penn).

29. "Stock on Hand," Horace Liveright, Inc., August 1, 1932 (Penn).

30. Upton Sinclair to TD, October 11, 1932 (Indiana); "Townsend," *American Spectator* 1 (June 1933): 2; and "Winterton," *American Spectator* 2 (December 1933): 3–4.

31. "Mathewson," *Esquire* 1 (May 1934): 20–21, 125, and (June 1934): 24–25, 114; and Margaret Tjader [Harris], *Theodore Dreiser: A New Dimension* (Norwalk, Conn.: Silvermine Publishers, 1965), 57–58. See also Joseph Griffin, "Dreiser's Later Sketches," *DN,* 16 (Fall, 1985), 1–13.

32. *HH,* 348.

33. George Jean Nathan et al., eds., *American Spectator Year Book* (New York: Frederick A. Stokes Company, 1934), 347–52.

34. I am indebted to Robert M. Dowling for some of this background; see also Michael Marcaccio, *The Hapgoods: Three Earnest Brothers* (Charlottesville: University Press of Virginia, 1977).

35. Hutchins Hapgood, *A Victorian in the Modern World* (New York: Harcourt, Brace, and Co., 1939), 429–31; Hapgood to TD, June 28, 1932; Evelyn Light to Hapgood, July 11, 1932; and TD to Hapgood, April 17, 1933 (Penn). See also Ernest Boyd to Hapgood, September 13, 1932 (Yale University Library).

36. Quoted in Hutchins Hapgood, "Is Dreiser Anti-Semitic?" *Nation* 140 (April 17, 1935): 436–38; and *L*, 2: 648–53.

37. Hy Kraft, *On My Way to the Theater* (New York: Macmillan, 1971), 74; Berenice C. Skidelsky, "America and the Jews," *Jewish Advocate* (Boston), February 5, 1920; "Clean Book Bill Slays Freedom," *New York Herald Tribune,* January 27, 1925; Sulamith Ish-Kishor, "Dreiser Looks at the Russian Jews," *New York Day,* February 10, 1929; and *L*, 2: 652.

38. Hapgood, "Is Dreiser Anti-Semitic?" 437–38.

39. Kennedy, *Freedom from Fear,* 383–84; and Gladys D. Mack to TD, April

12, 1935 (Penn). During the centennial celebration of the publication of *Sister Carrie,* at the University of Pennsylvania on November 7–9, 2000, the keynote speaker Joseph Epstein deplored Dreiser's anti-Semitism; see his *Partial Payments: On Writers and Their Lives* (New York: W. W. Norton, 1989), 259–79.

40. "Dreiser Denies He Is Anti-Semitic," *New Masses* 15 (April 30, 1935): 10–11; and *L,* 2: 714. See also Hapgood, *Victorian in the Modern World,* 266–74; and Mike Gold, "The Gun Is Loaded, Dreiser," *New Masses* 15 (May 7, 1935): 14–15.

41. TD to John Cowper Powys, November 21, 1932 (Virginia); and *L,* 2: 643.

42. "Dreiser Overlooks His Former Experiences with Hollywood, For Things Will Be Different in the Filming of 'Jennie Gerhardt,'" *New York World Telegram,* December 15, 1932; Hussman, "Squandered Possibilities," 194; Swanberg, *Dreiser,* 401; "Dreiser Says NRA [National Recovery Act] Is Training Public," *New York Times,* August 28, 1933; and *L,* 3: 789.

43. "The Epic Sinclair," *Esquire* 2 (December 1934): 32–33, 178–79.

44. "'Tobacco and Men,' Motion Picture Idea" (Texas). The film scenario later became the basis for Borden Dell's *The Tobacco Men: A Novel Based on Notes by Theodore Dreiser and Hy Kraft* (1965); Kraft wrote the foreword, in which he discusses his collaboration with Dreiser.

45. Richard Lingeman, *Theodore Dreiser* (New York: G. P. Putnam's Sons, 1990), 2: 384–85; and *Moods Philosophic and Emotional* (New York: Simon and Schuster, 1935), v. Privately, Dreiser would have hardly agreed with Ish-Kishor's comparison. Earlier when a journalist tried to flatter Dreiser by saying that his verses were "more musical" than anything she had read in Whitman, Dreiser exploded: "They can't touch Whitman . . . Not Whitman's poetry. Much of Whitman's writing was not poetry at all—it was beautiful prose-philosophy. But when Whitman begins to sing, he sings! Have you read Whitman? . . . Have you read his 'When I Heard the Learned Astronomer'? No. Have you read 'The Noiseless Patient Spider'? And there is one beginning, 'A child asked me what is the grass'" (actually a misquoted line, not the beginning, of "Song of Myself"); see Jean West Maury, "A Neighborly Call on Theodore Dreiser," *Boston Evening Transcript,* January 29, 1927.

46. Marguerite Tjader [Harris] to W. A. Swanberg, June 8, 1962 (Penn); *L,* 2: 710n; and Mandy See, "'It Was Written That We Meet': Theodore Dreiser and George Douglas," *DS* 34 (Summer 2003): 35–57.

47. "All ethnology, geology, zoology, biology, botany, history, painting, sculpture, architecture, letters, explorations, and what not demonstrate that the mind is nothing more than a sensory registration of endlessly repeated and most often related stimuli from matter-energy sources and structures compelled, directed, and controlled by whatever evokes, directs, and controls matter-energy" (*Notes on Life,* ed. Marguerite Tjader and John J. McAleer [University: University of Alabama Press, 1974], 65). These notes, which in manuscript consisted of eighty-seven labeled packages when delivered to the University of Pennsylvania archives

in 1952, date back to 1915, but most were written in the 1930s when Dreiser struggled after a formal classification of these thoughts. See John J. McAleer, "Dreiser's 'Notes on Life,'" *Library Chronicle* 38 (Winter 1972): 78–91, for a defense of Dreiser's achievement in these writings.

48. TD to Ruth Kennell, April 30, 1935 (Penn).

49. "Mark the Double Twain," *English Journal* 24 (October 1935): 615–27.

50. *DML,* 2: 570–71.

51. *L,* 2: 784–85.

52. *L,* 2: 629; and TD to Ruth Kennell, February 24, 1928 (Penn).

53. Eugene O'Neill to TD, December 3, 1936 (Penn); Faulkner quoted in Lundén, "Dreiser and the Nobel Prize," 229.

54. Richard Lingeman, *Sinclair Lewis: Rebel from Main Street* (New York: Random House, 2002), 279–82.

55. Kennedy, *Freedom from Fear,* 398–99; and undated press clipping about Dreiser's speech in TD to Marguerite Tjader [Harris], September 6, [1938] (Texas). See also Marguerite Tjader [Harris], *Love That Will Not Let Me Go: My Time with Theodore Dreiser,* ed. Lawrence E. Hussman (New York: Peter Lang, 1998), 82n.

56. *L,* 3: 807–10; and Louise Campbell, "Portrait of an Artist: What I Know about Theodore Dreiser," unpublished MS. [1931], 5; and *L,* 3: 810.

57. Marguerite Tjader [Harris], "John Cowper Powys and Theodore Dreiser: A Friendship," *Powys Review* 2 (Winter/Spring 1979–1980): 16–23. See also Robert P. Saalbach, "Dreiser and the Powys Family," *DN* 6 (Fall 1975): 10–16.

58. "To Oscar Wilde: Written in his one time cell in Reading Gaol" (Texas); and *L,* 3: 877–78.

59. D. B. Graham, "Dreiser and Thoreau: An Early Influence," *DN* 7 (Spring 1976): 1–4; and *Living Thoughts of Thoreau, Presented by Theodore Dreiser* (New York: Longmans, Green, and Co., 1939).

60. *L,* 2: 639–40; TD to Helen Richardson, August 19, 1938 (Penn); *L,* 3: 813–15; and "Spanish Civilians to Get U.S. Flour," *New York Times,* December 30, 1938. A year later Roosevelt once again invited Dreiser to visit him in the White House. Shortly thereafter, the president thanked Dreiser for inscribed copies of *Twelve Men, Moods,* and *Living Thoughts of Thoreau* (*L,* 2: 849–50).

61. *L,* 3: 816; TD to Thelma Cudlipp [Whitman], May 12, 1936; and TD to Hazel Mack Godwin, November 2 and 23, 1942 (Penn).

62. *L,* 3: 823.

SIXTEEN. FACING WEST

1. *L,* 3: 833–34.

2. TD, "Good and Evil," *North American Review* 246 (Autumn 1938):

67–86. See also his "Kismet," *Esquire* 3 (January 1935): 29, 175–76; and "The Myth of Individuality," *American Mercury* 31 (March 1934): 337–42, reprinted in *Molders of American Thought, 1933–34,* ed. William H. Cordell (Garden City, N.Y.: Doubleday, Doran, 1934). For Dreiser's early reading of Emerson, see *D,* 252, 370.

3. Thomas P. Riggio, "Dreiser on Society and Literature: The San Francisco Exposition Interview," *American Literary Realism* 11 (Autumn 1978): 284–94.

4. *L,* 3: 844; and Lillian Rosenthal to W. A. Swanberg, March 5, 1963 (Penn). In *A Place in the Sun,* the names of the characters were changed. Sondra Finchley became Angela Vickers, Clyde Griffiths became George Eastman, and Roberta Alden became Alice Tripp (Shelley Winters). The film, directed and produced by George Stevens, captured six Oscars in 1951, but seems antiquated today; see Eugene L. Huddleston, "What a Difference Thirty Years Make: *A Place in the Sun* Today," *DN* 15 (Fall 1984): 1–12.

5. Marguerite Tjader [Harris], *Theodore Dreiser: A New Dimension* (Norwalk, Conn.: Silvermine Publishers, 1965), 147; and *ML,* 276.

6. *DML,* 2: 651; and TD, "U.S. Must Not Be Bled for Imperial Britain," Columbia Broadcasting System radio program, November 9, 1940; printed in *People's World* (San Francisco), November 12, 1940.

7. *TDCR,* 651–54. The book was originally to be published by the Veritas Press, where its head, Oskar Piest, offered Dreiser a flat fee of $5,000. The original charge to Dreiser was to write a book "designed to show the futility of America getting into the war," but Piest broke the contract when Dreiser also indicated that American "salvation rests in communism" (William C. Lengel to TD, September 19, 1940). Lengel then arranged for the manuscript to be published by Modern Age Books (Lengel to TD, December 4 and 5, 1940 [Penn]). Other suggested titles for *American Is Worth Saving* were "Keep Out," "My Country Tis of Thee" and "Is Democracy Worth Saving?"

8. Tjader [Harris], *Dreiser: A New Dimension,* 174; and *TDCR,* 655–56.

9. FBI Report, October 15, 1941.

10. *L,* 3: 932–38; William C. Lengel to TD, August 16, 1940; and TD to Lengel, August 22, 1940 (Penn).

11. *L,* 3: 931. In 1942 Dreiser told Mencken: "I ceased following Hitler when in 1940 [*sic*] he attacked Russia—my pet. At first I thought he had a progressive program for a United States of Europe—a better intellectual & social Europe" (*DML,* 2: 691).

12. *L,* 3: 768–69; and TD, "Sherwood Anderson," in *Homage to Sherwood Anderson,* ed. Paul P. Appel (Mamaroneck, N.Y.: Paul P. Appel, Publisher, 1970), 1–2.

13. TD to William C. Lengel, May 6, 1939, May 28 and October 8, 1941; Lengel to TD, June 5, 1941; TD to Earle H. Balch, Vice-President at Putnam's,

December 4, 1941; TD to Lengel, May 6, 1939 (Penn), printed in Louis Oldani, "Dreiser and Paperbacks: An Unpublished Letter," *DN* 6 (Fall 1975): 1–9; *DML*, 2: 669; and *L*, 3: 946–48.

14. *L*, 3: 966; Hazel Mack Godwin to TD, April 5, 1936. Godwin is called "Sylvia Bradshaw" in two earlier biographies.

15. "Abuse for Britain, Dreiser's Contribution to Anglo-U.S. Amity," *Toronto Evening Telegram,* [September 21, 1942].

16. "Second American Tragedy: Novelist Dreiser Dodges Interview with Reporters," *Port Huron Times Herald,* September 24, 1942.

17. Unidentified clippings entitled "Dreiser Insult Seen to Merit Pay from Hun" and "Dreiser's Anti-British Bile Brings St. Louis Tribute to Britain" (Penn); Robert M. McIlvaine, "A Literary Source for the Caesarean Section in *A Farewell to Arms,"* *American Literature* 43 (November 1971): 444–47; and *New York PM,* September 27, 1942 (Penn); see also *L*, 3: 965–66.

18. TD to Thelma Cudlipp Whitman, October 16, 1942; *ML,* 275; Sara White Dreiser (Jug) to Mrs. Gray, March 19, 1919 (Penn); and Jug to Robert H. Elias, September 14, 1939 (Cornell).

19. *ML,* 287; and *DML,* 2: 685–87, 700.

20. Donald Pizer, *The Novels of Theodore Dreiser: A Critical Study* (Minneapolis: University of Minnesota Press, 1976), 313.

21. Edgar Lee Masters, *Across Spoon River* (1936; repr. New York: Octagon Books, 1969), 329–330; and Richard W. Dowell, "Dreiser and Kathleen Mavourneen," *DN* 2 (Fall 1977): 2–4.

22. Richard Lehan, *Theodore Dreiser: His World and His Novels* (Carbondale: Southern Illinois University Press, 1969), 233.

23. Jean West Maury, "A Neighborly Call on Theodore Dreiser," *Boston Evening Transcript,* January 29, 1927; TD to Rufus M. Jones, December 1, 1938 (Haverford College Library), quoted in Gerhard Friedrich, "Theodore Dreiser's Debt to Woolman's *Journal,"* *American Quarterly* 7 (Winter 1955): 385–92. See by Rufus M. Jones *The Later Periods of Quakerism* (London: Macmillan & Co., 1921), *Finding the Trail of Life* (New York: Macmillan & Co., 1926), and *The Trail of Life in the Middle Years* (New York: Macmillan & Co., 1934); copies of these volumes are in Dreiser's personal library at Penn, heavily marked up.

24. Anna Tatum to TD, [winter 1934] (Penn); and Gerhard Friedrich, "A Major Influence on Theodore Dreiser's *The Bulwark,"* *American Literature* 29 (May 1957): 180–93.

25. Anna Tatum to TD, October 23, 1932 (Penn).

26. *The Bulwark* (New York: Doubleday & Company, 1946), 316–17, 337.

27. R. N. Mookerjee, "Dreiser's Use of Hindu Thought in *The Stoic,"* *American Literature* 43 (May 1971): 273–78.

28. *L*, 3: 997–98, 1009–10. It has also been asserted that Hazel Mack God-

win may have written "Black Sheep No. Three: Bill," a pointless sketch about a man whose practical joking drives away his friends and one of two wives. See Richard Lingeman, *Theodore Dreiser* (New York: G. P. Putnam's Sons, 1990), 2: 442; Joseph Griffin, "Dreiser's Later Sketches," *DN* 16 (Fall 1985): 8–9; and Donald Pizer, Richard W. Dowell, and Frederic E. Rusch, eds., *Theodore Dreiser: A Primary Bibliography and Reference Guide* (Boston: G. K. Hall, 1991), 54.

29. American Academy of Arts and Letters declaration as quoted in *L,* 3: 1001; and *DML,* 2: 708. Ironically, Mencken inadvertently accepted a gold medal from the same organization six years later; see Terry Teachout, *The Skeptic: A Life of H. L. Mencken* (New York: Harper-Collins, 2002), 321–22.

30. Richard Duffy, "Prospectus: Collected Works of Theodore Dreiser," June 1, 1944 (Texas); Tjader [Harris], *Dreiser: A New Dimension,* 126–27; and her *Love That Will Not Let Me Go: My Time with Theodore Dreiser,* ed. Lawrence E. Hussman (New York: Peter Lang, 1998), xi. See also "My Creator" (dated November 18, 1943), in *TDS,* 324–29.

31. H. L. Mencken, "Theodore Dreiser," in *A Book of Prefaces* (New York: Knopf, 1917), 67–148; TD to Floyd Dell, June 6, 1928 (Newberry Library); and Tjader [Harris], *Dreiser: A New Dimension,* 139–40.

32. Tjader [Harris], *Dreiser: A New Dimension,* 135–36.

33. TD to Marguerite Tjader [Harris], June 12, 1944 (Texas); and *ML,* 300.

34. *ML,* 302–5; and *DML,* 2: 726.

35. "Theodore Dreiser Joins Communist Party," *Daily Worker,* July 30, 1945. For the most recent reexamination of the circumstances surrounding Dreiser's decision to join the party on the brink of the Cold War, see Donald Pizer, "'The Logic of My Life and Work': Another Look at Dreiser's July 20, 1945, Letter to William Z. Foster," *DS* 30 (Fall 1999): 24–34. Dreiser told Robert H. Elias on September 10, 1945, that he would speak his mind as in the past: "If the Party doesn't like it, it can throw me out" (quoted in John J. McAleer, "Dreiser's 'Notes on Life,'" *Library Chronicle* 38 [Winter 1972]: 88, n. 8).

36. Richard W. Dowell, "Harold Dies and the Dreiser Trust," *DS* 19 (Spring 1988): 26–31.

37. *L,* 3: 1035.

38. *ML,* 312–16; and Vera Dreiser, *My Uncle Theodore* (New York: Nash Publishing Co., 1976), 12. See also Helen Dreiser to William C. Lengel, February 22, 1946 (Penn).

39. *ML,* 321; Esther McCoy, "The Death of Dreiser," *Grand Street* 7 (Winter 1988): 73–85; and *AT,* 2: 367.

40. The stroke from which Helen died in 1955 occurred not long after the publication of *My Life with Dreiser.* Earlier, during the book's composition, her editor paid her a visit in Oregon, where she was then living with her sister, Myrtle. He was shocked to find Helen, whom he had remembered as "a charming, totally feminine woman, radiating sexuality," now "lying in a giant-sized crib . . .

unable to speak except to utter a peculiar cackle, or laugh, from the side of her mouth. . . . She had put on a great amount of weight and looked like a giant kewpie doll in her crib" (William Targ, *Indecent Pleasures: The Life and Colorful Times of William Targ* [New York: Macmillan Publishing Co., 1975], 72–74).

41. Charles Chaplin, *My Autobiography* (New York: Simon and Schuster, 1964), 435; *New York Herald Tribune*, December 29, 1945; and *New York Times*, December 29, 1945.

INDEX

Harris, Marguerite Tjader, 345, 359, 378, 384–85, 395–97; *Direction,* 377; editing of *The Bulwark,* 393, 397; model for "Lucia" in *A Gallery,* 350

Harris, Overton, 303, 377

Hart, William S., 288

Harte, Bret, 52

Hartford Courant, 161

Harvey, Dorothy Dudley, xiii, 96, 124, 143, 193, 269

Harvey, Henry Blodgett, 269

Hauptmann, Gerhardt, 209

Haviland, Fred, 85–86, 99, 179

Hawthorne, Julian, 195, 228–29; *Subterranean Brotherhood, The,* 229

Hawthorne, Nathaniel, xii, 10, 16, 129, 138–39, 152, 154, 257; "My Kinsman Major Molineux," 134; "Rappachini's Daughter," 142; *Scarlet Letter, The,* 138–39, 206, 290

Hays, Arthur, 357

Hays, Will, 320

Haywood, "Big Bill," 238, 338

Hazard, Bob, 57, 61

Hearst's International-Cosmopolitan, 122–23, 178, 278, 291, 295–96, 331, 347–48

Hearst, William Randolph, 91, 123

Heinemann, William, 208, 230

Hemingway, Ernest, 276, 335, 367, 389; *Farewell to Arms, A,* 385; *In Our Time,* 276; *Sun Also Rises, The,* 339

Henri, Robert, 254

Henry, Arthur, 72–75, 78–79, 110, 118–19, 130, 132, 137, 139, 141, 145, 151, 155–60, 162, 164–67, 169, 180, 188, 190, 230, 248, 277, 282, 330; character in "Rona Murtha" in *A Gallery,* 165–67, 368; contributor to *Ev'ry Month,* 100; death, 167, 397; "Doctrine of Happiness, The," 145; editing of *Sister Carrie,* 142–44, 150–52, 154; *House in the Woods, The,* 144, 167; *Island Cabin, An,* 144–45, 164–69, 180, 330; "It Is to Laugh," 110, 113; *Nicholas Blood, Candidate,* 72–74, 137; "Philosophy of Hope," 145; *Princess of Arcady, A,* 131, 141–45, 150–51, 156–60; *Unwritten Law, The,* 74, 330

Henry, Dorothy ("Dottie"), 130, 141, 167, 180, 330

Henry, Maude Wood, 72, 130, 137, 141–42, 145, 167, 180

Henry, Patrick, 72

Herget, John F., 259

Herman the Great, 118

Herrick, Robert, 222; *Memories of an American Citizen, The,* 222

Hersey, Harold, 262

Herzberg, Max J., 108

Hicks, Elias, 392

Hicks, Granville, 386

Higby, Roy C., 305

Hill, David Bennett, 49

Hill, Thomas E., 10–11; *Hill's Manual of Social and Business Forms,* 10–11

Hirschberg, Leonard K., 188; "Nursing Baby, The," 188

Hitchcock, Ripley, 204–5

Hitler, Adolf, 367, 370, 372, 377, 385–87, 390

Hogg, James S., 56

Holly, Flora Mai, 185

Holmes, Oliver Wendell, 257

Hook, Sidney, 255

Hoover, Herbert, 354–55

Hopkins, L. A., 20–21, 85, 89, 93–94, 97, 114, 172, 312; model for Hurstwood, 148–49, 221

Horton, George, 159, 161

Houston Daily Post, 186

Howard, George Bronson, 193–94

Howells, William Dean, 17, 110, 129–30, 153–54, 204, 223, 235, 251, 262; Dreiser's interviews with, 125–28, 130, 196; "Editha," 251; *Hazard of New Fortunes, A,* 126, 153; *My Literary Passions,* 126–27; reaction to *Sister Carrie,* 92, 127, 160, 185; *Rise of Silas Lapham, The,* 126, 206, 222; *Traveler from Alturia, A,* 127

Howley, Haviland, and Company, 85–86, 99, 113

Howley, Haviland, and Dresser, 179, 182

Melville, Herman, xii, 154, 257; *Billy Budd,* 382; *Moby-Dick,* 100

Mencken, Anna, 316

Mencken, Henry Louis, xii, 81, 131, 133, 143–44, 153–54, 171, 188, 190–91, 193–94, 199, 205, 209–10, 220, 226, 228, 236–37, 253–54, 256, 259, 266, 284–85, 292–93, 295–96, 311, 313–14, 326, 328, 333–34, 365, 371, 374–75, 388, 391, 395, 401; *Book of Prefaces, A,* 269, 273–75; comment on "Free," 280; "Decay of Churches, The," 197; disapproval of Dreiser's socialist friends, 48, 239–40, 261, 269–70, 289, 385; ghost writing infant care articles for *The Delineator,* 188–89; "In Defense of Profanity," 193; opinion of *A Gallery of Women,* 348–49; petition in defense of *The "Genius,"* 260–62; quarrel with Dreiser in 1925, 316, 318; review of *An American Tragedy,* 318–19; review of *The Financier,* 227; review of *The Titan,* 235; trip to Europe in 1916, 271; reviews of *Jennie Gerhardt,* 206–7

Metropolitan Magazine, 97–98, 113, 116, 119–20, 331

Mill, John Stuart Mill, 170

Miller, Arthur, 146

Miller, Henry, 317

Millier, Arthur, 384

Mills, Darius O., 173

Mills, R. P., 175–77

Mitchell, Tobias, 56, 62–63

Moers, Ellen, 110

Molineaux, Roland, 303–4

Monahan, Margaret. *See* Székely, Margaret

Monahan, Roy Phelps, 351

Montaigne, Michel de, 376

Moody, Dwight L., 26

Mooney, James D., 358; *Onward Industry!* 358

Mooney, Thomas J., 355

Moore, George, 206, 230; *Esther Waters,* 206

Moore, Mary Adelaide, 225

More, Paul Elmer, 317

Morgan, J. P., 194–95

Morse, Theodore F., 101; "The Arrival of the Bride," 101

Moses, Montrose J., 218

Muldoon, William, 173–77, 282, 303, 308

Munsey's Magazine, 116, 120, 130, 187

Mussolini, Benito, 372

My Gal Sal (movie), 383

Myers, Gustavus, 223; *History of Great Fortunes,* 223

Nathan, George Jean, 189, 194, 365–67, 371

Nation, 160, 370

National Association for the Advancement of Colored People, 359

National Committee for the Defense of Political Prisoners, 359–60

National Mine Workers, 361

Naylor, Joseph P., 31

Nearing, Scott, 340–41

Nelson, John, 172

New England Society for the Suppression of Vice, 140

New, Jr., Harry, 303

New Idea for Women, 187, 193–94

New Masses, 371

New Orleans Picayune, 185

New Republic, 253, 317

New York American, 205

New York Aurora, 104

New York Call, 179, 272

New York Clipper, 97

New York Commercial Advertiser, 161, 163, 368

New York Daily News, 179–80

New York Daily Tribune, 52, 120, 206

New York Evening Globe, 252

New York Evening Journal, 91

New York Evening Post, 218, 339, 346

New York Evening Sun, 90, 280; coverage of the Brown-Gillette murder trial, 306

New York Herald, 159

New York Herald Tribune, 316, 385, 400

New York Post, 169

New York Society for the Prevention of Vice, 256, 259

Text:	11.25/13.5 Adobe Garamond
Display:	Perpetua, and Adobe Garamond
Compositor:	Integrated Composition Systems
Printer and binder:	Maple-Vail Manufacturing Group